CW00827956

de Havilland

TIGER MOTH

Legendary Biplane Trainer

To Noni
Eternal Butterfly

De Havilland Tiger Moth:
Legendary Biplane Trainer

ISBN 1 85780 061 3

First published in 1999 by
Midland Publishing Limited
24 The Hollow, Earl Shilton
Leicester, LE9 7NA, England
Tel: 01455 847 815 Fax: 01455 841 805
E-mail: midlandbooks@compuserve.com

Design concept and editorial layout
© Midland Publishing Limited
and Stephen Thompson Associates

Printed by Ian Allan Printing Limited
Molesey Road, Riverdene Business Park
Hersham, Surrey, KT12 4RG, England

Worldwide distribution (except Nth America):
Midland Counties Publications (Aerophile) Ltd
Unit 3 Maizefield, Hinckley Fields
Hinckley, Leics., LE10 1YF, England
Tel: 01455 233 747 Fax: 01455 233 737
E-mail: midlandbooks@compuserve.com

North America trade distribution:
Specialty Press Publishers & Wholesalers Inc,
11605 Kost Dam Road,
North Branch, MN 55056, USA
Tel: 651 583 3239 Fax: 651 583 2023
Toll free telephone: 800 895 4585

Photograph on previous page:
Flying over the production facilities at Hatfield on 21st October 1981, G-AIRI and G-AOEI, two of seven Tiger Moths which flew in to celebrate the aeroplane's 50th birthday with a luncheon party attended by Alan Butler. *Reg Bonner*

Title page, opposite:
An impressive line-up at 7 ERFTS Desford during an inspection by the AOC Training Command, September 1938. The instructors in blazers and slacks, are at right. *via John Collier*

Photograph on page 6:
DH.60T Tiger Moth G-ABPH frolicking at low level in 1931. Later that year she was sold to de Havilland's Portuguese agent. *deHMC Archive*

Midland Publishing Limited is a member
of the Ian Allan Group of companies

de Havilland
TIGER MOTH
Legendary Biplane Trainer

Stuart McKay MBE

Midland Publishing
Limited

ACKNOWLEDGEMENTS

DURING the preparation of this manuscript, much assistance and encouragement was provided, often against short order requests, but always willingly and generously by those who responded. In some cases the answers were in handy reference files, but in others it was necessary to tease out long forgotten memories from still active minds. In having the privilege of stringing some of the facts together, I hope I have done adequate justice to this remarkable aeroplane, the Tiger Moth, and the men and women who flew her, and continue to do so.

My special thanks are due to Therese Angelo, Royal New Zealand Air Force Museum; Nigel Arthur, British Aerobatic Association; Captain David Becker, South African Air Force Museum; Lewis Benjamin, The Tiger Club; Garry Bisshopp; Bill Bowker; Philip Bremridge; Charles Caliendi; John Collier; Charles Cornish; Darryl Cott; Sheila Courts; Frank Cox; John Cunningham; Mel Davies; Roger de Mercado; Iain Dick; Colin Dodds; Gary Dolski, Bombardier Aerospace; Neville Duke; David Edwards, British Motor Industry Heritage Centre, Gaydon; Peter Elliott, Royal Air Force Museum; Joan Ellis; Ken Ellis; Gordon Evans; Pat Fillingham; Malcolm Fillmore; David Freeman; Ben French; Ken Fulton; Michael Geoghegan; Pamela Guess, British Aerospace Heritage Collection; Tony Haigh; Bernie Halliday; Patricia Hammond; Charles Hastings-Winch; Terry Heffernan; Peter Henley; Bertil Henrikson for translation services; Bill Hitchcock, The Tiger Club of Australia; Kenneth Holliday; Michael Hooks; Carol Horton; Fred Hotson; Stuart Howe; Michael Inskip; John O Isaacs; Cliff Jenks, Aviation Historical Society of New Zealand; John King, The Tiger Moth Club of New Zealand; Colonel Knut Kinne, Kjeller Flyhistoriske Forening, Norway; Ted Lawrence; Ted Leonard, de Havilland Moth Club of Canada; Wolf Letsch, for translation services; Tony Lloyd, British Aerobatic Association; Dr Ivan McLannahan; Jack Meaden; Michael Oakey; Bob Ogden; Anita Paalanen, Bombardier Aerospace; Desmond Penrose; Bo Vincent Petersen, for translation services; Eva Peverett for translation services; Staff of the Public Records Office, Kew; Melvin K Rees, The British Patent Office; Richard Riding; Bill Sarjantson; Gerry Schwam, US Moth Club; Commander Philip Shaw, RN; Colin Smith; Rusty Tack; Captain Fred Terry; David Tipper; Guy Tucker; Chris Tucker; United States Air Force Museum, Wright-Patterson AFB, Ohio; Michael Vaisey; Steve van Dulken, The British Library; Captain David Vernon; Monica Walsh, Royal Australian Air Force Museum; Bruce Winley; Christine Woodland, University of Warwickshire.

In addition, thanks to all who have contributed with letters, memories and photographs gathered together since the formation of the de Havilland Moth Club in 1975, much of which archive has provided valuable source material, and to those who today enjoy the unique opportunities offered by an association with the Tiger Moth, for they continue to extend a noble history.

Since the low point at the end of the aircraft's involvement in agricultural aviation in Australia, the Tiger Moth's fortunes have been completely revised to assume cult status. In this tidy line-up at Maitland, the nearest aircraft clearly has a revised geometry undercarriage similar to the Canadian model. via Bill Hitchcock

CONTENTS

A CONCERN FOR THE INSTRUCTOR

Everybody loves a Tiger Moth, to the exclusion of heartier beasts. Empire Air Day at Hendon, 1935, and a hands-on experience for many a starry eyed schoolboy. Keystone

ON 2ND FEBRUARY 1932, Mr Charles Power of Renfrew, Pennsylvania, USA, wrote to the Sales Office of the de Havilland Aircraft Company at Stag Lane aerodrome, Edgware, and requested details of the Tiger Moth.

The letter arrived on the desk of Business Director Francis St Barbe only eight days later, and as it was just a routine enquiry, one of the office staff replied politely to advise that they were enclosing a reprint from *The Aeroplane* giving full particulars of the company's Tiger Moth Military Training Machine, receipt of which it was hoped would be to Mr Power's satisfaction.

There was no hint that the correspondent from Pennsylvania should visit the company in London although that offer was undoubtedly made to Dr H J van der Maas from the Rotterdamse Aeroclub in the Netherlands. The Club board had suggested that a trial of the Tiger Moth would be required in advance of any prospective order, and Dr van der Maas was duly entertained by one of the de Havilland sales and demonstration pilots, Hugh 'Jimmy' Buckingham, on 28th June 1932.

While the de Havilland company was in a position to extract £5 per hour from the Air Ministry for Moth aeroplanes operated on behalf of the Royal Air Force Reserve, St Barbe's instructions to his salesmen were undoubtedly centred around minimum flight time or the least that could be considered polite. In the event Dr van der Maas was permitted to fly solo and the de Havilland reward was the sale of one Tiger Moth which was delivered, as requested, almost exactly a year later.

During his discussions with Jimmy Buckingham, the Dutch visitor had been assured that the current Tiger Moth was an improved version of the prototype, having been modified following extensive flight trials with the RAF. Van der Maas was probably comparing his demonstration aeroplane with the two DH.60T Tiger Moths which had been the subject of tests at the Aeroplane and Armament Experimental Establishment (A&AEE) Martlesham Heath, resulting in a modified airframe under the designation DH.82 in October 1931. An early production model of an RAF DH.82 had been actively engaged in experimental flight trials at the Royal Aircraft Establishment (RAE) Farnborough only the previous month.

Initially, the 'T' in designation DH.60T had identified the military trainer version of the popular metal fuselage model of the Moth, the DH.60M. When the standard 120hp Gipsy II powerplant was replaced with the inverted Gipsy III, (also120hp), the DH.60T was renamed Tiger Moth, but only eight aeroplanes were built before type designation DH.82 took claim to the title.

The Sales Office at Stag Lane was perhaps taken by surprise at the rapidity of the changes, or else instructed to exercise economy by the Business Director, for in an untypical and uncharacteristic practice, sales leaflets were distributed originally produced under the heading *de Havilland 'Moth' (Military Training Type DH60T),* badly amended by typewriter with the name *'Tiger'* inserted before *'Moth'* and the DH.60T nomination merely struck through.

The change of engine detail had been accomplished by the simple expedient of adding a further 'I' to the two existing Roman numerals. There was just sufficient space at the bottom of the page, tucked in between notification of colour options and the de Havilland trademark symbol, to advise interested parties that the price of the new aircraft was *'£1,045. Landplane Ex-Works, ready for Flight or Packing'*.

Under a sub-heading, the aircraft was again described as a *'Tiger'* Training Type Moth, and there followed a list of what a would-be purchaser might expect: standard instruments in both cockpits, mounted on a board, and supplied in what were described as 'English' or Metric units, and printed in any desired language. Items featured as 'Equipment' might well have been subject to query by anybody seeking a contractual definition of the aeroplane for they included fundamentals such as seats and 3-piece unsplinterable glass windscreens, controls and ignition switches, aerobatic harness and special wide doors for emergency exit. Particular reference was made to the Dunlop air wheels and low pressure tyres which were described very specifically as being 'fitted on ball bearings'.

Altogether it was a very uninspired document, liberally spiced with the considerable mis-use of capital letters, and ending with a statement clarifying the ex-factory colour schemes, advising that all covered surfaces would be, to quote, 'Alluminium', while 'Fuselage Strut and Undercarriage' colours were optional, excepting white or gold. But promotional matters were scheduled to change and heavy emphasis on the potential of the Tiger Moth *'As Supplied to the British Royal Air Force'* was soon reviewed in a three page brochure published early in 1932 which proclaimed the aircraft as: *'One machine adaptable for every branch of training'*. The copywriter must have been the same as that employed on the re-jigged DH.60T document because capital letters were liberally peppered within the short descriptive paragraphs under the headings of Flying, Fighting, Bombing, Photography and Wireless. Interested parties were advised that *'Fully illustrated literature will be sent upon request'*.

The Royal Air Force had been a supportive customer for de Havilland's DH.60 Moth series, from wooden aircraft with basic Cirrus engines and others specially adapted to take the Armstrong Siddeley Genet for display purposes. However, the vast majority of orders had been for the DH.60M Metal Moth with a 100hp Gipsy I and not placed until 1929/1930, five years into the aircraft's development. But in conciliation, it was the initiative of the Air Ministry that had established the Light Aeroplane Clubs in 1925 using DH.60 Cirrus Moths as their standard equipment, laying the foundation of flying facilities for the Reserve of Air Force Officers (RAFO) and upgrading with improved marks as they became available. Was it not an irony that Geoffrey de Havilland designed the DH.60 having excluded himself from the Air Ministry sponsored Light Aeroplane Trials of 1924, whose express purpose had been to formulate just such an aeroplane, except that the specifications had been hopelessly wide of any sense of practicality? The Air Ministry could have been dogmatic, even vindictive, but fortunately, they recognised the error of their ways.

The RAF took delivery of 135 DH.60M Moths between October 1929 and March 1931 under the terms of four separate contracts. While nearly all the British aero clubs used Moths for training, only the first eleven of the Air Ministry order were scheduled for school work.

DH.60Ms J9922 to J9932 (factory build numbers 1384-1392 and 1382-1383), were delivered to 5 Flying Training School (FTS) at Sealand between October and December 1929, although there were some late arrivals, posted in from temporary store at Henlow. Most seem to have left Sealand shortly after the last of the contracted aircraft were delivered into Air Force care from Stag Lane. J9922 (1384), was sold back to her manufacturer in June 1931, only ten months after arrival at Sealand, and joined operations with the de Havilland School as G-ABNE. J9931 (1382) had spun off her approach to land on 21st November 1929, only days after delivery, and J9923 (1385), crashed on 22nd April 1930 after the pilot's straps broke and he fell out of the cockpit mid-way through a slow roll.

Apart from those delivered to 5 FTS, none of the remaining aircraft was scheduled in the primary training roles, and they were scattered across Great Britain attached to Station Flights, fighting units, various trade schools, communications squadrons, practice flights, an anti-aircraft co-operation unit and the RAF Colleges at Andover and Cranwell. One aircraft was used to test an experimental seaplane hull, others went as vehicles of communication to Aden, Iraq and Malta. Six aircraft joined the Central Flying School (CFS) in 1931 and flew as a team at that year's RAF Pageant. In spite of the aircraft's non-intensive training role, her exposure within a practising, high mobility Air Force was wide, and senior rank officers had sampled her delights as both pilot and passenger, raising a catalogue of opinion both for and against.

de Havilland took note and developed the DH.60M into a multi-role trainer aircraft aimed specifically at the military under the designation DH.60T Moth Trainer:

'Throughout the design the importance of interchangeability, together with ease and simplicity of repair and replacement has been kept uppermost. All points which need periodical inspection are readily accessible and, if damage is done, repairs can generally be localised and new sections can be fitted without disturbing the main structure'.

Provision was made for dual control but more particularly for items such as camera guns, mapping, reconnaissance and wireless equipment, and practice bombs hung on an underfloor rack. The aircraft was heavier and stronger than the DH.60M; power was still provided by the 120hp Gipsy II, and an improved escape path for the occupant of the front seat was engineered by routing the exhaust system vertically down immediately behind the propeller, thus allowing deep doors to be provided on both sides of the cockpit. Crew abandonment had previously been impeded by the convergence of the rear flying wires at the root end of the lower rear spar; the geometry was altered to permit grouping of the cluster at the front spar root, ahead of the cockpit and away from the passage of anxious feet propelling parachute encumbered bodies.

Following flight trials at Stag Lane in April 1931, orders were secured for ten aircraft for the Royal Swedish Air Force (re-designated Sk.9 in their inventory), 40 for the Brazilian Government to be divided by the ratio of 3:5 in favour of the Navy, and one for China, two for Iraq and six for Egypt.

The decision to 'invert' the Gipsy II was taken in 1929, and the clean lines of the resultant Gipsy III made it an ideal powerplant for the DH.80 Moth Three (later named the

Puss Moth), the DH.60GIII Moth Major, and the DH.60T Moth Trainer.

Early in 1931 the Air Ministry called for design submissions for a new basic training aircraft. Particular emphasis was to be applied to the ease with which the instructor might escape from his front office. Armed with an ideal engine and experience of the revised airframe, the Stag Lane team was well placed to meet the challenge.

The venerable Avro 504N, whose core dated back to 1912, had been replaced in 1929 by the Air Ministry's pre-conceived ideal, the Hawker Tomtit. The fabric covered tubular steel fuselage frame, fitted with a 150hp Armstrong Siddeley Mongoose 5 cylinder radial engine, had been chosen partly on account of the dwindling number of RAF tradesmen capable of maintaining anything else. The Tomtit was built to specification 5/29 with an emphasis on simplicity and safety: slats were fitted to the top wings which were arranged with forward stagger to permit ease of evacuation; there were no brakes, but an adjustable rear seat was standard, and there was provision for a blind flying hood. Unhappily for many, only 25 Tomtits were built in the face of severe competition from Avro and de Havilland, and served only with 3 FTS at Grantham and the Central Flying School at Wittering.

Stag Lane aerodrome in March 1933, a hive of activity with DH.60 Moth, DH.82 Tiger Moth, DH.80 Puss Moth and DH.84 Dragon all clearly visible. Features, viewing from left (north) clockwise are private owner lock-ups, Service Department and London Aeroplane Club, Engine Division, Aircraft Company and Flight Test. Stag Lane can be seen running eastwards from behind the buildings of the Engine Division to join the Edgware Road immediately opposite the white fronted building with a three apex roof: de Havilland's local, the Bald Faced Stag. de Havilland Aircraft Co.

DH.60T Moth Trainer G-ABKM clearly illustrating how the occupant of the front seat could be enmeshed in rigging wires during parachute escape. Partial resolution of the port side clutter was achieved by routing the exhaust pipe vertically downwards just behind the propeller. This aircraft was sold to the Swedish Air Force in June 1931. deHMC Archive

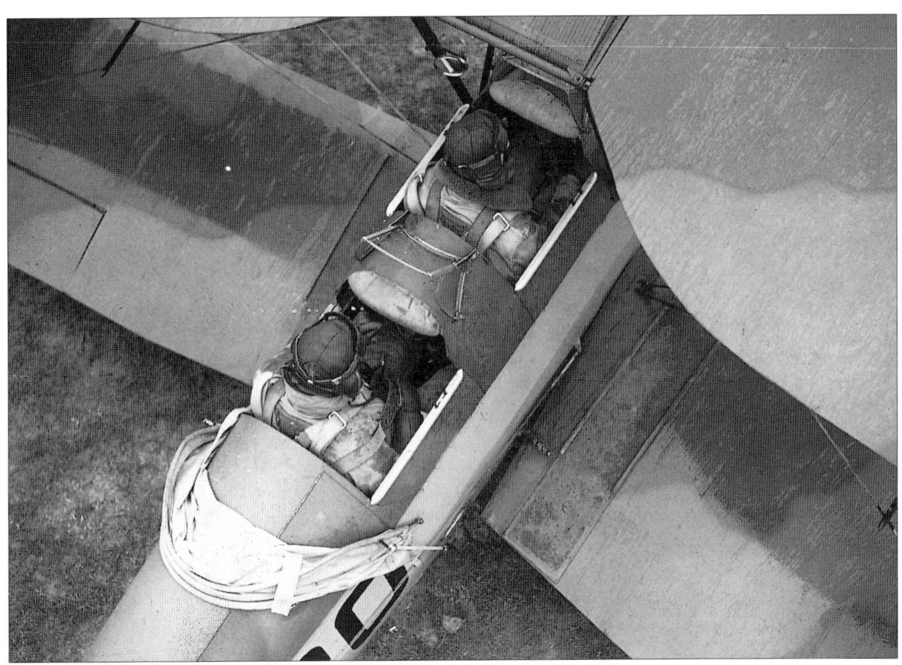

Clear egress for pupil and instructor was achieved by moving the whole of the centre section forward of the front cockpit. To compensate for the shift in centre of gravity, the wings were swept back, additional sweep being applied to the top wings. deHMC Archive

Ordered a year later against specification 3/30 was the Avro 621, which, when re-engined with the 240hp development of the Armstrong Siddeley Lynx, became the Tutor, improving on the performance of the 504N (also Lynx powered) by virtue of some extra 25hp. The Tutor was well equipped with mainwheel brakes, a tailwheel, adjustable seats and rudder pedals, variable incidence tailplane, leading edge slats and ailerons on top and bottom wings. The front cockpit was also free of obstruction, and although almost 400 Tutors were eventually in widespread and active circulation through-out the home based training establishments, at a time of financial constraint it was regarded as a relatively expensive aeroplane to operate.

Flying Officer Peter Heath, soon to become acquainted with the fruits of de Havilland's thinking on a new trainer, flew several hundred hours instructing on Tutors, and described it as a 'bad trainer'. *'It was far too forgiving and suffered fools too gladly. The result was that when the fools went on to more advanced types and tried things with which they had got away on Tutors, they were surprised when they killed themselves'.*

de Havilland's DH.60T with its new Gipsy III engine and revised rigging was considered a prime contender for the new basic trainer contract, especially so in view of the Air Ministry's recent heavy investment in the DH.60M. The commonality of engine, spares, and servicing requirements were all viewed with favour, but there was still one glaring problem: the biplane wing geometry of the DH.60T left the occupant of the front seat surrounded with cabane struts and a fuel tank immediately overhead. There were no solutions more obvious than to move the tank or the cabane structure or to delete the top wings altogether, but time and the need to utilise as much of the existing structure as possible in the bare interests of economy, were paramount if the tender was to be realistic in terms of delivery and price.

It is reasonable to say that this essential new training aeroplane was not so much designed by anyone in particular as evolved by a group of interested individuals, enlisting the skills of the shop floor specialists and their supervisors, who gathered round what has been described as a skeletal DH.60M airframe in a quiet corner of the Stag Lane factory where they were provided with all the facilities they needed.

There is some suspicion that the airframe might not have been that of a DH.60M but rather a DH.60T Moth Trainer, which would have been more logical. G-ABKS (1705) had been registered to the company in April 1931, the last of a limited batch of six. Whilst the other five (1700-1704), had all been sold to the Royal Swedish Air Force in June 1931, G-ABKS was retained as a test and demonstration aircraft but never aspired to a full certificate of airworthiness, and was finally cancelled against de Havilland's own description as having been 'reduced to redundant stock'. With the knowledge that an important new project was developing modelled on a comparable Moth Trainer specification, it is almost impossible to believe that the airframe would have been cast off as scrap, redundant or otherwise.

Chief Designer Arthur Hagg and General Manager Frank Hearle were on hand to assist company stalwarts Fred Plumb and Douglas Hunter to tackle the problem. Fred Plumb had joined the company soon after its establishment at Stag Lane with all the qualifications of a skilled aircraft woodworker and was personally responsible for much of the earliest Moth construction and manufacturing development.

As Superintendent of the Experimental Shop, he was closely associated with all subsequent prototype building, completing a high percentage of the work by hand, and was inextricably involved with the later DH.88 Comet and DH.98 Mosquito programmes. It was the need to adapt the Mosquito to limited production facilities that took him to Canada during the Second World War.

Assigned as project engineer, Douglas Hunter had joined the Stag Lane Drawing Office in 1925 where he had been closely involved with development of every project since. Like Fred Plumb, his expertise was eventually required in support of the Canadian Mosquito programme, and as Director of Engineering to de Havilland Canada, his responsibility in 1946 was to oversee the company's efforts in producing a successful replacement for the Tiger Moth.

At Stag Lane in 1931, the team's first task was to move the fuel tank forward, away from the Moth's front cockpit, and under Hunter's direction, rearrange the geometry of that specimen airframe, reversing the cabane 'V' strut effectively to provide the basis of a platform onto which the fuel tank could be re-positioned. The move proved to be 18 inches measured at the wing root, and the trial installation was shown to Captain de Havilland and test pilot Hubert Broad who tried the cockpit but was not totally convinced. After lunch, Broad is believed to have revisited the site to amplify his concern with the result that, according to Fred Plumb, the centre section was moved forward again by a further 4 inches. Based on a DH.60T fuselage sideframe, there would have been no braced pickup joint at this new position and the new position was only satisfied by local engineering.

The change in geometry successfully solved the problem of cockpit accessibility, but the aircraft was now seriously out of balance, and some simple method of re-establishing an equitable centre of gravity (CG) had to be agreed.

The only real option was to sweep back the wings, an exercise accomplished by shortening the spindled rear spars of each wing, and adjusting the fittings to suit. By calculation it was agreed that a sweep of 9in measured from the original position of the interplane struts should be sufficient to restore the CG to lie within a practical and workable range, but it proved not to be. The remedy, and most expeditious course, was to add extra sweep to the top wings only, and again using the interplane struts as a datum, a further 2 inches of sweepback was added at which the CG conditions were considered to be satisfied. *Flight's* correspondent, when introduced to the problem, believed that the solution was *'not altogether beneficial in the matter of looks, but having probably no other disadvantages'.*

Having established the basic geometry of the airframe, recording of the detail differences demanded by attachment fittings and other structural members could now begin prior to issue of manufacturing drawings. Following Stag Lane practice, prototype wings were built, attached to stanchions in one of the workshops, and sandbagged against a defined schedule of structural testing. The new geometry precluded the ability to fold back the wings, a major selling feature of all other Moth aeroplanes, but the market for this machine was perceived as being an almost exclusively military one, where hangarage and storage facilities would be amply provided.

A small production batch of aeroplanes built to the new formula was approved by the board, and in view of the competition for RAF orders, the aircraft was to be called DH.60T 'Tiger Moth', 'T' not only denoting 'Trainer', but acting in compliance with the Air Ministry's contemporary naming policy (Tomtit/Tutor).

Not all found favour with the new name. A correspondent who reported on his experience of flying the machine for *The Aeroplane* wrote:

'Personally we are inclined to be sorry that this name should be used again as a machine so utterly different from the tiny and fiery monoplane on which Mr H S Broad made, and still holds, the World's speed record for light aeroplanes in the Third Category. From the fanciful standpoint also, the name suggests something far less tractable than the new trainer'.

The first DH.60T Tiger Moth (1727), was delivered by Hubert Broad to the A&AEE at Martlesham Heath on 18th August 1931 identified by the manufacturer's Class II serial 'E.5', an alpha-numeric system allocated by the Air Ministry strictly for experimental flying. Civil registration G-ABNJ had been issued to the aircraft in June.

The general impression when investigative flying and assessment began four days

The first de Havilland aircraft to carry the name 'Tiger Moth' was the diminutive DH.71 of 1928. Test pilot Hubert Broad carries out a power check assisted by human intervention and under supervision of a practised eye probably assessing propeller tracking. de Havilland Aircraft Co.

DH.60T Tiger Moth G-ABPH was constructed with the typical stringer turtle deck, deep front door and air scoop for a rear mounted carburettor for the Gipsy III engine. This aircraft was the first to be tested with increased dihedral on the lower wings and is seen here indulging in a session of sustained inverted flight over Stag Lane. Note the angle of the elevators. deHMC Archive

later was favourable, except that in the opinion of the Establishment's test pilots, landing in a crosswind put the into-wind wing tip perilously close to the ground, and that when taxying across uneven territory, any down aileron was liable to make contact and trail across the surface.

An apocryphal story which circulated in and probably emanated from the bars of the Stag Lane factory's 'local', *The Bald Faced Stag*, suggested that part of an Air Ministry 'competition' was judgement of the time taken to remove all four wings.

A de Havilland engineer had picked up a snatch of conversation in an Ipswich pub, and in association with his colleagues on detachment, serviced the aircraft in the Martlesham hangar the night before the assessment, during which they removed all the necessary split pins, substantially reducing the clocked time and earning the aircraft top marks for maintenance accessibility.

At Stag Lane, a second DH.60T Tiger Moth G-ABPH (1732), was re-rigged to accept 4° 30' of dihedral on the lower wings only, an increase of 1°45'. over the setting of the top wings, adequately solving the problem of ground proximity, and in this configuration, the type was cleared at A&AEE having been delivered by Hubert Broad on 3rd September. Martlesham Heath reported that the change in rigging made no difference in handling when compared with recorded flight trials conducted on E.5 the previous month. In this new 'frozen' configuration, the design received A&AEE clearance as a military trainer acceptable to the Air Ministry.

Due to the introduction of sweep and revised lower wing dihedral, the distance between locating pin centres at the top and bottom of the front and rear interplane struts was now unequal by one sixteenth of an inch, the rear strut being the longer. Although the difference was minimal and had no marked effect on rigging, the difference was to prove the bane of many an engineer's life in the future.

Adding sweep to the constant chord wing of a DH.60 changed the relationship between the angle of the ribs and the airflow, resulting in a less efficient section. de Havilland viewed the prospect of modifying their jigs to accommodate realigned ribs, with some alarm. What would be the advantages if such an investment were made? The aircraft was designed as a trainer, not a high efficiency, long distance tourer or a racing vehicle, or a commercial aircraft reliant on good economics for survival. The RAF 15 (modified) wing profile, described by the Aerodynamics Department as 'a flat bottomed section', had been carefully chosen: when stalling, the lift fell off gradually and smoothly, not abruptly, and the spin was normal with immediate recovery. The company decided to make no immediate change to the layout of the wing. And they never did. The economics of the matter are summarised by the popular myth that the Tiger Moth was designed on the back of the proverbial brown envelope by Wilfred Nixon and Francis St Barbe, Directors of Finance and Sales respectively, who recognised what had to be done to secure the Air Ministry contract, sketched out the changes which could be accommodated involving the least cost, and handed their deliberations to Fred Plumb with a short but concise message: 'build that'. The myth developed into the Tiger Moth, but the analogy of the brown envelope and what Plumb and Hunter were asked to achieve was not far from the truth.

Eight aircraft were built to the DH.60T Tiger Moth specification: G-ABNJ (1725) was demonstrated to the Royal Swedish Air Force in December 1931 and taken on charge immediately following the presentation. G-ABPH (1732), was officially sold to Carlos Bleck, de Havilland's Portuguese agent, in December, having been delivered by Hubert Broad the previous September, and almost certainly joined the Portuguese military. G-ABNI (1726) was dispatched to Canada where she was registered CF-APL and operated as a demonstrator for barely a year, ending her days as an instructional airframe with Toronto Central Technical School during the Second World War.

DH.82 Tiger Moth prototype G-ABRC, first flown by Hubert Broad on 26th October 1931, survived until 1956 when she was broken up and burned at Croydon. Charles Holland

The remaining five aircraft, G-ABNY (1724); G-ABNG (1725); G-ABNK (1728); G-ABNL (1729) and G-ABNM (1730) were all sold to the Swedish Air Force in August 1931.

Following Martlesham Heath's approval, the Air Ministry placed an order with de Havilland (contract No 120255/31) for the supply of 35 aircraft to be built to specification 23/31, essentially the same as the build standard of DH.60T Tiger Moth G-ABPH. The first batch of 15 aircraft was to be air delivered to 3 FTS Grantham in November 1931, where they would be used as primary trainers, replacing the popular Hawker Tomtit. Each of the remaining 20 was required 'less engine' to be delivered by surface, as directed.

At Stag Lane during the summer of 1931, it was decided that a sufficient number of major alterations had been absorbed for the DH.60T Type Number to be amended. This was not a hasty decision for all design and stress calculations, modification summaries and flight test reports collectively formed the aircraft Type Record held by the Design Authority, the de Havilland Aircraft Company Ltd. The Type Record for a 'modified' aircraft, no matter how major the modification was considered progressive development of the same series, and in 1931 all de Havilland biplane Moth documentation was predicated on the standard of the DH.60X. In theory, the change of Type Number signalled an entirely new design of aeroplane, in which case authority, in the shape of the Air Ministry, could have argued and insisted that a whole new Type Record be established from scratch, a time consuming and expensive exercise, to be avoided if possible.

In the event, the option of a new Type Number was chosen: DH.82, one number on from the soon to be discarded DH.81 Swallow Moth, a victim of financial stringency as much as anything, but the Type Record continued to be referenced to the DH.60X, under whose protection it has remained ever since.

The Air Ministry awarded the company a contract for a single prototype DH.82 to be built against a unique specification, 15/31, fitted with a Gipsy III engine. Painted silver overall, the aircraft, work's number 1733, was flown from Stag Lane under marking 'E.6' on 26th October 1931 by Hubert Broad, who positioned her to Martlesham Heath for the standard acceptance trials on 11th November.

And how did Broad record the first flight of the DH.82 Tiger Moth in his logbook? There is no entry! de Havilland's chief test pilot was so committed to testing and demonstrating Moths and a miscellany of other aircraft that the events of 26th October 1931 were of no greater significance than those of any other date of that era. Admittedly, he did rely on the watch office for much of the detail he was obliged to record, and there is evidence that on occasion his logbooks were completed by third parties acting on his behalf.

An analysis of Hubert Broad's recorded work pattern for dates either side of 26th October is significant. Between 12th October and 6th November he test flew the DH.81 Swallow Moth on three occasions, made 16 test or demonstration flights in DH.80 Puss Moths, production tested two new DH.60 Moths and a reconditioned one, and flew five of the RAF's new DH.82 Tiger Moths, although three of these are listed as DH.60s. On 3rd and 6th November respectively, K2570 and K2573 were flown under the heading 'DH.82', the first such mention. The 20 minute test of 'E.6' on 4th November is listed as that of a DH.60.

Later registered G-ABRC, the prototype DH.82 Tiger Moth was fitted with a Gipsy Major engine early in 1932 and during the 1933 season was operated by National Aviation Day Displays before joining the Reserve School fleet operated by the de Havilland School of Flying at Hatfield.

The aircraft remained firmly in the grip of the military, taking on Impressment serial BB723 in October 1940, continuing to operate at Hatfield with No.1 Elementary Flying Training School (EFTS). Transferred to the Royal Navy in 1943 one of her many different bases was Heathrow where she stayed for six months from November 1944. Sold out of the service in 1951 as just another Tiger Moth, BB723 was not recognised for the treasure she surely was, and is believed to have been broken up for scrap and burned at Croydon in November 1956.

DH.82 Tiger Moth K2570 at Stag Lane illustrating the dissimilarity between the dihedral angles of top and bottom mainplanes. deHMC Archive

In his Foreword to the DH.82 Tiger Moth Maintenance Manual, Albert Brant of the de Havilland Service Department wrote:

'Guided by the accumulated experience of years, especially that since 1925, during which over 2,000 Moths have been built, mainly for training purposes, and kept in continuous service in every part of the world, the de Havilland Aircraft Company Limited is now producing the Tiger Moth, specially designed, arranged and equipped as a General Training and Practice type.

'There is one right and many wrong ways of doing most things and the operation and maintenance of an aeroplane is no exception. The object of these Notes is to point out the right way of doing the few small jobs necessary to ensure completely satisfactory and trouble-free operation. Due to its straightforward design and robust construction, the Tiger Moth needs a minimum of attention, but this very simplicity of maintenance must not be allowed to engender carelessness'.

What manner of machine was it that had been created at Stag Lane which was now called 'Tiger Moth'? By definition it was a simple biplane, built up on enhanced principles whose roots could be traced back to the First World War. There can be little improvement on the description penned by the manufacturer in 1931:

Main Planes:
The single bay biplane structure has a pronounced stagger and sweep-back achieving the visibility and ease of egress from both cockpits aimed at. Each plane consists of two heavy 'I' section spruce spars with leading and trailing edge and ribs of normal wood structure. The tip bends are of light alloy tubing. The drag struts are of steel tube, the lugs for the swaged rod and light tensile steel wire bracing being integral with the tube, completing a structure which is not affected by any slight shrinkage which might take place in the wooden spar. The interplane struts are of spruce with steel end sockets and the drag bracings are duplicated.

Fuselage:
The sizes of tubing to specification DTD.89.A used for round tubes in the construction of the fuselage, and DTD.113 for square tubes, are shown on Drawing M.1698. In addition to the above, there are the lower cross members terminating with attachment fittings for root ends of the lower planes, which are especially constructed parts. The various stiffening plates at the welded joints are mild steel plate to specification S.3.

The front fuselage, the sides of which are parallel in plan view, is constructed of two flat sides, the junction joints of the structure and diagonal members to the longerons being welded in a jig. All joints are reinforced with side plates welded on. All holes in these side units are also jig drilled, and the side forms a replaceable unit should the need arise. The side units are assembled with no welding by the bolted cross members, which complete the front fuselage framework.

The rear fuselage from the rear of the pilot's seat to the stern post, is a completely rigid welded-up unit, jig built, and is a replaceable unit. The four longerons are of square tube and struts, diagonals and cross members of round tubing. All joints are reinforced by side plates welded on. A small quantity of quarter inch diameter by 22G commercial quality steel tubing is also used as stays for the rear fuselage fairing formers. (This requirement was deleted when the ply turtle deck/rear cowl was introduced with the DH.82A model).

The engine bay structure consists of two side frames, each constructed of three square tubes in triangular form, welded flat in a jig at the joints. The joints are reinforced with steel plates welded on. The side units are assembled to the front fuselage section by bolted fishplates, and being jig made and drilled, form replaceable units. A stay tube from the right-hand rear engine foot to the bottom left-hand joint of the fuselage braces the structure against side loads. It will be appreciated from the foregoing description that in the event of major damage the replaceable section can be obtained and fitted with little or no constructional experience.

Empennage:
The empennage follows the normal de Havilland practice and is constructed of wood and fabric covered. The control surfaces have trailing bends of light alloy tubing.

The tailplane is not adjustable in flight, but longitudinal trim is attained by adjustable spring loading on elevators, which has proved so satisfactory on other Gipsy Moth types.

Undercarriage:
The undercarriage is of the divided axle type. Spring legs embodying rubber-in-compression springing are used. The top end is attached to the fuselage lower longeron and the other end to the wheel end of the cranked half axle, which terminates at a tripod fitting under the fuselage. The structure is completed by a forwardly inclined stay tube from the lower end of the leg casing to the fuselage.

[Coil springs replacing rubber-in-compression was one of the detail changes designed into the DH.82A. The new legs designed by Dowty were incorporated by students of the de Havilland Aeronautical Technical School into their own DH.60G Moth G-ABTS (1900), when it was rebuilt in June 1933 after it had landed on the roof of a house in Edgware the previous year, and the new system was considered to be worthy of comprehensive handling trials conducted by Hubert Broad at Stag Lane the following month. – Author]

Controls:
All machine control operating gear is housed in a control box running centrally along the cockpit floor, forming a unit which can be easily removed for periodical inspection. The controls in the front cockpit are quickly detachable, the control columns by withdrawing a safety locking pin, and the rudder by removing the connecting rod.

The two control columns connect with a shaft carrying a lever which transmits side movement to the ailerons by cables, and fore and aft movement by link tubes to a cross shaft behind the pilot's seat, from which cables run direct to the elevator levers. Rudder cables run direct from attachment on the outer end of the rear rudder bar to the levers on the rudder.

Unable to raise patents against the DH.82 Tiger Moth design, de Havilland were content to label each aircraft with a reminder that it carried three patented features:

GB 184,317. Improvements in or relating to aileron control-mechanism (aileron differential), registered in the name of chief designer Arthur Hagg and dated 1922.

GB 277,914. Improvements in or relating to air speed-indicators for aircraft (strut mounted ASI) registered in the name of Geoffrey de Havilland and dated 1927.

GB 297,541. Improvements in or relating to harness for airmen (three point seat restraint) registered in the name of Hubert Broad and dated 1928.

Reporting for *The Aeroplane*, Francis Bradbrooke wrote:

'In the new Tiger Moth the de Havilland Company has succeeded in producing a machine which has all the flying qualities of the Moth either unimpaired or improved, and at the same time incorporates a number of special features for Air Force training requirements which make it substantially a different aeroplane.

'The wings and bracing have been so stiffened up that the most violent aerobatics can be performed in these machines when they are in constant service and carrying parachutes, complete dual sets of instruments and controls, and various extras such as camera or machine gun equipment.

'The standard Moth cellule is simplicity itself compared with the new staggered and swept back arrangement, from the designer's point of view, but the complicated problems involved have been solved with remarkable rapidity by the drawing office, inspection departments and shops in turn'.

The first six of the RAF's DH.82 Tiger Moths, K2567-K2572, (1739-1744), were scheduled for delivery from Stag Lane to No. 3 Flying Training School (FTS) at Grantham on 9th November 1931, but the weather, very cold and accompanied by poor visibility, ensured the flight was postponed until the following day. The delivery pilots, drawn from 24 (Communications) Squadron based only a few miles west of Stag Lane at Northolt, were entertained by de Havilland staff and invited to thaw out after local flight testing by sampling freshly brewed coffee liberally laced with rum. While waiting, Flying Officer Peter Heath was moved to assess the crazy flying qualities of the DH.82 in comparison to the DH.60 with which he was already familiar, and believed his 20 minute low level routine proved that the new aeroplane was considerably more versatile. Peter Heath later recalled that nobody in the de Havilland organisation objected to his exhibition, but his own Commanding Officer was far from amused.

This 'ticking off' of an RAF Tiger Moth pilot occurred even before the aircraft had been delivered into service, but no official action was taken to impede Peter Heath's long career from which he retired with the rank of Group Captain.

Conditions had improved sufficiently the following day for the task to be completed: nothing was considered remarkable, the squadron pilots were merely delivering another batch of aeroplanes. Leaving Stag Lane at 0945 hours the flight to Lincolnshire took exactly 65 minutes. Having handed over his own machine, K2572, and received the necessary signature, he accepted Avro Tutor K1579 and flew her back to Northolt. It was all in a day's work.

At the time of the Tiger Moth's entry into RAF service, pilots were being trained under a number of different schemes as described in this contemporary appraisal:

'If a man joins the Reserve of Air Force Officers, he is taught to fly at one of the civilian training schools approved for the purpose by the Air Ministry, where the training methods are kept closely to the lines adopted in the RAF itself. If he joins the Auxiliary Air Force he is taught to fly in the squadron which he joins, under the care of the Adjutant, who is always a regular officer and a qualified instructor. Officers of the Special Reserve are taught at one of the civilian schools, while regular officers with short-service commissions are taught at one of the RAF Flying Training Schools. The permanent officers who have learnt elementary flying at Cranwell, Oxford or Cambridge, are also sent to a Flying Training School for further instruction before being posted to a squadron.

'There are four approved civilian training schools: the de Havilland school for London, the Bristol school for the West, the Blackburn school at Brough in Yorkshire, and Flying Training Services at Hamble near Southampton. The Flying Training Schools of the RAF are at Digby in Lincolnshire, Grantham, also in Lincolnshire, Sealand near Chester, and Abu Sueir in Egypt. At the Flying Training Schools officers who can fly receive instruction in aerial gunnery, photography and other necessary duties. They leave these schools fully trained pilot officers.

'Considerations of economy have often turned attention to the possibility of using a smaller and cheaper machine than the Avro for elementary training, for minor mishaps to undercarriages and propellers are bound to be not infrequent. A great deal of good training work has been carried out on the de Havilland Moth, and the Tiger Moth is now also used. The Hawker Tomtit is another type which has done good service. The exponents of the Avro type for training now admit that after so many years of redoubtable service it is time that the 504 type should go on the half pay list'.

The student pilots of 'A' Flight, 3 FTS, were all approaching solo standard on their Hawker Tomtits when the Tiger Moths arrived, bearing an order from the Air Ministry that type conversion was to begin without delay. In spite of protests, additional pre-solo hours had now to be flown by students and instructors, none of whom were seduced by the new aeroplane which they compared unfavourably with the Tomtit except in the arenas of price, economy of operation, reliability and baggage space, the latter proving a bonus for weekends away.

Of the residual nine aircraft from the air delivery schedule, a further six, K2573-K2578 (1744-1750), were flown to Grantham on 16th November; K2579 and K2580 (1751-1752) joined them on 2nd December and K2581 (1753),12 days later. All 20 aircraft ordered for delivery 'less engines', K2582-K2601 (1754-1773), were transported to the Home Aircraft Depot (HAD) at Henlow between 16th December 1931 and 4th February 1932, arriving singly or in pairs in 15 separate consignments.

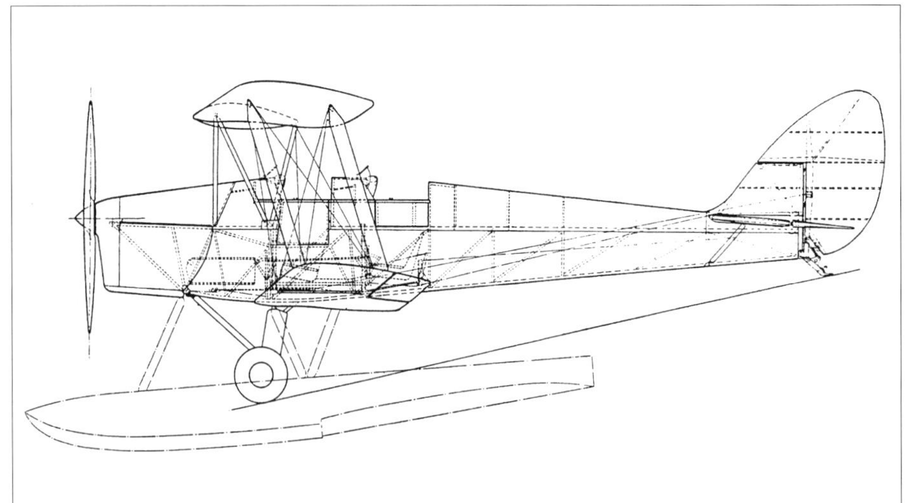

As part of its earliest sales campaigns in support of the DH.82 Tiger Moth, de Havilland promoted the type as a floatplane, following a company tradition. Trials conducted by the RAF, however, rejected the Tiger Moth as a type suitable for seaplane training.

DH.82 Tiger Moth K2573 wearing the chevrons and titling of No 24 (Communications) Squadron, RAF, after a short posting to Grantham. The distinctive DH trademark symbols applied to the interplane struts of all civil and military biplanes supplied pre-war, have been painted over or removed. Frank Bentley

The 1932 RAF Central Flying School Display Team, in the form of K2583, K2584, K2585, K2586 and K2587, at altitude in perfect formation, inverted. The top surfaces of the mainplanes and horizontal tail were painted in a large red and white chequerboard pattern for maximum visual effect when playing to the crowd. via Darryl Cott.

In 1927, the RAF Central Flying School had established a formation display team of six Armstrong Siddeley Genet I powered DH.60 Moths in support of that year's Royal Air Force Pageant at Hendon. For the 1932 season, six Tiger Moths were removed from store at Henlow, K2582-K2587 (1754-1759), and transferred back to Stag Lane in pairs on 4th, 6th and 8th April. The fleet was modified to permit sustained inverted flight, and a large red and white chequerboard colour scheme was painted onto the top surfaces of all mainplanes, tailplanes and elevators: those surfaces most generally expected to be on view to spectators on the ground.

Operating in a single seat configuration with the inverted fuel system hidden inside the front cockpit, the team was to display in a formation of five, leaving one aircraft in reserve.

K2582 was delivered to CFS on 26th April, and the remaining five aircraft joined the school at its new home at Wittering in May where the routines were perfected under the team leadership of Flight Lieutenant P M Watt. At Hendon on 26th June 1932, four of the five aircraft team (Flight Lieutenant L K Stokes, Flying Officers D D Christie and V R Moon, and Sergeant Pilot S J Mansell), engaged one another in a slow speed race, during which they were not permitted to lose height.

A contemporary report was headed 'The Tortoise Race':

'First the four Tiger Moths flew past at normal speed in line astern, then they flew over the aerodrome across wind in line abreast, each pilot checking his speed by a series of stalls. At first the third machine rapidly 'underhauled' his rivals, but lost altitude in his effort. Finally, No 3 machine fell behind in fine style with only a comparatively small loss in altitude. It was quite an interesting event, which certainly tortoised *a lot regarding the advance made in present-day flying with the help of automatic slots etc'.*

The team aircraft were returned to Stag Lane in mid-August for conversion to standard configuration, after which they were flown into storage at 2 Aircraft Servicing Unit (ASU) Cardington. Perhaps this was a questionable decision, for the Air Ministry moved all six back to de Havilland in March and April 1933, where the inverted systems were refitted, and the team reformed at Wittering on 9th May. But it was to be their second and last season: the aircraft were all delivered to Henlow on 24th July, standardised, and finally allocated to other less arduous duties.

Having ordered the type into service as a new trainer, the history of the Tiger Moth with 3 FTS might be described as brief. By August 1933, K2569 had been struck off charge at Grantham; three aircraft had been transferred to communications duties with 24 Squadron at Hendon, followed by a further five in 1934; four aircraft were transferred to the HAD at Henlow in August 1933 and had been broken up within a year, and another had been allocated to an Air Armament School where it was scrapped in the August of 1934. The previous May, K2570 (1742), was featured in a magazine article, photographed with the hood erected, 'for instruction in the art of blind flying', said the caption, whilst confirming that 'the particular machine illustrated' belonged not to a flying training establishment, but to No 24 (Communications) Squadron. K2586 (1758), was transferred to 24 Squadron at Hendon late in 1934 for a four year posting, during which time the aircraft was used to conduct civilian 'B' (commercial) cross country tests of about two hours average duration. Intended to become an instructional airframe in October 1938, K2586 was instead broken up for spares.

Remarkably, the first of the Grantham batch lived longest: K2567 spent several weeks at RAE Farnborough early in 1932, engaged on 'experimental work', instrument testing and as a communications aircraft. It is believed she was posted to 18 Elementary and Reserve Flying Training School (ERFTS) at Fairoaks before delivery to 12 Maintenance Unit (MU) Kirkbride in March 1940. Three months later she was converted into an instructional airframe (2049M), by 4 MU at Cowley, probably as an educational aid in support of Tiger Moth production which was just gaining momentum at the Morris Motors' works.

In reply to a criticism of the first aircraft completed at Cowley in April 1940, the Works' Superintendent had replied that the job had been copied from 'a de Havilland fuselage held at these works'. In July 1940, 2049M returned to Fairoaks where she remained with 18 Elementary Flying Training School (EFTS) until December 1941. After a service life of just ten years, the RAF's first Tiger Moth was cut up for scrap.

K2579 (1751), was withdrawn from Grantham in May 1932 and contributed to a programme of performance measurement at Martlesham Heath during which she was dived at speeds up to 225mph IAS.

Two major criticisms were expressed: the lack of an adjustable seat and the degree of the forced draught which was channelled into the rear cockpit from around the front windscreen. Some attempt was made to counter this by extending laterally the plywood framework in which the front seat was located. Under the hopeful title 'draught excluder', the spare parts inventory was increased to include delicately tailored strips of plywood which were glued and pinned in their strategic locations.

Permitted to solo one of the RAF's new Tiger Moths from Stag Lane prior to delivery, and in some soupy winter weather, Francis Bradbrooke, correspondent for *The Aeroplane*, touched on points with which later generations of Tiger Moth pilots might beg to disagree:

'When flying the machine has most of the standard Moth characteristics with all its sensitiveness on the elevators and lightness on ailerons. Like the other Moths it can be turned by the use of aileron alone without need for ruddering, but unlike the great majority of light aeroplanes it will fly a perfectly straight course with both hands and feet off the controls at cruising speed. When throttled down a slight swing to the left sets in.

'When the rudder bar is left alone the machine can be turned to the right quite readily by means of aileron and elevator but the left hand turn only begins after some sideslipping, presumably because the slipstream swirl imparts a right handed tendency which is overcome when the rudder is held solidly as part of the fin, but not so well when the rudder floats free.

'The slot locking device made possible a comparative experiment which we have never previously been able to make on a Moth, or any other machine with ailerons on the bottom wings only.

'The Tiger Moth can just be kept straight at 40 indicated mph with the slots locked shut. At less than this speed, with the rudder straight, a brisk right handed spin develops. An equally brisk left hand spin can be induced by the rudder.

'With slots free there is no difficulty in keeping straight at 35mph but the nose cannot be kept up to that speed except in successive pull ups, unless the engine is used to provide a little slipstream for the elevators. With extreme use of all controls a spin in either direction can be started, even with slats open, but we did not stay in to see what happened because too much right hand spinning makes us come all over queer abdominally.

'The windshields are quite as effective as usual but we should have preferred a sinkable seat so that when the excellent visibility is not vital, as on cross country flights, we could retire into seclusion out of the fresh air. We are becoming cabin conscious. When we mentioned this point to Mr Broad he said that this feature of up and down seats, adjustable while flying, was being incorporated'.

Writing a series of reminiscences 50 years after Francis Bradbrooke's contribution had appeared in *The Aeroplane*, John Fricker wrote of the Tiger Moth:

Like all de Havilland aeroplanes of the 1930s, the Tiger Moth is somewhat short of vertical fin area and directional stability. Application of the non-Frise and wide-chord ailerons on the lower mainplanes also results in generous amounts of adverse yaw, despite their differential action, calling for further and carefully co-ordinated use of the sensitive rudder.

In December 1932, K2578 (1750), arrived at Martlesham Heath to begin flutter trials, with the result that having dived the aircraft to 215mph IAS, mass balance weights were recommended for attachment to the ailerons. K2570 (1742), joined the programme in February 1933, spending additional time investigating the inverted envelope from 120mph to the stall which was recorded at 60mph.

K2583 (1755), one of the 1932 CFS Team, began trials on 13th November 1933 which resulted in a report the following January recommending mass balancing of the rudder, a feature not universally accepted, and never fitted to Tiger Moths later manufactured in Australia. At Martlesham Heath, Tiger Moth K2583 had been temporarily loaned the mass balanced rudder of DH.60M K1864 (1604), an aircraft posted in during September from communications duties on behalf of the Air Ministry's 'Air Defence of Great Britain' organisation, and herself scheduled for further flight investigation of DH.60 aileron control. The rudder was returned in good order to permit K1864 to take up a new post with 24 Squadron early in 1934.

de Havilland were particularly keen to sell into overseas markets, and their network of local agents and associated companies always had a demonstration aircraft on hand with which to entertain potential customers. The company policy directed from the Sales Office at Stag Lane and later at Hatfield required that agents bought their own demonstrators and payment was required prior to delivery, a policy not always appreciated, but one which safeguarded the business structure.

Where a large or prestigious order was in prospect, especially from an overseas government, it was not unusual for de Havilland to dispatch one of their own demonstration aircraft, flown by a pilot from the home team or possibly a dependable freelancer hired in for the occasion. In December 1931, in the depths of the Swedish winter, DH test pilot Hubert Broad drew the short straw, and flew DH.60T Tiger Moth G-ABNJ (1727), upgraded to the latest specification, to the military airfield at Barkarby, north of Stockholm and mid-way to Uppsala, where in conditions of extreme cold and deep snow, he demonstrated the open cockpit biplane over several days to government officials and Air Force officers. It was something of a change from the trials flown by this same aeroplane under designation 'E.5' at Martlesham Heath the previous August, but Broad's considerable talent as a sales representative in addition to his flying skills, assisted in selling the developed aeroplane, quite literally. G-ABNJ remained in Sweden, sold to the Air Force, with whom she operated under the designation Sk.11, and with serial Fv6562, until July 1934. It was an important sale which led to an order for 12 DH.82 Tiger Moths and licensed manufacture of both the DH.82 and DH.82A in pre-war Sweden.

Before the war, few would have denied that the most famous display of flying in Europe, was the annual RAF Pageant at Hendon. Following the 13th Pageant on the last Monday of June in 1932, the Air Ministry encouraged members of the Society of British Aircraft Constructors (SBAC) to set up shop at Hendon and to exhibit their latest airframes and engines to an exclusive list of guests specially invited from around the world.

de Havilland flew three aircraft into Hendon from Stag Lane, just a few miles over the hedge: Gipsy III versions of the DH.80 Puss Moth, DH.83 Fox Moth and DH.82 Tiger Moth. *Flight* thought it a capital idea allowing visitors to make the acquaintance of these new machines in the flesh, but in contrast to their effusive descriptions of the Puss Moth's 'comfort' and Fox Moth's 'obvious economy' leaving a marked impression on the visitors, no welcoming words were reserved for the new Tiger Moth.

In October 1932 at 30 years of age, Christopher Clarkson was already into his third year of retirement as a veteran instructor from the RAF Central Flying School. For this gifted pilot, retirement actually meant establishing the Aviation Department of the famous Selfridges' London departmental store, operating from the Heston base of old school chum and business partner Brian Lewis, later Lord Essendon.

Brian Lewis & Co Ltd had been appointed British agents for de Havilland aeroplanes in an interesting arrangement announced in March 1932, and which divided England into three business regions, although the agents' offices were all within a radius of 25 miles of one another: Brian Lewis at Heston, Brooklands Aviation at Weybridge and Phillips and Powis at Woodley. Stag Lane/Hatfield controlled sales in Northern Ireland, Scotland and Wales.

The CFS aerobatic team was part of an impressive show of RAF support at the opening of Portsmouth airport in July 1932. Dihedral on the Tiger Moth's top wings appears to have been reduced to zero or even minus, probably in the quest to improve the quality of sustained inverted flight. via Mike Jerram

When the manufacturer was called upon to demonstrate the Tiger Moth in Lisbon competing for a trainer aircraft contract for the Portuguese military, Christopher Clarkson was recruited as pilot nominee.

The contemporary demonstration aircraft was G-ABYJ (3137), registered to the de Havilland Aircraft Co Ltd on 14th July 1932 and issued with a Certificate of Airworthiness (C of A) eight days later. Apart from a long range fuel tank installed forward of the front cockpit, G-ABYJ had been fitted with an uprated version of the Gipsy III engine, the new Gipsy Major, production number 5003, and was listed in the de Havilland inventory as a DH.82A. She carried the legend 'Tiger Moth' inelegantly stencilled in six inch capital letters along the fuselage sides, coincident with the bottom hinge-line of the front cockpit doors. At least showing some consistency, all reference to the aeroplane in surviving de Havilland documents identify her as 'G-ABYT' due to nothing more sinister than bad hand-writing or third copy typed memos one suspects.

G-ABYJ was flown to Lisbon early in September, transiting via Paris, Tours, Biarritz and Burgos. On previous occasions a routing via Madrid had resulted in Clarkson using his hat as a petrol filter due to the primitive state of the refuelling facilities, but apart from that disincentive the city was not on the direct routing, and he had not been asked to make a diplomatic landing there.

On arrival in Lisbon three other aircraft were found to be competing for the same business: a Bluebird from Blackburn Aircraft flown by an old friend, Patrick Johnson, a Fleet Trainer and an Italian Caproni Ca.100, built with DH.60 parts supplied by de Havilland and which was soon eliminated in spite and because of, its confused pedigree, a situation richly exploited by the de Havilland team. The Bluebird went next because the military did not like the side-by-side seating arrangement, an ideal which to save trouble and expense, could have been transmitted to Blackburn before arrival. Johnson threw in his lot with the Tiger Moth, exhibiting a broad band of patriotism in an effort to unsettle the obvious pretensions of the American Fleet.

During exercises held over the next few days, Johnson climbed out onto the wing of the Tiger Moth in flight in an effort to prove the strength of the airframe after the pilot of the Fleet had been seen on the ground, jumping on and off his tailplane in an effort to demonstrate a similar point. A few days before an aerobatic competition which had been arranged at the local aero club, the Fleet went to Madrid for a presentation to the Spanish Air Force, but forced landed due to the loss of a cylinder during the return flight to Lisbon, and effectively was ruled out. But Fleet supporters managed to delay the contest by a week in view of the forecast weather conditions, which in spite of their prognosis, turned out bright and clear.

With the aid of the local agent, Carlos Bleck, authority was secured for the two British aircraft to fly a mild aerobatic display over an exhibition site situated on a hillside, followed by a loop and a roll over the local football stadium where the host country was to play Spain.

What happened after that is best expressed by Clarkson himself:

'All our long years of RAF training and discipline found their reward that sunny day in Lisbon. Never before and never again could such a thing happen. We worked out a beautiful programme. Johnson on the Bluebird and I on the Tiger Moth. Fix the exhibition first, we thought, then maybe stop the soccer match.

'The field was good and big and lent itself to some low flying. After that? Well, why not fly upside down in formation above the main street from the top of the hill to the harbour? It had a gentle slope which just about took care of the sinking speed of an inverted Moth or Bluebird. And so it was.

'In an effort to prove the strength of the structure'.

If it was enjoyed by the participants, it certainly was by the populace. All the populace, that is, except the protagonists of the Fleet who realised too late that we had got away with a publicity stunt of far, far greater value than the local aero club meeting. And for the participants, it was nice to think that they had at least been able to fly upside down along the main avenue of a European capital and not be clapped in jail. What we did not know, however, was that there were wires of some sort strung across our path. But we missed them.'

The promised aerobatic competition was held at the local aero club as planned, but the Fleet did not manage to get back to Lisbon in time, and the Tiger Moth in the hands of Christopher Clarkson took all the honours, securing the contract for de Havilland. Soon after, and at another venue, the engine of the Fleet Trainer failed again, during a low level aerobatic display, and the aircraft crashed, killing the pilot.

Tiger Moth G-ABYJ returned to a demonstration career with her makers at Stag Lane where she was modified in December to accept a revised exhaust system, a long tail pipe which curved gracefully back underneath the fuselage, terminating at the trailing edge of the lower wings. It was in this configuration that Clarkson was invited to display her at the Saint Germain Aviation Meeting on 22nd May 1933, an event held annually at the picturesque aerodrome situated a few miles south west of the centre of Paris, on the edge of the Bois de Boulogne, and within sight of the Eiffel Tower.

Following the flight of a 'chicken-coop' Farman which carried Miss Paris 1933 around the circuit, an 'International Stunting Exhibition' was opened by Gerhard Fiesler piloting his new biplane, the Tiger II, powered by a 420hp Walter engine which, should there have been any confusion over names, certainly distinguished it from the 130hp of de Havilland's Tiger Moth. Clarkson was introduced as 'the well known English aerobatic pilot' whose display was reported as *'... a novel exhibition of crazy flying. Side-slipping around the field, letting one wheel touch on the ground, then rising a short height, as if bouncing up, and again letting a wheel touch on the ground, Clarkson encircled the aerodrome, having his plane under perfect control all the time. All of his evolutions in the air, barrel rolls, loopings, nose dives etc., were all done in that smooth continuous manner that has so often been admired in the Royal Air Force displays'.*

Like all other demonstrators, G-ABYJ soon was passed on, making way for another factory fresh example. She joined de Havilland's fleet at White Waltham where she was operated on behalf of 13 ERFTS, by which time she had been fitted with a new Gipsy Major engine, No 5519. On 13th July 1936, a pilot with eight hours solo time was authorised to conduct forced landing practice at the Relief Landing Ground (RLG) at Winkfield. During one approach, excess height was lost by attempting gliding turns to left and right, but the aircraft stalled at low level and crashed causing damage from which the airframe failed to recover. G-ABYJ was replaced on the establishment of 13 ERFTS by G-AEMF (3514), delivered to White Waltham following issue of her Certificate of Airworthiness on 19th September, and fitted with G-ABYJ's Gipsy Major engine, No 5519.

At Stag Lane the Sales Department had redesigned their brochures and a standard Price List appeared in November 1931 under designation 'Form 253' which initially was re-published in a modified form every two months, not because the price was increasing at an alarming rate, but rather as the requirement to include extras and options for which verified prices to supply and fit could be quoted. Although Price List No 2 dated January 1932 had been subjected to a mild attack of updating by typewriter prior to publication of List No 3 in March, the changes reflected the rapid progression of modification, development and customer requirements.

The heading 'Equipment' as specified in the early and amended DH.60T leaflet had been revised to read 'Normal Standard Fixed Equipment' but still carried details of seats, harness and controls. The option for special wide doors had been deleted but replaced with a note that cushions could be supplied as standard but only if specified during the sales' negotiations. The information on colour remained as before, except the subject was referred to as the 'Normal Standard' colour scheme, and the spelling of 'aluminium' had been corrected. Whereas the price for supply and fitting of certain lighting electrics and instruments had been reduced, the cost of installing remote control gear for the Hythe Mk.IIIA camera gun had almost doubled to 15 guineas, reflecting the difficulties introduced by incorporation of the mechanism.

Hughes IIIA compasses were mounted on top of the control boxes in both cockpits, forward of the stick position, excepting when Marconi AD22 wireless (or as specified) was fitted in the front cockpit. In this configuration it was necessary to move the compass to a port side shelf where it effectively blanked off the low speed scale of the engine revolution indicator, but left the right side of the cockpit clear for installation of the wireless trailing aerial reel and winch.

Handley Page automatic slots had always been a feature of de Havilland aeroplanes scheduled for club or training duties, and were a safety device recommended by the manufacturer, at extra cost, especially so after Captain de Havilland's famously public accident during the demonstration of an experimentally slotted DH.60 Moth at Stag Lane in March 1928. The aeroplane was wrecked but the pilot walked away unscathed and the press was there by invitation, to report the event in graphic detail but not quite from the angle they had expected. Accident inspectors thereafter nearly always recorded whether the subject aircraft had been fitted with slots or not.

All Tiger Moths ordered by the Air Ministry were fitted with slots on delivery as part of the standard specification. Only the six aircraft operated by the CFS formation team during the summer of 1932, flew with the slots removed, and then only on a temporary basis.

Perhaps the de Havilland Aircraft Company was being honest with its customers when it quoted the cost of supplying and fitting slots to a Tiger Moth early in 1932 as £18.0s.0d with a further ten guineas required for a cockpit locking device. An *additional* sum of £38.11s.6d was to be paid to Handley Page Ltd as a royalty on each set fitted. There is every reason to suppose that this burden was the main reason why the company did not fit the devices to its own demonstrator aircraft until they were sold or re-deployed, when the cost could be recovered from the client.

Items of subsidiary equipment specified by an early export order to Persia, and which filtered into the first few issues of the price lists as an incentive to prospectives, included a drinking water tank and a ration box in each cockpit, neither of which could have been treated as anything short of emergency equipment, although as a subject of its own, that particular title was never used in any published schedule of spare parts.

The Persian order, booked against the name of the Imperial Persian Army Flying Corps, was for 20 aeroplanes, serialled 101-120, and which were allocated production slots 17-36, relatively early positions from which the customer could dictate specification and terms. But the manufacturer was not unhappy: the order for 20 unified aircraft had been won after mutually beneficial negotiations between Francis St Barbe with the assistance of the General Production Manager, Harry Povey, in Berne. The Persian delegation was impressed with the de Havilland approach to business which required cash payments in advance and the balance before delivery. St Barbe knew that other manufacturers had offered better terms including a promise to accept local produce as part-payment, a potentially disastrous spiral into which he refused to be drawn. It was a good start; there was the promise of additional orders, and design and stress work originated as a result could always be carried forward for 'off the shelf' availability to other potentially interested customers.

A modification to satisfy the Flying Corps' requirement for the aerobatic weight to be increased by 100lb to 1,750lb was achieved by strengthening the front spars of the top mainplanes by adding ash 'packing pieces' (cappings) and doubling up on some rib lattice slats. When introduced to the Tiger Moth in October 1931, *Flight's* correspondent had assumed that the next logical step in development would be an all metal wing, and this was perhaps the opportunity to provide one, but at no time as a result of any of the subsequent discussions regarding an upgrade of the aeroplane was a metal wing put forward as a subject for further investigation. The Persian Army also specified Fairey-Reed fixed pitch metal propellers to be fitted to their Gipsy III engines. Coincident with these changes and in order to publicise the multi-role military potential of the Tiger Moth, a 16 page booklet was published dedicated solely to this matter and for which performance figures for the new Gipsy Major powered DH.82A were available for inclusion.

Engineering practice and a degree of common sense ruled that the cylinders and heads of an aero engine should, perhaps, be

Some of the first batch of 20 DH.82 Tiger Moths ordered on behalf of the Imperial Persian Army Flying Corps in 1932 under construction at Stag Lane. Serial numbers appear to have been applied to the top surfaces of the upper mainplanes. *The Aeroplane*

One of the few pre-war British civil Tiger Moths, DH.82A G-ABUL, was used by Alan Cobham's National Aviation Day and in this photograph was displaying from a field at Skipton, Yorkshire, in June 1932. A propeller driven pump and a drain tube seen attached to the undercarriage are probably part of the kit to permit sustained inverted flight. Leonard Porter positioned above the crankcase, protected from the deluge of oil that surely would otherwise engulf them. But if the engine could be arranged to run efficiently when 'inverted' not only would the top cowling line provide a better forward view for the pilot, but the thrust line would be raised providing a greater ground clearance for the propeller tips or alternatively, an opportunity for blades of a greater diameter and higher efficiency. Major Frank Halford and his engine design team considered the problem and after relatively straightforward modifications were applied to a Gipsy II, the engine was persuaded to run 'upside-down' by Eric Mitchell in the Experimental Department at Stag Lane in 1929. The team had created the Gipsy III for an increase in weight of 7lb, and the engine was tested in a DH.80 Moth Three (later renamed Puss Moth), for which type in early production, it became the standard power unit.

Further development of the Gipsy III, which in the DH.82 Tiger Moth was inclined to overheat when the climb speed was too low, included an increase in bore from 114mm to 118mm, raising the capacity from 5.71 to 6.12 litres, and the maximum output by 10hp to 130hp, a figure achieved at 2,350rpm. The improved engine was initially designated Gipsy IIIA, but the military connection was considered vital, and the name Gipsy Major was adopted on full production in 1932. Unprecedented for aero engines of the period, the Gipsy Major I was introduced into service with an overhaul life of 450 hours, a 50% increase over the Gipsy I of 1927. By July 1933, the figure had risen to 750 hours, and by August 1937 the value had been extended to the accompaniment of universal acclaim, to the magic one thousand. And even that was not the end of the story.

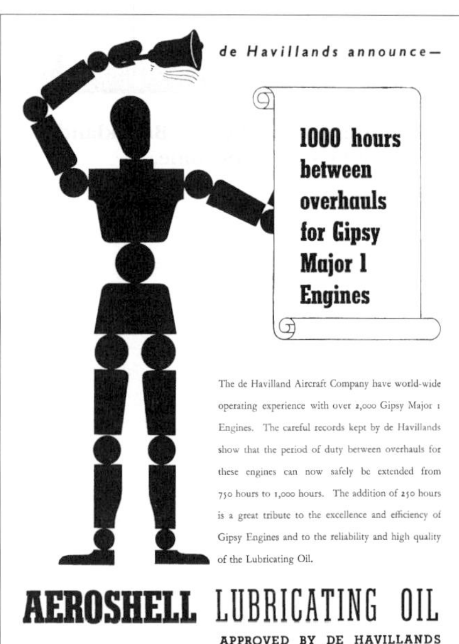

The Gipsy Major I overhaul life of 1,000 hrs was remarkable for the time, and a fact quickly recognised by the oil suppliers.

Until production of the Gipsy III was halted, potential customers were offered DH.82 Tiger Moths with a choice of either engine, although the Gipsy Major powered aircraft attracted a small premium of slightly less than 5%, increasing the ex-factory price to £1,095. And what could be expected for the money? At the same maximum permitted all up weight of 1,825lb, the performance variation offered by the extra power of the Gipsy Major was neither startling nor surprising. Maximum speeds at all levels up to 10,000ft were about 4mph greater than the Gipsy III model, 109mph quoted at sea level reducing to 99mph at 10,000ft, and the cruising speed of 93mph maintained the average difference. Petrol consumption had risen by 4 pints to 6 gallons per hour reducing the miles per gallon by slightly more than half a mile. Operating with a fuel capacity quoted as 18 gallons (later increased to 19 gallons), ultimate range was reduced slightly by little more than 4% to 279 miles.

In all other respects, the new engine improved basic performance as anticipated with a reduction by some 17 yards to achieve a take-off run of 156 yards measured from a standing start to lift off.

In 1933, performance was calculated against criteria defined by the Paris based International Commission of Air Navigation (ICAN), a necessary regulation which permitted easier acceptance of performance values obtained world-wide which could be judged against the same benchmark.

One curiosity of the system was in timing the take-off run. A Gipsy Major powered Tiger Moth at maximum authorised weight was clocked at 12 seconds for 'take-off' compared with just over 13 for the Gipsy III variant and 16 or 18 seconds for a similarly loaded seaplane. A parameter deleted from the system of performance analysis universally adopted in 1939 included aircraft height after take-off, measured 500 metres 'from rest'. Figures quoted as 119ft and 143ft respectively served to confirm the better rate of climb on 130hp: 673 feet per minute at sea level, an improvement of 15% over the Gipsy III.

For an aircraft designed primarily for circuit training, the thought of a service ceiling of 13,600ft operating at maximum weight behind the Gipsy Major might have seemed fairly academic, (12,100ft for the Gipsy III), or an absolute value of 18,100ft at normal weight (1,650lb) compared with 16,800ft. But de Havilland's main thrust early in 1933, and for some time to follow, was to promote acceptance of the Tiger Moth as a multi-role military training aircraft, under which heading bomb aiming and photographic reconnaissance from such altitudes would have been normal operational practice.

During the summer vacation of 1932, two young students, F Naish and F Page, using published data, constructed a formula from which the relative efficiency of a range of fully laden civil aircraft could be generated and the resultant 'unit values' compared. Although their endeavours were not intended to be anything but light hearted, the results were published in the aviation press. Several de Havilland aircraft were included but DH.82 analysis was limited to the Gipsy III powerplant:

DH.83 Fox Moth (Gipsy Major)	56.2
DH.83 Fox Moth (Gipsy III)	52.0
DH.60GIII Moth Major (Gipsy Major)	50.4
DH.82 Tiger Moth (Gipsy III)	46.2
DH.60G Gipsy Moth (Gipsy II)	45.3

Seriously intentioned or not, de Havilland might have been alarmed to see that in the complete list, the most efficient aircraft judged against the common formula at 59.7, was a Percival Gull powered by a Cirrus Hermes IV engine.

Upgrading of the basic DH.82 Tiger Moth into the Gipsy Major powered 'A' model was the result of natural development, allied to the considerable experience gained from operation of the 103 Gipsy III powered DH.82s listed in the de Havilland order of manufacture. The transition from DH.60T Tiger Moth (Gipsy III) to DH.82 Tiger Moth (Gipsy III) with DH.60T Moth Trainers (Gipsy I and Gipsy II) and DH.60M Metal Moths (Gipsy I and Gipsy II) on the factory floor at the same time, appears to have been handled by the progress clerks with some equanimity, but a greater clarity of order was introduced when the DH.82 Tiger Moth was issued with its own unique series of works' identification numbers commencing from No.3100, an unregistered aircraft shipped early in 1932 to Arnhold & Co, de Havilland's successful agent in Shanghai.

Although the first 'A' designated Tiger Moth is listed as G-ABUL (3107), the original airframe was merely re-engined with a Gipsy Major for use by Sir Alan Cobham and his National Aviation Day Display during the 1933 season.

The company demonstrator G-ABYJ and an aircraft ordered for the Deutscher Reichverkenes Ministerium in Berlin, (D-2357/3142), and to which a British certificate of airworthiness was issued in October 1932, were similarly, production DH.82 airframes fitted with the new engine. In contrast, the Bristol Aeroplane Company accepted delivery of a pair of basic DH.82 aircraft, complete with Gipsy III engines (G-ACZY/3315 and G-ACZZ/3316) as late as December 1934. These were the last of the Gipsy III powered Tiger Moths, and followed two others, G-ACVK (3224) and G-ACVL (3225), which had been delivered the previous July, no doubt to maintain standardisation of the Filton based fleet.

DEVELOPING MARKET SHARE

The facilities established by Brooklands Aviation at Sywell aerodrome, Northamptonshire, for operation of 6 ERFTS. Nearly all the buildings have survived, have been improved and added to, and are in current use.
Richard Riding

WITH THE INSTALLATION of the first Gipsy Major I engines in the summer of 1932, the opportunity was also taken to tidy up, standardise and refine the airframe. The fabric covered hoop and stringer arrangement which formed the rear fuselage top decking, was replaced with a single construction which encapsulated the production subtleties of bending a ply skin around three bulkheads, one front and one rear, both incorporating variable radii and differences in depth and width, while maintaining an unkinked curved surface which tapered and sloped over a length of eight and a half feet! Adding further complication was a cut-out for the luggage locker door situated just behind the rear cockpit on the starboard side. But de Havilland was a company rich with experience in designing and building wooden aeroplanes, and the new rear decking which, in unity with the wooden structures forward of each cockpit were known officially and confusingly as 'cowls', used less resource and a tiny fraction of that knowledge which soon would be focused on a unique racing aeroplane, a four engined transatlantic mail carrying airliner, and a military twin of sensational performance and adaptability.

The rear cowl was part of a series of improvements already on the drawing board in the spring of 1932, and which were progressively leached into the approval system. In the light of experience and for the sake of expediency, further changes were made to the top wings to introduce a standard maximum aerobatic weight of 1,750lb. Simple modifications to the front spar root end fittings reduced bending moments in the wing bays, and eliminated the requirement for the ash cappings first fitted to the Persian aircraft. On paper, the facility for adjusting the rear seat was removed although there are no references to one ever having been fitted. Hubert Broad once responded to criticism of the lack of an adjustable seat with a remark that implied the deficiency was being addressed. An extra gallon was engineered into the centre section fuel tank by

Seen at Baginton, Coventry, in 1960, in company with other stock British aircraft of the period, DH.82A Tiger Moth G-ADIA was then operated by Northamptonshire Aero Club at Sywell which explains the pseudo Brooklands Aviation colour scheme. Maurice Marsh

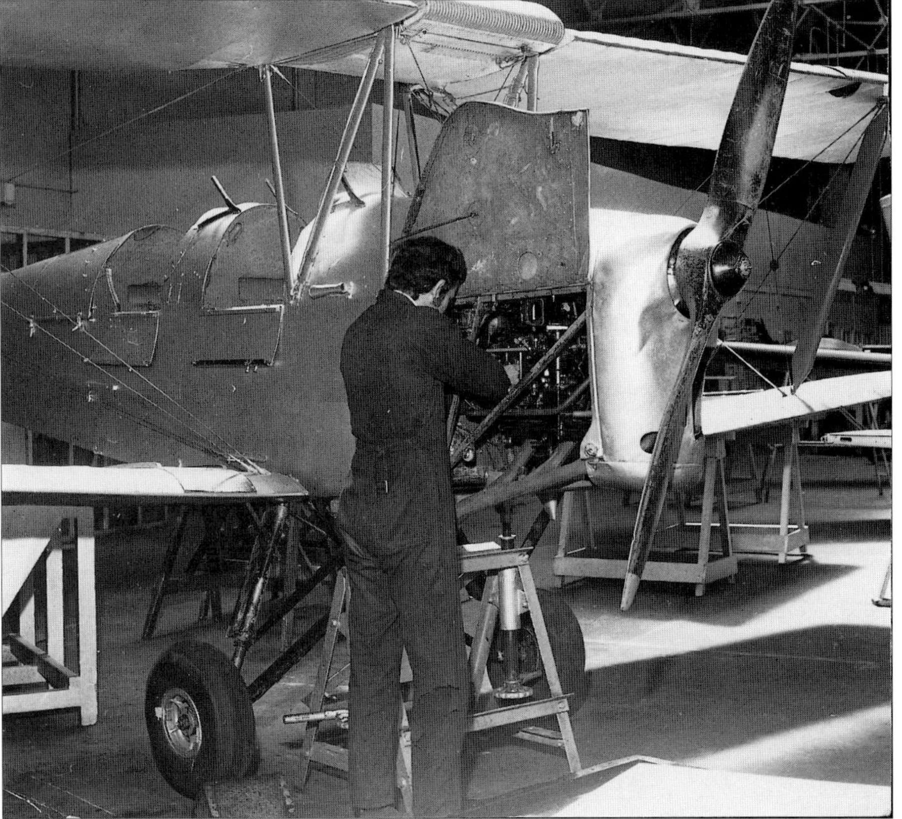

Maximum deflection on the side cowling of a Tiger Moth permits easy and unhindered access to the Gipsy Major engine. In the jacked up 'flying position' the tail has to be anchored to prevent the aircraft tipping forward onto her nose. *The Aeroplane*

rounding out the leading edge. First aircraft to take advantage of the new engine, revised weights and rear cowl construction was work's No 3148, supplied with the serial 33-1 to the Aeronautical Department of the Ministry of War in Madrid at the end of 1932.

The evident military connection between the civilian contractors and their Reserve School aircraft was maintained by an order from the Air Ministry in 1932 for seven DH.82 Tiger Moths for operation by the Bristol Aeroplane Company. The first of these, G-ACBA (3152), was delivered in February 1933 with white civil letters on her purple and black fuselage, (the wings were painted custard yellow), but a cockpit equipped for blind flying and provision for a camera gun, Aldis sight and a P.7 camera installation. There is no reason to believe the equipment was not still on board when G-ACBA collided with a Hawker Hart over Filton in May 1939 and was destroyed in the subsequent crash.

The request by Brooklands Aviation that provision for a floor mounted P14 camera, and installation of a camera gun and sight should be made in each of the eleven new aircraft scheduled for delivery to 6 Elementary and Reserve Flying Training School (ERFTS) at Sywell during the early summer of 1935 was answered by clearance of the equipment in the first of the batch, G-ADGS (3337), on 29th May. This was less than three weeks after a further nominal increase in the maximum permitted aerobatic weight had been authorised, rising by a mere 20lb to 1,770lb. The rise was necessary to accommodate the gently creeping increase in basic weight, and without physical modification was applied retrospectively and equally to all civil and service aircraft which currently enjoyed a 1,750lb aerobatic maximum.

G-ADGS provided faithful service at Sywell from June 1935 until 1944 when as BB705, an impressment serial adopted from September 1940, she was transferred to the Royal Navy. Surviving the war and the rigours of demobilisation in 1951, she was used as a source of spares by Rollason Aircraft at Croydon until with no more to offer, she was ignominiously burned on a Guy Fawkes bonfire at the Fiveways Night Club, Purley, in 1956.

A year after her unveiling, the DH.82's port and starboard front fuselage side frames were redesigned to delete the complications surrounding the deep door at the front cockpit position, now considered unnecessary in view of the greater ease of egress. The requirement had necessitated a massive kink in the natural line of the top longeron, and the tidied assembly effectively created a straight edge running from the front cups on the engine bearers to the top of the fuselage sternpost. Front and rear cockpit doors were thus standardised, for a short while at least, and certainly until instrument flying 'under the hood' became a greater part of the military's daily routine.

Final customers for the basic DH82 model, although fitted with the Gipsy Major engine, were the Portuguese Ministry of War in Lisbon who took eleven (3159-3169), all delivered without military serial numbers, and Haerens Flyvertropper, the Danish Army Air Corps. Their five DH.82 Tiger Moths (3170-3174), acquired at a total cost of £5,910.10s.10d, and identified on the Air Corps inventory as Type 1S (School aircraft, Trainer type), were shipped on board the SS *Margrethe* in March 1933. On arrival at the Flying School at Lundtofte, the aircraft were issued with serial numbers S-358 to S-362, changed a year later to S1-S5, coincident with a change of base to Vaerlose.

The first civil Tiger Moth built at Stag Lane which incorporated all the cleared design improvements in addition to installation of the Gipsy Major I, was No 3175. Registered G-ACDA to the de Havilland Aircraft Co Ltd at Hatfield on 6th February 1933, this machine is acknowledged as the first definitive DH.82A, and was one of a batch of ten scheduled for service with the de Havilland School of Flying, operating on behalf of the Royal Air Force Reserve. The new Tiger Moths were to replace weary Armstrong Siddeley Jaguar powered DH.9Js which had been operated specifically for advanced training alongside a dedicated 'Reserve Only' fleet of DH.60 Moths.

Before delivery to Hatfield, and immediately after qualification for her civil Certificate of Airworthiness on 10th March 1933, G-ACDA flew a series of trials at the Aeroplane and Armament Experimental Establishment (A&AEE) Martlesham Heath, not only as a matter of routine expected of all civil prototypes, especially in view of the number of changes incorporated since the type's last visit, but also with a view to the military future. Later that same year G-ACDA and her sister aircraft G-ACDB (3176), were used to test experimental wooden propellers of relatively fine pitch but principally of new construction. As an exercise, the Airscrew Company of Weybridge had built one propeller to de Havilland design 5220/H entirely from birch, and another with inner core of traditional mahogany, but outer laminations of birch. The material had been selected from a small sample of boards tested at RAE Farnborough in connection with airscrew research on behalf of the Air Ministry. The two Tiger Moths were chosen as test vehicles because of their expected high utilisation during Reserve School operations, such that a steady plot of condition could be maintained following regular 25 hourly inspections from October until the end of 1933.

While the first Tiger Moths at Grantham were being posted away and replaced on a temporary basis by the assuredly more expensive Avro Tutor, the Air Ministry was professing acute awareness of the constant need for economy, and in March 1934 announced an order for 50 DH.82A Tiger Moths, to be known as Tiger Moth Mk. II. Unlike the first batch, all were to be delivered by surface, less engines, to RAF Kenley, between November 1934 and the following February. Manufactured to specification T.26/33 under contract No 307395/34, the aircraft were to carry serial numbers K4242 to K4291 (3238-3287), and eventual allocation was to be throughout the Royal Air Force mostly not as trainer aircraft, but to serve with squadrons and station flights, communications units, practice flights, and an army co-operation unit.

In 1935 under a British Government initiative created in the Air Estimates of March the previous year, the Air Training Plan expanded the four civilian operated Reserve Schools at Bristol, Brough, Hamble and Hatfield to offer primary training in a pseudo-military environment, to large numbers of cadet pilots who either were streamed straight into a Royal Air Force career, or remained in their civilian occupations but joined the RAF Volunteer Reserve (RAFVR). From August the scheme required civilian pupils to complete their courses at the newly designated Elementary and Reserve Flying Training Schools (ERFTS) in eight weeks as opposed to 12 months at an RAF Service Flying Training School (SFTS). In addition to 50 hours flying, a mixture of dual and solo, each course included a comprehensive range of classroom studies. Nine more ERFTSs were established in1936 and a further 20 the following year.

DH.82A G-ACDA in the colours of the de Havilland School of Flying, picketed in company with an unidentified sister aircraft, Waco U1C G-ACGJ and other types at an away event, probably in 1934. Richard Riding

DH.82A Tiger Moth K4288 cavorting above the clouds when on strength with 18 ERFTS Fairoaks in 1938. Note the code number '3' painted unusually on the top decking behind the rear cockpit. deHMC Archive

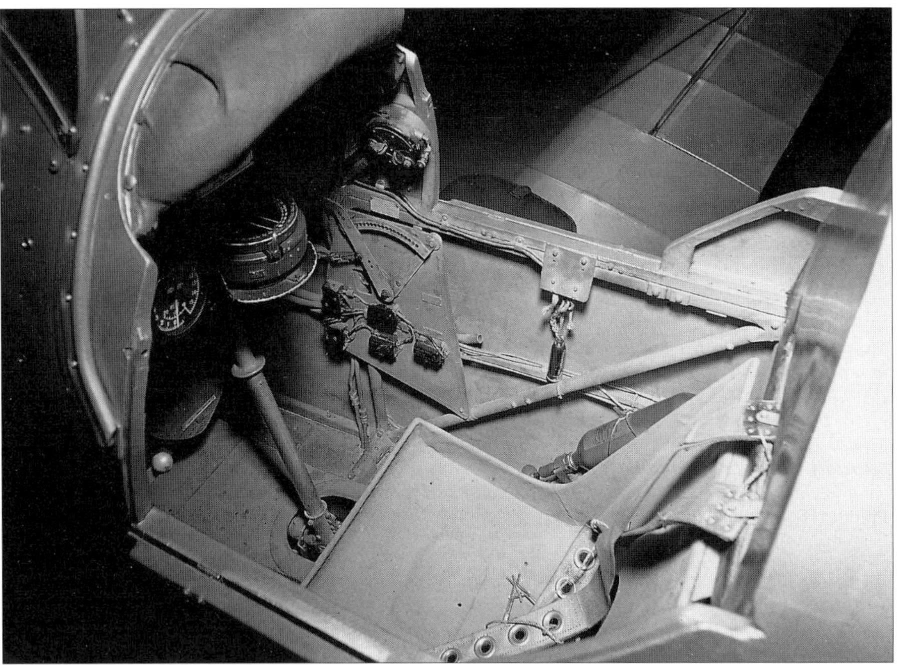

A general view of the rear cockpit of a post-war RAF DH.82A Tiger Moth showing the electrical fuse panel below the Morse tapper; junction box for the electric intercom with an RAF type socket; fire extinguisher; parachute seat pan and Sutton harness. via British Aerospace

The Tiger Moth Mk II military specification called for a number of detail changes and minor modifications in and around the cockpits which were drawn up between April and October 1934 as the result of substantial operational experience at de Havilland's Reserve School. K4242 (3238), was nominated for performance trials at Martlesham Heath in September and November 1934, and prior to delivery in December 1934, K4288 (3244), was selected as a representative aircraft for further tests: the blind flying hood attachment was modified to permit a greater tension in the elastic cords which held it in the erected position; the auto slot pulley brackets were revised and alterations to the safety harnesses were called up to conform to changing service requirements. The accumulator was repositioned to the front cockpit floor where it was held between the rudder bar supports on a plywood surface specially prepared against damage from anticipated acid spillage. It was the only position for the accumulator owing to centre of gravity limitations, and special protection was necessary when an auxiliary fuel tank was installed inside the wooden cowl just above it. It was not a totally satisfactory arrangement and all that de Havilland could argue was that they had made the accumulator lid and leads 'as petrol tight as possible'.

Additional changes were incorporated against Drawing Office Instructions (DOIs), by which method de Havilland could assess their suitability, or not, as the result of in-service use, prior to committing to approved drawings and the laborious procedure of subsequent amendment. Enduring changes made after October 1934 included spacer plates for the dualled external rudder cables, a board to mount fuse box and terminal block, deletion of the master switch and provision of an amazingly intricate thin brass frame screwed to the inside walls of the cockpit cowls, whose sole purpose was to house a compass correction card or performance data plate. In subsequent revisions, K4242-K4265 were all modified to accept navigation lights on the tips of both upper mainplanes and the trailing edge of the rudder, while all 50 aircraft were subject of petrol drain pipe modifications following engine installation by the RAF.

At a later date, two small modifications were introduced without which a Tiger Moth could almost be labelled an imposter. Square cut doors could not easily be opened by the occupant of the rear cockpit when an instrument hood assembly was fitted, but by the simple expedient of cutting off the bottom rear corners, and replacing them with amazingly complex and handed, curved fabrications in plywood and spruce, glued, pinned and screwed to the rear decking superstructure, and officially listed as 'fillings', the pilot regained his freedom. British built aircraft acquired the Mk. VIIA pitot/static head with its characteristic bend, (Mod No. 19), a feature intended to protect the system from the ingress of rain water.

Distribution of the 50 new aeroplanes from Kenley was extraordinarily protracted and especially so in view of the stated aims for economy: as a basic training machine, only three aircraft were posted to 1 FTS Leuchars between September 1935 and October the following year; one went to 14 ERFTS at Castle Bromwich on formation of the establishment at the beginning of July 1937, and six others to 16 ERFTS at Shoreham at the same time. Four aircraft were posted overseas: K4252 and K4255 to RAF Hinaidi, Iraq in January and March 1936 respectively, as replacements for a pair of DH.60M Metal Moths on charge with the Iraq Communications Flight, and K4253 to Singapore, but the aircraft appears to have been diverted to Aden where she was with 8 Squadron in June 1937, joining Vickers Vincents and Hawker Demons at Khormaksar.

Tiger Moth K4259 (3255), spent some time with 24 (Communications) Squadron at Hendon before a period of storage at Waddington, but in June 1937 the aircraft was loaned to the British Air Attaché in Paris for a month before returning to serve with 19 ERFTS at Gatwick. It was there during a sunny day in March 1939 that K4259 managed to taxy into Hawker Audax K7461 which was hidden in a shadow. The aeroplane completed a war service training career with a number of Elementary Schools and was one of the last operational Tiger Moths on the RAF inventory, honourably retiring from the Grading Unit at Kirton in Lindsey in 1953. As a civil aircraft registered G-ANMO, but painted in RAF camouflage, the aircraft was involved in a spectacular mid-air collision with Stampe SV-4 G-AYGR during an air display at Weston-super-Mare on 30th July 1972, and the wreckage was sold, subsequently to be placed in store as spares for prospective rebuilding projects in Oxfordshire, Northamptonshire and Ayrshire. Gathered together again from January 1987 by Ted Lay at Didcot, the aircraft was gradually re-assembled, and painted in the colours she wore during her last RAF commission, 'K4259' was flown again from White Waltham in July 1997.

K4284 (3280), was allocated to the use of the British Air Attaché in Berlin in December 1937 and the sensitivity of the posting required that the aircraft be operated in civilian guise. Registration G-AERM was allocated under the ownership of The Air Council for the ten month posting which ended with the aircraft's restoration to military markings with 24 Squadron at Hendon, where with some irony, she was destroyed during a German air raid on 8th October 1940.

K4268 (3264), on the other hand, appears to have been shuffled between maintenance units from delivery in February 1935 until she was sold for scrap from storage at Hullavington in 1950, with no recorded history of a day's active service in between.

Further feedback from the 'civil' fleet at Hatfield, an arrangement which provided excellent on-site flight development facilities, suggested that a slight alteration to the standard rigging of the control stick coupled with a 2 degree change to the aileron sprocket differential, would result in better handling during aerobatics and was particularly relevant to inverted flying. This was an interesting observation and may have referred to inverted time spent during the course of normal aerobatics, for with the exception of the six aircraft used by the Central Flying School (CFS) team which were modified for sustained but short duration inverted flight in 1932, and the civil National Aviation Day aircraft, inverted flying systems were not fitted to standard school machines.

Approved for experimental purposes was an adjustable trimmer set into the trailing edge of each elevator. Known as an 'elevator flap' the installation was in its third revision by the time it was flight tested on mass balanced elevators fitted to G-ACDJ (3183), in March 1935. For all its worth the system was complicated and infinitely more expensive than the simple spring loading of the control stick which was retained in preference. Drawings for the deletion of the trimmer and associated controls were issued the following October. Only when the Tiger Moth was adapted to Canadian conditions as the DH.82C and built in Toronto from April 1940, was a cockpit adjustable elevator trimmer incorporated as standard, although a similar system had enjoyed a brief flirtation with the experimental DH.82B Tiger Moth E.11 at Hatfield in the summer of 1939, an aircraft described in a later chapter.

de Havilland had developed the Tiger Moth as a military trainer and the majority of their effort in selling the type was directed towards that cause. A major promotion surrounded the ability of the aircraft to offer practical through-training from school to squadron, and the company carefully presented a reasoned argument in support of their case:

Training Methods:

Can a single aeroplane be produced which will by itself, give a complete training for all types of first-line aircraft from the single-seater fighter and the high performance day-bomber, to the large multi-engined night bomber?

The answer is that such an aircraft is actually in existence, but before discussing this 'one type' trainer it will be as well to examine the system of training which is to employ it.

In the British Royal Air Force great care is taken to select the best personnel, men of the highest physical and mental standards. This is the raw material of the air force. We may now see the process of converting this raw material into the competent, skilled and experienced service airman.

Two systems of training have been tried. Under the earlier system pilots began their training on slow 'nursery' machines of low power, then passed to a more powerful and slightly faster intermediate machine and thence to the first-line service aircraft. But this theory has been shown to be unsound, and the more advanced of the world's air forces have abandoned it in favour of the modern system, which uses one type of machine for the entire range of training, the pilot changing over to the first-line type of aircraft only for active service.

The advantages of this system are many. First of all, it allows a reduction in the number of different types which need to be borne on the strength of the air force; secondly it permits a reduction in the quantity and variety of spare parts which have to be carried; and, thirdly, it reduces considerably the wastage of personnel and material through accidents. Further, it allows pilots to obtain a complete mastery of the one type, which makes for confidence and all-round efficiency. Measured in any way whatever, the pilot who is fully trained and experienced on one type of aircraft is a better pilot than one partially trained to fly many different types.

Practical Service Flying:

It has been shown that the 'one type' system of training offers overwhelming economic advantages; it remains to be shown that it offers similar advantages from the viewpoint of practical service flying.

The art of flying is the same for all types of aircraft and it follows that the pilot who can fly one type of aeroplane of normal control and behaviour really well can fly any other aeroplane of similar control and behaviour. The days are past when a specialised knowledge of each one of many different types was required before they could be safely handled. Today, all aeroplanes, both civil and military, require a flying technique which is fundamentally the same, and a skilled and experienced pilot can handle any type of modern aeroplane just as a skilled and experienced motorist can handle any type of modern motor car.

With a verbal knowledge of stalling speeds, gliding speeds and general qualities, a pilot who has been taught to fly well in a good comprehensive trainer is able to pass direct to a new, high-performance type and to fly it safely. He will not, of course, feel completely at his ease immediately, but there will never be any doubt as to his mastery of the aeroplane.

It has, in fact, been demonstrated in the Royal Air Force that a pilot can pass direct from a training aircraft of 120hp to a 450hp first-line service machine, provided only that the 120hp trainer has suitable handling characteristics.

The One Type Trainer:

The essential attributes of a one 'type trainer' are:

a. Versatility, or adaptability to the varying uses to which first-line service aircraft are put.
b. Performance, or the capability of reproducing, on a small scale, the handling characteristics and performance of the different types of first-line aircraft.
c. Economy, in first cost, maintenance cost and running cost.
d. Strength, which involves reliability.
e. Safety.

Examination of the trainer aircraft now in existence shows that the de Havilland Tiger Moth embodies in balanced form all these essential features. It is a scaled-down edition of the full-size, high powered, high-performance military aircraft, and reproduces with remarkable fidelity the characteristics of the larger machine.

Moreover, the pupil who has never been in the air before can, on this one type alone, be thoroughly trained in every branch of aerial manoeuvre and pass direct from the Tiger Moth to any of the various high-performance types which he may be ordered to fly on service.

The Tiger Moth has been specifically designed as a one-type trainer. It is the outcome of the experience gained by the de Havilland Aircraft Company with over 2,000 Moths of other types in actual service, both civil and military, all over the world in extremes of temperature and humidity and under the most difficult operational conditions.

It was an over-worded and fairly thin argument, and just how successful the 'One Type' campaign was might be judged from the following figures.

Of the 400 Tiger Moths, DH.82 and DH.82A, built at Stag Lane and Hatfield between January 1932 and May 1936, distribution was to air arms, ministries of war or government departments in varying proportions: Austria 2; Brazil 17; China 4; Denmark 9; Germany 1; India 4; Iraq 7; Israel 1; Japan 1; Persia/Iran 69; Poland 1; Portugal 21; Spain 5; Sweden 16 and Uruguay 6.

A de Havilland publicity shot of Hatfield-based Tiger Moths and others awaiting delivery, taken in the late summer of 1935. In November, G-ADJB went to Phillips and Powis, civilian operators of 8 ERFTS at Woodley, but was written off the following March. via Richard Riding

The motives behind the single acquisition of aircraft 3116 by the Mosawa Company of Japan in July 1932 can only be surmised. Supplied in an airworthy condition and with a British Certificate of Airworthiness, the aircraft's subsequent history is completely unknown. But more than half the 400 were sold to the British Air Ministry: 51 directly into RAF service and 158 to the civilian operated schools at Brooklands, Desford, Filton, Hatfield, Prestwick, Perth and Reading.

A lead customer for the Tiger Moth, the Imperial Persian Army Flying Corps was as pleased to have their new aircraft equipped to the latest standards as was de Havilland to supply, and the spin-off in terms of publicity and prestige was as valuable as the knowledge gained in designing, manufacturing and fitting out the aircraft. In September 1932, Persian Tiger Moth 113 (3129), was the development aircraft at Stag Lane for a blind flying hood, B.S.2C bomb sight, arrangement of bomb gear, navigation lights, Holt flares and Very pistol, together with the mounting for a ten gallon auxiliary fuel tank. The following month, aircraft 104 (3120), was fitted with a nine gallon auxiliary tank of new design which replaced the approved ten gallon tank in this aircraft, almost certainly to create space for additional equipment. By November, 113 had been further modified to accept a second bomb rack with the associated bomb release gear, an Eagle III camera with electrical control equipment, and arrangements for mounting either Williamson Mk I or Mk III cameras.

As the result of experience operating from rough desert airstrips, by February 1936 when an order for ten DH.82A Tiger Moths for the 'Imperial Iranian Ministry of War ' was progressing through the Hatfield shops, 160 (3464) and 169 (3473), were supplied with special tailplanes incorporating plywood skins on the under surfaces, as a guard against damage from stones thrown up by the wheels. The Persian aircraft were the only ones ever to specify this modification which may not have found general favour on the grounds of extra weight, and its influence on the already critical aft CG position. At least for aircraft 160 and 169, the additional weight at the tail neutralised the nose heaviness induced by the mass of the Fairey Reed metal propeller, and tare CG was restored to a more comfortable situation.

The most radical of all modifications resulted in the Tiger Moth Fighter, 122 (3201), which was unveiled in October 1932. As far as the engineering approvals were concerned, Hatfield's Resident Technical Officer (RTO) reported on 11th October that regarding safety considerations, the installation of a machine gun mounting, cockpit control for the interrupter gear, and ammunition container had all been completed in conformity with the drawing schedule.

Shortly afterwards, the de Havilland sales office was moved to provide more information:

'We are now able to offer the Tiger Moth as a single seater fighter with a machine gun firing forward through the propeller, and also capable of carrying eight bombs of 20lb each. Fuel can be carried for a range of over 500 miles, with gun, gun sight and four bombs of 20lb each, but if eight bombs are carried, range would be reduced to approximately 250 miles, the range being limited by the all up weight of the aircraft.

The gun and mounting are easily removable, so that the machine can be readily converted to a training type aircraft, and for any other of the duties for which the Tiger Moth was primarily designed.

The Gun: *The machine gun is air cooled, weighs only 9.5kg, and is manufactured by the Czechoslovakian Arms Factory of Prague. The muzzle velocity is 839ms, and the maximum rate of fire 900 +/− 100 rounds per minute. The bore is 7.92 mm. A Pratt and Whitney synchronising gear is fitted, which is very light and efficient, the drive being taken from the top half of the rear cover of the engine, where provision for hand starting gear is normally allowed for.*

Location and mounting: *The gun is mounted in the front cockpit, and shoots directly over the top engine cowling. It is fixed to the machine mounting by two bolts only, the rear bolt incorporating a vernier adjustment for direction and elevation. The ammunition box, holding 200 rounds, and the cartridge chute, are fixed to the mounting itself, and the only connections between the gun, gun mounting and fuselage, are four holding down bolts. The mounting rests at four points on the two top longerons with one bolt at each of these points. No extra holes are drilled in the longerons.*

It takes one man fifteen minutes to install, or to remove the gun. With the latter operation the machine becomes a normal two seater. The whole installation is extremely simple and very effective, as only eight bolts have to be removed to take off the complete gun and sight. The cocking handle is connected only by a cotter pin to the lever which acts on the gun. In order to protect the workings of the gun it has been cowled in, which cowling is held by four butterfly nuts.

The trigger is located on the control column, and its action is conveyed to the gun by means of a Bowden cable. It is actuated very easily by closing the hand round the trigger and the handle of the control column.

Sights: *The Aldis telescopic gun sight is provided for long distance firing. The ordinary ring and bead sight for dog fighting can be fitted as an alternative, or together with the Aldis sight.*

Ammunition Box and chute: *The ammunition box can be taken out, refilled and put back, without disturbing the rest of the mounting or gun. The top chute is for the spent belt and the larger one below for the spent cartridges.*

Tests: *The results of the official ground and air acceptance tests were as follows:*

1. *Pulling over the propeller by hand, the first round penetrated the disc nineteen and a half degrees after top dead centre.*
2. *Dispersion throughout the entire speed range occurred between the angles of 45 and 86 deg., that is to say through an arc of 41 deg.*
3. *Propeller speeds varied from 800rpm to 2,400rpm.*

These results are absolutely satisfactory'.

A horribly gloomy day at 7 ERFTS Desford in February 1936, with over posed positions set up to simulate the height of the British summer. The photograph illustrates part of the pupil's mess which together with other facilities at the aerodrome, was designed by Squadron Leader George Reid. *The Aeroplane*

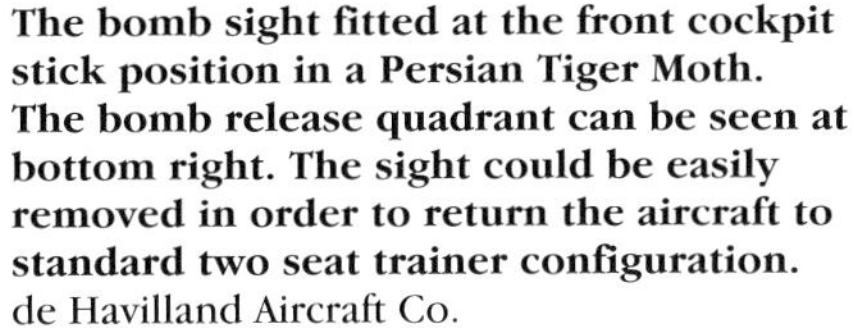

The bomb sight fitted at the front cockpit stick position in a Persian Tiger Moth. The bomb release quadrant can be seen at bottom right. The sight could be easily removed in order to return the aircraft to standard two seat trainer configuration. de Havilland Aircraft Co.

E.6, the de Havilland 'Class 2' markings used for test flying purposes, applied to a single seat fighter version of the DH.82A Tiger Moth developed for the Persian Government. A machine gun straddles the faired-in front cockpit, firing through the arc of the propeller. de Havilland Aircraft Co.

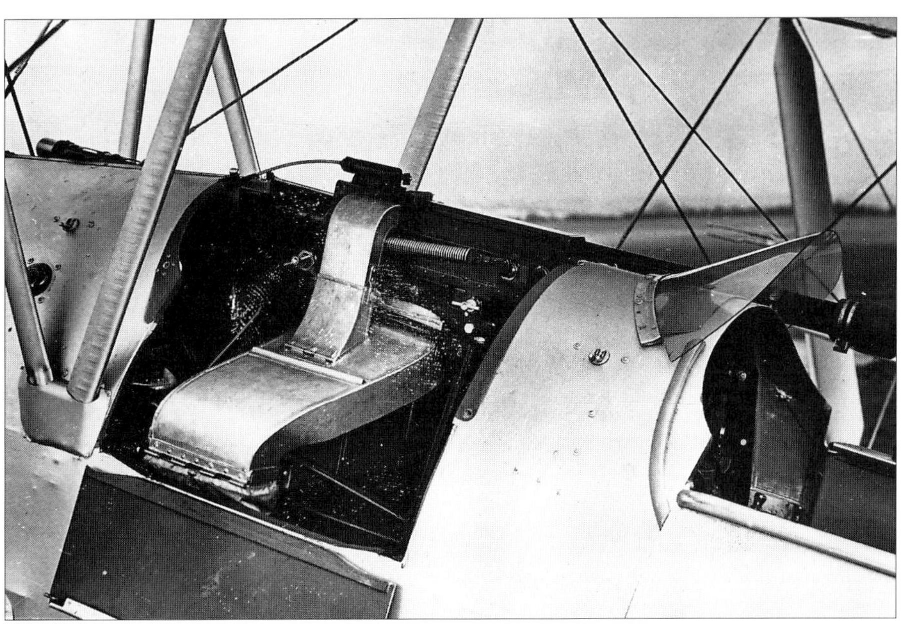

Machine gun and magazine installed in the front cockpit of a Persian Government Tiger Moth. Note the streamlined windscreen fitted for the pilot. The curved ply fairing below the screen was a simple device to prevent rain water running back along the decking and dripping into the cockpit. de Havilland Aircraft Co.

In none of the contemporary publicity material did de Havilland ever once mention the identity of their customer, and it was left to the aviation correspondents of the press to speculate, as predictably they did: *'The machine looks a very nice little job and should be very useful for ground strafing, for which purpose it was probably designed, more than for actual aerial fighting. A detachment of this machine has been ordered by a foreign government and has already been packed up for dispatch'.* Some years later, a connection was assumed between the fighter and the training on Tiger Moths at Panshanger and Wolverhampton, of many Iranian flying instructors. Yet another link was seen in the adaption of the Pratt and Whitney E-4 Gun Synchroniser which was believed to have been specified to standardise on such equipment in the Air Corps, and after Sydney Camm had rejected a proposal to fit Pratt and Whitney Hornet engines to his elegant Fury.

A DH.82A Tiger Moth was the first aircraft purchased by the official Jewish institutions in Palestine in 1934 when attempts were made to establish a joint Jewish-British-Arab Flying Club, 'The Flying Camel'. Although this attempt failed, a follow-up club, the Palestine Flying Club was set up as a wholly Jewish organisation. In the autumn of 1934, a group of Palestine officials who dealt with immigration matters in Poland, met with David Ben-Gurion, Head of the Jewish Agency, and obtained the necessary funds to acquire the Tiger Moth which was delivered in October.

Registered G-ACYN (3314), the aircraft operated with the Aviron Flying School in 1936 but was also used for military spotting purposes in addition to missions in support of national defence such as the protection of groups of workers engaged in building roads and other construction projects. She was also used for dropping essential supplies of food and ammunition to settlers, especially those in newly developed areas, when the winter was at its height. By the end of 1938 operations were so successful that it was decided to list the Tiger Moth in the Palestine Civil Register as VQ-PAN, but the aircraft crashed while operating from the Afikim airstrip in the Jordan Valley during the summer of 1939, and it was the British civil listing instead that was cancelled.

Two of a batch of 12 Tiger Moths registered to the Bristol Aeroplane Company in October 1935 (G-ADNW/3417 and G-ADNY/3419), were involved in a mid-air collision near Avebury, Wiltshire, on 3rd December 1938 while operating from Yate, a site often used as a satellite for Yatesbury and Filton. G-ADNW, abandoned by her crew, crashed in a cornfield while the two pilots descended by parachute. G-ADNY was successfully put down at Yate and survived her ordeal,

Yatesbury aerodrome, August 1937, and Tiger Moths of 10 ERFTS, operated by the Bristol Aeroplane Company are paid a visit by an unidentified DH.90 Dragonfly. The rudder of G-ADNY appears to be at variance with the remainder of the fleet whose house colours were purple fuselage and custard yellow wings. Richard Riding

Four Tiger Moths and a Hornet Moth of the London Aeroplane Club at Hatfield in April 1939. All the Club's Tiger Moths were sold by de Havilland to the Royal New Zealand Air Force. Note the camouflaged Tiger Moth taxying in and DH.85 Leopard Moth taxying out, in the background. *The Aeroplane*

for she was one of the entire Bristol fleet that was seconded to Indian 'military' service in 1940, although she retained civil markings (VT-AOB) until cancelled in August 1945.

One early civil Tiger Moth had been sold directly to the Netherlands, and another, G-ADSI (3423), to the Egyptian branch of the RAF Flying Club, although the aircraft was delivered to their Hatfield base in October 1935 and was written off in a crash at Nithsdale, Dumfries in 1938, almost certainly having never seen the waters of the Nile.

de Havilland also supplied their associated companies and agents: one aircraft was crated to Australia, a pair to South Africa and five to Canada. OA-CCH (3289), went to Peru in June 1934, OE-DAX (3494), to Nikolaus von Eltz, de Havilland's agent in Austria and LY-LAT (3493), to the Lietuvos Aero Club in Lithuania, both in April 1936.

The Marquess of Douglas and Clydesdale who received G-ADUC (3425), at Prestwick in November 1935, together with David McIntyre and A. Stewart Kennedy, had set up Scottish Aviation Ltd the previous August. This company was to manage the first civilian flying school in Scotland to become part of the Air Ministry's expanding ERFTS scheme and G-ADUC was operated by 12 ERFTS/12 EFTS until after the end of the war when she joined the Royal Navy. The de Havilland Aircraft Company supplied 16 Tiger Moths to Scottish Aviation at a price of £750 each, but astutely opted for a shareholding in the new business rather than taking a cash payment, an interest that lasted almost until the end of the war, when Kennedy joined de Havilland at Hatfield as part of a redeployment of top management following the retirement of Frank Hearle. Kennedy learned to fly at his own Scottish school, but on his first solo, the rudder bar contrived to jump off its bearing, leaving him with only one-way movement, committing him, as he put it, to skidding round the sky somewhat slowly.

Only 11 Tiger Moths were released into the UK civilian market between March 1932 and April 1936, four of which (prototype G-ABRC/1733; G-ABUL/3107; G-ACEZ/3186 and G-ACFA/3187), all operated with National Aviation Day Ltd, the flying circus organised by Sir Alan Cobham and based at Ford in Sussex. Each aircraft survived trial by bunt, loop and falling leaf to have a long career in aviation; hard daily use was a sure way of ironing out the bugs, and the best possible form of publicity for the aeroplane. de Havilland were quick to recognise and promote this exposure and those vital appearances of the RAF teams at Hendon, and encapsulated the detail in their subsequent advertising material:

'A training aircraft must of necessity be of exceptionally strong construction as it has not only to withstand the stresses of normal flying and landings, but also to the abnormal strains imposed by the performance of violent aerobatics.

'The exhibition of formation aerobatics at the Royal Air Force Display by the Instructors of the Central Flying School demonstrated beyond doubt that the Tiger Moth will stand up to any aerobatic manoeuvre which it may be called upon to perform. A further remarkable testimony is contained in a letter received by the de Havilland Aircraft Company from Sir Alan Cobham, who used a standard Tiger Moth for the demonstration of aerobatics in his 1932 propaganda tour of Great Britain. For six months this machine gave eight displays of aerobatics daily, including such violent manoeuvres as upward rolls and inverted loops. It performed a total of 2,520 landings, 345 half outside loops, 300 upward rolls, 1,440 loops, 1,080 rolls and upwards of 90 hours inverted flying in that period; it was never under cover, never failed to give its display and, when returned to the factory for overhaul, was found to be in perfect condition. Sir Alan expressed the opinion that this machine has put up a greater number of aerobatic displays than any other aeroplane in history'.

Not such a happy story surrounded G-ACDY (3189), which was delivered to the Scottish Motor Traction Co at Renfrew in April 1933. The brief was to perform public aerobatic displays as a means of promoting the company's internal Scottish airline services shortly to be flown with DH.83 Fox Moths, but G-ACDY crashed into the River Don at Aberdeen less than five months later.

Apart from G-ABTB (3101), which was registered to The Standard Telephone & Cable Co Ltd for almost two years from January 1932, and used in experimental work connected with development of airborne wireless transmission equipment on behalf of the Air Ministry until sale to the Netherlands, and G-ADWG (3492), which spent the 1936 season with C W A Scott's Flying Display Ltd before moving into Club use at Lympne, the remaining four civil aircraft were all operated by the London Aeroplane Club at Hatfield: G-ACSK/3223; G-ACWB/3226; G-ADLU/3357 and G-ADUK/3426.

de Havilland had bought the Club on the closure of Stag Lane and relocated it to their new aerodrome where it became one of London's centres of society and civil flying. Later still, the once fashionable London Aeroplane Club was adopted as the vehicle through which employees of the company could learn to fly at a rate which barely covered the cost of the petrol. In 1940, the Club's entire Tiger Moth fleet was packed into crates and shipped south, sold to the Royal New Zealand Air Force.

With the immediate requirements of the military appearing to have been met, the destinations of the 250 Tiger Moths built at Hatfield between April 1936 and August 1938 indicated that de Havilland had broadened their sales base, and their efforts in promoting the type as the natural successor to the DH.60 as a civil training aircraft were bearing fruit. The RAF took only 35 of these aircraft, mostly at the end of this audit, although they were but a prelude; the advance party of what shortly was to develop into a veritable avalanche of orders.

The supply of aircraft to the established ERFTS contractors accounted for 43 of the 250 manufacturing positions, 13 of which in ones and twos, possibly ordered as replacements, were unsystematically scattered though the period. No.1 ERFTS established at Hatfield flew 6,000 hours in 1935, and partly due to seven days a week operations, increased that to 9,000 hours in 1936 and 11,400 hours in 1937. Their sister organisation, 13 ERFTS at White Waltham, flew 7,500 hours in its first year and then beat the parent school with 12,300 hours in 1937.

As a measure of the expansion, in 1941, No.1 EFTS flew a total of 43,693 hours. During such utilisation there was bound to be wastage and a constant need for additional or replacement aircraft. By the end of 1937 the British schools' establishment was estimated to be 175 Tiger Moths.

A block of 30 aircraft laid down against civilian specification in June 1937 was purchased off the line by an Air Ministry acting with a degree of urgency. Carrying military serials, these hybrids were distributed amongst selected schools: four to Brooklands, seven to the new Airwork organisation at Castle Bromwich, three to Desford, four to the Bristol Aeroplane Company at Filton, and seven to Scottish Aviation at Prestwick. Five aircraft were delivered to the de Havilland school at White Waltham, while one of the batch, L6923 (3558), remained with the home team at Hatfield where she was exposed to intense air-to-air photographic coverage, much of which later appeared in promotional articles and advertisements.

All aircraft in the batch were gradually converted to military standard and L6923 subsequently led a varied life: she became part of Hatfield's 1 EFTS on the outbreak of war but crashed in September 1940 and was rebuilt by the de Havilland Civil Repair Organisation (CRO) at Witney, a job which began in early October but was not completed until Christmas, the aircraft transferring to 19 Maintenance Unit (MU) at St Athan on New Year's Day 1941. Allocated to 'A' Flight of 1 Anti Aircraft Co-operation Unit (AACU) in June 1941, L6923 crashed again in November and was repaired at the Taylorcraft CRO, Rearsby, before transfer to 5 MU at Kemble on the last day of 1941. A month later, the aircraft was delivered to 6 EFTS Sywell where she remained for the rest of the war until allocated to storage with 38 MU at Llandow for over four years, only to be cut up for scrap in 1950.

With the increase in training capacity, during the summer of 1937, the Royal Air Force took advertising space in the search for pilot recruits, emphasising the need for no previous experience:

Short Service Commissions:
Age limits 17½-25.
Appointments, in the first instance, are for four years on the active list, followed by six years' reserve service.
Gratuity of £300 payable after four years' service.

Reserve of Air Force Officers (Class A):
Age limits 18-25
Appointments are for five years' service in the Reserve, of which the first year is spent in continuous whole time attendance for training, followed by a short period of training in each subsequent year.
Pay is given during training and there is a retaining fee of £25/year after the first year.

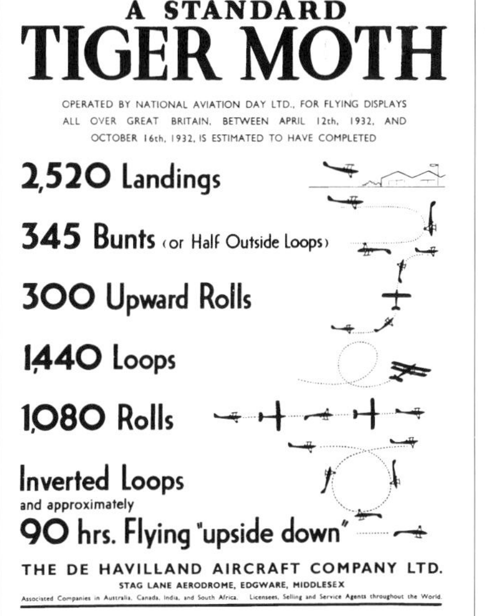

A de Havilland advertisement from late 1932 extolling the strength of the Tiger Moth as proven by the rigorous handling during time spent with Alan Cobham's National Aviation Day display. Pilots needed to be hardy creatures too.

One of the rare pre-war British civil Tiger Moths was DH.82 G-ABTB, registered to the Standard Telephone and Cable Co Ltd in January 1932, and used for air to ground wireless communication experiments. Aerials can be seen on the top of the port upper mainplane and just behind the rear cockpit, while the front cockpit has a non-standard rounded screen.

Volunteer Reserve (Pilot Section):
Age limits 18-25
Candidates are entered as airman pilots for five years' service. Training is carried out in the evenings and at weekends, with a con tinuous period of 15 days training each year. An annual retaining Fee of £25 is payable.

Respondents were advised that they should have received education to the standard of the Oxford and Cambridge School Certificate, and should now contact:
The Secretary, S.7.e/DP
The Air Ministry, Kingsway
London WC2

Brooklands Aviation operated not only a Reserve School at Sywell but a civil flying club from their Surrey headquarters, the famous motor racing circuit near Weybridge. For many years the Brooklands Flying Club had been a major user of DH.60 Moths and through their parent company acted as sales agents and a major force in the training of aeronautical engineers. Early in 1937 some of the DH.60 Moths were replaced by the purchase of six Tiger Moths, and after a year's activity the first of the new aircraft, G-AESA (3544), was taken in for overhaul. During her 12 month stay, the aircraft had accumulated 850 flying hours and 7,000 landings. de Havilland promoted the news that the cost of materials used during overhaul amounted to just £21, the most expensive single item being the provision of one new mainwheel tyre.

Doing his best to keep up the hours on the Tiger Moth fleet at £2 per hour, was Charles Nepean Bishop, who together with two fellow Club members organised a unique 'weekend' formation team of four and later six Tiger Moths. The team was only disbanded when several of the members qualified for their commercial licences, and went off to earn instead of spend. Started almost by accident in 1937 when a trio of aircraft would travel around the south of England 'in close proximity' attending the standard club Breakfast Patrols, matters changed in 1938:

'In April came our first really organised flight of this description, this being a special luncheon flight to Hanworth aerodrome at the invitation of the London Air Park Flying Club. Four Tiger Moths and a Gipsy Moth took off from Brooklands, and as the distance to Hanworth was only seven miles we made a slight (?) detour by way of Reading at which aerodrome we landed in formation, much to the consternation of certain military instructors at the resident FTS.

'Having calmed them down and refuelled ourselves we took off, again in formation, and headed for Hanworth. The Gipsy Moth pilot having found that he could not keep up when on the outside of a turn came along separately, so the four Tiger Moths were flown in diamond formation, this being the first occasion on which this particular formation had been tried out.

'At Hanworth the advent of our four machines caused quite a sensation, and by a modern miracle we all touched down at the same moment on landing. This made our stock quite high, and when we left, after an excellent lunch, we were asked to fly past for the benefit of the local photographer, which we did. All went well until the landing at Brooklands, when our leader glided in at no feet and very little speed with us behind him stalling visibly. In the end we landed quite safely, but after the flight the order came forth that in future we must not land in formation unless there was an instructor in at least one of the machines'.

An aircraft which spent her entire wartime life with Brooklands Aviation at Sywell was Tiger Moth R5042 (82943), delivered from Hatfield to 6 MU Brize Norton in March 1943, and arriving at Sywell six months later. During forced landing practice in February 1943 the aircraft collided with the airfield boundary hedge but most damage was restricted to the rear fuselage. It seems she was repaired on site, and probably at a time when Tiger Moth L6923 was also on jacks, for when G-ANEM (as R5042 had become) was stripped down for overhaul in 1992, irrefutable proof was discovered that her rear fuselage was that of the much photographed, civil specification, L6923.

Between 1932 and 1934, 39 DH.60T Moth Trainers had been sold in South America, followed by orders for 17 DH.82 Tiger Moths for delivery to Brazil and six for Uruguay. de Havilland's agents in South America, Walter and Company in Brazil and Morrison and Company in Chile, were directed by the company's 'Special Representative in South America' W T W Ballantyne, whose responsibility for the entire continent was effected

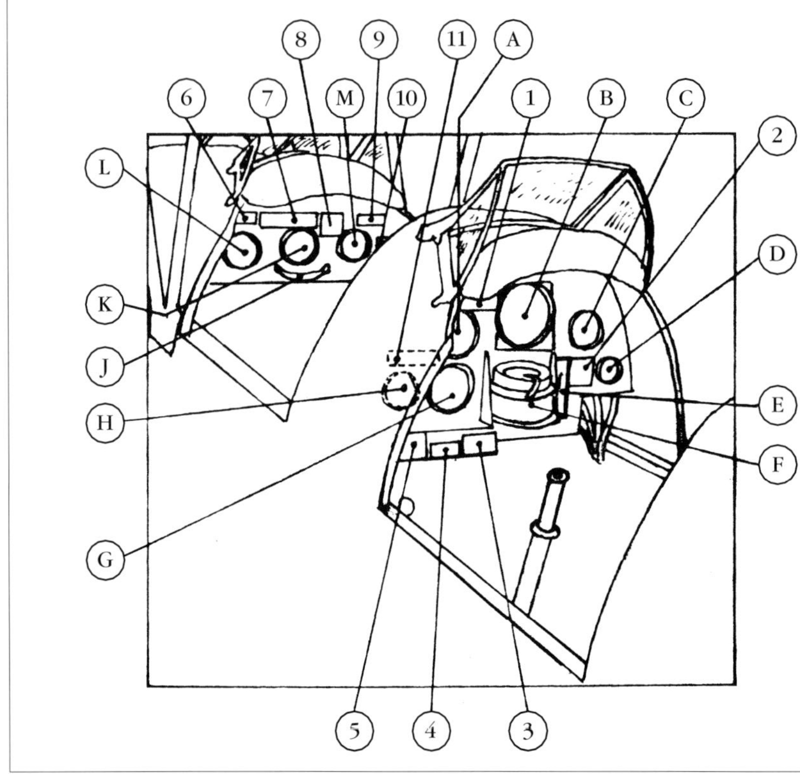

London Aeroplane Club
Tiger Moth cockpit layout, 1939.

1 & 7	*Running data for Gipsy Major engine*
2 & 8	*Technical specification for Gipsy Major engine*
3	*Owner's nameplate*
4 & 9	*'No Smoking' placard*
5 & 10	*Aircraft makers' name and individual build number*
6	*Engine starting procedure, switch and magneto configuration*
11	*Ignition switch and magneto check instruction placard*
A & L	*Tachometer*
B	*Turn indicator (top and bottom needle)*
C & K	*Air speed indicator*
D	*Oil pressure gauge*
E	*Inclinometer*
F	*Compass*
G & M	*Altimeter*
H	*Chronometer*

from the portals of the English Club in Buenos Aires.

Ballantyne was well qualified for what the company considered an important post, having joined the de Havilland School at Stag Lane as an officer in the Reserve, he qualified for his 'B' commercial pilots' licence before he could drive a car. Following a spell in the de Havilland Drawing Office at Stag Lane and on detachment with Arthur Hagg working in isolation on the DH. 61 Giant Moth in 1927, the increase in business activity found him promoted to the Sales Department in June 1929, where he became Technical Assistant to Francis St Barbe, and revelled in the opportunities offered to ferry and demonstrate the company's products.

The decision to set up a permanent office in South America and staff it from London, was something of a financial gamble, but Ballantyne agreed to take up the post as full time representative, visiting England as the situation demanded. On one occasion he returned to duties in South America by flying a DH.84 Dragon across the South Atlantic to Brazil, for delivery to VASP.

Ballantyne firmly believed that the company was ideally placed to exploit the market for trainer aircraft, and was greatly anticipating the new design from Hatfield proposed for 1936, and which at the suggested price of £1,850 for the stripped down basic machine was competition for the Waco and a new Wright Trainer. Pitched at its current level of specification, the Tiger Moth had proved generally unpopular throughout the region, and at home the Air Ministry was perceived as being positively unhelpful by prevaricating over a decision on whether or not to adopt the aircraft as an official training type for the RAF.

In spite of his best endeavours, only 12 more Tiger Moths were sold in the whole of South America pre-war, a repeat order for the Uruguyan Ministry of War. The aircraft, 3503-3505 and 3612-3620, were different from standard in that reverse action throttle controls were specified, and approval for the configuration was signed off after flight testing at Hatfield in June 1936.

On 20th November 1937, the country's 21st Anniversary of military aviation, 18 Tiger Moths of the Uruguayan Air Force assembled at Pando aerodrome, twelve miles from the capital, for the Montevideo Fiesta de Aviacion, and to mark the official opening of Pando as the Air Force's new training headquarters. Ballantyne was on hand as de Havilland Representative and was able to report that: 'the flying display did great credit to Major Gestido, organiser of the military school, and besides clean formation and aerobatic flying by the Tiger Moth trainers and the reconnaissance and day bombing types, (Potez and Breda), they demonstrated the Dragon Rapide ambulance which the military operate for the Ministry of Health'.

In all probability, the next and only other customer for throttle action of this type was the French Government which ordered a trio of Tiger Moths for delivery to a new civil flying school recently established in Indo-China. The aircraft were identified simply as '8', '9' and '10' and allocated Hatfield build positions 83364-83366. Four officials from the school visited Hatfield in April 1940, including two engineers, Chief Pilot Maurice Thoroval and the Commandant, Louis Costex. The Allied governments had agreed to the sale on the grounds that pupils were civilians, but the technical specification called for a deal of standard RAF equipment including blind flying instruments and navigation lighting.

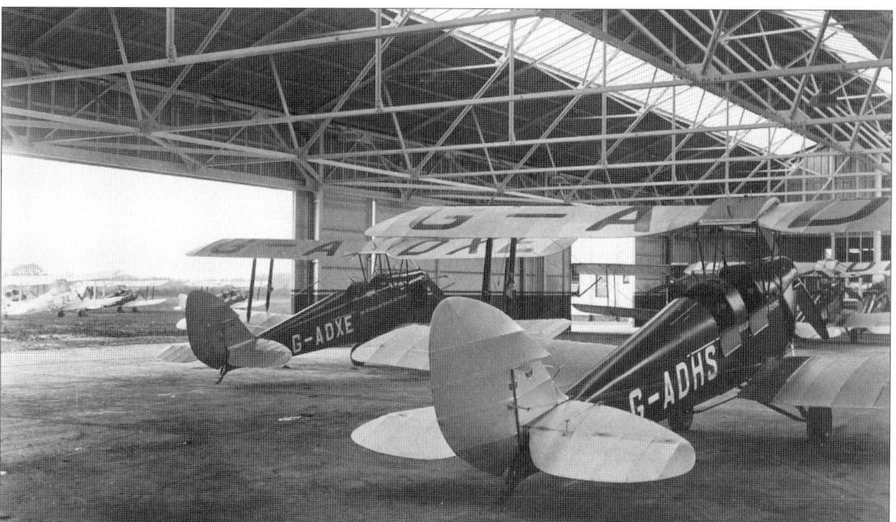

Aircraft of 13 ERFTS in the hangar at White Waltham, an aerodrome and associated facilities built and developed to de Havilland's own specification. Picketed outside is a visiting Tiger Moth from 24 (Communications) Squadron RAF, the only machine with both cockpits fully covered. de Havilland Aircraft Co.

Tiger Moth L6923 was one of 30 aircraft built to civilian specification but bought straight off the line by an Air Ministry seriously worried about its lack of Reserve training aircraft. The 30 were widely dispersed amongst the schools but L6923 was retained at Hatfield for publicity purposes before release to the home based 1 EFTS. de Havilland Aircraft Co.

Pat Fillingham flew 83365 on tests of ten and 15 minutes on 29th May 1940 and a civil certificate of airworthiness was issued on 4th June. But the delivery was frustrated by the changing pace of world events and eventually the aircraft were transferred to the RAF as T5883-T5885, when the reverse action mechanism was dismantled. All three served with the training schools, T5884 (83365), ending her career in Southern Rhodesia in 1950 as the result of an indiscretion when overshooting at No 4 Flying Training School, Heany.

But contradicting the slow rate of orders for South America, the de Havilland company in South Africa had taken 44 aircraft, with a further 16 shipped to New Zealand and 17 to Australia.

Closer to home, the British based private owners and clubs, having no affinity with military training contracts, took 26 aircraft, but precious few additional civil machines were to be completed.

Escalating Air Ministry orders filled nearly all the delivery positions, a degree of exclusivity which effectively closed the Hatfield line to outsiders from mid-1938.

As idyllic a scene as any. A red and black Tiger Moth with silver wings dipping in to land at a large grass aerodrome during an English summer afternoon in 1936. Could the photographer, Secretary of the Cycling Tourists Club taking a rest from his exercise, have realised that the pilot was being trained for war? Neville Whall

Tiger Moth 2-I-10 of the Brazilian Navy in the Museu Aeroespacial at Campo dos Afonsus. The aircraft as presented carries a number of non standard features: streamlined headrest; tailwheel, mass balanced elevator; redesigned chin cowl incorporating stub exhausts; additional air scoops on both port and starboard side cowls and an elongated oil tank. deHMC Archive

Tiger Moths of the Uruguayan Air Force together with Potez and Breda types lined up at Pando aerodrome, Montevideo on 20th November 1937 in celebration of the city's Fiesta de Aviacion. R Gatti via British Aerospace

The best, the only way to move a Tiger Moth single handed in the absence of a tail trolley: lift the tail until the aircraft is perfectly balanced and push. Hard work on grass and when negotiating a positive incline. London Aeroplane Club, Hatfield, summer 1939. de Havilland Aircraft Co.

CHASING THE EXPORT TRADE

DH.82 Tiger Moth S1675 fitted with Short floats, underwent manufacturer's trials from the River Medway in Kent in 1932. Service pilots later found against the suitability of the type as a vehicle for seaplane training. Short Bros.

De Havilland had always enjoyed a harmonious relationship with that particular section of the aviation fraternity who, by force of circumstance or out of preference, operated from water or any other precipitation covered surface. At one time or another, almost the entire Cirrus and Gipsy engined design range had been persuaded onto floats or skis for experimental or commercial purposes. It was no surprise then that from the earliest publication of brochures the company had alluded to the Seaplane version of the DH.82 Tiger Moth and, although they were specific with details of charges for packing and delivery from Stag Lane to the London Docks, *'£59 for a single Tiger Moth Seaplane or £93 for a pair, packed into three high specification wooden cases'*, the cost of a complete machine was never quoted. Prospective customers were advised that prices were available on application, and that the quotation provided for collection ex-works, ready for packing, or *'ex-Seaplane Station, ready for flight'* at extra cost.

A friendly and fruitful business relationship had always been maintained with Short Bros and it was their 'metal floats' that were specified for Moths built in England. Although de Havilland were unwilling to make a public revelation of prices for a float equipped Tiger Moth, the company did have sufficient experience to quote with confidence against a whole range of essentials for an aircraft operating in a marine environment. Special anti-corrosion treatment for engine and airframe was offered at just over £130, more than 12% of the basic purchase price; attachment fittings for the float chassis (but less chassis and floats) was £25 and the charge for supplying and fitting water rudder controls was an equal sum. The difficulties of hand swinging a propeller at a mooring were recognised by the offer to modify the engine and airframe to accept a handle activated, geared starter mechanism at a little over £85 extra. This was fitted at the same position occupied by the Pratt and Whitney E-4 Gun Synchroniser when the landplane fighter was developed for the Persian Air Force.

Additional Seaplane accessories were all available to assist the marine aviator: float bilge pumps, boat hooks, mooring cables, anchors and paddles, not to mention a beaching trolley. Floats and the float undercarriage were also referenced under 'accessories' and a note emphasised that water rudders, an essential device for taxying, were 'extra', but declined to quote by how much.

The Air Ministry dutifully ordered a pair of Tiger Moth Seaplanes in 1931 under contract No 113208/31, and built to specification T.6/33. The two Gipsy III powered aircraft, S1675 and S1676 (1774/1775), were erected for trial purposes at Stag Lane in March 1932, and later were delivered to the Short Bros factory at Rochester for water trials on the River Medway. S1675 subsequently flew with the Marine Aircraft Experimental Establishment (MAEE) at Felixstowe before a short posting to the Seaplane Training Flight (STF) at Calshot in May 1932.

The following year the aircraft was in Singapore, sharing space with the Hawker Horsleys operated by 36 Squadron from Seletar, but during a flight near Pasir Ris in Johore Strait on 14th August, she forced landed due to engine failure. S1676 also passed through the MAEE at Felixstowe and was last reported at Kai Tak, Hong Kong in December 1933.

Hubert Broad conducted Tiger Moth seaplane trials on the River Medway on 9th October 1933 when he flew two different aircraft under Class 2 markings 'E.2' and 'E.3'. Four days later further trails were flown in which the aircraft were listed as 3203/3204, identifying them as P125 and P126, two of a batch ordered by the Imperial Iranian Ministry of War. In view of the landplane deliveries to Ahwaz near Abadan, the Iranians possibly were considering the prospect of basing float equipped 'fighter' aircraft at the head of the Persian Gulf, although there is no evidence to suggest that they ever did.

Apart from the obvious differences of alighting gear, the Tiger Moth Seaplane was little changed from the Landplane, although the fundamental requirement to hoist the aircraft in and out of the water dictated modifications to allow attachment of slinging cables to the centre section. An auxiliary ten gallon tank was fitted as standard inside the front cockpit top decking, a measure considered necessary to combat higher consumption, a result of the extra drag of the float configuration rather than the anticipation of long duration standing patrols. Additional instruments conducive to low level operations over water were also specified, and a Turn Indicator and Fore and Aft Level were fitted to redesigned instrument panels; the occasion seen too as an opportunity to make provisions for a blind flying hood. Specification T.6/33 also called for complete engine and airframe protective treatment, and some element of stress analysis to ensure that the centre section attachment was adequate to support the entire weight of the structure when suspended by cables from the jib of a dockyard crane.

Undismayed by the general lack of enthusiasm for the Tiger Moth Seaplane, the Air Ministry ordered that five of the aircraft delivered into store at Henlow in January 1932 should be converted to Specification T.6/33. Aircraft serialled K2588-K2592 (1760-1764) were all allocated to de Havilland at Stag Lane on 20th June 1933 and by 29th March 1934 the five machines had each been signed off as a 'conversion of Landplane to Seaplane' at the new maximum weight of 1,825lb.

The quintet subsequently lead an unimpressive life: K2588 undertook trials at MAEE Felixstowe before delivery to Sealand in May 1934, where she was processed for shipment to Singapore the following month. It is not clear how long she served the colony as a Seaplane, but suspicions are that she had been converted back onto a wheeled undercarriage long before she was taken on charge by Tengah Station Flight late in 1939. K2589 also routed via Sealand in May and June, but her ultimate destination was Kai Tak, Hong Kong, where she survived to be broken up for spare parts in August 1937. This fatalistic decision might have been taken in support of K2592 which had accompanied her during the voyage to Asia. This aircraft was posted on from Hong Kong to Singapore, converted to a Landplane, and operated by 4 Anti Aircraft Cooperation Unit (AACU) before joining K2588 at Tengah Station Flight.

K2591 was another candidate for Singapore, shipped in June 1934 and almost immediately after arrival re-converted to a Landplane for service with 4 AACU. The machine was written off after suffering a take-off accident at Seletar the following November and was replaced by sister aircraft K2590 which, following conversion at Stag Lane, had been placed into temporary store as a Seaplane at RAF Kenley. Shipped to Singapore in January 1935 she too was re-converted to a Landplane on arrival. None of the aircraft survived the war.

The Norwegian Navy Air Force had rejected the Tiger Moth as a suitable candidate for a float mounted training aircraft in February 1934, but the British Air Ministry's apparent waste of money and resource during its flirtation with the Tiger Moth Seaplane was not yet at an end. In 1935, contract 419031/35 was signed for the supply of two further machines, K8336 (3500) and K8337 (3501), which were to be delivered less engines, and approved for operations at a maximum permissible weight of 1,875lb. At a tare weight of 1,350lb and assuming a combined crew weight with parachutes of 400lb, no more than 13.5 gallons of fuel could be uplifted, in addition to the essential oil capacity of 16 pints.

It is probable that K8336 and K8337 were used for trial purposes associated with finalisation of the DH. Queen Bee specification which had been laid down in 1933, although the prototype did not fly from Hatfield until January 1935. The Queen Bee programme flirted with the Tiger Moth almost until the target aircraft was withdrawn from service.

Both new Tiger Moth Seaplanes were taken on charge at 2 Aircraft Servicing Unit (ASU) Cardington, in October 1936, and on the last day of that year, the Air Ministry's Resident Technical Officer at Hatfield, W T Sandford, signed the approval for the increased operational weights. The next move seems to have been the transfer of both aircraft to 6 MU at Brize Norton on 30th January 1939, where they were re-categorised as Instructional Airframes (1506M and 1505M respectively), the former moving to Brighton Technical College and the latter to Stepney Mens' Institute, both transfers occurring in June. But the two airframes were soon re-united: 1505M was relocated to 3 School of Technical Training at Blackpool in November 1939 followed by 1506M the following month.

By April 1933, only 18 months after launch of the DH.82, and six months since introduction of the improved 'A' version, de Havilland were disappointed to receive criticism of the aeroplane channelled back from agents and field representatives. The new three seater Avro 640 Cadet was being discussed in the corridors as a 'formidable competitor' powered with a Cirrus Hermes IV, and arrangements were put in hand for Captain de Havilland to fly and assess one, probably with Scottish Motor Traction at Renfrew. In the event, only six Avro 640 Cadets were built in 1933, with another trio three years later, and although collectively the Cadet series did undoubtedly deprive de Havilland of orders, like the limited success of the Avian before it, ultimately the de Havilland team was able to shrug off the 'formidable competitor' as an irrelevance.

At their monthly meeting in June, the directors actively debated their concerns that an entirely new aircraft to replace the Tiger Moth might be required, but as an interim measure, and before any design work could be authorised, St Barbe's Sales Department was called upon to explore an amelioration of the criticism by offering agents a price reduction or the incentive of special rates of commission.

At the same time the Belgian agent, Jean Stampe, partner in the Stampe and Vertongen company, was suggesting that they might be allowed to market a machine similar to the Moth, a request that raised no objection on the grounds that locally manufactured aircraft would usually be given preference if customers were allowed a choice, and ought to provide additional opportunities for the sale of Gipsy engines, an argument exemplified at that time by the encouragement offered by the Dutch National Aviation School to design submissions made by the Koolhoven Company.

1933 ended with a flurry of proposals and considerations which in hindsight had little or no obvious effect on the long-term future of the Tiger Moth except that in making no firm decisions the company maintained the *status quo*, and permitted steady and uninterrupted production, the stability of which was vital for the slam acceleration that was demanded and achieved almost five years later.

Communicating with the managers of all the Associated Companies in November 1933, Francis St Barbe confirmed that the Gipsy Major powered Tiger Moth was 'of course' to be continued, and sold at the advertised price of £1,095. Although the aircraft was selling in a manner which he considered to be satisfactory, and a small price reduction was feasible, a view confirmed by analysis at the request of the management meeting in June, St Barbe was obdurate in his opinion that business negotiation, especially with foreign governments, was a costly exercise, often necessitating *'expensive demonstration exhibitions, certain terms of payment hazards, and other considerations which justify as comfortable a price as possible'.*

By coincidence, and at a time when St Barbe's November letter was still in transit, de Havilland were advised by 'a reliable source' that the Air Ministry were not entirely satisfied with performance of the Avro Tutor as a training type and in all probability would be seeking to replace it within two years. It was another blow to Avro, and the de Havilland board must have been delighted at the prospects. But the Tiger Moth was far from being the perfect replacement: it was certainly a more economical aircraft but had already been criticised by the military for having insufficient cockpit space, hardly enough performance and no facility for the training of observers or for air-to-air gunnery. Many of these points had been specifically tackled in the 1933 brochure which promoted the aircraft under such headings as 'The Foundations of an Air Force', and 'The One Type Trainer', apart from laying heavy emphasis on versatility, economy and performance.

K2593 (1765), one of the group delivered into store at Henlow in January 1932 was returned to Stag Lane in 1933 for experiments into the feasibility of heating front and rear open cockpits. A system had been designed in July to tap hot air from a muffler fitted to a long exhaust pipe running underneath the floor on the starboard side of the front fuselage. Heated air was drawn through a 3in pipe running vertically upwards inside the cockpit and connecting with another of half the diameter, about 4ft long, and secured horizontally to the fuselage side frame. The forward end was turned down to discharge warm air 12 inches above the front rudder pedals, a particularly cold area for a non-contributing instructor, or more probably, in view of the aircraft's limited contemporary use for training and preferential employment for communications, a lightly clad staff officer or minor official. In the rear cockpit the pipe was bent horizontally to form a 4 inch stub, discharging behind the rear instrument panel some 10 inches below the level of the top longeron.

The system was approved in April 1934 for service trials at Martlesham Heath, although there was criticism that the final installation did not fully comply with the original Design Memorandum, in that through-ventilation of the heater muffler was not provided in the event that both front and rear cockpit control valves were closed. An emphatic note also suggested that the installation was not to be considered for any aircraft carrying an auxiliary fuel tank in the front cockpit. Trials at A&AEE were flown in the late spring and early summer of 1934, which may or may not have been the best time of year to conduct such experiments, and the results were disappointing. The aircraft was returned to Stag Lane where modifications were made to the system during the winter, including a redesign of the exhaust pipe muffler and a seventh re-arrangement of the hot air feed into the cockpit. K2593 was flown again in May 1935 but all future developments in England were subsequently abandoned. By November 1936 the aircraft had passed into the care of 2 ASU Cardington before transfer the following February to 24 Squadron, for communication duties from Hendon.

The similarity of the Belgian SV-4 Stampe to the Tiger Moth renders it difficult immediately to identify the odd one out in this group. deHMC Archive

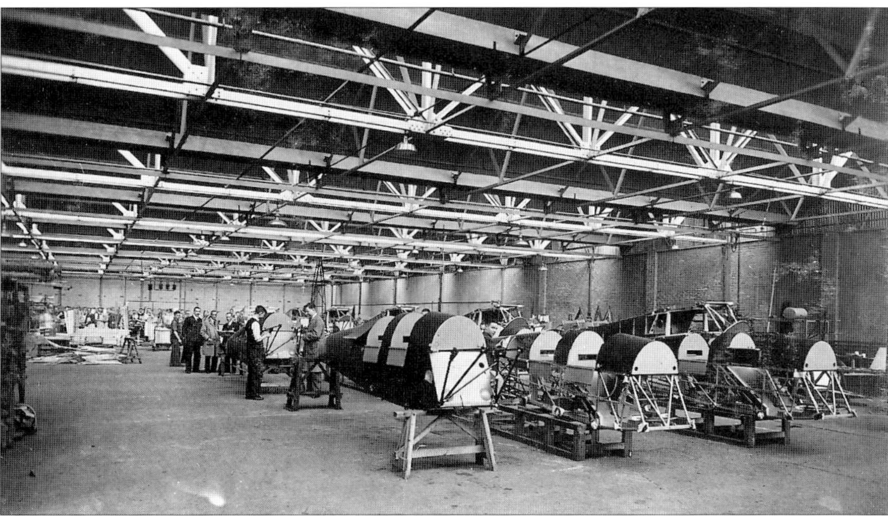

Stag Lane aerodrome closed in July 1934, but for some time before and after, airframe work was bled across to or initiated at the new factory site at Hatfield. This shot taken at Hatfield in 1934 appears to show a lethargic scene with Tiger Moth and DH.85 Leopard Moth construction running in parallel. For tidiness, the photographer has herded the majority of the workforce to the wing bay at the far end of the workshop. London and Provincial

Danish Army Air Corps Tiger Moth S-8 at Copenhagen. The aircraft was not fitted with slats or navigation lights and was operated under instrument conditions by day. The serial number is stencilled near the bottom of each interplane strut, no doubt as an aid to identification when re-rigging. deHMC Archive

Probably hoping for an instantly successful heater system were the seven pilots of the Danish Army Air Corps (Haerens Flyvertropper) who arrived at Hatfield in mid-March 1934, each to collect a new Tiger Moth. Senior Officer of the party, Captain C C Larsen, was to lead the flight from the comfort of his newly acquired DH.84 Dragon, a machine intended for troop transport, observation and general liaison duties. A photographic session held at Hatfield in the pouring rain was the perfect occasion upon which the engineers could display the Tiger Moth's tailored cockpit and propeller covers to good effect. The seven Tiger Moths (3196-3199 and 3209-3211), which joined up with the Dragon after take off for an immaculate formation flypast, were a follow-on order from the five DH.82s which had been delivered from Stag Lane by surface exactly a year previously.

The Danish Army Air Corps had decided that running a mixed Army Aviation School fleet of DH.60s and DH.82s was not efficient, in spite of the aircraft sharing a pedigree, and negotiations with de Havilland resulted in five DH.60 Moths being taken in part exchange for seven new DH.82A Tiger Moths and two DH.84 'Dragon Moths', against a cash balance of £12,480. The DH.60 Moths were immediately resold in Denmark by de Havilland's local agent to civil operators. Accompanied on their delivery flight by one of the DH.84 Dragons, the seven Tiger Moths arrived at Kastrup aerodrome, Copenhagen, on 24th March 1934 and were allocated military serial numbers S-6 to S-12.

During a training flight from Vaerlose on 11th August 1934, S-3 (3172), was abandoned by her crew who took to their parachutes, the aircraft crashing near Smorum. A replacement was purchased at a cost of £1,029 5s 0d, and delivered from Hatfield to Copenhagen by Captain Larsen on 20th February 1935, where serial S-13 was applied. In August the same year, during an instrument flying exercise, the crew of S-1 (3170), experienced a control lock in flight, and abandoned the aircraft over Amager. The student pilot, L M S Jacobsen, had parachuted from S-3 exactly twelve months previously.

Tiger Moth S-14 (3336), was purchased by the Haerens Flyvertropper in February 1936 at a price of £1,196.8s.10d, and delivered to Copenhagen by Premierlieutenant Michael Hansen. For her routing across Germany, the aircraft carried the spurious civil registration OY-DOK, although these letters were never officially allocated for the purpose, and were more legitimately worn by a DH.87B Hornet Moth (8065), delivered shortly afterwards to de Havilland's Danish agent Mr C Thielst. A month after the arrival of S-14, the first of the DH.82A Tiger Moths was lost when S-6 crashed at Stenlille, and was in turn replaced by the last of the pre-war Danish orders when S-15 (3611), was delivered by E B Meincke at exactly 1 o'clock on the afternoon of 16th October 1937.

A matter of days before an expedition was due to leave Copenhagen on board the MV *Gamma* in July 1938, bound for north east Greenland, funds became available for the hire of a spotter aircraft. The Danish Government agreed to loan Tiger Moth S-15 and after a set of suitable floats had been located in and collected from Stockholm, and fitted to the Tiger Moth at the KZ factory, Michael Hansen flew a series of trials from Copenhagen Harbour in the only Air Corps aeroplane ever to operate on floats.

The expedition proved very successful thanks to the efforts of the wireless equipped Tiger Moth and her pilot who was able to survey a passage free from ice, a task only possible from an airborne platform from which it was possible to report directly to the ship's captain. S-15 operated mostly at a height of 3,000ft and carried life belts, parachutes, flares, emergency rations for two days and fuel for two hours. On one occasion when the ship was difficult to locate due to its black hull, the Tiger Moth flew just above the surface from which position the *Gamma's* superstructure was spotted on the horizon.

Following the German invasion on 9th April 1941, eleven of the 12 surviving Air Corps' Tiger Moths were flown into storage at Avedore and the remaining one to Klovermarken. The whole fleet was confiscated by the Germans in August 1943 and offered for sale. With only 270 hours recorded, S-15 was sold to a Swedish company, Bjorkvallsflyg, early in 1944 for 6,300 Reichmarks, and registered SE-ADK on 29th February for operation by the Halmstad Aero Club.

In preparation for Michael Hansen's 1938 Greenland Expedition, Tiger Moth S-15 is towed across Copenhagen Harbour with a stabilising weight on the top surface of the upwind lower mainplane. deHMC Archive

During take off on 8th September 1946 with a glider on tow, the aircraft crashed and was written off.

Plans were drawn up in December 1942 for the loan of four Tiger Moths to Det Danske Luftfartsselskab in anticipation of the isolation of several small islands due to severe winter conditions, and registrations OY-DBA, OY-DBE, OY-DBI and OY-DBO were earmarked, but the scheme did not materialise.

Following the disbandment of the Danish Army in August 1943 and until June 1944, correspondence was exchanged between the Berlin office of the German Ministry of Aviation (Business Group, Overseas Department) and an address in Dessau, concerning the sale of ten Tiger Moths then based in Denmark. On 10th June 1944, the Luftwaffe High Command in occupation in Denmark, was advised by Doctor Pesch on behalf of the German Government, that the aircraft had been withdrawn from sale pending their allocation to other duties. Pesch made no mention of what these duties might have been or where, and although there is some suspicion that the customer might have been the Governments of Portugal or Spain, the ultimate fate of the Danish Tiger Moth fleet remains a mystery.

Within the space of six months, late in 1934, the de Havilland Company had rejected the idea of a substantial redesign of the Tiger Moth in favour of a review of prices for the existing model, but now found themselves being shepherded however unwillingly, into a major policy change in the wake of substantial re-equipment by the Royal Air Force. Most obvious requirements were likely to be a more powerful engine, and the six cylinder Gipsy Six was the natural candidate with which to replace the Gipsy Major. Good take-off and climb performance was necessary while speed was of little consequence. The aircraft should have more spacious cockpits, facility for a manoeuvrable observer's gun to the rear and a synchronised forward firing machine gun.

Immediate thoughts were that the new design should have a fabric covered metal frame fuselage and wings, and would sell at between £1,600 and £1,800. Furthermore, the type would be termed 'experimental' and a company funded prototype could be constructed relatively quickly, leading to the prospect of an Air Ministry development contract. The board agreed just before their 1934 Christmas holiday that the opportunities offered by provision of a new service trainer aircraft were very substantial.

Early in January 1935, shortly before delivery of the 1,000th Gipsy Major engine, the directors declared themselves to be divided in their opinion on whether a bigger, all-purpose development was after all preferable to a modified version of the standard Tiger Moth, the front fuselage suitably adapted to provide more spacious cockpits and other refinements, whilst retaining the Gipsy Major powerplant. Whatever the final decision, capacity was not available for any further progress to be made until after May 1934, but even that was conditional on the decision whether or not to proceed with a four seat cabin type replacement for the DH.83 Fox Moth, or the 'very cheap' light aeroplane which was considered even more essential. The production of Gipsy Major engines was scheduled to remain at 13 per week, although the weekly output of Gipsy Sixes was to be increased by one to a total of eight.

One of two unidentified Tiger Moths in this photograph caught in severe European weather during the Second World War. Traces of a civil registration under the wing, a long exhaust pipe and glider towing hook point towards an Austrian civil aircraft delivered pre-war and impressed after 1939. de Havilland Aircraft Co.

The matter had still not been resolved by April when Frank Hearle proposed that in order to reduce the necessity for the company to hold up to 18,000 part numbers in support of the current product range, (he quoted that in the USA, Waco held less than 4000), the DH.83 Fox Moth (selling at £995) should be phased out after current orders had been fulfilled, and that the DH.60GIII Moth Major at £695, should be dropped when the new DH.87 Hornet Moth was in production. A 'General Purpose Advance Trainer' Tiger Moth replacement was still under consideration, and although the military Tiger Moth selling price had been reduced by £50, the estimated cost of the proposed new trainer had risen to between £1,850 and £2,000.

During the spring of 1934, the Students of the de Havilland Aeronautical Technical School were working on the scheme to install a Gipsy III engine in their successful T.K.1 biplane in addition to finalising the layout for T.K.2, a low wing monoplane racer with an enclosed cockpit. In the workshops, and registered G-ACPS against one of de Havilland's 'special' build numbers, 1993, stood a Tiger Moth, built from scratch by the students and scheduled for service with the London Aeroplane Club at Hatfield. The aircraft qualified for a Certificate of Airworthiness in April 1934. In order to maintain momentum, a second Tiger Moth was laid down, registered G-ADGO (2262), to the London Aeroplane Club in May. A year later the aircraft spun into the ground during exuberant but not well executed low level aerobatics at Dunstable, but was repaired to live on. Perhaps it was the unexpected effort required in repairing G-ADGO that resulted in the School's third Tiger Moth production, G-AEVB (2264), not appearing until April 1937. This aircraft was registered in the name of the de Havilland Aircraft Company, and was immediately employed as part of the Reserve School establishment at Hatfield.

With the third Tiger Moth safely delivered, G-ACPS was sold to the Aero Club de France in Paris and registered F-AQDP in October 1937, but appears not to have survived the war. G-ADGO is believed to have crashed in March 1940 before impressment, and G-AEVB took up military markings as BB739 in October 1940 but was burned out after a take off accident at Hatfield the following September.

The opinion of the company's Special Representative in South America that training aircraft were vital, but the Tiger Moth was probably not the machine for the local market, was confirmed during the summer of 1934 when the Brazilian Government passed over de Havilland's proposals for 45 Tiger Moths in favour of 15 Curtiss Wright Primary Trainers and Waco F.3s. By the mid-'thirties, Brazil had discovered with others, that pilots of high performance military aircraft required a stepped level of training. If de Havilland were to remain competitive, a new aircraft was required sooner rather

One of a number of devices invented by countries where harsh environmental conditions could be a hazard to engine health, especially during start-up. This portable furnace is supplying hot air directly into the engine bay of a ski equipped Tiger Moth operated by the Royal Swedish Air Force.
via British Aerospace

than later, now with an emphasis on speed and capacity for armament training rather than manoeuvrability. An improved Tiger Moth with a Gipsy Six engine and variable pitch (VP) propeller was a prospect, or a completely new design, complementing the standard DH.82A which would then continue in the role of primary trainer. The company believed the Air Ministry was bound to announce soon an interest in an advanced training type and that their own promotion of the Tiger Moth as the 'one-type' trainer could no longer be substantiated.

Undeterred, Hatfield continued to exercise development effort on behalf of the DH.82A, and in October 1935 an experimental exhaust manifold was authorised for flight trials. The following month G-ADUC (3425), an aircraft purchased by the Marquess of Douglas and Clydesdale in support of his initiative to form a local airline based at Prestwick, was fitted with a full set of Demec navigation lights to a similar standard of installation as that employed two years previously on Lindsay Everard's DH.60GIII G-ACBX, a machine used for all-weather operations from his private airfield at Ratcliffe.

Before delivery, G-ADUC received a 6in Harley landing light: the unit was housed in the floor of the front cockpit, situated between the runners of the rudder bar support. Bowden cables operated by a small winch adjacent to the throttle controls in the rear cockpit permitted the lamp to be lowered or retracted into a position flush with the underside. The beam was directed 15 degrees off-centre rather than straight ahead and under the nose, eliminating the nuisance of flickering propeller interference and providing the pilot with a better chance of seeing it in contact with the ground, although the position of the port lower wing may have blanketed most meaningful reference.

In addition to their Reserve School at Desford, the Reid and Sigrist Company manufactured aircraft instruments, the most famous and perhaps widely appreciated being the ubiquitous 'Turn and Slip' indicator which took centre place in many instrument panels, not the least of which was the Tiger Moth.

In 1935 the company designed a new instrument, the Gyorizon, described as a combination of a rate of turn indicator with a visible horizon created using coloured fluid. By the simple expedient of allowing a pair of wings to sprout at the pivot point of the turn indicator needle, the lateral relation of the aircraft could be represented against an imaginary horizon. Since this horizon was itself affected both by gravity and by centrifugal force, the pilot was given an easily understood diagrammatical picture of the angular motion as well as the attitude of the aeroplane.

Early in 1936 the Gyorizon was installed and flight tested in a Desford Reserve School Tiger Moth, G-ADPD (3394), and at the end of February it was arranged that a practical demonstration of the safety potential of the device should be given to the press. This would be in the form of an aerobatic routine by a solo pilot flying from the rear cockpit and under the blind flying hood; probably the first time in the world that the aircraft had been flown in such a configuration. A contemporary report of the proceedings at Desford duly appeared in *Flight:*

'After only half an hour or so of practice under the hood with George Lowdell, Chief Instructor, in the front seat, Flight Lieutenant H A Howes took off by himself, lowered the hood and proceeded to carry out a series of very presentable slow rolls interspersed with odd half minutes of inverted flying.

'The sensations cannot have been too pleasant when another machine was known to be formating close by. Flight Lieutenant Howes suffered a bad ten seconds or so when his engine blew back with such force that he felt convinced that the photographic machine had touched his. He admitted that his only real difficulty consisted in stopping the roll in a squarely inverted position so that the machine would not fall out at once in one direction or another'.

As if to confirm the attitude prevailing in South America, in November, 'Jimmy' Buckingham reported back from the Initial Training School (5th Air Corps) of the Royal Swedish Air Force at Ljungbyhed where he had been demonstrating a DH.89 Dragon Rapide, that the Tiger Moth had fallen into disfavour. Instructors believed the aircraft was too small and too easy to fly, and that the cramped cockpits were not compatible with a pilot encased in a winter flying suit. Clearly, during contract negotiations, somebody had failed to raise the subject or had chosen to ignore it. Neither the aircraft nor the natural environment had changed since the first sales in 1931, and Sweden continued to build Tiger Moths under licence until June 1937.

Swedish debate on the likely specification of an improved aircraft was in tune with de Havilland's own thoughts, but of more immediate concern to Hatfield was that a Focke-Wulf Stieglitz with a 150hp Siemens engine had already been delivered to Ljungbyhed for assessment and Swedish authorities confirmed that another British aircraft was also being considered, almost certainly a trainer from Avro. Both types could offer *ab initio* and a degree of advanced training. Should either be recruited, de Havilland stood to lose the advantage for follow-on commercial aircraft orders which had proved to be so beneficial. The company's fears were realised in December when the Swedish Air Force announced an order for 12 Stieglitz and the prospect of more to follow.

Within nine months, Nikolaus von Eltz, de Havilland's agent in Vienna, raised almost identical criticism of the Tiger Moth as addressed to him by the Austrian Air Force. Von Eltz had suggested that a crashed aircraft, probably A-81 (3191), a previous de Havilland demonstration aircraft sold second hand in 1934, might be replaced by a new Tiger Moth, but he was advised that the DH.82 was an old design; in 1936 nobody had control cables running outside the fuselage and stretched across a non-adjustable tailplane. The aircraft had no mainwheel brakes, nor a tailwheel, and was, according to the Air Force, not very good at aerobatics.

Apart from the reliability of the Gipsy engine, reported the Austrian agent, his customers perceived the Tiger Moth and her sisters the Leopard Moth and Hornet Moth as old fashioned and uncompetitive. If the developing policy of buying from a near neighbour, due to ease and reliability of delivery and subsequent support was to be challenged, then it could only be as the result of a higher quality product offered at an appropriate price. The Austrian Air Force had declared itself in favour of the new Bücker machine which at about the same cost as the Tiger Moth, was more economical on fuel and a greatly improved acrobatic platform. The message from Nikolaus von

Eltz was clear enough: if the Tiger Moth was not modernised, nobody would buy it.

The gauntlet flung down in Vienna was picked up by de Havilland at Hatfield. The company was only too aware that it had a serious problem on its hands. A massive effort spent on designing, building, delivering on time and selling (at a huge predicted loss) the trio of DH.88 Comets which distinguished themselves in the 1934 MacRobertson Race; the major effort with the DH.91 Albatross, including new 12 cylinder engines, and modernisation of the DH.89 Dragon Rapide into the elegant but already dated DH.92 Dolphin biplane, had caused the company to neglect the trainer programme and the private owners and clubs upon whose support the very foundation of the company had been laid. 'Drifting away from the Training markets' is how St Barbe described it, with other companies offering new designs (notably Miles Hawks and Percival Gulls) and some even considering alternative powerplants. Phillips and Powis, the de Havilland West Country agents at Woodley were openly courting the prospect of manufacturing the American Menasco engine in support of its Miles aircraft production, not only to relieve its dependence on de Havilland, but to cream off a greater share of the revenues.

In April 1936, St Barbe admitted that had it not been for those other recent preoccupations, the Tiger Moth would have been replaced some time previously, but on Captain de Havilland's initiative, some consideration was now being given to setting up a semi-independent unit to address the whole issue of trainer aircraft. An alternative was to buy a controlling interest in a competitor offering an appropriate design. He considered the Tiger Moth to be 'on its last legs' and at the current price of £1,100, unlikely to attract any more orders. St Barbe's decision was to cut the price to £850, a figure at which the aeroplane could be produced at 'no loss', with his salesman's belief that the move would revive interest in the type, 'leading possibly to the construction of two or three hundred more'.

By the end of 1936, the company was considering a three year plan during which design capacity was to be allocated to a Tiger Moth replacement, probably from April 1937, but only after the development of a trainer of a different kind had been well established: built to Air Ministry specification T.6/36, and excessively 'improved' by interfering official dictate, the DH.93 Don finally emerged as a total inadequate, soaking up much precious effort before and after its first flight on 18th June 1937.

In December 1936, the same month that brought confirmation of the Swedish Air Force order for the Stieglitz, 40 Tiger Moths were ordered by the Air Ministry for distribution amongst the expanding Reserve. The contract called for delivery by 1st April 1937, a situation demanding a re-organisation of the production programme. Capacity had already been sold until mid-March and only 16 machines were scheduled from then until the end of April, following which production of four Tiger Moths per week were anticipated until the middle of July.

Ballantyne reported from Buenos Aires that following a deal of hard bargaining, there was a prospect for another 35 Tiger Moths for South America: ten each from Argentina, Brazil and Chile with five for Uruguay. In the event the optimism largely evaporated although Uruguay's Ministry of War did place a repeat order for nine aircraft in 1937, serialled 10-18 (3612-3620), which were shipped in September after an initial and temporary difficulty in effecting payment had been overcome, and with the capable Ballantyne taking passage home on board the same vessel.

In January 1937, the prospective Argentinean order was reported lost to the American Fleet in a deal which included six spare Kinner engines, and at a price quoted by Consolidated Aircraft said to be greater than the de Havilland proposal. Just over a year later, the Inspector General of Aviation in Peru called for a tender against training aircraft to be based in Lima, but to be fitted with Wright engines, a number of which were held as surplus on his spares inventory. As the Tiger Moth was not a suitable candidate, Ballantyne passed the enquiry on to Avro, anticipating the normal introductory commission. Money as much as anything was a factor behind the Austrian Air Force's eventual order for the Stieglitz. In a transparent display of political economics, the Austrian Finance Minister was reported as having instructed the Air Force to buy German aircraft not only as a good propaganda exercise but due to unmatchable terms for long term credit.

An enquiry from Portugal suggested a further eight Tiger Moths might be required, but there were grounds to believe that the Portuguese were also interested in acquiring licensed manufacturing rights. Arrangements were made for the Portuguese agent, Carlos Bleck, to accompany a government delegation to Hatfield, arriving in early June. There was little further news until October when a contract for the eight aircraft as predicted (3645-3652), was signed on behalf of Oficinas Gerais de Material Aeronáutico, in an arrangement which included purchase of a manufacturing licence. The eight aircraft were amongst 13 delivered from Hatfield in December.

At the beginning of 1937, the company was still soul searching, believing that in spite of a slight acceleration in interest, probably assisted by St Barbe's price reductions, the Tiger Moth was near to its end and accepting that a replacement was long overdue. The image of a wooden winged biplane was not compliant with a once universally perceived view of excellence and imagination in the company's designs, they admitted. But enquiries continued to arrive at Hatfield and in January and February were received from Turkey and Egypt whilst deliveries were made to South Africa, Ceylon, Iraq and Malaya. Orders were also confirmed for 13 Tiger Moths for the Reserve Schools at Bristol, Sywell and Desford, including one for the Airwork syndicate's school at Castle Bromwich, signifying the last of the Air Ministry's current round of interest.

In April a Reserve aircraft scheduled for delivery to the Newcastle upon Tyne Aero Club, G-AEWG (3589), was tested with a Rotax K625 signal navigation light installed under the floor, part of a continuing development strategy. In spite of having now sold practically all of its sanctioned Tiger Moth build positions, the company sensed that

Tiger Moth A-78 was a direct export to de Havilland's Austrian agent, Nikolaus von Eltz in 1934. She was registered OE-DAM to the Austrian Aero Club in 1935 but joined the Austrian Army that same year. Hugh Evans

Tiger Moths of the Egyptian Air Force being inspected by a party of officers who appear to have arrived at their desert airfield in the unidentified aircraft to the right of the corrugated iron hangars. Hugh Buckingham

Peter de Havilland (left) and Hugh Buckingham with Tiger Moth G-ACJA, during one of their ranging sales and demonstration tours on behalf of the de Havilland Company. Hugh Buckingham

the Reserve requirements were still not completely satisfied and laid down a further 'small' batch, all in the face of increasing Air Ministry orders for Miles Hawk Trainers from Phillips and Powis, to whom Hatfield continued to supply Gipsy Major engines.

With the continuing trickle of orders, an analysis of the production cost was called up in May 1937, and concluded that per pound of empty weight (1,125lb quoted) the price of aircraft materials amounted to three shillings and a halfpenny and the labour content to two shillings and a halfpenny. Against these economics, it was considered prudent to make an upwards adjustment in the currently advertised price from £875 to £925, still more than 11% below the 1931 listing, although by September the figure had been amended again to read £1,095, an amazingly brash move which took it to within £5 of its highest ever quoted price.

Since the introduction of the DH.82 Tiger Moth, examples of all models had been purchased by the Persian authorities following their approval of the de Havilland business ethic outlined during contract discussions in Switzerland. It was the Persians who had initiated many of the earliest military modifications, culminating in the fully fledged Tiger Moth 'Fighter' in 1932.

Their support of the order book was satisfyingly constant, but each contract would appear to have been negotiated under a different bureaucracy:

1932: 3117-3136 (20), serials 101-120
Imperial Persian Army Flying Corps.
1934: 3200-3208 (9), serials 121-129
Imperial Iranian Ministry of War.
1934: 3228-3237 (10), serials 130-139
Le Ministere de la Guerre,
Imperial de Perse.
1934: 3290-3309 (20), serials 140-159 (?)
Imperial Persian War Ministry.
1936: 3464-3473 (10), serials 160-169
Imperial Iranian War Ministry.
1939: 3930-3934, 82005-82009, 82047-82051, 82092-82096 (20), serials unknown
Imperial Iranian Army.

In 1933, Hugh Buckingham spent time training the Tiger Moth force at Ahwaz, five miles north of Abadan at the head of the Persian Gulf, travelling out by DH.83 Fox Moth G-ABZN, which he delivered to a customer in Cairo on the way home.

The Sales Department made a surprise announcement in June 1937 that seven Gipsy Major engines had been sold to Iran (Persia) and were to be fitted to Tiger Moths built under licence in that country, but there is no evidence to suppose that a single aircraft was ever built there, quite to the contrary: 20 additional aircraft were supplied from Hatfield in 1939 making a total of 89, together with five engines which were ordered very specifically as 'spares'.

Added to the commercial aircraft business through the supply of DH.89 Dragon Rapides, and the knowledge that with some regularity, groups of Iranian pilots were being coached in the art of flying instruction by de Havilland at Hatfield and Panshanger until at least 1944, the importance of the first diplomatic contacts in Switzerland can be appreciated.

In August 1937 the company returned to its earlier sales philosophy and released another brochure extolling the multi-role virtues of the Tiger Moth, 'The One Type Trainer' with the sheer reliability of the Gipsy Major engine:

'Possessing adequately high performance to permit instruction without loss of time in securing height, reproducing perfectly the handling characteristics of first-line aircraft and having ample accommodation for the installation of all forms of military equipment, the Tiger Moth is equally recommended for ab initio, intermediate and advanced flying training as well as for instruction in specialised military duties.

'The adoption of Tiger Moths spells absolute standardisation in training aircraft, eliminates completely the need for a variety of different types for individual phases of military instruction and ensures the most economical training of an efficient Air Force personnel'.

It was a fairly lightweight document compared with the solidity of the 1932 booklet although the message was substantially the same, and the promotion very much in line with St Barbe's business instinct that irrespective of criticism, a renewed interest and requirement was beginning to emerge. The brochure was a reminder to all that the aircraft's capabilities were already well recognised in air arms and civil organisations around the world.

The recent substantial increases in price had little or no connection with any rise in production costs; there was no follow-on aircraft, no updated Tiger Moth to sell or to buy, and the Business Office had little to lose in exercising its talents to achieve those 'two or three hundred' predicted sales of the aircraft which they had already declared to be 'on its last legs'.

The price list which followed in September 1937 was greatly expanded and included details of all the 'subsidiary equipment' which had previously been supplied to individual customer specification, not unnaturally with a heavy bias towards military installations. No firm commitment to price was offered on items such as machine guns, bombing sights or wireless, all of which depended on the operator's choice of supplier, although de Havilland revealed that they could offer two alternative types of inverted flying conversion kits: £58 would buy the three minute system, but an extended period of ten minutes was available at £73.15s.0d per aircraft, supplied and fitted.

In a report to the board, the Business Department was able to record that 108 Tiger Moths had been sold during the 12 month period until 30th September 1937, but at an average price allowing for variations in equipment and commissions of only £780 each, and that an allowance for 50 sales might be made for 1938. There was no projection beyond that in anticipation of a new, low priced practical two seater that might be expected to fulfil the roles of both the Tiger Moth and the generally unpopular Hornet Moth. In prospect was a new advanced light trainer for 1941, doubling in an alternative model, as a high speed civil tourer.

The publicity drive caused no immediate impact on sales: during the last quarter of 1937, only 18 Tiger Moths were ordered: three for the associated company in South Africa, one each for India and New Zealand, and the anticipated eight aircraft order from Portugal. Five were ordered for private owners by French agent Costa de Beauregard, operating from his offices in the Champs Elysées, followed by a further five early in 1938. This second order had been accepted against a spring delivery in the confident expectation that the French authorities would present no difficulties, but by the end of February when eight aircraft had been completed, import licences for only three had been granted, and the group sat somewhat disconsolately in the Hatfield factory, just recovering from the effects of a fortnight's strike, and still awaiting paperwork to authorise delivery. All was resolved by mid-April when a third batch of five aircraft was ordered for delivery in June.

Once safely in France, 14 of the 15 aircraft were re-registered in the name of the Société Française de Transports Aériens and all but two were eventually delivered to the Spanish Republican Army. Documentation for the 15th aircraft, F-AQOS (3677), registered to Roger Levy at Neuilly, was cancelled in London during August 1938 and the eventual fate of the aircraft is unknown. de Havilland records indicate that only ten of the 15 aircraft were delivered to France: two in February 1938, one in March, four in May and three in June. It was a sensitive issue and perhaps not best recorded.

St Barbe must have been heartened to receive from the Chinese Government, an invitation to tender for 60 Tiger Moths, but equally frustrated that he could not offer a reasonable delivery schedule. Advised that Chinese contacts had re-focused their attention on the Fleet, Hatfield immediately revised their schedule but it was too late and nothing further was heard.

Eastern Europe had proved to be a profitable trading area for de Havilland since the company chairman Alan Butler toured the area extensively in his personal DH.37 G-EBDO in 1924 seeking government contracts and licensing agreements.

When in October 1937 the Government of Bulgaria asked de Havilland to tender for 20 Tiger Moths, the company was dismayed to be advised that their usual terms of business were not acceptable. The proposal was for 50% of the total value to be paid only after all the aircraft had been delivered to Sofia, where they would be regarded as in 'temporary reception' for six months, after which the remaining 50% would be negotiated for 'definite reception'. In common with competing British and American manufacturers, de Havilland refused the terms which they were later advised by 'informed sources' were part of a ploy to ensure that the order went to Germany. The intelligence was not without foundation, for in May 1938 it was announced that the Bulgarian order had indeed been placed as anticipated.

Although St Barbe would rarely view a lost order with anything but disappointment, contemporary systems of international control and transfer of currency could create uncertainty and possibly danger for the unwary business dabbler. de Havilland's Business Director was both worldly and wise and had only recently rejected the opportunity to tender for a Turkish order, purely on the grounds of what he perceived to be a bad long-term currency situation. At the first opportunity following advice that Bulgaria was in a position to place Sterling in London, he appointed an agent in Sofia. It was a shrewd move: in August 1938 only months after the loss of the government order to Germany, and against all predictions, there arose the slightest prospect for an order for Tiger Moths. de Havilland were anxious enough to send Lee Murray to Sofia to enter into discussions, and Major Ivan Nojaroff led a Trade Mission to Hatfield in January 1939, during which visit he said that much as he liked the Tiger Moth, he preferred a low wing monoplane made from wood, suitable for manufacture under licence in Bulgaria. The Tiger Moth order did not materialise.

The Roumanian agent, Mr A Mano, called from Bucharest in January 1938 to seek confirmation of prices and terms for between ten and 20 Tiger Moths. The Roumanian Government had recently purchased 25 Nardi trainers from Italy, powered by Gipsy engines licence built by Alfa Romeo. Hatfield knew from past experience involving the sale of DH.89 Dragon Rapides, that negotiations were liable to continue for many months. The enquiry itself almost certainly resulted from Clem Pike's demonstration of Tiger Moth G-ACJA (3191), in Bucharest three and a half years previously, but in spite of his warm welcome and an enduring relationship between the two countries and their aviation interests, no order was received.

In July 1938, funded by a donation from the Abe Bailey Aviation Coronation Gift, and a small subsidy from the Government of Southern Rhodesia, Tiger Moth VP-YBW (3701), was test flown at Hatfield and shipped to the de Havilland associated company in South Africa where it was prepared for delivery to the 'Travelling Flying School' recently established in Southern Rhodesia.

A line-up of Tiger Moths photographed in Spain during the Civil War, none of which appears to have slats although several are complete with long exhaust pipes. These are probably some of the aircraft nominally ordered by private owners in France in 1938, all of which were immediately re-sold south of the border. John Pothecary

Under the big sky in Africa, Tiger Moth VP-YBW of the touring Southern Rhodesia Flying Training School. Operations were confined to early mornings and late afternoons due to heat and turbulence. *The Aeroplane*

Representatives of the Southern Rhodesian Government and of the de Havilland Aircraft Company, which was already operating flying schools at Salisbury and Bulawayo using DH.60 Moths and DH.82A Tiger Moths, had visited several towns to discuss with local flying clubs how to overcome the financial problems of maintaining facilities, for what would always be a limited number of members. As a result, the Southern Rhodesia Flying Training School was inaugurated at Que Que on 25th October 1938, consisting of: *'Tiger Moth VP-YBW, complete with slots and a fixed pitch metal propeller, an instructor, Mr D D Longmore, an A and C licensed ground engineer, Mr T H Gundry, a tent, a box of tools and spares, and half a dozen sets of helmets, earphones and goggles'.*

Que Que was the first town visited where seven members of the flying club were helped to obtain their 'A' licences. The next move was to Gatooma where on 7th January 1939 nine members of the club started their flying training in climatic conditions that seriously limited the number of hours available for useful instruction. It was usual to start flying as early as 5.30am but finishing by 8.30am and then starting again after 4.00pm when the heat of the day had diminished and with it, the turbulent conditions that *ab initio* pupils found impossible to cope with. In company with other civil aircraft in the region, VP-YBW was impressed into the Southern Rhodesia Air Service just eight months later.

The subject of de Havilland's new *ab initio* trainer had been raised again during a review of the company's design programme conducted by Frank Hearle and Lee Murray in October 1937. The new 'cheap aeroplane', the DH.94, was first flown at Hatfield on 23rd June 1937, but first deliveries were not expected before October 1938, and more realistically, six months later than that due to difficulties in development of its new engine, provisionally named the Gipsy Junior. The trainer project was now being referred to as the DH.96, but due to pressure on the overall programme, a further postponement was suggested, unless the responsibility could be switched to the new department specially created to work on the DH.94. On their own initiative, they were already attempting to fit a Gipsy Major engine into that airframe and would need high level direction to delay that project indefinitely in favour of the DH.96.

The review concluded that money and effort expended on the current level of design and development in both Engine Division and Aircraft Division was too high. Priorities would need to be identified and adhered to, and the new trainer was high on the list. Should there have been doubt, word came from Belgium that the Military Flying School had rejected the Tiger Moth on the grounds that both construction and performance were below the current level of their specification, which equally had eliminated both the Bücker Jungmann and the Gipsy Major powered Stampe SV-4B, a type submitted by de Havilland's Belgian agents. The company hoped that as no firm decision had been made, the competition would remain open until after the DH.96 had been launched. Preliminary drawings revealed the DH.96 to be an open cockpit, tandem two seat monoplane, looking for all the world like a Miles Magister.

The unnamed DH.96 might have replaced the Tiger Moth after de Havilland finally acknowledged that change was necessary, but world events moved too rapidly and the project progressed no further than the drawing boards at Hatfield. deHMC Archive

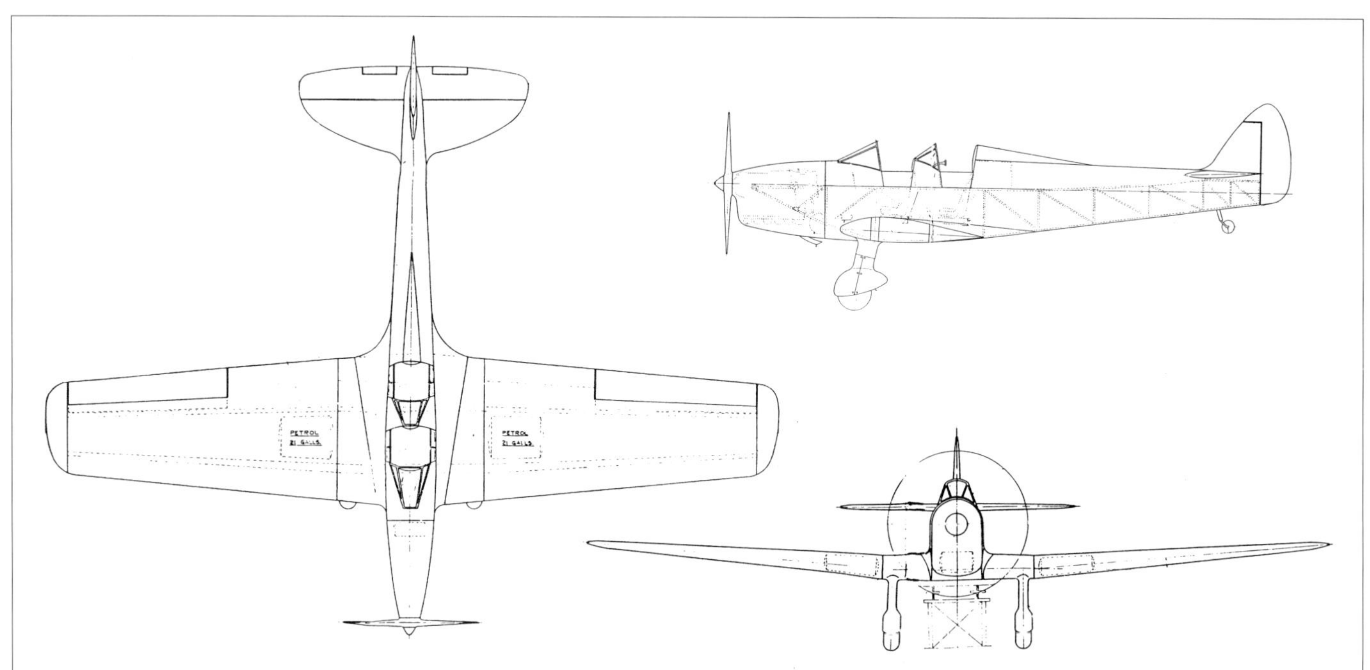

A TIME FOR DECISIONS

The Stag Lane factory site in 1935, marooned within a sea of actual and pending housing development. Engine production was housed in the block nearest the camera. Most of the buildings survived until final demolition in 1997, to be replaced with more houses.
de Havilland Aircraft Co.

IN VIEW of his most recent sales promotions in support of the Tiger Moth, Francis St Barbe must have been surprised to take a telephone call in February 1938 from the Directorate of Aeronautical Production (DAP) at the Air Ministry, asking whether the company was still in a position to supply Tiger Moths! On hearing that they were, the Director confirmed that a further order was being considered. Possibly, it had been brought to his attention that the Gipsy Major engine had just been approved for a 1,000 hour overhaul life, a figure without precedent. In March, officials from the DAP visited the Stag Lane engine factory on two occasions to enquire after the company's position if large numbers of additional engines should be required at short notice in the event of a national emergency?

The Air Ministry was already critical of de Havilland for not maintaining contracted Gipsy Major deliveries for Magisters, forcing some aircraft to be accepted into storage less engines, but Frank Hearle was confident that all current obligations would be honoured by October 1938.

At the current rate of production, the factory was able to provide 20 Gipsy Major engines per month, although they would have preferred to offer 25. To increase production significantly it would be necessary to invest heavily in a new range of tools and jigs which, for civil orders alone, could not be justified. It was a serious problem that only government money together with de Havilland effort could hope to resolve.

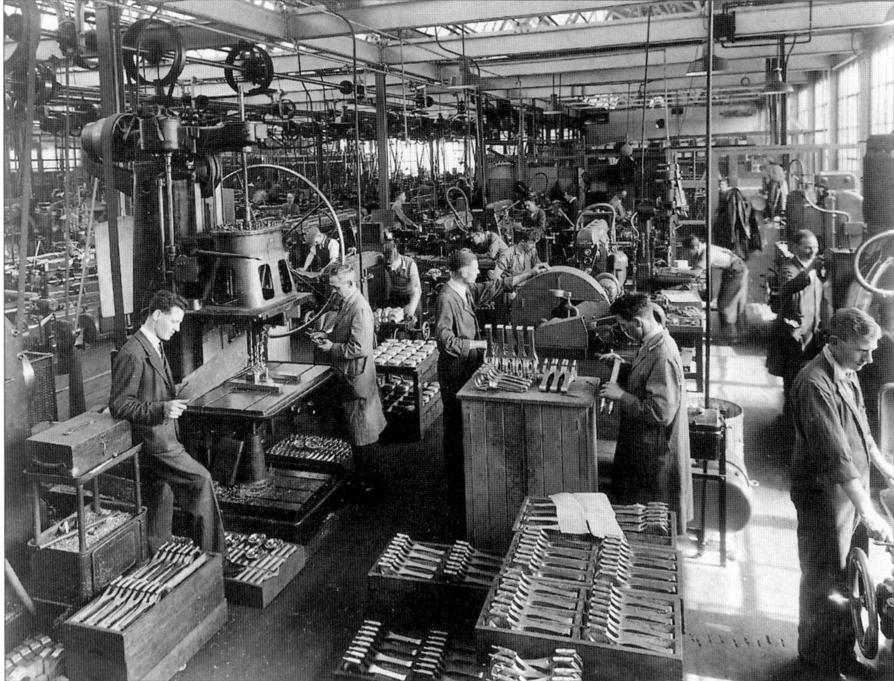

A corner of the de Havilland Engine Division shops at Stag Lane, an area specialising in connecting rods and pistons and at the time of the photographic session, busy with throughput for the 12 cylinder Gipsy King. via British Aerospace

It was the only argument and resulted in the Engine Division's immediate authority to proceed with a major re-development of the production shops at Stag Lane, following which it was expected that an additional 120 engines per month could be supplied.

It was the engine situation too which initiated a review of Tiger Moth production. de Havilland had been tasked to build Airspeed Oxfords on the grounds that Hatfield could offer both facilities and capacity. There was what some believed to be a lesser need for more Tiger Moths, and for the time being, the Air Ministry was reasonably content to accept delivery, without engines, of airframes intended for storage as strategic reserve. The paradox was that while Hatfield was building urgently needed Oxfords, and Tiger Moths were regarded as a second priority, before Oxford production reached a peak, capacity for the urgent output of more Tiger Moths might only be found outside de Havilland's own factory.

The Air Ministry became embroiled in an interesting round of correspondence in April 1938, when Air Service Training (AST), ordered a trio of Tiger Moths for operation either at Hamble with 3 ERFTS or Ansty on behalf of 9 ERFTS. The Ministry advised de Havilland that in their tender to operate a Reserve School, AST had stipulated the use of Miles Magisters, and asked Hatfield not to supply Tiger Moths against the threat of a refusal to recognise them. AST countered that their submission had been against 'aircraft of an approved type'. The Tiger Moths were not delivered.

The loss of an order for three Tiger Moths might have caused greater concern had not Frank Hearle reported to his fellow directors on 27th May that the company was to be in imminent receipt of a contract to supply 400 Tiger Moths to the Air Ministry, the last of which was to be delivered by 30th September 1939. Notice of confirmation of no additional requirement beyond 400 was to be posted not later than 31st March. A large coincidental order for Miles Magisters resulted in the Engine Division receiving an immediate contract for the supply of 780 Gipsy Major Is.

At a required average monthly production rate of 25 aircraft, it would be difficult for Hatfield to fulfil the contract without assistance, and the Air Ministry agreed to allow the de Havilland factory at Downsview, Toronto, to assist with the provision of metal parts, assuming the need not to increase its own workforce. In the event it was agreed that Canada should contribute 200 complete fuselages, while Hatfield sourced a major woodworking company who, under de Havilland control and supervision, could produce high quality sub contract work, graduating towards manufacture of complete aircraft.

As an interim measure, the Air Ministry placed an order with de Havilland in May 1938 for the supply of 50 Tiger Moths to be built against contract 778402/38, and extended this the following month by an additional 400 machines against a schedule which would deliver 20 in December 1938, 30 in January 1939, 36 in February and each month thereafter until completion, and assumed Canadian participation.

Frank Hearle advised the Ministry that the aircraft with Canadian components would be 30% to 40% more expensive than a pure Hatfield product on the grounds of freight charges alone: an estimated airframe cost of about £800 against £600. This revelation brought only another question: 'can you make 50 Tiger Moths a month?' The Air Ministry was now looking towards an estimated requirement for 896 more training aircraft in addition to those already contracted, and were beginning to believe that such numbers would give an ample margin over the current de Havilland capacity to be of real interest to an outside contractor.

Hatfield was pleased to have the immediate order for 50 Tiger Moths as it plugged a gap in the schedule of work and prevented a prospective loss of labour which even on a temporary basis at a time of growing crisis was barely imaginable. An order for 200 Oxfords for delivery by March 1940 was also secured in May 1938, much to the displeasure of Airspeed who adopted an uncooperative attitude. Hatfield was permitted to increase floor space by the addition of a new shed of 80,000sq.ft. at the same time as deciding to abandon any further thought of developing the DH.91 Albatross as a bomber. The additional Tiger Moth orders also appeared to put an end to speculation that the Air Ministry was considering purchase of the Curtiss Wright NA16. The government's own advisors had already suggested that at such a time, the British aircraft industry would hardly welcome any further interest in that direction.

Such momentous activity made the Coventry Aeroplane Club's order for a single Tiger Moth, G-AFHI (3682), delivered to Whitley in May, look rather insignificant, but the Air Ministry eventually had that too, impressed into military service just over two years later.

G-AFHT (3695), was another refugee from the immediate pre-war flying club movement, just managing to drag itself out of recessionary times to re-equip. Delivered to the Merseyside Aero and Sports Company Ltd in July 1938 for operation by Liverpool Aero Club from Hooton Park, and painted in the traditional colours of yellow fuselage with silver wings, the aircraft joined the RAF exactly two years later, survived the war, including eight years with the Royal Navy, and was sold to New Zealand in 1952 where she crashed after only ten months' activity.

Encouraged by the Air Ministry's massive order against a strict timetable, the company put up its own proposal for a follow-on run of 500 additional Tiger Moths and also solicited further enquiries from any quarter. Although the political situation in the world at large was deteriorating, it could equally well improve, and the civil and commercial lines of business had to be maintained. The London Aeroplane Club and Liverpool Aero Club both enquired after additional Tiger Moths in July, and from Syria a request to tender against the provision of 20 touring aircraft was met by the offer of civil specification Tiger Moths, and refused. Hatfield admitted that even with the current level of commitment to the Air Ministry, it could still squeeze in one 'independent' order each week.

Tiger Moth G-ADLZ (3362), fresh from the factory and with a C of A dated 16th August 1935, left Hatfield in the early hours of 23rd August 1935 bound for Lympne. The famous grass aerodrome on the south coast of England had, in course of its rich history, dispatched and received many record breaking flights, and provided a safe haven for ever optimistic or totally exhausted light aeroplane pilots. G-ADLZ was using Lympne as a stepping off point before crossing the English Channel bound for Brussels, Cologne and Frankfurt where pilot Hugh Buckingham was scheduled to spend the night. The following day the aircraft flew via Linz, Vienna and Budapest to Belgrade, and on the third day, 25th August, travelling via Skopje and Salonica, she touched down at her destination, Athens, after a total flight time of 21 hours.

During the course of the next six weeks, Buckingham lived in the Air Force Mess where he was introduced to some extraordinary drinking games, but managed to accumulate more than 28 hours of test and demonstration flying. The end result was nothing; the authorities decided to buy the Avro Cadet instead.

Having travelled deep into the Balkans, G-ADLZ was required to fly on to Turkey, demonstrating at Ankara on 10th October and flying more than ten hours at Eskisehir during a week's stay. No sales resulted. The aircraft was delivered back to Heston rather than Hatfield, arriving on 31st October operating from Frankfurt via Brussels in two sectors of more than three hours each. In spite of the pilot acting as his own operations staff and engineer, it was an expensive trip, logging 100 flying hours alone, costs that would of necessity find their way into the prices of subsequent sales from Hatfield, as the Business Director was very much aware.

G-ADLZ joined the de Havilland fleet at White Waltham operating in support of 13 ERFTS until she was impressed as BB752 in October 1940. In June 1941 the aircraft was transferred to 21 EFTS Booker, and on 28th January 1942 suffered engine failure during take off from the Relief Landing Ground (RLG) at Garston, stalling into the ground from 30ft and sustaining damage which was not considered economical to repair.

Hugh Buckingham's demonstration in Athens did leave one good impression. Amongst the Tiger Moths ordered in July 1938 was one listed under 'Private Club Greece'. SX-AAK (3721), had been sold to Squadron Leader Stephan T Zotos of Athens, a retired Greek Air Force officer, and although the British airworthiness certificate was dated 27th September 1938, there are no records to confirm that the aircraft was ever delivered, although she was reported to have been seen in Paris in August 1939 and in a dismantled condition at Hatfield the following October. In April 1940, the registered ownership was changed to Technical and Aeronautical Exploitations Ltd (TAE), a company owned by Stephan Zotos, and through which he was trying to persuade the Greek Government to establish a fully fledged Air Force Reserve based on the operating principles established by the British. Zotos knew the Greek Air Force was keen to be rid of its expensive-to-run Avro Cadets, an aircraft not liked by instructors, and which could easily be replaced by more economical Tiger Moths.

de Havilland backed the plan as a valuable entree: Zotos was a most valued ally, having bought his own demonstration aircraft, and there was no coincidence in the fact that he and the company's Greek agent, Mr Coutroubie, were at Hatfield together when the Tiger Moth order had been placed. They returned to Greece in Squadron Leader Zotos' new Hornet Moth SX-AAI, also destined for ownership by TAE before her impressment into local and emergency service with the RAF in 1941. Any record of SX-AAK held on file in Athens was lost after the Italian invasion in 1940. The Greek Air Force did receive Tiger Moths, eventually, although they had to wait until after the war was over.

Stephan Zotos would still have been on his protracted four week journey back to Athens, meandering across Europe in his Hornet Moth during the summer of 1938, when the British Air Ministry announced that 300 more Tiger Moths were to be added to the 450 of the current contract. At Hatfield, the de Havilland sales team was also receiving orders for the DH.94, now named Moth Minor, and inviting clubs and other bodies participating in the Civil Air Guard scheme, to come and fly the new aeroplane, although due to its uncertificated state, this would have to be within the boundary of the airfield.

Although it was August, the Hatfield works was hardly on holiday, but only two Tiger Moths were delivered that month, one to New Zealand and the other to the Aero Club de Suisse. HB-OKU (3702), was written off in a crash at Saleve within a few weeks of arrival, and was not replaced.

The political situation in Europe in September 1938 resulted in mixed fortunes for Hatfield. While the Air Ministry ordered hundreds of Tiger Moths, nobody else did, save for a pair booked to the associate company in South Africa. Much attention was being paid to the new DH.94 Moth Minor and 111 delivery positions were reserved during the month, all but five from the home country. Two Tiger Moths reserved for India were subsequently cancelled due to problems with payment: the customers it seemed, had no money. Meanwhile, Costa de Beauregard, not in the least diverted by his sale of Tiger Moths nearly all of which had flown on to the conflict in Spain, was negotiating with the French Naval Air Service for the provision of 30 more, but the quoted delivery dates may not have been acceptable and no firm order was placed.

Through the Royal Canadian Air Force, the Air Ministry had been making representations to the Canadian Government on the prospect of providing facilities for a substantial pilot training programme, and news soon reached the redoubtable Phil Garratt, de Havilland Aircraft of Canada's General Manager. Garratt had received a copy of an RCAF specification for a proposed new training aircraft which, because of limited

One week before war was declared in 1939 and the sun shines brightly down onto a line of yellow painted Tiger Moths awaiting engine runs at Hatfield. The spinner of each aircraft is loose fitted back to front to draw attention. Note the TK2 parked behind the nearest Tiger Moth.
de Havilland Aircraft Co

Note quite in alphabetical order, three new Tiger Moths for the Midland Aero Club await delivery to their base at Castle Bromwich on 4th February 1939. The site would soon be more famous as a massive factory under The Nuffield Organisation, building Supermarine Spitfires and Avro Lancasters. de Havilland Aircraft Co

design facilities at Downsview, he had forwarded to Hatfield, suggesting that it was very close to the company's own proposals in the shape of the DH.96. By reply, Garratt was informed that in view of the workload then being experienced in England, the DH.96 had been dropped. Garratt believed this was a serious mistake and confirmed that Fleet Aircraft were working on a Trainer designed around the Air Force specification and which would, if successful, undoubtedly secure the Canadian market. He suggested that the company had invested too heavily in the DH.91 and DH.95 leaving him with little to sell for immediate delivery except the prospect of a few Moth Minors, and that for many reasons the DH.96 was urgently required. But his pleas were to no avail; at Hatfield the decision had been made and all work on the new trainer had been brought to a halt. As it transpired, none of the aircraft designed and built in Great Britain to the same specification as the proposed DH.96 was accepted by the Air Ministry. Following a series of service flight trials, all were rejected as unsuitable and the specification was allowed to lapse.

The year 1938 ended with a flurry of orders and deliveries: during the last quarter, 34 Tiger Moths were ordered including 20 part-built machines scheduled for completion in Australia, and 102 were delivered of which 80 were for the Air Ministry. British based flying clubs continued to show interest, as did those in New Zealand and India where a scheme of subsidy was being proposed. The Iranian Army said it wanted another 20 aircraft and placed a firm order in January; the Port of Spain Aero Club booked two for operation under the blue skies of the Caribbean. The Midland Aero Club at Castle Bromwich asked for a reservation on six on the grounds that they were unable to wait for delivery of Moth Minors, but a month later when confirming the Tiger Moth order, they declared their intention to take five Moth Minors too.

In January 1939, New Year discussions revolved around the company's 1940 programme. Following enormous increases in unrecovered development costs incurred by the Aircraft Division for the past several years, a situation likely to be balanced only by the huge Air Ministry contracts currently going through the shops, it was planned to launch a major civil aircraft sales campaign which would absorb 70% of available production capacity, and fill the remaining 30% with Air Ministry orders against a limited but guaranteed profit. Sights were set on the sale of 50 DH.95 Flamingos, 12 DH.91 Albatross, 40 DH.89 Dragon Rapides and at least 250 DH.94 Moth Minors. Continuance of a current production contract for Airspeed Oxfords would be sought, although the type was on the prohibited export list which restricted any extension to sales, other than to the Air Ministry. The Tiger Moth remained in the mind of the company very much as a 'military contract' aeroplane, and was useful to balance the loss of Oxford export business. *'From that point of view it is very desirable that we should maintain a good production of Tiger Moths or its successor'*, wrote Lee Murray, General Manager at Hatfield. It was essential that an early decision be made regarding the 1940 programme, he urged the Directors, both from a production point of view and in formulation of design policy.

Encouraged by the Directorate of Civil Research and Production, by mid-February the company was actively considering involvement in another new project, a small twin to accommodate perhaps eight or ten passengers, and the study had already been allocated an identity: DH.97. Much as he was in favour, and concerned that a rival manufacturer might take up the specification and compete in the markets currently and adequately satisfied by the Dragon Rapide, St Barbe still believed that for business reasons amongst others, a new training aircraft was more urgently required.

During the late summer of 1938, the Canadian company had asked Hatfield to investigate prospects for the installation of an uprated engine for Tiger Moth operations in Canada. The basic Gipsy Major I had already been developed into the 1C version specifically for Canada: domed pistons raised the compression ratio from 5.25 to 6:1, and aluminium alloy heads were fitted, a revived form of the old Gipsy I and Gipsy II heads, but with an improved technique for inserting the valve seats. The engine was in most other respects identical to the Gipsy Major I, except that it could burn leaded fuel without fear of damage to the valve seats, and maximum power output was raised from 130bhp to 142bhp at little increase in turning speed and with a reduction in weight.

On 18th November, approval was received for Hatfield to begin flight trials of the Tiger Moth fitted with a Gipsy Major Series II and Fairey Reed fixed pitch metal propeller. A review of airframe stressing suggested no changes were necessary except that the mounting had to be moved forward by 2 inches to provide clearance between the engine back cover and the fireproof bulkhead. Compared with a basic Gipsy Major I, the Series II engine had grown in weight by about 14lb and the metal airscrew was 18lb heavier than its wooden counterpart, but perversely, the increases were beneficial to the position of the centre of gravity (CG) which, other than in a fully loaded Tiger Moth, was near to the permitted aft limit.

As the result of research and laboratory analysis of vibration, many of the components in the Series II had been redesigned, and the new, stiffer, crankshaft had been specified with a splined nose which could accept in addition to a fixed pitch propeller, a two pitch or constant speed unit. High compression pistons and new aluminium heads with increased finning were fitted to permit a higher cruising output, and the crankcase was cast from Elektron magnesium alloy rather than aluminium in an effort to save weight. The timing gear cover on the back of the engine had been redesigned to accommodate a vacuum pump, double scavenge pump, a constant speed unit (governor) and a small generator. The forward shift of the mounting necessitated fitting a V bracing in the engine bay to cope with side and tortional loads, which replaced the single diagonal brace acceptable on the Gipsy Major I. Other minor modifications were made to the oil system and exhaust manifold and the whole new installation was approved on 16th January 1939.

The New Year order book was expectant when news was received that five Tiger

Moths were required in Java (Netherlands East Indies) for the earliest possible delivery in 1939, and the de Havilland agents in Bandoeng, Rous and Meeuwenoord, were cabled from Hatfield offering one delivery position in March, April and May and two in June. In return, Hatfield was advised that Bücker in Germany were offering delivery three weeks following receipt of order and their quotation was 30% below de Havilland's published list price. Nothing more was heard until March when Hatfield was advised that the order would definitely not be theirs but would be placed with Bücker on the grounds of better delivery, price and payment terms. The Bücker offer had resulted in an affordable order which for the same cash sum would now provide six machines.

But the East Indies were to have Tiger Moths: five aircraft were delivered to the Northern Aviation School and Club at Barton in August 1939, two weeks before war was declared: G-AFTI (82233); G-AFXZ (82234); G-AFYB (82593); G-AFYC (82594) and G-AFZD (82595). All escaped immediate impressment but were sold to aircraft brokers W S Shackleton Ltd, operating from their London office in Piccadilly. G-AFZD was flown to the de Havilland Civil Repair Organisation (CRO) at Witney on 6th July 1940 where she was converted to South African Air Force specification and crated for dispatch in September. The remaining four aircraft from Barton were shipped to the Netherlands East Indies, arriving in August 1940, two months later than planned due to problems with the issue of export licences. Assistance in this matter was volunteered by Jonkheer Krayerhoff, one time chairman of the Soerabaja Flying Club, and conveniently positioned in London working with Royal Dutch Shell.

The aircraft were scheduled for operation by flying clubs scattered through the islands and had been paid for by the Netherlands Indies Aviation Fund. Three aircraft had been sought but the Fund was adequately solvent and provided finance for four. More than 50 additional Tiger Moths were ordered from Australia in 1941, and subsequently led dramatic lives.

With the continued growth of the de Havilland Company, John Parkes was promoted to the position of General Manager of the Engine Division at Stag Lane and Lee Murray to a parallel situation within the aircraft factory at Hatfield. Frank Hearle was appointed Managing Director of the Company with effect from the beginning of 1939, in time to inherit guidance of the DH.95 Flamingo programme, the prototype of which had flown on 22nd December 1938 and was the subject of intense promotional activity.

At the same time, the DH.91 Albatross was in the spotlight too, but as the result of an undercarriage failure at Croydon and subsequent temporary grounding of the fleet. Maintaining composure, the Public Relations Office reported that it had supplied 'photographs of a Tiger Moth (with girl)' at the request of a printing house to illustrate a calendar which hopefully was scheduled for 1940 publication. The Sales Department bagged a pair of Tiger Moths, one each for India and New Zealand, in addition to the orders for the Midland Club and Iran (28 for the month) and was delighted to take deposits on a total of 67 Moth Minors.

Planning stability was vital to Lee Murray's perception of the company's programme for 1940 and he teased out some of the views of the Aeronautical Inspection Directorate (AID) at a meeting in March.

Although discussions were wide ranging, considerable time was spent on the subject of the Tiger Moth: development or replacement? Colonel Harold Outram, Director of AID, commented that prospects for the continuance of the Tiger Moth programme would be greatly enhanced if the company could offer a version with a bigger cockpit and an improvement in the efficiency of its production.

The possibility of a larger engine was also discussed, a six cylinder in preference to the Gipsy Major, or perhaps the Series II which was then engaged in flight trials.

No trace seems to have survived of records surrounding experiments with a rocket propelled Tiger Moth which were conducted in Scotland by a group of model aircraft engineers some time after 1934, most probably in 1938 or 1939. Their interest had been kindled by reports that a schoolboy living in Glasgow had in 1920, flown a 4ft span model aircraft a distance of three miles in one minute: an average speed of 180mph.

The powerplant was a crude rocket motor mounted on a cardboard tube fuselage, and the implications of the feat had been largely ignored until the group of five engineers, one of whom had been working on a military rocket programme, combined their talents and were able to use sparsely inhabited areas of Sutherland and Cumberland, testing devices on bicycles, rowing boats and float equipped models, operating from the surface of Loch Lomond. They even laid a concrete track with a diameter of 60ft for captive trials on which speeds of up to 2,000 mph were claimed to have been achieved.

The group turned its attentions to full size aircraft when they proved to their own satisfaction that skilfully designed and made 'ejectors' were more efficient than airscrews, and that it was perfectly possible to scale up their experiments, either to consider aircraft operating at very high speed (over 1,000mph) when rocket propulsion was at its most efficient, but sadly outside their level of resource, or to harness thrust to provide what they described as 'really useful acceleration'.

Against this latter principle, a re-usable rocket motor and ejector were designed for trials to accelerate a Tiger Moth into the air. The device was 11 feet long and 22 inches in diameter, and weighed 34lb including a 1lb charge of explosive fuel. Measured thrust was 150lb up to a speed of 50mph, falling to 100lb at 100mph. Cost per launch was estimated at about 1s.8d. There is no evidence to assume that the motor detached after its fuel was exhausted.

Conducting a vibration check on a running Gipsy Major engine at Hatfield. The aircraft is painted in the accepted pre-war style of semi-camouflage with large areas of 'sunshine' yellow dope to signify 'trainer'. de Havilland Aircraft Co.

Regrettably, no performance figures have been found, nor other details of any modifications to the basic Tiger Moth airframe which allowed it to absorb the slam accelerations which it obviously endured. Who sanctioned the rocket assisted take-off tests, where were they undertaken and whose aeroplane was used? The questions remain unanswered, but the experimenters are reported to have said that when faced with the test results in 1939, the Air Ministry classified them as being of 'low value'.

The views of the AID were evidently taken to heart for during 1939 the company prepared a scheme for a DH.82B Tiger Moth which incorporated answers to all the major criticisms of the DH.82 and DH.82A. The fuselage was widened by about 4in to offer more shoulder room for the crew and a larger fin and horn balanced rudder were designed to provide inherent stability. Elevator trim tabs and horn balances were installed to improve aerodynamic fore and aft trim, replacing the crude but cheap and effective method of control column spring tensioning. The most important airframe upgrade was perhaps the design of a Hornet Moth style undercarriage, offering a wider track and with the wheels set further forward to permit functional cable operated brakes, augmented by a tailwheel, a configuration long sought by the overseas agents.

At a time of considerable development within the Engine Division, and continuing investigation of the Gipsy Major Series II, another experimental powerplant was chosen: the Gipsy Major IIA, forerunner of the Gipsy Major III, which produced 160bhp at 2,500rpm, and was different in having both magnetos mounted on top of the Elektron crankcase. Had the project reached maturity, the Gipsy Major III, a four cylinder engine and predecessor of the supercharged military specification developed for use in the Saunders-Roe Skeeter helicopter, might have been chosen for the new airframe against the trend which always advocated a six cylinder powerplant. The moderate increase in power but lower price of the Gipsy Major II or III series engine, regarded only as two thirds of a six cylinder layout anyway, being considered sufficient for the immediate needs.

The Gipsy Major IIA was described in a secret document dated 15th September 1942, and written by Hatfield's Public Relations Manager, Martin Sharp, as a *'lash-up to obtain the power output of the proposed Gipsy Major III but using modified Gipsy Major II components'*. The Gipsy Major IIA engine had been civil type approved to permit Phillips and Powis to fly it in Miles M.18 and M.28 trainer prototypes, and a third engine had been installed in Captain de Havilland's DH.85 Leopard Moth. Apart from those few and the engine fitted to the DH.82B, it is believed only one other unit was built.

The installation required mounting the engine 8in further forward when compared with the standard Gipsy Major I, not only in an effort to restore or improve fore and aft balance, but to accommodate the redesigned timing gear cover. Production aircraft were planned to carry a larger capacity fuel tank to maintain endurance otherwise reduced by the increased consumption of the new engine.

Very little is known about the DH.82B Tiger Moth, a designation often and erroneously applied to the DH.82 Queen Bee. One prototype aircraft was allocated a construction number (1989), built against the company specification in 1939 and tested at Hatfield using the Class II markings E.11. Under this identity the aircraft was flown by de Havilland test pilot Lionel 'Wilf' Clark on 1st October 1939 who clearly labelled the aeroplane as a DH.82B in his log book, and added the note 'Production test. Elevator'.

As a young man from the Aerodynamics Department, David Newman remembers watching the DH.82B as it landed after its first flight. One of the elevators had broken up due to what was assumed to have been flutter, and the aircraft touched down with an elevator reduced to a spar and some stumps of the rib caps. Chief Aerodynamicist Richard Clarkson subsequently worked on a layout for a revised Tiger Moth empennage, although he recoiled from the suggestion that he had designed it. The chances are that he was investigating the reasons for the elevator problems which might have been associated with the introduction of the trimmer.

In other respects, trials are believed to have been considered successful, although there is only one further entry for the type in Wilf Clark's logbook, that for 8th May 1940 when the note reads 'Experimental. To 12,000ft'.

Improvements over the standard Tiger Moth were certainly considered worthwhile, but the more pressing need for immediate, high volume production of a primary trainer overtook the need for refinement. The eventual sub-contract to Morris Motors coupled with acceleration of the Mosquito programme brought the DH.82B project to a premature end in 1940.

Although there is no positive proof, it seems likely that components of E.11 might have been reduced to the standard of a mere DH.82A, and slotted back into the production line.

In hindsight it would appear that Lee Murray was not entirely convinced of the need for an improved trainer, Tiger Moth or otherwise, especially when the factory was already working at almost full capacity, for he queried the real need for wheel brakes and tailwheel, coupe top and cabin heater. The Air Ministry had not said they would stop buying the current aircraft unless and until it was improved, neither had they confirmed additional orders if it was. Should the refinements be considered necessary, he proposed a Canadian example be imported for test purposes. No evidence suggests that this was ever done. As if to emphasise the point of the argument to leave well alone, a record number of 65 Tiger Moths was delivered during March 1939, 51 of which were for the Air Ministry, and eleven new orders were received, all for overseas customers.

Tiger Moth G-AJOA shortly after delivery to Universal Flying Services at Fairoaks in 1947. At some stage she acquired a Canadian-built fuselage. Bob Andrews

Unpainted Tiger Moths and Queen Bees covering the assembly floor at Hatfield, summer 1939. Note DH.89 Dragon Rapides against the far wall, and Airspeed Oxfords to the right. The three aircraft nearest the camera have airframe and engine numbers chalked on the rudders: 82115/82517; 82116/82511 and 82117/82515, just to prove how confusing the similarity in block serials could be. British Aerospace

Not all the 200 fuselages ordered by Hatfield from the Canadian factory as part of the required production boost, were delivered, or at least not supplied in a state to be immediately built into complete aeroplanes. 94 build positions cannot be accounted for in the 1939 allocation (82599-82692), which were reserved to accommodate the imports, and although somewhat haphazard, the known sequence of engine allocation tends to confirm that the slots were not taken up.

During the mid-'eighties, the fuselage of a dismantled Tiger Moth was exported from Australia to Canada. The frame carried a plate identifying it as 'E75', one of the Downsview built components, which may have arrived in Australia as part of the 100 aircraft consignment shipped from RAF stocks in 1940. In November 1990, a major overhaul of G-AJOA (83167), revealed a docket lodged in the rear fuselage which proved the unit to be of Canadian manufacture and originally allocated to N6588 (3889), a Hatfield assembled aircraft of February 1939. In his logbook entries for 1939, amongst 79 individual Tiger Moth production test flights, de Havilland test pilot 'Wilf' Clark noted 'DH.82C' against just three: N9266 (82367), N9305 (82386), and N9452 (82506). Had the Flight Test foreman tipped him off about Canadian components or was the 'C' just the slip of a busy pen?

In April 1939 the Air Council decided that following a general review of the state of the aircraft industry, de Havilland required more orders to be placed for Tiger Moths or Oxfords, using as its gauge for commitment, a date some nine months prior to completion of current contracts. The orders would be part of an immediate £30M production plan authorised by the Treasury in a bid to provide 1,000 aircraft prior to the prospect of war breaking out in 1940. The Treasury had agreed in 1938 that as far as budget sanctions were concerned, a Tiger Moth and other trainers should count only as half of one aircraft unit. By July 1939 the 1,000 aircraft production plan had been increased to 2,400, of which 650 were anticipated to be trainer types.

Over a period of some years, the Air Ministry had championed the cause for heavy sub contracting of all aircraft component parts, ensuring that manufacturers received supplies from more than one source at least. As early as 1933, de Havilland had been required to approve an alternative supplier for Tiger Moth undercarriage compression legs (shock absorber struts) and new internally sprung units were eventually sourced from Aircraft Components Ltd, a Dowty-owned company based in Cheltenham. The new multi-spring legs replaced the original design of rubber blocks in compression, a feature revived when purity and simplicity was being sought in support of the DH.98 Mosquito design programme.

The Munich Agreement signed in September 1938 provided a year's grace during which in addition to the thousands of aircraft, 16 new battleships were commissioned. The Royal Air Force structured a Reserve Command with the responsibility of refreshing active reservists.

A school was formed at Gatwick with an establishment of nine instructors and 16 Tiger Moths to train personnel from the Royal Navy Air Branch. Secret meetings held by the Air Council Committee on Supply were to agree that Hatfield had a major role to play with its current products, and that more Tiger Moths built to the standard specification, out of date, uncomfortable, under powered, lacking performance, and on its last legs, were needed as quickly as possible.

Two days before war was declared, the Air Council was advised that Tiger Moth production capacity under current circumstances could not be greater than 90 aircraft per month. Three weeks later the same body was reviewing the requirements of trainer aircraft by types for inclusion in a total production programme of 2,000 aircraft per month supplemented by 250 aircraft per month supplied by the Dominions.

On 23rd September 1939 they decided that an immediate order should be placed on de Havilland for the supply of 1,000 Gipsy Major engines.

To clear their own decks for receipt of Air Ministry contracts, de Havilland nominated Morris Motors as a company capable of accepting the mantle of sub-contractor to the British Tiger Moth programme, not merely to make components, but to take responsibility for manufacture and assembly of whole aircraft. Why should not the principles of mass motor production, or at least some of them, be applied to the quantity and quality construction of a basic aeroplane too ?

With war declared, the camouflage scheme applied to Tiger Moths ex-factory deleted the all yellow tail surfaces and wing tips. Three aircraft await collection from Hatfield on a frosty morning, 10th January 1940. de Havilland Aircraft Co.

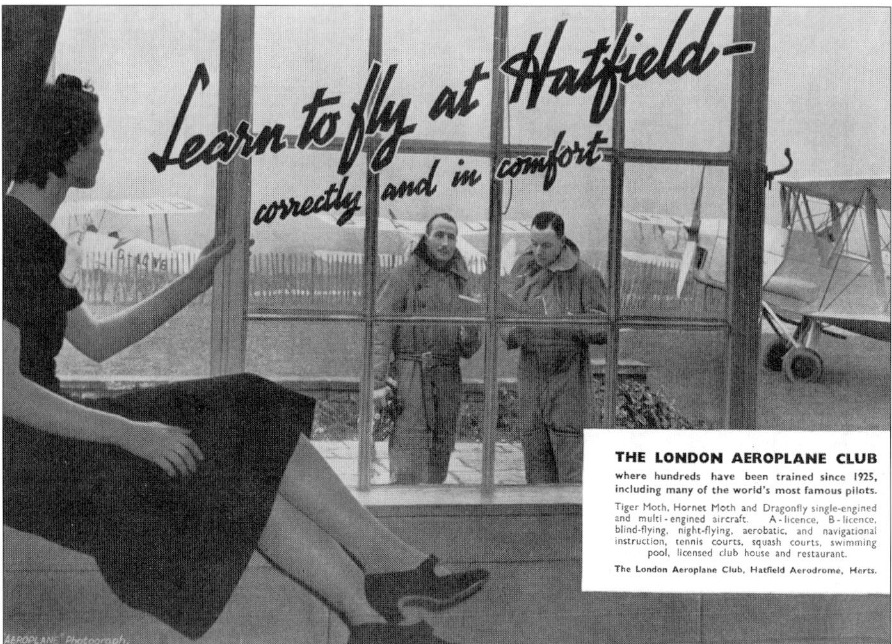

Learn to fly at Hatfield –

where hundreds have been trained since 1925, including many of the world's most famous pilots.
Tiger Moth, Hornet Moth and Dragonfly single-engined and multi-engined aircraft. A-licence, B-licence, blind-flying, night-flying, aerobatic, and navigational instruction, tennis courts, squash courts, swimming pool, licensed club house and restaurant.

de Havilland advertisement for the London Aeroplane Club placed in 1938. With increased use by Reserve and off-production aircraft, the Public Use Licence of Hatfield aerodrome was allowed to lapse almost exactly a year later and Club membership was limited to de Havilland employees.

Serious
FLYING ENTHUSIASTS
BROOKLANDS is the club for you !
N.B. For those who wish to take advantage of C.A.G. terms for financial reasons, but still appreciate instruction of a particularly high standard, the C.A.G. sections of our Provincial Clubs at Sywell and Shoreham have special attractions. Write to the Secretaries for particulars.
NO C.A.G.
NO WAITING
NO RESTRICTIONS
FULL FACILITIES FOR ADVANCED INSTRUCTION, NAVIGATION, BLIND FLYING, GROUND INSTRUCTION, AND EVERYTHING ELSE THAT MAKES A GOOD PILOT.
B LICENCE INSTRUCTORS AND TIGER MOTH MACHINES ONLY
BROOKLANDS
Nearest Station WEST WEYBRIDGE
WEYBRIDGE SURREY
Telephone:- BYFLEET 456-7-8
THE HOME OF BRITISH CIVIL AVIATION

Brooklands Flying Club at Weybridge had standardised on 'Tiger Moth Machines' by March 1939, and was keen to direct applicants to the Civil Air Guard scheme (CAG) elsewhere. Through a heavy government subsidy, members of the CAG flew for five shillings per hour and at some establishments created embarrassment as they swamped limited facilities.

A CHANGE OF COLOURS

10 EFTS Yatesbury, April 1940. Apart from one, all these civil registered aircraft are wearing the pre-war camouflage scheme. At least 14 Dragon Rapides, used for wireless training, are dispersed alongside the hangar on the far side of the airfield. This photograph was taken on a wet day from a low flying Tiger Moth. *Flight*

THE immense effort of Hatfield's DH.91 Albatross programme had resulted in a total of seven aeroplanes; the DH.95 Flamingo reached 16. Both aircraft types served their country well, and the Flamingo would, without doubt, have been a commercial success had its arrival on the scene not coincided with a world in turmoil. The DH.93 Don was unsuited to most of its specified tasks and the anticipated order for 250 was reduced to 50, and 20 of those were delivered as incomplete and engineless shells for technical training purposes. The Hatfield workforce was seriously concerned about a large scale layoff, and when 30 of the shop floor staff were given notice on the grounds that they were 'not required', representations were made in July 1939 directly to the Air Minister, Sir Kingsley Wood, citing any 'discharge of labour' as having very serious repercussions at a time of gathering uncertainty. Had none of these programmes been so demanding, would an improved Tiger Moth have been developed, or possibly an entirely new aircraft designed as a replacement, both options discussed so often at the Hatfield board meetings? Would either or both have been available for accelerated mass production when the need arose?

When a state of war was declared between Great Britain and Germany on 3rd September 1939, some 1,300 Tiger Moths had been built in eight years at Stag Lane and Hatfield, the Hertfordshire factory delivering 660 in 1939 alone. Until September the Air Ministry had administered 35 Elementary and Reserve Flying Training Schools (ERFTS) operated under contracts let to civilian companies throughout the country, and which under a preconceived plan, were immediately re-organised into 20 Elementary Flying Training Schools (EFTS) where all operations were conducted in accordance with King's Regulations. Instructors took RAF rank and uniform and aeroplanes with civil registrations were 'impressed' into Crown service and allocated military serial numbers under Air Ministry Directive 364041/34/CH8(d).

Distinctive civilian school colours gradually disappeared under coats of camouflage dope, often hastily applied by brush during periodic hangar checks.

To assist the Airspeed Company with production of wooden Oxford twin engine trainers, de Havilland had accepted an Air Ministry contract to build the aircraft at Hatfield, and completed an initial batch of 150 in 1939. Towards the end of the year, contracts for the supply of large numbers of Tiger Moths were being discussed, and de Havilland recommended that Oxford production be transferred to a new shadow factory established at their Scottish aerodrome

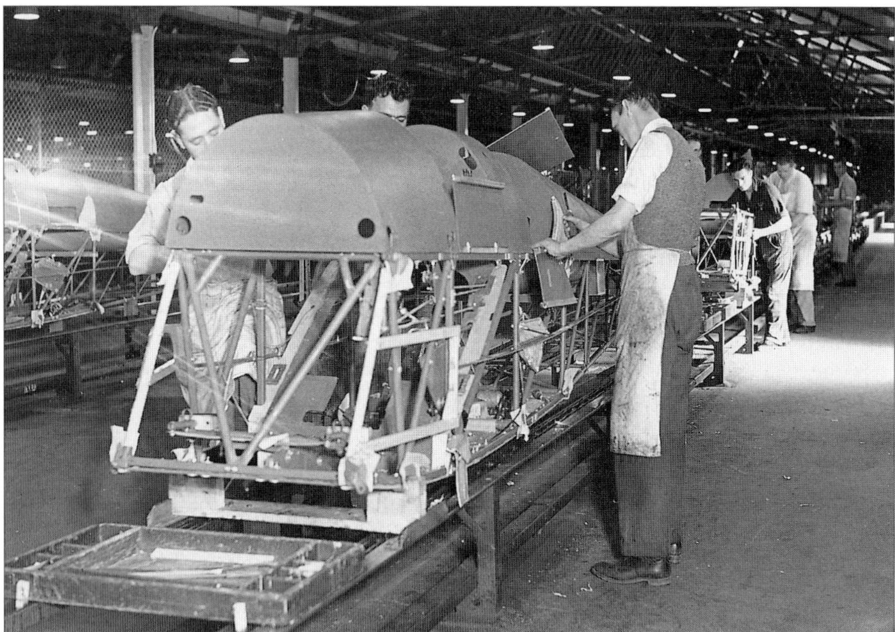

A basic Tiger Moth fuselage in the final stages of fitting out at Morris Motors, Cowley. The first Cowley aircraft were built in 'F Block', part of the North Side factory. *The Aeroplane*

Following declaration of war, and technical inspection, all civil registered Tiger Moths found suitable were gradually 'impressed' into military service, including the aircraft previously operated by the Reserve schools. Painted in the camouflage contemporary scheme, civil registrations were later changed to military serial numbers allocated from the batches created for impressed machines. G-ADWM was on establishment with 12 EFTS Prestwick where camouflage of the buildings was treated just as seriously. C Nepean Bishop

at Grangemouth, mid-way between Edinburgh and Glasgow. The offer was rejected, and the company built a further 1,290 Oxfords at Hatfield before their place was taken by a wooden twin of greater potency. From May 1940 Hatfield was in receipt of damaged Hawker Hurricanes and Rolls-Royce Merlin engines at an increasing rate, all seeking rapid and urgent repair and return to service. Moth Minor production had already been shut down and materials, tools, jigs, engines and incomplete aircraft packed off to the Australian company at Mascot near Sydney.

In 1938, millionaire motor magnate Sir William Morris was elevated to the Peerage, and as Lord Nuffield, headed the 'Nuffield Organisation', a huge motor engineering conglomerate akin to de Havilland's worldwide 'Enterprise'. One of Nuffield's companies, Wolseley Motors, had dabbled with aero engines, but never quite managed to bracket power, size and weight with the rapid developments taking place in the airframe industry.

From the mid-'thirties, implementation of government initiatives to disperse production by the creation of 'shadow factories' was gaining momentum. Nuffield's Organisation was approached to supervise the erection of a new plant at Castle Bromwich, there to organise the production of Spitfires. He was reluctant to do so having developed a poor relationship with the Air Minister, Lord Swinton, as a result of receiving no recognition and no orders following considerable work on the development of the Wolseley Aero Engine Company's Scorpio and Leo. The factory was eventually built following persuasion from his own top management team, but Lord Nuffield refused absolutely for the Castle Bromwich works ever to be referred to as a 'shadow' factory, and in all official communication it was never called anything less than the Castle Bromwich Aeroplane Factory.

In 1940, after a change in personalities at the Air Ministry and creation of the Ministry of Aircraft Production (MAP), Lord Nuffield was offered and accepted without remuneration, the post of Director General of Repairs and Maintenance for the Royal Air Force, with offices in London, but he soon tired of the bureaucratic life-style and removed himself to his own office at the Morris Motors plant at Cowley, Oxford. His responsibilities as Director General were for the organisation of repair of aircraft and ancillary equipment for the RAF, and as far as facilities were concerned, his brief was 'to make the fullest and most efficient use of industrial undertakings not engaged on essential production'.

The first unit of the Civil Repair Organisation (CRO) had been established at Cowley in September 1939 specifically to cater for fighter and trainer aircraft, and a number of badly damaged airframes were shipped in at an early stage for educational purposes. With normal business falling off, Cowley's 5,000 workforce had already been reduced by 2,000, and for the survivors, major re-direction was as welcome as it was inevitable. With Lord Nuffield's personal interest in tanks, aeroplanes and aero engines, and the clearest brief on industrial efficiency and essential production, the Morris Motors' Cowley works was a most appropriate site at which to provide facilities for Tiger Moth manufacture when the necessity was evident.

The Air Council promised Lee Murray in October 1939 that de Havilland were shortly to receive a contract for the supply of 2,000 new Tiger Moths, and reservedly agreed that 1,000 of these could be sub-contracted to Morris Motors, but reminded the company of their current obligations for Oxford aircraft and completion of the last contracted Flamingos. It was suggested too that de Havilland should not lose sight of the provisioning of spare parts.

Hatfield, confident of its productive capability and anxious to retain as much business for itself as was practical, requested that it retain the right to export any production in excess of that required by the Air Ministry's contracted delivery schedule. This was agreed by the Air Council subject to the surplus production being no greater than 10% of the planned output, and that no exports would be permitted until the Air Ministry requirement had been satisfied. It seemed to be a polite way of saying 'home team first'. St Barbe took up the matter again in November when his request that the Morris allowance be reduced to 900 aircraft was agreed. As events unfolded and changed situations were experienced with increasing frequency, the total Hatfield contribution after 3rd September and until Morris Motors took complete charge of manufacture from June 1940, was restricted to only 795 machines.

Two weeks after the declaration of war, Alan Butler in his capacity as Chairman of the de Havilland Aircraft Company Ltd, was minded to bring to the attention of the Air Minister that Hatfield aerodrome and works had been provided with no defensive armament. The reason quoted by official channels for this apparent oversight was that the factory was 'only making training aircraft'. Alan Butler stressed the opinion that Tiger Moths today could become fighters and bombers tomorrow should vital production facilities elsewhere be 'knocked out', and this was the greatest possible case for a strong defence. Sir Kingsley Wood replied that there was an acute shortage of guns, but that he was looking into the supply of some light automatic weapons.

In the event, Hatfield aerodrome was attacked, but on only one occasion: 3rd October 1940. An opportunist Junkers Ju 88 bounced four bombs from low level into the workshops recently vacated by the Moth Minor, and then full of Mosquito parts. The '94 Shop' was destroyed and 21 people killed, but the intruder paid the price and was shot down by local defences, crashing into a field three miles to the south. In passive resistance, and with the intention of drawing attention away from the real site, the Relief Landing Ground (RLG) at Holwell Hyde, later known as Panshanger aerodrome, was converted into a 'dummy factory' with the creative aid of the film industry, and to add an air of authenticity, a number of requisitioned DH.60 Moth aircraft were picketed out but did not survive the English climate.

While design office capacity was available and desperately in need of a project, shop floor space was severely limited. Oxford production was to be given priority, and with suggestions that the company might build Armstrong Whitworth Albemarles, later changed to an agreed monthly output of 300 Vickers Wellingtons, the Second Aircraft Group was founded with headquarters at a new site known as Watford aerodrome, Leavesden. In order for Hatfield to concentrate wholly on Mosquito matters, for which de Havilland were awarded a contract for a prototype and 49 production models in March 1940, the company agreed to a total transfer of all Tiger Moth production on a sub-contract basis to Morris Motors. The aircraft were to be built at the company's car factory at Cowley, just south of the university city of Oxford, commencing immediately. Eight aircraft were required to be completed during April 1940.

When allocating works' construction numbers, the new de Havilland Aircraft Company Ltd had, upon commencing operations at Stag Lane in September 1920, not unnaturally started at No.1. Strangely, this was a Hendon (Airco) built DH.18, G-EARI, fitted with a Napier Lion engine for service with Air Transport & Travel Ltd (AT&T), and first flown under the test markings E.52. It was wrecked a month before the de Havilland Company opened its doors for business!

Dark earth and green camouflage and removal of the white segment of the roundels on the upper mainplanes allowed aircraft so painted to merge into the British country background at most times of the year. It was a difficult task spotting camouflaged Tiger Moths from above in a crowded circuit. *The Aeroplane*

In fact G-EARI was the fourth aircraft in the order book: first was a Condor-engined DH.9 G-EAAC, listed against the build number H.9277, an ex-AT&T aircraft purchased by de Havilland for refurbishment and their own use, and scheduled to remain in active service until 1933; second and third were both booked as DH.14s, E.44 and E.45, unfinished military projects inherited from Airco at Hendon.

As additional shop floor projects were commissioned the numerical listing continued, taking in a range of DH.9 variants, and a miscellany of other DH types until No.168 which was allocated to the first DH.60 Moth in 1925. From then until No.400, DH.60 Moths took the lion's share of positions, occasionally making way for a substantial run of DH.9 work, and including DH.56, DH.61, DH.65, DH.66, DH.71, DH.72, DH.75 and DH.80.

Apart from numbers 704-710, allocated to a DH.9J, five DH.75 Hawk Moths and the unique DH.80 based autogyro, DH.60 Moth build numbers run consecutively and uninterrupted until 1739, the first nominated DH.82, and from 1740 to 1927, the last DH.60G.

Numbers 1988-1999 were allocated separately to 'special' projects: DH.100 light twin; DH.82B experimental Tiger Moth; DH.81 Swallow Moth, a Jaguar engined DH.9J, a quartet of DH.88 Comets, DH.87 Hornet Moth prototype, and the Technical School T.K.2 and a hand made Tiger Moth.

With the new 'types' becoming established, it was decided to split the numbering sequences into easily recognisable groups, just as the basic DH.60 line conveniently petered out. The 2000 block was allocated to the DH.80 Puss Moth (DH.86 from 2300 and Airspeed Oxford from 2400); 3000 to DH.82 Tiger Moth; 4000 to DH.83 Fox Moth; 5000 to DH.60GIII Moth Major and Queen Bee; 6000 to DH.84 Dragon (DH.89 from 6250); 7000 to DH.85 Leopard Moth (DH.90 Dragonfly from 7500); 8000 to DH.87 Hornet Moth; 9000 to DH.93 Don and 94000 to the DH.94 Moth Minor.

When DH.82A Tiger Moth production reached build number 3999, the opportunity was taken to start a new series, and the selected figure was 82000. Oxford production just kept on, and from 2400 it reached 3914, re-using the initial Tiger Moth sequence.

Gipsy Major engines manufactured by the Engine Division began their numeric sequences at 5000-5999, and 8000-8999 before adding a digit and starting again at 80000. This latter means of identification was to cause some confusion, especially during later civil operations when ex-military aircraft were occasionally and erroneously registered against their engine numbers. Engine production being faster than airframe, the allocation quickly 'caught up' with the Tiger Moth build positions, and RAF aircraft N9498 (82525), for example, was fitted with Gipsy Major I, engine number 82524.

Acting in the capacity of sub-contractor to de Havilland, Morris Motors were obliged to continue the numerical progression. It was agreed that the first Cowley aeroplane would be constructed against drawings supplied by Hatfield, aided by component parts delivered from de Havilland and other major sub-contracted sources. The first Morris Tiger Moth was to be 83176, serial T7011, available for inspection from the beginning of April, and eight aircraft in total were expected to be cleared that month. Cowley was to take sole responsibility for production from June 1940.

Some of Cowley's first efforts in the manifested form of T7013 (83179) were the subject of critical analysis at Hatfield after the aircraft had been delivered by road at the beginning of April. The Cowley line had been established and initial manufacture supervised by Hatfield staff with additional assistance drafted in from nearby Witney, and the report from A H Povey at Hatfield and addressed to Mr S V Smith, Works' Superintendent at Cowley, indicated that every inch of T7013 had been examined in minute detail, resulting in 67 observations worthy of comment.

Harry Povey, de Havilland's General Production Manager had joined the Stag Lane Drawing Office in 1926 where he was responsible for the design of teak production jigs for the DH.60 Moth, a move not supported by the then Works' Manager, Frank Hearle, until the scheme had proved spectacularly efficient and effective.

In 1928 Povey succeeded Arthur Morse as Chief Inspector, and it was his ideas that were developed into concrete moulds for the manufacture of Mosquito half fuselages. His value to the company was recognised by promotion to the board of the Aircraft Company in 1951. It was Harry Povey's lot to advise S V Smith, a man with an iron fist reputation within the motor industry, of the Hatfield assessment. Smith received the report with reasonable humour and replied to each of the 67 points by letter on 24th April, quoting A F Houlberg, Chief Inspector from the Aeronautical Inspection Directorate (AID) as his mentor. This was evidently a prudent move as the Works' Superintendent had already caused some dismay among the de Havilland advance party in claiming that the assembly of an aircraft should be treated no differently from that of a motor vehicle. Perhaps the eventual smooth output of 3,210 Tiger Moths from Cowley vindicated this philosophy to some degree, and assisted in his promotion by 1946 to the post of General Manager.

AID at Cowley agreed that in order to clear the eight aircraft due for delivery in April, 43 of the 67 points identified by Povey's team would be addressed immediately. These mostly concerned the absence of clips and chafe protection for electrical wiring, missing washers and misaligned installation of moving parts which caused fouling, under- and over-tightened bolts, badly aligned greasers etc. Cowley undertook responsibility to revise other points but only on account of expediency; they would ensure that the steel bolts holding the compass brackets were replaced with brass ones, but in mitigation revealed that

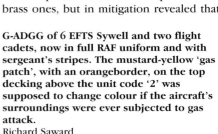

G-ADGG of 6 EFTS Sywell and two flight cadets, now in full RAF uniform and with sergeant's stripes. The mustard-yellow 'gas patch', with an orangeborder, on the top decking above the unit code '2' was supposed to change colour if the aircraft's surroundings were ever subjected to gas attack.
Richard Saward

Location of the propeller and a check on the starboard slat completes the task in assembling NL913 at the Cowley works in November 1943. Manoeuvred clear of the pillars and into natural daylight, engine checks await. Morris Motors

both steel and brass nuts and bolts had received a cadmium finish making it difficult on sight for the operatives to distinguish between the two. The engine nose cowling, according to Hatfield, had been poorly finished and badly fitted, and incorrectly drilled holes had been filled with rivets. Cowley replied that while they did not disagree, the standard of the cowling as supplied left much to be desired.

In response to Hatfield's claim that the anti-vibration leather strap looped around the torque tube in the control box was too loose, Cowley responded with an accusation that straps fitted to a Hatfield built fuselage they had inspected were not to drawing, and that extra holes had been cut by erecting shop staff to facilitate their installation. *'This would appear to be a point to be cleared up by de Havilland as well as here, if a standard is to be ensured'*, suggested AID.

Regarding other matters, Cowley believed that misalignment and distortion might have been caused during transportation of the aircraft by road to Hatfield.

On a further 12 points, AID confirmed that manufacture had proceeded strictly in accordance with the current issue drawings, and the criticism levelled from Hatfield was because the drawings were either wrong or contained insufficient detail or guidance, and their suggestion was that such matters should be corrected without delay. Perhaps it was the classic case of Hatfield being too close to the wood to see the trees: Canada had expressed similar views on drawings when contracted to build 200 fuselages in 1938, but errors and omissions were easily circumvented by the Hatfield workforce who had absorbed all the necessary production changes as a matter of daily routine, irrespective of the state of validity of the drawings.

Cowley was not in the least vexed by the criticism: where they had been in error they recognised and admitted to the fault and took immediate steps for correction. It was a remarkable achievement that they had been able to adapt to the delicate complications of building light, fabric covered structures involving many processes so different from motor manufacture, and to harness them so efficiently to almost instant mass production. They were not averse to offering advice either. On the matter of fuselage side frames they put forward an honest and practical opinion: *'we think that during manufacture we could eliminate a number of drilled holes which we understand were for both RAF and civilian requirements in the past, and as this machine is now to be used expressly for the Air Ministry, will you please confirm and modify the drawing accordingly'*.

To conclude his response, Mr Smith underlined AID's belief that Hatfield were building some parts of the aeroplane to a more practical or convenient standard by local agreement, rather than to detail shown on the drawings, and Cowley was in receipt of unfair criticism for simply following the approved path. In respect of Hatfield's assertion that inspection tabs on control cables should be turned to enable the inspection stamps to be clearly seen, the Works' Superintendent and his AID Chief Inspector were agreed: *'this is a matter of opinion and not a fault,'* they replied.

When a large batch of Tiger Moth spares was imported into England from India in 1980, it was found that the hinge pin holes drilled in the rudder posts were half an inch off centre. The inspecting engineer was beginning to form the impression that it was a manufacturing error when coincidentally he was asked to assist with the upgrade of a Morris Motors built Tiger Moth in fairly original condition, which had been retrieved from France. Much to his surprise the rudder post was drilled in an exactly similar manner. Was it a production error, misinterpretation of the drawings, incorrect drawings or a local modification tied in with tugging target sleeves or gliders?

The first of the Cowley built aircraft to fly was T7011 (83136), transferred to Witney and test flown from there by Guy Tucker on 15th May 1940. The aircraft was eventually posted to 3 EFTS at Watchfield and later Shellingford, and spent her entire working

Setting up NL911 on the camouflaged concrete base adjacent to Cowley airfield ready for swinging both bowl compasses. Two Supermarine Spitfires and the nose of what possibly is a Dragon Rapide can just be seen on the left edge of the picture.
Morris Motors

life with the unit until sold into obscurity in 1951. Guy Tucker, inevitably known as 'Tommy' or 'Tiger', was a de Havilland test pilot drafted in from Hatfield who took up residence at Cowley, test flying production Tiger Moths and later repaired Spitfires from the barely adequate grass airfield. A further 18 aircraft experienced maiden flights from Witney while the aerodrome at Cowley was being prepared, the last being T7028 (83309), which flew on 24th June. Three days later, Guy Tucker flew T7029 (83310), from Cowley's own fair acres.

In early June, T7013 was returned to Cowley from her brief expedition to Hatfield, and the catalogue of shared errors was corrected, following which she was moved to Witney and test flown from there. The aircraft was allocated to 24 Maintenance Unit (MU) at Stoke Heath on 25th April 1940 and delivered on 13th May, probably for a detailed acceptance inspection. There she remained until allocation to 12 Elementary Flying Training School (EFTS) Prestwick, on 20th September. Prior to closure of that establishment in April 1941, T7013 was transferred on 14th March to 19 EFTS Sealand where she remained until transfer on paper to 24 EFTS which re-formed at Sealand on 7th February 1942. Cowley's much inspected Tiger Moth crashed at Sealand on 10th June 1944 when a pilot on his second solo flight held off too high and stalled into the ground. The pupil's instructor received the blame for permitting him to fly a one hour session and become fatigued. The considerable damage caused when the undercarriage collapsed resulted in T7013 being officially written off nine days later.

In its initial stages, production at Cowley was sited at the southern end of 'F Block, North Side Factory', a single storey red brick building typical of the inter-war period, under a blacked out northlight truss roof. The line was set up in what appeared to visitors to be a corridor running east-west, abutting a vast floor space devoted to the manufacture of Bren Gun Carriers. The woodmill and sub assembly area was at the eastern end of the block, and fuselages were built up on wheeled dollies running in floor mounted guide rails, which gradually were processed towards the west, shifted manually as required. These mobile jigs have given rise to a popular myth that Cowley's mass production motor methods included a continuously moving assembly line. This was never the case, and at a productive rate of about 40 Tiger Moths per week, was never required.

Following completion, accumulated groups of six red doped fuselages were pushed on their own wheels on a southerly heading out of F Block and to the end of a wide covered passageway between C Block to the right and GK vehicle paint and finishing lines to the left, now assembly areas for torpedoes and armoured cars. Headed due east as far as the end of L Block, it was necessary to turn sharp right to head south again, past the P Block trimshop and the wages office, through Gate 16, across the busy Garsington Road, and immediately right into R Block of the South Side Factory. Wings and camouflage paint were added here together with the Gipsy Major engine, and the aircraft was weighed before engine runs and final checks were signed off prior to test flying.

The tiny airfield which had been used on at least one occasion pre-war by a DH.51 visiting from Stag Lane for reasons that can only be imagined, hosted thousands of maiden and post-repair flights, not only by Tiger Moths in the hands of resident test pilot Guy Tucker, but Geoffrey de Havilland Jr and Pat Fillingham who flew down from Hertfordshire in a company communications aeroplane, staying for three week assignments to assist with a seemingly endless backlog.

Flight Lieutenant Richard Jones was occasionally loaned from similar duties with repaired Tiger Moths and Spitfires at Witney. Richard Jones had been posted to de Havilland in April 1941 for a 'rest' from operations with 19 Squadron and their Supermarine Spitfire 1s operating as part of the Duxford Wing commanded by Douglas Bader during the summer of 1940, and stayed at Witney as resident test pilot until 1945. He enjoyed flying Tiger Moths, remembering that his first solo in 1937 was in a Miles Magister which carried a label on his instrument panel, written in bold red letters, which said: 'This aircraft will not, repeat will not, come out of a spin'.

Export orders from Cowley were crated and sent out via the factory's own railway branch line. Domestic collection and delivery was handled by civilian pilots of the Air Transport Auxiliary, an organisation with pilot 'Pools' established in different parts of the country. These lady pilots of the ATA were introduced to the press at Hatfield in January 1940.
de Havilland Aircraft Co

Alex Henshaw squeezed in and out of Cowley testing Spitfires which had been attended to by the resident CRO, and John Grierson, 'Cloudy Joe' to his chums, flew mended Hurricanes.

Pat Fillingham remembers the days at Cowley as very routine, but the social life was good. He and Geoffrey de Havilland Jr would stay with Guy Tucker in his cottage at Old Marston and try to enjoy their time off duty as much as wartime shortages and an annual salary of £175 would permit. In such dark times, every effort was required and the Cowley test pilots found space in their busy schedule to join the Oxford Local Defence Volunteers (LDV), the Home Guard, with whom they were engaged on night patrols by launch along the River Thames, armed with ancient rifles, seeking parachuted spies.

Between 3rd July and 24th July 1940, Fillingham made 97 test flights on Tiger Moths, including a batch of civil aircraft destined for the Indian Government. It was fair game when the wind was right, to fly between the two tall chimneys of the power house which still bore the traces of wartime camouflage paint over 50 years later before demolition, but happily no scars from wingtip scrapes.

Many Air Transport Auxiliary (ATA) pilots completed their first assignments by delivering Tiger Moths to RAF MUs from the holding area at Cowley, situated next to one of the country's two biggest reclamation and salvage dumps, where they were held under the authority of Hatfield nominated Chief Inspector Terry Dunworth. Flying in gaggles of three or four or more at a time, the numbers were probably reflected by the carrying capacity of the taxi Avro Ansons. Fillingham once took off on a routine production test flight during the late summer of 1940 as six new Tiger Moths were being taxied out by ATA pilots. His brief was standard: a routine test lasting between ten and 20 minutes during which he was scheduled to check engine performance, general handling, especially with respect to trim and setting of the aileron differential. Occasionally it was necessary to change a rogue propeller or an oil gauge if the indications looked bad. Climbing between 500ft and 1,000ft Fillingham happened to glance back to see six Tiger Moths climbing after him. When he turned, they turned, and it soon became clear that they were trying to formate on him, wrongly suspecting him to be their group leader. Not wishing to prolong their agony, he took evasive action and hurriedly returned to land.

In order to join the ATA, pilots were required to fly an 'acceptance' test with the chief instructor, A R O MacMillan, flying Tiger Moth G-AFSX (82004), at Whitchurch aerodrome, Bristol. The aircraft had originally been assigned to RAF care as N6731, but was re-directed to 'The Secretary of State for Air' and allocated to the Director

Engine runs, adjustments and determination of fuel flow were completed in the shadow of some fancy camouflage design and construction on the outside of Cowley's R Block. Having built Tiger Moths all day, male workers were compelled to spend two nights every week patrolling the factory roof, on fire watching duties.
Morris Motors

General of Civil Aviation. The first tests were completed on 6th September 1939 as the result of which 26 pilots acceptable to the ATA were invited to fly a North American Harvard at the RAF Central Flying School, Upavon, and so qualify to ferry all RAF single engine aircraft.

In view of their experience and following interview, the flight test was almost a formality for most, and usually consisted of little more than a wide circuit and landing. Selection and training later moved to ATA Headquarters at White Waltham although an Initial Training Unit was eventually established using Tiger Moths and based at Barton le Clay, near Luton, Bedfordshire.

The original flight acceptance aircraft, G-AFSX, was delivered to No 3 Ferry Pilots Pool at White Waltham in February 1940 and took on the military serial AX856 the following July, but evidence of her hard life style was revealed during a major inspection in August 1942, and she was scrapped.

With an increased operational need, ATA pilots later were called upon to ferry Spitfires from at Cowley too. One such was Diana Barnato Walker whose father had raced Bentley cars at Brooklands. It was almost inevitable that she should join the Brooklands Flying Club in 1936 where she learned to fly on Tiger Moths at a cost of £3 per hour. Her family was not amused and cut off her allowance which meant she was not in flying practise at the beginning of the war and took up duties as an ambulance driver. She joined the ATA in 1942 and her first delivery flight was on 25th March when she ferried Tiger Moth DE410 (85418), on a 40 minute trip from Cowley to Hullavington. An ATA Avro Anson returned Diana Barnato Walker and her colleagues back to Cowley the same day after which she flew DE569 (85536), to Kemble, and was airlifted back for tea at White Waltham in the Anson again.

Having been invalided out of the RAF, Anthony Phelps returned to civilian life as a Fleet Street journalist, but was persuaded to join the ATA. A few days after his flight test at Whitchurch he was welcomed to a snow covered White Waltham aerodrome from where he was immediately invited to deliver a brand new Tiger Moth, a feat he described in his book *I Couldn't Care Less*:

'Apart from my short flight test I had not flown a Tiger Moth since before the war started, and, forgetting just how cold they could be, especially when the temperature at ground level is two degrees below, had neglected to attire myself suitably.

'For the first few minutes after taking off I could hardly breathe. It was just like diving into an icy cold pool. Then I became wildly exhilarated. To be flying again, on a real job, when I had given up all hope of flying until the war finished. The wind whipping my face was like champagne that had been on ice for a long time.

'Like champagne too it was not long before the exhilaration began to wear off, until finally I was conscious of nothing except that I was cold.

'I glanced at my compass. Yes, I was on the course. Then I looked at my map and was not so sure. I had another look and became equally sure that I was not.

'Now aerial navigation is one of those many things in which the theory at times seems somewhat far removed from the practice. Also, of course, there is a vast difference between navigating a light aircraft like a Moth and modern service types for which the drift is much less. Furthermore, the fighter pilot often has very little time for serious navigation and tends to rely more and more on wireless.

'Hence, although my theory was sound, my practice (may I admit, never brilliant), was a little rusty. To add to my difficulties,

the entire country was covered with snow, which renders many landmarks difficult of recognition.

'I began to get a little worried, but stuck grimly to my course, I think I must have been frozen to it anyhow, until a certain town came into view, and I heaved a sigh of relief. I realised that the low ground speed of the Tiger Moth had fooled me and in consequence I had been navigating somewhat ahead of myself. Furthermore, I had been guilty of neglecting my watch, which would have told me that everything was in order.

'All this of course is very elementary, but it really is surprising how easy it is to get out of the habit of navigating, and I was terribly nervous of making a mess of my first job: even a simple one like a Tiger Moth. I know my luck.

'For nearly two hours after that all I had to do was to sit like a piece of chilled mutton waiting for the refrigerator door to open. When I saw my destination I was too cold even to feel happy about it. Had the machine started to break up in mid-air I would not have cared. All I wanted was to get it over'.

Although 154 ATA personnel died in the service, often the result of accidents caused by bad weather, only one pilot was killed when ferrying a Tiger Moth amongst the 171,934 single engine delivery flights completed between February 1940 and November 1945. As a grand total, the ATA pilots delivered 309,011 aircraft during which they achieved 414,984 flying hours.

Tiger Moth G-AEEA (3495), was part of the establishment of 11 ERFTS Perth at the beginning of the war, and took on military markings BB691 in September 1940. During landing practice at Buttergask relief aerodrome on 19th November 1941, BB691 had undershot and collided with a wall. Damage was severe, and the aircraft was routed to the de Havilland CRO at Witney where, following repairs, she was test flown by Richard Jones on 27th December.

Second Officer J A Nathan had joined the ATA in April 1941 with a total of 72 hours experience. On 8th February 1942 he was engaged on his 66th single engined ferry, during the course of which his total flight time had increased to 188 hours. Nathan's aircraft was BB691, assigned to Prestwick, and he took off from Witney in the early afternoon bound for RAF Ouston near Newcastle upon Tyne, where he was scheduled to stop for fuel. The aircraft arrived at 1530 hours and landed normally, but swung badly when taxying clear such that it re-entered the active runway and was rammed by a Spitfire which had landed immediately behind, wrecking the Tiger Moth and killing the pilot.

The entire production facility at Cowley was set up around a shop foreman (Mr Coles) and chargehand (Percy Saunders) in a cell of about 50 employees. These included some Morris Motors' male permanent staff, and others with woodworking skills recruited from the building industry and augmented by a number of local women and girls. The group worked long hours, 7.30am to 7.30 pm, six days a week, and occasionally seven, (there was no night shift), or for as long as parts and supplies were to hand. In addition there was a compulsorily rostered fire watching duty on two nights per week for each male employee. The F Block men patrolled their own roof, operating from a small hut inside the Block where they could brew tea and sleep in rotation.

As a 19 year old, Les Gurl (Snowball to his workmates) assisted Archie Penn in fitting control boxes, and on a daily basis was required to lift a tail to push a fuselage complete with empennage, on the half mile journey through the factory and across the public road to R Block. It was a tough physical exercise and the one way push took about 15 minutes. The covered walkway had to be navigated with care as the factory had taken on emergency assembly of thousands of American Mack and White army lorries, diverted from France and delivered in kit form to fill every vacant corner of the site. Les Gurl left Cowley in the late summer of 1940, part of an emergency draft redirected to work at the Cunliffe Owen company at Eastleigh where his talents were employed in assisting to accelerate the production of Spitfire wings. From there he joined the Royal Navy, and was therefore, not part of the Cowley team which moved out of F Block in 1942, and consolidated the whole of the production and assembly process more efficiently in R Block, leaving the vacated space for the assembly of Horsa gliders.

With the military training machine in top gear at home and overseas, the immediate requirement for a continuous supply of new Tiger Moths diminished from February 1944 and increasing numbers of complete but dismantled aircraft were delivered by road into hastily secured 'Purgatory Stores' in and around Oxford, all under the authority of 15 MU Wroughton. From June to October 1945, many were routed back to Cowley where they were updated, customised, erected, test flown and delivered to MUs at Aston Down, Colerne, Little Rissington and Llandow, prior to sale or gift-in-aid to the Air Forces of Belgium, France, the Netherlands and Yugoslavia.

At Witney, every square inch of available hangar floor space had been utilised for the repair and overhaul of Spitfires and Tiger Moths. Additional storage was requisitioned in the adjacent Blarney Garage and Tower Hill Garage, and dismantled Tiger Moths were stored in the basement of the Haines' repair workshop at Staple Hall. Dent's glove factory at Charlbury was the site of major wood repairs and fabric work including the recovering of the majority of reconditioned Tiger Moth wings.

The last Tiger Moth to be wholly constructed at Cowley was PG746 (86632). Taken into care by 15 MU Wroughton on 24th July 1944, PG746 was routed to 38 MU Llandow, a major Tiger Moth refurbishment centre near Cardiff, on 8th July the following year, and on 12th September 1946 she was transferred to 47 MU, a specialist packing unit based at Sealand. It seems astonishing that instead of air delivery to the Royal Netherlands Air Force, to whom the aircraft had been sold, PG746 along with several others, was dismantled, crated, transported to Dagenham Docks from Cheshire, and ferried across the North Sea on board the SS *Ponto* to take up duties with the Air Force at Woensdrecht, and later the Navy at Valkenburg. Withdrawn from use in December 1965 and sold in January 1966, the aircraft is thought to have been purchased as a source of spare parts by a naval gliding club in the Netherlands.

For Morris Motors, building Tiger Moths was just another mass production job to be completed against a high specification and to a strict timetable and price agreed under conditions of national emergency. The company was not involved in promoting any form of development or experimental flying. Miles Thomas, a senior executive with the Nuffield Organisation, makes not a single mention of the Tiger Moth in his otherwise meticulously detailed autobiography. Apart from a series of photographs taken in F Block in January 1941, a further sequence covering detail work and assembly in R Block was not recorded by Morris Motors until October 1943, after which the negatives were misfiled for over 30 years. Five decades after the last Tiger Moth had flown away from Cowley, an exhibition held in Oxford and which included a major feature on the contribution made by the Cowley site in times of war and peace, failed to acknowledge any association with Tiger Moths.

After the war the British motor industry underwent massive changes both in company identity and organisation. In latter days Cowley was operational under the banner of the Rover Group, a company purchased by an irony of politics and economics by British Aerospace who deliberately ran down the works before closing the whole of the North and South factories, to embark on a planned and systematic programme of demolition. F Block and R Block went down to the bulldozers in 1993, together with Lord Nuffield's historical office block. So too did all the post-war additions to the South Factory, releasing for a short period, the outline of a dusty patch of a one time airfield from which more than 3,000 Tiger Moths first took wing.

With dispersal of production and the establishment of new facilities across the country, some of the aircraft manufacturers discovered that it was impossible to move key personnel, test pilots, drawings, spares or urgently needed supplies with any alacrity. The railway service throughout the British Isles was liable to disruption and long road journies were tedious.

Westland Aircraft were the first to raise the subject of production companies using 'communications' aircraft when early in 1941, they were faced with regular liaison between their Somerset factory and 263 Squadron RAF operating Whirlwind 1s from Montrose in Scotland. Other companies were soon anxious to be included in any realistic scheme which could be devised, and the civil service went into top gear establishing committees to study the appropriate rates for aircraft loan and flight time, depreciation, insurance, maintenance, and even the operational competence of the company personnel who would fly the government's property.

It was recognised at an early stage that aircraft 'hire' charges made by the Ministry of Aircraft Production (MAP) or on behalf of the Director General of Research and Development (DGRD) would only be included in company overheads and recovered by the manufacturers in due course, so the basics of Third Party insurance, fuel, oil, servicing and repairs were agreed as the maximum contribution which could realistically be expected from the users.

Westland had asked for a multi-seat transport, a DH.89A Dragon Rapide for example, but currently these were all fully occupied, and supplies of the alternative Avro Anson were all earmarked for export. Vickers, MAP decided, were to be given priority anyway, with dispersal factories and operational squadrons occupied with Vickers Wellingtons and Supermarine Spitfires. In June 1941, the company was allocated a G.A.L. Monospar, Percival Vega Gull, Miles Falcon and a pair of DH.90 Dragonflies, AV992 (G-AEDJ) and AV993 (G-AFRF), which after clearance of all the necessary paperwork by 41 Group at Andover, were to be collected from the Ferry Pool at White Waltham. Thereafter and until further notice, the fleet was to be the responsibility of Vickers. In its submission for the allocation of a communications aircraft, the company had included the Morris Motors aerodrome at Cowley as a base of operations, hinged to the requirements of the CRO Spitfire salvage and repair programmes.

Short Bros were invited to inspect DH.90 DJ716 (G-AEWZ), lying at 39 MU Colerne, for suitability; not only did the aircraft service their requirements faithfully throughout the war, but the company bought and maintained her on the civil register from 1946. Hawker Aircraft were offered another DH.90, AX855 (G-AECX), which was quoted to be under repair at White Waltham, and which they put into service in August, but for only four months before the aircraft was posted to Northolt. Westland were eventually allocated their DH.89A when X7321 (6494), joined them in October 1941, the first of a batch of new Dominies built at Hatfield against a 1940 Air Ministry contract, and another was authorised for the Lockheed Aircraft Company with a request from MAP that 41 Group should choose a suitable candidate and advise accordingly.

In common with all British based motor engineering companies, the Rootes Group became heavily involved in military aircraft production, and by June 1941 their association with the Bristol Blenheim occupied facilities at Shawbury, Stoke, Burtonwood and Speke. The company complained that test pilots were having to rely on the good offices of the RAF Overseer to be chauffeured around the network in his duty Miles Magister. Perhaps Rootes did not have the same political clout as Westland which resulted in allocation of their brand new Dominie, for DGRD's committee thought that a Tiger Moth could be made available after all the formalities had been approved. And having received the green light, a Tiger Moth was allocated, but not until June 1943 when T7842 (84207), was delivered to Standard Motors from 10 MU Hullavington, and remained on charge with the company until January 1945.

Following more than three years of training activity with 11 EFTS / 11 RFS at Perth, T7842 was declared surplus and took up an agricultural appointment in New Zealand until she was grounded and dismantled in 1963. The aircraft was acquired by the Croydon Aircraft Company of Mandeville and rebuilt to her 1942 configuration for Mark Zipfell, an ex-RAF English Electric Lightning pilot, who returned her to the luxury of a private landing ground in Suffolk during the summer of 1995.

The availability of light aircraft, especially Tiger Moths, after the early pressures had been removed from the UK based training programme were evidenced by the allocation of communications Tiger Moths to Airspeed, Short Bros, Power Jets, Westland, Vickers, Vosper and Bristol. Although de Havilland did operate Tiger Moths for company communications they much preferred the extra speed and comfort of the Leopard Moth, Hornet Moth and Dragon Rapide. Tiger Moth PG624 (86533) was delivered across the hedge from Cowley to de Havilland at Witney in March 1944, officially for 'modifications', and nominal ownership passed to the government's Controller of Research and Development in August 1945. Under de Havilland control she was extensively flown during the course of communications and weather observation duties until she was purchased outright by the company in April 1946, registered G-AHIZ, and posted to the London Aeroplane Club at Panshanger, in whose colours she continues to operate *ab initio* training flights from Cambridge.

Pauline Gower, an experienced and popular pre-war pilot, who is credited with much of the effort that resulted in ATA acceptance of women, and who rose to a position of considerable responsibility in the organisation. via British Aerospace

Before the war and under civil contract, The Air Operating Company Ltd flew missions over the British Isles on behalf of the Home Office to identify sites which would be best protected by camouflage in the event of a national emergency.

'On the outbreak of hostilities all civilian flying was stopped and the Camouflage Flight was taken over by the RAF, moved to Hendon and operated by 24 Squadron by virtue of arrangements with RAF Fighter Command. Subsequently, it was taken over by the RAF completely to be known as No 1 Camouflage Unit, and was instructed to commence operations at Baginton, Coventry, on 9th October 1939'.

The Unit flew a variety of aircraft including at least two Leopard Moths and a variety of Dragon Rapides and Dominies. The first of two Tiger Moths was on strength for general duties from 19th July 1942 after the CO had been delivered to High Ercall to collect one from 222 MU, a packing unit more associated with sending Tiger Moths out of the country than to grassy British aerodromes like Stapleford Tawney. T7723 (84100), had been on strength briefly with 55 Operational Training Unit (OTU) at Annan before allocation to the Unit, but was written off as the result of a landing accident at Stapleford Tawney on 13th April 1943. With 23 hours solo time on Tiger Moths, the pilot had approached to land in a steep sideslip but had misjudged his recovery, probably due to failing evening light, touched down heavily, bounced and dived into the ground. 'Careless and over confident' was the Station Commander's assessment!

The second aircraft, T7604 (84001), was delivered on the last day of July with only test and ferry time logged. Both aircraft were heavily involved with communications and air experience flying with Air Training Corps cadets as much as anything else, which may explain why, after a stay of only five months, T7604 was posted in January 1943 to 167 Squadron flying Supermarine Spitfire Vcs at Ludham, and was not replaced. Six weeks later, the aircraft joined 164 Squadron as they moved into Middle Wallop with Hawker Hurricane IVs, and is believed to have remained with them during a re-equipment programme which saw the introduction of the Hawker Typhoon 1B, and 19 changes of airfield, including forward bases on the Continent. Retired to 39 MU at Colerne in November 1944, T7604 aircraft was held in storage until declared surplus in 1950 and cut up for scrap.

The Ministry of Home Security established a wartime unit at Leamington Spa from where schemes were raised to disguise everything of strategic value, and the flying unit was tasked with the job of photographing and reporting. All aircraft factories and aerodromes were divided into categories and the Morris Motors works was classified as '2A', a site in which the Air Ministry specifically, had no direct interest, although a plethora of other government agencies would have. In consequence, the Ministry of Home Security was responsible for the design, execution and maintenance of the whole scheme. Painting a wall in brown and green drab was fairly basic, but three dimensional devices were permitted only as long as they were removable at 24 hours notice, and consultations on their possible effect on the normal operation of the factory or aerodrome were to be held between the Ministry and the Superintending Engineer of the site. Having erected any such devices on facilities such as those in the Cowley category however, and their ultimate removal was regarded as the responsibility of the Air Ministry.

Manufacturers became uneasy when the airfields at some production sites were selected for training-related activities. They believed the inevitable high rate of utilisation would draw unwelcome attention. Phillips and Powis were still applying the finishing touches to a new shadow factory built at South Marston near Swindon in 1940 for the production of Miles Masters, when news reached them that the airfield was to be added to the list of Relief Grounds already established for the Elementary Schools which proliferated throughout the area.

During construction of the factory, and with nearly all the steelwork for the main assembly hall already erected, the Air Ministry themselves had decided that the site was too attractive a target, and two thirds of it was dismantled and rebuilt into two additional and separate units elsewhere in the locality. Having insisted on such an expensive and disruptive measure, added to which the company had planted trees for screening and made further efforts to disguise the taxyways leading from factory to aerodrome, Phillips and Powis made vigorous protest to the MAP after which plans for access by the training schools were cancelled.

The inherent dangers of a high utilisation aerodrome were experienced to some extent by the proximity of Luton Corporation's airfield at the top of the town, overlooking the hat factories and the Vauxhall motor plant. On the airfield, the Percival Aircraft Company had been joined by the Miles Magisters of 29 ERFTS in August 1938, contracted to Birkett Air Services Ltd, an organisation with roots at Stag Lane. This unit had been a casualty of the September 1939 reorganisation, and had closed down, reforming with Tiger Moths for the training of pilots for the Fleet Air Arm at Clyffe Pypard two years later. On 22nd July 1940, the void was filled when 24 EFTS was transferred to Luton from Belfast, and the Percival company immediately expressed their feelings of nervousness. Percival had complained in a letter addressed to the MAP that the intensive flight training operations at Luton was drawing attention to the airfield and consequently to the aircraft factory, quite apart from the other local activities in support of the war effort. The camouflage experts at Leamington were drawn into the argument and presented a report in December 1941 which was critical of the RAF Station Commander and OC 24 EFTS, Wing Commander Chambers. Although the camouflage of the buildings was satisfactory, an enormous muddy scar had been allowed to develop on the grass manoeuvring area, the result of intensive ploughing in a confined space by Tiger Moth tailskids, a situation exacerbated by the movement of support vehicles, refuelling bowsers etc.

The aerodrome manager Mr Rushton, acting on behalf of Luton Corporation, had asked that the area be fenced off and reseeded to allow the healing process to take due course. The camouflage agency had agreed that this was necessary and easily accomplished. The Station CO had retaliated by reiterating that he was duty bound to produce target results in the form of hours and pupil accomplishment, and had positively refused to co-operate. This was before he had even read the report which suggested the scar was associated with one of the 'usual problems of an EFTS; lack of proper control over taxying aircraft etc.' There might have been more than just coincidence in the closure of the Luton based school and transfer to Sealand only two months later. Sited on a permanent military airfield, the units busily engaged in the business of packing and shipping of aircraft to the outposts of the Empire, were less likely to be drawn into the argument.

The whole business of flying training operations conducted from MAP airfields was considered very seriously, and at the height of the Luton dispute, the Ministry published a list of aerodromes at which they declared themselves 'very anxious' not to accommodate or offer facilities to training units. Included were Morris Motors at Cowley and de Havilland at Watford aerodrome (Leavesden). There was no mention of Hatfield or Windsor (Smiths Lawn) where Vickers maintained a shadow installation and the polo fields were used extensively as a Relief Landing Ground by Tiger Moths operating beyond the circuits of White Waltham and Fairoaks.

A visiting Dragon Rapide, staff and two Tiger Moths (G-AFGJ and G-AFGT) posing for the press at the opening of the Luton Flying Club in 1938. The Tiger Moths of 24 EFTS which took up residence in 1940 were willed off the site the following year. via British Aerospace

A MATTER OF DESPERATION

Bombs fitted to underfloor carriers on Tiger Moth T5610, 1940 style, photographed at RAE Farnborough with the aid of some strategically placed cardboard sheets. RAE Farnborough

TIGER MOTH bombers were the secret ingredient of a clandestine anti-invasion plan devised by the Air Staff in the spring of 1940, probably as the result of representations by No 2 School of Army Co-operation. The plan resulted from Training Command Operational Order No.1 issued on 23rd May 1940 for the Command, in a time of declared national emergency, i.e. invasion, to reinforce Bomber Command. As originally devised, the overall scheme was called 'ZZ' and known as *The Julius Caesar Plan* by Army Co-operation, but was renamed *Banquet* on 27th May. Between 179 and 247 miscellaneous bomber training aircraft were expected to be deployed at 14 Bomber Command airfields. At the same time, the factor of light primary training aircraft was added to the equation. This extension to the Plan was coded *Banquet Light* and dictated that improvised striking forces, a 'cooks and butchers air force', raised from within the elementary training establishments, would be allocated to stations where Army Co-operation Westland Lysander squadrons were located. There, they were to come under the jurisdiction of the local RAF operational commander, and were to attack targets allocated by the Army or Corps headquarters. As many of the assembly sites were likely to be remote from prospective action, aircraft were scheduled for re-deployment as necessary to advanced landing grounds, where they would be fuelled and armed and maintained at full alert.

Additional *Banquet* plans included the use of civil transport aircraft *(Banquet Civil)* although the perceived requirement for extensive modification and subsequent training and maintenance, not to mention a greater usefulness in their transport role rather than deployment as night bombers, tipped the balance against the idea which was dropped. *Banquet Comm* was intended to relieve Communications Flights of their Tiger Moths and Magisters, but the idea was also abandoned in the face of realisation that good and flexible communications in an emergency situation would be equally critical. *Banquet CB* involved integration of some 251 obsolescent bombers of the Hawker Hart variety of which 174 had already been earmarked at storage units for service overseas, but which could be retained and integrated as part of the Training Command contribution. *Banquet Master* was intended to employ the Miles Master trainer as a fighter, but the fitting of Browning machine guns had caused such disruption during manufacture that Lord Beaverbrook, Minister of Aircraft Production, had agreed to an abandonment of the concept.

At the end of May, the Deputy Director of Home Operations asked for a quantification of the light aircraft immediately available and was advised that 663 RAF Tiger Moths could be mustered together with 410 light civil aircraft. *'In the last resort they might enable us to hit the enemy,'* he wrote. The civil aircraft were identified as Gipsy Moth 12; Moth Minor 11; DH.60 Moth 5; DH.60A Moth 1; DH.60G Moth 119; DH.60M Moth 23, DH.60N Moth 1; DH.60X Moth 23; Tiger Moth 69. With several spurious entries the author of the accompanying note could hardly have realised the unintended irony: *'It is impossible to say how many of these are in serviceable condition or, in fact, really exist at all, until they have been inspected, as the records kept have been found to be very inaccurate'*.

At about the time the Tiger Moth Coastal Patrol Flights (CPF) were being re-equipped with Westland Lysanders and Avro Ansons, the Assistant Chief of the Air Staff, aware that *'DCAS has laid on a scheme for arming a number of Moths with light bomb racks'*, advised his colleagues that they should bear in mind *'the Coastal Command Moths of which there are Flights of six at ....'.* But those particular birds had already flown.

On the basis that an Elementary Flying Training School (EFTS) may have two or three or four Flights (some had more), it was considered that the strength of the light bomber force should be drawn in proportion: a four Flight EFTS would provide 30 aircraft for example, while a two Flight school would allocate half as many. Fifteen of the 24 Avro Cadets of 3 EFTS at Hamble were to be included as no reason could be seen for excluding them, providing bomb racks could be fitted, and five more schools were to allocate a total of 120 Miles Magisters. The remaining 13 schools, all equipped with Tiger Moths, were scheduled to release a total of 350 aircraft. At this time the active training fleet was assessed at 756 aircraft, but a drawback was in pilot strength; for the 485 operational light bombers, only 378 instructor pilots could be mustered.

One solution to the shortage of pilots was to consider withdrawing students who had recently joined Service Flying Training Schools (SFTS) and who could be regarded as competent on recently vacated light training types; another was the redirection of more senior pilots over the age of 30, and then 40, who were involved in administrative duties.

In April it had been discovered that the Magister was capable of carrying only an old style 20lb Cooper bomb, and by June it was admitted that modifications necessary to convert the aircraft into a light bomber were seriously interfering with production, and that after the 28th job, the programme had been stopped. While the converted aircraft would be available for use, a much greater reliance would now be placed on the Tiger Moth.

On 25th June 1940 an urgent request from the Air Ministry was received by the Deputy Director of Operational Requirements: *'Please signal number of Moths fitted with bomb racks as at 1200 hours June 25 1940, rate of fitting, and number still to be fitted',* it asked.

Instructors from the schools were allocated 'after hours' flying sessions in which they were to practise low level flying at maximum speed. It was regarded by many as a welcome relief from their normal day in which six hours of instructional flying divided into 45 minute sessions was routine. Although each station had its own prescribed low-flying area, the instructors made the most of their opportunity to indulge in authorised and legitimate hedge height inspection of the English countryside during transit.

Exercises with army units were encouraged and pilots from 3 EFTS Watchfield were invited to hurl make-believe bombs at troops positioned with camera guns around their detachment headquarters in the manor house at Coleshill. More seriously, during the early summer of 1940, 15lb smoke bombs were dropped onto targets set up on the Salisbury Plain ranges. Pilots were gathered together at Old Sarum and taken by bus to assess form as Army Co-operation Westland Lysanders attempted to lob practice bombs into the target circle. Returned to Old Sarum by road, the Tiger Moth crews were given their heads, and a stream of biplanes was let loose at 90mph,

At the start of another day. Just part of the post-war establishment of 6 EFTS Sywell viewed from the roof of the flight cadet's mess. Ken Ellis collection

operating below the tree line, with the object of achieving a maximum score at the end of a shallow diving approach. It was all good fun and a break from the responsibilities of formal training, but then the only aggression was offered by army referees armed with nothing more lethal than their cameras, clip-boards and Very pistols.

Part of the administrative task of civilian clerks employed in the watch offices at the school aerodromes was the regular update of flying logbooks and aircraft technical records, but instructors found that details of their practise sessions were not being recorded as a matter of official policy, almost certainly a dictate resulting from the near tangible levels of secrecy and security being imposed on Plan *Banquet* at the time.

The high level of alert was reflected in the fact that some senior personnel remained on station for long periods during the Battle of Britain; Flight Lieutenant Monty Cox, CFI of 13 EFTS White Waltham, set up domestic and sleeping arrangements in his new office immediately after taking over from Squadron Leader Bob Reeve in August 1940. The new CFI would have viewed the prospect of action with a greater clarity than most, having bombed and strafed the enemy from a Sopwith Camel during the latter days of conflict on the Western Front in 1918, operations which combined with other duties resulted in the immediate award of a Military Cross.

It seems unlikely that bomber flights would have been authorised for anything but an all-out assault on the invasion beaches, but local provision seems to have been made at some schools for a last ditch attempt to inflict maximum damage on their own assets and facilities, even though such destruction might have been more efficiently wrought by demolition teams working on the ground, supposing time was available to set the charges.

At 1 EFTS Hatfield, volunteer engineers were called for, to position with a pre-allocated pilot to the assembly point, and to be ready to service the aircraft and bomb-up whenever the call should come. Ben French ran his finger down the list of names which had been presented to him and selected Flight Lieutenant V R Moon whom he regarded as a 'steady type'. Reggie Moon knew a thing or two about Tiger Moths. In 1932 as a Flying Officer he had been one of the five pilots from CFS who had flown formation aerobatics at the RAF Pageant at Hendon, a display which included sustained inverted demonstrations in close order.

In June 1934, Flying Officer Moon was one of a pair of instructors from the de Havilland School of Flying who had taken part in the display organised by the Royal Air Force Flying Club at Hatfield. Before an audience which included HRH Prince George, the future King George VI, Marshal of the Royal Air Force Lord Trenchard, and the Director of Civil Aviation, Lieutenant Colonel Shelmerdine, Flying Officers G S King and V R Moon were credited with *'a lurid and very hair raising exhibition termed on the programme "Eccentric Aerobatics". They were! Their Tiger Moths were put into every conceivable position which, had we not known who they were, would have condemned them as the world's worst and most dangerous pilots'*.

On Empire Air Day 1938, George King, 'Whizzy' to his friends, put on a show for the public who were invited into Hatfield aerodrome to inspect the School facilities. Whizzy gave a display of crazy flying operating from the rear cockpit with the blind flying hood pulled down. The public was not aware that small wooden blocks prevented the hood from fully closing, allowing the pilot some visual reference. The finale of his display was to fly across the aerodrome skipping from one mainwheel to the other. Unfortunately, one touchdown was too heavy which caused the port side front fuselage frame to buckle, although he taxied in cheerfully enough to the accompaniment of loud applause from the crowd. Eager to see action, he joined a Blenheim squadron in 1939 and was shot down and killed in one of the first raids of the war.

From 1941, Reggie Moon instructed on Night Fighter Bristol Blenheims at Church Fenton where he was awarded a Bar to his Air Force Cross earned at Hatfield. Promoted to command 219 Squadron, he returned with the rank of Wing Commander to an appointment as CFI with 1 EFTS which had long since moved to the Hatfield satellite aerodrome at Holwell Hyde, (Panshanger). It was from there that he acted as instructor to Don Stoneham in Tiger Moth DE836 (85734), in the first sortie flown by the renamed No 1 Reserve Flying School (RFS) on 13th June 1947.

All volunteer *'Banquet'* engineers were issued with a standard service flying kit: Sidcot suit, parachute and leather helmet, in addition to the obligatory tin hat, gas mask and cape, all of which were stored in steel lockers inside the school hangar. Each volunteer was advised to prepare an overnight bag and rations for two days and was read The Official Secrets Act. Nobody outside of their immediate circle of fellow travellers was to be allowed the slightest hint of the plans.

The establishment of every EFTS included a civilian armourer, and in the summer of 1940 the post at 1 EFTS was filled by Len Gaskin, later to remuster in the handsome Hatfield tower as an air traffic controller. The technician was called upon to provide essential instruction in loading the bomb racks while maintaining the highest standards of safety. This aspect was high in the minds of the pilots and engineers as dummy drops were made onto a carpet spread on the hangar floor. Rumours had filtered down from the Experimental Department that the prototype trials had been made with a live round included amongst the clutch.

While Hereward de Havilland continued with release and delivery trials near the carefully tended woodland on the north eastern perimeter of the aerodrome, the scene of seasonal shooting parties organised by the de Havilland directors in happier days, the school instructors were emulating their colleagues elsewhere and flying along the hedges in their designated low level zone at Wheathampstead. Touch-and-go forced landings at No Man's Common were practised with a new relish.

Ben French was on permanent standby to contact all personnel who were not on site when the balloon went up. He was authorised to fill the petrol tank of his motorcycle and call on the names and addresses provided against a secure list. His sole message was to be *'Banquet Light'*; all other communication was forbidden. If the intended recipient was not at home, a message was to be left asking that they should telephone the chief engineer as soon as possible. But the call to arms was never necessary, and all the temporarily loaned equipment had been returned to stores by the late summer of 1941.

In addition to what might be considered the conventionality of bomb racks, Tiger Moths were involved in two other bizarre anti-invasion schemes in 1940. Although its origins have been dimmed, the aircraft was fleetingly involved in a plan to spray invading forces with a poisonous bright green insecticide called Paris Green. In powder form this was to be carried in a tank installed in the front cockpit and dispensed through nozzles situated under the wings, or more likely the fuselage floor. No details of the installation or of its sponsors appear to have survived.

The 'Paraslasher' was, on the other hand, tried and tested, but not taken up in spite of impeccable credentials. The idea was originated by George Reid of the Reid and Sigrist company, who apart from being the contracted civil operators of 7 EFTS and its Tiger Moths at Desford, were designers and builders of aircraft parts and equipment. A garden scythe attached to an 8ft pole was stowed underneath a Tiger Moth fuselage, pivoting about the knuckle joint of the split undercarriage. In the extended position, it was intended to trail the scythe through massed ranks of descending parachutists, ripping canopies and causing mayhem.

Jack Bentley, chief engineer at MRC Ltd (Teleflex Controls), was ordered to Desford with great urgency in March 1940 to liaise with Reid and Sigrist's chief designer Chas Bower, a talented engineer previously involved with the Hawker Hart, and later responsible for the twin engined Desford.

The urgency, he discovered to his surprise, centred on how the paraslasher pole could be shifted through a 90 degree arc, controlled by Teleflex cables.

George Reid obtained permission for the conversion of one aircraft, G-ADPG (3397), and the system was demonstrated at Braunstone aerodrome, Leicester, on 12th June 1940 by the CO of 7 EFTS, Squadron Leader George Lowdell, a pre-war air display pilot. Through his contacts at the Air Ministry at which institution he had variously been a member of the Air Inventions Committee and Training Departments, George Reid arranged for a further trial to be conducted for officials on 7th July, following which his offer to attack weighted parachutes descending over Henlow was rejected. In spite of his submission that the device was cheap, effective, non-intrusive to training duties, and required no back-up service or maintenance, the scheme was dropped, according to official belief that pilots less competent than George Lowdell would be unable to wring out maximum benefit. Another reason might have been that the time between troop transports appearing overhead and parachutists touching down was probably a lot less than the warm-up time for a recently started Gipsy Major engine.

Unconnected with the low level 'paraslasher' experiments when on occasions the scythe had been menacingly trailed across the ground at high speed, G-ADPG levelled out too high and stalled from 10ft when being flown by a pilot with three hours solo time, during landing practice at Desford on 27th September 1940, and was written off as a result of the damage sustained in the near vertical arrival.

The apparent vagaries of the postings system had moved one *Banquet Light* bomber pilot from 1 EFTS where he had graduated from pupil pilot to full instructor, via 601 Squadron to 134 Squadron operating Hawker Hurricane IIs at Vaenga in Russia. As commander of 'A' Flight, Flight Lieutenant Vic Berg was one of several RAF Hurricane pilots who apart from the appalling weather, had already suffered the unnerving experience of hearing his engine cutting out and back in again during cruise, a phenomenon attributed to the low octane fuel then available. The precarious state of the airfield surface was the cause of many ground manoeuvring incidents but nothing as tragic as the accident which occurred in September 1941 when Berg inadvertently took off in his Hurricane BD825 with two members of the groundcrew, who were attempting to prevent the aircraft from tipping onto its nose, still weighting down the tailplane. The aircraft stalled at 50ft and the resulting crash killed both men and put Berg on the sick list for a year during which time he was a frequent visitor to 1 EFTS, looking up old friends amongst the engineers and staff. He became fairly dextrous on his crutches before full fitness permitted him to return to operations with a vengeance, joining 222 Squadron in 1942 to fly Supermarine Spitfires and Hawker Tempests.

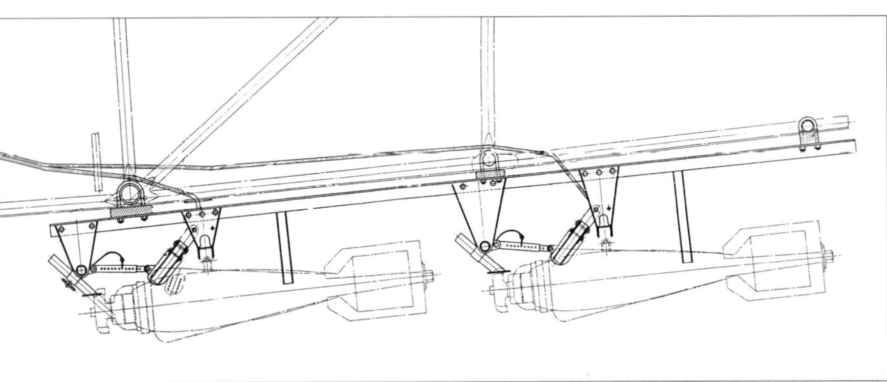

Bombs and racks located with respect to the lower longerons of a Tiger Moth fuselage. Bombs were rarely carried; racks and rails were often retained during training sorties. de Havilland Aircraft Co.

Regarded as an emergency and hopefully temporary measure, proper testing of the Tiger Moth with her military ordnance still had to be completed to an agreed schedule, and questions answered for the record. How would this trainer aircraft behave with up to 250lb of small bombs slung underneath the rear seat, and just as relevant, how would she handle with empty cradles? The Aeroplane and Armament Experimental Establishment (A&AEE) at Boscombe Down was tasked with the job of finding out.

Early in 1940, against the prospect of a German invasion, the de Havilland Aircraft Company had been urgently required to assess the practical implications of converting innocuous Tiger Moth training aeroplanes into front line light bombers. It was a case of back to the wall offensive defence, and every option had to be considered in dissuading the would-be occupiers from landing on British beaches. If the kitchen sink had to be thrown, so be it. A scheme to carry a single 250lb bomb was considered, and Major Hereward de Havilland flew a trial installation at Hatfield, but the dummy bomb fell off and embedded itself in open ground near the main factory buildings, fortunately without damage or injury. Geoffrey de Havilland Jr was co-opted into the trials and dropped a 250lb bomb over the airfield which test pilot 'Baron' Cross and Charles Caliendi were detailed off to recover, but in spite of intensive searches, no trace of it was ever found.

An installation to accept eight Cooper or 'F' type bombs of 20lb each was approved on 12th June 1940. Hereward conducted release trials near the northern perimeter of Hatfield aerodrome following which 1,500 sets of racks (carrier, bomb, light series, type B, de Havilland), were ordered. The first 100 sets were delivered to 25 Maintenance Unit (MU) Hartlebury at the beginning of July for distribution amongst the elementary flying schools of Training Command, and the remainder followed at the rate of 200 sets per week. 240 sets of 'old type carrier' were already in stock.

The scheme was not exactly original. As part of their sales campaign dating from early 1932, de Havilland had presented the Tiger Moth as a machine with great military versatility, and aircraft were configured to include camera guns and telescopic sights, wireless sets for telegraphy and telephony, electrically operated photographic equipment, long range tankage, a bomb sight in the front cockpit, and the capacity to carry eight 20lb bombs capable of release from either seat, implying no perceived problem with operational weight or centre of gravity (CG) position. In January 1932, a 'Light Series Bomb Rack and Release Control (less Bowden Cable)' was being advertised in lists of subsidiary equipment available to customers: racks could be supplied at a cost of £24.0s.0d plus a fitting charge of £9.15s.0d each. Alternatively, the aircraft could be prepared for later installation for just ten shillings less.

While the Royal Air Force as lead customer chose to ignore most of the options, allocating its first Tiger Moths to basic flying training, a formation display team and a communications squadron, the offer of an aggressive Tiger Moth was far from shelved, but rather refined. In October 1933 the company had unveiled their Tiger Moth Fighter which in addition to carrying a machine gun mounted over the front seat position, was scheduled to carry eight 20lb Cooper bombs mounted on racks beneath the rear cockpit floor.

Drawing on this experience in 1940, de Havilland were able to provide early detail for manufacture of kits of the 38 individual component parts required for the bomb racks and their installation, including the plumbing of release gear up into the front cockpit.

The kits were distributed from Hartlebury, together with detailed instructions on how to undertake the conversion. Unlike some instruction leaflets, AP.1449B/C.2-W could only have been compiled by a secretary noting every action during a trial installation at Hatfield. *'If necessary, bend the pitot tubes to clear the aileron cables'*, mechanics were urged, no doubt as a result of such a requirement being discovered during the 'on the job' modification.

A total of 15 man hours was required to complete the conversion of each aircraft in the field, but was applicable only to Tiger Moth IIs held at certain Home Units which effectively meant all the Elementary Schools. Some of the modifications necessary to accept the installations were embodied on production aircraft at Cowley from October 1940 where T7266 (83764), was the first. The production standard saved ten hours of in-service engineering time, and although updated instructions on how to complete the job were still being published as late as December 1941, the greater urgency had passed.

To maintain the CG when bombs were carried, and equally after they had been dropped, under the 1940 de Havilland scheme it was necessary for the pilot to operate solo, and from the front seat. Included in the 38 piece kit was a placard: *'When bombs are carried, rear cockpit must be empty'*. Fixing the label was the very last action on the conversion instructions, which said it should be positioned to the top left-hand corner of the instrument panel and screwed in place with two ⅜in x No. 4 round-head nickel-plated woodscrews. Nobody could have been left in any doubt.

It was anticipated that instructors would be operating the aircraft during their raids, who were more used to the front seat position and which many preferred anyway, believing it to be less draughty than the rear cockpit.

Bomb release was activated by a pair of Bowden cables routed up through the floor on the starboard side, and then outboard of the fuselage side frame, to run between that and the fabric covering. Both cable outer sleeves were secured to the frame's mid-depth wooden stringer before looping up and back to link onto a pair of long throttle-type levers assembled in a quadrant and clamped to the structure near the slat cable pulley. A single plain split pin acted as safety guard and prevented inadvertent operation of the levers which were pulled backwards for release: the longer, outer lever for the rear salvo and the semi-arched inner lever for the forward four. There was no provision for dropping the small bombs singly, not that any prospective bomber pilot would have wanted a choice other than to drop the whole load on one pass and get on his way.

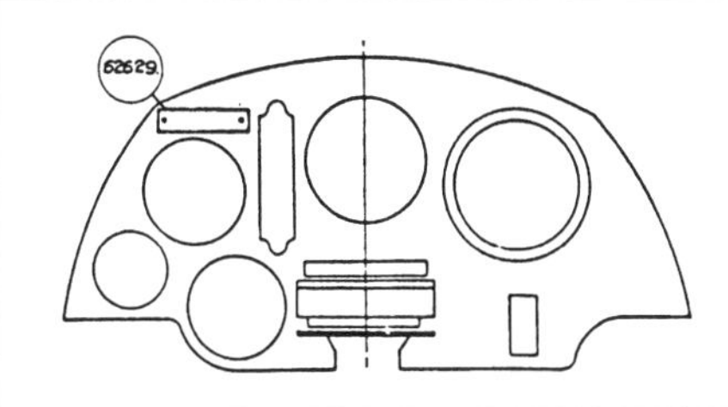

When converting a Tiger Moth to her bomber role, the final item on the checklist was a precise instruction on how and where to screw label, Part No 62629 onto the instrument panel. And the legend? *'When bombs are carried, rear cockpit must be empty'*.

The two levers were grouped for ease in releasing both salvos together, controlled by the pilot's right hand, and assuming the throttle to have been pre-set for maximum power, with the stick in his left. This was an unnatural situation for any instructor or long term habitué of the front cockpit of a Tiger Moth.

The bomb 'rack' was a box which could easily and quickly be fitted to a pair of fixed parallel rails situated under the floor of the rear cockpit and unlike the inflexible installation on the Magister, were designed to accommodate either eight 20lb or 25lb bombs arranged transversely in two rows of four.

There was some debate at Chief of Staff level on whether, once fitted, bomb carriers should remain on the aircraft.

One school of thought was that carriers should be removed and stored until the Plan *Banquet* force was called to readiness. It was decided however, that it would be better to leave them permanently fitted *'provided they did not seriously affect the performance of the aircraft in its role as a trainer'*. One senior staff officer was moved to point out that it would be uneconomical to leave bomb carriers attached as they would be written off every time an aircraft was crashed. A fellow officer consoled him with the view that very few aircraft were damaged at the Elementary Schools!

It was inevitable that some schools flew the aircraft with the carriers permanently attached while others removed them for training during the working day, refitting the selected aircraft to coincide with the instructors' practice sessions after normal hours. While it was simple enough to schedule modification of the 69 Tiger Moths confirmed by the RAF to be in reserve storage on 1st June, conversion of the working aircraft had to be integrated into the school programme. For minimum disruption, slave aircraft were rotated through the system, enabling establishment Tiger Moths to be temporarily withdrawn and modified on site.

Two Tiger Moths, N9454 (82508) and T5610 (83303), were delivered to A&AEE in the summer of 1940 to become the responsibility of 'A' Squadron, Performance Testing Squadron. N9454 had been built in November 1939 and although allocated to storage at 20 MU Aston Down, may have been retained by de Havilland as a trials aircraft. T5610, a brand new machine in the June production batch, was fitted with bomb racks and after a prolonged one hour flight test by de Havilland test pilot Pat Fillingham on 28th July, during which he encountered no peculiarities in handling, was dispatched to Boscombe Down. The initial briefing was to investigate 'Handling and Diving', but at the request of Flying Training

The Home Command markings and serial batch of this Tiger Moth are evidence of a deception. The aircraft is EM836, the place Hatfield aerodrome, and the date, 2nd June 1944. Attaching the bombs is believed to be Hereward de Havilland. The scene was set up by Merton Park Studios and incorporated into the classic de Havilland film biography of the Mosquito.
de Havilland Aircraft Co.

Command the remit was widened to include spinning.

A series of flight tests at varying weights and CG positions, with the pilot operating in either front or rear cockpits, showed the aircraft to behave much as expected, but in level flight at an extended aft CG position, it was noted that there was insufficient trim to allow hands-off flight at full throttle. This may have been considered a serious deficiency in view of the revised control layout of the bomber cockpit conversion.

The diving tests were conducted at one third throttle setting or less in order to limit the engine to its maximum permitted rotational speed of 2,350rpm, which otherwise was reached very rapidly. At engine speeds of 1,500 to 2,000rpm, and dive angles of 50 to 55 degrees, indicated airspeeds of 160 to 170mph were recorded operating from 5,000ft, speeds which it was considered would be difficult to better within a reasonable loss of height due to the extra drag effected by the racks and bombs.

'A' Squadron reported that they were satisfied with the aircraft's diving performance and control, and proceeded with bomb release tests conducted when in level flight, a prolonged dive, and from a dive following a half roll. Spinning trials were flown only with bombs removed, and with solo pilots again operating from the front seat and then the rear seat. At each loading situation, spins of eight turns were made both to the right and to the left, during which it was noted that the control column tended to move in the direction of the spins which were described as being steady and of a normal attitude. The aeroplane responded to the standard method of spin recovery which resulted in spins stopping within half a turn of control reversal. Height lost during the eight turn sequence amounted to about 2,000ft. Boscombe Down's secret report concluded that in their opinion, the behaviour of the Tiger Moth II in general handling, diving and spinning, was satisfactory.

Cartoonist Charles Hall ('Holly') did not believe in cruelty to Tiger Moths and claimed this creation was based on an unpublished sketch found in a de Havilland dustbin. Charles Hall

However, Training Command's concerns on spinning with the racks in position had been noted, and on 16th August 1940, the Hatfield-based Service Manager of the de Havilland Aircraft Company, Albert Brant, wrote to all Elementary Schools to advise them that to improve flying characteristics during training, the entire bomb rack or at least the rear crutch boards fitted in accordance with modifications Tiger Moth II/73 and 77, should be removed. The Air Ministry confirmed the detail of the letter by signal to all units on 25th September 1940, and the instruction was re-emphasised in an Air Ministry circular, although this was not published until the following April.

The two trials' aeroplanes went their separate ways. In November, N9454 flew from Boscombe Down into a period of 18 months storage at 10 MU Hullavington before allocation in June 1942 to a detachment of 2 Squadron RAF, operating their North American Mustang 1s from Gatwick. Within a month the aircraft had been broken and was routed through the locally based Southern Aircraft Civil Repair Organisation (CRO). After a few weeks with 1424 Flight, N9454 crashed on 1st December 1942, and having been repaired by Taylorcraft at Rearsby, passed through Hullavington again enroute to the packing unit at High Ercall, from where she was dispatched for service in South Africa. During passage in convoy LS33, her freighter, the SS *Djambe*, was attacked and sunk.

T5610 fared better. The aircraft was returned to de Havilland at Hatfield by the end of 1942 where she was used extensively during the next two years in development of improved 'suction' systems, especially with regard to night flying instrumentation, and occasionally for the airborne inspection of the factory camouflage scheme, both exercises often flown by Pat Fillingham accompanied by Resident Technical Officer (RTO), Ray Fitch. The aircraft was eventually posted to Scotland, and spent a few weeks with Station Flight at RAF Kirkbride early in 1945 before heading south again, and final disposal from 5 MU Kemble in July 1947, when she was acquired by BOAC. Registered G-AKCM the aircraft was based at White Waltham, but sold to Airwork only a month later and delivered to Saudi Arabia in October 1950.

But all was not well in the world at large, and training units were advised to mark the boards with the serial numbers of the aircraft from which they had been separated. In addition, the tireless engineering staff were encouraged to ensure there would be no delay in the event of a national emergency, by periodically refitting the crutches in position on the racks.

No documentation can be traced which details the authorised installation or use of bomb racks fitted under the *wings* of Tiger Moths based in Great Britain, but the number of sightings and reports would indicate that such a provision may have been made as the result of local initiatives when necessity once again proved to be the mother of invention. The habit of one prominent test pilot closely involved in spinning trials with bomb racked Tiger Moths in referring to 'wing' racks in all written communication on the subject, has done nothing to lift the veil of confusion.

At least one Tiger Moth with a pair of 25lb Cooper bombs fitted to racks carried under each lower wing was observed by the Spitfire pilots of 603 Squadron to be operational for a few days in January 1940 at Dyce aerodrome, Aberdeen. This was an aircraft from 1 Coastal Patrol Flight (CPF), a unit which had been established as unarmed reconnaissance patrollers in December 1939, and whose crews were probably moved to emulate the more aggressive role of their near neighbours during discussions on tactics while thawing out in the mess.

The on-site modifications may have preempted what was already being considered elsewhere and are unlikely to have received approval from anywhere but within the unit. Much to the consternation of the Spitfire air and ground crews, not to mention the CPF pilots, the bombs were inclined to fall off the racks when manoeuvring on the ground, particularly during touchdown, and apart from familiarisation, only two operational sorties are believed to have been flown before the experiment was halted and the racks removed.

Possibly the idea for wing mounted bomb racks migrated with ex-CPF aircraft to 11 EFTS at Perth during the late summer of 1940. A pupil pilot recorded, long after retirement as a Consolidated Catalina captain and Station Commander based in India, that during his initial training at Perth in August and September of that year, some of the establishment's Tiger Moths were fitted with what he clearly described as bomb racks fitted 'outboard of each landing wheel' and that each rack was capable of carrying 4 bombs. In the evenings, the instructors were seen carrying out practice dive bombing attacks on a target set up in the corner of the airfield.

While wandering around the dispersals at 13 EFTS at White Waltham in August 1940, pupil pilot Neville Duke noticed that the aircraft of one Flight were fitted with what appeared to be racks under each lower wing capable of carrying four bombs. The school's recently appointed CFI, Flight Lieutenant George 'Monty' Cox MC, advised his instructional staff that when armed, these aircraft should only be flown solo. A misinterpretation of this order seems to have been that 'with a full bomb load and two up, it is not possible to carry full fuel'.

No. 13 EFTS was operated under contract by the de Havilland Aircraft Company and

A pleasing study of Tiger Moth R4922 in flight with the instrument hood erected. The Holt flareholder can be clearly seen trailing beneath the starboard lower mainplane, and often confused with underwing, as opposed to under-fuselage, bomb racks. Note the negative angle of the elevator in level flight. deHMC Archive

although administered as a completely autonomous body, ultimately reported back to the Enterprise at Hatfield. The de Havilland technical archive makes no mention of any modification which involved fitting bomb racks anywhere except underneath the fuselage, and although it may appear improbable that an operational establishment so closely tied to its manufacturing parent would effect such a radical modification at a local level, August and September 1940 were desperate times calling for dramatic initiatives.

As recently as 3rd July 1940, a Dornier Do217 had attacked the airfield at White Waltham, laying two sticks of small fragmentation bombs across the dispersal, destroying six Tiger Moths and damaging 25 more. A year later, 13 EFTS was closed down and the premises vacated for use by the Air Transport Auxiliary, a move which greatly displeased de Havilland who had planned and built the site for maximum efficiency, although they would have preferred to have been based at nearby Benson anyway. As compensation the company was tasked with organising 90 Tiger Moths for 17 EFTS at Peterborough until the unit was disbanded in May 1942.

What chance that underwing racks may have been confused with single point Holt flare carriers bolted through the lower pick-up bracket for the forward interplane strut? The carrier arms were designed to fold backwards when not in use, an additional safety feature intended to prevent them hooking onto obstructions during landing. The flare carriers were not easy to see on casual inspection when standing near a Tiger Moth and their location at 8ft from the root end was not in conformity with the opinion of most observers which put the racks close to the fuselage sides, and definitely within the first bay.

In the intervening years, restorers opening up wings for structural inspection prior to application of new fabric, have occasionally reported the presence of apparently redundant fittings. The lack of part numbers stamped on some of them would indicate local modification, and their absence certainly hampered any serious investigation of what might be just another red herring.

At 22 EFTS Cambridge in November 1940, pupil pilot Idris Griffith was sent solo in a Tiger Moth which he described as having been subject to 'considerable usage'. The pre-flight inspection was inadequate, the pilot paying greater attention to his cockpit drill and the prospects of what lay immediately ahead. After what appeared to be a normal take-off, the aircraft refused to fly straight and level, and it was with great difficulty that the first soloist managed to land back, only to be met by an exasperated instructor, not with a congratulatory smile but a demand to know what had happened to standard technique. A closer look at the aircraft revealed that the 'bomb rack' underneath the starboard lower wing had been removed, but perhaps the arrival of the NAAFI wagon had interrupted the mechanic's schedule, and the aircraft had been presented to the flight line with the port side unit still firmly attached.

No.116 Squadron was disbanded in 1918 and its Handley Page 0/400 bombers struck off charge. From the nucleus of 1 Anti-Aircraft Co-operation Unit, the squadron was re-formed at Hatfield in February 1941, operating Westland Lysander IIIs, but moved to Hendon in April of that year where Hawker Hurricane Is were inherited. The squadron was headquartered at a number of different airfields all located around London until disbandment in May 1945, by which time DH Hornet Moth, Airspeed Oxford II and Avro Anson I and XII had all been part of the inventory.

The nature of the squadron's business, partly the provision of flying services for anti-aircraft gun and radar alignment in various areas of the country, necessitated the regular deployment of small detachments. In July 1942, Detachment D5 equipped with Lysander IIIs was stationed at Church Fenton, Yorkshire.

Mindful of the continuing and crucial need to economise on fuel, the Air Ministry believed that D5's non-fighting role could equally well be achieved by substituting the Mercury engined Lysanders with Gipsy Major powered Tiger Moths, consuming about a quarter of the precious liquid for the same basic end result. Tiger Moth DE680 (85621), was one of a total of 34 brand new aircraft allocated to 116 Squadron on 1st July 1942, and was delivered a few days later by a pilot of the Air Transport Auxiliary (ATA), positioning from 38 MU Llandow. On arrival the Detachment crews were astonished to discover what to their minds were tiny bomb racks fitted to the undersides of both lower wings, and the fighting potential of the aircraft was the matter of much discussion and playful demonstration.

The Commanding Officer of D5, Pilot Officer Jenkins, freely discussed the options: in case of an invasion, still a possibility in July 1942, he and his fellow pilots Warrant Officer Morgan and Sergeant Evans, would fight with the Lysanders, leaving the Detachment's two Wireless Operator/Air Gunners Kydd and Hawkesworth to fly the Tiger Moth. Jenkins repeated his philosophy so often that Kydd and Hawkesworth realised he was not joking at their expense, especially when the tactics to be employed at hedge top height were debated and briefed.

Sergeant Hawkesworth's first 'training' flight took place on 16th July 1942 and he logged a total of almost 18 hours with the squadron pilots on 'familiarisation' work plus additional unrecorded sorties. But the invasion did not come, the crisis was eased, and DE680 was transferred in May 1943 to 486 Squadron, a New Zealand unit operating Hawker Typhoons from Tangmere.

With the Japanese on the rampage throughout the Pacific, even New Zealand was vulnerable to their unwelcome attentions, and the Tiger Moth was immediately considered part of a greater effort to develop the best line of defence: offence! Group Captain Michael Keogh, Director of Repair and Maintenance, Royal New Zealand Air Force, had been trained as a pilot before joining the Engineering Branch, and had been awarded the Albert Medal for rescuing a pilot trapped in a crashed and burning aircraft. Taking a leaf from the Japanese book on tactics, it is alleged that Micky Keogh proposed to the Air Staff that Tiger Moths carrying bombs, and flown by the more elderly officers and men who had previously received some form of pilot training, such as himself, should be deliberately crashed into ships carrying the invading hordes.

That may have been the version which filtered down through the ranks, but the Air Staff did take the matter seriously enough to draw up plans in December 1941 for every available training aircraft to be converted to a fighter or a bomber, including a force of 80 Tiger Moths. 'Light Series Mechanically Actuated Bomb Carriers' were fitted under the fuselages, initially with a capacity for four 20lb bombs, later increased to eight. Due to weight and balance limitations, the aircraft could only be flown solo and from the front seat. Not for the Tiger Moth was the prospect of a machine gun equipped rear cockpit to emulate the Hawker Hinds, Vickers Vincents, Fairey Gordons and Vickers Vildebeeste, or a forward firing gun which converted North American Harvards and Airspeed Oxfords into potent fighter bombers.

Hugh Buckingham, General Manager of the de Havilland Aircraft Company of New Zealand's factory at Rongotai, Wellington, was asked to design in great secrecy, a bomb rack system which could be fitted to the underside of each of the country's civilian owned DH.89 Dragon Rapides, and his basic but practical suggestions were conveyed to Hatfield for approval. In the event the Dragon Rapides were not armed and in accord with British belief, were considered to be of greater value in a transport configuration.

The Tiger Moth fleet was accorded the lowest priority in provisioning of offensive equipment, not least in view of their primary and continuing role of training new pilots. Courses of 55 pupils continued to join the Elementary Schools every four weeks.

The New Zealand Defence Plan as approved by Air Commodore R V Goddard, Chief of the Air Staff, was issued under the 'secret' classification from Air Force Headquarters in Wellington on 17th January 1942. Known as the FAFAI Scheme (Forces Available For Anti Invasion), the Tiger Moth element was clearly defined. Four operational light bomber squadrons of 'Moths' were to be formed (41, 42, 43 and 44 Auxiliary Squadrons), provided from the resources of 1, 2, 3 and 4 EFTS, together with 51 Auxiliary Squadron from the Central Flying School. Each squadron was to have an initial establishment of 18 aircraft and instructor pilots, later increased to 24. Administered as 'paper' squadrons within their host organisations, each school was required to nominate a Squadron Commander and conventional chain of authority for flying, maintenance and administrative duties. Officers with recent operational experience were appointed by Air Force Headquarters to advise school commanders on the best tactics to be taught during squadron training. From July 1942, the eighth week in each course was dedicated to concentrated operational training for the instructors, either on a local basis or as dictated by exercises organised from HQ, during which the local hedges were subject to constant low level review.

Each of the new Moth auxiliary squadrons was initially divided into two Flights of nine aircraft each, with a Pool Reserve composed of all remaining aircraft on the establishment strength, and fitted with whatever leftover equipment could be made available. The Chief Flying Instructor was usually appointed Squadron Commander, and it was the Station Commander's prerogative to nominate Flight Commanders and other officers with a similar authority within the Pool Reserve.

Due to a shortage of practice bombs, the CFI/Squadron Commander was advised to arrange training on the most appropriate ranges with aircraft operating in sections of three or by Flights, when imaginary bombs

The only Tiger Moth known to have carried under wing bomb racks, and for which incontrovertible photographic evidence exists, is A17-330 of the Royal Australian Air Force, converted to the specification called up by John Kingsford-Smith in 1942. RAAF Museum

A clear view of the underwing bomb rack positions on A17-330. The de Havilland factory at Mascot and other interesting hardware can be seen in the background. via Bruce Winley

Bomb release T handles on the port side of the rear cockpit of A17-330, together with an illustrated placard indicating what does what. via Bruce Winley

The Australian underwing bombs could be armed or made safe in the air via an arrangement on the starboard side of the rear cockpit, utilising the top rail of a Tiger Moth cockpit door. via Bruce Winley

would be dropped against a pre-arranged signal to simulate the attack window. Methods of ordnance delivery were the subject of discussion between squadrons, and for their declared role of beach reconnaissance and troop harassment, a low level shallow diving technique using the cross-over of the centre section bracing wires as a reference, was considered to be the most productive, endorsing what had been discovered in England during the tense days of 1940.

A trainee pilot at 2 EFTS New Plymouth said after the danger was past, that on all solo flights except when aerobatics were expected, pilots flew with a clutch of four anti-personnel bombs attached to the aircraft which were to be dropped on invading troops, after which instructions were quite clear: *'we were to fly inland, land somewhere, take off our uniforms, camouflage the aircraft, and get the hell out of it'*.

Tiger Moth bomber squadrons were allocated to pre-planned airfield and satellite locations dotted around the major cities which were considered the most obvious enemy targets, and stocks of bombs, spares and fuel sufficient for 20 flying hours per aircraft were scheduled to be laid down. In the event, neither of the code words required to spring the trap were ever broadcast. 'FAFAI' would have brought units to a four hour state of readiness with all flying training stopped in favour of essential test flying only, and the immediate equipping and provisioning of aircraft. 'LAFRAF' was the signal to bomb-up and for armouries to issue the available supply of revolvers and tin hats. 'Fly-off to rendezvous' instructions were then tensely awaited from Air Force Headquarters.

Although the FAFAI scheme was never tested in anger, the plan was conceived with the best of motives, was well organised and the aircrew thoroughly briefed and trained. Their period of legal low level activity was considered a welcome break from the exigencies of circuit discipline, much like their British counterparts who had already discovered the delights of authorised hedge-hopping.

'Holly' added an underfloor cannon and a second pilot to his battleworthy Tiger Moth, ideas which even by 1940's emergency standards would have been considered optimistic. Charles Hall

No.44 Auxiliary Squadron was disbanded along with 4 EFTS on 9th March 1942 when the aerodrome at Whenuapai was handed over to operational squadrons. The aircraft and trained staff were absorbed by the three remaining units, all of which were located by design in South Island, and whose establishments were subsequently increased to at least 55 Tiger Moths each. CFS renounced its anti-invasion status in July 1942 when 51 Auxiliary Squadron was stood down, and 41, 42 and 43 Squadrons were formally disbanded on 5th April 1943.

In 1942, Australia too was concerned about the prospects of a Japanese invasion, and for what protection could be provided had moved most of her slender defence resources to the areas of most immediate danger in the north. But supposing the Japanese invasion fleet merely bypassed the obvious landing sites and their defences, and hit hard straight at Sydney and the extensive beaches on the eastern seaboard? What was left in the country's armoury?

The answer was a few armed Commonwealth Aircraft Corporation Wirraway trainers and Lockheed Hudsons which could operate only from a small number of adequately large airfields, and about 700 Tiger Moths with nearly 1,000 experienced pilots, mostly instructors, stationed at the Elementary Schools. One such instructor, a Flight Commander at 4 EFTS Mascot, was John Kingsford-Smith, a nephew of Sir Charles Kingsford-Smith, the legendary 'Smithy'.

John Kingsford-Smith devised a plan to fit stocks of redundant under-wing bomb racks to Tiger Moths at the schools scattered throughout Victoria and New South Wales. He had discovered nearly 100 bomb rack sets originally designed for Westland Wapitis in store at Richmond, together with others from DH.9s and Hawker Demons. Additional racks were later discovered at Laverton.

The proposal for the emergency arming of Tiger Moths was submitted to the Commanding Officer of Eastern Command Headquarters at Port Piper, Air Commodore Lachal, who was impressed sufficiently to stand down Kingsford-Smith from his instructional duties, probably coincident with the closure of 4 EFTS in April 1942 anyway, and to appoint him to head a small team to develop the scheme.

The installation was designed by two friends of Kingsford-Smith, both of whom worked for de Havilland at Mascot: Johnny Larkin and Norm Lennon. The pilot's bomb controls were divided between port and starboard side of the rear cockpit: the 'safety' device was cable operated, using as a locator the top rail of a Tiger Moth door bolted with a slight nose down bias, just below the slat operating quadrant on the starboard sideframe.

Bomb release was effected by cables connected to a pair of T handles operating in a nearly vertical orientation on the port side, forward of the trimmer quadrant and below the combined throttle/mixture levers. The starboard bombs were released by the handle in a lower and more rearward position when compared to the port control, a configuration which permitted a firm grip on both handles at the same time to encourage a simultaneous drop. If the pilot forgot which release was appropriate to which rack, a diagrammatic scheme was stencilled onto an adjacent facia.

Unlike their British counterparts, however, and those across the Tasman Sea, the aggressive Australian Tiger Moth was not intended to double as a trainer after conversion.

The aircraft was designed to be flown solo from the rear cockpit with the front instrument panel and windscreen removed and a fairing secured over the void. In this configuration and with her bright yellow training colours hidden under a faded camouflage scheme, Tiger Moth bombers were to be deployed to their operational sites, and scheduled to remain there for as long as was considered necessary.

The de Havilland Aircraft Company at Mascot was formally involved with the trials conversion of Tiger Moth A17-330 (DHA349), a judicious decision considering the clamour for conversion kits which might be expected if the balloon were to go up!

A17-330 had been based with 4 EFTS on home ground at Mascot before transfer to 2 Communications Flight, also at Mascot, remaining with that unit until May 1942 when the Flight moved to Wagga Wagga.

However, perhaps by coincidence, the aircraft was re-allocated to 3 Communications Flight which formed at Mascot just as soon as their predecessors had shifted their kit, and was retained for what was officially described as 'photographic duties'.

Although this was a euphemism driven by security for 'bomber conversion trials', the aircraft was featured in a number of official photographs released after the war in which a 40lb bomb is displayed in each cradle, adjacent to a placard warning that the maximum design load for the configuration under normal conditions, was never intended to be greater than a 30lb bomb in any one position.

Having established the credibility of the mechanism, it was necessary to test the concept, and release trials were conducted at Richmond where it was established that remarkable accuracy could be achieved when operating at high speed and at low level. Kingsford-Smith had already given considerable thought to the theoretical disposition of this new offensive defence force, and ideal sites were considered to be the 52 golf courses situated within a 15 mile coastal band between Newcastle and Wollongong. Assisted by two other RAAF pilots operating standard aircraft, Kingsford-Smith and his team surveyed each site and rejected only four as unsuitable for operational use.

Flight trials were conducted from all the selected fairways much to the consternation of some club officials. The secretary of the Royal Sydney Club at Rose Bay suffered a fit of apoplexy when he saw the damage being inflicted by the Tiger Moth's tailskid, and a popular rumour has it that he was doubly outraged to discover that the responsible pilot was not a member. But it was just a rumour. Having threatened police action and complaints directed at the highest seats in government, the secretary was told to expect ten aircraft to arrive for trials the following day on the authority of the same government.

From the trial fitting of the first rack to completion of the 52nd site survey, only four weeks had elapsed. The plan had proved feasible and de Havilland were immediately commissioned to produce 800 sets of standard conversion kits which would include the sets of bomb racks previously discovered in store.

Plans were in hand to issue location maps and to provision each fairway with a 44 gallon barrel of petrol and a supply of anti-personnel bombs when the cavalry arrived in the form of two squadrons of American Curtiss P-40 Kittyhawks, posted into the area. Tested and ready for action, the Tiger Moth bomber project was shelved.

A17-330 was delivered into store at Canberra the following year, perhaps as an insurance, but having been stripped back to her standard configuration she joined an Air Ambulance Unit in Queensland in June 1943. Following spells with 8 and 9 EFTS and another period in storage, the aircraft was sold for £305 in April 1946 to the Royal Aero Club of Western Australia in Perth, where she was broken down for spare parts.

GETTING INTO A SPIN

DH.85 Leopard Moth CH-368; DH.60GIII Moth Major, probably CH-369; a DH.60M Moth and DH.82A Tiger Moth G-ACJA together with some splendid carpets and 'office' furniture, represented the de Havilland Aircraft Company at the Geneva Aero Show in April 1934. P Geiselhard

POSSIBLY the first recorded Tiger Moth spinning accident, one which involved a civilian aircraft, occurred on 15th December 1933, near to Hatfield aerodrome, when G-ACJA (3191), failed to recover from a spin initiated at about 1,500ft, and fell into trees just outside the airfield boundary. The pilot was a recently qualified student of the de Havilland Aeronautical Technical School who was working towards his 'B' commercial pilot's licence. G-ACJA was an almost new aeroplane, a demonstration model on loan to the London Aeroplane Club and with only 115 flying hours logged since the previous August, most of which are thought to have been accumulated during a demonstration tour to the Middle East, possibly as far as Syria. After taking off from Hatfield the previous afternoon the pilot had flown to Stag Lane and engaged in the exuberant low level antics of a man with 97 hours experience, a display for the benefit of his ex colleagues which earned him what was politely termed 'a caution' from a member of the de Havilland staff.

The following morning G-ACJA returned to Hatfield and indulged in a further series of indifferent aerobatics. The left hand spin was intentional but in the opinion of the accident inspector, it was a dangerous error of judgement to spin from such a low altitude, during which manoeuvre the pilot failed to make proper use of the controls to effect a rapid recovery. The report included a note to the effect that G-ACJA was not fitted with Handley Page automatic slots, an optional extra attracting a heavy royalty.

Nine days before Christmas 1933, Tiger Moth G-ACJA spun into trees just outside the boundary of Hatfield aerodrome, assisted by the pilot, according to the accident inspector's report. Four months later, G-ACJA was an exhibit at the Geneva Aero Show. deHMC Archive

At the time of the accident, the aircraft was painted in a style most unlike any de Havilland demonstration aircraft with the fuselage displaying a broad two-tone spiral which required some letters of the registration to be painted in one colour and others in the opposite hue.

Following repairs, G-ACJA was displayed in an overall silver scheme, looking pristine and with a blind flying hood in the raised position, at the Geneva Aero Show in May 1934, when she shared stand space at the indoor exhibition with DH.85 Leopard Moth CH-368 (7045) and a DH.60GIII, almost certainly CH-369 (5069). Soon after her static appearance in Switzerland, the aircraft was photographed at an unknown location overseas with a metal propeller and in the colours of the de Havilland School of Flying.

In September 1934, G-ACJA was sold to Austria, joining the Luftschutzkommando as A-81, but only three months later she was lost in unrecorded circumstances, and the entry was cancelled.

Operating from Hatfield in 1936, the London Aeroplane Club's G-ADGO (2262), a Tiger Moth built as a practical exercise by members of the de Havilland Aeronautical Technical School, and not fitted with slots, was seen to dive towards the Dunstable clubhouse of the London Gliding Club before climbing away to perform two loops. At the end of the second manoeuvre the aircraft commenced a spin from less than 1,000ft, but recovery was very late and during the pull-out the aircraft flew into the ground.

An embarrassed pilot afterwards admitted that the second 'loop' was a failed attempt at a stall turn to the left, and the aircraft had spun off. In this case the accident inspector expressed no opinion, other than that the aeroplane appeared to have suffered no pre-crash defects or failures. Given just another 10ft perhaps, G-ADGO might have survived to prove that she was docile enough to be safely extracted from an unintentional spin at low level.

Before the critical need for offensive equipment had even been contemplated, an instructor from 1 ERFTS Hatfield experienced a fright when spinning a Tiger Moth with a pupil early in 1938. Until now he had regarded the type with great respect, and was confident enough in the structural integrity to have tried a bunt, a half outside loop. After four turns of a planned spin with recovery due to be effected following the appearance of St Albans Cathedral for the seventh time, the aircraft appeared to lose momentum before quite suddenly rearing up into a climbing attitude to enter what was described as a fast, unbanked turn with the wings parallel with the horizon. The instructor, John Nesbit-Dufort, 'Whippy' to close friends, reported no skidding sensation; he considered that he was sitting above the vertical axis of rotation and that the aircraft had no forward speed whatsoever, a fact verified by the needle of the Air Speed Indicator (ASI) flickering around the lowest graduations on the dial.

Realising he was in a flat spin, the instructor took control and at first attempted normal recovery action, but the controls appeared to be stuck fast, and he was suspicious that the pupil pilot was still clinging on. Following a burst of high volume communication via the Gosports, the pupil exposed both gloved hands simultaneously, but the stick remained obstinate, forced back against the stop as the elevators were deflected upwards with the rapid descent of the aircraft. On the point of ordering abandonment at 1,000ft, Dufort remembered he had not enlisted the aid of the gently ticking engine, and in a last chance effort slammed on full throttle. With some elevator power restored, the Tiger Moth almost instantly flipped into a normal spin from which a standard recovery was made at 150ft. 'Whippy' Dufort later wrote that his post-flight report was treated with some disbelief and soon after he was posted to Central Flying School (CFS) to attend a re-categorisation course, after which and with two and a half hours of night flying experience, he was judged sufficiently qualified to teach others.

On 13th September 1940, Tiger Moth N6948 (82198), an aircraft reported as being fitted with 'bomb racks', operating with 7 EFTS from Desford, was conducting spinning tests with a pupil, but in spite of all efforts was unable to recover into stable flight. The instructor, Flight Lieutenant F W Moxham, ordered his pupil to abandon the aircraft, immediately after which control was regained, and the Tiger Moth safely landed solo and from the front seat.

Bill Oliver, a DH.60 Moth pilot from Stag Lane days, and inventor of a banned flick manoeuvre which quickly became known as 'the Oliver Twist', was 'B' Flight Commander at 31 EFTS Elmdon during the summer of 1940. He initiated a deliberate spin in a Tiger Moth equipped with bomb rack rails close to the airfield boundary at 3,000ft, and was surprised that in spite of applying all known methods of recovery, absolutely nothing happened. Continuous pumping of the throttle resulted in sudden and unexpected recovery at a height to quote Oliver, 'down amongst the bird's nests'. Having mentioned the incident to fellow instructors, Oliver was astonished at the incredulity and derision which resulted and allowed the matter to pass. Soon after he was posted overseas and unable to pursue his concerns, only learning of the possible causes more than 40 years later.

As a trainee, Geoffrey Alden flew 17 different Tiger Moths at 10 EFTS Weston-super-Mare between 3rd August and 28th September 1941, and remembers that bomb rack rails were still fitted to some of the unit's aircraft. One of them, R5129 (83011), was considered to be a rogue. A ban on Tiger Moth spinning had been imposed by Flying Training Command as the result of a series of accidents early in 1941, but was later lifted. On the same day, R5129 was involved in a delayed recovery and had been grounded, only to feature prominently in Boscombe Down's further investigations into spinning characteristics shortly after. Meanwhile the spinning ban had been reimposed.

At Weston-super-Mare, trainees were advised that in the event of an invasion, selected senior pupils would be expected to fly Tiger Moth bomber conversions into battle. This was a story leaked by instructors (who were already allocated to the task) perhaps in the hope of improving standards. It was not unusual for a pupil to be advised that he would have nothing to worry about: when the invading hordes saw the way this pilot flew, distressed enemy troops would drop their weapons and run back into the sea.

In spite of Albert Brant's letter from Hatfield dated August 1940, where a proportion of 1 EFTS aircraft always operated with complete racks attached, by mid-summer 1941, Flying Training Command was continuing to receive complaints about the randomly poor performance of a few Tiger Moths during spinning demonstrations. Specific aircraft appeared to behave more erratically than others, and spin recovery had proved difficult for both seasoned instructors and solo pupils. In some cases failure to recover from spins had resulted in abandonment or a crash with fatal results.

An engineering check was carried out on Tiger Moth N9437 (82491), of 4 Service Flying Instructors School at Cambridge in April 1941 after the aircraft had entered a flat spin at 4,000ft and recovered at 800ft. The rigging was considered to be satisfactory, but the port elevator was found to be warped and both port and starboard surfaces were changed. An air test which included spinning to left and right, reported no difficulty in recovery from up to one and a half turns, but after three turns 'there was a little tendency for the spin to flatten'. The control column flicked over to the side in the direction of the spin and required sheer brute force to centralise. Several spins from different methods of entry all led to the same result but it was found that if, instead of moving the control column to the centre and then forward, it was moved forward and then to the centre, as the aircraft came out of the spin the pressure on the control column was quite gentle. N9437 was restricted to non-spin training until after its next scheduled maintenance during which a new set of wings was fitted and the tailplane stripped and reassembled. A check on the alignment of the fuselage proved it not to be twisted and following reintroduction to service, no further difficulties were experienced.

Instructors of 1 ERFTS Hatfield in 1936. L-R back row, John Nesbit-Dufort; Michael Daunt; Lieutenant Commander Morgan; George Weighill; Bill Wilson. Front row, Reggie Moon; Eddy Fulford; Clem Pike (CFI); George King and Gordon Carey. A formidable pool of talent. via Ben French

In July 1941, officials of the Ministry of Aircraft Production (MAP) based at Hatfield wrote to Flying Training Command authorising return to the factory of Tiger Moth components, especially wings, which it was thought might have a bearing on the bad spinning habits. Mainplanes salvaged from T5692 (83407), arrived at Hatfield on 9th July from 2 EFTS Staverton where the aircraft had crashed on 24th June. It had been a classic case: at 5,500ft with instructor and pupil on board, the aircraft had been eased into a right hand spin and after about seven turns full left rudder was applied with no result. Opening the throttle had only increased the speed of the spin which also flattened, at which point the crew had bailed out.

More wings were in prospect from N9464 (82518), which had experienced difficulties in recovering from a spin at 10 EFTS Weston-super-Mare on 11th July. After landing, the instructor had demanded an engineering inspection, during which it was discovered that the trailing edge and the extremities of all the ribs of the starboard upper mainplane were warped, the effect being that the rib ends were curled upwards by approximately 20 degrees, carrying with them the trailing edge section. In addition the aileron cables were slack and the rudder cable 'very slightly' slack. The defective wing was removed and replaced with a serviceable unit, but before a comparative flight test could be arranged, Flying Training Command had imposed a ban on all Tiger Moth spinning exercises, and the opportunity was lost.

In his signal reporting the incident to the MAP Overseer at Hatfield, the Commanding Officer of 10 EFTS confirmed what would eventually be discovered during the investigations at Farnborough. 'The trouble is always rectified when the control column is moved right forward'.

On 21st July Albert Brant visited 2 EFTS at Staverton and was introduced not only to a pilot who had already bailed out of Tiger Moth N9464 (82518), but to another recalcitrant aeroplane, T8240 (84513).

A serious degree of briefing being exercised at 10 EFTS Yatesbury early in 1940 while the Gipsy Major engine ticks merrily away in an unattended aircraft not hindered by chocks. Richard Riding

This aeroplane had flown barely 15 hours since manufacture at Cowley, and the only defects which the Hatfield Work's Manager could determine was a warped rudder due to very tight fabric which had twisted the trailing edge by about half an inch along its length, and a stern post which was on the top limit of permissibility for being out of plumb. It was also noted that the setting of the tailplane was about half a degree above the authorised maximum.

In chasing every possible cause for the spinning problems, Albert Brant was also moved to report back to Hatfield that he had discovered that the slat locking device had been wired up to make it inoperative, 'meaning that aerobatics have been indulged in with the slots free. It has also been observed that the machine collected from Ansty for tests at Hatfield has the slot locking device made inoperative, meaning that they too are indulging in aerobatics without the slots being locked'.

A second series of spinning investigations was programmed for Boscombe Down, from where test pilot Allen Wheeler considered that instructors and pupils alike might unwittingly have developed a culture of not allowing normal recovery action to take effect before trying a different control configuration. Also, a developed spin is likely to rotate faster and at a steeper angle just before recovery, a situation that may have been misinterpreted.

Conducted again by 'A' Squadron on behalf of the Director General of Research and Development, the brief was to establish a reason for the normally docile Tiger Moth becoming, on occasions, an aggressive old dog, and biting. Although dangerous spins may have occurred before, only after bomb rack rails were fitted did the volume of complaints increase, and the new appendages were easily the most natural target for further investigation. It was recognised that both centre of gravity and moments of inertia had been changed only slightly, leaving disturbed airflow over the rear fuselage and tail unit as probable causes.

Flying without a helmet and goggles but wearing normal glasses, and clearly solo, Prince Bernhardt of the Netherlands flying N6919 near Hatfield. deHMC Archive

Why were only some Tiger Moths subject to dangerous spin characteristics? Rigging errors had been investigated and discounted. The CG position was not a primary issue either. Had the blind flying hood and bomb rack rails together caused a new reaction? Flying Training Command nominated three aircraft reported to have bad spin characteristics: N5468 (3736) and N6621 (3922), both from 9 EFTS Ansty, and R4760 (82701), from 10 EFTS Weston-super-Mare. Each report received was carefully analysed, and in addition to the fuel and baggage loads, crew composition and nature of the exercise, one column of information was reserved for the identity of the maker.

N5468 had refused to recover from what developed into a flat spin on 16th June, and according to the Ministry of Aircraft Production's Directorate of Technical Development, had been abandoned by the crew after the controls became unresponsive following two turns of an intentional spin commenced at 4,500ft. The MAP Overseer at Hatfield requested that de Havilland receive and inspect the aircraft 'which was finally landed with only slight damage and is being repaired by the EFTS at Ansty'.

The full story was that having given orders to abandon the aircraft, the instructor bailed out, but partly because of a loose helmet, the pupil, who was a qualified pilot undertaking a refresher prior to attending an Instructor's Course at the Central Flying School, could not hear what was said. He was astonished to see the instructor jump over the side, at which point the Tiger Moth recovered from the spin. Still not sure about the nature of the problem, but with the engine and controls still apparently functioning normally, N5468 was immediately landed in a suitable field, a safe arrival marred slightly by the experience of breaking the port front interplane strut on a wire obstruction, and denting the engine cowling undertray. Subsequent inspection concluded that all controls were functional, the rudder was not warped, bomb racks were not fitted, the petrol tank was half full and there was no significant weight in the rear locker. N5468 was eventually flown to Hatfield and arrived on 18th July where the tailplane was re-fabriced after several broken ribs had been repaired.

Operating from Lulsgate Bottom on 6th February 1941, R4760 had entered a conventional spin at 3,800 ft which had quickly flattened, and the aircraft had been extracted at 600ft only after extensive use of the throttle. An engineering check showed that the rigging was almost symmetrical and within limits, but the rudder hinges were very slightly out of alignment as was the rudder trailing edge. Bomb racks, it was noted, were not fitted.

The incident which booked N6621 a place in the trials was very similar to that of N5468: a conventional spin commenced at 4,000ft had gone flat after fewer than two turns, and the instructor could get no response from the controls which he later described as 'sluggish'. At 2,000ft the instructor ordered the pupil to bail out, but before he could, and while the instructor also was preparing to abandon the aircraft, the spin stopped, and the pupil regained control at about 1,000ft.

Both N6621 and R4760 were delivered to A&AEE in July 1941, neither with racks nor rails fitted, where 'A' Squadron concentrated their initial attentions on operations with the blind flying hood stowed or removed, and with one or both of the leading edge slats locked. Each aircraft was spun on 33 separate occasions.

While these intensive trials were in progress, on 9th August another aircraft from 10 EFTS, R5129 (83011), an aircraft built at Hatfield in March 1940, was added to the programme when she was delivered to A&AEE by the CFI. Instructors agreed that R5129 was not a good aircraft for spinning training as almost five turns were necessary to effect recovery.

The aircraft had arrived at Boscombe Down with what was described as 'bomb racks' fitted, although they were almost certainly just the rack rails attached to the lower longerons under the cockpit floor. The first three in a series of seven programmed spins were conducted by the 'A' Squadron Commander with the rails remaining in place, after which they were removed. The blind flying hood had been eliminated as a potential source of significant disturbance and was not fitted at any time during the programme. The test pilots discovered that recovery from a right hand spin was quite normal (a half turn), but exit from left hand rotation was delayed, even when standard methods of entry and recovery were used, with an average of about four turns required. Removal of the port navigation light made no apparent difference and two subsequent left hand spins had still resulted in four and five turns before full recovery.

It was quickly realised that spinning characteristics were very sensitive to aileron setting and flatter spins resulted from the input of small amounts of out of spin aileron, varying in degree between individual aeroplanes. R5129 was found to require only one inch of sideways control stick deflection to change the spin incidence by between 40 and 50 degrees.

In such tests, accurate counting of fractions of turns was essential, and with a need to record a number of additional parameters, the test pilots relied not on visual reference beyond the nose, but on the angle of the sun shining into the cockpit, where the instruments were illuminated long enough for a full scan, and afforded the opportunity to note the altimeter readings.

Boscombe Down's report forwarded to the Ministry of Aircraft Production, dated 22nd August 1941, was distilled from analysis of the flight tests and said in part:

'The tests made by us on three aeroplanes show that a different number of turns were required to recover, varying from three quarters to four and threequarter turns. Because of this discrepancy on three aeroplanes tested, one might reason that recovery from spins on some Tiger Moths might be impossible and in consequence that spinning should be banned until some remedial action has been applied to make recovery more consistent and in general, quicker. Though we accept this reasoning, some considerable time may elapse before the present investigation being conducted by the RAE is completed and a further period will be required before remedial steps can be taken to make recovery quicker on all Tiger Moths in Flying Training Command.

'In the interim, therefore, much valuable spinning instruction will be lost if spinning on the type is banned. With this in view, we consider that spinning should still be allowed on the type and in order to reduce accidents to a minimum we now propose that the minimum height at which recovery is initiated be increased from 3,000ft, previously recommended, to 4,000ft. Also, in order to provide sufficient height for spinning instruction to be given, the minimum height at which spinning should be started should be increased from 5,000ft, previously recommended, to 6,000ft. In addition, we propose that the number of turns during spins should not exceed three.

'We feel confident that most, if not all, of the accidents will be eliminated if the above procedure is followed until such time as a more permanent solution to the problem is found'.

The A&AEE report published for internal circulation on 15th September 1941 and classified 'secret', concluded that one test aircraft did not behave in a manner properly associated with Tiger Moths in which it was usual for recovery from spins to be effected immediately rudder was taken off, and that the reason for this misbehaviour was unknown. In the case of N6621 and R4760, delayed recoveries had only been induced by artificial means, and when using the standard method of entry and recovery, both aircraft had reacted normally with a maximum delay of not more than two and a quarter turns.

R5129 was considered not to be a satisfactory aircraft for training purposes and was to be retained for further investigations, while N6621 and R4760 were both thought certain to recover from spins no matter how unconventional the entry configuration and subsequent use or mis-use of the controls, provided the standard method of recovery was eventually applied.

N6621 rejoined 9 EFTS on 28th August where she remained in harness for most of the next three years. R4760 was routed through the Civil Repair Organisation operated by Lundy and Atlantic Coast Airlines at Barnstaple in August 1941, probably for routine maintenance, and was posted to training duties with 4 EFTS Brough on 10th September.

Allen Wheeler recalled that his Squadron Commander at A&AEE was very excited after analysis of the first results showed there to be a positive link between the bomb rack rails and a change in the aeroplane's behaviour. He subsequently became almost totally committed to the programme, experiencing about 120 rotations, but the job was still not finished.

Four Tiger Moth IIs drawn from RAF sources were co-opted into the continuing test programme and all had been assessed by Aero Flight at RAE Farnborough by the end of 1941:

N5468 (3736), from 9 EFTS Ansty which had been posted into the care of the de Havilland Company at Hatfield on 18th July was fitted with an anti-spin safety parachute on the tail and test flown by Pat Fillingham on 6th/7th August and 18th September, and also by Geoffrey de Havilland Jr before referral to the RAE.

During the trails at Hatfield, spins were completed at varying positions of Centre of Gravity, and operating at the aftmost limit, N5468 was entered into a 14 turn spin to the right from which recovery was described as being 'excellent'. In a report to Richard Clarkson in the Aerodynamics Department, Geoffrey de Havilland Jr wrote: *'During this sequence of tests the machine did not show the slightest tendency to flat spin or to become uncontrollable in any way'.*

The aircraft was never again used for flying training: following nine months in store with 33 MU at Lyneham, N5468 was operated by 1483 Flight before she was moved to RAF Halton and converted to a ground instructional airframe (4439M) in December 1943. By March 1945 the aircraft had been relocated to RAF Locking where she was scrapped in May 1947.

R5180 (83042), from 10 EFTS Stoke Orchard had been considerably spun during her 12 month training assignment and had shown no dangerous tendencies when recovering. It is not clear whether she returned to Stoke Orchard, but from July 1942 she was posted to 16 EFTS Burnaston where she remained for three years. In July 1945 she was placed in store with 8 MU Little Rissington and remained there until March 1950 when she was sold for scrap.

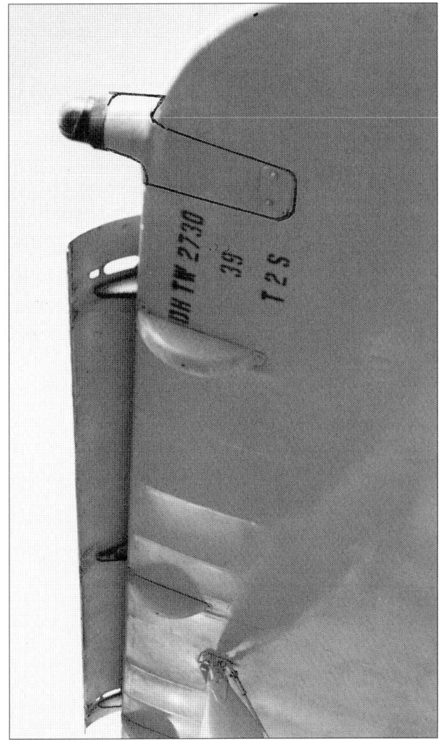

A view of the port upper mainplane showing the fairing and lens of the navigation light, leading edge slat in the extended (open) position, and the shroud at each of the three slat hinges. Darryl Cott

T6035 (84214), from 26 EFTS Theale was a brand new aeroplane, with her home unit for exactly a month before delivery 15 miles across the open fields to Farnborough on 3rd September. Following the trials T6035 spent seven months in store with 33 MU at Lyneham before transport to 222 MU High Ercall where she was packed for dispatch to South Africa in September 1942.

T6615 (84929), a brand new aeroplane, was allocated directly to Farnborough. No.26 EFTS had formed at Theale on 20th August 1941, and after the trials, T6615 was posted to that unit, arriving ten days after the commencement of operations, and remaining until the school closed in July 1945. Posted to Woodley, she continued in service with 8 EFTS and the post-war Reserve Flying School (RFS) until May 1948 when she crashed on landing and was written off the following month.

In addition, BB727 (3178), described as a 'reconstructed civil type Tiger Moth' but fitted with wings incorporating some Mk. II features, was made available to join the investigation at a late stage and was to provide direct comparisons with the performance of Mk II specification airframes. In civilian life, BB727 had been registered G-ACDE to the de Havilland School of Flying at Hatfield where she was operated as part of the establishment of 1 ERFTS, 1 EFTS from the outbreak of war. The aircraft received a coat of camouflage to obliterate her maroon and silver house colours, and with her impressed military serial allocated from 30th October 1940, continued with her daily tasks much as always. The aircraft arrived at Farnborough on 13th September 1941 and remained until the end of October.

As a result of the aileron mass balance trials with K2583 at Martlesham Heath in 1933, all aircraft were built to accept them. The RAE had targeted them as a possible cause of trouble: a lead weight attached to a lever arm and weighing just under 4lb each. The spinning characteristics of a slightly staggered biplane deteriorate with an increase in the rolling moment of inertia, and the removal of the mass balance served to reduce or improve the longitudinal moment (A) by 5% and the vertical (normal) moment (C) by 3%.

To create a Tiger Moth II and permit unrestricted aerobatic operations at a new maximum weight of 1,770lb, an increase of 120lb, a number of modifications to the Mk.I wing had been approved from January 1937. These were designed to permit all aircraft to be brought to a common (improved) standard, and whilst factory-new wings were manufactured with the modifications incorporated, aircraft in the field were subject to longer term retrofit action. The 1937 upgrade was extensive, affecting both top and bottom mainplanes, and called for new spars; aileron gearbox structure and mounting; strengthened ribs at the control box, root end and walkway; special aileron hinge bolts to accommodate the aileron mass balance (and increased from three to four in accordance with the post trial requirements); new wing tip bows; trailing edge and associated wiring plates; modified fittings, stiffening struts and support tubes.

These were additional to other airframe changes which filtered through to constitute the current in-service specification of the aircraft: rudder mass balance; slot locking gear; strengthened undercarriage; navigation and identification lights; flare holders; an electrics panel; first aid box and amended instrument fit and layout; improved treatments for protection of the wing panels; revisions to aileron differentials; a blind flying hood and camouflage dope scheme.

All had contributed to a not insubstantial increase in tare weight (over 113lb), and to moments of inertia, 'A' by 10% and 'C' by 7%. Bomb rack rails and associated release cables, guides and levers accounted for an additional 30lb.

The reasoned removal of the aileron balance weights would go some way toward restoration of the known situation. de Havilland calculated that compared with a standard civil flying school Tiger Moth, the RAF 'Contract Tiger Moth' showed an increase in weight of 223lb.

The opportunity of test flying the nearest equivalent civil Tiger Moth BB727/G-ACDE was a bonus. The results indicated that even with some Mk.II features in her wings, spinning properties were very similar to the best of the standard RAF aircraft. The civil aircraft's wings were subsequently loaded with lead weights to simulate a full Mk.II version and bomb rack rails were fitted to the lower longerons, after which a further flight test resulted in a spin of eight turns before recovery, a situation comparable with the worst of the military machines.

As a precaution, R5129 had been fitted with an anti-spin tail parachute which Hatfield was anxious to reclaim immediately after the trials had been completed, as some of the component parts had been borrowed from other firms. This was deployed once to good effect when during a trial with rails and mass balances in position, the aircraft failed to respond to any pilot induced recovery action, and control was regained only after 13 full turns had been completed.

Further trials with the aileron mass weights removed (but with bomb rails in position) indicated a marked improvement in recovery no matter what mispositioning of the ailerons, averaging about four turns. With ailerons held in the neutral position, recovery was effected after two and a half turns.

R5129 was then subjected to a series of tests with as many of the Mk.II modifications deleted as was practical. Normal recovery was again achieved after about four turns. However, little further improvement was registered when neither aileron mass balances nor bomb rack rails were present on the same test. Equally, the effects of removing the 2lb 4oz lead rudder balance were small, as were the effects of changing aileron differential ratios and sprocket angles.

During the course of the trials, service Tiger Moths were still earning their daily crusts and on 19th August 1941, N5455 (3718), entered a left spin at 5,000ft near Booker where she was on the establishment of 21 EFTS. After the application of normal corrective action, the instructor, whose favourite aeroplane this was, found there was no resistance to application of the rudder, and in spite of 'rocking' the control column without resorting to bursts of full throttle, the spin merely increased in speed and the aircraft tended to go over the vertical. Then without warning, the Tiger Moth snapped out of the spin with a jerk having lost 3,000ft. A post flight engineering check confirmed that the rigging was within limits and apart from warping at the top of the rudder and the tip of the starboard aileron, the aircraft was serviceable. Bomb racks were not carried and the luggage locker was completely empty.

Having *identified* what was believed to be the root cause of the spinning difficulties, and believing that references to 'flat' spins in accident reports were misleading, A&AEE recommended that the current ban on spin training should be lifted. More attention was now to be paid to the prospects of *correcting* the situation. At a meeting convened at Hatfield on 22nd September 1941, one of a series which had been held throughout the summer, Richard Clarkson and Percy Bryan of de Havilland accompanied by the Aeronautical Inspection Directorate's (AID) Resident Technical Officer (RTO) R W Fitch, were joined by Messrs Stevens (Air Ministry), Lyons and Finn (RAE), with a brief to agree a programme of alternative modifications in order to investigate an improvement in Tiger Moth spinning performance.

As the aircraft currently displaying the worst spinning characteristics, R5129 was to be routed to Hatfield as soon as possible for de Havilland to incorporate two specific modifications: detachable strakes fitted to the top of the fuselage immediately forward of the tailplane leading edge and an increase in the depth of the rear fuselage immediately below the tailplane effected by installation of a detachable fairing.

Farnborough was tasked to design a method of increasing the rudder area by filling the gap between the rudder and the hinge line at the bottom of the finpost; airframe modification was to be completed at the RAE if required. It was also agreed that Farnborough would design and manufacture a rudder of revised outline which effectively shrouded the tailskid cut-out and increased the surface area. In addition a revised dorsal-like fin fairing would be sought, but no installation or any trials were to be authorised without presentation first to de Havilland, affording them the opportunity to check the integrity and strength of the proposals.

Perhaps this was the most crucial of all the meetings between de Havilland and government scientists that summer. As a result of the post trial report written by D J Lyons with R H Francis, spin strakes were adapted throughout the RAF. Percy Bryant had advised the Hatfield gathering that strakes were by far the easiest of the proposed modifications to fit retrospectively, and that very careful consideration should be given before fitting any of the other suggested devices.

Richard Clarkson revealed to the meeting that de Havilland had previously studied prospects for a Tiger Moth Mk.III, the elusive DH.82B, and a rudder similar to that now proposed by the RAE had been built and flight tested. He would endeavour to find the rudder somewhere in the Experimental Department, he promised, or at least have copies of the drawings forwarded to Farnborough.

Based on the knowledge that spin characteristics of some other aircraft types had been varied by changing rudder angles, flight tests were conducted with a conventional empennage but with a 10 degree reduction in pro-spin rudder and 4 degree increase in anti-spin rudder, but both entry and recovery were found to be substantially unaltered. Only slight improvement resulted from the increase in rudder area effected by the de Havilland modification to fill the gap at the bottom of the finpost.

The conclusions drawn from the Farnborough report were that all the Tiger Moths sent to the RAE as part of this investigation had spun correctly and recovered quickly when the controls were centralised as prescribed. A mishandled Tiger Moth II could spin dangerously; if the control column was not held central, flat spins could be effected. The greatest difficulty in recovery was obtained with full opposite aileron, and with full pro-spin aileron the spin was again flat.

Agreeing that a considerable number of modifications had been incorporated into the aircraft since the type had last been tested by the A&AEE or RAE, there remained little doubt that the spin would become safer if aileron mass balance weights and bomb rack rails were removed.

There was no evidence to suggest that the six Tiger Moth Mk.I and 87 civil Tiger Moth Mk.II then operating with the military and not fitted with aileron mass balances, had ever experienced difficulty, but in association with the removal of the balances on RAF aircraft, a reduction in the diving speed from 210mph to 170mph was recommended, which together with the maintenance of regular inspections of the rigging and control circuit were considered a sufficient guard against flutter. The Air Staff was to be approached over the matter of the bomb racks; de Havilland were to prepare modification drawings for the removal of the mass balances, a job which they estimated at about an hour, and the advisability for proper centralisation of the control column during recovery was to be made clear to all users through Flying Training Command. In the revised configuration, it was also recommended that the restriction regarding the commencement of spins at a height of not less than 5,000ft be removed.

It was still considered that a greater improvement in spin characteristics would be obtained as a result of the modifications agreed between de Havilland and the RAE on 22nd September, especially the fitting of strakes at the rear fuselage. Their incorporation was considered a worthwhile insurance against any future non-training demands that might be under consideration for the aircraft. Strakes had been used previously to improve the spinning characteristics of other types and they were thought likely to be especially effective with the fuselage cross section employed on the Tiger Moth.

In her modified form, de Havilland had promised that Tiger Moth R5129 would be ready for further testing from 1st October.

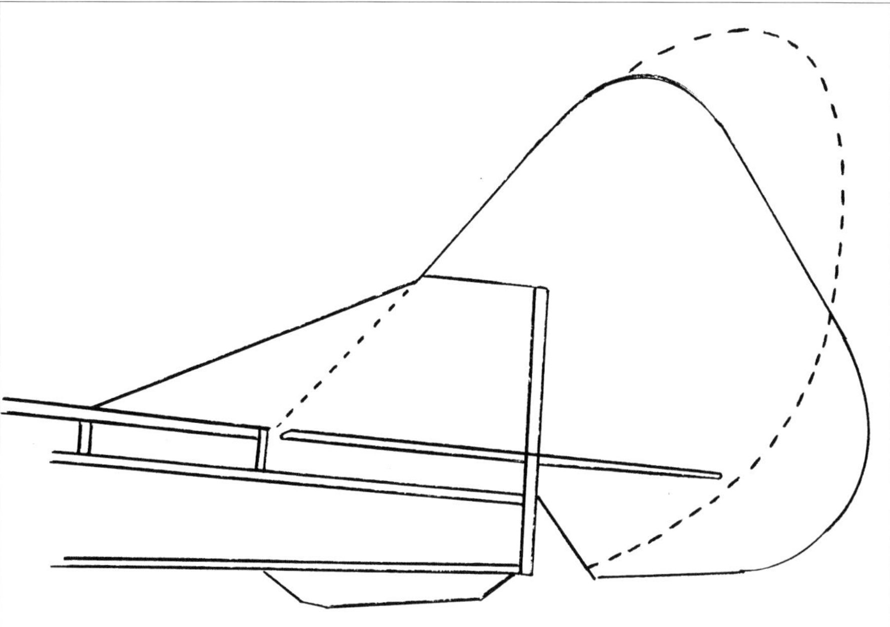

A basic drawing of one proposal for a new empennage for the Tiger Moth, possibly the Mk.III, which has been attributed to Richard Clarkson. The dashed line represents the outline of the standard fin and rudder fitted to the Tiger Moth. deHMC Archive

Results of the British flight tests had been transmitted to de Havilland Aircraft of Canada where in the late summer of 1941, an exhaustive series of normal and what the company referred to as 'crossed aileron' spinning tests was completed on a DH.82C model Tiger Moth. Towards the end of October, the report landed on the desk of Managing Director Phil Garratt:

'Tests were carried out on the aircraft with and without navigation lights being fitted. No appreciable difference was noted during the spins or at the time of recovery although some slight rudder flutter was noted on machines fitted with navigation lights.

'All spins were maintained for a minimum of seven turns before recovery was commenced and several tests were undertaken which included a maximum of 12 turns.

'Using the normally accepted method for spinning to the left or right, recoveries were immediate in every case. Specifically, 'immediate' should be read to indicate a maximum of three quarters of a turn. Some increase in the speed of normal spinning can be obtained by applying full inside aileron. The spin continues normally although somewhat steeper and faster. This procedure has no effect upon normal recovery.

'When a spin is made to the left or right with crossed ailerons the spin becomes quite flat, the nose rises quite appreciably and a very definite whipping occurs once in each revolution. The spin is unpleasant and would tend to alarm an inexperienced pilot. Recovery can be effected in the normal way, that is to say, the usual procedure as laid down in the Air Force Manual of Training is sufficient to produce a normal dive. However, it should be noted that the time for recovery is much longer and takes a minimum of one and a half turns and a maximum of

Tiger Moth R5082 was photographed at Hatfield on 27th December 1941 with strakes in position. The units were screwed through the ply top decking into anchor nuts glued to the underside. No other structural modifications to the tail were applied anywhere until the post-war Fokker conversions in the Netherlands.
de Havilland Aircraft Co.

two and a half turns. Furthermore, it will be found that when applying opposite rudder to recover from the spin it is necessary to exert quite a considerable pressure on the rudder bar over and above that usually necessary to recover from a normal spin. Pilots should be informed that an earlier recovery from the 'crossed aileron' spin can be effected by applying inside aileron or, in other words, uncrossing the ailerons towards the direction of the spin.

'There is an average altitude loss of 150ft per turn on the 'crossed aileron' spin and 250ft per turn on the normal spin. Exhaustive tests have shown that spins to the right require a little longer to recover than spins to the left.'

Copies of the de Havilland Canada report were sent to the RCAF Director of Training, Air Vice-Marshal E W Stedman, and to Lee Murray at Hatfield. In its conclusion it was fairly specific on how the matter of spinning should be treated during pilot training:

'Allowed sufficient height there is no more difficulty in recovering from the 'crossed aileron' spin than from the normal spin but in the case of the 'crossed aileron' spin, additional altitude should be allowed. In other words, Elementary Flying Training Schools should be instructed that 'crossed aileron' spins should not be made on Tiger Moths under an altitude of 2,000ft. Also, it might be as well for instructors to inform their pupils that there is no cause for alarm arising out of the peculiar attitude or behaviour of the aircraft during the 'crossed aileron' spin, since it is apparent that crossing of the ailerons changes the nose position and at the same time brings on an unpleasant whipping motion which can be dampened out immediately'.

As far as the DH.82C Tiger Moth was concerned, there appeared to be no spinning problems but Lee Murray was moved to remind his colleagues that the Canadian Tiger Moth did have *'a large fitted canopy, undercarriage moved forward for brakes and a tailwheel'*. And much else besides.

R5129 was subjected to a further programme of intensive spinning checks at A&AEE in November 1941. A series of 27 spins was completed without aileron mass balance weights but with bomb rack rails fitted under the fuselage and strakes forward of the tailplane. The blind flying hood was discounted again, but a tail parachute was carried as a precaution, otherwise apart from the various modifications agreed the previous August, the aircraft was to current RAF standard Tiger Moth II configuration.

The biggest single improvement in spin recovery resulted from the fitting of the strakes: light alloy extensions of the tailplane running forward onto the rear fuselage top cowl, and picking up on captive nuts that were attached to the underside. Strakes were flight tested on R5129 with and without aileron mass balances and bomb rack rails, and in both cases the spinning characteristics were considerably improved. With centralised ailerons the spin stabilised at 20 degree incidence and flattened only marginally with application of opposite aileron, in which configuration spins were arrested in less than two and a half turns. Standard recovery was effected in less than one turn.

The addition of strakes had moved the CG rearwards by 0.6 of an inch, and tests were conducted both at the normal load case and at the 1% Mean Aerodynamic Chord (MAC) extension to the new aft limit. Both slats were either locked or left free, and a sequence of normal aerobatic manoeuvres was flown. The tests confirmed a vast improvement in the spin recovery performance of R5129 while maintaining the general handling characteristics of the type, although it was reported that aileron snatch could occur at about 80mph, accentuated by turbulent air conditions, and also during inverted flight.

The Establishment's earlier recommendation that R5129 was unsuitable as a training vehicle was heeded, even after her absolution. The aircraft was posted from Boscombe Down to 15 MU Wroughton and issued to 654 (AOP) Squadron for barely three weeks towards the end of August 1942, immediately before the unit's new Taylorcraft Auster Is were delivered. She spent the next several years shuffling between Maintenance Units until September 1946 when she was sold to a civilian owner for operations with the Nottingham Flying Club at Tollerton. Sold to India in 1949, the aircraft was destroyed by fire at Safdarjung, New Delhi, after an Indian Air Force DH.100 Vampire collided with her hangar.

Inevitably, every production run using identical jigging could spawn a rogue aeroplane: the sum of all the minor differences in degrees of straightness, thickness, weight distribution and alignment. Bad rigging had never been a perceived problem, but A&AEE and RAE test pilot Allen Wheeler had nagging doubts throughout his involvement with the trials that the bomb racks and their fittings were the *sole* cause of the Tiger Moth, a docile old friend, turning into a vicious animal. Why were *all* Tiger Moths not affected, and why did the bad ones *gradually* degenerate?

Having taken ten turns to recover from an intentional spin initiated at 8,000ft, an instructor at 10 EFTS, Weston-super-Mare, had ordered Tiger Moth T7047 (83417), to be removed to a hangar where his suspicions of mis-rigging or bad load distribution were not substantiated. The aircraft was returned to service with a cautionary note attached blaming the climate for a temporary distortion of the structure. The CFI later flew the aircraft and carried out an extensive spinning exercise without any recovery problems, followed by the original instructor, again with no difficulties.

Rapidly expanding flying schools in Great Britain did not always have facilities at main base, not to mention satellite fields, to keep these open cockpit, fabric covered airframes under cover, and immune to climatic attack. The aircraft establishment at 6 EFTS Sywell was 140 Tiger Moths by the end of 1940, most of which were forced to endure the English climate picketed at dispersal. No matter how securely covered, it was almost inevitable that rainwater and the effects of condensation were likely to accumulate in the rear fuselage, adding weight at the rate of 10lb per gallon, and causing gross distortion of any calculated CG position. A modification which removed corrugated aluminium clips originally designed to segregate fabric bagging from the fuselage bottom longerons, was found necessary after the clips were proved to provide a series of perfect reservoirs for the retention of moisture. Checks on the level of corrosion suffered by the rear fuselage lower longerons subsequently became a matter of major concern when aircraft were recovered or rebuilt in later years.

Drain eyelets were occasionally found not to have been opened up after fabric re-work or new painting, and were especially critical in the tailplane and elevator where they might equally have become blocked with mud or grass during basic or extraordinary manoeuvrings on the ground. At altitude, trapped moisture could freeze, spraying out in the relative warmth of the lower levels as the result of centrifugal force, permitting eventual but worryingly delayed recovery from spins, and leaving no obvious trace for subsequent investigation. Pre-war colour schemes had been hastily covered with camouflage dope, often by mechanics wielding brushes, and coupled with patched repairs, weighty layers of paint estimated in some quarters to be as heavy as 60lb had been gradually propagated.

In May 1940, *Flight* published an article on flying training with the Royal Air Force, which carried a specific passage dedicated to spinning:

'A lot has been said about spinning during the past year, particularly by the non-flying public who can hardly know what it is all about. One of the early lessons in flying is in how to recover from a spin, having purposely got into it. From the safety point of view, which is most important in a trainer, the Tiger Moth, representative of biplane trainers, is ideal in this respect. A Tiger Moth will, in fact, recover from a spin unaided. Certainly, it is sufficient on all occasions to centralise controls. This method is not, however, suitable for getting the majority of monoplanes out of a spin. It is essential, if the practice is to be valuable, at least to hold on sharply full opposite rudder and then ease the control column well forward to dive the aeroplane to full flying speed. This practice seems rather to trouble pupils, and only with the greatest difficulty can they be persuaded to put on more rudder than is required for recovery on the Tiger Moth. Spinning is considered important enough to be a compulsory practice each week, and is the only manoeuvre outside straightforward flying which is taught previous to a first solo. Later at a Service FTS, pupils are taught other or extra movements to facilitate recovery from spins. These include the use of throttle'.

By December of the same year, the correspondent was writing an amended story:

'The control technique for getting out of a spin has now been slightly altered. Previously it was to put on opposite rudder and then, about two seconds later, to bring the stick forward. Not too far forward, as this leaves the aeroplane in a steep dive after the spin has been stopped, a decided disadvantage if near the ground. Now it is to put on opposite rudder and stick forward simultaneously, and with no apologies, as the instructor said. It is permissible to put the stick right forward, although this is not necessary on a Tiger Moth. The reason for the change seems to be that the procedure is necessary with some of the advanced trainer types, the North American Harvard, for example, and so it is taught right from the start. A Tiger Moth loses about 300ft per turn in a spin, but a Harvard between two and three times that height. A safe height for a spin in a Harvard is to start at 9,000ft'.

Allen Wheeler suspected not only the spin recovery techniques employed by some pilots, but also the position of the centre of gravity which would be different for every individual aircraft. In 1954, Air Registration Board (ARB) surveyor Michael Inskip was checking the weight schedule for a civil Tiger Moth and was amazed to find that the basic centre of gravity (CG) was so far aft that it would be impossible to load the aircraft and stay within the prescribed limits. He then checked through 90 other weight schedules and found that only ten were satisfactory for flight where no spin strakes were fitted, 73 needed strakes to stay within limits and the remaining seven were well outside the envelope. Inskip wrote a paper on the subject which was circulated within the ARB on 24th March 1954, AW/151, all traces of which have disappeared from official files.

The major points of issue could well have read back to 1940:

1. It is imperative to rig the stagger of the centre section to the foremost limit, on the dot, and square with the fuselage.
2. Accurate weighing is essential and must be completed with the tail up 4° rather than in a horizontal position which would be more usual. A 1° difference will result in significant inaccuracies in the measurement of lever arms.
3. A build up of additional weight in the tailskid shoe will move the CG aft.
4. Too many coats of paint on the rear fuselage structure allied with too many coats of dope on the covered rear fuse lage and tail unit. Two full coats of dope in these areas will move the CG aft.
5. Be aware of the night flying lamp on the rudder, not fitted to all Tiger Moths, and the lead mass balance weight in the rudder horn.
6. Monitor the load carried in the baggage locker. A 20lb load will move the CG aft 0.78in when the aircraft is flown dual and 0.92in when flown solo.

An additional factor to be considered in relation to wartime production was a possible variation in the radius or gauge of the steel tubes supplied batch upon batch, for building into rear fuselage structures. Was there no difference at all between the fuselages supplied from Canada and those built at Hatfield in 1938 and subsequently, and those manufactured at Cowley?

At the time of Michael Inskip's survey there were more considerations, all of which tended to shift the CG to the aft position: a glider tow hook at 3lb moved the CG 1.16in; aluminium cylinder heads fitted to a Gipsy Major engine moved the CG 0.31in; replacement of a Schwartz covered wooden propeller with a modern lightweight example, radio kit and wiring situated in the rear fuselage, and removal of slats and mechanism from the upper mainplanes, all resulted in an increased 'positive' moment.

The official capacity of the rear luggage locker has varied across the range of manuals published since 1931, and actual contents of the lockers of RAF aircraft involved in spinning incidents and accidents in 1940 were carefully analysed. In Australia the initial limit of 60lb, later amended to 40lb, was further reduced to 30lb when operating with two crew. Air Publication (AP) 1449B, the standard RAF work of reference for dimensions, weights and tolerances, makes no mention at all of locker limitations.

de Havilland admitted post-war that the Tiger Moth had imposed practically no workload on design staff during the conflict: it was considered a straight production job. However, the operational behaviour of the aeroplane was always considered a prime DH responsibility, and the company maintained a close liaison with all owners, users and servicing units.

Two projects which did consume drawing office time covered the 'mandatory' removal of Tiger Moth aileron mass balance weights (Mod.103), which also imposed a restriction on the 'never exceed' speed (Vne) of 170mph, a reduction of 40mph, as a precaution against aileron flutter. Modification 112, published on 17th October 1942 as 'desirable', was applied to all RAF Tiger

Moths and became the subject of continuing debate.

Drawing M7685 was the vehicle which conveyed detailed instructions for the application of Mod.112; the light alloy pressings, Part Nos 62976 and 62977 (left and right hand) which formed the core of the strake modification, and which had been conceived and fitted to R5129 a full year previously. Including pins, screws and washers, 304 individual parts were called up to complete each field modification kit. From unlacing the under fuselage fabric for access to the inside of the rear cowl, assuming that the bootlacing had not been replaced by a stretched fabric skin as a matter of expediency during an overhaul or repair, to the final licks of green and dark earth paint, the job was estimated at eight man hours per aircraft.

Aircraft in production on the Cowley line were fitted with strakes from September 1942, nine months after a trial batch of conversions on aircraft with 1 EFTS at Hatfield, including R5082 (82977). This aircraft had been repaired at Witney in April 1941 following an accident at Church Fenton and the strakes could have been fitted then, but the 'system' was not yet in gear. Displaying her new appendages, R5082 was subjected to an official photographic session in the pouring rain at Hatfield on 27th December 1941.

A story circulating at 6 EFTS Sywell late in 1941 where there was knowledge of strakes, suggested that they had been invented as a morale booster in the light of the reported spinning accidents, and the idea had been pinched from the Miles Magister. It is doubtful whether the Air Ministry had communicated any part of the 'secret' reports being compiled at Boscombe Down and Farnborough at that time, and the tales remained a matter of pure conjecture.

A more malicious rumour suggested that only the Morris Motors built aircraft were affected, a fact that was blatantly untrue. Following some initial criticism of the quality of the Morris product, de Havilland test pilot Guy Tucker who was responsible for testing the vast majority of Cowley built Tiger Moths, refuted absolutely suggestions that quality was inferior in any way to products of the parent company.

One Cowley built Tiger Moth did come under scrutiny in the late summer of 1941 when operating with 17 EFTS Peterborough. In the rear seat, the pupil pilot heard a loud crack and watched bemused as the starboard lower wing detached from its root end pickup on the lower longeron. The instructor only realised his pupil had bailed out when he saw the descending parachute, at which point the aircraft broke up and he too abandoned what had become a spinning fuselage, which devoid of all wings, landed on a house in Peterborough town alongside the engine which had already buried itself in the garden.

The salvage recovery team reported that when they reached the site, they found the fuselage covered in jam, the product of an industrious British housewife and not in any way connected with the theme of an enduring First World War song describing the last moments of a bold aviator.

Flying at 17 EFTS was suspended for two days while the fuselage tie rods of the entire fleet were examined in detail, partly by engineers wielding magnets. There was some suspicion that during assembly or later maintenance, tie rods manufactured from dural instead of high tensile steel had been installed or substituted, and the whiff of sabotage as much as carelessness in quality control was prevalent, although the engineering staff were never advised of the outcome.

Philip Bremridge, a Flight Commander with 3 EFTS Watchfield (later Shellingford) during 1940-1942, clearly remembers strakes being fitted to the School's Tiger Moths, but with equal clarity he recalls never having been advised of the reason. As an instructor at Yatesbury with the pre-war 10 ERFTS from October 1938 until he was promoted

Air Commodore Allen Wheeler owned a number of Tiger Moths after his retirement from military flying duties. His last, G-ADGV, restored in the pre-war colours of Brooklands Aviation, and seen here refuelling during the 1979 Famous Grouse Rally, was regularly aerobatted and spun without strakes. deHMC Archive

Wing Commander and posted away from his appointment as Chief Flying Instructor (CFI) at 22 EFTS Cambridge in May 1943, and having spent six months as Deputy CFI with 21 EFTS Booker in the meantime, Philip Bremridge can recall no spinning incidents of any malevolence involving Tiger Moths, and only discovered in 1997 that strakes had resulted from the Farnborough investigations called for by his own Command.

Inevitably, and for some considerable time, all schools flew Tiger Moths both with and without strakes, and no obvious attempts appear to have been made to segregate non-straked aircraft from spinning exercises which continued relentlessly, an essential part of the daily training programme.

Modification 112 was never incorporated into DH.82A Tiger Moths built in Australia or New Zealand, nor into the DH.82C rolling off the line in Canada and aircraft in the field were never retro-fitted as was the case in Great Britain. Tiger Moths used extensively for training in Rhodesia, an amalgam of English and Australian factory output, were regularly spun from only 3,500ft. When operating from the high elevations of the base airfields, it just took too long to climb any higher. Spin recovery was never considered a problem although it was noted that Tiger Moths flying here solely in support of *ab initio* training, did not require heavy wingtip navigation lights, neither did they have occasion to carry bomb racks.

For Tiger Moth G-AKXO (83548), 13th March 1964 was not a good day. She spun off a climbing turn at 500ft after taking off from Shoreham airport in the late afternoon, and the rotation was checked only as the result of colliding with the roof of a house in Buckingham Road. The accident inspector concluded that the fatal spin had followed a stall, and there was evidence to indicate that the amount of alcohol found in the pilot's blood could have resulted in a diminution of attention and a reduction in both judgement and efficiency.

Clearly, whether the aircraft was or was not fitted with strakes was of no consequence on this occasion, but after the war, the whole question of Tiger Moths operating with or without spin strakes was raised again, notably by the Dutch Government who requested assistance from the British Air Registration Board (ARB) following a series of accidents which had occurred with newly imported ex-RAF Tiger Moths during the summer of 1946.

The ARB called upon one of its expert consultants, none other than Air Commodore Allen Wheeler, test pilot during the Tiger Moth's wartime trials at Boscombe Down and later Commanding Officer of A&AEE's Performance Testing Squadron and RAE's Experimental Flying Department. Accepting Allen Wheeler's first hand experience and advice, the Board's considered reply was fairly unequivocal:

'The horizontal stabiliser modification was incorporated at the instigation of Flying Training Command but whether it was really necessary is doubtful.

'The reason for the modification was to decrease the time taken for spin recovery but it has been suggested that although they fulfil this function, they also may slightly increase the tendency to spin when near the stall.

'Although this modification was classed as essential by RAF Flying Training Command it was not considered so by the Air Registration Board and is not included in the list of essential modifications which must be incorporated for the issue of a civil certificate of airworthiness'.

DH.82C Tiger Moth CF-CTB was one of a pair operated by the Aviron Company, later the Palestine Aero Club at Remleh in 1947. This aircraft caused concern when deliberately spun with the canopy removed. George Nelson

In 1982, the Civil Aviation Authority, successor to the ARB, issued a certificate of airworthiness to a British civil registered Tiger Moth which in the small print declared that aerobatics were prohibited unless spin strakes were fitted. By coincidence, the aircraft had been imported from South Africa where at much the same time an unstraked Tiger Moth, ZS-DFM (84478), an RAF import from 1941, was regularly recovering from 28 turn spin demonstrations at air displays flown by her owner, Dr H J Coetzee, a pilot with only one leg. When challenged to explain their decision, imposed without any consultation, the CAA referred back to the Farnborough test reports and quoted the RAE's recommendation that strakes were a 'desirable' modification, a grading which they would not challenge, but clearly using an interpretation different from that of the test pilot turned consultant. The CAA's reply continued:

'Our conclusions are that as anti-spin strakes are a desirable *modification, backed by a considerable body of evidence, then they should be fitted to Tiger Moths certificated for spinning. As we also argue that aeroplanes intended for aerobatics must be cleared for spinning - this rule is applied rigorously to British aeroplanes - then if a Tiger Moth is to be aerobatic, it should have anti-spin strakes.*

'Just because one Tiger Moth can be spun for 25 to 30 years without strakes, it does not follow that all Tiger Moths will behave in the same way on all occasions with all pilots. That is the reason now, with hindsight, for restricting spinning and aerobatics without spin strakes'.

The term 'anti-spin' strake used by the CAA was, perhaps, misleading. In all contemporary discussions between de Havilland, RAE, A&AEE and RAF, the part in question was never referred to as anything but a strake, and Tiger Moth part numbers 62976/62977 refer to 'strake, fairing, port (or starboard), Mod 112' and are listed under the 'aerofoils, arrangement of tail unit' section of the Schedule of Spare Parts, rather than 'fuselage' which is where most owners would tend to look first.

Allen Wheeler's personal views on the matter were expressed not only with the first hand knowledge of his own military test flying, but also as the owner of a number of Tiger Moths at different times, one of which, G-ADGV (3340), was an aircraft he had regularly flown and aerobatted since restoration in 1978. Operated in the 1935 colours of the aircraft's first owners, Brooklands Aviation, G-ADGV would not have been authentic with spin strakes and so none was fitted.

Wheeler considered that whether or not strakes were fitted, the matter was entirely by choice of the owner, whom he assumed would not be carrying bomb racks, and would take care with any weight liable for distribution along the wings. His own enquiries of the CAA were answered by a reply which put the emphasis on flight safety in the modern age and with which there was no argument. '*... we accept that particular pilots may have considerable experience and skills ... (but it is advisable) ... to increase the level of safety for the average pilot ...*'

Unfortunately, these views were expressed almost simultaneously with publication in 1973 of an article by an anonymous hand in the General Aviation Safety Council's *Flight Safety Bulletin*, under the title 'Beware Tiger', which implied that all Tiger Moths Mk.II had never been safe until strakes were fitted. The article was severely criticised by another anonymous hand described as being in an official position enabling judgement of the statements to be made realistically:

'From the evidence it can be seen that the presentation is far from accurate in many respects. Some of this is due to a lack of knowledge of Ministry procedures and some to misinterpretation of the evidence'.

Pressure from the Tiger Moth owning fraternity resulted in the CAA granting dispensation which permitted aerobatics to be flown by non-straked aircraft following application on an individual basis, but in 1983 the system was changed again. An Airworthiness Directive (AD) was issued listing the fitment of strakes under 'Mandatory Modifications' with an Information Leaflet available for those who required amplification. Under the new rules, applications for aerobatic certificates of airworthiness for private aircraft not fitted with strakes would only be considered after flight testing of Tiger Moths on an individual basis, by a CAA test pilot, and at the owner's expense.

This concession was further amended in June 1992 when the CAA issued a revised version of their Information and Procedures Leaflet which prohibited aircraft operating in the Transport and Aerial Work category from spinning and aerobatics unless strakes were fitted, and in order to qualify for a Transport Category certificate at all, the individual aircraft was to be subject to a spin recovery check performed by a CAA test pilot.

Owners and operators were left wondering what difference a piece of paper with an official stamp on it, and left in the filing cabinet, could possibly make to the airborne capabilities of a Tiger Moth, and conditional upon whether or not the pilot was being paid to fly her. It was a classic case of compromise, but opened up the spectre of dual standards and provided plenty of ammunition for a continuing debate.

Prompted by the British AD of 1983, the Airworthiness Division of Transport Canada was stirred into action. Shocked owners of Tiger Moths bearing Canadian registrations were advised that under the Directive effective from 9th September 1985, no DH.82C Tiger Moth would be permitted to fly aerobatics or to spin unless strakes were fitted, and that cockpits were to be placarded to this effect. Companies engaged in commercial operations with the 82C model were to fit strakes as a mandatory modification. British built DH.82A Tiger Moths registered in Canada were already subject to the conditions laid down by the British CAA, and enforced by the Canadian authorities.

The reasons for implicating the DH.82C model, reported Transport Canada, was because neither British Aerospace, inheritors of the de Havilland technical archive nor the de Havilland Aircraft of Canada could shed light on any aerodynamic differences which could lead to a variation of spinning characteristics between the 'A' and 'C' models.

The DH.82C was an innocent, and the thousands of hours which had been flown without complication when training pilots in Canada for over 40 years, seemed to have been forgotten. But the views of the owners supported by the Moth Clubs of Canada, USA and Great Britain were soon well voiced in the corridors of power, following study of which Transport Canada were roundly applauded for their early and complete acceptance of the fact that they had made a mistake. In their own words:

'Subsequent to the initial issue of this Directive, sufficient new information has been received which leads Transport Canada to believe that the configuration differences and Canadian service experience are such as to conclude that the unacceptable spin recovery characteristics of the DH.82A do not warrant airworthiness action on the DH.82C'.

'Unacceptable spin recovery characteristics of the DH.82A' was an unwarranted comment, but if it helped to establish the DH.82C as an independent force, and free of the strictures of the misguided AD, it was acceptable. Those in Canada and Great Britain who had inherited the archive data relating to the Tiger Moth may have proved there was no aerodynamic difference between the British and Canadian models, but they also showed a significant ignorance of history.

Was Transport Canada aware that in 1947, two DH.82C Tiger Moths, CF-CJA (DHC1747) and CF-CTB (DHC1653) were operational with the Aviron Company, later the Palestine Aero Club, in Tel Aviv? Both aircraft operated for a time in their original configurations, complete with yellow colour schemes and Canadian registrations, but in the summer heat, flying with the huge canopy closed was found to be barely tolerable. The situation which resulted in one aircraft, CF-CTB, having its canopy removed on a trial basis, coincident with local registry as VQ-PAU, leaving a wide fixed windscreen and long bath-like open cockpit behind it.

A Club pilot and one of the engineers flew the aircraft in this configuration, and from a good altitude tempted her into a spin. It proved to be a frightening experience for all concerned, not least the bathers on the sun drenched beaches below, but after three full turns the aircraft recovered, having taught another lesson which was not to be repeated.

During the production life of the Tiger Moth in New Zealand, 15 local modifications of consequence were introduced between April 1940 and May 1944 which were identified separately from those called up by the Royal Air Force or the parent company in England. Although Mod NZ104 dated 28th October 1941 called for removal of the aileron mass balance weights, there was no suggestion that spin strakes should be fitted, and none of the aircraft imported from England for local assembly nor any of those manufactured at Rongotai, was ever modified. After the war, the New Zealand airworthiness authorities insisted that strakes be fitted to all Tiger Moths in use by aero clubs, but the mandatory requirement was lifted after substantial input of pilot opinion suggested the strakes made no appreciable difference to the spin characteristics.

A programme of performance testing for agricultural Tiger Moths to judge the effects of 'excrescences in the form of hopper tanks' was conducted between 9th April and 9th May 1952 when ZK-ALK (3795), was hired from the Wellington Aero Club and flown in various configurations, including with and without strakes, to measure amongst the usual parameters, longitudinal stability, stalling and spinning. The results were later reported in the Journal of the Aviation Historical Society of New Zealand:

'The spinning tests involved four turns in each configuration, one in which three turns were made before beginning recovery, and one for eight turns, each of these being carried out both to the left and to the right. The aircraft was at 1,675lb, and with the centre of gravity fully aft.

'The results were interesting. For all spins to the right, the excrescences had no effect, but to the left they improved recovery characteristics for three turn spins, and were the same or slightly worse for eight turn spins.

'What were more interesting were the spins performed with the aircraft in a clean (unmodified) configuration and with no spin strakes. For eight turn spins to the right, removing the strakes had no effect, but to the left the number of turns to recover and the height lost were greater than with strakes. For three spin turns, however, removal of the strakes had improved recovery characteristics for spins in either direction'.

The protectionist powers of the Tiger Moth might be judged from an incident that occurred in the United States in 1980. A flying instructor who claimed experience in Moth aircraft from the 'thirties and 'forties, persuaded the owner of a recently imported

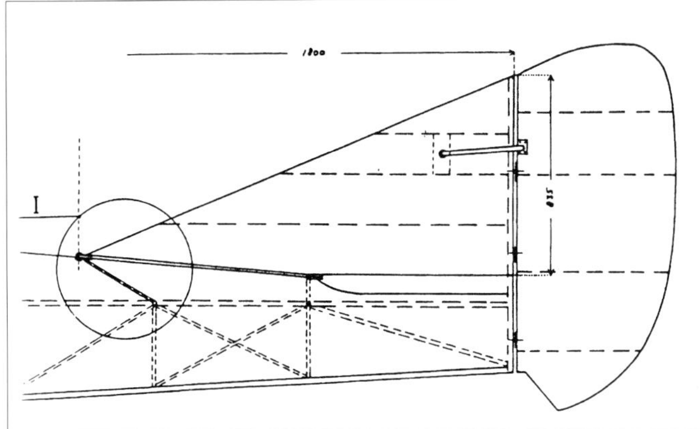

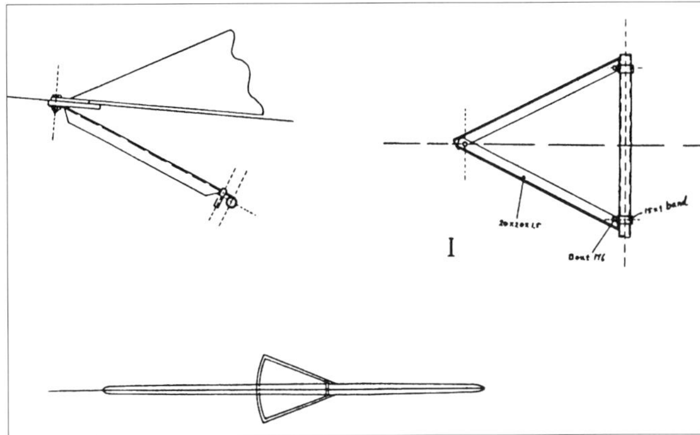

A drawing for the Tiger Moth's Fokker designed tail as approved by the Dutch RLD in September 1947. The modification increased the area of the fixed fin at the expense of the rudder and introduced a limiter for rudder deflection.

Tiger Moth to allow him to fly it. With the owner in the front seat and no method of communicating with the rear cockpit, the aircraft took off to fly a standard circuit, but the first landing was a disaster: the Tiger Moth was dropped in from 10ft and witnesses on the ground said they could see the wings deflect. Without stopping to inspect the aircraft, the instructor immediately took off again. At a point where the aircraft would normally expect to be 600ft-700ft it was at 200ft and continued to climb, struggling to 400ft with a horrified owner powerless to intervene. Having reached 400ft the aircraft was banked into a left turn but immediately entered a spin which was only arrested when the Tiger Moth hit the ground. The owner suffered a back injury as the result of failure of a shoulder harness, but was fit again within a month; the instructor sustained a minor cut on his arm. The FAA Investigator commented that the chances of anyone surviving a similar impact in a modern light aircraft would have been slim indeed. As it was, the Tiger Moth protected her charges and was herself rebuilt.

During the period from immediately after the war until the early 1950s, the RAF sold off the majority of its still considerable stockholding of now obsolete Tiger Moths, by which time all had been fitted with Modification 112. Aircraft sold or gifted as aid by the British Government to overseas air arms, were already fitted with strakes and these were retained no matter what new duties the aircraft were expected to perform. In most cases the Tiger Moths were used to supplement or even modernise emerging air force training schemes, but glider tugging was an important task in post-war France where about 200 Tiger Moths were employed at one time, some serving the sport well for almost 30 years.

In the Netherlands, the bad spinning habits reportedly developed by the wartime Tiger Moth were noted by the authorities. Ex-RAF machines delivered to the Government Aviation School (RLS) and National Aviation School (NLS) were found to have an increased angle of rudder deflection when compared with the trio of Dutch civil registered examples from pre-war days: N V Avon's PH-AJO (3101); PH-AJD (3188), owned privately by J Montauban van Swijndregt from May 1933, and PH-AJG (3190), the aircraft originally used as a test vehicle for Dutch certification.

In the late 1920s, the Rotterdamse Aeroclub had been selected to train Dutch civil air line pilots, effectively becoming the first National Aviation School, and by December 1930 had a growing requirement for improved equipment, favouring a local manufacturer if one could be found. Of three prospective candidates, Fokker would only build a minimum of 12 aircraft while Pander and Koolhoven were essentially prototype constructors. Koolhoven was willing to design to the school's requirements, but was slow in delivering promises and completing what eventually became the FK-46, a tandem seat, open cockpit biplane.

During this time of uncertainty, the school sent Dr H J van der Maas to de Havilland at Stag Lane where he flew a DH.82 Tiger Moth accompanied by Hugh Buckingham at first, and then solo with 40lb of ballast lashed down in the rear locker. In his report to the school board, Dr van der Maas made specific reference to the controls being heavier than he was used to, and that *'spinning is positive and quick and easy to recover from: nose slightly down; rudder in centre for a quick response. The aircraft can be regarded as very promising'.*

Other virtues openly discussed included low initial cost due to series production; the immediate availability and low cost of spare parts; incorporation of improvements resulting from an ordered test flight programme, and the fact that deliveries could be fulfilled almost immediately. He recommended that the school should buy two Tiger Moths without delay. In fact, bowing to some opposition from officials who still preferred to buy locally, only one aircraft was ordered, and PH-AJG was delivered to Waalhaven on 1st July 1933 where it was subjected to intensive flight trials in an effort to alleviate a major concern still being expressed over the use of the rudder and entry to the spin.

PH-UAI was operated in single seat configuration during the 'sixties, almost certainly for banner towing duties. Note the cable fairleads anchored to the lower longeron and what appears to be an outsize silencer box under the engine cowling. P Martyn

A post-war formation of three yellow painted Tiger Moths of the Royal Netherlands Air Force. Supplied from RAF surplus stocks in Great Britain with Mod 112 incorporated, no attempt was made to remove strakes from Dutch military aircraft and replace them with Fokker tails. via Herman Dekker

Koolhoven flew their promised FK-46 on 18th August 1933, and re-engined with a Gipsy 1 in January 1934, the aircraft proved to have a very impressive performance. A Gipsy Major was installed early in 1935 which transformed the aircraft and the NLS board honoured their intention to buy locally by ordering five aircraft with no further orders in prospect for de Havilland except the supply of engines and spares.

Tiger Moth PH-AJG was hangared at Schiphol on 10th May 1940 where she was destroyed in an air raid. The Koolhoven works at Waalhaven were destroyed at about the same time.

Although the two other Dutch registered Tiger Moths had returned to Great Britain pre-war, PH-AJD to the Cinque Ports Flying Club as G-ACGE in March 1936 and PH-AJO to Brooklands Flying Club as G-ABTB the following June, the Dutch authorities had created an extensive technical file on the type which they dusted off in 1946 in order to make comparisons with the new intake.

The RLS commenced flying training at Gilze-Rijen airfield in March 1946 but four major crashes were experienced that summer and the loss of PH-UAK (86303), in a landing accident on 26th August in which the 19 year old pilot was killed, is believed to have been caused by spinning off an unbanked turn at slow speed during the approach to land. This accident triggered the investigative research which resulted in major modifications to the areas always viewed with deep suspicion: the fin and classical de Havilland rudder.

An increase in the degree of rudder movement compared with that afforded PH-AJG in 1933 was considered to be a contributory factor in post-war spin related accidents. In addition, all the Gilze-Rijen aircraft which had crashed had been fitted with spin strakes, and these were blamed to some extent. Assistance requested from Great Britain resulted in the opinion of the Air Registration Board that strakes were not really necessary and may have increased the tendency to spin when near the stall.

The Tiger Moth was subjected to yet another series of official tests, this time under the authority of the Dutch Department of Civil Aviation (RLD) and which were conducted by Captain H J van Overvest of the National Flying Laboratory (NLL) on 5th and 9th September 1946. The subject aircraft, PH-UAM (86536), was one of several brand new Tiger Moths which had been upgraded by de Havilland early in 1946, and with civil letters painted over their RAF camouflage, delivered with British export certificates of airworthiness. PH-AUM was registered to the RLD on 9th May 1946 and prior to the trials was modified to restrict the range of available rudder movement. The structure of the fin and rudder was altered also: the area of rudder forward of the hinge line was deleted and substituted with an exactly similar area added as an upper extension to the fixed fin. The aircraft was found to perform normally in a straight and level attitude but showed her wrath by developing bad stall characteristics, especially during turns.

The NLL report (V.1388) was finally published on 9th December 1946 and said in summary: *'in its present form the aircraft is considered less suitable to be used as an initial trainer'* and concluded *'the aircraft could be improved and made safe by further aerodynamic underbalancing of the rudder and enlargement of the fin'*.

A further series of test flights by Captain J K Hoekstra resulted in another report (V.1406) which in turn was responsible for major surgery on de Havilland's trademark empennage. Three stages of development were tested by Captain Hoekstra using PH-UAM. On 21st March 1947, the aircraft was flown with a dorsal fin added to the existing modified fin, superimposed along almost the entire length of the strakes which remained in position, then on 9th April the same tests were flown with the strakes removed. Finally, a new dorsal fin was fitted which enlarged the fin area by almost half a square metre. In this configuration PH-UAM was flown on 22nd April.

The greatest improvement in spin control was achieved using the configuration which embodied the larger of the dorsal fins and no strakes, a situation which tended to confirm opinions expressed on the validity of the strakes. The publication of report V.1407 confirmed that spinning was entered 'calmly' and a more vertical position was held while height was lost at almost 295ft per rotation: a rate of one turn in about two seconds. Two bonus situations arose as might have been expected: the CG aft limit was extended rearwards by almost 2%, and landings on hard runways or grass were achieved without problems in cross wind speeds of up to 19mph, somewhat different from the manufacturer's recommended limit of zero.

Two suggestions were made in the final report in addition to the recommendation that the revised fin and rudder be adopted, providing its lightweight structure could be made strong enough to permit aerobatic manoeuvres, and that the revised rearward CG was acceptable. Mr T van Oosterom, investigator from the NLL, recommended deletion of the Tiger Moth rudder balance area and its static balance weight, and that spin strakes should be removed too.

The Royal Netherlands Air Force was not obliged to conform to this civil aviation report, and even after their camouflaged aircraft had been dismantled and re-painted yellow overall, the fin and rudder shape remained pure de Havilland. None of the military aircraft had their strakes removed. All Tiger Moths operated by both the RLS and NLS were modified with the ugly fins and rudders which were known locally as 'Fokker Tails'. All civil Tiger Moths registered in the Netherlands during the next 40 years were required to carry this modification, the most compelling reason for imports and restorations during the period to be registered at convenient addresses in Great Britain, Belgium and the USA, although flying on a daily basis, and without undue difficulty, through Dutch skies. Realising that the rules applied only to a handful of privately owned Tiger Moths, and not the great fleet of aircraft maintained to provide a new generation of pilots for the national airline, the Dutch authorities were encouraged to fly a further series of trials in 1985 as the result of which they removed the requirement for the modified fin and rudder.

An enquiry made of RLD in 1998 to explain why the authorities had changed their views, was answered only with copies of correspondence dating from 1946 explaining why the Fokker modification was to be mandatory, accompanied by a metaphorical shrug of the official shoulders. It is believed the 1985 tests had shown there to be very little difference between the new results and those recorded 50 years previously.

In Australia strakes were not fitted to aircraft of local manufacture, and the 100 Tiger Moths imported from Great Britain between February and September 1940 for service with the RAAF, all of which retained their RAF serial numbers, were not retrospectively converted. Strakes were never carried by the 345 Tiger Moths built by de Havilland in New Zealand, and the modification was never called up during the FAFAI Scheme early in 1942.

Out of interest but also for the greater understanding and benefit of all those involved with the growing phenomenon of ownership and operation of Tiger Moths in Australia, it was decided by a few friends in 1992 that a civil aircraft should be subject to a thorough flight test under peacetime conditions, and the results freely published. The candidate aircraft was VH-SSK (DHA885), a standard Tiger Moth built at Mascot in 1942, owned by Ken Broomhead, marked in RAAF Training Yellow as A17-468, and resident as a flying exhibit in the RAAF Museum at Point Cook.

The trials were to be the responsibility of Flight Lieutenant Antony Morris, an RAAF pilot assigned to fast jet duties at the Aircraft Research and Development Unit, and a graduate of the Empire Test Pilots' School, then based at Boscombe Down in England. Tony Morris had experience on over 40 different types of aircraft, and volunteered to conduct the trials as a civilian. The results were purely out of private interest and would have no official standing in the eyes of authority. The assessment was conducted at Point Cook between 1st-8th January 1993 against the following brief:

'... to produce a document outlining the recommended operating techniques and describing the aircraft's handling characteristics both on the ground and in the air. The existing Pilot's Notes for the aircraft (based on RAAF Training Notes dated 1948) are brief and do not describe major flight characteristics such as stalling and spinning, nor is any guidance given for recommended operating techniques for ground handling, take-off, aerobatics or landing. This report seeks to rectify that deficiency by providing guidance to pilots converting to the Tiger Moth who have little or no biplane or tailwheel experience ...'

Tony Morris asked readers to consider his report as a complete document rather than a series of isolated parts, but his investigation into the spinning characteristics of the Tiger Moth are of specific interest here:

'After the completion of the first turn the aircraft was defined as being in a steady state spin. The steady state spin was characterised by a 60 deg. nose-low attitude, with no detectable oscillations or hesitations in roll or yaw rates. The time per turn was

A fully camouflaged Tiger Moth of the Royal Netherlands Air Force shortly after delivery, with national insignia applied to wings and fuselage, but still carrying RAF serial T5820. The aircraft later became 'A-11' at Woensdrecht. via Herman Dekker

The classic situation when arrested by the ground after an unrestricted spin from 2,000ft. The Royal Australian Navy officer operating A17-700 from 1 FTS Point Cook on 6th March 1950 was almost unhurt. The Tiger Moth was cut up for spares. RAAF Museum

quick (approximately 2-3 seconds), however the motion was quite smooth and no disorientation was experienced. Altitude loss was between 200ft and 300ft per turn. The forces required to hold the pro-spin controls were light to moderate (with outspin force required to keep the aileron neutral), and no stick or rudder buffeting was observed. During the spin the pilot remained firmly restrained, and determining spin direction from outside reference was easy. The engine rpm remained stable throughout the spin and no rough running was noticed. Airspeed during the spin was observed at 48 knots indicated (KIAS) and 36 KIAS for left and right spins respectively. No other significant differences were observed between left and right spins. The aircraft remained in the steady state spin while the pro-spin controls were applied and no tendency to transition to a spiral dive was noted. Only small differences between the slots locked and unlocked case were observed, although the slots deployed symmetrically during the spin when unlocked.

'Recovery from the baseline spin was made from both the incipient and steady-state cases. Incipient recovery (which merely required centralising the controls) was rapid, with yaw and roll ceasing within a half a turn after recovery control application. Full power was then applied and the wings levelled. Height loss from the application of recovery controls to wings level, climbing flight at 58 KIAS was approximately 250ft. Once the spin had progressed to the steady state phase, recovery was effected by applying full deflection rudder opposite to the direction of spin, and simultaneously moving the control column forward to the elevator neutral position, maintaining neutral aileron. Following the application of recovery controls, the rotation ceased abruptly (within one turn), providing the pilot with a good cue to centralise the rudder. Full power was applied after the rotation had ceased, and the wings levelled. Height loss from the application of recovery controls to wings level, climbing flight at 58 KIAS was 300ft. The recovery technique was straightforward to fly and only required moderate control forces. Once the rotation had ceased, prompt centralisation of the rudder was required to prevent departure in the opposite direction.

'To establish the recovery technique providing the minimum altitude loss, four additional recovery variations were examined. The baseline spin entry technique was used in each case:

'Controls central recovery: *The effect of centralising the rudder and control column (longitudinally and laterally) was examined during one left and one right spin. From a left spin, this technique resulted in a recovery 2.5 turns after the centralisation of the controls, consuming significantly more altitude than the baseline recovery. Similar results were observed during the right spin.*

'Controls free recovery: *The effect of abandoning the controls during the spin was examined during one left and one right spin. For each direction of spin, releasing the controls did not effect a recovery after a further four turns, and a standard recovery was then made.*

'Pro-rudder recovery: *The effect of maintaining full rudder deflection in the direction of spin, while applying forward control column was assessed during one spin in each direction. In both cases the aircraft failed to recover and standard recovery action was required.*

'Aft stick recovery: *The effect of applying full rudder deflection opposite to the direction of spin, while maintaining full aft control column was examined during one spin in each direction. In the case of the left spin, after applying the opposite rudder the spin rotation ceased after less than one turn. For the right spin, the recovery was slightly slower, requiring 2.5 turns.*

'Minimum altitude recovery: *In all cases, minimum altitude loss for the spin recovery was achieved by applying full rudder opposite to the direction of spin and moving the control column forward. This is the recommended spin recovery technique.*

'The effect of introducing aileron during the spin was evaluated for both the in-spin and out-spin cases during the left and right spins. Lateral control column displacement in both directions generally increased the rate of rotation, but did not inhibit recovery if inadvertently applied while moving the stick forward. Lateral control displacement was not required to maintain a stable spin'.

Military flying training post-war was dedicated towards creation of an 'all weather air force' which was so vital an ingredient in the safe and efficient operation of the new generation of aeroplanes, especially low endurance jets. Pilots of the RAF Volunteer Reserve who maintained their flying skills on Tiger Moths into the early 'fifties, were expected to cope with instructor induced 'unusual attitudes' under the blind flying hood. John Fricker, reminiscing in 1982, wrote:

'Unusual attitude training included spin recovery (under the hood) on primary instruments, which is a pressing invitation to vertigo and air sickness if you are that way inclined. A spin is fairly easy to identify on instruments since the needles stay in line, although way off centre, and the ASI remains steady at a bit above the normal stalling speed. The bottom needle is centred, unusually, by rudder in the direction of its displacement, and the wings are then held level by maintaining the turn needle in the middle. All controls are neutralised before easing out of the ensuing dive, remembering to relax back pressure on the stick momentarily if excessive 'g' causes the bottom needle to precess into a sudden maximum rate turn indication'.

So, was the Tiger Moth an inherently dangerous beast, ready to ensnare pupil and seasoned instructor alike, or were her unpredictable moods of savagery a direct result of creeping military overload and lack of appreciation? Were the remedial measures of 1940 and later adequate or even necessary? The arguments are guaranteed to continue whenever the nose is high with the ASI showing barely 35kts.

A JOB TO BE DONE

Flight Lieutenant Richard Jones RAFVR, took a break from flying Supermarine Spitfires with the Bader Wing at Duxford, to become resident test pilot with the de Havilland CRO at Witney, flight testing Spitfires and Tiger Moths. 'Nichi' the bulldog belonged to Witney's much respected General Manager, Philip Gordon-Marshall. deHMC Archive

EVEN at an estimated cost of only £5 per flying hour for RAF Tiger Moth pilot training in 1940, the high rejection rate of would-be pilots at the flying schools was not only bad economics, but the unsuccessful candidates were slowing the passage of waiting recruits and consequently the flow of competent pilots to operational squadrons. The problem was exacerbated with the establishment of the Empire Air Training Scheme, when pupil pilots transported to overseas schools, and there found to be unsuitable material, had by that time already been subject to high levels of expenditure and logistical support.

A correspondent of the day was partially right in his assessment of the situation: *'We are practically mass producing pilots for the first time in our history. In the First World War, a man became a pilot by grit and a good modicum of luck which gave him time to complete his flying training while on actual service. This time a pilot who has passed through elementary, intermediate and advanced schools, and has sampled squadron work, can call himself experienced. It is unlikely that anyone who is unsuitable for active service will get past the elementary stage'.*

In order to reach the elementary stage in the first instance, pilot recruits passed through an indoctrination process at an Initial Training Wing, and were required to undertake both written and mechanical aptitude tests in addition to a stringent medical, before even getting close to a Tiger Moth weeks later. In Great Britain, aircrew cadets were mustered as Aircraftmen 2nd Class (AC2) with pay at the rate of two shillings per day during training. Those going on to become pilots were promoted to Leading Aircraftmen with pay raised to five shillings per day with an additional two shillings on account of 'flying instructional pay'. It was important to score good marks at the end of the EFTS course as these dictated possible reclassification and certainly promotion. A sergeant pilot could expect a rate of twelve shillings and sixpence a day.

In Great Britain the length of time spent at EFTS, eight to 12 weeks, depended on the season of the year initially, although course duration varied as the war progressed, and depended on global location and the urgency or otherwise for speeding up or slowing down the throughput. Working to a standard syllabus, the trainees operating Tiger Moths could expect to fly for 50 hours of which five hours would be under the

The top picture was released on behalf of the Admiralty in March 1940, accompanied by the following statement: *'The Fleet Air Arm, the speedy infant of the Royal Navy, plays an important part in modern warfare. At the Elementary Flying Training School where this picture was taken, the Rating pilots undergo ten weeks intensive training in all branches of aeronautics.'*

During the early part of the Second World War Tiger Moth circuit training in Great Britain was almost continuous, often in marginal weather, by day and by night. The introduction of the Grading System and opening of schools in The Commonwealth, considerably eased the home situation. via Richard Riding

blind flying hood, coping with instruments, five hours navigation work including a first solo cross country exercise, and at least 25 hours dual.

Precious to the memory of every trainee was the number of the 'Exercise' and the order in which they progressed:

1 Air Experience
1A Familiarity with cockpit layout
2 Effect of controls
3 Taxying
4 Straight and level flight
5 Climbing, gliding and stalling
6 Medium turns
7 Taking off into wind
8 Powered approach and landing
9 Gliding approach and landing
10 Spinning
11 First solo
12 Side slipping
13 Precautionary landings
14 Low flying (with instructor only)
15 Steep turns
16 Climbing turns
17 Forced landings
18 Action in the event of fire
18A Abandoning the aircraft
19 Instrument flying
20 Taking off and landing out of wind
21 Restarting the engine in flight
22 Aerobatics.

The 'Grading System' introduced into the RAF in November 1941, and based on a points score for ability and aptitude awarded at each of ten phases, functioned as an integral part of the Elementary School programme, where selected pilot candidates were allowed up to 12 hours of instructional flying, during which at 6 hours and 12 hours, their suitability or not, to go forward for further training, was assessed by the CFI according to the points total. Pupils were not expected to achieve solo standard although many did and were sent off for their never-to-be-forgotten ten minute circuit. Some instructors held back pupils just on the edge of solo standard to prevent the prospect of a bad solo flight 'score' spoiling an otherwise exemplary course result.

But achieving a high standard at Grading School did not guarantee further advancement. Elementary School places matched to the availability of berths on sailings to Canada or southern Africa, or to a sudden increased demand due to heavier than expected casualties, dictated how many successful 'graded' trainees could be accommodated, and the percentage of the total was never constant, varying from as little as 5% to 40% or more.

The Grading System had an unforeseen secondary effect. By providing a stream of higher quality trainees, the wastage rate on EFTS courses was significantly lower, resulting in qualified EFTS pupils queuing for vacancies at Service Flying Training Schools

(SFTS). To counter this, the result was a corresponding reduction in the intake of EFTS pupils, and towards the end of the war when the training machine was running down, a total cancellation of options against modest compensation.

Grading was scheduled to be swiftly and efficiently completed within 14 days, but could be a victim of circumstances. Don Roskilly flew solo on Tiger Moth T7472 (83901), during grading at 15 EFTS Carlisle on 28th February 1944, having received 11 hours 15 minutes dual instruction on 18 sorties, in ten aircraft with eight instructors spread over seven weeks. Prior to issue of proper log books to those scheduled for further instruction, flight times were preciously recorded on log sheets (Form 4148). Fortunately, dates of birth were not recorded, for in spite of the delays, Don Roskilly soloed at 17 years of age, having persuaded the recruiting officer that he was a year older.

Another famous form was 'A25', designed to record details of all military flying accidents. Fleet Air Arm pilots, graded in an identical manner to their counterparts in the RAF, except that all FAA training was completed in Great Britain, composed a song about the Form A25, one verse of which went:

They taught me to fly in an old Tiger Moth,
A fantastic contraption of wood, string and cloth,
The take off is great and the climb is fantastic,
A bloody good show for some string and elastic.
Chorus:
Cracking Show, I'm alive,
But I still have to render my A25.

Derek Piggott made remarkable progress during his Grading course and his instructor was willing to allow him to go solo after only four hours' dual. He relished the experience, noting especially the improved performance of the Tiger Moth without the mass in the front seat. Piggott later learned that the Flight Commander had mistakenly believed he was already an accomplished glider pilot, (he did become a world class glider pilot and instructor after the war), and had encouraged his progress, but the overheard discussions had actually concerned flying model gliders. Nevertheless, with a natural ability and 'above average' assessment, within the 12 hour allowance he managed several hours solo and some spinning exercises.

A legendary instructor at 24 EFTS Booker had recorded 500 flying hours in his first logbook which was dated 1915, and was still adding hours in his tenth when the total had passed 17,000. He looked casually at the names chalked on the flying rota together with achieved hours, and called out a student listed for some dual. After two circuits, the instructor climbed out of the front cockpit, tidied up the straps, offered a word of encouragement to the prospective soloist, and shambled back to the hut. Enter the Flight Commander, scheduled to fly with the same student, only to be told that he had just been sent off solo. Now somewhat concerned, the instructor looked again at the chalked hours to read 1 hour and 15 minutes and not 11 hours 50 minutes as he had believed. The student managed to land the Tiger Moth safely and in one piece, on his sixth attempt.

Neville Duke, another naturally talented pilot, had flown his first RAF familiarisation trip at 13 EFTS White Waltham in Tiger Moth N6790 (82060), on 20th August 1940, before the Grading System had been established. On 6th September 1940, at the height of the Battle of Britain, he flew solo after eight and a half hours dual, and two days later, such was the pressure, that he flew seven sorties between dawn and dusk, of which four were solo. He described the whole experience of solo flight as 'exhilarating'. Following a successful career as an RAF fighter pilot, Squadron Leader N F Duke DSO, OBE, DFC and 2 Bars, AFC, became the holder of the world air speed record in 1953.

The Grading System remained an essential part of the military selection process after the war, and a fleet of RAF Tiger Moths was maintained for the purpose at Digby and Kirton in Lindsey until the type was finally withdrawn from service. Long after his short association with Digby, one pupil revealed that when taxying out in the morning, the instructors would sit on the leading edge of the Tiger Moth's lower mainplanes, spotting for mushrooms. On one occasion, the pupil taxied his Tiger Moth into the tail of the preceding aircraft, causing considerable damage, but both Tiger Moths were spirited away for repair and nothing further

A figure of perfection. Not a scratch on her; everything new and serviceable. Chocked on a dispersal area at Hatfield in 1940, Tiger Moth T6297 survived all tutorials to become a civilian in 1951.
de Havilland Aircraft Co.

Most instructors tried to remain impassive having sent a pupil off on his first solo.
Iain Dick

was heard of the incident. The trainee believes he was removed from the prospect of a pilot's course and remustered as a navigator, not because of the mushroom hunting accident, but due to getting lost on his first solo and putting the Tiger Moth down again on a different aerodrome.

By mid-1947 the Tiger Moths at 15 EFTS Carlisle had been fitted with battery operated electric intercom, replacing the original Gosport systems which remained in the aircraft. Iain Dick recalls that when flying south of Carlisle over the hills towards Shap Fell, it was possible to pick up the BBC Overseas Service in the headphones which created a pleasant interlude. The down side was that the intercom required the pilot to wear a face mask, from which the oxygen tube had been removed. During the course of flights in winter, condensation would drip out of the mask and promptly freeze on the compass. All crews found it handy to carry some small sharp tool to chip away the ice.

In November 1941, the Hatfield factory, ever mindful of the importance of communication, introduced a pocket sized newsletter for fortnightly circulation within the local workforce. It was inexpensively produced on cheap wartime utility paper and the first edition of eight sides carried three photographs, none of which showed the image of an aeroplane, a cartoon, and a short report under the heading 'Our stinger on show':

'Some hundreds of people who are very close friends of ours came to the aircraft factory on Saturday and saw something they are all helping to make'.

The 'close friends' were all sub-contract suppliers and the 'Stinger' they had come to see fly was the DH.98 Mosquito, which it did, capably demonstrated by Geoffrey de Havilland Jr, although the report totally refrained from saying so.

Entitled *Our Job*, issue 1 of the new publication carried the title-page sub-heading: *'which deals informally with matters of interest to everyone in the de Havilland organisation'* and on the reverse side, a warning: *'Published for private circulation only. The contents are not to be communicated to anyone not in the employ of the de Havilland Aircraft Co Ltd.'*

By issue 13 dated 16th April 1942, those policing the paper control regulations had warned de Havilland that their title page wasted too much space on the heading (four square inches) and all future editions appeared with a mere 10 point header: *'Memorandum of Information to all de Havilland personnel'* followed by an OJ number and numeric date.

There were always remarkably few photographs, almost none of which were of current company products although a few historic aircraft pictures appeared on an occasional basis, but there were some thinly veiled propagandist cartoons and a few advertisements for national effort. Frequency of publication gradually declined as the war wound wearily on, with only four issues between November 1944 and July 1945.

Perhaps it was something of a relief for the editor to be able to include real aeroplane facts in issue 34 dated 11th February 1943, for hidden amongst the continuous text which allowed not a blank line for fear of infringing the paper regulations, and which included news of fund raising for Merchant Navy Week, the Aircraft Division Sports Club, the need to save fuel in the factory heating system and distribution of prime cuts from the Pig Club, not to mention the call for editorial contributions of the right material, was a choice piece entitled 'The Ubiquitous Tiger'.

The editorial spoke of four Tiger Moths which were in service at an Elementary Flying Training School (EFTS) in the West Country, which between them had amassed a total of nearly 13,000 flying hours, and were still going strong. Curiously, for a publication of limited circulation which had been concerned enough about security in its first issue not even to mention the name of its own company product, the reporter quoted the serial numbers of all four air-

Pre-war Reserve Tiger Moth G-ADXT survived her time at Desford and elsewhere and was featured by the de Havilland in-house publication 'Our Job'. The aircraft was rebuilt at Shoreham and restored to the post-war civil register in 1979.
John Pothecary

craft. To have achieved an average of over 3,000 hours even by mid-1942, each Tiger Moth would surely have required substantial investment in pre-war activity to have boosted her totals, and so it proved to be.

BB694 (3340), had operated as G-ADGV before military impressment with 6 ERFTS, contracted to Brooklands Aviation at Sywell since May 1935. BB791 (3382), was another Sywell aircraft, having joined 6 ERFTS in August 1935 as G-ADJF. BB742 (3182), was the ninth production DH.82A and the veteran of the piece, having been delivered to the de Havilland administered 13 ERFTS at White Waltham in February 1933 as G-ACDI.

The youngest of the quartet was BB860 (3436), delivered to Reid and Sigrist on behalf of 7 ERFTS Desford as G-ADXT in December 1935; she was probably also the most fortunate of the group to have survived for inclusion in the *Our Job* list. On 22nd September 1939, her pupil pilot choked the engine during an attempted overshoot, stalled and crashed, causing substantial airframe damage. On 4th January 1940, without assistance from the pilot, the engine failed just after take off and during the inevitable straight-ahead landing, BB860 ran into a concealed ditch which wrecked the undercarriage and caused a re-arrangement of the engine bay. But as if that was not a sufficient indignity, during circuit activity on 17th June 1941, Tiger Moth R4776 (82720) managed to land on top of her. BB860 was conveyed to the de Havilland Civil Repair Organisation (CRO) at Witney where she was eventually wheeled out to be test flown on 5th September by resident RAF test pilot Flight Lieutenant Richard Jones.

When not flight testing Spitfires which were also routed through Witney for repair, or helping with standard production testing of new Tiger Moths from the nearby Morris Motors' factory at Cowley, Jones was kept busy with a constant flow of Tiger Moths each of which required a standard flight check after overhaul or repair. By coincidence he had been featured in *Our Job* issue 2 dated 20th November 1941 when a close-up photograph of him appeared seated in the rear cockpit of an unidentified Tiger Moth. In the front seat was Nichi, a bulldog owned by the General Manager at Witney, Philip Gordon-Marshall.

Nichi was a much travelled air passenger and a dog with great character, much loved by all at the CRO. Among his many claims to fame, apart from being photogenic, was the occasion when he attacked the black and tan terrier accompanying Professor Lindemann's party during an official visit. Wartime Prime Minister Winston Churchill relied on Lindemann for technical guidance, and there was speculation amongst staff at Witney on the future course of the war had Lindemann been so shocked at Nichi's ferocious attack to have suffered a seizure and died. On another occasion Nichi had leapt at the spinning propeller blades of a Spitfire, only to be hurled away cruelly injured and carried off in the belief he was dead, but he was only unconscious and had recovered sufficiently within a few days to attack the white cat mascot of a locally based army regiment. The Colonel later made a bid for Nichi but the offer was refused.

de Havilland's support organisations always prided themselves on their direct links with operators in the field, and it must have been a sharp eyed representative at 29 EFTS Clyffe Pypard who had recognised the depth of experience in the school fleet. Perhaps he should have realised the contribution of three of his brood earlier, but then maybe he had, only to discover there was no published vehicle to carry his observations until the editor of *Our Job* cast his net more widely.

The arrival of BB694 in July 1942, posted in to 29 EFTS from Sywell, was fairly typical of the general scheme of movements. Some aircraft remained at one location for a few weeks only; others for several years continuous service, broken only by the need for major maintenance or accident repair.

BB742 was delivered to Clyffe Pypard following a major inspection at a CRO in Devon on 28th September 1941 and remained there until November 1947, only leaving then due to her 'obsolete' tag and sale out of the service. BB791 was at 20 Maintenance Unit (MU) Aston Down for only a few days, taken back into store after accident repairs at Rearsby, before she was delivered to 29 EFTS on re-establishment of the unit. Following her repairs at Witney, BB860 was another aircraft drafted in to establish the unit at its Wiltshire base, a county which many would find difficulty in recognising as true West Country as labelled by the correspondent in *Our Job*.

By one of those probably pre-arranged coincidences, both G-ADGV and G-ADXT survived the war and much else, to be reunited as members of the de Havilland Moth Club's Diamond Nine formation team, flying close alongside each other from 1995, a manoeuvre probably not included in the Clyffe Pypard syllabus 50 years previously.

In addition to the four old stagers, the *Our Job* editor highlighted a further four Tiger Moths in his 34th issue, each of which was involved in an unpublished story every bit as interesting as the morale raising facts appearing in print.

BB675 (3402), was declared to be a 'redoubtable veteran' with 2,600 hours since her registration as G-ADOI on 11th October 1935, and posting to Perth for duty with 11 ERFTS. By the time news of her status was published in *Our Job* early in 1943, she had been repaired in Devon twice, firstly after a major landing accident at Perth and then following a mishap at Yeovilton while serving with Station Flight at RAF Hawkinge. At the moment of publication, BB675 was with 16 EFTS Burnaston, and remained there apart from terminal leave at 9 MU Cosford until sold, ironically to the de Havilland Aircraft Company who refurbished her at Witney prior to sale in Ethiopia.

DE241 (85287), was hailed as the first Tiger Moth to be fitted experimentally with a full blind flying instrument panel, 'and the experiment has proved a success'. The aircraft was delivered to 22 EFTS Cambridge in January 1942 where a pupil made three attempts to land during his first night solo, and on his final approach dragged the aeroplane in low and slow but collided with a blister hangar near the perimeter track. Following repairs at Llandow, the aircraft returned to operate at Cambridge until 1950.

T6683 (84983), collided with another aircraft when landing at Clyffe Pypard, a fact willingly acknowledged in the *Our Job* report, but it was very much a case of the other fellow coming off second best; while T6683 suffered a broken top wing and damaged fuel tank, repairs to which kept her off the circuit for only two days, the second aeroplane was said to have been cut in half. But shortly after the publication of issue 34, on 6th May 1943, T6683 is reported to have 'crashed' and was sent to Taylorcraft at Rearsby for repairs. Damage must have been severe for her incapacitation lasted for an almost unprecedented eight weeks before she was positioned to 5 MU Kemble, and nine weeks later allocated to the Pilotless Aircraft Unit (PAU) at Manorbier, five miles south east of the flying boat activity at Pembroke Dock in West Wales, where on 22nd November 1943 she was allocated for conversion to a Queen Bee.

Why was what is assumed to have been a perfectly serviceable Tiger Moth removed from the training programme when production of new aircraft was scheduled to continue at Cowley for another eight months, and be slated for conversion after lengthy repairs? And what form of conversion was contemplated: a completely new wooden fuselage or merely the installation of basic wireless apparatus into the standard Tiger Moth cockpit? Whatever the rationale, T6683 was spared. A fortnight later she was posted to the Glider Pilot Exercise Unit (GPEU) at Shrewton, Wiltshire, and a week after that to the Operational and Refresher Training Unit (ORTU), but only on account of the fact that the Unit had changed its name!

Was there something odd about Tiger Moth T6683, something that had been discovered during that extended repair schedule at Rearsby? Had she developed a personality disorder after her accidents at Clyffe Pypard when the de Havilland publicity machine had described her as being 'sturdy'? After spending more than five years in storage with 10 MU Hullavington from January 1945, the aircraft was sold for scrap.

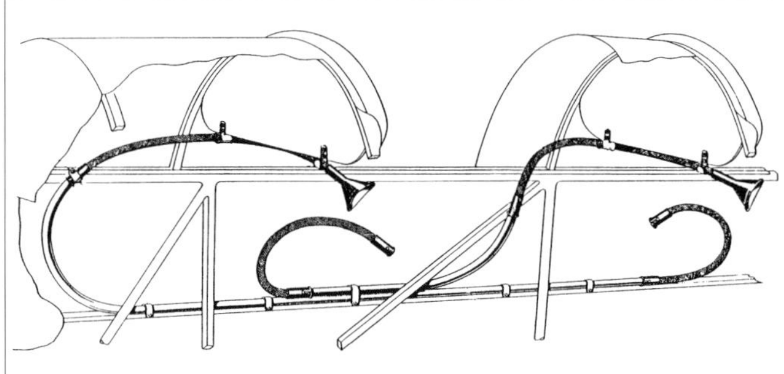

The crude but reliable and effective 'Gosport' dynamic tube communications system which remained the only contact between student and instructor until electric intercom was installed post-war. If ever a student chose to shower retribution on an unfriendly instructor he could choose to be sick into the mouthpiece, and blow!

'A bit murky and rather cool, but the wind is down the runway, the forecast is better and the aeroplane is serviceable. Shall we go, gentlemen?' **Flight Lieutenant Godfrey Bremridge (top left), a member of the pre-war Brooklands Aviation sales team based at Weybridge, joined the instructional staff at 6 EFTS Sywell, where he was later killed when his Tiger Moth collided with an Airspeed Oxford during a weather check overhead the airfield.** Richard Sayward

The lightweight Brown Two Stage DNF Hood, developed by Flying Training Command at RAF Hullavington and flight tested at A&AEE Boscombe Down in 1943. Crown Copyright PRO

The final aircraft of the batch chosen for publicity was R4962 (82771), another Tiger Moth based with 22 EFTS at Cambridge. *'A cadet pilot making his first night solo trip was suddenly confronted by a Nazi swooping from the cloud. Although the enemy attacked fiercely and the British pilot was wounded, he succeeded in evading his formidable opponent and brought his unarmed machine safe home'*, read the report.

In truth the action was much more serious. R4962 was operating from Caxton Gibbet, one of three satellite airfields for Cambridge's main aerodrome at Teversham, and where night flying facilities were available. At 0230 hours on 16th July 1941, the Tiger Moth was attacked in the circuit by a German prowler, thought to have been a Messerschmit Me 110, lurking with just such an intent. Against a blacked-out background, the appearance of a lighted flarepath was an obvious draw and training aircraft showing navigation lights as they flew sedate circuits made easy and attractive targets for enemy intruders. R4962 received two bursts of machine gun fire which badly damaged the tail, but the pilot, LAC Hassall, was praised for the confidence he displayed when forced to crash-land the aircraft in the darkness. His personal injuries amounted to a cut on his neck which received one stitch. 'Safe home' it might have been, but the Tiger Moth was classified as having been shot down as the result of enemy action and was written off.

Just as interesting, but not for publication in 1941, was the fact that the enemy aircraft also dropped 10 delayed action bombs across the landing ground. An area of some 250 yards radius around each was cordoned off, and training continued unabated by day and by night for the next four days, at which point the Bomb Disposal Squad removed them from the site.

Caxton Gibbet was the source of another interesting story which circulated amongst the stations of Flying Training Command. Pupils from one Flight, intent on demonstrating their abilities to fly in formation, but denied the opportunity by the CFI, are said to have locked their instructors into the crew room one day and enjoyed a brief and unauthorised interlude in close harmony.

Flying Training Command's reaction to intruder incidents had been to launch a thorough investigation of night flying techniques which could be adapted to safer daylight conditions, and these resulted in the simple and effective Day/Night Flight (DNF) systems of Two Stage Blue, Two Stage Amber and Two Stage Brown. Invented by the brothers Wood, professional photographers from Bradford, and developed by Wing Commander Philip Bremridge and his teams of the Day/Night Flight and Flying Training Research Flight, part of the Empire Central Flying School (ECFS) at Hullavington, the two-stage system became the standard method of converting pilots into night owls during the hours of daylight.

To permit 'day/night flight' (DNF) training in a Tiger Moth, a new version of the blind flying hood was designed which incorporated a transparent blue panel sewn into the fabric and acting as a windscreen. Known as the Brown Two-stage DNF Hood, the tent-like device was of much lighter construction than the heavy canvas covered blind flying 'pram hood' then in daily use, and following flight trials conducted with Tiger Moth T7809 (84187), at Boscombe Down on 18th/19th June 1943, it was recommended that for aerobatic flight, and to prevent damage, the hood should first be removed on account of what was described as 'its relatively flimsy construction'.

Do NOT use the Gosport tube

'What did I tell you about doing that?' Gordon Evans

At Boscombe Down T7809 was flown with two crew and tested with the hood erected when it was found difficult to engage the locking catch, or folded down, transiting between the two positions in the air without difficulty. In the folded position, the crew noted that the hood lifted about 12in from the rear decking in a dive at 140mph, but remained in that position with any further increase in diving speed up to 155mph. Unlike the standard blind flying hood, the lightweight construction of the Brown DNF Hood caused it to buffet when erected, transmitting an intermittent shudder through the airframe. In all other respects, the hood caused no significant difference to the handling characteristics of the aeroplane which was stalled, aerobatted and spun without difficulty. In view of their previous association with Tiger Moth spinning trials, the Boscombe Down test pilots were pleased to report that with the hood either up or down, behaviour in three turn spins left or right, was perfectly normal, recovery being effected after half a turn.

At the time of the trials T7809 was operational with the Empire Central Flying School, conveniently placed within 30 minutes' flight time of Boscombe Down at Hullavington, and remained on strength there until September 1948 when she was posted to 10 MU, just across the airfield, and listed for sale. In February 1949 the aircraft was acquired by W A Rollason Ltd at Croydon and civilianised as G-AMEG, but ironically rejoined the military when she was sold into the employ of the Royal Thai Navy.

Soon after the Grading System was introduced, 22 EFTS Cambridge was asked to conduct an experiment to train six pupil pilots of average ability, to fly a Tiger Moth to and beyond solo standard, entirely at night. The six were to be divided into two groups: one to be trained solely with the aid of visual references and feel, and the basic instrumentation of a Tiger Moth, and the second to work with instruments as the primary guide aided by visual indications. Three instructors were selected, each taking one pupil from both groups. Four Tiger Moths were fitted with artificial horizons in front and rear cockpits, and Holt flares on the wingtips, and were scheduled to operate at the main base at Teversham aerodrome and Caxton Gibbet Relief Landing Ground (RLG) where single electrically lit flare paths were available. As the flying experiment progressed, and in order to achieve maximum practical value, the aircraft were converted to accept full blind flying panels in both cockpits, and a twin flare path was introduced.

To coincide with maximum darkness and also by definition, the coldest conditions, flying training started in January 1942. Oliver Wells, a 19 year old flying instructor at 22 EFTS was an interested observer, but even now cannot be clear about the reasons for the experiment, except perhaps as a scheme to accelerate the supply and quality of night fighter pilots:

'The flying started with the instrument cadets being given experience of the feel of the controls and instrument reactions to their use. The visual cadets were given experience of the effect of the controls, straight and level climbing, gliding, stalling and medium turns. Reference was made to stars and landmark beacons and sometimes a faintly visible horizon or bank of clouds allied with reference to the artificial horizon. Recovery from a spin could not be taught due to the unsuitability of the Tiger Moth battery fittings for such a manoeuvre, apart from any other considerations, so emphasis was placed on familiarity with the stall and recovery, both with and without the engine, and the attitude and feel of this manoeuvre. There was a tendency for cadets to be unconcerned by unusual flying attitudes or speeds since darkness cloaked the fact that the ground was in the wrong place or rushing up to meet them, but they were firmly taught to avoid steep turns or violent manoeuvres'.

All six cadets went on to complete their first solo flights at night after an average 16 hours 30 minutes dual instruction, having never flown in daylight. They enjoyed certain advantages in being alone in the circuit, not troubled with the need to avoid up to 30 other active aircraft for example, and the flare path was always laid into wind. After 25 hours dual and six hours solo, all at night, the six cadets were introduced to daylight flying and soloed after an hour's dual instruction and detailed briefings on what to expect in the real world. Their experiment had proved that it was possible to teach a pilot to fly safely by night using instruments and visual references, and although wheel landings were taught, everybody agreed that a tricycle undercarriage would have saved time and reduced the risk of accidents.

Woefully short of equipment, the RAF was required to subscribe an 'Air Component' to the British Expeditionary Force which set off for France in September 1939. In anticipation, an 'Avro Tutor Communications Squadron' was established on paper, utilising aircraft drawn from the University Air Squadrons, falling back on an organisation, no doubt, when Tutors had operated briefly between November 1931 and October 1932 with No 24 Squadron on communications duties from Northolt. When inspected, however, only about four aircraft were considered to be in any fit condition to go to war, and they were replaced at very short notice in August and September by brand new Tiger Moths delivered to Andover from RAF MUs. The assemblage eventually formed from 28th August 1939, the Air Component 'Tiger Moth Communication Squadron'.

The Squadron's medical officer, Dr V P Geoghegan recorded the following memories:

'I found a mixed lot of commissioned pilots posted from various squadrons and not very pleased at finding themselves in what they naturally regarded as a second class outfit, and four or five NCO pilots, two of them qualified instructors, with similar feelings. There was a veteran Flying Officer from the Reserve who had done some of his early training on Bristol Fighters and had joined his first Squadron in 1927, but had not been in an aircraft for five years. He arrived shortly before the Air Party was due to leave for France and when told he was to fly a Tiger Moth over there in a couple of days, he mildly suggested that a few circuits and bumps might be a wise preliminary. One of the instructors took him up for an hour and he coped perfectly well, becoming a tower of strength from then on.

'During the first two weeks of September the plans for our move to France began to emerge. There were to be three parties: the Air Party divided into 'A' and 'B' Flights would fly to France in true RFC tradition with a fitter in each front seat; the Road Party would be shipped with all the vehicles from Southampton and the Main Party would also cross from Southampton. Security was tight: nobody knew where we were going or how long it would take, and it was 43 years later that I discovered we were a small part of Operation Violet.

'There were about a dozen 3-ton Crossley 6-wheelers and as many 4-wheeled trailers all pre-packed with the necessary spare parts, engines etc. for yes, Avro Tutors. The Engineer Warrant Officer lost a lot of hair in the ten days or so before embarkation, trying to persuade Equipment Officers in Maintenance Units up and down the country to swap Lynx engines for Gipsy Majors and Avro Tutor airframe spares for Tiger Moth. He was largely successful, but we still arrived in France with some of the wrong bits.

'The CO, Squadron Leader George Ashton would not agree to 'A' Flight flying in formation: he decided the aircraft would fly in line astern with Flying Officer Bevis as tail end Charlie, Flight Sergeant Carver leading with the CO tucked in behind him. Bevis was advised to watch out for any machine that went down into the drink, and if it did, to mark the spot, and fly around until help arrived. In reply to his question 'And what if I go down?' he was told; 'that's your bad luck!'

'The CO had very little idea of navigation, or on what course the aircraft should all be flying. Carver, the most experienced pilot, flew in front and was to be seen signalling his CO to go left or right when he veered off course. The Flight refuelled at Shoreham and crossed the Channel to Le Tréport before heading for Poix. Getting close to their destination, the CO made no attempt to lose

height or make an approach. Carver waved at him and pointed downwards emphatically, whereupon the CO went into a steep dive and landed straight off the bottom. When the aircraft stopped, well out in the field, he was seen throwing off his Sutton harness and parachute, leaping out and having a long pee by the tailplane. Meanwhile two of the junior officers dutifully followed their Squadron Commander and landed down wind while Carver led the remainder round the circuit to land into wind, a performance which resulted in Tiger Moths landing in all directions, but nobody hit anybody else and the aerodrome authorities did not turn a hair'.

'A' Flight moved on to Montjoie by the end of September where they were joined by 'B' Flight on 6th October, detaching elements to Arras, Abbeville, Poix and Metz. On 21st November 1939 the Tiger Moth Communications Squadron was formally listed as No 81 Squadron with Headquarters at Montjoie, a few miles north east of Amiens, although the unit recalls that it was not advised of its new name until 1st December, which is the date it records as that of its formation.

The squadron had previously disbanded in January 1920 when operating S.E.5as at Shoreham, and under the reformation acceded as the only RAF squadron ever to be solely equipped with Tiger Moths. For a brief period in December 1939, the Tiger Moths were uniquely joined by a Cierva C.40 Autogyro, 'the whirling spray', a device which was said to have frightened the life out of some high ranking Staff Officers.

Dr Geoghegan recalls some of the Squadron's unique operations in France:

'During the Phoney War which lasted until 10th May, 81 Squadron sat at Montjoie, survived the cold spell when the temperature fell as low as zero degrees Fahrenheit, and provided a minicab cum postal service for the Air Component and GHQ. There was a daily milk run to Arras, navigated by following the HT wires from Amiens and it was whispered that staff officers were occasionally flown to Le Touquet on golfing weekends. Machines were detached to various aerodromes: 57 and 59 Squadrons, both with Bristol Blenheim IV were at Poix or Crecy, and others were at Rosieres where we used to fly for Sunday lunch, returning in the afternoon, more or less in formation.

'At Montjoie the circumstances were ideal for learning to fly: Tiger Moths with dual control and a number of qualified instructors. On one occasion under instruction, the aircraft was taken off smoothly and climbed gently as I kept my hands and feet well clear of the controls. My instructor who was sitting in the back seat then asked quietly at about 500ft whether I might flatten out and pay attention to the speed. We discovered that the aircraft had climbed away quite happily without human interference.

'When a new pilot was posted in, he was introduced to the daily routine by taking the front seat on the morning mail run to Arras. On return to base the pilot in command confessed that the man could not fly, although he had claimed to be just out of current practice. After some persuasion he was forced to admit that he had joined the RAF in 1918 and after a few hours instruction, the war had ended and he was sent home. In 1939 he had re-enlisted and managed to convince the chain of authority that he was a qualified pilot, but all his records had been destroyed. When the CO was confronted with the story he decided that the best method of escaping the inevitable deluge of forms and trouble was to teach the man to fly at Montjoie, which is what happened. When the Squadron returned to disband in England, it is believed the pilot was transferred to another squadron thought to be flying Hurricanes.

'When the shooting war started some of the pilots encountered the enemy and quickly found that by flying low and as slowly as possible, they were moderately safe. Johnny Sayer described how he saw coloured balls coming from astern and passing between the upper and lower mainplanes. He managed to shake off his attacker by making a tight turn at low level. Another pilot was advised that the Squadron had moved from Montjoie and relocated to Abbeville, but when he landed there he found the airfield had been captured and he and his Tiger Moth were taken prisoner. One Tiger Moth landed near a farmhouse where the pilot, Flying Officer Gautier was asking for directions as a German motorcycle combination complete with machine gun arrived in the field. Fortunately, the Gipsy Major had been left ticking over, and the aircraft took off on a direct heading for England, but ran out of fuel in mid-Channel. The pilot managed to parachute into the sea near a passing French navy destroyer and was picked up safely'.

A signal delivered by motor cycle was received at Montjoie instructing the Squadron to reassemble at Boulogne 'with all dispatch'. The serviceable aircraft left for home and two unairworthy Tiger Moths were disabled and abandoned together with some of the transport. After some noisy and nervous days in and around the port, the personnel of 81 Squadron returned to Dover Harbour on board the SS *King George V,* a MacBrayne steamer from Oban, whose inbound cargo of ammunition they had helped to unload at full speed. Although some of the aircraft returned to Andover, 81 Squadron regrouped at Hendon, to be officially disbanded there on 15th June, only to reform on 29th July 1941 equipped with Hawker Hurricane IIBs in preparation for a posting to Russia.

The evacuation of the unique Tiger Moth Squadron from France had been agreed by Air Vice-Marshal Charles Blount, AOC of the Air Component, after his Command had all but ceased to exist. The Air Marshal was persuaded to fly himself home in a Tiger Moth found abandoned amongst a collection of Bristol Blenheims and Westland Lysanders after the basic controls of the aircraft, a type he had never flown, had been explained to him, and an army greatcoat squabbed into the seat pan to replace the unavailable parachute. His overall emotions on landing safely at Hawkinge can only be imagined.

For its initial allocation, 18 new Tiger Moths were posted to 81 Squadron, all of which are thought to have served in France. A further 10 aircraft were posted in during March and May 1940 which permitted five of the first batch, N9154-N9158 (82273-82277), to fly back to England for servicing at 6 MU Brize Norton.

One of the replacement aircraft, N9433 (82487), collided with a tree on arrival in France on 11th March and was written off before handover. Eleven other aircraft were lost during the Expedition including two that were written off as the result of operational accidents, two that were deliberately burned at Arras, and one that went missing during operations on 20th May 1940, and might well have been the aircraft captured at Abbeville.

Three of the squadron aircraft survived their battle training and subsequent exposure to wartime conditions in England: N6847 (82102), was refurbished at 39 MU Colerne in July 1940 and took on standard duties with Flying Training Command until declared surplus in 1953. In 1958 and registered G-APAL, the aircraft was converted into the 16th Jackaroo at Thruxton, but was converted back into a Tiger Moth at Gransden in 1984. N6946 (82196), was operated by 24 Squadron at Hendon from October 1940 and served with various units until sale in 1955. Registered G-AOEI, for some years the aircraft has been operated on a Public Transport Certificate, uniquely offering *ab initio* training in company with G-AHIZ (86533), with the Cambridge Flying Group, based at the old 22 EFTS aerodrome, Teversham, now Cambridge airport.

N6965 (82203) also served with 24 Squadron at Hendon immediately after she was relinquished by 81 Squadron, and then completed the rounds: Northolt Station Flight, 418 Squadron with their Douglas Boston III at Bradwell Bay, and 488 Squadron with de Havilland Mosquitos at West Malling. N6965 maintained her Mosquito connection when she was posted to 13 Operational Training Unit (OTU) at Middleton St George in December 1945. In conditions of drizzle and poor visibility on 11th March 1946 the aeroplane was being flown by the unit's Senior Air Staff Officer (SASO), Christopher Paul:

'The Tiger Moth became my early morning jaunt: it was my custom, after my morning half hour, to land the aeroplane on the small patch of usable grass outside the hangar in which she was kept. When the SW wind was right this could be done neatly, so that a slight swerve at the end of the minuscule landing run, and by cutting the engine just before finish, resulted in our arrival neatly, with engine stopped, just inside the hangar doors. It was of course sheer showing off, but the crew enjoyed it, and I was not above the belief that a little showmanship of the right kind can sometimes help in a Service which likes to see its commanding officers flying and enjoying it.

'This arrival at the hangar doors required a nicely judged approach over the roof of the hut in which the radar operators did their ground training. This produced no problems until one day they had erected a co-axial cable suspended between two low masts along the whole length of the building; as I afterwards found it ran about three feet above the top pitch of the roof. I found it by hitting the cable in such a way that it slid over the top of the Tiger Moth landing wheels, and acted as a splendidly efficient arrester cable; the only trouble was that it brought the Tiger Moth to a standstill about 20ft up, from which height it descended nose first.

'The immediate results were dramatic. The crash alarm went, the ambulance, fire crews and rescue teams sprang into lightning action, and the senior air traffic controller in the tower immediately rang my wife in our married quarter, and gave her a running commentary on proceedings. I myself, having descended with a bump had only one thought, which was to get out of the cockpit fast in case anything went on fire; in fact I was able to watch from a comfortable distance the very efficient operation of all the fire and rescue services which we took great pains to keep at concert pitch, for a Mosquito, for example, could go up, if things went wrong, very quickly.

'But the most serious immediate effect was that, by some means which only an electronic genius could explain, the radar people's co-axial cable had become tied up with the perimeter telephone circuit which went all round the airfield, and was in some way linked up to the station Tannoy system. We were all to become aware of this when the Tannoy began to recount to us, all over Middleton, in clear girlish voices, the conversation of two young women describing in uncensored detail their previous night out in Darlington. This incident happened when the AOC was away on leave; as Station Commander it was my duty to write on the accident report my opinion as to the reason, and responsibility. On this one, having got all the detail filled in, I wrote my own comments: "The pilot was showing off and is entirely to blame".'

Tiger Moth G-AOEI of the Cambridge Flying Group about to touch down in the classic three-point attitude. In military service as N6946, the aeroplane was a member of 81 Squadron in France during the opening phase of the Second World War. Norman Rivett

N6965 was sold by the RAF in 1947 and registered G-AJTW was operated by Short Bros from their factory at Rochester. The aircraft subsequently passed through a number of different hands until eventually she was allowed to go derelict. Rebuilt to qualify for a new C of A in 1988, G-AJTW's former history was recognised when the aircraft was painted in the wartime colours of 81 Squadron.

One of the most bizarre tasks Tiger Moths were called upon to perform, occurred between December 1939 and May 1940. In spite of the massive programme of re-armament embarked upon in 1938, the shadow factories and tens of thousands of new aircraft contracted by the multifarious government committees under the co-ordination of the Ministry of Aircraft Production (MAP), RAF Coastal Command had little in the locker with which to effect anti-submarine patrols within the vicinity of some of the country's biggest, busiest, most vital and vulnerable ports. It was known that Germany had pre-positioned its submarine fleet, and the sinking of the liner SS *Athenia* on the day war was declared, was a sobering reminder of the prospects for the future.

In an act of near desperation, a theory was devised which it was hoped would keep prowling submarines below periscope depth where they would be blind and relatively harmless. Working on the belief that any submarine commander would submerge at the sight or sound of an approaching aircraft, Coastal Command proposed to establish a number of units strategically stationed around the British coastline which would operate as non-aggressive, unarmed spotters and nuisances. It was appropriate that somebody coined the name *'Scarecrow'* to cover the proposed operations. There was precious little equipment to chose from, but given the nature of the task and the immediate availability of suitable aircrew from the Auxiliary Air Force and Volunteer Reserve, it was confirmed that there existed a stored adequacy of one type: the Tiger Moth.

The prime object of the units was the detection of submarines; their additional brief was to record the fullest details of all shipping and coastal movements. At first it was believed that resident Coastal Command squadrons would absorb the intake of new aircraft and assume the role. The planned locations reflected that view: Aberdeen, Dyce aerodrome, 612 Squadron (Avro Anson 1); Belfast, Aldergrove aerodrome, 224 Squadron (Lockheed Hudson); Liverpool/Birkenhead, Hooton Park aerodrome, 206 Squadron (Avro Anson I), posted in from Bircham Newton to supplement 502 Squadron, already on site sharing facilities with the Supermarine Spitfire Is of 610 Squadron. 217 Squadron (South West England and South Wales) was based at St Eval in Cornwall with a detachment of Avro Anson 1s at Carew Cheriton. Their brief was to cover the southern coast of the Gower Peninsula and much of the Cornish Peninsula within a 100 mile radius of Newquay. While the northern units would be watchful of the sea lanes leading to and from their major port facilities, those situated in the south west would be on the alert for submarines taking advantage of the shelter afforded by the myriad of coves and bays, conveniently situated adjacent to the North Atlantic ocean lanes.

Although the allocation of Tiger Moths was initiated on the disposition of Squadrons in September 1939, plans quickly changed, and instead of detachments, new, self contained units were formed to be known as Coastal Patrol Flights, with the exception of the addition of Glasgow, their operating bases remaining as forecast:

No.1 CPF - Aberdeen (Dyce)
No.2 CPF - Glasgow (Abbotsinch)
No.3 CPF - Hooton Park
No.4 CPF - Belfast (Aldergrove)
No.5 CPF - Carew Cheriton
No.6 CPF - St Eval

And what of operational equipment and policy? Each Flight was to operate with an establishment of nine Tiger Moths, all new and drawn from RAF Reserve storage. The only exception was No.6 CPF which was allocated ten impressed Hornet Moths, capable of longer duration exploratory flights around the rugged coastline and in considerably more comfort. There was no wireless, no offensive equipment with the exception of a Very pistol which together with a standard downward facing signalling light were the only method of communication. As additional emergency equipment, the Tiger Moths were to carry semi-inflated rubber rings in their lockers and two carrier pigeons in a basket strapped to the front seat. In the event of a ditching, the pilot was expected to record his position, attach the scroll to a thimble tied to a bird's leg, and release one or the pair before the aircraft sank, leaving the pilot to wallow in his Mae West and rubber ring.

With little time available and much to achieve, an element of confusion and awakening of the system had to be expected. Five officer pilots and five airmen were posted in to Abbotsinch from St Athan on 9th October 1939 with little knowledge of their purpose and no idea of the name of their unit. Nine days later, the Station Adjutant gave verbal instructions for the formation of No.2 Coastal Patrol Flight, although the Flight still had no aircraft. By 22nd October seven more airmen had arrived and the following day written instructions were received outlining their duties which were amplified by further instructions two days later.

In order to establish some degree of formality, and set up a Headquarters, the Flight requested paperwork and publications, but Abbotsinch refused to recognise their lodgers, believing them to come under the administrative authority of Leuchars. That station subsequently returned all requisitions, not recognising the Flight either, and suggesting it direct its enquiries elsewhere.

On 3rd November, three pilots travelled to 6 MU Brize Norton to collect a trio of Tiger Moths which were delivered on 6th November having spent the previous night at Hooton Park. Three more Tiger Moths were delivered from Brize Norton on 9th November and the final three, collected from 10 MU Hullavington on 19th November arrived at Abbotsinch the following day, having operated via West Freugh.

Meanwhile, a meeting with the Senior Naval Officer, Clyde, had identified duties and established the most appropriate areas in which No.2 CPF should operate: anti-submarine patrols in the Clyde Approaches and escort to the passage of armed merchant cruisers through the same waters.

The Flight's Commanding Officer, Pilot Officer Tillett, had his nine aeroplane establishment but no operational equipment, and sent urgent signals on 23rd November which resulted in the arrival and practical test of a consignment of Very pistols and cartridges three weeks later. With the end of the month looming and the Flight still non-operational, it was decided that in view of their wide area of responsibility, accurate fuel consumption figures would be essential for individual aircraft, and each was subsequently flown for one hour at 75mph and again at 90mph. With little else to do, Tillett advised all concerned that 'as there is time during the week to get in all the practice flying needed, the Flight is closed on Sundays'.

Two additional pilots arrived before the end of the year, directed straight from the Reserve system: Sergeant Perkins had flown 1,400 hours in Moths as a civilian instructor, and had attended an RAF elementary instructors' course, and Sergeant Carter could claim 200 hours. Neither had been awarded an RAF pilots' brevet, and both required instruction in formation flying and the daily routines expected of a Sergeant pilot posted to an operational unit.

In working up towards their first serious operation on 17th December, location of a convoy (which they failed to find) when detached to Prestwick, the CPF pilots were all encouraged to fly locally and familiarise themselves. Knowledge of landmarks could make all the difference between returning safely home and perhaps landing out, or worse. Abbotsinch was greatly affected by industrial haze and smoke generated by the nearby city of Glasgow, and November and December had already demonstrated how prone the area was to lingering shrouds of mist and fog.

Each CPF worked to the same basic plan under the operational title of 'AS' (Anti-submarine patrol). How this was achieved efficiently and economically was left to the initiative of the local commander, bearing in mind the limitations of the Tiger Moth as a patrol aircraft, and the scandalous lack of equipment. While all Flights operated each patrol with two aircraft, one to remain overhead the contact but making attempts to interest any conveniently positioned naval vessel by firing off recognised flare patterns, and the other to scurry back to base or the nearest facility in order to report, No.2 CPF put up three aircraft on each sweep. With an establishment of only six pilots, the scheme was impossible to maintain, but the theory was right: two aircraft were to remain on patrol for two hours whilst the third returned after an hour and a half. The returning pilot then briefed the second patrol as to the expected position in which to establish contact with the two aircraft still airborne, and waiting to be relieved. It was the only practical solution to having no wireless communication.

Unlike the pilots at Abbotsinch, amongst whom the Flight aircraft were rotated as required, the Aberdeen based pilots of No.1 CPF maintained close contact with individual aircraft, and always hunted in pairs. Their operations began on 14th December when Tiger Moths N6664 (3968) and N6800 (82070), took off at 1350 hours local time and landed an hour and 28 minutes later, having consumed 30 gallons of petrol to reach and return from a point some 25 miles south of Aberdeen. Absolutely everything seen then and on all subsequent patrols was noted in meticulous detail: every vessel of whatever size, patches of oil, floating debris. Two or even three patrols were undertaken every day: the early afternoon sweep was expected to be fairly routine, but it was during the dawn and dusk patrols that submarines were more likely to be found on the surface.

Only nine days after their initial operation, the Flight's Commanding Officer, Pilot Officer Child, together with Pilot Officer Hoyle, had been on early morning patrol for 20 minutes when from a point about one mile off shore, Hoyle noticed what appeared to be a flashing light. He turned the Tiger Moth towards the source and as he approached the light disappeared to be replaced by a much brighter light nearby which was exposed and extinguished several times, and appeared to be transmitting 'S' in Morse Code. Hoyle took N6841 'TA' down to 25ft, and having established the source as a house, flew round it several times noting its position, layout and identifying features such as the shape of the roof and chimney stacks, all of which detail was passed on to the local police after landing.

It was Pilot Officer Hoyle who answered the challenge of a patrolling Avro Anson at 0800 hours on Christmas Day by firing off the colours of the day, but on 25th January 1941 he used his Very pistol in anger for the first time. Having sighted what seemed to be a drifting line of oil on the water, Hoyle established that its source appeared to be bubbling up from below the surface. By firing off green flares and repeatedly diving on the spot, he managed to attract the attention of a destroyer 'F22' which arrived overhead the source 20 minutes later and dropped a pattern of depth charges. The explosions resulted in the appearance of considerably more oil accompanied by large air bubbles, and shortly after the destroyer signalled 'AAA', (proceedings now at an end), at which point the circling aircraft returned to Dyce.

Tiger Moths 'TA' and 'TJ' (N6845), were back on early patrol the next morning. Some of the Flights worked a roster which required the late patrollers to sleep at dispersal and fly the dawn patrol too, after which the crews had a whole day to themselves, to be disturbed only in the case of an extreme emergency. Tiredness and monotony are believed to have lulled two pilots from Abbotsinch into momentary sleep. One of them hit the sea with both mainwheels causing waterspouts which were observed by the coastguard on the shore, and a belief that the aircraft was dropping bombs. On another occasion an aircraft returned to base with ribbons of seaweed wrapped around the tailskid. Neither pilot could remember anything about either incident.

The first northern winter of the Second World War was one of the worst on record and even the hardened Tiger Moth pilots of the CPFs were grounded for days on end. No patrols could be flown from Dyce between 27th January and 7th February. The nights were so cold that engines could not be started, and on one morning at Hooton Park, the engineers started swinging at 0830 hours and finally succeeded in running up at 1100 hours. Abbotsinch decided to leave arc lights near the aircraft all night to provide security and a source of directable heat.

No.3 CPF at Hooton Park and No.4 at Aldergrove had evolved into operational units along much the same paths as those experienced in Scotland. No.3 CPF flew its first patrols from Hooton Park at 0800 hours and 1350 hours on 1st December, and apart from authorised shipping had nothing to report. Bad weather caused strings of cancellations: fog and snow and intense cold all took their toll. Engines could not be started and aircraft standing in the open at dawn were susceptible to complete coating in rime ice. There was no flying at all during the first week of February when the aerodrome disappeared under deep snow drifts. The engineers busied themselves with a programme of engine runs and also tried to alleviate the problem of sea spray freezing on the aircraft by applying a proprietary Kilfrost paste to all leading edges. Although this had some benefit if it was renewed on a routine basis, the chemical reaction damaged alloy parts and on 26th February, N6779 (82043) was fitted with a new oil tank and N6780 (82044), with a pair of new slats.

Six Tiger Moths had been delivered to Aldergrove from Little Rissington on 13th November for use by No.4 CPF, but two weeks later they were still operationally ineffective due to the lack of equipment, quite apart from the state of the aerodrome surface which rendered it completely unserviceable. A change of policy resulted in the entire Flight moving to Hooton Park in December where they maintained their identity but operated in parallel with No.3 CPF very much on the basis of a squadron. The six new Tiger Moths which had never flown an operation were ferried to Silloth on 4th December but due to poor visibility, low cloud and heavy rain, they put down for a convivial night in Blackpool.

Still nominally non-operational, No.4 CPF loaned pilots on a short term basis to Aberdeen whose manifest gratitude was exemplified by the loan of equipment to get two aircraft into an operational condition on 18th December, on which day No.4 CPF's last three establishment Tiger Moths were delivered, all arriving from Little Rissington.

The New Year started badly when the first patrol of 1940 took off into poor visibility which suddenly deteriorated even further. The pilot of N6722 (3995), lost sight of the aerodrome and attempted to land in a ploughed field whose surface was heavily disguised by snow. The Tiger Moth turned over, breaking all four wings, the rudder, centre section and propeller. It was considered expeditious to effect repairs on site, although the necessary spares did not arrive until 18th January.

All CPF pilots complained about the insidiously creeping cold and the constant draught experienced in their open cockpits. The front windscreens were removed as an experimental measure and although this did reduce the turbulence around the rear cockpit, it also steered an icy blast more piercingly into that same position. Circulating draughts also picked up the loose contents of the carrier pigeon baskets and channelled them into the pilot's face, causing cases of sickness due to sore eyes and throats. Just after take off from Dyce on 21st May, Pilot Officer Cole received the full impact of wood shavings and droppings, some of which managed to evade the protection of his goggles and affected his eyes, forcing him into an immediate return to land. The pigeon passengers were the cause of the denial of a request to allow the front cockpit to be faired over, a simple enough exercise which would have improved conditions immensely.

The wide spread of flying experience amongst the hastily assembled pilots was demonstrated by an incident on 27th February when two crews from No.3 CPF were returning to Hooton Park after their uneventful evening patrol. Pilot Officer Hodgkinson and Sergeant Galt encountered conditions of practically zero visibility, and Hodgkinson immediately put down in a small field on the coast. Galt made six attempts to land in the same field but a lack of experience in the necessary forced landing technique prevented a safe touchdown. Hodgkinson recognised the problem and took off again, shepherding the other aircraft back to Hooton Park in near blind conditions, and a safe landing just after dark.

The sun was just setting at Aberdeen on 14th April as Pilot Officer Child landed back in his N6664 'TB' after a patrol of two hours and 20 minutes, but with nothing to report. The action had started with Pilot Officer Hoyle taking off on his afternoon patrol at 1350 hours in N6841 'TA' and observing a periscope. Having fired off his green Very lights he sighted a second periscope, and both remained tantalisingly above the surface while he continued to circle completely impotent for 15 frustrating minutes. Having been alerted, Pilot Officer Burgess in N6800 'TH' took off to join 'TA' for about 40 minutes before Hoyle returned to base. Burgess was in turn joined and relieved by Pilot Officer Boyes flying N6711 'TD' before Child arrived to round off the day. Hoyle, Boyes and Child each uplifted 15 gallons of petrol on return to Aberdeen, but the refuellers were able to deliver the maximum capacity of 19 gallons to the tank on 'TH', somewhat to the concern of her pilot.

The exercise proved a number of points. The endurance without long range tanks was insufficient, although whether or not the crew could have coped with longer patrols, especially in poor conditions, was open to debate. The need to fly Tiger Moths in pairs to maintain some degree of flexible communication and security whenever possible was valid. Had the enemy now been advised that they were in no danger from Tiger Moths with no teeth? On 14th April two probable targets had been allowed to escape. CPF pilots had always been aware of the impossibility of sighting a submarine once it had slipped below the surface of the waters surrounding the British coastline, and in spite of a positive double sighting and intensive effort, nothing further was ever heard.

Having suffered some of the most atrocious weather conditions ever experienced on the north west coast of England, the CPF pilots based at Hooton Park received an issue of electrically heated Sidcot suits on 10th March 1940. Their standard mode of protective dress was described as a Sidcot, a monkey suit, three pairs of gloves, a balaclava under the helmet and a Mae West and parachute harness. In 1942, David Masters wrote quoting the Commanding Officer of No.1 CPF saying of his duties: *'It was exceptionally hard to turn one's head let alone get at the signal pistol and flares, but all this difficulty was well worth while because the uninterrupted view from the back seat of a Tiger Moth could not be beaten, and the aircraft could be flown slowly'.*

The arrival of heated clothing was somewhat ironic in view of a decision taken to supplement Nos.3 and 4 CPFs with impressed civilian DH.87B Hornet Moths which began to trickle through from 22nd January, much to the astonishment of Pilot Officer E H Fuller of 4 CPF who received G-ADKH on 14th February.

Retired from RAF training duties at Woodley in 1946, N9241, formerly of No.2 CPF and the Torpedo Training Unit at Abbotsinch, moved a few miles along the Great Western main line, to White Waltham, where as G-AIRK with the West London Aero Club she remained active on the training fleet until 1960. Raymond Rayner

The Thanet Aero Club at Lympne received G-AHLT in 1946, once N9191 on the establishment of No 6 CPF Carew Cheriton. Damaged in 1957, restoration to airworthiness took 40 years. Charles Holland

Following serialisation as W5747, application of camouflage and installation of a First Aid satchel, Fuller flew the first *Scarecrow* Patrol by a Hooton Park Hornet Moth on 16th March. In civilian life, Edward Fuller had owned the same aircraft at Heston.

No. 1 CPF made a final patrol on 28th May 1940 after which duties were assumed by armed Westland Lysanders and an increased fleet of Avro Ansons of Coastal Command, aircraft with longer range and provision of some degree of comfort for the crew. No. 2 CPF stood down at Abbotsinch at the end of the month, like her sister unit at Aberdeen having operated only Tiger Moths through the worst of the weather until the spring when eight DH.87B Hornet Moths requisitioned for *Scarecrow* duties had been allocated to them. Although more comfortable than a Tiger Moth and with a considerably extended range, the Hornet Moths were not well received in the *Scarecrow* role due to the blanketing effect on downward vision caused by the proximity of the lower wings and the semi-opaque nature of scratched windscreens and side windows. Tiger Moths were never withdrawn during the lifetime of the *Scarecrow* operation.

Hornet Moths in greater profusion were taken on charge with Nos.3 and 4 CPFs at Hooton Park and 22 of the type eventually worked alongside the establishment of 18 Tiger Moths until both units were disbanded in May 1940. The weather in late March had seen a procession of deep Atlantic depressions sweeping across the country bringing low cloud, heavy squalls, poor visibility and gale force winds. The Hornet Moths were thought better able to survive in such conditions, and Tiger Moths were banned from operating whenever a gale warning was in force.

A famous party trick exploited by barnstorming circus pilots and hard bitten instructors alike was the ability to hover a biplane when headed into a strong, steady wind. While learning to fly at Carlisle, Iain Dick well remembers the performances which took place during the early morning weather check. Almost immediately after an apparently normal take off, the Tiger Moth seemed to stop and maintaining its climbing attitude, was lifted vertically upwards. At about 500ft the pilot levelled out and the aircraft flew backwards against the wind, its airspeed being less than the wind speed, until it reached the down-wind boundary when it dipped down and landed on the spot alongside a group of airman who had been pre-positioned to catch the wingtips.

Carew Cheriton had received its establishment of nine Tiger Moths for No.5 CPF by 21st December 1939, although N9337 (82424), had been lost on 15th November when the aircraft was ditched into the sea off the South Wales coast at Tenby during her delivery flight, and was almost immediately replaced by N9441 (82495), which arrived on 2nd December. The Tiger Moth strength was eventually increased to eleven and these were joined by six Hornet Moths in mid-January and another trio in March, all of which attempted to operate in pairs for standing patrols timed at 0530 hours, 1000 hours and 1930 hours every day. They meshed with the activities of No.6 CPF based at St Eval across the Bristol Channel, and although nine new Tiger Moths were allocated only three weeks before the unit disbanded on 27th May, it is unlikely they were ever delivered. No.6 CPF flew ten impressed Hornet Moths around the coastline on five pre-determined routes from early February 1940.

During the six months of operation, although there had been some engine problems, not surprisingly in view of the environmental conditions in which the aircraft were dispersed and expected to fly, and in spite of the very high percentage of flight time spent cruising at relatively low level, no Tiger Moth or Hornet Moth was lost at sea. But two of the Scottish based aircraft were lost, over land, on consecutive days, and within a relatively few hours of the Flights' disbandment.

On 26th May, Tiger Moth N9202 (82319), of No.2 CPF left Abbotsinch in darkness just after 0400 hours in order to be on station at dawn. Heading out over Ladyland Moor, the pilot took late evading action to avoid entering a low lying cloudbank, and the aircraft's wingtip hit the ground. The pilot was injured but the aircraft was wrecked. The Commanding Officer thought that the pilot, a relatively senior officer who had trained at Cranwell, should, with his experience, have decided to fly round the cloud somewhat earlier.

The following day, Tiger Moth N6785 (82055), up from Dyce, was engaged in an afternoon's exercise of forced landing practice near Fintroy, when she stalled off a steep gliding turn and flew into the ground, killing the pilot. Another CPF Tiger Moth flew over the scene shortly after the accident and her crew reported very severe downdraughts which were thought to have contributed towards the accident.

David Masters summed up the Coastal Patrol Flights in his 1942 book *So Few*:

'There was nothing spectacular about the Scarecrow Patrols, nothing to win high honours. Of the six pilots who formed the first flight, three alas are no more. But the amateur pilots who joyfully risked their lives without question for day after day flying far out to sea, sitting in open cockpits exposed to all the rigours of a terrible winter, until fully-armed aircraft were manufactured to take up the task, won, by their quiet confidence and their physical endurance, a worthy place in British history'.

Having relinquished them to the distribution system, the subsequent rate of attrition amongst ex-CPF aircraft was no worse than for any other group, and they suffered their share of accidents during the next decade. N6719 (3992), previously with No.4 CPF at Hooton Park was posted to No.1 Anti-Aircraft Co-operation Unit and with great irony was lost when she hit the sea in January 1942 when low flying off the Norfolk coast at Weybourne, a Queen Bee launch site. Another Tiger Moth from No.4 CPF N6722 (3995), was actually converted into a Queen Bee but crashed on landing at her control centre at Manorbier in June 1944. Two Tiger Moths from No.3 CPF were abandoned in flight: N6724 (3997), during an aerobatic sortie when operating with 29 EFTS at Clyffe Pypard in January 1943 and N6726 (3999), when she suffered a control jam in April 1945, also on the establishment of 29 EFTS at the time.

One time Carew Cheriton Tiger Moth N6798 (82068), dived into the ground at Croy, Inverness-shire, in December 1942 when serving with No.2 Air Gunners School, and another machine not to reach an EFTS, which may not have served as a CPF aircraft at St Eval either, Tiger Moth N9196 (82313), was abandoned overhead that same airfield in January 1941 as the result of bad weather when operating with No.1 Photographic Reconnaissance Unit.

And what of the remaining Tiger Moths which had spent the first six months of their active lives gallantly defending the British coastline? Twenty were relocated to 11 EFTS Perth after overhaul at 45 MU Kinloss and six more found their way to 4 EFTS Brough. The remaining 25 were scattered around the system: 14 went to British based flying schools and the others joined a miscellany of Flights, Squadrons and Units. A total of 21 ex-CPF Tiger Moths survived their military service to be sold 'as standing' in conformity with the prevailing disposals policy, and seven of those subsequently endured almost half a century of civil ownership:

N6720 (3993), No.4 CPF Hooton Park, served with 11 EFTS Perth and a number of University Air Squadrons before recategorisation as an instructional airframe (7014M) in 1953, and served with Air Training Corps squadrons for almost 40 years. A rebuilding programme to airworthy condition was begun in 1993 at Gransden, Cambridgeshire.

N6730 (82003), No.3 CPF Hooton Park, served with a number of training units until 1951 and was one of the last active Tiger Moths in RAF service, retiring from No.2 Grading Unit at Kirton in Lindsey in June 1952. Converted for the German civil market in 1961, the aircraft was resold to Sweden in 1976, and as SE-FNA is currently a non-flying exhibit at the Svedinos Bil Och Flygmuseum at Ugglarp.

N6779 (82043), No.4 CPF Hooton Park, suffered a number of accidents during service at 11 EFTS Perth, but ended her RAF career with two years at Station Flight, West Raynham. She was acquired by the Wiltshire School of Flying at Thruxton in July 1954, and was one of 15 Tiger Moths sold at £80 each to Peter Schulte in West Germany. Registered D-EDON and used by the Flugsportvereinigung Speyer at Birkenheide until 1969, the aircraft was rebuilt to static condition, painted in camouflage colours as DE623, and has been on display at the Auto Techniks Museum at Sinsheim since 1988.

N6849 (82104), No.1 CPF Dyce, spent the remainder of her RAF career at 11 EFTS Perth, and was one of the first Tiger Moths in April 1946 to be sold into the civil market via the Royal Aero Club. Registered G-AHRV and operated by a number of owners until 1967, the aircraft was sold to Denmark as OY-DNR in December 1968. The engine failed on take off during a filming session for a Swedish television channel in November 1974, and the damaged aircraft which was not repaired, was put into store at Greve Strand until sold to an airline pilot based in Israel at the end of 1998.

N9128 (82247), No.5 CPF Carew Cheriton, was sold in the 1946 disposal having spent over four years with 11 EFTS Perth and a few months at Cranwell. Registered G-AHLT and operated by the Thanet Aero Club at Lympne, she crashed into trees near Hythe in June 1957 and was not repaired. Acquired by Roger Bailey in 1974, a complete restoration was completed for the aircraft to fly again in 1997.

N9191 (82308), No.6 CPF St Eval, was probably never delivered, and instead spent time at Duxford and Sealand before joining Technical Training Command at Locking for two years from October 1941. After six years in storage with 20 MU Aston Down, she was sold in March 1949 and registered G-ALND to lead a varied life as a professional school trainer, group owned aircraft and circus

One of a number of different casualty evacuation conversions applied to Tiger Moths, in which fuselage space under the rear decking, sometimes including the rear cockpit, was re-engineered to accept a stretcher. This RAAF conversion dates from September 1945. RAAF Museum

This ambitious conversion to ambulance role included provision of a new fixed windscreen and enclosed cockpit for the pilot. RAAF Museum

performer. Severely damaged in an accident on take off in March 1981, the aircraft was sold as a long term restoration project in 1990.

N9241 (82336), No.2 CPF Abbotsinch, joined the Torpedo Training Unit at Abbotsinch before transferring to training duties at Woodley and eventual sale in August 1946, to become G-AIRK with the West London Aero Club at White Waltham, an organisation founded very largely by ex members of the ATA. Converted for use as a crop-sprayer in 1961 and a film prop for *The Blue Max* in 1965, she was sold to a small group in Suffolk in 1966, under whose guiding hand she remains fully operational.

Andover aerodrome was used to the sight and sound of itinerant Tiger Moths by May 1941. Station Flight was host to two examples already, including T7359 (83669), which later went on to a Pilots' Advanced Flying Unit (PAFU). She was sold onto the civil market as G-AHRX in 1946, ending her days with the Oxford Aeroplane Club in 1953 when she lost the argument with a fence during take off from Kidlington. R5135 (83017), arrived to join Station Flight on 23rd May and N9386 (82456), touched down four days later. Together with the resident Miles Magisters, the Station Flight aircraft were required to operate regular patrols within an eight mile radius of the airfield seeking out 'action of an obvious nature by enemy agents'. Trying to locate the proverbial needle in the haystack might have been easier, but no doubt the occasions provided some relief to the crews. R5135 moved on to 15 PAFU in company with T7359 on 21st June 1943 where she was damaged beyond what was then considered to be economical repair on 20th September 1944. N9386 served with No.7 Anti-Aircraft Co-operation Unit and 289 Squadron from the end of 1943, supporting Miles Martinets from Catterick until the Squadron re-equipped with the Vultee Vengeance in May 1945 and moved to Acklington. N9386 was sold from 12 MU Kirkbride in 1951 and was almost certainly used as a source of spares in Blackpool.

Unlike the pilots of the British Coastal Patrol Flights in 1940 amongst whose enemies were extreme cold and frustration, obstacles of a different nature confronted the patrolling Tiger Moths of No.5 Coastal Defence Flight (CDF), Royal Indian Air Force Volunteer Reserve, in October 1942. Based at Cochin on Willingdon Island, South India, the Flight's establishment of two DH.86s and a pair of Westland Wapities was allocated to shipping and anti submarine sweeps while two Tiger Moths flew regular beach patrols searching for signs of Fifth Column infiltration. Many other coastal areas were shadowed by CDFs operating Tiger Moths and a veritable mix of additional aircraft types. The Tiger Moths of No.5 CDF were ideally suited to their task, and on many occasions were able to put down on the sandy beaches when faced with ferocious storm activity which brewed sullenly over the Arabian Sea.

Patrols ranged equidistantly about 125 miles north to Cannanore and south to Trivandrum. A task on 1st October was to fly a naval officer to Trivandrum to interview the captain of the SS *Camilla*. The ship had been discovered drifting and ablaze by another aircraft from the Flight a few days before, and together with lifeboats had fetched up on the beach where an aerial survey conducted by low flying Tiger Moth had confirmed her to be a total loss. The ship's crew was later to explain how they had been attacked by gunfire from a surfaced submarine.

The coastal storms were, on occasions, so severe that the aircraft were forced to take shelter on the nearest beach for hours at a time to allow torrential rain to move away. Forced landings following attempts to resume patrols interrupted by weather and unserviceability due to water in the carburettor were common occurrences. A brief diversion on 21st November was the carriage of spare parts almost 200 miles inland to Salem where a Wapiti had forced landed. It was a passing interlude for only five days later the Tiger Moths were flown over 1,200 miles to join a Communications Flight in Calcutta, while Cochin was formalised as an RAF Station, and the coastal defence duties were taken over by detachments of 353 Squadron flying Lockheed Hudson IIIAs.

The evacuation of wounded troops from positions close to the front line has always demanded priority, and the prospects of operating light aircraft into forward strips with a view to airlifting out serious cases was viewed with interest as the Allied armies moved forward during the latter stages of the war in Asia. Two schemes to employ Tiger Moths in this role were developed after 1944, almost certainly independently of one another, but following exactly similar methods.

While Tiger Moths in standard configuration could cope with wounded soldiers capable of sitting normally, it was those who were completely incapacitated that had to be moved quickly, and therefore the aeroplanes chosen required conversion or modification to the total satisfaction of that need. With careful remodelling of the Tiger Moth decking aft of the rear instrument panel and deletion of the rear cockpit, it was possible to create a platform on the tapering rear fuselage frame, using the top longerons, capable of accepting a stretcher. Protection of the patient was then possible by design of a new superstructure which hinged, or unbolted completely, for ease and care of loading.

The Australian Army required an aerial evacuation system towards the end of 1944 when they returned to the offensive in New Britain and New Guinea, where Tiger Moths could be operated at low level into small airstrips hastily hacked out of the jungle within sight of the enemy.

The first full conversion of a Tiger Moth to the ambulance role undertaken on behalf of the RAAF was relatively simple. A17-57 (DHA 54), was modified by removing the first six feet of rear decking, including the luggage locker, and building a lightweight tapered frame with cross webbing, a Norcom Stretcher, which filled the entire created space including that of the redundant rear cockpit. A modified rear decking built to the original profile was then latched down onto the top longerons. The patient's head was left exposed at a cutout where the rear instrument panel would have been, and he was restrained by a wide webbing belt laterally across his thighs, and a four strap Sutton harness placed conventionally across shoulders and stomach. The system was crude but effective although A17-57 appears to have been used for Australian based trials only, selected as a willing volunteer possibly, during a nominal allocation to storage at Temora.

The best known ambulance conversion was A17-450 (DHA655), which had passed through Laverton in April 1945. Following the installation of long range tanks at Breddan, the aircraft had been dismantled and shipped to Nadzab in New Guinea for service with No.8 Communications Unit (CU) based at Madang, an organisation formed from what was previously No.1 Rescue and Communications Squadron (RCS). The Unit operated eleven different Tiger Moths in its time and A17-450 was one of the last four, sold locally for £200 in April 1946. No.9 Communications Unit at Port Moresby in New Guinea, and later Lae, flew a total of eight Tiger Moths from November 1943 until November 1944 when their last aircraft, Mascot's much publicised A17-565 (DHA1,000), was returned to storage in Australia.

A17-180 (DHA181), was converted into an air ambulance at Laverton in June 1945, the final touch being to spray her 'foliage green' overall, but following installation of a long range fuel tank at Breddan in August the aircraft was placed into storage without allocation, and sold for £100 in September 1946. Acquired by Connellan Airways at Alice Springs and registered VH-BAA, she was operated as a civilian air ambulance in company with a similarly converted Tiger Moth, VH-BIW (DHA978). This second aircraft, formally A17-543, used the same basic principles of a stretcher mounted on the top longerons, and a detachable rear decking, but a more spacious hinged hood with windows which completely enclosed the patient and front seat pilot, mating with a tall wraparound windscreen. The aircraft had preceded A17-180 from conversion at Laverton to Breddan, also for long range tank installation, but was delayed there, placed into storage, and sold for £100 in September 1946.

A17-450 would have been starting her tour of duties in New Guinea as both A17-180 and A17-543 were receiving their extra tankage at Breddan, and the reasons for the change of plan which directed both ambulance aircraft into storage are unknown. Eleven possible reasons were that A17-450 was found to be unsuited to operations in the field, always a possibility, even considering the versatility of the aeroplane and the period of trialling in Australia. The ten other reasons were the Tiger Moths which had received long range tankage at Breddan, but probably little else by way of ambulance conversion, and had been flown as a group, shepherded by an Avro Anson, 2,500 miles north, heading for Jaquinot Bay in New Britain.

It was a grand adventure: the aircraft left Breddan on 3rd April 1945 and nine of them arrived near their destination 49 days later. At the last minute the group was re-routed further north to Tadjj due to the uncertainty of whose troops held the landing strip. The tenth aircraft, A17-506 (DHA929), had been abandoned at Atkinson Strip, near Milne Bay in New Guinea after turning over during transit for refuelling, and was later dismantled for spares at Port Moresby. The aircraft had probably been intended to reinforce Nos.8 and 9 CU, although No.33 Squadron RAAF also operated a total of 18 Tiger Moths at various locations in New Guinea between December 1942 and January 1945.

A17-489 (DHA912), operated by 12 Local Air Supply Unit (LASU) based at Aitape, New Guinea from April 1945, and coded TA-L, was commissioned to fly the Japanese Commander, Lieutenant General Hatazo Adachi, from Cape Wom to Kiarivu on 14th September 1945, following the surrender of Japanese forces in the region.

Elsewhere, as the South East Asia campaign moved into Burma, the need for casualty evacuation from the front line was equally well recognised by the RAF, and a similar arrangement to that employed by the Australians in the conversion of A17-57, but pre-dating it, was applied to six Tiger Moths in India late in 1943. The whole of the rear decking was reconstructed to shield a patient strapped onto a plywood baseboard, occupying space from the stripped out rear cockpit towards the tail. The aircraft was flown from the front seat which maintained its open cockpit configuration.

The conversion and trials flying were completed at the RAF's Research and Development Unit at Cawnpore, and the Tiger Moths were operated by 224 Group Communications Squadron, notionally based at Chittagong, and in some reports referred to as the Air Ambulance Detachment of the 3rd Tactical Air Force Communications Squadron. Exactly which six aircraft were converted is not recorded, but DG456 was photographed at Cawnpore during trials, and is believed to be one of a group of Indian civil aircraft requisitioned in 1941, and struck off charge without explanation in December 1944.

Her sister aircraft DG455, had remained with 1 EFTS at Begumpet since impressment and was not selected for ambulance duties. During an aerobatic sortie on 22nd May 1945, the engine fell out. The pilot managed to regain some measure of control but the aircraft crashed at Shaikpet and was written off.

RAAF Tiger Moth ambulance A17-543 was commissioned in June 1942 and remained in that configuration following civil acquisition by Connellan Airways in 1948, operating an essential community service centred on Alice Springs. Neville Parnell

DG493, another conversion from an impressed civil aircraft is known to have overshot a forward landing ground at Bongya on 11th November 1944, damaging the undercarriage and causing the aircraft to be abandoned on site.

A year after the action around some of the remote reaches of the River Kaladan in Arakan, a report published in Great Britain coincided with the award of the Distinguished Flying Medal to Flight Sergeant J K Davies of Yorkshire, and the Distinguished Flying Cross to Warrant Officer M L Cecil of Western Australia:

'The story behind the work of these pilots began early in 1944 when the West Africans made their advance along the Kaladan and evacuation of the wounded became a problem. The answer lay in employing Tiger Moths and Fox Moths, modified to take stretcher cases. As the West Africans advanced, they built small landing strips in paddy fields or on dry river beds. These strips were never more than a few hundred yards from Japanese positions, and were almost continually under mortar or machine-gun fire. During engagements with the enemy a call would be sent back, and the ambulance pilots at once set out to pick up the casualties. Their journey, a little over 50 miles there and back, was mostly over enemy territory and entailed a double crossing of a 3,000ft high range of hills. Sergeant Davies and Warrant Officer Cecil flew an average of ten hours a day to evacuate wounded. Sergeant Davies flew over 100 sorties.

'At one position where casualties were being evacuated the enemy made an attack and the West Africans withdrew to another point. Wounded still remained to be evacuated, and the pilots flew in to pick them up until they were forced to stop. Even on that occasion, Warrant Officer Cecil insisted on his last run and taking in a pilot to fly out a damaged Tiger Moth, he collected the last casualties from the deserted strip under mortar fire, a few minutes before the Japanese arrived.

'Between 16th February and 8th May 1944, over 2,000 casualties were brought out to forward bases, where they were put into hospital or transferred to Dakotas and flown to the rear'.

The eventual withdrawal of the Tiger Moth from her primary role in the Royal Air Force in 1952 was the occasion for many to vent their opinions for and against what had become an institution, this clutter of technology with roots in the era of the First World War. The following thoughts were expressed by an RAF pilot who with thousands of others, had trained on Tiger Moths:

'The Tiger Moth will be missed chiefly, of course, by the old air dogs, those tough, nerveless instructors who were so much a part of their aircraft that they positively preferred to impart their instructional patter while hanging upside down in the straps. One could not but admire their ability, developed through long years of practice, to roll the Tiger Moth about a very small dot on the horizon; but for the novice, the slow roll was the grimmest trial of the lot. Mental preparation was useless, for by reading up beforehand the mechanics of the roll, outlined in half a page of close print detailing the succession of stick, rudder and throttle movement, the pupil was apt to be conditioned in a mood of despair before even attempting the manoeuvre. The time for doing aerobatics was usually chosen by the instructor to be in that part of the day when the morale and metabolic rate of the pupil was at its lowest; that is to say, immediately after breakfast, or after a long day's flying. It must be admitted that the condition of the pupil after five hours of bumpy flying was such as to excite compassion. His nerves, jarred by the incessant vibration, had gone completely numb. His brain was dulled by the scream of the wind about his head; and in his ears there was the high singing note left by the roaring of the engine. He was now entitled to a little quiet and relaxation. At this point the kindly instructor, who possessed a cast iron stomach, would gently insinuate himself into the consciousness of the pupil, and quietly suggest an hour's aerobatics before tea. He would ask his pupil what he was looking so glum about: Do you not like aerobatics? The pupil would choke back an oath, and restrain himself from yelling at his tormentor that the mere thought of them filled him with such a fierce loathing that to give proper expression to his feelings would entail resort to the use of language rivalling the most vitriolic excesses of an eighteenth century pamphleteer. Instead, he would merely crawl out to the Tiger Moth again. The system had him in thrall'.

Nostalgia being a marketable commodity, perhaps it was surprising that it took until 1984 for enterprise to surface at Staverton aerodrome, Cheltenham. The glossy brochure advertised a Nostalgia Holiday in the form of: *'Full board for the week in a purpose built Sergeant's billet (£145) or for an extra £100 per week languish in luxury in Officers' quarters. A full week's course of flying instruction on a Tiger Moth starts at £195. Sample the same sizzle of bacon and eggs before flying briefing, and the same tankards of fiery local brew after the sun has set and the Tiger Moths are silent'.* The business did have takers, but not enough to go into a second season.

Although designed, sold, bought and operated as a pilot training aeroplane, during the Second World War the Tiger Moth was enrolled into a wide diversity of essential military activities, all of which were, seemingly, accomplished with a minimum of effort. Such dexterity added immeasurably to the type's universal appeal, popularity and lasting affection: the very stuff of legend.

Student pilot Cyril Saward and much patched Tiger Moth N6983 of 6 EFTS Sywell about October 1939. All three Tiger Moths which appear in the photograph are at different stages in the camouflage change-over programme. Richard Saward

PERPETUAL PHOENIX

Just one more shot! After the official poses at Yatesbury early in 1940, there was time for another pass by the photographic Tiger Moth which took in the whole panoply of the station and the urgency of frail, frozen humans to seek the comforts of the NAAFI wagon. *Flight*

WITH THOUSANDS of Tiger Moths in use all over the world, operating in a variety of climates and under the guiding hands of every calibre of air and ground crew from polished professional to the newest recruits in 'the cooks and butchers air force', so described by a senior RAF Staff Officer, it should be no surprise that incidents and accidents occurred almost on a daily basis until the very end of the Tiger Moth's service life. There were many reasons: first solo and low time pilots bouncing their landings, ballooning and stalling into the ground with or without an undercarriage; pupils straying off the centreline of the flarepath during night training and colliding with other aircraft in the air or waiting to take off, and even vehicles and buildings shrouded by the darkness; aircraft being blown over after landing or during unaided taxying in strong winds or behind other larger aircraft with turning engines.

Forced landings as the result of getting lost, running out of fuel, engine misbehaviour or simply unauthorised practice, frequently resulted in Tiger Moths turning over after touching down on soft or otherwise unsuitable surfaces. Low flying, approved and not, letting off steam or relieving boredom, accounted for the disappearance of miles of telephone wires and electricity cables and the tops of trees and hedges all over the Empire.

Pilots used to higher performance aircraft were sometimes prone to take the Tiger Moth very much for granted, and as something of a toy, attempting to take off with most of the available runway behind them for example, or with extraordinarily heavy loads on board, and realising too late the approaching hedge could not be cleared, could do little but shut off the engine, metaphorically apply the brakes, and rely on the decelerating powers of the enveloping foliage. In post-war days, the cockpits of Tiger Club aeroplanes carried an additional placard: 'All aeroplanes bite fools'.

Ground crews were occasionally taken to task for bad handling when assisting with parking or taxying and the enduring problem of turning a propeller with the switches on, or mostly off, only to receive a crack over the hand, or worse, as the engine fired and the blade came powering round. And although they did their best in times of forecast gales and filthy weather, the engineers sometimes could do little but watch as aircraft were tossed into the air, picket lines flailing, as huge gusts, cyclones, 'willy willies' and revolving storms hit the dispersals, the damage compounded, especially in Australia and southern Africa, by torrents of destructive hail. In many cases it seems, whole replacement aircraft were easier to obtain than spare parts with which to apply the magic fix.

Ben French had been involved with Tiger Moths at Hatfield's Reserve School from the time the new type joined the establishment, and in 1939 when the aircraft were eventually forced to admit they were in the pay of the military, and took on coats of camouflage to disguise their distinguished colours of maroon and silver, French and colleagues were obliged to apply the first coverings

A not entirely unexpected occurrence at any time during the working day of a Reserve School. Tiger Moth G-ACDC over and out at Hatfield in 1938, sustaining standard damage in the process: undercarriage, rudder, propeller, cowlings and fuel tank. Ben French

using brushes and buckets of dope, and without dismantling any parts of the aircraft, such was the urgency. The undersides of the lower wings were painted by engineers lying on their backs on the hangar floor underneath the trestled airframes.

It was the duty of the senior engineers each evening to taxy some aircraft into their dispersed positions around the aerodrome, and at Hatfield, a favourite site was close by the shelter of a wooded area on the northern boundary. The practice was not without its local perils as Ben French explained:

'Dispersing the Tiger Moths gave rise to some fast taxying with tail up and only when the undercarriage began to bounce did warning bells ring and it was time to throttle back. Also at that time, a ridge ran across the aerodrome and it was imperative that speed was reduced before going over the top. With no brakes, a ditch and a wire fence awaited the unwary.

'We had an engineer, Fred, an ex Royal Flying Corps mechanic. To us youngsters, Fred was ancient and so short in stature that when sitting in the cockpit he could hardly reach the rudder pedals and could not see over the coaming. It was during one of our taxying trips when I was in formation with another engineer, that we were overtaken by a Tiger Moth on our starboard side, apparently pilotless and going at great speed. Suddenly the cockpit door dropped and we were greeted with a grinning Fred giving us a two finger salute. In his jollity Fred had forgotten the ridge, and as we taxied over the top we saw Fred having switched off the engine, endeavouring to evacuate the cockpit to throw himself over the tail. Unable to do so, his machine careered on towards two already parked machines. There was a loud crunching noise as the port and starboard wings took the tops off the rudders of the parked pair, causing extensive damage to all three.

'Fred claimed the throttle had stuck but the excuse was not accepted, and after spending unpaid overtime in trying to reduce the extent of the damage, assisted by some of his colleagues, Fred was handed his cards and shown out of the gate'.

Engineers at 14 EFTS Elmdon were also encouraged to disperse their Tiger Moths in the face of occasional hit and run attacks by lone enemy aircraft roaming the Midlands. Malcolm Carlisle flew his first solo at Elmdon although he was not allowed to log it as he was a civilian in a service aircraft, and the wheels should have remained on the ground:

'When we heard the alert, factory workers downed tools and took to the shelters. Myself and a few colleagues, instructors and senior pupils would scramble the parked Tiger Moths to disperse them around the airfield boundary. Engineers soon became dab hands at high speed taxying and after a number of such trips we had our tails up and ran on the mainwheels. We then progressed further by lifting the aircraft slightly off the ground! Our unorthodox taxying seemed to go unobserved except for one instance when we tried a return in Vee formation, and that manoeuvre earned us a blast from our Chief'.

Tiger Moth L6936 (3571), was involved in a collision with Hawker Hind K6669 at Prestwick on 23rd June 1939. The pilot of the Hind, surprised by the sudden appearance of a Tiger Moth under his nose, confused his engine ignition and bomb release switches and flipped the wrong one, fortunately without dropping live cookies and blowing everyone up.

At 17 EFTS Peterborough, the civilian ground crews were subjected to a verbal explosion by the Commanding Officer on 24th February 1942 when their uncoordinated ground handling managed to persuade the pilot of L6936 to taxy into parked Tiger Moth T7356 (83666). In 1943, L6936 was one of a number of Tiger Moths selected for conversion to Queen Bee configuration, and the aircraft was moved to the Pilotless Aircraft Unit at Manorbier in September. Although not converted, she suffered 'substantial damage' in November which took a month to repair in Barnstaple, and she subsequently returned to training duties with 21 EFTS at Booker from January 1944. The aircraft survived the war and as G-ANPK, a well publicised attack on a sea wall near Clacton in 1996. She is believed to be one of only four survivors of the 30 civil specification aircraft bought off the Hatfield line in 1937.

The entry into RAF service of Tiger Moth N6972 (82210), was less than auspicious. Delivered from Hatfield to Brize Norton on an English summer's day, 19th July 1939, the aircraft taxied onto a wet and slippery tarmac where she was hit by a gust. The ferry pilot could do nothing except wait for the inevitable as the aircraft skated over the surface and collided with a pair of petrol bowsers, watched by the ground crew who claimed the aircraft had arrived unexpectedly. Although badly damaged, N6972 was taken onto the books the following day but was not allocated to 18 EFTS Fairoaks until 22nd November 1940.

At school, life was full of incident. N6972 was waiting to take off on 11th April 1942 when another Tiger Moth, T5718 (83439), landing in poor visibility, undershot and fortunately for all concerned, collided with just the wingtips. Only four days later a 16 year old civilian was injured during a propeller swinging incident which caused the Station Rules to be re-written.

N6972 landed in a field at Effingham on 4th April 1945 and hit a post which caused the undercarriage to collapse. The pilot claimed he had been forced to land to satisfy the call of nature, and the station medical officer confirmed that the pilot did have a bladder problem and the claim was probably genuine. The aircraft was retrieved and temporarily housed in a blister hangar at the bottom end of the airfield alongside NL828 (86286), when a Bristol Beaufighter Mk X, NE347, operating with 455 Squadron, landed on the short runway in a light wind, skidded on the grass due to heavy braking, and ran into the hangar. N6972 survived the ordeal and after repairs, continued to fly for another two years when she was downgraded to an Instructional Airframe (6317M). On 1st August 1947 she left Newcastle on board the SS *Bonn*, bound for Oslo, a gift to the Royal Norwegian Air Force Collection at Gardermoen Air Force Base.

All thoughts of the war must have been far from the minds of two RAF officers as they enjoyed a spot of recreational flying in their Tiger Moth in the late afternoon sunshine of a day in mid-October 1939, meandering over the Firth of Forth. What subsequently occurred after a heavy aircraft buzzed them was described by A B Austin in his wartime salute to RAF Fighter Command:

'Probably the other pilot was being sportive. Entering into the fun of the thing, the pilot of the Tiger Moth dived on the big black aeroplane, zoomed up and dived again. It was rather like a wren playing tig with a hawk. But the stranger pilot did not seem to be so playful after all. Indeed he appeared to be moody, even a vicious fellow. As the Tiger Moth dived, something spat out of the black fellow's tail, and bullets whined past. Startled, the Tiger Moth turned sharply away, whilst the German bomber disappeared into a cloud. Probably the German crew were puzzled about the behaviour of the little British aeroplane which dived in true fighter fashion, and yet did not bother to fire'.

A single bomb fell onto the hard standing by the hangar at 14 EFTS Elmdon early in the war, but instead of exploding on contact, it ricocheted into the middle of the grass aerodrome and harmlessly blew a hole in the ground. One engineer expressed thanks for his salvation by suggesting with great seriousness, that he had been spared in order to continue stitching and patching the school Tiger Moths. To sound the all-clear, the duty officer strode to the middle of the tarmac with a Very pistol which he raised to full elevation and fired. Many eyes watched the coloured ball of flame as it soared skyward and then descended, still blazing.Unerringly, it fell into the rear cockpit of a parked and soon to be flaming Tiger Moth.

All the lights that were permitted to burn were suddenly extinguished in Henley-on-Thames one night early in 1940 as the result of a Tiger Moth pilot parachuting onto the local mains supply cable. The aircraft had been engaged in a night exercise from Woodley, and was using the Relief Landing Ground (RLG) near Shiplake. The ailerons had locked when a drive chain jumped off its sprocket in the wing box and jammed the system.

The problem had occurred before, and several modifications were made to British built Tiger Moths to improve the aileron control system, including Mods 56, 101, 125 and 138. Wing boxes built into Australian-made wings were never changed from the original design. Not until May 1945 at the request of the Ministry of Aircraft Production was Modification 134 raised, to seal the aileron gearbox and improve inspection facilities. The reasoning, said MAP, was quite simple: 15 cases of foreign bodies entering or being left in the aileron gearbox had been reported; jamming of the aileron and loss of control were the results!

The thrill of a first solo was, in the opinion of a pupil at 15 EFTS Carlisle, something to be savoured and exploited to the maximum. He made the excuse that a slightly imperfect three-point landing after his first solo circuit had prompted him to go around. During his second approach, the pilot became aware that the layout of the airfield and boundary appeared to have changed and he was only sure of his own position by the reassuring sight of the hangars and parked aeroplanes where he thought they ought to be. After landing and a ticking off by his instructor, the pilot discovered that while he was airborne, dummy hedges and shadows had been painted on the grass as part of an overall camouflage plan which had nearly caught him out.

Operating with No. 1 School of Army Co-operation at Old Sarum, N6856 (82111), was engaged in a triangular cross country flight around the Marlborough Downs on 27th September 1940, an area not renowned for navigational landmarks. The pilot, an escapee from Poland, became unsure of his position and when attempting a precautionary landing at Frobury Farm, Kingsclere, he became temporary confused and fully opened the throttle on landing, driving the aeroplane full tilt into a hedge. He explained later that throttles on Polish Air Force aircraft operated in the reverse sense. The aircraft was repaired at nearby Witney and banished to Perth where she remained operational with 11 EFTS until declared surplus in 1952.

Civilianised as G-ANLR and later operated by a co-ownership Group as a glider tug, instructional machine and tourer, the aircraft was intended to be flown during a Battle of Britain display at Wyton in September 1963 with a soldier standing in the front cockpit, restrained by a specially adapted long harness and firing blank cartridges as part of a spoof target shooting demonstration. During the take off run the soldier stood up but knocked off the ignition switches and the unexpected return to earth precipitated a bounce from which the aircraft cartwheeled and turned over. Reminiscent of her RAF days, in April 1966, G-ANLR was landed in a Norfolk field to allow the captain to ask his whereabouts, and although the landing was completely successful and the required information identified him as being only a few miles from his destination, the aircraft veered into a hedge when attempting to take off again and was substantially damaged.

In 1968, a survey of the Seaplane Club's Tiger Moth G-AIVW (83135), revealed a heavily corroded fuselage. The storeman at Rollason's Croydon hangar had just the thing as a replacement, and wheeled in the complete fuselage of G-ANLR. The rejuvenated Sea Tiger enjoyed another 14 years of a unique lifestyle on the south coast of England until August 1982 when in murky conditions which merged sky with the surface of the sea, she hit the water at Rye, Sussex, during a turn at low level, and the salvaged remains were rebuilt for static display at the Robertsbridge Aviation Society.

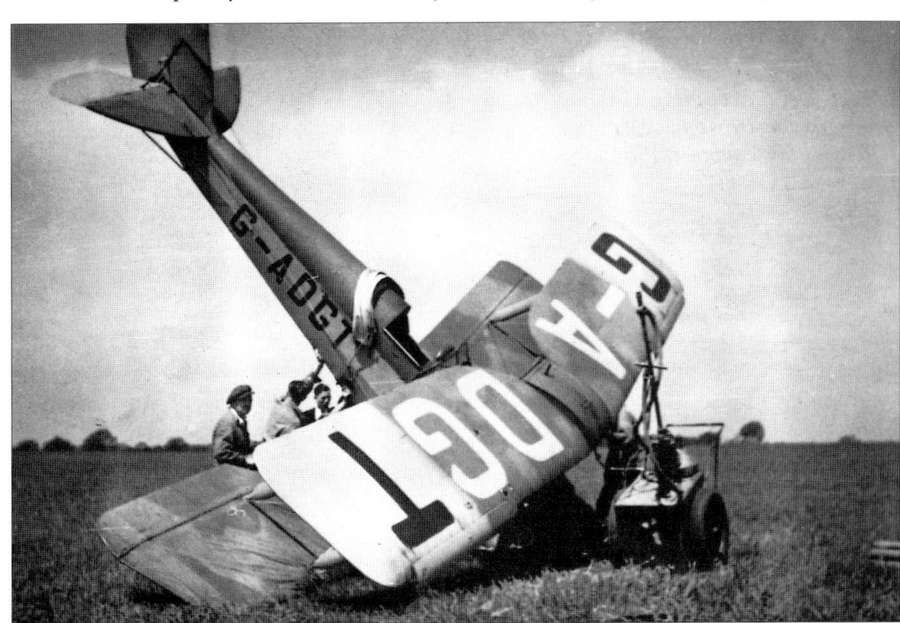

In the quasi-camouflage scheme of the day, Tiger Moth G-ADGT is very much nose down at Sywell, 31st May 1939. The rig on the right is defuelling the petrol tank while the civilian ground crew decide how the aircraft should be moved. deHMC Archive

With covered accommodation used only for maintenance, military Tiger Moths were mostly left out in the weather, and in Great Britain, the threat of invasion or surprise attack on airfields needed to be countered by night guards posted among the picket lines. At Sywell, Hatfield and other establishments, scrap cars were towed out onto the airfield at night to act as mobile obstructions, and pupil pilots were detailed off as guards and issued with ancient rifles complete with bayonets, but no ammunition. During one particular period at Sywell, it was believed aircraft were being sabotaged when each morning a number of innocent Tiger Moths were found with slashes in the fabric-covered undersurface of the top main-planes. Only after thorough investigation was it realised that the damage was being caused by bayonet tips when rifles were carried over the shoulders of the defending troops.

An all night guard utilising the services of reluctant pupil pilots was mounted at 15 EFTS Carlisle where armed patrols were also undertaken without the benefit of ammunition. During storm conditions one night, the guards could only watch as Tiger Moths picketed nose to wind, dragged their wing restraints out of the ground, but still secured by the tail, took off and landed on their backs. One pilot clung on to a propeller as the Tiger Moth was lifted bodily into the air, but let go just before the aircraft flipped over. About a third of the fleet was damaged that night before further assistance arrived from the main camp, and by morning it could be seen that a number of aircraft had suffered not only from the effects of the wind, but also from the efforts of the ground crews in attempting to claw them out of their airborne positions.

Pity the poor ground crew, working all hours to present serviceable aircraft when training was an urgent necessity. Engineers at 21 EFTS Booker, an airfield at high elevation on the edge of the Chilterns in Buckinghamshire, worked through the winter of 1940 carrying out daily inspections in an unheated T-type hangar, muffled up to their eyebrows in layers of clothing. Outside, the airfield was covered in snow and frost as the Tiger Moths were trundled to the tarmac ready for engine runs. The cold got into the engines and the propellers were hard to pull over. Rather than sit in the aircraft, the engineer on the switches stood alongside the cockpit with head and shoulders tucked well inside. When the engine fired and began running, he would adjust the throttle to a fast tickover, tighten the friction nut and stand well clear of what was an icy blast. A full power run-up was carried out as expeditiously as procedures would allow.

Taxying a Tiger Moth in a strong wind without outside assistance has, due to the geometry and load distribution of the aeroplane, always been hazardous, and in standard configuration quite impossible on a hard, smooth surface. Pity the pilot of DE315 (85349), taxying in a gusting wind at 25 EFTS Hucknall in February 1945 who thought a main wheel must have dropped into a hole. The moment he climbed out to investigate he could only watch in dumb horror as the aeroplane was lifted bodily by the wind and turned onto her back.

The pilot of DE715 (85645), taxying on tarmac in strong winds at 16 EFTS Burnaston in June 1942, waved away the wing walkers and was promptly blown into Miles Magister V1074. Post war on the establishment of 12 RFS at Filton, the same aeroplane, flown by a pilot who was unsure of his position and suffering from severe airsickness in turbulent conditions, put down at the first aerodrome to come into view: it was Exeter and unfamiliar territory. Too exhausted to await assistance after landing, DE715 was taxied slowly towards habitation until a gust picked her up and blew her over.

The following advice was penned by an accomplished Tiger Moth pilot with experience of operating the type in all conditions in most parts of the world:

'It is seldom realised that steering the aircraft is down to the helpers when there is wing tip assistance. If you are wing-walking a Tiger Moth watch the rudder and you will get a good idea where the pilot wants to go'.

Why was a pilot landing DE615 (85569), into a 40 knot wind at Fairlop in October 1942? Having touched down he waved away the handlers, took off again, landed on another runway and was promptly blown over. When the pilot was carpeted by his Commanding Officer, he was reprimanded against a charge of taking off (again) without permission!

For a comparison of wind speeds against experience the following is a reasonable summary:

- 0-5 knots: Suitable for all, especially if the wind is straight down the runway.
- 5-10 knots: Suitable for all but be alert for the possibility of wind shear.
- 10-15 knots: Suitable for experienced Tiger Moth pilots and low time pilots providing the wind is not gusting.
- 15-20 knots: Start to watch it. The aircraft rocks on the ground and slats pop out if they are left unlocked. Operate into wind only. When you taxy the aircraft, get help.
- 20-25 knots, with gusts: Now you have your hands (and feet) fully occupied. There is a good chance of being blown onto a wing tip. Get help.
- 25-30 knots: A situation for aces, idiots and emergencies only. Put the aeroplane back in the shed. It should not have been outside anyway.
- 30 plus knots: Get a quote in advance for major damage repairs.

Flying from 18 EFTS Fairoaks in July 1940, just after take off, Richard Davies and his instructor spotted a parachute in an adjacent field, attached to what appeared to be a cylinder. They circled and flew low over the object then returned to base to report their sighting. Later that afternoon while waiting for another sortie, the assembled crews witnessed a tremendous explosion: the object over which the Tiger Moth had made several low, slow passes in the morning, had been a land mine dropped during the night, and fitted with a delayed action fuse.

When a survey revealed that the fuselage of Sea Tiger G-AIVW was subject to salt water corrosion, the remedy was to replace it with the fuselage of Sea Tiger G-AIVW ! See page 105 and the story of N6856 / G-ANLR (82111). M J Hooks

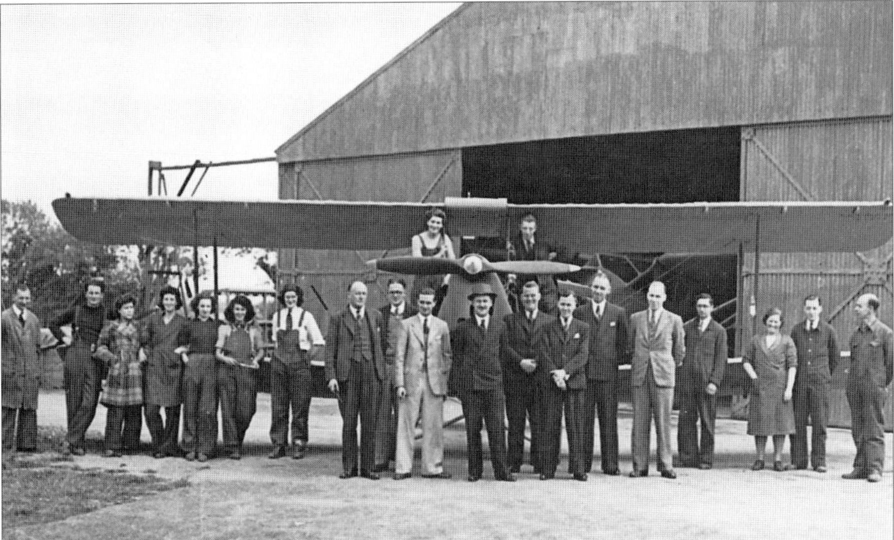

Civilian contractor W Mumford repaired RAF Tiger Moths in a hangar sited just outside the boundary of Roborough aerodrome, Plymouth. Visible in the mouth of the hangar is a visiting Heston Phoenix. via Dick Gliddon

RAAF Tiger Moth A17-114, damaged at 8 EFTS Narrandera on 6th December 1940, was routed to The Clyde Engineering Co Pty Ltd, at Clyde, NSW, a civilian organisation which worked on a wide range of military aircraft during the war and continued into the immediate years of peace. Bruce Winley

18 EFTS was the scene of another near disaster featuring a Tiger Moth, details of which were released in 1942. According to the official reports, the aircraft had been operating in an authorised low flying area when the cloud ceiling suddenly dropped to 200ft, requiring the Tiger Moth to be climbed up into the overcast to enable it to clear a range of hills between its present position, presumed to be south of the South Downs, and Fairoaks. For security reasons, the censor would not identify the location of the aircraft's base. During transition, the Tiger Moth hit a suspended barrage balloon with its wheels; the fabric bag was punctured by the propeller and escaping hydrogen gas ignited against the hot exhaust from the Gipsy Major engine.

Instantly enveloped in a ball of flame, fabric on the starboard upper trailing edge, inboard of the interplane strut, starboard lower trailing edge inclusive of the aileron, and complete upper surfaces of the starboard tailplane and elevator, all caught fire. The flames were extinguished only by an instinctive and violent sideslip to port in an effort to keep them away from the crew and the petrol tank as much as anything. Finding that the aircraft continued to fly, albeit with crossed controls, the crew elected to return to base where the Tiger Moth was landed normally.

The coincidence of the descent onto a golf course of a blazing barrage balloon and the appearance of a heavily singed Tiger Moth landing at a local aerodrome had to be explained. The release of the story as told, placated those for whom it was intended and attracted welcome publicity for the amazing survivability of the aeroplane. But in reality, and behind closed doors, it was admitted that the crew of a Tiger Moth operating above a cloud layer had spotted the silvery manifestation of a balloon suspended and apparently motionless, and hidden from all observation by the furry carpet of vapour, had indulged in the well known practice of airborne spot landing. On this occasion the 'landing' had been firm or slightly off target. Fortunately, although the balloon had been ruptured and exploded, all had survived. T6188 (84636), the aircraft involved, was repaired and remained part of the post-war establishment at Fairoaks until finally struck off charge in May 1950.

Mary de Bunsen learned to fly at Woodley and her first solo was on an overcast day in November 1930 when she guided a Cirrus II Moth, G-EBUS, around the circuit. She flew several other Moth types during the next ten years and in the frantic summer of 1940 was a member of the London Fire Brigade when she volunteered for duties as a ferry pilot with the Air Transport Auxiliary (ATA).

On 19th June 1940, Mary de Bunsen failed her ATA selection flight test undertaken on Tiger Moth R5130 (83012), operating from Hatfield, due to a condition described by her examiner as 'rusty, very rusty', and she returned to her duties at the fire station. Within three weeks she had been contracted to deliver Tiger Moth G-AFZD (82595), from Barton, where the aeroplane had been accepted into the Northern Aviation School and Club less than a year before, to de Havilland at Witney. By her own account the trip was memorable in that she was uncertain of her position for almost half the two hour journey; the Air Ministry refused her any proper maps and had cancelled her preferred routing just prior to take-off. And it was her first solo flight for 364 days. The Tiger Moth had been acquired by brokers W S Shackleton and the nearly new G-AFZD was militarised and shipped to the South African Air Force as 1547, the following September.

In August 1940, de Bunsen became Chief Test Pilot to Lundy and Atlantic Coast Air Services, a Civilian Repair Organisation (CRO) based in Devonshire and contracted to specialise in Tiger Moth engineering. In her diary for 17th August, she wrote:

'All pilots who are not maimed, halt and blind being usefully employed elsewhere, I am the only pilot on the premises and my pronouncements seem to carry considerable weight. I have done 79 hours 40 minutes solo in the past ten years. I wonder how you test aeroplanes? Test this one on the principle that if it and I come down together in one piece, the aeroplane is all right. Ten minutes later: report aircraft nose heavy, but everybody seems delighted with what, it appears, is their first effort. "They said we could not rig a Tiger Moth etc etc." they told me. I feel tempted to reply "They said I could not fly one!" From now on, all Tiger Moths inspire me with the greatest confidence'.

Having become far less 'rusty', Mary de Bunsen was accepted into the ATA in October 1941 and a little over two years later was ferrying DH.98 Mosquitos.

Hatfield built N6457 (3787), was delivered into storage at Dumfries in November 1938, but when 34 ERFTS was established at Southend on 16th January the following year, she was posted hundreds of miles south again. By October, the aircraft was back at Hatfield, operating with 1 EFTS. Flying near Alconbury on 16th September 1941, the pilot became unsure of his position and in an effort to locate familiar landmarks began a search pattern during which the aircraft ran out of fuel and crashed as a consequence of a misjudgement of the forced landing. At the subsequent enquiry it transpired that the aircraft's clock was broken and that the flight endurance had been stretched to almost four hours. In addition the pilot had been operating without a map due to a critical shortage in supply!

Flying with no clock at all was T7798 (84176), airborne from 5 RFS Castle Bromwich on 12th July 1949. Running short of fuel and uncertain of his position the pilot formated on another aircraft which maintained course without recognition. An attempt to read the local road signs proved a disappointing failure, and a precautionary landing in a field ended with the aircraft turning over, after which the pilot was pleased to be told he was at Bridgnorth.

N6532 (3845), was with 22 EFTS Cambridge when operating from Bottisham on 18th May 1941. The pilot removed his leather gauntlet to make a throttle adjustment but the silk inner on his left hand picked up in the quadrant and while trying to disentangle it with his right hand, the aircraft stalled and crashed. After extensive repairs completed on site, the aircraft remained at Cambridge until sold as surplus to the Darlington and District Aero Club in 1954. Registered as G-ANTS, but remaining unconverted, the dismantled airframe was acquired for the Strathallan Collection in 1968, and an assembly of parts catalogued as G-ANTS was sold at the slimming down auction conducted at Strathallan in June 1981.

In a partially restored condition the aircraft was re-sold to Sweden in September 1991, but meanwhile a further clearout at Strathallan following the decision to close the museum, yielded another fuselage clearly marked 'G-ANTS' which was sold at auction in 1985, and disappeared into obscurity.

Aircraft accident reports were usually copied to the Ministry of Aircraft Production (MAP), for use perhaps in the profit and loss account and as a determinant in the size of prospective contracts. One such, addressed to the Commanding Officer of 6 Flying Instructor School (FIS) Staverton, concerned the accident to a Tiger Moth in February 1942, and was cited by the MAP recipient as one of the finest examples of the art of aircraft accident reporting he had encountered during his very long career:

'I was ordered to carry out exercises with Pilot Officer X, and after spending some time on the circuit, we went away from the aerodrome to practice aerobatics. After both of us had carried out a considerable number of rolls, loops and rolls off the top, the aeroplane started to do a series of dives, stalls and stall turns, starting at about 2,500ft to 2,000ft and gradually getting lower and lower. At this time I thought Pilot Officer X was piloting the aircraft and although I did not like the manoeuvres that were being carried out, at that altitude anyway, as he was an officer and already had his flying badge, which I had not, and moreover had, I knew, flown many more advanced types than I had, I assumed he knew what he was doing and accordingly sat tight.

'As he several times said he did not like doing crazy flying of this description near the ground and I was still under the impression that he was flying the machine, for some reason I got the impression that he was trying to scare me and consequently just sat in front and said nothing, as I was waiting for him to get tired of what I thought was just an exhibition of unauthorised low flying for my benefit.

'Eventually the aeroplane hit a hedge and crashed. I was out first and whilst trying to assist Pilot Officer X, I was astounded to hear him blaming me for the accident, and told him so. As he was, and I believe still is, under the impression that I had been piloting the aeroplane at the time, he naturally thought I was trying to put the blame on him. I also jumped to the conclusion that he was trying to put the blame on me and as a result we spent the following two hours not speaking to each other very much.

'I telephoned Worcester aerodrome and spoke to Squadron Leader Y and in view of this misunderstanding with Pilot Officer X was reluctant to discuss the matter over the telephone, but on being pressed, stated what I believed at that time, that the accident was due to 'low flying'. Later I spoke to Squadron Leader Z and again stated that I was reluctant to discuss the matter until I had an opportunity for an interview with him. After I had arranged for a police guard for the aeroplane, Mr A brought us home in a van in which he had been sent to pick us up.

'While in the van and just prior to arriving at Staverton, the thought crossed my mind that possibly neither of us had been piloting the aeroplane during the 20 minutes preceding the accident, during which times the stalls and dives had been going on. I mentioned this fact to Pilot Officer X after he had seen the medical officer, and he not unnaturally, being under the impression that I had first of all tried to blame him, does not hold the view that this was the case. I should like to state that I was definitely not using the controls during the time that these dives and stalls were made, and that I do not now hold the opinion that Pilot Officer X was either. I think personally that the accident was caused because it did not occur to either of us that the other was not piloting the aeroplane, and because we were both under the impression that the other was showing off.

'I would also like to make it quite clear in order to exonerate completely Pilot Officer X, that I was in the front cockpit and therefore, though of lower rank, nominally in charge of the aeroplane. It was for this reason that I carried out the telephoning and arranging for the guard afterwards'.

Donald Smith was posted away from the Supermarine Spitfire Vs of 72 Squadron in July 1942, and was required to travel just a few miles from his former base at Biggin Hill to join 116 Squadron, whose detachment at Croydon was operating Tiger Moths and Airspeed Oxfords in support of gun and searchlight calibration duties. Set courses at heights up to 10,000ft were flown as determined by signals displayed on the ground, after which the cold and tedium of the whole exercise was tempered by the occasional chance to land back at Croydon having slipped round the famous control tower to touch down and stop within the confines of the concrete apron.

Returning from an East Anglian sortie one afternoon, the weather closed in, obliterating all signs of Croydon aerodrome, the control tower and even the local cooling towers which were used as an outstanding landmark. A few snatched glimpses of the ground revealed nothing familiar until Donald Smith suddenly spotted two Tiger Moths parked on a grass airfield. He spiralled down to discover he was over Hanworth, and while taxying in after an uneventful landing, the engine coughed and stopped. This sortie had lasted over two and a half hours, and the fuel tank had run dry.

Under similar conditions a 116 Squadron Tiger Moth flown by a Canadian bad weather specialist, Nobby Clark, was heard overhead Croydon, but the engine note diminished as the aircraft appeared to head towards the west, leaving those on the ground in no doubt that he had diverted. In conditions of low and lowering cloud and poor horizontal visibility, all further flying was abandoned. Half an hour after most other pilots had settled into the mess, Nobby Clark appeared in full flying kit with a story that he had flown over a railway station and by counting the number of platforms had deduced it was East Croydon, from where he had followed the road to the airfield. Gliding in to land on the side furthest from control, nobody was aware of his safe arrival, after which the fog settled and he could not see to taxy. Abandoning the aircraft in the middle of the airfield, another successful mission by 116 Squadron had been completed on foot.

Fog too was one of the problems experienced during winter training at Kirton in Lindsey on the east coast of Lincolnshire. Bob Palmer was airborne for a half hour session of steep turns when his instructor observed red Very flares being fired off from the control tower and the reason was soon obvious as both pilots saw a wall of sea fog rolling inland at amazing speed. The instructor immediately took control, dived for the airfield and put down nearly into wind, to be enveloped in mist as soon as the taxy run back to dispersal was completed. Later arrivals were not so lucky and several aircraft were stranded on the airfield. Taxying the Tiger Moths in fog with the constant need to swing the tail to ensure some modicum of forward visibility, resulted in crews getting hopelessly disorientated. They were forced to switch off the engines and listen for the approach of help in the form of the station Jeep, and hopefully not another Tiger Moth which might collide on the ground or even worse, attempt to land on top of them.

Feet were the subject of a lesson in flying taught by a pre-war instructor with 12 ERFTS at Prestwick. The pupil had been practising forced landings under instruction on Ayr racecourse, and due to the wintry conditions had elected to wear his heavy flying boots. These had reduced his dexterity on the rudder bars, and his instructor was becoming frustrated at the lack of co-ordination. Finally putting the aircraft down on the snow covered racetrack, the instructor told his pupil to take off his boots and stow them in the locker, and then to get back into his seat. Although his feet were frozen, the following session was considered productive and worthwhile due to the extra sensitivity transmitted through the pupil's soles.

Thirty years later a similar tale told in New Zealand could have had fatal consequences. Dr Bernie Gunn remembers a pilot who used to fly a Tiger Moth from Tauranga to visit friends at Kawerau, and on one occasion had suffered the embarrassment of getting a new flying boot jammed between the end of the rudder bar and the fuselage side frame. The experience had caused the pilot to investigate control with bare feet and on one sunny and unusually mild winter's day he took off without footwear and clad in just a shirt and shorts. Soon feeling very cold, a brief session of aerobatics did nothing to relieve the creeping numbness, and the situation was not improved when he found Kawerau shrouded in fog and almost landed in a field off the aerodrome by mistake.

Some time after a safe touchdown, club members found the pilot still sitting in the aircraft with the engine running, unable to taxy or to speak. They switched off the ignition and managed to lift him out of the cockpit, but it was only after half an hour in front of a gentle heater that he recovered the powers of speech. More drastic action to relieve a classic case of hypothermia, said Dr Gunn, could have resulted in death.

N6924 (82168), had been involved in a number of skirmishes since posting to 22 EFTS Cambridge in September 1939. Mostly these were forced landings due to pilot disorientation, but on 27th June 1942 her pupil pilot ignored a red light on finals to land at night at Caxton Gibbet RLG, and bumped into N6971 (82209), which was ahead of him. N6924 was operating near Northampton on 10th February 1943 when the solo pilot saw a Lockheed P-38 Lightning catch fire in the air, followed shortly after by the sight of the pilot bailing out and descending by parachute only to land in a tree. The Tiger Moth was immediately put down in an adjacent field with the thoughts of her pilot tuned to the prospect of rendering all possible assistance, but the aircraft ran into soft earth and only succeeded in standing on her nose, hopefully out of sight of the Lightning pilot who was left suspended in his harness. Following more landing damage sustained at Caxton Gibbet in June and repaired by Lundy and Atlantic Coast Airlines, the grandiose and deliberately confusing title of the CRO in Barnstaple, N6924 served until 1945 with two Polish squadrons operating North American P-51 Mustangs: No.316 at Friston and Coltishall and No.306 at Andrewsfield. Sold in 1951 and registered G-APHZ in 1957, the aircraft was converted into the ninth Thruxton Jackaroo in 1958 and operated initially as a cropspraying demonstrator.

A 'communications' Tiger Moth serialled in the DE700 series, complete with shark's teeth, a steely eye, and USAAF fuselage insignia, photographed at RAF Metfield in 1943. Having completed 300 hours in P-47s, USAAF pilot Herbert Field was due for posting, but with D-Day imminent, he volunteered for an extension of service and was killed in action on 7th June 1944.
via Colonel Sid Tucker

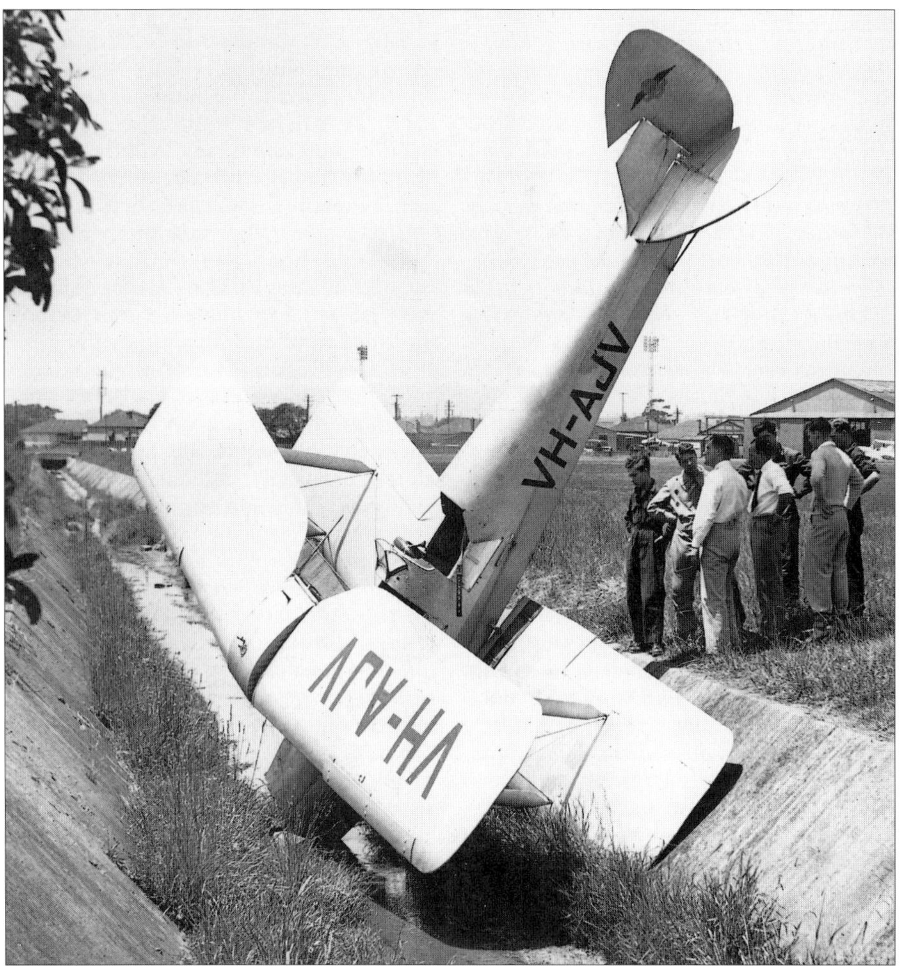

Tiger Moth VH-AJV suffered this embarrassment through her inability to stop (no brakes!) before the grass ran out during landing at Orange, NSW in 1953 and she nosed down into a mud filled culvert. The aircraft was retrieved, repaired and flew again. J A Burns

Sold in Canada after the owner emigrated there in 1970, the Jackaroo was fitted with a forward raked and braked DH.82C undercarriage, and is maintained in concours condition at Guelph.

At least 16 Tiger Moths were loaned to the United States 8th Air Force in Great Britain during 1942-1945, principally for communications duties, although some degree of 'recreational' flying was enjoyed. The aircraft retained their RAF camouflage and serial numbers, but the fuselage roundel was changed to a star in a circle or a star and bar insignia, and others were repainted with dark green upper surfaces (olive drab) and neutral grey undersides.

Not surprisingly, the loaned fleet was involved in a number of incidents and several aircraft were lost including DE826 (85724), allocated to the 'Mighty Eighth' on 12th October 1942 and written off following a crash near Wadebridge, Cornwall, on 4th April 1943, when operating from Heston. DE745 (85675), was officially allocated to the 336th Bomb Group on 7th October 1942, but was actually on charge to the 353rd in February 1943 and named *Dorothy*, when a squadron aircraft put down in an East Anglian cabbage field. The unit commander, Colonel Duncan, landed DE745 alongside the victim without incident, but on take off managed to turn the Tiger Moth upside down causing considerable damage and embarrassment, after which the benign *Wizard of Oz* titling was changed to *El Pisstopho Jr.*

The detachment of DE935 (85806), lasted barely six weeks before she was written off in unknown circumstances; six more were lost in 1943, three in 1944 and one the following year. Of the two aircraft known to have been returned to the RAF, DE262 (85308), was allocated to 3 EFTS Shellingford on 3rd August 1944 and written off on 3rd September; DE560 (85527), joined 11 EFTS Perth in November 1944 and exactly a year later, stalled and crashed during forced landing practice.

Although the USAAF operation of Tiger Moths both in Great Britain and to a lesser degree in Australia was organised through official channels, there is every possibility that aircraft were liberally swapped amongst host units. A senior USAF officer admitted long after the war to knowing of 'Reverse Lend Lease' agreements sealed with a couple of bottles of whisky, including one deal which resulted in a pilot securing a Rolls-Royce built Merlin engine for his North American P-51 Mustang.

The Hawker Typhoon 1Bs of 181 Squadron spent almost the whole of June 1943 at Appledram, a forward airfield close to the eastern extremities of Chichester Harbour. When taxying their warhorses to and from the runway, the squadron pilots soon realised that an abundance of game, mostly partridge, took absolutely no notice of them, but were off at high speed at the sight of a man strolling around the dispersals without evil intent. A communications Tiger Moth was enlisted into the task of supplying supplemental rations, and while the aircraft was taxied from the front cockpit, the occupant of the rear seat brandished a loaded shotgun. Results were not spectacular as on uneven ground the soft-sprung undercarriage created a poor platform for gunnery. Performance was slowly improving with practice when on 3rd July 1943 the squadron was ordered to pack its tents and relocate to the barren acres of Romney Marsh. But the game birds of Appledram were left to multiply in quiet isolation for less than a year before five squadrons of Supermarine Spitfire IXs descended upon them.

On detachment to 17 EFTS Peterborough, engineer Ben French was called upon to change a propeller on a Tiger Moth which had landed away at a new aerodrome at Wing in Buckinghamshire. An instructor had taken the aeroplane 'home for the weekend' but had had the misfortune to taxy off the runway and into a hidden gully running alongside, breaking the propeller and denting the cowlings in all the usual places. French was chauffeured to Wing in a Tiger Moth with the replacement propeller strapped to the side of the fuselage and in the near certainty that it would fit. (A pilot who flew a DH.60 Moth to Australia with a spare propeller lashed to the fuselage side was fortunate not to have needed it whilst en-route. Reaching Australia unscathed, he discovered that the spacing of the bolt holes in the hub was different from those on his engine, and the propeller was completely useless!) Without brakes, after landing French's Tiger Moth rolled down the new runway, which was soon to host Vickers Wellingtons on circuit training. The engineer was then required by his pilot to render assistance on the wingtip to help taxy back to the threshold and dispersal. Having found the victim of the gully, the breathless white knight was able to get on with his job: remove the broken propeller and its hub; clock the crankshaft (was it bent?); change the front rockerbox cover which was squashed; dress out the bottom cowling; fit the new propeller; check the tracking and run the engine; pack up and fly back to Peterborough. It was all in a day's work, completely routine, but these were unusual times. What excited French most was that during his unscheduled trip he came to realise how much effort the war was taking, for at no time during the flight was he out of sight of a new aerodrome.

Somewhat earlier, Jack Franklin had been operating in the same area during the course of learning to fly with the de Havilland Reserve School at Hatfield:

'The time came for my first solo cross-country to Abingdon. Carefully trying to hang on to my correct course, I soon lost the pencil line across the map, and when the ETA came up I could not see Abingdon. It was slightly hazy, and then I did the worst thing: wandered about in the air trying to find it. At last I decided I would stop and ask, and soon an obliging large and flat grass field came into view. I duly landed and touched down almost on top of a dozing fox which hurriedly departed.

'Not seeing anybody I got out of the Tiger Moth and then met some children who told me that Abingdon was about seven miles away. I walked back to the aeroplane, donned my parachute and then pondered how to start the engine on my own and with no chocks. Suddenly I remembered that I had once seen someone swing a propeller from behind, so, although being rather cumbersome wearing Sidcot suit and parachute, I turned on the engine switches, opened the throttle slightly, and took up my position between the leading edge of the lower wing and the propeller. I gave it one or two swings but still being warm, the engine refused to oblige. Ah! I thought, a little more throttle is needed, and got back to the cockpit and slightly opened it.

'I repeated this laborious pantomime about three times, and at the next swing the engine burst enthusiastically into life at what may well have been about half throttle. The aircraft waddled aimlessly off, and I desperately tried to get back to the switches, only to get my parachute pack wedged against the rigging wires.

'The waddle speed was fairly constant: we were nowhere near airborne, but after some distance the wheels must have hit a clump of grass or some uneven obstruction, and the Tiger Moth stood very neatly on her nose, the propeller immediately becoming nothing better than quality firewood.

'Discarding my parachute I then had about a half mile trudge, wearing my Sidcot, to a largish house where I hoped to find a telephone. By now my thoughts were becoming almost adventurous, and I was conjuring up visions of meeting a glamorous blonde etc, but it was not to be. I found the house alright but the sole occupant was a mean, wizened old lady, who grudgingly let me use the telephone and made me pay for my call. On instructions from Hatfield, I walked back and waited by the aeroplane. They were going to fly a new propeller out to me. In about two hours a School Tiger Moth appeared, circled the field twice and landed. The aircraft was being flown by George Cox, one of the School instructors and a pilot from Royal Flying Corps days, and in the back seat was Maintenance Manager Sid Weedon, sitting with a propeller between his knees, sticking vertically out of the cockpit. It was soon fitted, engine run up, and I was told to take off and circle the field and wait for George to join me. All this went according to plan and I followed him back to Hatfield to land in the failing light of a February evening'.

Pilots, posted from the rigours of operational flying where they would say somebody on the 'other side' was trying to kill them, often were remustered for 'rest' as flying instructors at the elementary schools where they would say that somebody from their own side was trying to kill them. Frustration was vented in all manner of different ways, especially it seems through flying low and as fast as a Tiger Moth would permit, or even slowly when the occasion demanded. On his first familiarisation flight, one pupil was conducted on a low level tour of the area surrounding the Solway Firth, when his instructor pointed out all the spots where parts of a body had been discovered during a murder inquiry.

Early in 1944 at low level and high speed, a Tiger Moth was seen to fly through a blister hangar at Alton Barnes RLG near Devizes. The eye witness report stated, perhaps unnecessarily, that the aircraft achieved this feat without touching the sides of the hangar, and that the heavy tarpaulin curtains were open. The pilot who was a resident instructor, must have enjoyed his time with the school, for the act of bravado followed receipt of his notice of posting.

At 28 EFTS Wolverhampton in 1944, the instructors were coping with groups of Iraqi, Iranian and Turkish students, all under some pressure from their respective governments to achieve distinction. Somebody discovered that while the British Government was responsible for the costs of training Turkish pilots, Turkish navigators were being funded by the Luftwaffe.

It was a Turkish officer who landed Tiger Moth '98' after an exercise prescribed for spinning and aerobatics, and who was completely bemused when his propeller flew off the hub as he applied power to taxi crosswind. The pilot was so astonished at the lack of performance that he sat for several minutes behind the engine, still rattling under power, before a member of the emergency services switched off the ignition.

Despite a comprehensive review, nobody could determine the reason why all eight hub bolts had sheared until a chance remark made by a visiting Boulton and Paul test pilot led to a complete revelation. He had been testing a locally built Barracuda, flying level at 180mph, when his aircraft had been subjected to a fighter style attack by a Tiger Moth which had broken away in a dive at an estimated speed of about 200mph. On the nose of the Tiger Moth the test pilot distinctly remembered reading a unit code: '98'. The Turkish officer later confessed to an irrational mock attack on what he had believed to be an enemy aircraft. Apart from the engine change, the unit Engineering Officer immediately ordered a second and thorough inspection of the airframe which failed to reveal any indication of damage or stress.

Returning to Southampton from Ceylon late in 1945, troops from all three services were embarked on an ancient Royal Mail ship which had hardly cleared the dockside at Colombo before it was subjected to a series of low level attacks by a Tiger Moth. The pilot, identified as the Wing Commander Flying and his bomb aimer were both observed to be wearing full mess kit, and assumed to have recently left the all-night farewell party. The aircraft bombed the ship with tins of 'tickler', Royal Navy cigarette tobacco, attached to yards of bunting which carried rude messages. There was only one direct hit but the exercise was appreciated by everyone.

Victor Pederson, a Captain in the Salvation Army, flew his own Tiger Moth around the areas of the Northern Territories of Australia which constituted his parish in 1945, and would regularly call at Darwin to pass time with the engineers working in the claustrophobic heat of the hangars. The Captain always carried a fold-up bicycle in the front cockpit which he used to good effect on the many substantial and remote airfields when visiting his congregation. Pederson had taken delivery in August 1945 of the first Tiger Moth to be civilianised from surplus RAAF stock after the war, but the aircraft was lost to a freak blowback of a signal fire after a forced landing in Western Australia in 1947.

A similar freedom was enjoyed in the less arid countryside in England 20 years afterwards. Bill Hardy, a professor at Reading University, would fly south in the Calleva Group's Tiger Moth G-APRX (85302), operating from a small strip near Newbury, and land in a Dorset field near Shaftesbury where his daughter was at school. Her chums might have been surprised (the first time) after being told that her father was flying down for the day, to see a besuited gentleman wearing a black beret appear at the school gates on a fold-up bicycle.

Alex Smith was stationed at RAF Northolt awaiting call-up for aircrew training at a time towards the end of the war when the system had already created a surplus, and recruits were being found a diversity of things to do just to mark time. The station commander volunteered all such chaps to plant vegetables between the runways and alongside the perimeter track, and to keep their enthusiasm at fever pitch, all plantings were logged: 1,000 cabbages entitled each volunteer to an hour's flight in the station Tiger Moth.

During his earned hour, Smith was flown via Ruislip Lido, where the wheels were subjected to their obligatory skim of the water's surface, and on towards Heston, by which time the visibility had deteriorated to such a degree that the pilot elected to land at the first airfield which hove into view. Which is exactly what they did. After touchdown both pilot and passenger were astonished at their encounter with so much contractor's plant and mounds of sand and gravel, and were even more alarmed as they climbed out of the aircraft to see a party of workmen advancing towards them with anything but a welcoming attitude. All was revealed soon enough; the Tiger Moth had touched down in the middle of the expansion of RAF Heathrow, soon to be London Airport and the world's busiest international terminal. The next movement by a Tiger Moth at Heathrow was 20 years later when G-AMIU (83228), an aircraft purchased as a tug for the British European Airways' Silver Wing Gliding Club, was overhauled at the Corporation's engineering base and afterwards flown out, non radio, to Booker.

The services have always paid particular attention to sport and offered encouragement to participants in all the popular team games through the legendary Wednesday afternoon sessions set aside for endeavour on the station playing fields. Inter-service rivalry could only be matched by inter-Command or station or unit competition, and therefore the briefing that was held behind closed doors at 7 EFTS Desford on 25th March 1946 would have been serious and secretive. The School's rugby team was scheduled to play a needle match with their rivals from 16 EFTS Burnaston on 27th March and the briefing at Desford was more than a discussion on tactics. The Chief Flying Instructor, Squadron Leader Wardell, was detailing his pilots to their positions in a formation of 36 Tiger Moths that was to arrive overhead Derby precisely on time and in sharp order; a reminder of the talent that was routinely available at Desford. The rugby match was another problem altogether and although the result is not known, was there significance in the fact that the following day 7 EFTS was inspected by the AOC?

In order to move a Tiger Moth single handed, the most efficient way is to lift the rear of the aircraft by the tailplane strut, at least to normal shoulder height, at which point a Tiger Moth is balanced on her main wheels and can be manoeuvred quite successfully at ground level. In this configuration on a rough surface or where an upslope is encountered, the load becomes marginal for an ordinary mortal but is still a perfectly reasonable proposition for two people, the best reason for private owners operating from remote aerodromes always to have an athletic passenger for the first or last flight of the day.

Tiger Moth N6754 (82032), had served as a training aircraft since allocation to 18 EFTS at Fairoaks in October 1939, and from June 1947 she was part of the Cambridge University Air Squadron (CUAS) fleet lodging with 22 RFS at Teversham. During the night of 16th January 1948, a man later identified as an escaped German Prisoner of War, broke into the hangar and moved the aircraft nearest to the door, N6754, onto the apron outside. It was his intention to position the Tiger Moth as far from the buildings as possible to allow time to familiarise himself with the aircraft, start and warm the engine, and take off at first light, creating no unnecessary attention. The plan might have worked had it not been for growing fatigue and loss of orientation and a gust of wind which unbalanced the arrangement.

The following day in the cold light of a January morning the Air Squadron engineers were astonished to find N6754 lying on her back in the middle of the aerodrome. Repaired and maintained in service until 1953 the aircraft emigrated to New Zealand the following year, but within two days of the completion of major work at Rotorua on 31st March 1981, the hangar burned down, allowing only a few Tiger Moth parts to be salvaged from the ashes.

A sister Tiger Moth from the same Hatfield batch created in the early summer of 1939, N6797 (82067), was another survivor of wartime training released to the civil market in 1953. Sold to the Association of

Professor Bill Hardy landing the Calleva Group's Tiger Moth G-APRX in a Dorset field, carrying his fold-up bicycle in the front cockpit. deHMC Archive

Provided the balance is right, a Tiger Moth can be manoeuvred on the ground with single-person-power. On grass, or an uneven surface, or against an up-slope, the task is hard work for two. John King

During an air race at Rochester in July 1967, Tiger Moth G-AOBX not only crossed the winning line but managed to hit it at speed. Rollason Aircraft effected the necessary repairs by injecting a lot of spare parts. Norman Rivett

In the middle of a large grass aerodrome, under blue skies in the full light of day, with all concerned weaving and observing in order to avoid just this situation, two Tiger Moths of the Royal Newcastle Aero Club became locked in a non-fatal but otherwise lethal embrace. Bill Hitchcock

British Aero Clubs (ABAC) on behalf of the Defford Aero Club for a mere £25, the aircraft was rough rigged at Cosford and flown home to RAE Defford where she was registered G-ANEH in September 1953, and qualified for a Certificate of Airworthiness under the hand of club engineer Cyril Pugh in July 1954. At the same time the Club bought a second Tiger Moth from Cosford at a price of £75: R5065 (82960), had logged test flight hours only following a complete overhaul. In 1950, the Club had purchased four Tiger Moths from Sandown, Isle of Wight, at £60 the lot, from which two good aircraft were rebuilt and eventually sold.

Following incidents with a number of subsequent owners, G-ANEH was discovered in a semi derelict condition in a barn near Kemble in 1968 by none other than Pugh who took ownership in December that year, and undertook a complete rebuild in the gliding club hangar at Nympsfield where he was then resident engineer. On 6th May 1973 with the part time restoration of G-ANEH about 75% complete, some guttersnipe thought it incredibly amusing to set the hangar on fire, and as a consequence, just like her old stablemate 82032, Tiger Moth 82067 was reduced to a collection of parts singed round the edges. Also lost in the fire was the gliding club's own Tiger Moth G-AODX (83437), salvaged parts of which later were sold to the USA.

The rebuilding scheme passed through a number of hands and proved a financial nightmare when a restoration company collapsed taking all the up-front funds with it, but the project endured and the aircraft was finally completed by Ben Cooper at the Newbury Aeroplane Company in 1995 to an outstanding, award winning concours condition.

During a Battle of Britain flying display at Ternhill on 18th September 1948, Tiger Moth T6774 (85061), a resident aircraft with 6 FTS, was conducting a mock attack on a cardboard fort when the luggage locker flapped open, distracting the pilot, who subsequently flew into the ground but managed to recover to land on one wheel. The aircraft was declared a write-off, sold to Wolverhampton Flying Club and registered G-ALNA in April 1949. In January 1986, having suffered a traumatic civil life, the aircraft was reported to have suffered a rudder control problem, and involuntarily sideslipped into a flooded gravel pit near Clacton. The occupants were rescued with difficulty from the sheer sided workings by a man and his dog who heard cries for help. The aeroplane was rescued too, dried out and restored to airworthiness.

DF159 (85908), a 1943 Morris Motors model, was scheduled to spend the first year of her life in a 15MU Purgatory Store before erection and test at Cowley and issue to a training system already in contraction. As part of the establishment of 1 Radio School, Cranwell, DF159 was operating from Spitalgate in July 1951 on what was officially described as 'ground strafing practice', but the pilot took off with a faulty intercom, the occupant of the front seat clutching a lapful of primed flourbag bombs. During the first run in, the front doors were let down to permit visual signals to be given to the pilot, but some of the flour which had escaped from the bombs blew up into his face causing loss of control at low level. The port lower wing of the Tiger Moth struck an RAF Regiment officer who was standing near the target judging hits, injuring his thigh, but with a damaged mainplane and pasty faced pilot, the aircraft was landed safely at Saltby. In 1955, registered G-AOAA, 85908 was the first Tiger Moth to be assigned to the fleet of the Tiger Club at Croydon, and was later converted to become *The Deacon,* one of the unique quartet of Super Tigers, much refined to boost the aerobatic qualities of the basic aeroplane.

Tiger Moth DE141 (85212), was based at RAF Coltishall during the summer of 1952, appropriately enough in the care of 141 Squadron, although nobody admits to any knowledge of the reason why. When not operating their Gloster Meteor NF.11s, the squadron pilots were encouraged to use the aeroplane to hone their basic flying skills, and were permitted to take DE141 away for weekends at a charge of 5s.0d, payable to squadron funds. Everybody agreed that this was a splendid arrangement and enjoyed by many, but it could not possibly last. While inspecting a cereal crop from low level on 22nd July 1952, the undercarriage became entangled with the ripening ears, and the flying career of DE141 came to an abrupt end. The pilot escaped the crash and his subsequent court marshall unscathed, but the unit funds and weekends away were destined never to be the same.

The Royal Navy was a quietly prolific user of Tiger Moths, and apart from supplying the RAF with an example for their Museum at Hendon after the original exhibit suffered an arson attack, even before the facility had been opened to the public, the Senior Service bought back four aircraft from the civil market long after the type had been declared obsolete.The Tiger Moths were to provide air experience flying at minimum cost to officer cadets at Plymouth, and during summer camping expeditions to Scotland. As part of the Air Day organised at Lossiemouth in 1959, a Tiger Moth Air Race was scheduled, each aircraft carrying a coloured pennant mounted on the tail skid, and a Wren in the front seat wearing a coloured jumper to match. After three laps the aircraft were to land to allow the girls to jump out and race through an obstacle course to reach the control tower. The rules for the race permitted full power until the leader was overtaken, at which point the engine was throttled back to 1,800rpm until in due course the new leader was overtaken.

On the day all went well with the three Tiger Moth entrants until at the end of the race it was time to land as near to the control tower as possible. Only then was it realised that the prospective touchdown area was meshed with lengths of anchor cable, all part of the arrester training system. No undercarriages were lost but the ladies had a longer sprint than had been anticipated.

Flushed with the exuberance that can only be the result of captaining a Tiger Moth at the age of 17, an Air Training Corps cadet flying under the provisions of an Air Ministry Scholarship scheme in 1957, overstepped the mark near Petersfield, Hampshire, after which he was prosecuted for flying below 500ft (fined £5), and for 'flying an aeroplane in a reckless manner' for which he was fined a further £5. These indiscretions were highlighted because the Tiger Moth was damaged when it collided with the ground.

At a little over 17 years of age, Paul Barton was flying a Tiger Moth at Cambridge, also the beneficiary of an RAF Flying Scholarship, although he later transferred allegiance and retired after a successful career as a pilot in the Fleet Air Arm. On his solo cross-country he reached Luton safely, but a wind change on the second leg, to White Waltham, put him off track and he landed in what proved to be a rough surfaced field in order to ask the way. The firm three pointer broke off the tailskid, although he was not aware of that until, after a take off which scraped the top of the surrounding trees, and a landing downwind at White Waltham where he misread the windsock, he found taxying the aircraft more difficult than he could remember.

The lack of brakes on his Tiger Moth was forgotten as he approached the fuel pumps: *'A veritable brainstorm of a decision, they being surrounded by a concrete apron. Moreover, this apron sloped ever so gently down to a set of gates in the airfield perimeter fence, beyond which lay a public highway. Once on the apron there was, like the engineer's big wheel, no way of stopping it. So off we trundled down the slope with a depressing inevitability that totally scuppered my previous euphoria.*

'Luckily though, the gates were open and there was nothing immediately in the way, so there seemed little point in adopting the standard emergency procedure (jump out) and in any case we were soon going rather too fast. Luckily, the laws of gravity, having been gently responsible, with me, for starting this debacle, elected to terminate it by means of the camber in the road, which is where we stopped, right in the middle. So there, like a lemon, I sat in my flying machine, holding up the traffic until help arrived.

'As a precaution I joined the Fleet Air Arm to continue my flying career as a helicopter pilot. The Navy seemed to have a rather more liberal understanding of the foibles of the youthful aviator than most; besides, it was obviously going to be very much easier to stop and ask the way!'

Taxying downwind on concrete with a steerable tail trolley under the skid requires an officer or two to act as brakes. Royal Navy Tiger Moth T8191 wearing the Culdrose code, striking down at Yeovilton. deHMC Archive

The caption attached to this photograph of a camouflaged T8191 in an 'unusual attitude' reads *'The Tiger Moth was not designed for arrested landings and with the barbed wire firmly wrapped round the port undercarriage, the old girl came to an abrupt halt and tipped gracefully onto her nose'.* HMS *Heron*

VARIATION ON A PROVEN THEME

Norwegian Army Air Force DH.82 Tiger Moth 159 was fitted with a float chassis and tested by the Norwegian Navy in a series of trials lasting 22 hours in 1934. A prospective seaplane trainer, the type was rejected as unsuitable for naval service. Kjeller Flyhistoriske Forening

NORWAY proved to be a good customer for de Havilland products and the government owned aircraft factory at Kjeller near Oslo (Haerens Flyfabrikk) had negotiated a licence for production of the DH.60M, known in Air Force parlance as the 'Standard Moth', in 1930, after which ten aircraft had been constructed the following year.

Welcomed as a visitor to Stag Lane in 1931, Norwegian Army Air Force Captain Richard Clason was invited to fly the new DH.82, with the result that he recommended to his superiors that no more 'Standard' Moths should be constructed, and that efforts should be concentrated on the Tiger Moth instead. He was particularly impressed by the versatility of the aircraft in the military roles of reconnaissance and observation as much as the type's primary function as a basic trainer.

In February 1932 it was announced that an agreement between the de Havilland Aircraft Company Ltd and the Norwegian Government acting on behalf of the State Military Aircraft Factory at Kjeller, would result in licence production of the DH.60M being discontinued in favour of local manufacture of 17 DH.82 Tiger Moths, and for each of which, British built Gipsy III engines would be supplied from Stag Lane. Information provided to the press spoke only of 'training duties', a description which covered most military prospects in addition to circuits and bumps.

The de Havilland licence had been procured at a fee of almost 16,000 Norwegian Kroner (Nkr), and every effort was made to build the aircraft as economically as possible. Much of the production tooling required for the DH.60M could be used again with little or no modification for the manufacture of DH.82 parts, although an investment of Nkr 14,500 was necessary for additional jigging.

All 17 aircraft were completed by the summer of 1933 at a total manufacturing cost of Nkr 215,348 plus an additional Nkr 132,320 spent with the de Havilland Engine Division for the supply of 20 Gipsy III engines. The entire fleet was paraded at Kjeller before allocation to duties: 13 were scheduled for the Army Air Force Flying School and some other operational units before 1st July 1933, two would join the Flying School after 1st July, and two more were to be retained for use by the factory as communications, liaison and development aircraft. Kjeller issued build numbers 149-165 to which the Army Air Force allocated serials 127-159 but using only the odd numbers in sequence; even numbers were reserved for the Naval Air Force. Before delivery of the DH.82 Tiger Moths, the Norwegian Government voted funds for construction of a further 20 aircraft to be built to the DH.82A specification.

First of the Kjeller built DH.82 Tiger Moths, Army Air Force 127, was tested on aerodynamically shaped skis during the winter of 1933. Kjeller Flyhistoriske Forening

These new machines were to take second place to a batch of ten Fokker C.V-D and -E reconnaissance and bomber aircraft under construction at Kjeller, but the de Havilland aircraft were given priority when the military immersed itself in indecision regarding the choice of a suitable engine for the Fokker airframes. However, all aeroplane construction was substantially interrupted when the authorities decided in favour of a major programme of factory repair and refurbishment in 1934, very much with a view to creating modern facilities for the future mass production of a new fighter. It is also suspected that an extended trainer production schedule was necessary to maintain continuity until the site was again fully functional, and the fighter project on the factory floor.

An allocation of funds was made to purchase Gipsy III engines for the DH.82A fleet, but negotiations with Stag Lane proved difficult and de Havilland refused to consider lowering their contract price. It was probably part of a preconceived business strategy, for with the Gipsy III soon to make way for the Gipsy Major, the Norwegian Government found they were offered a better deal on the new engine. The contract called for just 20 units to be delivered, one for each airframe, and no extras for reserve. In February 1935 the Inspector General of the Army Air Force announced that when the 20 aircraft were complete in the spring, three years after the line was laid down, six aircraft would be allocated to the Army Air Force Flying School at Kjeller, ten to the operational units at Kjeller and the remaining four to the unit at Vaernes.

The DH.82A line was identified by build numbers 171-190 and Army Air Force serials 161-199, odd numerals only. Having described the DH.60M as the 'Standard Moth', the DH.82A was to be known somewhat erroneously as the 'Moth Major' to distinguish it from the Gipsy III powered DH.82. Allowing for revised jigging, each of the new aircraft had cost a little under Nkr 19,000, about 10% per unit less than the DH.82, essentially a function of lower pre-production costs. A further financial saving per aircraft was made by the decision not to fit leading edge slats, thus depriving the Handley Page Aircraft Company of a potentially handsome royalty.

The Norwegian military were strong proponents of the de Havilland philosophy of a 'one type trainer' as indicated by their widespread deployment of the Tiger Moth. In addition to a machine gun equipped operational trainer which was transferred to the front line in 1940, the winter exercises at Kongsvinger in 1934 unveiled DH.82 129 (150), in the role of bomber, with a rack of four under-fuselage bombs, each of which could be released individually. Zeiss camera guns were fitted to several aircraft in addition to long range fuel tankage of ten, 20 or even 35 gallons, installed in the front cockpit, the greater endurance requiring larger capacity oil tanks to be fitted to aircraft with the Gipsy III engine.

Blind flying panels and hoods were standard for instrument training which continued throughout the year, and night flying equipment included a wind driven generator fixed to the undercarriage V strut and an accumulator in the luggage locker. Although not equipped with landing lights, night landings were accomplished with the aid of floodlit touch down zones rather than flarepaths which could be seen at high altitude from very long distances.

On behalf of the Department of Meteorology at the University of Oslo, the Flying School at Kjeller provided facilities for research and data collection. Beginning in June 1933, Captain Normann, Commanding Officer, flew DH.82 149 (160) several times a week to altitudes in excess of 15,000ft. In recognition of the conditions met during these ascents, the pilot's cockpit was fitted with a turn indicator and a fore and aft level, while barographs were strapped to the interplane struts. The role was assumed by DH.82A 163 (172), for six months from September 1936, and DH.82 151 (161) later in 1937.

On 29th March 1936, Norwegian built DH.60M LN-BAE (139), of the Widerøes Flying School, formerly Army Air Force No 111, was written off after an accident at Grorud. As replacement, the Widerøes school was offered Army Air Force DH.60M No 109 (138), which was registered LN-BAT in their name at the company's Oslo base on 7th April, only eight days after the accident. As No 109 had been transferred from the Army Air Force Flying School at Kjeller, an organisation which now needed its own replacement, DH.82 No 157 (164), one of the two factory communications aircraft, was nominated.

The sale of DH.60M No 109 had raised Nkr 7,300, money which was paid to the factory account. In consequence, a single new DH.82A Tiger Moth was commissioned on 2nd April 1936, and a Gipsy Major engine was delivered from England on 30th September. The new Tiger Moth (193), was allocated Army Air Force serial 201, and fitted with a metal propeller which gave it a distinctive sound, mainwheel brakes and a castoring tailwheel. She was delivered across the workshop floor on 1st October 1937, largely for use by the Commanding Officer of the Factory, Captain Eckhoff, the 38th and last of the type to be built locally. The improved stopping capability was welcomed during the autumn of 1939 when 201 operated from an abbreviated strip at Stavern when on detachment to tug targets for anti-aircraft gunnery practice.

The Kjeller factory had suffered its share of difficulties spawned by incorrect drawings, but mostly the errors had been identified and corrected before the DH.82A was put into production. In December 1934, several spare sets of front fuselage side frames were constructed, and following the demise of the first Norwegian built DH.82A 161 (171), after a crash at Aurland on 29th July 1935, with only 95 hours logged, the Gipsy Major engine was removed and during the Autumn of 1936 installed in No 159 (165), the second of the factory's DH.82 communicators.

During the engine conversion, the opportunity was taken to upgrade the aeroplane for the personal convenience of the Inspector General of the Army Air Force, Colonel Trygve Klingenberg, an officer who had been left with a stiff leg following an accident as a young pilot. The Tiger Moth rudder bar was modified to accept a clamp on one side instead of a conventional pedal, which arrangement allowed the Colonel to pull with his good leg in addition to pushing as normal, and to retain complete authority over an otherwise standard control.

On 27th May 1937, Colonel Klingenberg led seven Tiger Moths and four Standard Moths from Kjeller to the opening of the new airfield at Sola, but weather conditions were so bad that only two aircraft arrived. Two Standard Moths, 107 and 117 crashed en route, and one of the pilots was killed when he bailed out.

Tiger Moth 159 had been the subject of marine investigations in 1934 when she had been loaned to the Naval Air Force for evaluation as a float equipped trainer. Purchase of a pair of Short Bros floats had been sanctioned in November 1933 and in February 1934, Lieutenant K Ostby flew the ski equipped 159 from a snow covered Kjeller to Lake Borrevannet where the float chassis was fitted. Trials were completed at the Norwegian naval base at Karljohansvaern where after almost 22 hours flight time the Naval Air Force pronounced that the type was not suitable for its purposes, and 159 was flown back to Kjeller, alighting on the River Nitelva which normally flowed half a mile from the airfield, but which in May 1934 was in flood, creating a lake immediately adjacent to the airfield buildings.

The Kjeller factory had been responsible for the design and manufacture of skis for all Norwegian military aircraft since January 1916 when flight trials had been conducted on a locally built Maurice Farman MF.7 Longhorn (Kjeller FF.1). The first director of Kjeller Flyfabrikk, Captain Einar Sem-Jacobsen, had adapted a normal 'domestic' ski, and fitted one pair to each side of the FF.1 with remarkable results. As a matter of course, all Norwegian land based military aircraft later operated during the six month long winters, on skis designed, developed and manufactured at Kjeller. The Tiger Moths were provided with two types of narrow width skis with round or squared off ends, fore and aft, or a broader laminated ski which was less likely to 'straighten out', a configuration which could cause embarrassment on touchdown. Equipped with skis, Tiger Moths were restricted to a maximum diving speed of 165mph.

With the exception of laminated skis, all others were smeared with Tento, a propriatory wax, and some were fitted with bullet shaped aerodynamic fairings to help lessen the drag.

Operating on snow covered ice with a ski equipped aircraft was hazardous, even for experienced pilots, until the engineers devised a simple but very effective solution. By bolting a steel strip to the outer edges of each ski, they created skates on which the aircraft could, with practice, be controlled on the slippery surface with both verve and precision.

During the summer months, as everywhere, the cast iron tailskid shoe would wear thin due to the abrasive nature of dry grass runway surfaces or concrete hard standings and taxy tracks. Loose or wet ground was easily excavated by the ploughing qualities of the skid as it fulfilled its primary functions of steering and braking. Trials proved that leaving the winter kit's mini-ski on the tailskid arm all through the summer in preference to the iron shoe, not only preserved runway surfaces with very little difference in braking capacity, but reduced the frequency of attention and replacement.

Tiger Moths flew as target tugs in support of the anti-aircraft schools, and the experience was later put to good effect when towing gliders or advertising banners. In the reconnaissance role during the Russo-Finnish War of 1939-1940, the aircraft routinely patrolled the country's northern borders in defence of Norway's neutrality.

To ensure uninterrupted operations under the severest weather conditions in winter, oil was drained from the engines immediately on shut down after the last flight of the day and heated almost to boiling point before the tanks were replenished, and the engines started immediately afterwards. To ensure there was no misunderstanding, oilless engines were placarded with red triangles, and both pilots and engineers were required to sign log books before attempting to start up. When aircraft were required on a stand-by basis in severe weather, cowlings were shrouded by a Dalli Apparatus, under which heating elements the size and shape of a brick and housed in a perforated container, were suspended below the engine.

Three elements were sufficient to maintain warmth in the bay for 12 hours throughout the night. An alternative system was the provision of heat by a small portable furnace, from which hot air was fed into the cowlings along flexible ducting. Apart from these precautions and the choice of landing gear appropriate to the surface conditions, there were no concessions to the climate.

For the crews, it was necessary to be dressed in fur lined boots, flying suits, helmets and gloves, with face masks to prevent frost bite. Operating under such conditions, the inadequacy of the fuselage width was revealed when pilots were obliged to fly with the cockpit doors hinged down in order to improve working space, but it was not until after the winter exercises of 1938 that serious thought was given to the procurement of a training aircraft fitted with a canopy, and then only in preparation for the arrival of the new Gloster Gladiator fighters as much as anything else.

DH.82A Tiger Moths 183 (182) and 185 (183), were modified at Kjeller in 1935 to carry machine guns, but only on a temporary basis. Experience gathered from these and previous installations led two Air Force officers to develop a new system of gun synchronisation driven by the engine camshaft, and in preference to other hydraulically operated arrangements which were prone to leakage. The synchronisation was proven by firing a bullet from a Colt .303 machine gun, mounted with a sight above the front cockpit, through a hole in one blade of the propeller, which had itself been fitted several degrees off its normal orientation.

Standing on her ski chassis, Norwegian DH.82 Tiger Moth 129 is fitted with a concrete practice bomb. A rack underneath the fuselage floor was designed to carry four bombs of up to 10kg each.
Kjeller Flyhistoriske Forening

Five DH.82A Tiger Moths of the Norwegian Army Air Force operating from a frozen lake during pre-war manoeuvres in northern Norway. 189 escaped to Sweden on 15th April 1940; 185 was lost in a crash in southern Norway on 20th April 1940; 181, 187 and 191 continued to fight in the north until 7th June 1940. via B Olsen

DH.82A Tiger Moth SE-ANL, previously Norwegian Army Air Force 151 and an escapee in April 1940, was sold by her last Swedish owner to the Norsk Flyhistoriske Forening in 1971 for display at Haermuseet, Oslo. Ole G Nordbo

The system was installed on DH.82A Tiger Moth 165 (173), which was used for gunnery training by student pilots in the summer, and experienced officers during winter exercises. The Army Air Force was pleased enough to award the two inventors an extraordinary payment for their work, and funded conversion of another four aircraft in the winter of 1939. While 165 was detached to the Jagervingen, (Fighter Flight), operating their new Gloster Gladiators from Fornebu in the spring of 1940, she was destroyed there by enemy bombing on 9th April. The other four aircraft had already been disarmed in support of the spring pilot training programme at a time when they were needed most of all.

Several other Tiger Moths were early casualties of the German invasion, destroyed in bombing raids at Sola and Fornebu. At Kjeller it is believed that five Tiger Moths were on station with two fighter units, and a further three Tiger Moths and three DH.60M Moths were in the factory undergoing maintenance and repairs.

At first light, 167 and 175 left Kjeller and landed at Steinfjorden. 171 is known to have been destroyed on the ground and another Tiger Moth took off in the dark but collided with a Fokker C.V-E. The previous day, 15 Tiger Moths of the Army Air Force Flying School had been flown to Oyeren where they landed on the ice and were immediately camouflaged. On 10th April at dawn, they flew to Rena leaving behind one machine whose engine could not be started and which was immobilised. Later that evening the Army High Command ordered the aircraft to move to Nordre Osen in the eastern province of Hedmark, close to the Swedish border, where a gathering of 23 aircraft was hidden in woodlands along the edge of Lake Ossjoen.

Following a decision to evacuate the flying school aircraft to Sweden, on 15th April seven Tiger Moths accompanied by four Fokkers flew north again to Horrmundssjoen, but one aircraft became detached from the main group during a heavy snowstorm and landed on a small frozen lake; another touched down in a bog and was later recovered in a dismantled condition, eventually joining the other six at Ostersund in Sweden where they had arrived on 18th April.

The seven escapees were DH.82s 127; 131; 137; 151 and 157, and DH.82As 163 and 185, all of which took civil letters on the Swedish register and continued operating much as before in the varied roles of trainer, target and glider tug. In April 1971, SE-ANL (Air Force 151), was acquired by the Norwegian Aviation Historical Society and returned for permanent display at the Military Museum established at Akershus Castle, Oslo.

On 16th April 1940, Group R was formed in southern Norway to which all available aircraft were attached, and on whose behalf the remaining Tiger Moths were extensively used for communications duties. An attempt was made by four Tiger Moths to escape through northern Norway to Finland in June 1940. It seems likely that each had been hurriedly disguised as civil aircraft, but only one, Air Force 159 (165), the Kjeller factory machine, posted to the Army Air Force Flying School since July 1937, was successful, disguised as LN-BDD. The aircraft subsequently saw service with the Finnish Air Force as MO-159, but her fate is unrecorded.

DH.82 Tiger Moth Air Force 145 (158), had spent her entire career with the operational unit at Vaernes, and had recorded 1,814 flying hours by December 1939. At the end of April 1940, the crew escaped when No 145 crashed at Dovrefjell mountain during evacuation operations from Lake Lesjaskogsvatn. Substantial remains of the aircraft were recovered by local inhabitants and hidden, and post-war, some of the rudder fabric complete with vertical colour stripes was discovered at the crash site. At the time of the accident, the aircraft had been fitted with the same Gipsy Major engine installed on manufacture at Kjeller, and this was traced in 1993, having been recovered during the war, hidden locally, and re-sold several times since. With the approval and co-operation of the Armed Forces Museum, as much of the original structure that survived has been grafted into a static model intended for local exhibition.

Once the fighting in southern Norway had stopped, German forces took control of all surviving aircraft. DH.82 129 (150), was dismantled at the flying school at Lesja and removed; the engine and fuselage of DH.82A 187 (184), which had crashed during take off from Koppang in April were also confiscated. It is not known what happened to the remaining aircraft which were serviceable or nearly so. At least one was photographed at Kjeller in full Luftwaffe colours bearing the code 6M+OS, but her previous identity and subsequent fate are unknown.

The Norwegian Tiger Moths and others confiscated in Denmark were not the only examples to see wartime service with the Luftwaffe. It is believed that at least some of the aircraft abandoned in France by 81 Squadron in 1940, were made serviceable and flown in German markings at least until the lack of spares rendered the situation untenable. Four previously civil registered Tiger Moths based at the Austrian Air Force Air Training School at Parndorf in October 1939 were reallocated to Flying School A/B24 at Olmutz where at least one was known to have been written off in a landing accident during training operations that continued until October 1940. It was a situation immersed in irony bearing in mind the opinions expressed on the suitability of the Tiger Moth by de Havilland's Austrian agent, Nikolaus von Eltz, in 1936.

In 1953, the Norsk Aero Club (NAK) bought Tiger Moth SE-AWO from Birger Nilsson at Falkoping in Sweden, a DH.82 (Sk.11) built by ASJA at Linkoping as works number 44 in May 1935. The aircraft had served with Nos 6, 7 and 8 Air Corps but carrying serial Fv.512 had been retired from operations with the 5th Air Corps at Ljungbyhed on 23rd May 1947, having reached 2,000 airframe hours. Registered to NAK as LN-TVB on 19th August 1953 and operated as a glider tug, the aircraft was sold to the Royal Norwegian Air Force in December 1955, although NAK was commissioned by the new owners to manage the aircraft on their behalf. The arrangement worked well until 14th June 1958 when during a glider towing sortie, the aircraft ran out of fuel and was almost destroyed in the subsequent forced landing. The Air Force advertised the wreckage for sale on 16th October but emphasised the impossibility of restoring any part of the salvage to airworthy condition.

Cementing their good relations with de Havilland through the company's Swedish agent Sven Blomberg of Aero Material in Stockholm, a company also acting as representative in Latvia and Finland, and demonstrating their faith in the integrity of the British built airframes and engines, the Swedish Air Force bought ten of the first batch of 12 DH.60T Moth Trainers during the summer of 1931, ordered on their behalf by the Flygstyreisen office in Stockholm, and redesignated Sk.9, serials Fv5103 to Fv5112. It was almost inevitable that as a major customer for de Havilland products, the Air Force would progress to newer models as they became available, and following the emergence of the DH.82 Tiger Moth as a next step development from their still new Sk.9s, the type was soon subject to serious investigation.

Following demonstration of DH.60T Tiger Moth G-ABNJ by Hubert Broad at Barkarby in December 1931, and subsequent purchase of that aircraft, orders were placed on Stag Lane for June 1932 delivery of 12 DH.82 Tiger Moths with Gipsy III engines. These would be classified with G-ABNJ, formally taken on Swedish Air Force charge on 9th February 1932 as Fv6562, as type Sk.11. Aircraft 3108-3115 and 3138-3141 would become Fv5563-Fv5568 and Fv5591-Fv5596 respectively. In the event, delivery was spread through the year: 3108 and 3109 arrived during the last week of April while 3110 and 3111 were delivered on 6th May. 3112-3115 were received in the middle of July, and the final four, 3138-3141, were not taken on charge until 25th October.

Four of the aircraft, 3112-3115 had been ordered by Aero Material as civil aeroplanes (SE-ADE to SE-ADH), for a reason which is not obvious, but may have been directed by budgetary constraints and alternative methods of funding or some associated political rationale. Following delivery, all were cancelled from the civil register and allocated the Air Force serials Fv5567, Fv5568, Fv5591 and Fv5592.

The new aircraft were posted to the 5th Air Corps Flying School at Ljungbyhed near Malmö, where they were used for *ab initio* training during courses which included 170 hours of elementary and advanced flying training spread over a 12 month period. Markings carried on the aircraft changed progressively between 1932 and 1944, and it was as 4-74 that aircraft 3139, crashed at Bydalen in March 1945 with only 2,062 hours flight time logged in 13 years. The very substantial remains were sold and the parts stored until 1997 when they were rediscovered by Mats Roth and transferred to the Aeronautical Engineering College at Vasteras for restoration to airworthy condition. As Fv568, 3113 survived two major accidents during her Air Force career, but was sold in an airworthy condition in February 1947 and registered SE-ATI to Hans Peterson at Orsa who occasionally operated her on a float chassis. In April 1949 the aircraft was acquired by the Royal Swedish Aero Club (KSAK) for glider tugging duties at the Central Gliding School, Alleberg, and remained operational in that capacity until 1985 when she underwent a major overhaul and restoration to her Air Force configuration. By consent of the authorities, the original registration SE-ADF was restored in June 1987, and painted in her wartime colours, panzergra (nearly black) and orange, the aircraft took up residence at the Alleberg Gliding Museum near Falkoping where she is maintained in airworthy condition.

In the mid-1930s it was customary for Sweden to build under licence most of the aircraft required for her own defence forces, a practice which enabled the services to match airframes with appropriate engines of their own defined choice. Apart from the Tiger Moth and Raab Katzenstein, a single seater used for advanced training and fitted with a Walter Castor engine, all other operational aircraft were matched to Bristol Aeroplane Company engines built in Sweden by NOHAB at Trollhättan.

Stag Lane built DH.82 Tiger Moth 5563, type Sk.11 of the Royal Swedish Air Force, on floats at Vasteras Centrala Flygverkstaden (CVV), a Tiger Moth repair station which licence-built the rival Focke Wulf Stieglitz (Sk.12) between 1939 and 1945. via Mats Roth

DH.82 Tiger Moth SE-ADF was delivered new to Sweden in 1932 and immediately taken on charge by the Air Force as 5568. Registered SE-ATI in 1947, the aircraft was operated as a glider tug by the Royal Swedish Aero Club. Original registration SE-ADF was restored in June 1987. This aircraft is the world's oldest surviving Tiger Moth of any marque and is maintained in airworthy condition. KSAK

While de Havilland were experiencing an increase in demand for the Tiger Moth there was a selective willingness to permit local production and it was agreed that three additional DH.82s ordered by the Swedish military were to be built under licence by Aktiebolaget Svenska Jarnvagsverkstaderna (ASJA) at Linkoping. Allocated build numbers 38-40 and military serials Fv597-Fv599, the three aircraft were taken on charge on 15th March 1935, two of them almost certainly replacements for aircraft of the original Stag Lane order which had been written off, and the third against predicted attrition.

First to be lost was Fv6562 (1727), the DH.60T Tiger Moth delivered after Hubert Broad's demonstrations in December 1931. The aircraft crashed on 16th April 1934 after 631 flying hours, and was struck off charge on 10th July. Next to suffer was Fv5595 (3140), which crashed at Ugerupsfalter on 20th September 1934 and was struck off on 16th October with even less recorded time at 593 hours. By 6th September 1935, Fv5567 (3112), had accumulated 1,010 hours when she came to grief at Eket, and was judged to be a total loss on 4th October.

Although the military serial numbers remained unaltered (a four digit number was displayed alongside the fuselage insignia on the otherwise all silver scheme, except for national colours of blue and yellow worn as vertical rudder stripes, the M/32 system), after 1935 all the aircraft adopted and displayed code numbers indicating to which Air Corps each belonged. By far the most numerous was 5- when the majority of Tiger Moths were employed for basic training duties at 5th Air Corps, Ljungbyhed, but in later life the survivors were scattered through other divisions, and allotments had reached 18- by 1944. Colours changed to the high visibility red and yellow in 1935 (M/35); low visibility panzergra/armour grey and orange in 1940 (M/40), with dark green replacing the near black panzergra in 1944 (M/44).

With the introduction of the improved Tiger Moth airframe married to the Gipsy Major engine early in 1933, it was apparent that any further production at Linkoping would need to be to the DH.82A standard. An order for ten such was placed with ASJA with delivery scheduled for the summer of 1935, the first to be taken on charge only two months after the last Sk.11. The new aircraft were designated Sk.11A and build positions 41-50 were allocated with Air Force serial numbers Fv519, Fv520 and Fv511-Fv518.

ASJA designed a number of improvements to cater for all-year operation in a widely variable and generally harsh environment. Pickup points for a float chassis were included as standard, and several aircraft were eventually operated in this configuration, including the Sk.11s imported from Stag Lane. Pilots were advised that should engine failure occur when operating float equipped aircraft over snow covered territory, an enforced landing should be treated like any other marine touchdown, and was likely to be much smoother and relatively uncomplicated, providing there

were no obstacles. Brackets were also fitted to enable a pair of skis to be carried along each fuselage side, a most practical measure born from experience to help crews cope with landings, scheduled or otherwise, away from base.

The Sk.11A retained the simple rubber block in compression system for main undercarriage damping, rejecting the greater complication of the steel multi spring Dowty legs introduced with the British DH.82A, and spin strakes were not fitted either during manufacture or retrospectively. Navigation lights were not carried, but an electrics panel accommodated on the re-designed instrument board, controlled a pitot heater and variable throat venturi. The crew enjoyed no visual interference from brass channel edging around either windscreen.

The Royal Swedish Air Force was well into its third full season of winter operations with the Tiger Moth when complaints were fed back to Hatfield via Hugh Buckingham that instructors believed the cockpits were too small for comfortable operation in heavy protective clothing. Undeterred, ASJA was contracted by the authorities to complete a second batch of ten Sk.11As in spite of the 12 Focke Wulf 44 Stieglitz which had been ordered in December 1936, just as Hugh Buckingham had signalled as a real probability 12 months previously.

Ten Gipsy Major engines were ordered from Stag Lane by Aero Material between December 1936 and June 1937, to coincide with the second batch of Sk.11A, Nos 66-75 (Fv509-Fv510, Fv546-Fv550, Fv553 and Fv589-Fv590), delivered in January (5), February (2) and June (3). Meanwhile, the first Sk.11A taken on charge, Fv511 (43), had flown only 77 hours between 21st May 1935 and 10th January 1936, when she came to grief at Barkarby.

The arrival at Ljungbyhed of the Stieglitz, Sk.12 on the Air Force inventory and licence manufactured by Vasteras Centrala Flygverkstaden (CVV) at Vasteras, in the same factory where most Tiger Moth overhauls and repairs were completed, released a number of the surviving Sk.11 and Sk.11As from training to other duties, and they were subsequently distributed amongst Air Corps' bases to be employed as communications aircraft and glider tugs.

DH.82 Tiger Moth 5595 in pre-war silver with vertical rudder stripes of blue and yellow, and typically bearing the 'Tiger Moth' star on the fin and 'DH' trademark symbols on each interplane strut. Note the reinforcement around the footstep below the rear cockpit. deHMC Archive

This glider tow hook arrangement fitted to a Swedish Tiger Moth is completely independent of the conventional tailskid assembly. Darryl Cott

Of the Linkoping built aircraft, only three have survived: Fv515 (47), remained in service until January 1952 when she was sold and registered SE-BYM. Operated by the Stockholm and Roslagen Aero Clubs, the aircraft was later sold to SAAB, refurbished and repainted in the pre-war M/35 high visibility colour scheme, and put on permanent display in the Royal Swedish Air Force Museum at Linkoping.

Fv517 (49), was struck off charge in March 1948 with a total of 1,561 hours flown in 13 years. The aircraft was acquired in a poor condition by Mats Roth of Vasteras who also traced the wings of Fv599 (40), which had been operated by the Skovde Aero Club since sale to the KVAK in May 1958. Rebuilt and registered as SE-AMR, '49' flew from Vasteras in September 1985 and is painted in the M/40 wartime scheme of panzergra and orange.

Another resident at Vasteras in M/35 colours, Sk.11A Fv553 (73), was retired from Air Force communications duties in November 1952, and together with Fv550 (72), was sold to the KSAK's Central Gliding School at Alleberg. Registered SE-BYL in May 1953, the aircraft was withdrawn from service in 1960, stored, and eventually sold to Peter Billing at Lidingo in 1983. The fuselage was sent to England in 1986 for restoration by Henry Labouchere at Langham and returned to Sweden where the post restoration flight on locally rebuilt wings took place on 4th April 1988.

A year after production of the Sk.12 began at Vasteras, the Swedish Air Force advised de Havilland in May 1938, that it had no requirement for any further Tiger Moths, and that licensed production at Linkoping would not be revived. By a strange twist of irony, notes and photographs covering Tiger Moth operations with the Swedish Air Force had only just been sent by de Havilland's Public Relations Department to Leonard Bridgman, respected staff member of *The Aeroplane* and Editor of *Janes,* to assist in compilation of an article on behalf of the American magazine *Popular Aviation.*

Following cancellation of the licence there came a request from KSAK to Aero Material that same year enquiring after details of price and delivery for five Tiger Moths to be supplied from Hatfield for distribution amongst affiliated Clubs. The resultant offer was not pursued, almost certainly for reasons of delivery position rather than price. Ultimately, the Club was obliged to wait until 7th May 1942 when a Norwegian built refugee Tiger Moth (164), was assigned to the Club as SE-ALK, although it crashed a year and two days later. Another Norwegian built Tiger Moth (172), was posted in as SE-ALM in July 1942 and survived to become a permanent exhibit at the Alleberg Museum. The two aircraft had been authorised for transfer to the Swedish civil register during the war following contact with and agreement from the Norwegian Government which had set up in exile in England. The Club acquired additional Tiger Moths in 1947 (1), 1952 (2) and 1958 (2).

In July 1938, ASJA test pilot Lennart Segerqvist paid a courtesy visit to Hatfield, but there was to be no more Tiger Moth production from the erstwhile railway factory at Linkoping for him to test. Sven Blomberg, the de Havilland agent with Aero Material, was appointed General Representative for Sweden, Norway and Denmark in 1946, and was closely involved with the introduction of DH.100 Vampires into the region in the early post-war years. He was also actively concerned with the inauguration of the Swedish National Aircraft Factory, Svenska Aeroplan AB (SAAB), which took over the facilities offered by the old Tiger Moth factory at Linkoping.

Very little is known of the activities of the Tiger Moth in Portugal. Like the similar situation in France, Portuguese military records are not open to public scrutiny, and those who may have details have proved unwilling or unable to communicate.

Through the efforts of the de Havilland agent in Portugal, Carlos Bleck, aided by the demonstration flying of Christopher Clarkson, the Portuguese Government contracted to purchase 23 Tiger Moths: a DH.60T Tiger Moth, G-ABPH (1732), and a DH.82, G-ABSK (1796), in December 1931, followed by 3159-3169 and 3212-3221, ordered by the Ministry of War, Lisbon, and delivered without serial numbers in 1933 and 1934. A further batch of eight aircraft, 3645-3652, was delivered at the beginning of 1938, consigned to Oficinas Gerais de Material Aeronáutico (OGMA), the government aircraft factory at Alverca.

During manufacture of the last eight Portuguese Tiger Moths at Hatfield in December 1937, the factory was visited by a delegation of military officers from OGMA, led by Major Beja, whose brief was to study manufacturing facilities and requirements. de Havilland had previously signed a licence agreement with OGMA and at the time of the visit, production had already begun.

Stag Lane was somewhat embarrassed to receive an order for 12 Gipsy Major engines in March 1938 as production capacity was allocated for the next three months, but the Engine Division promised to endeavour to supply at the rate of four engines a month from June 1938. In April an order for a single engine was received directly from the Portuguese Naval Air Service, a clue perhaps to the allocation of at least some of the British built aircraft. In the event, Stag Lane dispatched seven engines in June and five in July.

A second batch of Tiger Moths was laid down at Alverca early in 1939 and an order was placed on Stag Lane for the supply of ten Gipsy Major engines, eight of which were delivered the following month. It is believed production at OGMA continued into the early 'forties, and eventually reached a total of 91 aircraft.

As a neutral country during the Second World War, the Portuguese Government was at liberty to organise military supplies from whichever source it saw fit, and in September 1943, the British Government supplied 20 new Tiger Moths, followed by a further ten in December 1944.

One aircraft was civil registered in 1940, CS-ADS, but cancelled in 1947 having offered no clues to previous identity or use. CS-ADH joined the register in 1948 but crashed in June of the same year without revealing her secrets. CS-AAA was listed to the Department of Civil Aviation, Lisbon, in 1946, identified as 3650, one of the last batch bought from Hatfield. The aircraft was maintained in an airworthy state after presentation to the Portuguese Air Force Museum and was painted in military colours with serial '111'. Damaged in 1978 but repaired to static condition, the Tiger Moth is currently displayed at the Museu do Ar at Alverca. It is possible that Portugal was the intended or actual customer for Tiger Moths confiscated by the Germans in Norway and Denmark, but there is no hard public evidence to support the theory.

Between 1957 and 1961, 48 Tiger Moths were registered in Portugal and Mozambique of which 16 quoted manufacturer's serial numbers allocated by OGMA, and four were identified as wartime imports from Great Britain. Twelve others quoted numbers from a series allocated following major rebuilding or repair. One of these, DHTM.3A, believed to be P1, the first licence built Tiger Moth, was registered CS-AEF to the Aero Club de Porto in 1957, but the registration was cancelled in 1970 when the aircraft appeared in the Portuguese Air Force Museum painted with serial '102'. Moved to storage at Sintra in 1978 and to the OGMA factory in February 1989, the Tiger Moth was restored to airworthy condition on behalf of the Portuguese Air Force Historic Flight. On 20th May 1996, 102 represented the host country at Beja during the regular NATO Forces' 'Tiger Meet', and carried an ungainly legend, triple banked in large capital letters along the length of the fuselage:

'Once a Tiger . . . Always a Tiger!'

Portuguese built Tiger Moth P.12 was civilianised as CS-AFC in 1959 after service with the Air Force, and suffered a number of major mishaps before relegation to storage on behalf of the Museum at Alverca. deHMC Archive

Marked as '111' when displayed at Alverca, this Tiger Moth was part of the last batch delivered to the pre-war Portuguese Government from Hatfield. Listed to the Department of Civil Aviation in 1946 as CS-AAA, she had been presented to the Portuguese Air Force Museum as an airworthy exhibit by 1968. via Stuart Howe

ADVENTURE IN CANADA

8905, part of the middle third of the last batch of 350 DH.82C Tiger Moths delivered to the RCAF between March and September 1942. Production averaged 51 aircraft per month throughout the run and peaked at 75 aircraft per month at the end of 1941. deHMC Archive

THE proposal to establish a Canadian branch of the de Havilland Company grew after a visit to Stag Lane in 1927 by Captain Roy Maxwell, acting on behalf of the Ontario Provincial Government. He was permitted to fly a conventional Moth, and acting upon his suggestion, the company made hurried arrangements with Short Bros at Rochester to fit a DH.60 with a float chassis, and to fly trials from the River Medway. The subsequent purchase of four Cirrus Moths by the Provincial Government to be employed as fire spotters, and their immediate and popular acceptance, was reason enough for Business Director Francis St Barbe to travel to the Dominion that same year to view the prospects for further business.

In January 1928, Bob Loader arrived in Toronto, sent out from Stag Lane with a brief to set up the de Havilland Aircraft of Canada Ltd, a task which he quickly and efficiently achieved. By February a disused warehouse had been acquired at Mount Dennis to act as a reception and storage facility for Moths which were already en route in their packing cases from London, accompanied by Arthur Robins carrying the necessary lore and experience on a temporary posting from his duties in the Stag Lane erecting shop. By March the company was fully incorporated and a small aerodrome had been established at de Lesseps Field on part of the home estate of Frank Tretheway, an enthusiastic member of the Toronto Flying Club. By the end of 1928 a total of 62 Moths had been processed and sold by the new company, a level of business which warranted a change of premises, and accordingly in the spring of 1929, work began on the erection of buildings and preparation of an aerodrome site at Downsview, which was ready to be occupied in September.

The company continued to flourish and booked sales of the DH.61 Giant Moth, re-engined to accept a Pratt and Whitney Wasp radial in deference to local requirements. Competition from other manufacturers was fierce and forced de Havilland into adapting their designs to cope more realistically with the Canadian environment, especially the winter conditions. In 1931, the company lost an order for 20 primary trainers required by the Royal Canadian Air Force to the Fleet Fawn, an aircraft of American origin assembled in Canada, and which in many respects St Barbe admitted was better than the DH.60M. When in 1936 the RCAF was struggling to understand what a Gipsy Major powered Tiger Moth really was, they bought another ten Fawns, and further increased their establishment after that. The DH.80 Puss Moth was also facing a severe challenge from Stinson who were offering a 215hp four seater equipped with electric starter, tailwheel and brakes for less than £1,000.

Drawing on his operational experience and an increasing exposure to competing designs, the Director of the RCAF advised St Barbe during a second business visit in April and May 1931, homeward bound to England at the end of his world tour, that the Air Force would buy no more DH.60 Moths for training until and unless both emergency egress and the view from the front cockpit were improved. The message was clear and echoed those precise sentiments being expressed at home. At Stag Lane the re-engineered DH.60T Tiger Moth emerged from its corner of the workshop only five months later with both problems resolved.

The 1931 Christmas letter distributed to shareholders and signed by the Chairman of the Canadian board, W R Parker, drew attention to the company's new model.

'The Tiger Moth is a new type of training machine which has been specially designed to meet the requirements of the Royal Canadian Air Force, and from the tests which have been completed, your Directors are satisfied that this should prove another successful type to be added to the Company's lines'.

During his report to the Annual General Meeting of the de Havilland Aircraft of Canada Ltd, held on 8th January 1932, Bob Loader, introduced against his North American title as Company Vice President, praised the virtues of the Puss Moth and Bert Hinkler's flight to England, announced that Downsview was to become the Canadian centre for Bellanca aircraft production and refurbishment, and that three other manufacturers in Canada had chosen Gipsy engines. He ended his review by saying: *'We have recently demonstrated to the Dominion Government a new type of training aircraft known as the Tiger Moth, which we believe to be definitely superior to any other craft for similar duties in existence. This type has already been purchased in quantity by the RAF and the possibility of it being accepted as the standard training type is, I understand, exceedingly encouraging'.*

Canada's first Tiger Moth was one of the eight aircraft built to the DH.60T Tiger Moth specification: G-ABNI (1726). The British registration was cancelled in June 1931 and she was shipped to Toronto where she became CF-APL in September, known affectionately as 'Apple'. Operated by the company as a demonstrator on both a wheeled undercarriage and floats, the aircraft was acquired by Leigh Capreol, the company test pilot, when he left Downsview in 1933 as part of an economy measure, and set up a charter business on the Toronto waterfront partnered by Chuck and Jack Austin. Test piloting duties subsequently became the responsibility of the versatile Lee Murray, an Australian by birth, who had arrived from England that year to assume the post of General Manager in succession to Bob Loader who returned to promotional activities with the Business Office at Stag Lane.

The 'Apple' subsequently passed to Walter Deisher, a private owner based in Ottawa before sale to the Toronto Flying Club and ultimate donation in 1942 to the Central Technical School in Toronto, where the airframe was eventually scrapped. It was hardly the 'exceedingly encouraging' start which Bob Loader and his chairman had anticipated at the end of 1931, and it was not until August 1935 that the Canadian company took delivery of another Tiger Moth from England, a fully developed DH.82A.

Build No 3348 was a conventional model but with an extra fuel tank installed on the floor of the front cockpit and a plumbed in system which permitted sustained inverted flight. Intended as a new demonstration aircraft for the British company, she had been built with a batch of aeroplanes scheduled for the Reserve Schools, and modified for aerobatics at the approved higher gross weight of 1,770lb. The registration letters G-ADHA were allocated but never carried.

In 1984 at a time when the British registration authorities were more generous in their attitude, the letters were re-allocated to a DH.83 Fox Moth imported into England from the USA, which had been a direct export to New Zealand exactly 50 years previously, and which was in need of a 'period' registration. In Canada, the letters CF-AVG were issued to 3348 on 24th August 1935.

Having taken heed and 'winterised' the open cockpit DH.60 Moth, and generally adapted the type to the Canadian environment, there were more than several astonished to find that 3348 had been built to European standards and delivered with no apparent attempt to offer any form of winter protection. A sliding canopy was soon fitted which replaced both conventional windscreens and was found to be generally easier to install due to the revised geometry of the centre section. In this configuration CF-AVG was widely demonstrated by the immensely capable Lee Murray; included in his itinerary was the RCAF in Ottawa and at Camp Borden, and every flying club within a reasonable radius.

As a result of his tour, Lee Murray was officially advised that although the new aircraft met all the criteria laid down by the Air Force, there was no budget to buy a single one, and only four sales in total resulted from the exercise. The quartet was dispatched from Hatfield in July 1936 less engines

The first Tiger Moth delivered to Canada was a type DH.60T, G-ABNI, registered CF-APL in September 1931 and known to the workforce as 'Apple'. Note the configuration of the open front cockpit door. Bombardier Aerospace

A view of a Canadianised DH.82A which highlights some of the features adopted to create the 'C' model: low chord steel interplane struts; lagged oil tank with new filler and drain necks; rudder cable shroud; new instrument panels and canopy with sliding mechanism. The blind flying curtain can just be seen folded down on the starboard side of the rear canopy. It was deployed by the pupil who pulled it up and over his head, the curtain running on two rails which followed the contours of the canopy frame. Don Long

which were to be installed at Downsview, together with sliding canopies, and each aircraft was subsequently registered to the Department of National Defence for operations by the flying clubs at Moose Jaw (3478/CF-CBR); Calgary (3481/CF-CBS); Hamilton (3479/CF-CBT) and Kingston (3480/CF-CBU). CF-CBR was donated to the Director of Youth Training in 1941 and CF-CBS went to Saskatoon Technical College in the same year, both re-classified as ground instructional airframes. CF-CBT was destroyed by a fire which originated in the engine compartment as the aircraft was being started at Hamilton on 16th April 1940. CF-CBU remained a civil registered aircraft throughout the war, transferring from Kingston to Toronto Flying Club in January 1941, and to the Department of Transport the following October. In May 1944 she was operating in Winnipeg and from 1946 in Arborg, Manitoba. Landing on snow at Elliott Lake on 20th February 1946, she overturned and was abandoned on site. CF-AVG continued in use for occasional demonstrations but spent more time as a company communications aeroplane in and around the Province.

In May 1936 after a three year commitment, Lee Murray returned to England to take up the position of General Manager at Hatfield. He was replaced in that same capacity at Downsview by Phillip Garratt, a Toronto born man who had been studying medicine when the First World War broke out, the reason which caused him to become a fighter pilot instead. Although the owner of a chemical company, Phil Garratt had been recruited as a test and demonstration pilot for de Havilland in Canada on an enthusiastic *ad hoc* basis, and was invited to join the board of directors in 1935.

The new manager immediately campaigned to sell demonstrator CF-AVG to the Air Force at a price of $5,000, insisting that the aircraft had been respecified to their requirements and already had cost the company $6,000. Four months of correspondence finally resulted in recognition and appreciation by Ottawa that the new aircraft was fitted with the Gipsy Major engine, an improved version of the Gipsy III, an example of which they already held in reserve for a Puss Moth. To save money, the Air Force suggested that they might fit their spare Gipsy III if the Tiger Moth airframe alone could be secured for a reasonable sum. Before the matter could be pursued, Garratt received a letter from the Director of Contracts dated 24th September 1936, in which he stated the concern held by some elements of the Air Force, who still believed they were faced with acquiring a single engine of a new design.

Phil Garratt was still convinced that the Tiger Moth should become a primary trainer with the Air Force which added more Fleet biplanes to its inventory early in 1937. His persuasive lobbying of Ottawa, discussion on design improvements, and offer to build the aircraft in Toronto, resulted in the issue of specification C/11/36, and a contract for the supply of 28 Tiger Moths was signed on 12th March 1937. The order itemised 27 brand new aircraft built to the basic British DH.82A design but re-engineered locally to conform to the issued specification, and to be known as type DH.82A(Can) Tiger Moth. Demonstrator CF-AVG was included in the sale as the 28th aircraft, but first it was completely disassembled for every part to be drawn and used as a working pattern.

Don Long was promoted Chief Designer and W E Ledingham was hired as his assistant only three days after the contract signature, to be joined on the programme by Peter Gooch on 3rd May. CF-AVG was nominally accepted on behalf of the Air Force and immediately returned to de Havilland for remodelling. To provide essential assistance, a complete set of working drawings was received from Hatfield on 14th May.

Under Don Long's experienced eye, the Drawing Office called up its considerable knowledge and experience gained as the result of Moth operations throughout the Dominion during the previous ten years. Unlike some customers who required multi-role Moths, the RCAF expected their Tiger Moths to be used only as primary trainers, but on wheeled or ski equipped undercarriages and in severe climatic conditions.

The main changes which led the transition from DH.82A to DH.82A(Can) were listed by the Chief Designer:

- Wide plywood walkways located on lower wings adjacent to each side of the fuselage, finished with a granulated cork non slip surface.
- Plywood leading edges on the upper surfaces of both lower mainplanes.
- Re-inforced hand holds at the tip bow position on both lower mainplanes.
- Mass balanced ailerons.
- Streamline section steel interplane struts replacing the wider chord wooden struts.
- A covering of 2in thick Dunlopillo foam rubber over the instrument panels to act as crashpads in preference to normal headroll.
- A new canopy, similar to that fitted to the imported DH.82A Tiger Moths, but with an aluminium frame rather than steel tubing, ball bearing track rollers and a transparent fairing built into the rear-most of the three sections. The canopy over the rear cockpit included provision for a blind flying curtain. As a complete unit, fitted to the aircraft, the canopy employed 838 individual parts in its manufacture.
- A cockpit heating system fed from a muff on the long exhaust tailpipe.
- A differential action built into the elevator spring trimming system to improve feel.
- Fire extinguisher, watch holder and document pouch all provided against standard RCAF specification.
- Engine cowling to be constructed in three pieces only rather than five, opening from a central hinge line running fore and aft along the top cowling, permitting instant access to left, right and underside of the engine.

- Enlarged filler necks with quick action caps, on fuel and oil tanks, and with an enlarged drain on the oil tank which was fitted with quilted lagging for winter protection, easily removed for more temporate conditions.
- Fuel tank vent and bonding tabs to standard RCAF specification.
- The Borden Safety Harness also designed to RCAF specification comprised two shoulder harness straps attached to a transverse cable, but joining at the crutch position from where a single strap attached to another transverse cable at floor level.
- Heavy duty main undercarriage axles to cope with operations on skis.

The new Tiger Moth line was identified with build numbers C301-C330 to accommodate 30 airframes. CF-AVG (UK build No 3348) was allocated RCAF serial 238; C301-C320 became RCAF 239-258; and C322-C326, RCAF 275-279. Positions C321, C327 and C329 were built as civil aircraft, CF-CFJ, CF-BNF and CF-BNC respectively. C328 and C330 were never completed as whole aeroplanes and may have been sacrificed as test specimens.

At lunchtime on 21st December 1937, a miserably cold day, and with the aerodrome covered in snow, Phil Garratt test flew C301 (RCAF 239), operating from the rear cockpit, and dressed unobtrusively in his city overcoat and trilby hat. From contract to first flight the programme had consumed less than 10 months, and 239 was delivered to the RCAF at Trenton, at that time Canada's newest and biggest flying base, on 18th January 1938. The remainder of the order followed as agreed and was complete by 12th April.

In her new guise as RCAF 238, Hatfield's 3348 was taken onto military charge on 28th February 1938, but by June 1939 had been civil registered CF-CGZ on behalf of the Department of National Defence. Until May 1941 when she re-mustered into the Air Force, the Tiger Moth was operated for approximately six months each by the Aero Club of British Columbia; Edmonton and Northern Alberta Aero Club and Moose Jaw Flying Club. In February 1944 '238' was finally struck off the inventory having been reduced to spare parts at No 6 Repair Depot, Trenton.

CF-CFJ (C321), is believed to have been fitted with a Gipsy III engine and delivered to the Kitchener-Waterloo Flying Club in February 1938 on behalf of the Department of Transport. Transferred to the Toronto Flying Club in December 1940, ownership passed through several Ontario based organisations until November 1946 when the registration was cancelled as 'lapsed', probably a reference to non-renewal of the Certificate of Airworthiness (C of A).

CF-BNC (C329), was registered to the manufacturer in October 1939 and delivered to their flight hangar at Downsview on 7th May 1940. She may have been used for development activity between the two dates. In June the aircraft was sold to the Hamilton Flying Club where she remained until 1951. Last registered to a private owner in Toronto, the C of A lapsed in June 1955 and the allocation was finally cancelled two years later.

Having established a good production base, Phil Garratt was keen to ensure that the Air Force purchased more Tiger Moths in preference to any other type, especially as Ottawa had declared early in 1938 that following delivery of the first order, no more RCAF DH.60 aircraft would be overhauled or rebuilt, neither would Gipsy I or Gipsy II engines be re-lifed once they had become time expired. To some extent, the engine situation had been catered for by the creation of a workshop which was accepting Gipsy Major engines from Stag Lane supplied in kit form. Nine sets had been dispatched from England in July 1937 followed by six more in August.

A general review of the situation surrounding Canadian built Tiger Moths appeared in the February 1938 edition of *The de Havilland Gazette:*

'Without sacrificing the essential characteristics of the Tiger Moth as a trainer of up-to-date orthodoxy, several interesting detail modifications have been introduced to suit Canadian conditions. The aircraft have interchangeable wheel, ski or float chassis and must operate as efficiently and conveniently in the severest cold of winter as in the heat of summer.

'A sliding transparent coupe top affords cabin protection without restricting vision or ease of exit, and incorporates a blind flying hood of instant actuation. The instrument panels cater for all primary and blind flying instruction and are covered with moulded rubber pads for protection in the event of minor accident. The special RCAF fighting harness is fitted in both cockpits. Trim has to cover all conditions of summer and winter operations and a differential spring loading on the elevator control affords a comfortable longitudinal trim, thumb operated ratchet levers being provided in both cockpits for trimming the tail.

'The ventilation system supplies heated air to the cockpits in winter or cool air in summer, and another special winter provision consists of quickly attachable masks and covers to reduce the amount of engine cooling and oil tank cooling.

'For convenient maintenance, particularly in seaplane use, a three piece engine cowling similar to that used on the Dragonfly has been adopted. The tanks have quick acting bayonet filler caps and there is a special cap to expedite oil draining in winter. A pressure type fire extinguisher in the engine bay may be operated from either cockpit or from outside the aircraft at a point convenient to the person cranking the engine.

'The contract for the new Tiger Moths was secured at the end of April last, and since then all the jigs and tools have been built and the entire aircraft have been constructed there, the only imported items being standard parts such as bolts, instruments and wheels. The Gipsy Major I engines have been assembled and tested in Toronto.

'The staff has lately been increased, two new hangars have enlarged the factory, and new plant including sheet metal formers and machines, has been installed, while the older welding and finishing shops, stores, airframe and engine assembly departments have been much augmented'.

Perhaps it was a lack of awareness that their new trainer was equipped with a canopy that led an unknown RCAF uniformed hand to pen an ode to the biplane:

It's a practical craft, a biplane,
Its beauty is not all that you gain,
The upper wing's gift
Is additional lift,
Besides which
It keeps out the rain.

With Hatfield-supplied DH.82A Tiger Moth RCAF 238 (ex CF-AVG), and locally built C302 (RCAF 240) standing by, preparations are made at Downsview to launch DH.82A (Can) C301, RCAF 239, on her maiden flight four days before Christmas, 1937. Fred Hotson

The third production DH.82A(Can) Tiger Moth, RCAF 241 (C303), was quickly introduced to the flight test programme, taking advantage of the seasonal conditions to explore the type's performance with a ski undercarriage.
Don Long

Once the new facilities at Downsview were available and space was plentiful, each of the aircraft of the March 1937 contract could be rigged *in situ*. One of the three civil aircraft called up and allocated a late production slot, CF-BNF (C327), is on the left of the picture ahead of the fleet.
Bombardier Aerospace

In July 1938, de Havilland Aircraft of Canada placed an order with Stag Lane for 50 more Gipsy Major engines to be delivered as sub-assemblies, and suggested that a further 50 were in prospect. Deliveries were promised from September starting at two engine sets per week but soon rising to four. Stag Lane was already considering its plans for streamlining production when the Air Ministry increased its Gipsy Major order in August 1938 from 810 to 1,020. Slightly later than forecast, the first 15 kits for Canada were dispatched in October with 15 more the following month.

The engine orders were placed in anticipation of a contract for 100 Tiger Moths expected shortly to be confirmed by the Canadian Government. At the beginning of August, Phil Garratt was in discussion with Hatfield concerning the prospects of his currently under-utilised factory capacity assisting with large orders for Tiger Moths then being contemplated in England, and it was suggested that for practical assistance, Downsview could supply 200 fuselage frames built to the British specification. A Canadian order, should it come, could not be satisfied concurrently from existing facilities, and on 19th August, Garratt cabled Hatfield in anticipation to request a substantial cash loan in order to undertake immediate plant extensions, the loan to be serviced by the shipment of fuselage frames to England.

Hatfield was already showing some concern over the financial state of the Canadian company and were interested to learn whether they were intending to make a profit on the prospective government order, and if so how much. When the order was completed, would they find themselves with a surplus of personnel and other commitments? Lee Murray and Hatfield Chief Designer R E Bishop visited Canada to see for themselves and the agreement for 200 fuselages and additional metal parts was eventually confirmed, plus the approval for considerable modification and expansion of the plant into a facility which was described as having the capacity to produce 300-400 aircraft per annum. The building extension work was begun in September 1938 and completed in time for a Christmas dinner party and dance in one of the new shops on 23rd December.

Build numbers E1-E200 were allocated to the fuselages scheduled for export from the autumn of 1938. A photograph which appeared in the *de Havilland Gazette* for November 1938 was accompanied by a caption which indicated that the aeroplane sized wooden crate being prised open in the rain by an extraordinarily tall man (for the benefit of the photographer no doubt), was the *'first of many packages received from Canada containing Tiger Moth metal components'*.

Hatfield probably absorbed the frames into their production schedules for 400 aircraft built between November 1938 and June 1939 (commencing 3773); 300 aircraft between July 1939 and January 1940 (commencing 82227), and another 400 aircraft between December 1939 and May 1940 (commencing 82551). Hatfield build positions 82599 to 82692 inclusive were never allocated any identity, giving authority to the belief that the order for all 200 fuselages was never fulfilled, and the supposition must be that the effort required to build the last 94, all of which would have been required towards the end of 1939, was diverted back into the next major contract from the Canadian Government, anticipated for over a year, but not actually received until February 1940, five months after the declaration of war.

The Canadian fuselages were manufactured against British drawings when pattern parts from CF-AVG were not available. Inspection of the first units on arrival in England brought forth howls of anguish and pages of snag sheets which were expeditiously communicated to Downsview.

Not unnaturally, Canada was far from amused, and Chief Designer Don Long was sent to Hatfield in December 1938 to defend his company and explain the situation. Six months later, similar problems arose when Morris Motors suffered slings and arrows after building fuselages to drawings supplied from Hatfield.

Having got production of the Canadianised DH.82A under way as the DH.82A (Can), the Downsview Drawing Office sought to add even more refinements in advance of the next prospective order. A significant improvement was provided by the installation of cable operated Bendix mainwheel brakes, a system identical to that on the Puss Moth, and a fully castoring tailwheel with pneumatic tyre. The brake was activated by a hand lever fitted in both cockpits, and mechanically modulated by the rudder pedals for steering on the ground. The undercarriage radius rods were shortened to permit

The tail wheel assembly of the 'C' model was constructed along identical lines to the basic skid. Steering on the ground was assisted by a pair of ears bolted through the lower front member of the rudder. deHMC Archive

Clearly identified by the radius of the middle cowl (decking) are these fuselages for DH.82C Tiger Moths under construction at Downsview. Seats and engine bearers can be seen in the foreground whilst rear fuselage pylons are stacked vertically at top right. Bombardier Aerospace

revision of the angle of the compression legs, sweeping them forward, guarding against any tendency for the aircraft to lift her tail when brakes were applied. The decking between the cockpits was reduced in radius and height, a change which when combined with smaller instrument panels, cut 3 inches off each side, enabling direct forward vision from the rear seat. New American sourced instruments of smaller diameter were recessed into the foam rubber covered panels, and the layout completely revised.

The apparent difficulties experienced with the elevator trimmer fitted to the DH.82B at Hatfield in 1939, clearly did not deter Don Long and his design team, and a tab was set into the trailing edge of each elevator, to which mass balances were introduced. The trimmer was capable of precision setting by finger tip control exercised in either cockpit.

Before delivery to Hamilton Flying Club in June 1940, Tiger Moth CF-BNC (C329), had been used by de Havilland as a test vehicle for both brakes and trimmer, but the first serious brake trials were credited to the third of the civilian DH.82A(Can) aircraft, C327, which was first flown as an unregistered test aircraft by Phil Garratt on 9th December 1938, and was to continue in service for some time as an important trials machine.

The improvements to the DH.82A(Can) continued with the choice of the Gipsy Major IC as standard engine, rated at 140hp for take off as compared with 122hp for the basic Gipsy Major I, and to which the Air Force insisted on fitting a pressure system fire extinguisher. Another user requirement was for battery powered navigation and signalling lamps and modifications to the canopy which would permit it to be jettisoned. Although de Havilland argued that the canopy rolled back very satisfactorily to allow either occupant freedom to step over the side, the modification programme was insisted upon and proved to be extremely awkward and frustrating to satisfy.

Following the delivery of the last DH.82A (Can) on 12th April 1939, the factory closed down the Tiger Moth line without receiving the 100 aeroplane order for which engines had already been delivered in anticipation. Downsview accepted an unexpected order from the Air Force to refurbish 12 DH.60 Moths which were to be supplied to civilian flying clubs as part of a government sponsored training scheme. The contract allowed the workforce to be maintained without layoff, and as the last overhauled DH.60 was delivered in August, the Dominion found itself only days short of involvement in a world war.

The British Commonwealth Air Training Plan was announced on 10th December 1939, and in February 1940 the de Havilland Aircraft of Canada Ltd received a government order to supply 404 Tiger Moths embodying all the modifications and improvements which had been authorised under specification AP/3/39. The number of aircraft exactly equalled an order recently placed with Fleet for their Canadian built Finch trainer. The new type designation was to be DH.82C, 'C' for Canada, and owing no allegiance whatever to the system of identification which had been established elsewhere. The first aircraft built to the specification, C331 (RCAF 4001), was erected almost immediately, flown by Bruce Douglas on 12th March and handed over to the RCAF on 10th April 1940.

Until the submarine menace in the North Atlantic had been finally addressed, the shipping of materials and supplies in easterly or westerly directions was hazardous, and the Canadian company quickly realised how dangerous their situation could become should they find themselves isolated from their sole source of engine supply. Propellers were the least problem supplied from Laidlaw in Toronto and 'S and S' in Winnipeg. On mainland North America they sought and found an alternative powerplant: the D-4 Pirate engine designed and built by the Menasco Manufacturing Company of Los Angeles, California.

During the 1930s, de Havilland engines were in daily use all over the world, supported by a thriving airframe industry and first rate publicity machine. Overseen by Frank Halford's enthusiastic and capable design team and the boundless energies of the Business Director, output was substantial and profitable. The Canadian company's concern was that an interruption of the supply line, for whatever reason, could result in a factory full of engineless airframes. In England in 1936, Phillips and Powis, Woodley based manufacturers of Miles aircraft designs, realised that as far as their powerplant requirements were concerned, de Havilland held a virtual monopoly and could vary speed of supply, price and development potential at will. The success of the Miles Hawk range of touring and racing aeroplanes had boosted the image of the Gipsy engine, but posed a simultaneous threat to the continued success of the airframe side of de Havilland's business.

The Miles design team was looking for improved performance which they wrongly believed was not a priority at Stag Lane, and in order to achieve greater independence, approached Menasco in California with a view not only to using their engines, but to build the range under licence in England. Examples of 'B' and 'C' series engines were delivered to Woodley during the year, and plans were agreed to import American manufacturing jigs and tools. Al Menasco, Chairman of the company, visited the Phillips and Powis factory on at least two occasions in 1936, carrying a C-4 Pirate engine with him on the first visit. In July 1937, with licences signed, contracts placed with suppliers and construction of an engine test rig all but complete, Charles Powis suddenly resigned from Woodley following a dispute over policy and the Menasco company was advised shortly after that the project would not be continuing. Phillips and Powis continued to work on their Hawk Trainer, soon to be built in hundreds for the RAF as the Gipsy Major powered Magister, and early in 1938, Al Menasco too resigned from office in Los Angeles and enlisted in the United States Army Air Force.

There was some irony in the contact now made between a company bearing the de Havilland name, and an engine supplier whose practical ideas, had they been developed in England, might have caused commercial embarrassment. On offer to Phil Garratt was an engine from the Menasco D series, the -4 Pirate, physically similar and with a performance almost identical to the Gipsy Major IC.

The Menasco D-4 Pirate was rated at 130 hp on take off: 10hp and 100rpm less than the Gipsy Major IC, and was heavier by about 50lb complete with all accessories. Distinguished by a crankcase of stove enamelled dark blue, both air and ground crew needed to be aware that the propeller rotation was in the opposite sense from the Gipsy Major which turned in an anti-clockwise direction when viewed from the cockpit. The first installation (of a C4 model) was made in Downsview's development aircraft C327, CF-BNF, and test flying by Bruce Douglas began on 30th June 1940.

Deliveries of the 404 DH.82Cs ordered in February 1940 and fitted with Gipsy Major IC engines provided by the British Ministry of Aircraft Production, began on 10th April 1940 (C331-C734, RCAF 4001-4404), and all had been placed on charge by 12th March 1941 when further contracts were already under discussion. Ten aircraft with Menasco Pirate engines and ordered for delivery between 15th May and 11th June 1941 were re-designated DH.82C2 by de Havilland and Menasco Moth by the Air Force (C735-C744, RCAF 4935-4944). The continuing supply of engines from Stag Lane promoted orders for another 428 DH.82C specification aircraft (C745-C974, RCAF 4946-5175; C975-C999, RCAF 5800-5824, and C1128-C1302, RCAF 5825-5999), which were delivered progressively from April to December 1941. These followed a second batch of Menasco Moths which had entered service as wireless trainers in the first half of 1941 (C1000-C1127, RCAF 4810-4812, 4830-4934 and 4945), excepting airframes C1125 and C1126 which were not completed and may have been siphoned off for structural test or major damage repair.

DH.82C4 Menasco Moth 4861, built as a wireless trainer and powered by the Menasco D-4 Pirate engine, a type chosen as insurance against potential losses of imported British built Gipsy Major engines. Tell-tale sign of a Menasco under the cowling was the right hand rotation of the propeller. Gerald F Schwam

The wireless trainers were designated DH.82C4 (Menasco Moth II) and appeared ideally suited to the task on account of the engine driven generator system. The rear cockpit was stripped of its instrument panel, crash protection and inter-cockpit decking, and received instead a complement of obsolescent wireless equipment shipped in from Great Britain, complete with wind-up trailing aerials. For the task the aircraft were overloaded and under powered, and although they served with the four wireless schools at St. Hubert, Guelph, Winnipeg and Calgary, all were replaced as soon as practicable, and converted back to standard Menasco Moth trainers. In order to salvage some credibility, a Gipsy Major I Wireless Trainer designated DH.82C3 was proposed, but never progressed beyond initial planning.

The Menasco development aircraft C327 was registered CF-BNF to Leavens Brothers Air Services of Toronto, on 7th September 1940, a company chosen by Ottawa to administer a major repair and service centre for the Tiger Moth. Leavens Brothers converted CF-BNF back to Gipsy Major power and in September 1941 she was re-registered to the de Havilland Aircraft of Canada Ltd at Postal Station L, Toronto, where she became the personal transport of company director and General Manager Phil Garratt. Sold in January 1948, the sixth owner from 18th January 1957, but for only six months, was Leavens Bros. of Toronto. Sold twice more to owners in Hamilton and Exeter, the aircraft was acquired by Frank Ball of St. Mary's, Ontario in November 1962. Preserved in airworthy condition, Canada's oldest Tiger Moth is operated in the open cockpit configuration of an original and unique DH.82A(Can).

This batch of DH.82C Tiger Moths under construction at Downsview was taken onto RCAF charge from late in 1941. 5935 was transported by surface to the Reserve Depot at Calgary, erected and air delivered to 33 EFTS Caron on 6th January 1942. Captain Bert Davis

Menasco Moths in service at the flying training schools were generally not popular due to their comparatively poor performance, flight characteristics which differed from the more numerous DH.82C, resulting from the opposite rotation of the engine, and the requirement for the engineers to stock duplicates of all engine spares. Following the second contracted batch, no further Menasco Moths were ordered, and the next 200 aircraft manufactured under the Mutual Aid programme on behalf of the United States, were all specified to receive the Gipsy Major IC.

These aircraft were scheduled for operations by the United States Army Air Force, although exactly where is not clear. For induction into the American military, the DH.82C became the Pursuit Trainer type PT-24, and anticipating full integration, the Air Service Command at Wright Field published a preliminary manual: *Operation and Maintenance Instructions, Model PT-24 Airplane* dated 10th February 1942. The designated aircraft (C1303-C1502) were allocated USAAF serial numbers 42-964 to 42-1163 and each manufacturer's plate carried the concise individual details including a date of clearance for test.

But the complexity of economic agreements cast in wartime and tied firmly to political decisions concocted far away from aeroplane factories and flying training schools, meant that the PT-24s were never to wear Uncle Sam's colours. The whole consignment was donated to the Air Training Plan, which might have been the intention all along, and were allocated RAF serial numbers FE100-FE266 and FH618-FH650, running consecutively. In turn the RAF consigned the fleet as an integral part of the Training Plan, and in the field the aircraft wore the standard yellow and black trainer colours of the RCAF, with serials 1100-1299 stencilled on their sides. Deliveries began on Christmas Eve 1941 and the last aircraft, C1502/42-1163/FH650/1299, was signed off from Downsview on 23rd March 1942, and was delivered on 8th April.

A further 350 DH.82C Tiger Moths were delivered to the RCAF commencing on 3rd March 1942 and ending with the last on 9th September: C1503-C1652, (RCAF 3842-3991); C1653-C1801, (RCAF 8851-8999), and C1802-C1825 plus C1827-C1853, (RCAF 9645-9695). Airframe C1826 was not completed and may have been extracted from the line and grafted onto an active aircraft as part of a major repair.

From April 1940 until September 1942, the factory at Downsview maintained an average output of 51 Tiger Moths per month, reaching a peak of 75 real aircraft per month at the end of 1941. With Tiger Moth production likely to be in decline from that heady time, a contract first for the assembly of imported aircraft previously used by the RAF in Great Britain, then gradual introduction to complete manufacture of Avro Ansons had been accepted, a standard twin for the Air Training Plan. By 1943 the Mosquito was soaking up huge productive effort, aided and abetted by Fred Plumb and Douglas Hunter, part of the team who had nurtured the first Tiger Moth at Stag Lane 12 years previously. Downsview built 1,549 Tiger Moth airframes in addition to the kits sent to Hatfield. Phil Garratt and his team could feel satisfied that their early lobbying had paid off.

DH.82A(Can) Tiger Moth No C327, registered CF-BNF in September 1940, was the flying test bed for the Menasco D-4 Pirate. Re-engined with a Gipsy Major, she became Phil Garratt's personal transport. In 1971 the aircraft was rebuilt by Watt Martin to open cockpit configuration. Watt Martin

From within the last batch of 20 DH.82C Tiger Moths built at Downsview in August 1942, 9680 (C1838), with a conventional undercarriage, cruises over a snowscape stretching as far as the eye can see. Note the bird attacking the engine cowling. via Watt Martin

At the very end of DH.82C production in September 1942, Geoffrey de Havilland Jr visited Downsview to attend to matters Mosquito, but was persuaded to sample the delights of what must be the ultimate marque of Tiger Moth. deHMC Archive

INDUSTRY FOR THE ANTIPODES

The unmistakable figure of John Neave clad in long leather coat, preparing for another day's work testing Tiger Moths. In the background, some of the 20 aircraft imported from Australia and erected at Rongotai late in 1941. RNZAF Museum

THE AUSTRALIAN BRANCH of the de Havilland Company, the de Havilland Aircraft Pty Ltd, was incorporated in Victoria on 7th March 1927 following a visit to the country by Major Hereward de Havilland the previous year. Stag Lane had decided that in order to better promote exports, it was imperative to offer a good local after-sales service, and the Australian Dominion was considered to be rich in prospects.

The business was established in a rat infested warehouse in south Melbourne and prospered until the recessionary times beginning in 1929, after which sales gradually declined and a number of customers, especially outback farmers hit by the poor state of the economy exacerbated by drought conditions, approached the company in the hope of selling back their aircraft.

The aviation activity in New South Wales, in and around Sydney, tempted the company to relocate and a new facility was purpose built at Mascot aerodrome where several machine tools were installed, the investment reckoned to offset the cost of transporting every requirement from England, but more importantly, establishing a local skills base which was considered essential for future development. Metal fittings and wooden wings were produced immediately after the new factory was opened in February 1931: the complexity of jigging for welded steel tube structures encouraged the continuing import of fuselages from the parent company for the time being.

During his world tour of de Havilland outposts in 1931, the company's Business Director, Francis St Barbe, had met Major Alan Murray Jones at the Australian Directorate of Civil Aviation . The two men had established an immediate rapport and Murray Jones was soon offered the post of Managing Director of the Sydney based company, a move which released Hereward de Havilland to return to England where he became a development pilot and production trouble shooter at Hatfield. Murray Jones was to prove a competent production test pilot and capable administrator.

The Mascot works was soon busy not only with sales, servicing and assembly of DH.60 Moths, but was also in receipt from England of DH.83 Fox Moths, DH.84 Dragons and DH.86s, commercial transport aircraft which assisted in bridging the gap in the private owner market left by the lingering effects of the depression.

Some of the Australian aero clubs recognised the advantages of the new Tiger Moth but were not prolific customers for the type even after British export authority had been approved. The first aircraft received, VH-UTD (3320), was not registered until May 1935, sold to the Newcastle Aero Club, a major flying training organisation closely associated with the type until the present time. The aircraft was named *Halcyon* during a ceremony at District Park aerodrome attended by 2,000 people on 3rd June. What might the crowd have believed had they been told that the 1,000th Tiger Moth to be assembled in Australia would roll out of the factory at Mascot only seven years later, a gifted aeroplane, purchased for £1,200 by the good folk of Kuringai, NSW, and the centre-piece of a ceremony in which she was handed over to the RAAF by Lady Gowrie, wife of the Governor General? Two more Tiger Moths VH-UVZ (3508) and VH-UXC (3515), were received late in 1936 respectively for Airflite Ltd, a training organisation based locally at Mascot, and the Whyalla Aero Club situated in South Australia.

The Royal Aero Club of New South Wales received VH-UYJ, VH-UYK and VH-UYL (3593, 3598 and 3600), in August and September 1937, which were followed by a pair for the Royal Victorian Aero Club at Essendon (VH-UYP/3622 and VH-UYR/3621), in November. Two Tiger Moths marked VH-UYO and VH-UYP were photographed for a Melbourne newspaper flying in close harmony over the mouth of the Yarra River a few days later, at which time it was noticed that the letters VH-UYO prominently displayed near the camera, had been allocated to a DH.87B Hornet Moth five months previously. The Tiger Moth should have been masked for painting as VH-UYR, a situation that was quickly remedied. Another for Newcastle (VH-UYQ/3623), was also delivered in November and seven further Tiger Moths were imported from Hatfield, erratically spread through 1938, before the persistence of Murray Jones was rewarded with the first major government order.

Australia's first civil registered DH.82A Tiger Moth, VH-UTD *Halcyon*, imported by the Newcastle Aero Club in 1935, photographed at Broken Hill in 1938.
Neville Parnell

In common with the economic juggling practised by many governments pre-war, the aero clubs were considered to be useful in that most could provide cheap rate basic flying training and financial inducements sponsored at official level could dictate their choice of equipment. Australia was no exception, and early in 1940 many clubs and schools operating mostly DH.60 Moths and some Tiger Moths, were formally contracted to provide elementary training to RAAF pilot recruits. Due to difficulties with the administration of payments, not to mention RAAF dissatisfaction with the quality of some instruction, the arrangement was cancelled the following April and by August all the aircraft had been impressed and absorbed into the rapidly expanding network of the RAAF's own Elementary Flying Training Schools (EFTS).

As a logical progression from its still strong association with the DH.60 Moth, of which 74 had been delivered to the Air Force between 1926 and 1936, and a further 48 civil aircraft impressed into service in 1940, de Havilland Australia tried on several occasions to interest the RAAF in standardising on a new basic trainer by purchasing versatile DH.82A Tiger Moths. But the Avro 643 Cadet was chosen instead after an evaluation which had included the Tiger Moth, a type rejected on the grounds that at £1,000 each less engine, plus a 5% commission demanded by the business office at Mascot, it was too expensive. Moreover, its performance was inferior, and delivery quoted at 20 weeks was almost twice as long. de Havilland had also made it clear that they would not entertain the thought of building the Tiger Moth in Australia until a minimum of 36 aircraft had been imported from Great Britain. Paradoxically, a total of 34 Avro Cadets was delivered between 1935 and 1939 but the order for an additional 20 aircraft was cancelled, and the negotiated licence to build the type in Australia was never taken up.

Two major de Havilland presentations had been parried before 21st November 1938 on which date the Australian Air Board at last placed an order (A37202), for 20 Tiger Moths, its first for an Australian built aeroplane of any type, at a total cost of £33,660. The deal allowed fuselages to be imported from England and these were dispatched from Hatfield in January 1939 (6); February (6) and March (8). Wings and empennage were built at Mascot where engines manufactured at Stag Lane were installed and the aircraft assembled, test flown and cleared by the Australian authorities.

Coincident with assessments made in Canada, Australia believed operation of the Tiger Moth would benefit from the advantages of the Gipsy Major Series II engine but without a controllable pitch airscrew. Twenty such engines had been ordered from Stag Lane in November 1938 with the intention of fitting them into the British made fuselages, probably with metal propellers which had also been a specification raised in Canada in July 1938, the de Havilland Engine Division had already announced that production of the Series II was to be discontinued, on a temporary basis, and no further business would be sought. The last few orders which were to be honoured included a pair required by Handley Page for their experimental HP.75 tailless pusher. In the event several more engines were built and eight Gipsy Major Series II engines were dispatched to Australia in February 1939 with eight more the following month. After incorporation of a number of Hatfield approved modifications to accommodate the extra ancillaries on the back of the crankcase, the engines were fitted as fixed pitch units into the imported Tiger Moth airframes.

Fuselages supplied by Hatfield were identified by de Havilland in England as build numbers 82555 to 82574, to which Mascot added their own identities DHA1 to DHA20, and the RAAF allocated serial numbers A17-1 to A17-20, the 17th aircraft type to have been included in their inventory. Murray Jones made the first test flight of A17-1 from Mascot on 8th May 1939, and she was delivered into RAAF charge at Richmond eight days later. The aircraft was extensively used for training until February 1942 when she crashed at Maryborough in Queensland while in service with No 3 Wireless Air Gunner School (WAGS). All 20 aircraft had been delivered to the RAAF by October 1939, 13 by the outbreak of war, and apart from some initial use by communications squadrons, each aircraft was used almost exclusively thereafter for elementary training purposes, an experience survived by 15 of the original fleet, all of which were sold into the civil market in 1946 and 1947 with the exception of A17-11 (82565/DHA11). This aircraft was converted into an Instructional Airframe as early as October 1940 and used by various technical establishments based at Wagga Wagga until June 1957. Under a series of registration letters applied by different civilian owners, the aircraft has remained airworthy, based in Queensland since 1967.

Having secured their first RAAF Tiger Moth order, de Havilland pressed for more, not only on the grounds that the world was re-arming, but in an attempt to maintain continuity of supplies and the expertise of labour. Their approaches were answered with an order for 50 DH.94 Moth Minors placed by the Department of Supply in October 1939, on the grounds that there was now a serious shortage of trainer aircraft and the Moth Minors could be provided quickly. The majority of these (A21-1 to A21-50) were delivered in March and April 1940 from kits of unfinished aircraft hastily evacuated from Hatfield at the beginning of the year together with all production tooling and jigs. Three Moth Minors are known to have been built locally from scratch using materials entirely sourced in Australia, probably in an effort to satisfy the contract. In the event only 42 aircraft were constructed altogether.

Recognition of the inevitable resulted in an order for a further 350 Tiger Moths being placed on 10th October 1939, a month after the outbreak of war. All were to be built locally using Gipsy Major engines scheduled to be manufactured in Australia under the terms of a licence already held by the Commonwealth Aircraft Corporation.

The total order was valued at £800,000 and the aircraft were to equip nine additional Elementary Schools established under the provisions of the Empire Air Training Scheme (EATS).

While de Havilland Aircraft Pty Ltd was re-organising itself and expanding into facilities at Mascot previously used by Australian National Airways and Butler Air Transport, and arranging for supplies from sub contractors who would soon number 150, the British Government provided 100 new Tiger Moths from Reserve stocks which were shipped to Australia in staggered batches: 25 aircraft (all 'N' serials) arrived between February and March 1940; 41 ('R' serials) were taken on charge in June and July. The 34 aircraft ('T' serials) which were delivered between July and September were near to the last production from Hatfield before the line was finally relocated to Morris Motors.

Eighty aircraft were routed to No 1 Air Depot (AD) Laverton near Melbourne and 20 to No 2 AD Richmond, north of Sydney, where they were erected and mostly air delivered with the exception of five which were simply transferred in their packing cases to Adelaide and 20 others redirected in a similar condition to Tasmania. A pair of Laverton imports, N6901 (82145) and N6905 (82149), were immediately allocated as Instructional Airframes and posted to the Engineering School at Ascot Vale on 24th February.

Although these 100 aircraft were generally regarded as a gift from the British Government, a theory strengthened by the fact that all retained their RAF serial numbers, only after the war when asset realisation was being encouraged, was it revealed that the Australian Government had paid for the aircraft, but 200 Gipsy Major engines had been gifted as assistance towards early completion of indigenous airframes. Although the ebb and flow of war caused agreements to be made and frequently cancelled or renegotiated, at the commencement of the EATS, it had been expected that Great Britain would supply or provide funding for 223 CAC Wirraways, 336 Fairey Battles, 591 Avro Ansons and 486 Tiger Moths. Whoever paid for what, the RAAF eventually took on charge 1,028 Ansons and 861 Tiger Moths, of which 712 were built at Mascot.

Bruce Winley, an engineer with 5 EFTS at Narromine, was given occasional instructional flights at the station, but during his previous posting with 2 EFTS at Archerfield, and before the training scheme was in full cry, there were more instructors than pupils, and he was taught to a standard at which he was permitted to fly solo in a civil registered DH.60 Moth. Winley was resident at Narromine when at least four British built Tiger Moths joined B Flight in September 1940. While the locally built aircraft were all-over yellow, the RAF Tiger Moths were in camouflage, and being of slightly lighter construction offered better performance at the cost of a greater risk of ground handling damage.

A feature which was quickly appreciated by instructors engaged on night flying tuition was that the British aircraft all had wing tip and rudder lighting installed in addition to the downward facing identification lamp, whereas the locally produced aircraft were fitted only with quartered lights at the root end of the port upper mainplanes. Electrical power was provided by a battery clamped to the floor aft of the front cockpit rudder bar pivot. About one third of each School's establishment was fitted out for night flying and the battery boxes were fitted by the groundcrew only when the aircraft were detailed off for night operations. At 7 EFTS Western Junction, Tasmania, the British aircraft were described as being 'religiously reserved' for night flying training in preference to the Australian models which during night circuits were believed to be 'perspectively inferior'.

Landing lights as such were not carried on military Tiger Moths, although they had been fitted to one aircraft supplied from Hatfield to a British private owner pre-war and several others had been delivered to the Government of India. If it proved necessary for the pilot of a night flying Tiger Moth to illuminate the ground around him, usually as the result of an imminent forced landing, he fired off a Holt flare, suspended under the lower wings from a spring loaded pylon mounted below the front interplane strut. The flares were similar in appearance to large Roman Candle-like fireworks, had the same disadvantage of a once-only performance, and were activated from two push buttons placed alongside the Morse tapper

A17-1, first of a 20 aircraft contract for the RAAF, assembled at Mascot using a fuselage imported from Hatfield, Gipsy Major engine from Stag Lane, and wings and tail unit built locally. The aircraft was delivered into RAAF care at Richmond in May 1939. Robert Veitch

on the starboard wall of the rear cockpit. The units were a standard fit on almost all operational and nightflying biplanes of the day, and the intensity of the burning flare was shielded from the pilot's view by a simple fore and aft blanking plate which doubled as a flame guard to prevent the wing fabric from catching fire.

Working to maximum capacity in its enlarged facilities at Stag Lane, the de Havilland Engine Division was only just coping with orders for Gipsy Major engines for home produced Tiger Moths and Miles Magisters, and was now required to continue the large scale supply of Canada, New Zealand and Australia. Some of the workforce had even queried their value to the war effort and had had to be reminded that without initial training, there would be no new pilots to operate the more aggressive machines. Canada was already researching the Menasco engine and although New Zealand would always be reliant on imports from somewhere, Australian industry was thought capable, with assistance, of building a creditable monthly output of Gipsy Major engines using its existing resources, and without the benefit of sophisticated equipment routinely available to accelerate processes and procedures within the British industrial base.

In October 1935, the Commonwealth Government had announced its intention of entering into aircraft manufacturing through the Department of Aircraft Production and exactly two years later, the de Havilland Aircraft Company, working through Stag Lane, licensed the Commonwealth Aircraft Corporation (CAC) of Melbourne to build Gipsy Major Series I and Series II engines. Coincidentally, a licence had been offered to Japan although that seemed less likely to materialise as rights to build the French Renault engine had already been secured for a quarter of de Havilland's requisite £20,000 fee. The Australian licence was extremely modest in comparison at £2,500 with an additional annual service fee of £250, and de Havilland were pleased to have entertained CAC's new production manager, Mr Shipper, straight from Pratt and Whitney in the USA, during a planned visit to Stag Lane.

The licence was not activated until November 1939 when an order for 500 Gipsy Major I engines was placed by the Australian Government, and in January 1940 General Motors (Holdens) Ltd, a major shareholder in CAC, was appointed co-ordinating contractors for engine manufacture with the brief that production standard engines should be available for installation in Mascot built Tiger Moths as quickly as possible. It was fortunate that Holdens were still in business; the company lost £600,000 in 1930-1931 and a further £200,000 during the next 18 months, and remained solvent only by the intervention of the parent company, General Motors, supporting it from the USA.

It was a challenge. The Australian automotive industry was based on units of Imperial measurement whereas with its origins in French Renault powerplants dating from the First World War, the Gipsy range, historically, was founded on the metric system. Before there was the remotest chance of production, every drawing and specification had to be closely examined: 41,500 dimensions required conversion, and where identical materials were not available, the closest alternative specification needed sourcing and testing for approval.

Apart from the difficulties experienced with the differences in units of measurement and the necessary adaptions to tooling and manufacturing equipment, the drawings were found to be very much for home factory consumption rather than subcontract, and where some were already obsolete, others had not been amended or upgraded since the licence agreement was drawn up in 1935. Literal interpretation was made more precarious when it was discovered that some aspects referred only to the special needs of the Tiger Moth Seaplane and Queen Bee.

To assist Holdens, two de Havilland engineers were seconded from Stag Lane and arrived with a pair of production Gipsy Major engines, both of which were subsequently dismantled, one complete set of parts being retained by Holdens, while the other was fragmented and distributed amongst the 57 sub-contractors as appropriate.

There was no time to source, order and await delivery of imported equipment to improve the efficiency of manufacturing and especially inspection processes, and whatever specialist tooling was required was designed and built locally. Each contracted supplier eventually provided 20 sets of component parts from which just two were selected, one to be maintained by Holdens for reference and the other for return to the manufacturer as a master pattern.

Less than three months into the massive effort of Australianising the programme the Australian Government, through the Air Department, expressed their concern that the cost of locally built Gipsy Major engines was going to be unacceptably high, and suggested that their preference would be for a continuation of supply from Great Britain. At an Air Council meeting held in London on 26th February 1940, the Air Department officially requested a quotation for the urgent supply of 500 engines. The arrangements made with General Motors had not allowed sufficiently for the immensity of the pre-manufacturing preparation required, and de Havilland at Mascot were expecting the first 100 locally built engines to be delivered at the rate of 20 per month from April 1940.

In reply, the Air Department was advised that the major limitation on engine manufacture was in the machining of the crankshaft. To ease pressure on British production, de Havilland had agreed that from October 1940, the Standard Motor Company would build 20 Gipsy Major engines per month, rising to 100 per month by February 1941, subcontracting crankshaft, camshaft and propeller hub production to Austin Motors. Although the manufacturing methods for automotive engine assembly were not the same as those currently practised by the aircraft industry, discussions on the matter between de Havilland, Standard and Austin had resulted in a complete and satisfactory agreement.

Holdens were aware of the situation concerning crankshafts as confirmed by a report published by the Aviation Historical Society of Australia in 1981:

'Crankshaft machining of the type required was an unknown art in Australia. Overseas, the job was done on special crankshaft lathes. Here it was done on motor car engine reconditioning equipment. The machining dimensions were extremely critical; the crankshaft itself was so relatively flexible that intricate fixtures were needed to ensure absolute rigidity during machining. The finished shafts had to be held to extremely close limits of dynamic balance, to measure which it was necessary to import a crankshaft balancing machine, which, incidentally, was the only specialist machine imported for the whole job. In the machining, the weight of the forging was reduced from 70lb to 32lb. The crankshaft final check required 250 measurements, and some surfaces, such as journals, would have at least ten to 12 checks made of each dimension'.

From the end of 1939, de Havilland had been supplying parts directly to Holdens in an effort to expedite production. By the end of February 1940, 100 complete crankshafts had been shipped together with 430 blank forgings for machining locally. By agreement, 50 camshafts, 500 carburettors, 510 pairs of BTH magnetos and all necessary ball bearings had already been dispatched. *'The relief from any further obligation to supply parts would be of immediate and substantial benefit to home production'*, declared the Air Council.

Having expressed their views and pending a decision from Australia, all further shipments of engine parts were suspended, but on 16th March 1940 the Air Department announced that it had elected to continue with domestic manufacture.

In Great Britain, the proposed supply of engines from Standard Motors never did materialise. At the very last moment, the Ministry of Aircraft Production decided that the facilities could be better allocated to projects with a 'higher priority'.

The first Tiger Moth wholly constructed in Australia, A17-21 was delivered to the RAAF in June 1940. In this photograph taken at Mascot, A17-31 in the foreground is complete but less rudder. Activity in assembling other fuselages appears to be less than frenetic. de Havilland Aircraft Co Ltd.

Tiger Moths off production at Mascot awaiting flight test and allocation, mid-1940. The man who painted the company name on the hangar facade needed a steady nerve. RAAF Museum

After seven months, the first test engine was assembled at Holdens' plant at Fishermans Bend near Melbourne, and due to the extreme nature of the programme and the material specification differences, a full 50 hour running type test was considered necessary. It was essential to establish absolute credibility, for in service, in Australia or in southern Africa or India or wherever, the Australian parts had in every way, to be interchangeable and compatible with those manufactured and supplied from any other source. The first of 1,300 Holdens' built engines costing about £610 each was installed in RAAF Tiger Moths at Mascot in December 1940, and the whole of the batch of 18 aircraft exported to the Governments of India and Burma in January 1941 was similarly fitted. One enduring difference was the decision to fit Bendix-Scintilla magnetos imported from the United States, which were considered superior to the standard BTH magnetos which remained in service elsewhere.

On introduction in 1932, the overhaul period for a Gipsy Major I was 450 hours, extended to 750 hours in July 1933 and to 1,000 hours in August 1937. A year after the introduction to service of the Holdens engines, the British Air Ministry announced that the life had been extended to 1,260 hours with no intermediate top overhauls and in May 1945 this was again extended to the unprecedented figure of 1,500 hours. One reporter was prompted to write: *'This quite exceptional figure represents about double the overhaul period for the average aero engine, and that despite the fact that the Gipsy Major operates under the most arduous conditions that aviation can impose on a power unit, the conditions of the elementary flying schools which involve endless repetitions of taking off, climbing on full power, gliding, taxying and cooling down, this embodying a great deal of handling by inexperienced pupils. Its faithful dependability has meant much to the building up of their confidence in the air'.*

Delivery of the first Tiger Moth airframe to be wholly constructed in Australia was accomplished on 21st June 1940 when A17-25 (DHA21) was taken on change at 2 Air Depot (AD) Richmond. Allocated to 5 EFTS at Narromine on 12th July 1940, A17-25 worked until August 1944 when she was overhauled at Mascot then consigned to storage at Bankstown and later Cootamundra. In February 1946 the aircraft was sold to the Royal Queensland Aero Club at Archerfield, Brisbane, but their £250 investment was damaged beyond economical repair at Toowoomba on 13th October, only six months after registration.

Murray Jones had recognised the need for an Australian based propeller industry, and with the approval of the parent company following another visit by Francis St Barbe in 1938, a new factory was established at Alexandria, NSW, which opened for production of wooden blades in March 1940.

The threat of war and disruption of supplies had encouraged Mascot to stock up on raw materials and spare parts to the extent of having an estimated two year's requirement on hand by September 1939, a far sighted policy which provided an essential buffer before total self-sufficiency could be achieved, but as the training programme ground inexorably on and aeroplanes were heavily utilised and damaged, some of the civil Maintenance and Repair Units established across the country, suffered constant shortages of spare parts, and were often forced to rob one aircraft in order to establish serviceability of another.

The need for more floor space at Mascot, not only for production and assembly, but for maintenance, repair and packing of export orders, resulted in additional facilities being taken over at Alexandria where all component metal work was subsequently completed.

Steady progress evident at Mascot in January 1941. Note that vertical rudder stripes are still being applied as part of the RAAF insignia at this date.
via British Aerospace

The Australian Aircraft Production Commission also approved and provided additional space at Mascot purely for the overhaul of RAAF aircraft and in which five Tiger Moths were destroyed by fire on 3rd May 1944, although a considerable number of parts were salvaged and recycled.

In June 1940, as the result of a conference to determine future training needs, de Havilland was authorised to order raw materials for a further 300 airframes, and Holdens to provide 75 spare engines, figures based on what proved to be the pessimistic recalculation of wastage estimated at an annual rate of 90 aircraft and 72 engines. The package was valued at more than £570,000 within which the utilisation of existing jigs was expected to reduce the unit cost of an airframe to £1,170 and an engine to £500.

To complement the four second-hand Tiger Moths supplied to the Netherlands East Indies by British aircraft broker W S Shackleton late in 1940, four more (DHA 141,143, 144 and 145), were supplied from Mascot in October 1940 after representations at government level. On arrival in Batavia, the aircraft were painted blue, and joined by the British imports in a red colour scheme, and four Bückers painted white, they flew a combined formation at an air display representing the colours of the Dutch flag.

Throughout the Netherlands East Indies, the flying club movement was heavily supported by the government, operating as a civil reserve for the military. In view of the world situation and very much in accord with what was being practised elsewhere, the scheme was considered ready for necessary and immediate expansion. A formal request for more Australian built aircraft was rejected early in 1941 on the grounds that all production was allocated, but in March and April 1941 the delivery of 48 additional aircraft was approved, one of which, PK-BPP (DHA507), was to be supplied with provision for the attachment of a float chassis. By September 1941, approval for 62 Tiger Moths for export to the Indies had been granted.

Following Japan's entry into the war, many of the Dutch colony's training aircraft had been consolidated into an intense flying programme at Tasik Malaja, but plans for their continued operation from there were abandoned when the islands were invaded by Japanese forces, and with the grim prospects of no shipping space available for evacuation, the fleet was ordered by the Dutch authorities to be destroyed. Six Tiger Moths were hastily dismantled at Surabaya where they were in store prior to formal acceptance by the Naval Air School, and anticipating delivery of Edo floats from the United States. The aircraft were hurriedly loaded on board the SS *Tjinegara* which sailed on 19th February bound for Adelaide, South Australia. Although records of the original identities of the six had become confused, all were adopted by the RAAF, allocated serials A17-621 to A17-626, and operated by 1 EFTS at Parafield, a school which specialised in the training of pilot candidates of Dutch extraction.

The Prime Minister of Australia, Robert Menzies, led a mission to London in January 1941 part of whose purpose was to encourage the British Government to increase its purchase of Australian war supplies. These were already considerable, and involved almost everything from felt and serge cloth dispatched directly to Egypt, to bombs, machine guns, ammunition, tank tracks and food all shipped to Great Britain.

The aircraft industry in Australia was developing along proven lines and although no major complaints had been received in England, a complex industrial programme to build the Bristol Beaufort in considerable numbers was already running late due allegedly, to many of the drawings supplied by the Bristol Aeroplane Company being inaccurate. One report said that many of the notes on the drawings, such as could be read, carried so much mis-information that they were best ignored.

Prior to the Prime Minister's visit, his office had been in contact with the Air Ministry to offer Australian assistance to the Tiger Moth programme. In September 1940, London received an appreciation that the Mascot factory would complete its current order book for 650 Tiger Moths by the end of 1941 and that by early the following year, planned production would exceed all anticipated requirements. The report surmised that in view of the British Government's possible needs, there was every justification to authorise de Havilland Australia to proceed with the manufacture of at least another 200 Tiger Moths, plus spare parts.

By 31st December 1940, Mascot had delivered 208 aircraft and production reached ten Tiger Moths per week, a rate which it was possible to raise by half as much again. 200 engines had been received from Stag Lane; 500 were on order from General Motors (Holdens) and 89 had been received. Manufacture was at the rate of 40 engines per month, a figure which could easily be increased.

At the end of November 1940, the Air Ministry suggested to the Australian Air Board that it would be prepared to take 25 Tiger Moths per month after the end of April 1941, and if a higher rate of production was possible, the additional aircraft would be gladly accepted for delivery to flying schools situated in Africa and the East. It was made clear that Great Britain could not provide engines, nor could it assist with the provision of any factory equipment, machine tools or personnel. Five weeks later, Australia replied that providing an early decision was taken with respect to materials, Mascot would be capable of supplying 420 Tiger Moths for export in 1941 and a further 650 in 1942, all to be fitted with Holdens built engines.

The provision of Tiger Moths from the Southern Hemisphere to the schools of the expanding Empire Air Training Scheme in Africa, together with reinforcement of the Air Force in India, would lift the pressure off production of training aircraft in Great

Britain and the associated shipping requirements, resources which could be immediately released to other urgent needs. It was even suggested early in March 1941, that with Australia's development of an indigenous 'Intermediate Trainer', the RAAF might be persuaded to release additional Tiger Moths from the home based schools. In the meantime the whole of the 420 aircraft output promised for export delivery in 1941 could be absorbed, agreed the Air Ministry, plus any additional machines that might be manufactured after the RAAF demand had been satisfied.

Of major concern was the provision of aircraft quality timber and plywood, neither spruce nor birch being native to the Dominion. The prospect of an interrupted supply was a problem which had been identified more than ten years previously during which time a programme of progressive investigation into the properties of some 30 native species had been conducted. Although not as ideal as spruce, hoop pine and bunya pine were available in commercial quantities: both had good properties, but also deficiencies which could only be accommodated through detail redesign in an effort to redress the loss of strength. Scented satinwood was chosen for the manufacture of plywood as its qualities were almost the equal of birch, and the estimated annual availability of 2,000,000 sq ft could all be released to the standard required for airworthiness. In the event, with the careful distribution of supplies amongst several ships and convoys, it is believed the arrival in Australia of regular and sufficient supplies made the fallback onto alternative materials unnecessary. Meanwhile, concerns about the supply of imported aircraft quality Grade A spruce, specified as main spar stock, had been ameliorated to some extent by the approval of Grade B spruce (Modification 59) and even multi-laminated spars (Modification 80), in an effort to use every available cubic inch.

Tiger Moth production at Mascot was continuous from June 1940, reaching a peak of two aircraft per day by March 1941, until August 1942 when the line was halted. Japan's entry into the war in December 1941 had caused a deal of reappraisal in addition to a temporary halt to the export of Tiger Moths to southern Africa, and 119 aircraft ready for shipment were stored in and around Sydney pending a decision on their future. Eighteen of these aircraft were released from May 1942 for use by the United States Army Air Force in Australia pending delivery of their own communications types, and 101 were directed into RAAF service, obviating the immediate need for further manufacture at Mascot.

The aircraft released to the United States 5th Air Force were identified only by their Mascot build numbers, and were painted in matt green, displaying an American white star on either side of the fuselage. One (DHA907), was returned to RAAF service in August 1945 and another (DHA964), was loaned to the RAAF for a seven month detachment with 36 Squadron at Garbutt from August 1943. Apart from the loss of DHA963 which suffered a mid-air collision with a Bell P-39 Airacobra in September 1942, the fate of the remaining 15 aircraft is unknown.

A further eight Tiger Moths were allocated late in 1942. DHA917 was damaged during transit through Brisbane in December the following year and DHA918 was seemingly cannibalised on site to provide spares, and then abandoned to the administrative machinations of the RAAF's No.1 Technical Supply Depot. DHA917 eventually served in New Guinea with an American fighter squadron and was later adopted by a bomber group, but her ultimate fate is unknown. DHA1044 was damaged during her positioning flight to Archerfield in November 1942 and was never officially handed over, and nothing is known of the operational careers of the other five.

Transferred to local use was DHA870, intended to be DX838 in southern Africa but taken on to the RAAF inventory as A17-640. The aircraft crashed on take off from Mascot on 20th August 1943 during her delivery flight to the nearby Air Park at Bankstown, and her arrival there was delayed by some eleven weeks. A17-640 later remained in service with the RAAF until 1956 when she was sold for agricultural use, and was recovered from long term storage in Western Australia in 1990.

In September 1944 the Mascot line was reopened to provide a further 60 Tiger Moths at a cost of about £1,200 each, assessed as necessary by a review which had been adopted over two years previously. The new production at Mascot was authorised in spite of an offer to supply Tiger Moths from Great Britain where for some months already, Morris Motors had been delivering aircraft straight into store. By February 1945, 35 of the new Australian aircraft had been delivered, but the remainder of the order was subsequently cancelled on the grounds that all training was being run down, and the aircraft were simply not required.

The Aviation Historical Society of Australia reported in 1982 that the last Mascot aircraft A17-759 (DHA1090), undergoing overhaul, had been found to carry an inscription scribbled onto the ply beneath a cockpit panel: *'The last of the tribe. W Sullivan. 3/1/1945'*. A17-759 was delivered to 2 AD at Richmond on 5th February 1945 and remained in active service until 1957 before sale to the Royal Victorian Aero Club at Moorabin. Registered VH-COA and painted in RAAF Pacific area colours, the aircraft has been based near Canberra since 1981, the 1,070th and last all-Australian aeroplane of the 1,090 Tiger Moths assembled at Mascot.

In November 1943, 700 Tiger Moths were listed on the RAAF inventory, and 648 remained when peace was finally declared in 1945. The last two remaining in service, A17-671 (DHA821), part of a frustrated delivery to southern Africa, and A17-616 (DHA1051), an aircraft paid for by residents of the shire of Oxley, were sold on 23rd April 1959. DHA821 was registered VH-SNP to Townsville Aero Club in Queensland, and was last with a private owner at Home Hill on whose request the registration was cancelled in 1963. DHA1051 simply disappeared into the civil system and was probably used as a source of spares.

Built at Mascot in June 1942, A17-558 led a fairly standard life until July 1945 when she was removed from reserve storage at Benalla to serve with the Netherlands East Indies Personnel and Equipment Pool, then based at Canberra. Robert Veitch

Above: **For a brief period of the war, some RAAF Tiger Moths were finished in camouflage but with broad yellow trainer bands. A17-619 served with No 1 Air Observer School at Cootamundra in September 1942.** Robert Veitch

Below: **The Royal Australian Navy operated Tiger Moths using the same serial sequence as the RAAF, but with the addition of naval identification. This picture of A17-692 was taken post-war when civil aircraft VH-NVT was based at HMAS *Albatross* at Nowra.** David Foote

Very much a standard Tiger Moth equipped with a tailskid but no mainwheel brakes, and neither an inverted system nor a self starter, aircraft manufactured in Australia were subject to a number of modifications, some of which like the motives of their Canadian cousins were an inspired attempt to hold the local environment at bay, or to improve the aeroplane by subtle changes which the Mascot management considered desirable or necessary.

None of these was ever fed into the British line at Cowley where the aeroplane was regarded simply as a repetitive production job, with only the minimum number of essential modifications and changes sparingly agreed.

In May 1931, Francis St Barbe completed a 20 week world tour on behalf of the de Havilland Aircraft Company Ltd, during which he visited clubs and private owners, associated companies and agents in the course of travelling 22,000 miles by ship, 6,000 miles by air and 3,000 miles by train. On his return to England, he was pleased to report to the board that the whole exercise had cost the company not more than £950.

Furthest from Stag Lane was his visit to New Zealand agent F D Mill whose business, The Air Survey and Transport Company, employed four engineers at their base at Hobsonville near Auckland, a Royal New Zealand Air Force (RNZAF) station with seaplane facilities attached. St Barbe was delighted with what he saw: the servicing arrangements, spare parts supply, and ability to cope with anything up to and including major repairs. *'I am satisfied that our affairs are in very good hands,'* he reported. He was also pleased to add that during his eight day stay he had flown over 900 miles around North Island in the agent's demonstration DH.80 Puss Moth, and that all his official expenses had been met by Mr Mill. *'My visit to New Zealand did not cost the company one penny,'* he wrote gratifyingly.

Due to the initial limit imposed on the supply of civil Tiger Moths from Stag Lane and Hatfield by military precedence, it was not until July 1937 that the company could acknowledge its first order for the type from New Zealand, booked to F D Mill. Two aircraft were required and ZK-AFN (3629), and ZK-AFO (3630), were subsequently shipped in October on board the SS *Port Campbell.* Reaching Auckland on 20th December, they were delivered to Hobsonville, erected, inspected, test flown on 12th January and fully inspected again by the authorities in view of their differences from a standard DH.60 Moth which was familiar to them, finally reaching the Auckland Aero Club on 15th February 1938.

At the suggestion of the Air Force, a revised scheme of training for Civil Reservists and Air Force direct entrants was introduced in 1937 which progressed each stream, very much on the lines of the British Elementary and Reserve Flying Training School (ERFTS) system, through an existing and efficiently organised civil club channel, to A licence standard. 100 pupils were to be trained each year under contracts let from April 1937. A year earlier, four military DH.60 Moths had been transferred to civil clubs to assist with *ab initio* training of RNZAF pilots, and in August 1937, the government introduced an interest free loan scheme, with repayments spread over three years, to encourage clubs to buy the most modern and appropriate equipment. The delivery of Tiger Moths ZK-AFN and ZK-AFO to Auckland in February 1938 was a direct result of this initiative.

ZK-AFN survived her subsequent enforced Air Force career as NZ719 and was sold in February 1947 to W H Johns of New Plymouth, where she was operated by the local Aero Club under a new identity: ZK-AOL. The aircraft suffered engine failure near Mangere and crashed on 10th January 1959, sustaining damage considered uneconomical to repair. Stablemate ZK-AFO, the first Tiger Moth ever to fly in New Zealand, also joined the military, and as NZ720 had no distance to travel to enrol with the Flying Instructors' School (FIS) at Hobsonville where it is believed she spent her entire war service. Issued as a free gift to Hawera Aero Club in June 1948, the registration ZK-ASA was allocated but the aircraft was not used, and in April 1950 she was sold for agricultural conversion to Air Contracts of Masterton with whom she survived a catalogue of near terminal disasters. Passing to Aerial Advertising at Nelson in 1957, ZK-ASA was withdrawn after her final flight on 13th April

1958, having logged 7,203 flying hours. Dismantled and stored, the aircraft was acquired by John Galpin of Te Puke in August 1981 after his own Tiger Moth ZK-BFG (82032), had been destroyed in a hangar fire at Rotorua. In November 1981, registration letters ZK-AFO were re-allocated, and the aircraft embarked on a long programme of restoration to airworthiness.

Less blind flying hood, the price of a 1938 model Tiger Moth delivered to New Zealand was quoted at £1,547.10s.0d, and under the government loan scheme, by August 1939, Auckland Aero Club's monthly repayment for ZK-AFO amounted to a few shillings less than £40. Seven more aircraft ordered by Air Survey, dispatched from Hatfield in November and December 1937 (3638-3644), and delivered in February, collectively cost £7,680, just over £2 each more than the published list price, to which packing and shipping costs would surely have been added. The price tag of £1,708 affixed to the Marlborough Aero Club's ZK-AHH (82052), a one-off order placed by the Air Survey and Transport Company in 1939, reflected Hatfield's exclusive right to call the tune, a figure which almost certainly included increased shipping and insurance rates determined by a political situation which was rapidly deteriorating.

By 3rd September 1939, a total of 21 Tiger Moths was in use by New Zealand's civil clubs. Three others, ZK-AHO, ZK-AHM and ZK-AHR (82230-82232), were painted in civil colours and awaiting delivery from Hobsonville, but following declaration of war adopted military marks instead, and were diverted straight into the Air Force as NZ716, NZ714 and NZ715 respectively, slated to catch up with formal military colours at a convenient date in the future.

With the country on a war footing, all flying club equipment was requisitioned and the aircraft previously provided against 'free loans' were compulsorily purchased by the government. Following inspection, an agreed level of compensation was due, the figures dependent to some extent on the amount of the loan left outstanding.

Since her introduction the Tiger Moth had proved herself to be almost ideally suited to New Zealand's training requirements, and with an established base at Hobsonville offering service and support, the RNZAF decided it would happily standardise all its primary training needs on the type.

In his 1931 report to the board, de Havilland's Business Director clearly stated his opinion of future prospects: *'We can be fairly satisfied that we shall get the lion's share of the business in New Zealand'*. Based on that judgement, the satisfactory performance of the five existing overseas companies, and the extended supply line even beyond Australia which would always be subject to possible disruption, Alan Butler,

Rongotai aerodrome, Wellington, New Zealand, and the de Havilland factory set in scenic conditions but with little between it and Antarctica. Hugh Buckingham

Martin Sharp developed a distinctive 'house style' for the de Havilland Company based on the 'Times Roman' typeface, somewhat different from the fashionable 'Broadway' type, used on the facade at Rongotai. The streaming flags enforce the reputation of 'Windy Wellington'. Hugh Buckingham

Chairman of the Company, announced at the 19th Annual General Meeting on 7th February 1939, that a de Havilland Associated Company was to be established in the Dominion of New Zealand, with offices and workshops situated near Wellington.

Hugh Buckingham, one time de Havilland Aeronautical Technical School student and company sales and demonstration pilot, was married on 30th March 1939, and a few days later with his new bride, Pamela, was on board the RMS *Queen Mary* taking a first class passage to New York, a wedding present from the de Havilland Company. He took the opportunity to fly a Moth at the Canadian branch in Toronto before travelling overland to Los Angeles to board the SS *Maraquesa* on 26th April, bound for Australia and New Zealand. At the age of 29 he was to take up duties as General Manager of the newly created de Havilland Aircraft Company of New Zealand.

The firm had been registered in Wellington on 6th March 1939, the sixth de Havilland overseas company, while the Manager was still *en-route*, and followed initial organisation by St Barbe paying a second visit, during which he must have liaised closely with the Air Survey & Transport Company, detailing Hatfield's intentions. All but one of the 20,000 shares were to be held by the parent company; the odd one was registered to Major Alan Murray Jones, Managing Director of the Australian company, with a brief to lend a helping hand in addition to keeping a fatherly eye. Murray Jones was in Wellington on 28th March to review progress pending the arrival of Hugh Buckingham, and on 24th May construction of a new 200ft by 100ft workshop was commenced at Rongotai aerodrome.

Writing in *The Aeroplane,* Editor C G Grey expressed his tacit support of the venture and particularly that of the new manager. *'He is well known as a demonstration pilot and has flown all over Europe on the company's business. He is well liked everywhere he has been. He should do great things.'*

According to Alan Vause, an early employee who had transferred locally from Wellington Aero Club, it was hard to believe this was considered the ideal place at which to produce a large number of light training biplanes, on the eastern boundary of Rongotai aerodrome, wide open to the frequent southerly gales ripping in straight from Antarctica. The building had few windows: the main light source was through the glazed North Light Truss rooflights, quite correctly facing south and away from the sun, but as a result the shop floor was dark, miserable and freezing in the winter. It was believed locally the building and layout had been designed in Great Britain against a misconception and after the first year it was found necessary to install a substantial system to provide basic heating.

The policy of the company, dictated by Hatfield, was clear: *'Give the close attention and service to the Dominion Government, the air lines and other commercial undertakings, the flying clubs, schools and private owners which are demanded in the present growing state of civil and military aviation in the Dominion and which must be governed very largely by the policy of the New Zealand Government'.* First business was to be construction of Moth Minors and Tiger Moths for local distribution, initially working under the direction of eight staff posted on a temporary basis from England, including John Johnston who was to take up the position of Work's Manager, Jack Balls, in charge of metalwork production, Fred Betts, woodworking department, and Bill Gilbert. Ted Whitehouse arrived later to set up the jigs for making fuselage frames and instruct some of the workforce, including a number of pretty girls, in the art of welding. The factory relied on Hatfield for the supply of almost everything to begin with, but gradually became self reliant. The exceptions were always proprietary items: wheels, tyres, instruments, rigging wires, some specialist airframe parts and Gipsy Major engines.

Negotiations between de Havilland and the New Zealand Government had already resulted in the understanding that more Tiger Moths would be required for the RNZAF, but due to the economic situation, as much local input as practicable would be necessary. Construction in New Zealand was the obvious answer, and the prospects had been further discussed during a visit by the United Kingdom Air Mission in April, soon after incorporation of the new company. Buckingham was aware that following the Munich Crisis of 1938, de Havilland had been advised by the British Air Ministry to initiate Tiger Moth assembly at suitable overseas 'dispersed' sites, and the coincidental establishment of pre-war production in Canada, Australia and New Zealand was probably beyond the basic projection of normal commercial strategy.

Only nine weeks after de Havilland had sanctioned construction of the new factory at Rongotai, the Prime Minister of New Zealand announced to Parliament that the government had agreed to order 100 Tiger Moths at a total delivered cost of £155,000, all aircraft to be manufactured at Wellington, the last aircraft to be delivered by February 1941. The timing of the announcement may have been unexpected as a temporary halt to the building programme had been called while plans were urgently approved to add a further 5,000 sq ft of floor space, and makeshift office and workshop accommodation was secured in municipal facilities themselves awaiting completion.

To initiate the 100 aircraft contract it was intended to import batches of partially assembled aircraft kits from Hatfield and to complete them to civilian standards for *ab initio* pilot training on behalf of the Air Force, which would continue to be undertaken by the flying clubs. But in the event, and as a result of changed circumstances, all Tiger Moth work at Rongotai was to be for exclusive sale and delivery directly to the RNZAF.

Hugh Buckingham's voyage to Wellington had been broken in June by a visit to the Australian Company at Mascot where he took the opportunity to tour the local area in a demonstrator Puss Moth in addition to test flying several new production Tiger Moths. Following arrival at Rongotai he flew Percival P.10 Vega Gull to Palmerston North on 20th October, recording the flight under civil registration ZK-AFI, although officially the aircraft had been requisitioned from the Wellington Aero Club on 15th September and allocated Air Force serial NZ571. He retraced his steps some days later in a Waco UOC Custom, logged as ZK-AEL, yet another aircraft from the Wellington Club fleet impressed as NZ575, and based locally under the auspices of the Rongotai Communications Flight. From the beginning of November he made a number of test flights and local visits in DH.94 Moth Minor ZK-AHL, an aircraft sent from England in August intended for his personal use, but also destined to join the military as NZ595.

On 22nd December 1939, as the finishing touches were still being applied to the factory, Buckingham, known as 'Jimmy' since Stag Lane days, but answering to 'Hughie' in his new post, took off from Rongotai for a 25 minute test flight in Tiger Moth NZ740 (82296). This aircraft was amongst the first batch of 12 (82294-82298; 82344-82347 and 82393-82394), to be sent from Hatfield which had simply to be unpacked, erected, inspected and tested before offer to the RNZAF. Serial numbers NZ738-NZ749 were allocated on arrival, but not in any logical sequence. By the end of January, NZ738-NZ743 had been tested, and on 9th February, 'Hughie' flew NZ744, NZ747 (twice), NZ748 and NZ749.

Refuelling time at 3 EFTS Harewood for a gaggle of RNZAF Tiger Moths of mixed parentage: part built at Hatfield or wholly built at Rongotai. The three aircraft nearest the camera eventually went to civil flying clubs in New Zealand. RNZAF Ohakea

Not until 8th March was NZ746 tested, and it is probable that NZ745 was left for young Peter de Havilland to tackle as an introduction to his new role as production test pilot, a position which he filled between April 1940 and early 1942.

Peter de Havilland's arrival was to allow the General Manager administrative breathing space, but Buckingham remained in flying practice throughout 1940, testing DH.94 Moth Minors ZK-AHJ (94061) and ZK-AHN (94071), in March, both delivered from Hatfield against orders placed on an agency basis by F D Mill and the Air Survey and Transport Company. Neither aircraft retained its civil letters for long: both were impressed into military service (NZ591/NZ592), and were test flown by the General Manager on 8th April and 16th April respectively, although on both occasions he logged their type identity as 'Tiger Moth'.

In order to expedite pilot training while the production facilities at Rongotai were being organised, the British Government gifted 90 unused RAF issue Tiger Moths manufactured at Hatfield against pre-war contracts, in a similar fashion to the 100 aircraft shipped to the Royal Australian Air Force. Unlike the RAAF who retained the original RAF serial numbers, the RNZAF allocated its own identities, and over a period of several months post-delivery, obliterated the standard RAF green and brown camouflage scheme, known affectionately in some quarters as 'slime and sewage', with an overall coat of familiar 'trainer' yellow.

The first batch of aircraft dispatched from 36 Maintenance Unit (MU) Sealand arrived on board the SS *Somerset* in April 1940 and six were transported directly to the RNZAF base at New Plymouth where they were erected and flight tested. Although the aircraft arrived in random order, RNZAF serial numbers were applied in strict sequence as each was processed, the New Plymouth aircraft becoming NZ851-NZ856, respectively ex-RAF N9456; N9142; N9457; N9185; N9183 and N9410. These were followed at approximately monthly intervals on board the freighters *Rangitane, Wairangi, Rangitikei, Rangitata* and *Opawa,* by more new aircraft drawn from reserve storage at various RAF MUs in England. RNZAF serial allocations for ex-RAF 'N' and 'R' aircraft continued consecutively from NZ857 to NZ900; and from NZ656 to NZ689 for all 'T' serialled aircraft supplied direct from the Morris Motors' factory at Cowley.

Buckingham test flew the first of the ex RAF aircraft routed to Rongotai, N9249 (82350/NZ857), on 30th April, followed by the next six, (NZ858-NZ863), all within the first week of May, after which the job became the sole responsibility of Peter de Havilland, 'Pete the Pilot' as he was affectionately known. A similar job of erection and test flying was required for the entire eight aircraft Tiger Moth fleet of the London Aeroplane Club which had ceased operations at Hatfield following the embargo on civil flying imposed on the outbreak of war. The well used aircraft were all shipped to Wellington, probably as a matter of convenience and commercial opportunism, where they were prepared for service with the RNZAF as NZ730-NZ737, and taken on charge between 9th June and 16th August 1940. Integrated in the erecting shop with the brand new camouflaged aeroplanes arriving from England, they appear to have been allocated a lower priority in view of the greater amount of pre-delivery preparation required by each, and were found space in the system when available manpower permitted. According to the engineers who received them, working under the direction of Chief Inspector Bill Brazier, the London Club aircraft had every appearance of being packed up immediately after a day's flying, and were still streaked with oil and generous plumes of Hatfield mud.

With the influx of dismantled aircraft just requiring assembly and rigging, arrangements were made for an overspill to be accommodated in the Centennial Exhibition Buildings on the opposite side of Rongotai aerodrome, where de Havilland had planned to be a major independent exhibitor earlier in the year, although there is no evidence to prove that they actually were.

The second batch of 12 Tiger Moths to be assembled from Hatfield kits was ready in July (NZ751-NZ762). Five of the aircraft (82395-82397 and 82713-82714), had been sent from England complete with engines, but the remaining seven (82715 and 82836-82841), were scheduled to be united with part of a consignment of 21 Gipsy Major engines which had arrived in February as an anticipated prelude to greater participation in the local manufacturing programme.

The allocation of RNZAF serial numbers was again completely haphazard, and further confusion was caused when the factory allocated local build numbers (DHNZ1-DHNZ12), again on an apparently indiscriminate basis, on the grounds that all the wooden parts of the mainplanes together with dope and fabric work (Stage A of the Rongotai production programme), had been completed on site. These 12 aircraft were regarded as the first part of the order for 100 home produced Tiger Moths announced to Parliament on 1st August 1939, and called up against de Havilland's internal contract reference 8200.

New Zealand's first aircraft recognised as having a significant local content was NZ762 (DHNZ12), which was taken on Air Force charge on 18th July 1940 following flight testing by Peter de Havilland. Most official documentation has been lost, but local historians believe this may have been 82395, or possibly 82841. In spite of being the last of the DHNZ numbered build sequence, it was the first aircraft to be completed to delivery standard. NZ751 (DHNZ1 and either 82397 or 82395 or even 82713, which is most likely), was test flown by 'Hughie' Buckingham on 25th July and handed over four days later. NZ755 (DHNZ5) and NZ757 (DHNZ7), were flown by the General Manager on 20th and 21st August respectively, but the Air Force acceptance date for NZ755, quoted as 1st August 1940, adds to the uncertainty of the real identities.

Stage B of the integrated building schedule covered the second batch of 12 unassembled kits, (82944-82949 and 83077-83082), all received engineless from Hatfield, which in an ordered sequence (had the manager waved a big stick?) were allocated local build numbers DHNZ13-DHNZ24, and Air Force serials NZ763-NZ774. In addition to the mainplane woodwork, Stage B required Rongotai to build control surfaces and to provide all metal parts for the wings with the exception of drag struts, internal bracing wires and fabricated wiring plates. Buckingham considered the step forward to be of considerable significance and test flew the first aircraft, NZ763, on 11th September.

The problem of raw material supply in a non-industrialised country with few natural resources was only solved by staking a complete reliance on imports. Although local timber sources were investigated, none was found to be satisfactory, and baulks of spruce and ash, sheets of plywood, round, square and streamline section steel tube, plate and bar, fabric and even certain ingredients for the manufacture of dope were all bought in from sources in Great Britain and Australia. Stocks of raw materials were consistently maintained to a 'more than adequate' level for the programme in hand, and new supplies always managed to get through. Apart from one centre section cross spar which indulged in a brief flirtation with an American specification round tube, later found to be below strength, and which necessitated some subtle re-design, all Tiger Moth production at Rongotai complied with material specifications tried and tested at Stag Lane and Hatfield.

Fuselage tie rods fitted to British models were specified with a fine pitch metric thread and supplies were manufactured in Great Britain and shipped to Wellington. On an occasion when stocks had run surprisingly low, possibly due to a loss during shipping, rods imported with an urgency from Mascot were found to have the standard BSF threads acceptable for Australian standards. During later overhaul of Tiger Moth NZ881 (Hatfield manufactured 82971), the rod threads were misidentified and incorrectly treated, resulting in the nuts stripping off and catastrophic separation of the wings during aerobatics at Kaiapoi on 11th September 1941.

New Zealand elected to build standard pattern engine cowlings for its Tiger Moths rather than follow the Canadian example which was less complicated.
RNZAF Ohakea

Stage D of the development of New Zealand production included one of the most complicated parts of a Tiger Moth, the centre section petrol tank.
RNZAF Ohakea

Morris Motors supplied all major component parts for the next 24 bare fuselages (83202-83207 and 83379-83396), to which Rongotai added their own identification DHNZ25-DHNZ48, Air Force serials running consecutively from NZ775 to NZ798. The first 12 were completed to production Stage C (all as previously agreed plus Rongotai responsibility for the engine cowlings), and the last 12 conformed to the requirements of Stage D which added a locally built centre section with fuel tank, and the complete chassis system (undercarriage), with the exception of the tailskid.

Stages E and F were phased in during construction of the next 52 aircraft which bore only local build numbers. DHNZ49-DHNZ60 (Air Force serials NZ799-NZ810), represented Stage E which called for manufacture of the whole fuselage frame including controls, control box, top deckings (cowls), seats, instrument boards, bulkheads, oil tank and pipe connections, ignition wiring, external fittings, exhaust manifold and engine installation kit. By Stage F, apart from non-de Havilland proprietary items, special forgings, castings and pressings which included items like seats imported from Australia, the whole aircraft was to be a product of the Wellington factory. This happy state was met by NZ811 (DHNZ61), which was subject to a 30 minute test flight by the General Manager, to his great satisfaction and delight, on 19th April 1941. Much had been achieved in a short time by a small team working up from nothing but a green field site.

While the remainder of contract 8200 was being fulfilled (DHNZ62-DHNZ100, serialled NZ812-NZ850), with the last aircraft accepted by the military on 24th October 1941, it was recognised that the provisioning programme which progressively had been losing time, was eight months behind schedule, and in an effort to alleviate some of the shortfall, Buckingham made exploratory contact with his Australian shareholder Murray Jones at the Mascot factory near Sydney. The result was the supply by Australia of component parts which were integrated into New Zealand production from March 1941, followed by the provision of 20 complete aircraft (DHA487-DHA506), which were allocated RNZAF serials 1401-1420. The Australian built Tiger Moths were erected at Rongotai as the last of the first batch of home produced aircraft were being assembled, and apart from their Air Force serials adopted no amended form of builder's identity to cause the same degree of confusion afforded to earlier imports from England.

Aircraft consigned from Mascot had arrived with ten spare engines, Australian built Gipsy Majors manufactured by General Motors (Holdens). At a package price of £42,000, the 20 aircraft and spares were more expensive per unit than the local product, but the British Government agreed to contribute 50% of the total cost as part of their obligation to the Empire Air Training Scheme (EATS).

Buckingham continued to share test flying duties but on a much reduced scale, concentrating on the establishment of aircraft and engine overhaul facilities, raising staff levels from the initial 60 to about 400, and converting the old Electrolux factory at Evans Bay into a first class propeller workshop, capable of the manufacture of wooden blades for all airframes scheduled to pass through the Rongotai workshops, including the ubiquitous Airspeed Oxford and Supermarine Walrus.

The engine overhaul facility was to play a vital part in maintaining the flow of new airframes, for apart from a small residual stock of new engines which had been previously delivered from Stag Lane, and an almost similar number supplied from Australia, most airframe production from 1942 until the last aircraft built in 1944, relied on re-lifed engines acquired from many sources including service write-offs, estimated at a monthly wastage rate of three airframes and two engines. So important was the repair and overhaul of airframes and engines that the de Havilland Aircraft Company of New Zealand expanded into the unheated but elegant Centennial Exhibition Buildings on the western side of the aerodrome on a permanent basis and recruited extra civilian staff not only to relieve the pressure on Air Force maintenance shops as working aircraft became time expired, but to create one centrally located Tiger Moth support facility. Initially, the overhaul schedule at 1,000 hours flying time reduced a Tiger Moth airframe to a pile of component parts, less fabric, each of which was examined in minute detail. It was a curious course of action for an establishment cradled with British expertise since no such policy was encouraged by de Havilland's Service Department, or actioned at RAF Maintenance Units.

Somebody, somewhere, soon realised that in the best interests of time, economy, and the lingering danger of self-inflicted damage, much less dismantling combined with systematic visual inspection was entirely satisfactory. The 'somebody' may have been a government auditor who calculated that the cost involved under the strip and overhaul policy was greater than production of a new aeroplane. Fortunately for all concerned, by September 1944, the airframe overhaul life had been extended progressively and by degrees to reach 1600 hours.

It may have been due partly to the expense of this policy in both time, effort and cost, which caused Hatfield to issue a first rebuke to their New Zealand General Manager, but the final straw perhaps, concerned Buckingham's attempt to beautify the factory surrounds by planting daffodil bulbs. Having seen a number of different varieties in flower, he had unwittingly chosen one which he considered outstanding and ordered 500 bulbs, only to discover after planting that they were a rare species, a factor reflected by their price. Quite embarrassed, the invoice for £1,500 was forwarded with apologetic trepidation to Hatfield where upon receipt, Wilfred Nixon was said to be 'very unhappy'. Meanwhile, 'Hughie' awaited the storm he knew was brewing.

Having established a fully functional and competent industrial organisation from a standing start, Buckingham test flew the last of the Australian supplied aircraft, NZ1420 (DHA506), on New Year's Eve 1941, and three overhauled Tiger Moths the following week. On 19th January 1942 he made a final flight around the local area in a Miles M.11 Whitney Straight NZ579, the impressed ZK-AFG, late of the Wellington Aero Club, before returning to England, but certainly not into obscurity. 'Jimmy' Buckingham, a DH personality from the early Moth days at Stag Lane, remained with the company and continued flying on their behalf until 1951, succeeding Aubrey Burke as Executive Director of the de Havilland Engine Company in 1955, and remaining at its head until his retirement. Forty years after his departure from New Zealand he could still chuckle over the story of the daffodils.

The new General Manager at Rongotai was Nicholas Higgs, New Zealand's Technical Representative for Bristol Aeroplane Company engines since 1939. Other members of the original Hatfield team had already left, and Peter de Havilland also returned to England at this time to join brothers Geoffrey Jr and John who were fully engaged with Mosquito work at Hatfield. Test flying duties at Rongotai were taken up by John Neave, recruited from flying DH.83 Fox Moths for Air Travel (NZ) Ltd to and from primitive strips along the West Coast. His was to be a daily diet of new and reconditioned Tiger Moths until the end of the war when he left the company to take up the position of Chief Flying Instructor with the Canterbury Aero Club.

There had never been serious difficulties with new Tiger Moths at Rongotai, but during Neave's time one batch of aircraft was fitted with carburettors carrying an insert made necessary to salvage them from a manufacturing error committed elsewhere. Although test bed and ground running all went well, on at least three occasions the insert came loose in the air, generally during the climb out immediately after take-off, causing the engine to shut down. It was only the pilot's skill that allowed the aircraft to be landed deadstick back on the aerodrome.

A further 36 Tiger Moths were ordered early in 1942 (DHNZ101-DHNZ136), which were scheduled for delivery at the rate of three aircraft per month from the beginning of March, although signature of the contract was delayed until April. Wearing serial numbers NZ1426-NZ1456, the order was satisfied by November although NZ1447 (DHNZ 127), accepted onto Air Force charge at Rongotai on 8th October, never did reach her destination at Harewood. Flying in a strong north westerly wind on 28th October, conditions had become increasingly turbulent on the leeward coast of Motunau Island, North Canterbury, and the pilot descended to 200ft to find relief, but there was none and during the climb to regain altitude the aircraft became uncontrollable and fell inverted into the sea. The pilot swam ashore and the Tiger Moth minus its engine remained afloat long enough to be salvaged, but was written off after inspection as a complete loss. On 6th May 1943 delivery of the first of a further batch of 36 aircraft ordered under government contract A/129/42 was commenced (DHNZ137-DHNZ172, serialled NZ1457-NZ1492), and in July 1943 another 36 were contracted for delivery at the agreed rate of three aircraft per month throughout 1944.

Rongotai's dependence on imported parts whose local manufacture had never been contemplated (streamline wires, castings and forgings), was challenged when severe production shortages were experienced late in 1943 due to late deliveries principally from Mascot; the same shortages that held up numerous repair jobs across Australia. Some new aircraft at Rongotai were only completed for acceptance as a result of robbing spares from dismantled aircraft awaiting repair or overhaul.

The last of the first batch of New Zealand built Tiger Moths under final assembly in September 1941, eight months behind schedule. Ready erected is NZ1404, one of 20 Tiger Moths purchased from de Havilland Australia in an effort to redress the shortfall on deliveries.
Hugh Buckingham

As the programme slipped further back, contract A/129/42 was terminated following delivery of only 27 aircraft. The July contract (A/132/43) specifying 36 deliveries in 1944 was cancelled completely. It was an administrative effort to get the programme right on paper, for the aircraft were still required, and consequently an entirely new contract was drawn up in February 1944, A/133/44, requiring 45 Tiger Moths, the residue of the earlier contracts, to be delivered by 3rd December that year. These would include the nine aircraft originally scheduled to become NZ1484-NZ1492 (DHNZ164-DHNZ172), plus NZ1493-NZ1528, (DHNZ173-DHNZ209).

Although it was the seriously delayed delivery of nine aircraft that caused a major renegotiation of contracts, the last of the order was not handed over until mid-June, more than six weeks later than the new target. At about the same time there was realisation that Air Force serials NZ1501-NZ1528 duplicated those previously allocated to extinct Hawker Hinds, but still resulted in substitution of serials NZ1601-NZ1628. With a run-down in the training programme and an attrition rate lower than forecast, the final 27 aircraft were cancelled in September 1944 leaving the last of the Wellington built Tiger Moths, NZ1493-NZ1500 and NZ1601 (DHNZ173-DHNZ181), to be taken on to Air Force charge by the end of February 1945.

Tiger Moths built at Rongotai were essentially the same as those created from identical drawings held at Hatfield, Cowley and Mascot, but locally inspired modifications never became universal. The New Zealand built aircraft were more akin to the British product; improvements spawned at Mascot, practical and genuine, were not adopted at Rongotai, even after the New Zealand experience of assembling Tiger Moths built in Australia and enjoying the unique benefit of direct comparison between those and others supplied from two different sources in Great Britain.

The British spin strake about which the RAF had made such heavy representation and which had been thoroughly investigated at Farnborough and Boscombe Down, trials which had been followed by a massive 'on production' and retrofit programme, was never copied across to Australia or New Zealand where essentially the same aeroplanes were occupied by exactly the same commitments, even to the extent of carrying bomb racks. Details of the strakes were studied by the New Zealand factory late in 1941, and a set was fitted to a Tiger Moth and flight tested by John Neave early in 1942, but upon his recommendation, the modification was considered unnecessary and was never fitted to production aircraft. Assessment of the British spinning trials however, did result in universal removal of aileron mass balance weights.

Modification occasioned by a tragic local experience may have been regarded less emotionally in the corridors of authority thousands of miles away, which is why, perhaps, modification NZ101 dated 17th April 1940, was never adopted elsewhere. On 12th March 1940 a pupil and his instructor were engaged in aerobatic training at 3,000 ft near Mangere. Going inverted during the demonstration of a slow roll, the instructor checked forward on his stick, when the flange at the lower end of the handgrip caught behind the cord attached to the safety harness spring clip, withdrawing the locking pin. The straps were released instantly and to the horror of the pupil the instructor fell out of the aircraft. Contrary to training policy elsewhere, parachutes were not standard equipment at the time of this incident. When parachutes were later issued as a matter of routine, the seat anchorage was considered to be inadequate and modification NZ106 dated 12th November 1941 sought to remedy the perceived deficiency.

During the early 'fifties, an Australian pilot in a borrowed civilian aeroplane was flying inverted along the top of a square loop, when a safety harness clip fell out and shot earthwards past his startled eyes. Instinctively he grabbed the seat at the same time as pulling hard back on the stick, causing the Tiger Moth to half loop and return to normal flight. When he was calm enough to run his hand down the harness webbing he discovered the clip was still firmly in its place, and the one that had fallen out in the inverted position had been carelessly dropped down inside the bowels of the aircraft at some unknown time, where it had cunningly lodged until exploding like a timebomb.

Thirty years later, a fire extinguisher fell out of the cockpit of a British based Tiger Moth during an inverted manoeuvre. The incident was considered serious enough to result in a full accident enquiry, not on behalf of the owner of the empty field into which the device harmlessly fell, but in respect of what might have been the outcome if the pilot of the Tiger Moth had been incapacitated as a result of collision with the unguided missile.

It was fortunate that the Centennial Exhibition Building was both adjacent, suitable and available for Tiger Moth overflow. Note the DH.94 Moth Minor in the right foreground, and the port wings of a DH.90 Dragonfly. deHMC Archive

A display of aircraft on the establishment of the Central Flying School, RNZAF Tauranga, about 1943. The CFS Tiger Moths were distinguished by their red rudders and engine cowlings. RNZAF Ohakea

The COLOURFUL WORLD OF TIGER MOTHS

John Beattie and DH.82A Tiger Moth G-ADPC outbound from Guernsey to Somerset. Flying low over water has always held a fascination. Some wartime instructors were known to have vented frustration by running wheels across the surface. The open cockpit experience above clear blue water is unique.
Geoffrey P Jones

The Royal Air Force Central Flying School painted the top surfaces of their Tiger Moths in a red and white chequerboard to improve the crowd's appreciation of which aircraft were inverted at any one time. In 1995, John Pothecary's restored G-BJAP made her first appearance at Woburn Abbey in an identical scheme.
Mansfield Spong

Mike Russell used an amalgam of Tiger Moth parts to assemble a DH.82 style airframe registered G-MOTH and painted to represent K2567, the first of the marque delivered to the RAF in November 1931.
deHMC Archive

Painted in the colours of a Royal Swedish Air Force DH.82A Tiger Moth (SK11A) as delivered in 1933, '6550' is in reality SE-AMG, ex-RAF, built by Morris Motors and registered in Sweden in 1988. Lars Lundin

'5882' was a post-war civil import sold from Sweden to the USA in 1977 and is seen here painted in the high visibility colour scheme (M/35) adopted by the Royal Swedish Air Force for trainer aircraft before the Second World War. Lars de Jounge

Panzergra and Orange (M/40), the adopted wartime colours for Royal Swedish Air Force training aircraft, applied to SE-AMR, Swedish built SK11A No 49, which served in the military between 1935 and 1948. Ian Oliver

Built at Mascot in August 1940 for the RAAF, A17-63 served initially at Tamworth and later Narromine. She was sold for £100 in September 1946 but remained in store and unconverted until a certificate of airworthiness was issued in November 1990. David Freeman

de Havilland Tiger Moth and arch rival for the 1931 RAF trainer contract, the all-metal, side-by-side seating Blackburn B2. In the event only Blackburn's Reserve School at Brough was equipped with a fleet of B2 aircraft, later superseded by the Tiger Moth. DH.82A G-ANCS and sole surviving airworthy Blackburn B2 G-AEBJ were photographed at Brough. via Roger Reeves

Dennis Neville in a patch of sunlight over Booker, watching for traffic which might oppose his tight turn in camouflaged Tiger Moth G-ANMV. via Dennis Neville

The dark green scheme of the pre war Norwegian Army Air Force was broken only by national insignia carried at the tail and wing tips. LN-MAX, masquerading as Army Air Force '127', can be identified as a post-war import by the carriage of spin strakes. Ivar Windingstad

Tiger Moth G-ACDJ suffered a damaged rudder when being towed by a car in June 1995 and in order to attend the Woburn Abbey Rally that year, the fin and rudder were borrowed from G-ANTE, then in long term store at Chester. Peter Henley

Photographs on the opposite page:

The unsung hero: the flying instructor. In all weathers and under every operational condition, the flying instructor sat patiently in the front seat dispensing wisdom and experience. He became a familiar and comforting sight to the pupil pilot until solo stage when his referencing bulk was no longer there and the trim of the aeroplane was altered. Pim Van Dam

Once painted in the chequerboard colours of the RAF Central Flying School, Tiger Moth G-AMLF retained the scheme on export to the USA but took up the markings of the Brooklands Flying Club's G-ADNV after a major overhaul in California. David Watson

Representing the prototype DH.82A Tiger Moth in pre-war service with the de Havilland School of Flying, the aircraft marked 'G-ACDA' at Old Rhinebeck, New York, is in reality N3529, a late production by Morris Motors, exported new to the French Air Force in 1946, and sold to the USA in 1971. Barry Dowsett

After years in storage at Farnborough, Tiger Moth G-AHVU emerged bravely in its former guise of T6313 painted in a pre-war light tint camouflage scheme, although more surfaces should have been yellow, and the spin strakes deleted. In the lower photograph it can be seen that by 1990 even the concession of the yellow rudder had been abandoned. Barry Dowsett

Above: **John Beattie who bought his own Tiger Moth following retirement as Commanding Officer of the Royal Navy Historic Aircraft Flight, demonstrates how refuelling a Tiger Moth from a jerry can needs strength, cool nerve and a head for heights.** via John Beattie

Left: **Going up. But only just. Dennis Neville seeking earth orbit in G-AGPK poses for the camera before the inevitable break away and descent. Note the angle of the rudder and elevator.** John Dibbs

Below: **Green leaves, blue sky, a mown grass runway and a German registered Tiger Moth, D-EEAJ, engaged in tugging duties on behalf of a vintage glider, all varnished wood and doped fabric. Summer magic.** via Michael Dressler

One time de Havilland School of Flying Tiger Moth G-ADCG restored with a red rudder, caught in the stubble of de Havilland field, Seven Barrows, only a few days after her return to airworthiness in September 1986. In 1993 the aircraft joined a privately owned collection of vintage biplanes based at Wevelgem in Belgium. Jim Hitchcock

When frozen to a clearly defined specification, the Schwarzsee in Switzerland situated at 3,000ft, provides an operational area of 1,000 metres by 500 metres for an almost unique gathering of invited aeroplanes. Flown by Bruno Vonlanthen, Tiger Moth HB-UBC based at Ecuvillens, was one of 20 visiting types in February 1998. Bruno Vonlanthen

Bottom left: **In the sunshine against a blue sky, a Tiger Moth wearing colours of the de Havilland School of Flying. Only the black hills, tailwheel and full span American registration N459DE (ex-RAF DE459), identify the aeroplane as the fruits of a 25 year restoration programme completed by Tom Kewin in California in 1997.** Tom Kewin

Bottom right: **G-ANZZ, a typical Tiger Club aeroplane provided by Rollason Aircraft during the mid-'fifties. A Rollason trademark was the registration ending in the letter 'Z' together with rudder and engine cowlings painted in the same colour.** A J Jackson Collection

The rolling hills, enclosed fields, villages and stone churches act as backdrop to this camouflaged Tiger Moth operating out of a grassy British aerodrome perhaps? Once based at Desford as part of 7 EFTS and later civil registered in Switzerland, N82GS was acquired by Gerry Schwam, later Chairman of the American Moth Club, in 1975, and has operated in and around Pennsylvania ever since. via Gerry Schwam

Cloud chasing in an open cockpit biplane on a summer's day is one of life's pleasures that has no equal. Tricia Neville

Sitting on the ground in an open cockpit biplane with the rain pouring down is not an ideal way to spend a Sunday morning. Interlocking low aspect ratio umbrellas are an essential part of summer kit for British based Moth owners. John Beattie

Immediate post-war colours for RAF Flying Training Command Tiger Moths based in Great Britain was a coat of 'trainer yellow', (officially 'Golden Yellow' BS381C-356), usually applied over the concealing properties of the redundant camouflage scheme at a cost of extra weight.
Peter Bogue

The right to fly a Dutch civil registered Tiger Moth through the skies of the Netherlands wearing a fin and rudder designed by de Havilland, was a concession won from an airworthiness authority in reaction to Tiger Moths based locally but registered outside the country and seemingly operating without difficulty.
Marien van Schie

Caught in an isolated patch of sunshine near High Wycombe, Tigerfly's camouflaged G-ANMV/T7404 displays a late wartime scheme featuring yellow tips to the upper mainplanes, yellow tank and engine cowling side panels. Some units added a broad yellow band around the fuselage at the position of the roundel.
Tricia Neville

On the declaration of war in 1939, RAF Reserve School aircraft adopted the camouflage scheme of the day whilst retaining civil registration letters. By 1991, when she was caught slipping in to land over the lakes at Woburn Abbey, this adopted scheme had already been worn by G-ARAZ for several years. Don Conway

In June1994, Tiger Moths G-ANRN and G-APLU embarked on a 6,000 mile round trip from London to North Cape. The flight included extensive sectors over the sea, fjords and lakes. Nicholas Bence-Trower from G-ANRN

Built at Hatfield early in 1939 and exported to Los Angeles on board a 747 Freighter in 1988, N555XB was painted in this unusual red and blue scheme by her new owner, but retained British civil registration G-ASXB on the fuselage. Tim Jacobson

Flying low over the sea or a beach has its attractions especially if the sun is warm and the pilot keeps an eye on the height of the rollers. ZK-BUO frollicking near Daroaville, New Zealand. via Henry Labouchere

Amongst her many claims to fame, seen here taking a quiet tour of the Norfolk coastline, Tiger Moth G-ANOH was one of the Glasmoth Trio which flew from London to Moscow in April 1989. Henry Labouchere

One of the prettiest sights (and nostalgic sounds) is a 'shower' of biplanes in close harmony processing over summer fields. An early outing for the Diamond Nine in the days when the team was augmented by an occasional straight winged guest. deHMC Archive

Only the tailwheels superimposed against the high cumulus identify the location of these two 'RAF' Tiger Moths as United States rather than United Kingdom. Bob Curtin and Walt Kessler once formed part of a show trio in Wisconsin. via Walt Kessler

DH.82C Tiger Moth C-FGTU (RCAF 4319), was restored to airworthiness in 1996 and is employed in Canada on a Public Transport certificate as a professional joyrider. This view illustrates maximum extension of the oleos when not loaded and the bulk of the heater muff surrounding the long exhaust pipe. Eric Dumigan

During her time with the Royal Navy Historic Aircraft Flight, Tiger Moth T8191 was operated in a naval camouflage scheme of two tones of grey with yellow undersides, not the most inconspicuous when operating over browns and greens of the rolling countryside. R J Wilson

In August 1986 the Reynolds Aviation Museum in Wetaskiwin, Alberta, put up a representative formation of Second World War trainer biplanes: Boeing Stearman (1943); Fleet 16 Finch (1938); DH.82C Tiger Moth (1943) and a 1942 'C' model Tiger Moth operating in an open cockpit 'A' configuration. Reynolds Museum

During their flight to North Cape in June 1994, pilots Jonathan Elwes and Michael Vaisey in Tiger Moths G-ANRN and G-APLU experienced all weather conditions expected at such latitudes, and the opportunity to fly in broad daylight over Norwegian fjords with the clock well past midnight. Nick Bence-Trower from G-ANRN

Tiger Moths sold cheaply in southern Africa set a pattern for later disposal sales and allowed clubs to re-establish their pre-war status. Morris Motors built VP-YOI photographed at Induna, Bulawayo in October 1980, was previously with the South African Air Force and remains airworthy at Gwanda, Zimbabwe. Dave Becker

Tiger Moth PH-UDK of NLS, the Dutch National Aviation School, recently off a maintenance check, displaying the Fokker tail, single seat configuration and 'last two' on the fuselage side. M J Hooks

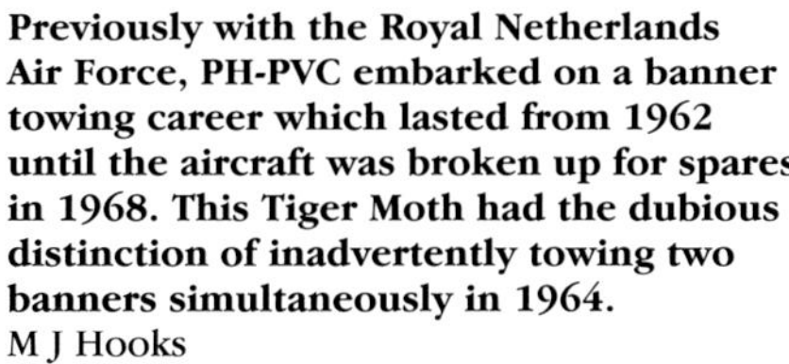

Previously with the Royal Netherlands Air Force, PH-PVC embarked on a banner towing career which lasted from 1962 until the aircraft was broken up for spares in 1968. This Tiger Moth had the dubious distinction of inadvertently towing two banners simultaneously in 1964. M J Hooks

No matter how intricate the design of colour schemes or considered the application of high technology finishing materials, the classical lines of the Tiger Moth airframe cannot be disguised. Rollason exported I-MOMI to Italy in 1959 in the standard finish of the day and decidedly not as photographed in June 1986. Gregory Alegi

When registered G-ASKP to Rollason Aircraft in 1963, ex RAF N6588 was unusual in that the civil letters did not end with a 'Z', a trait that became an acknowledged Rollason trademark. Equally non-standard was the colour scheme: the port side colours were the direct opposite of those on the starboard side, eye catching and effective but an engineer's nightmare. M J Hooks

Pastel blue is not a colour much associated with Tiger Moths, but operating under the sunlit skyscape of South Africa, Tiger Moth ZS-DNG, ex SAAF and of Australian origin, proves colour and airframe are in complete harmony. Dave Becker

Tiger Moths G-ANRN and G-APLU in good company at Petrozavodsk aerodrome near Lake Onezhskoye, 200nm north east of St Petersburg, Russia, on 18th June 1994, outbound from England to North Cape. Nick Bence-Trower

The final colour scheme adopted by the last Tiger Moths operational with the Royal Navy was silver overall with the addition of then fashionable peel-off 'day-glo' tape, stuck on to engine cowlings, rear fuselage and fin. Mike Longden

Tiger Moth PG651 never saw RAF service, but was delivered ex-storage at Colerne to the French Air Force in 1945. Returning to Britain in 1971, as G-AYUX she was based at Booker and camouflaged in the style of an aircraft previously established there with 21 EFTS. She was sold to Italy and ferried to Parma in April 1987. Stefano Rusconi

Bearing the legend *Spirit of Sky Harbour* DH.82C Tiger Moth C-GCVE (RCAF 4198), was rebuilt in December 1986 for John Hindmarsh, and based at Goderich on the same site where the owner had been a resident Tiger Moth instructor with 12 EFTS in 1944. Martin Lee

Blending into a background of parkland and mature oak trees Tiger Moth PH-TYG circles to land at Woburn Abbey in 1994. The aircraft is painted in the finite camouflage colours of the Royal Netherlands Air Force with yellow upper surfaces to the lower mainplanes. Pim van Dam

Rebuilt by students of Northbrook College at Shoreham airport and rolled out in 1997, G-AMNN had been used for student flying tuition at a previous base at Redhill until relegated to the workshops following an accident. The aircraft is named *Spirit of Pashley* after the legendary Shoreham founder and instructor Cecil Pashley. British Aerospace

Removal of the canopy and all-over yellow cannot disguise the fact that Tiger Moth N4030E is a Canadian built 'C' version instantly identified by the narrow chord steel interplane struts, raked landing gear and large tailwheel. Art Armstrong

Watt Martin's multi-functional DH.82C Tiger Moth CF-CKF in standard configuration at Guelph Air Park, a centre of Tiger Moth activity in Canada. Bombardier Regional Aircraft

Exercising over the appropriately named Mud Bay, British Columbia, Bill Teague and DH.82A Tiger Moth C-GWET *Old Harry*, an aircraft which emigrated from South Africa with her owner in 1976. Terry Elgood from DH.82C CF-ATG

On the opposite page:

Not a place for a forced landing. HB-UPP, the 1,000th Tiger Moth assembled in Australia reached Switzerland via the USA and Great Britain and with some trepidation was detached from her heavy canopy but not her colour scheme. Eric Gandet

A Tiger Moth restored in New Zealand gets her tail up at Chalmington Manor, Dorset. Out of picture at left, the ground slopes steeply down, requiring all arrivals to be towards the house. Gordon Bain

One of a trio of DH.82A Tiger Moths once owned by actor Cliff Robertson and upon whose initiative the aircraft qualified for Type Approval in the USA, N524R is operational in California carrying an impressive avionics suite and a deck mounted strobe. via Bill Lusk

When the crew of G-AYUX reported at home base prior to joining the Famous Grouse Rally at Hatfield in June 1979, they found the Tiger Moth's rudder had been damaged in her hangar. Astonishingly, the local maintenance organisation had a complete unit overhauled to the red dope stage in their stores. deHMC Archive

Flying low over the sea has always held a compulsive attraction, and when the sun is shining and sand conditions are ideal, a friendly shadow will dance along too. Tiger Moth ZK-BRM inspecting the surf in New Zealand. Gordon Bain

Sea and coastline will always provide some of the best possible background for air-to-air photography. Tiger Moth G-BFHH was captured flying against the exposed chalk of the South Downs near Beachy Head in Sussex, before January 1999 when a chunk of it fell into the sea. Gordon Bain

Australian built, British registered and resident in Switzerland, Tiger Moth G-BCRD was re-covered with lacquered lightweight fabric in 1976 at the beginning of an eight year sojourn in the USA. The Wackett canopy remained undisturbed for some years after her move to Europe. Richard Dent

A rear seat view of the Swiss Alps taken from under the Wackett canopy fitted to Richard Dent's Tiger Moth G-BCRD. The superstructure was later cut off with a handsaw to return the aircraft to standard open cockpit configuration. Richard Dent

Professional joyrider Bruce McGarvie has a fleet of Tiger Moths operating along Queensland's Gold Coast where temperatures all year round guarantee a steady stream of willing passengers. VH-WAP, a frustrated wartime export to southern Africa, was operated by the RAAF instead and acquired by the current owner in 1966. via Bruce McGarvie

During an extensive tour of North America in his British built, New Zealand registered Tiger Moth ZK-BFX in 1975, Ian Bennie visited the de Havilland factory at Downsview, Toronto. Broken and rebuilt on several occasions during the two year adventure, the Tiger Moth was sold to an owner in the USA in 1977 and wrecked during low level aerobatics in 1985. de Havilland Canada

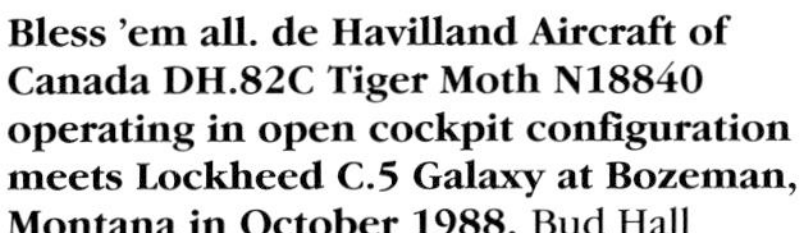

Bless 'em all. de Havilland Aircraft of Canada DH.82C Tiger Moth N18840 operating in open cockpit configuration meets Lockheed C.5 Galaxy at Bozeman, Montana in October 1988. Bud Hall

Bless 'em all. de Havilland Aircraft Pty Ltd. DH.82A Tiger Moth N10LW operating in Woody Woodpecker markings meets Avro Lancaster and Antonov An-124 at Oshkosh in July 1989. Stuart Hawkins

DH.82C Tiger Moth C-GMFT, an outdoor exhibit sharing space with assorted vehicles at the Museum of Flight and Transportation in British Columbia, experiencing a heavy accumulation of snow during a winter storm on Canada's Pacific coast. Ed Zalesky

A trio of time expired Indian Government Tiger Moths, VT-DOX, 'DOZ and 'DPB, parked on a weed encroached concrete apron at Madras. Painted yellow overall with green 'trainer bands' the three aircraft were part of the consignment delivered to England in 1979. Bob Wall

Formerly in service with the SAAF and SRAF, after 14 years under civil ownership in Southern Rhodesia as VP-YKB this aircraft was sold to South Africa in 1966. Rebuilt in 1986, ZS-ECI was caught frolicking in the mid-day sun, probably near Margate, where she was awarded championship honours the following year. Cliff Modlin

Following a visit to the Woburn Abbey Moth Rally, Barry and Carol Markham returned home to Western Australia, to name their airstrip 'Woburn Field'. In 1998, Barry Markham flew his Tiger Moth VH-NOV from Perth to Cambridge, England, leaving the hangar temporarily unoccupied. Barry Markham

Kurt Hofschneider and his Tiger Moth N39DH were welcomed into the team when they met the USAF 'Thunderbirds' at the Atlantic City Trans-Fair in 1978.
Kurt Hofschneider

Following the formation of the Diamond Nine Team in 1987, it was decided to put up all participating members together during the Woburn Abbey Moth Rally two years later, flying a unique Diamond Sixteen for a single north-south pass.
Mike Jerram / Ian Oliver

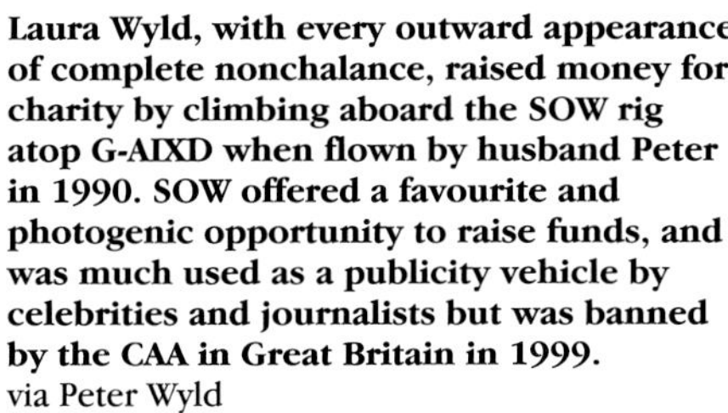

Laura Wyld, with every outward appearance of complete nonchalance, raised money for charity by climbing aboard the SOW rig atop G-AIXD when flown by husband Peter in 1990. SOW offered a favourite and photogenic opportunity to raise funds, and was much used as a publicity vehicle by celebrities and journalists but was banned by the CAA in Great Britain in 1999.
via Peter Wyld

Piloted by Ray Vuillermin with Peter Lawson-Hanscombe on the rig, Tiger Moth VH-SSI made the first authorised SOW flight in Australia on 6th February 1990.
via Ray Vuillermin

With some interestingly erratic farmland gridlines as reference, the assorted colour schemes of the 1988 Diamond Nine Team displaying at Badminton, inadvertently illustrated most episodes of the Tiger Moth's professional career. deHMC Archive

Part of the dispensation from the Air Navigation Order permitting this British registered Tiger Moth to fly under the hoop at the Woburn Abbey Moth Rally in 1997, was clearance to operate the aircraft to a minimum height of three feet above ground level. Darryl Cott

The advantage of a formation leader not smoking is evident in this shot of the Italian Tiger Moth Team 'Le Tigri' during their participation at the Redhill Air Show in July 1987. Smoke generation of such generously billowing proportions is generally difficult to achieve from an engine the size of a Gipsy Major. Don Conway

Formation take off at Rendcomb in 1994 ensures the two wingmen are safely established in flight and concentrating on the leader who remains anchored in the roll until satisfied. Peter Jackson

Rebuilt in Great Britain in 1986 from the wreck of an aircraft imported from the USA, G-AHAN took up vacant markings and was photographed with new owner Lloyd Owens over Gransden. The rear door is not disturbed by airflow when opened in flight and the configuration is often considered 'more comfortable' by broad shouldered pilots operating solo from the rear cockpit. via Lloyd Owens

Wearing blue and white chequerboard markings to illustrate her one time attachment to 19(F) Squadron RAF, when operating Gloster Meteor F.4s from Church Fenton in 1951, DH.82A Tiger Moth C-FFDQ emigrated to Canada with owner Dr Jeremy Johnston in 1972 and was aerobatted extensively until a growing family necessitated her replacement in 1984 by a Beech Staggerwing. via Jeremy Johnston

Following in the wake of chivalry when a gentleman picked up a dropped handkerchief, Royal Swedish Air Force jet fighter pilot Par Cederqvist has demonstrated the gentle art many times flying Tiger Moth SE-CWG. Once part of the establishment of White Waltham's de Havilland Reserve School, the aircraft was sold to Sweden in 1963. via Par Cederqvist

Australian built Tiger Moth DHA428 is unusual in that it is one of three aircraft of the same type to have carried the registration VH-ASC. Acquired in 1976 by Neil Cottee, the charismatic owner of a mail-order film processing company, VH-ASC was painted very cleverly to represent the stripy camouflage of a four legged beast. via Bill Hitchcock

A one time regular sight at Coventry when operated in the house colours of the Sir W G Armstrong Whitworth Aircraft Flying Group, Tiger Moth G-ALWW, known affectionately as 'Wearie Willie', has taken on see-and-be-seen colours and a satisfyingly busy occupation as glider tug at Bidford. Barry Dowsett

The concentration of the pilot is surely transmitted from this shot of Australian built ex-agricultural Tiger Moth VH-PSD operating at low level. Note the position of the elevators (down) and both leading edge slats (open). deHMC Archive

Red, white and blue sunburst, stars and a chequered rudder: not a scheme usually associated with a German owned Tiger Moth registered in the late 'sixties, but one highlighted by sunshine when set against a dark forest background near Frankfurt. Michael Dressler

Following sale in 1979, Tiger Moth VH-ASC replaced her tiger stripes for representation of a First World War scout, complete with sculpted cockpit and dummy machine gun. In conventional configuration but wearing the same colours, VH-ASC later operated aerial tours of Sydney Harbour under the title of Red Baron Scenic Flights. via David Voight

On the opposite page:

Photographed in April 1977 when based in Queensland, the bright red fuselage of Australian built Tiger Moth VH-BRM highlights the minimum structure and maximum glazing of the canopy, all of which was subsequently removed. Peter Keating

The 180hp engine fitted to Hannu Riihela's much modified Finnish Tiger Moth OH-XLA provided a phenomenal improvement in climb performance amongst much else, but remains the only such conversion in the world. Hannu Riihela

Previously registered OH-ELA, a 1951 import from Great Britain, the rebuilt Tiger Moth was obliged to carry 'Experimental' identification OH-XLA from 1977 due to the major modifications incorporated, none of which was acknowledged by the Design Authority. In addition to the Lycoming engine, some undercarriage components and electrics were sourced from a Beech Musketeer. M J Hooks

Tiger Moth OH-XLA was configured for wheel and ski undercarriage, as a glider tug and lake hopping floatplane by her creator during his four years of ownership. Hannu Riihela

Given the right circumstances, it is possible to manoeuvre a Tiger Moth on the ground single handed. A rough surface and a slope help to create conditions difficult even for a quartet! Following release from the RAF in 1955, D-EMUS was sold to a flying group based in Nürnberg. M J Hooks

The power of the tailskid as a braking factor on firm sand was amply demonstrated when beach landings were called for during production of a film on Queensland's Gold Coast in 1985. *Soft* sand is to be avoided at all costs. Chris de Vere

Stepping backwards off the trailing edge of the starboard lower mainplane, a sport parachutist is in the ideal position to free fall. Steve Plank, dropping away from Pete Colman's throttled G-AKXS, closed the front cockpit door during the run in. Peter Jackson

Once carrying the red and silver livery of the London Transport Flying Club and based at Fairoaks, Tiger Moth G-AIIZ was purchased by David Baker, son of the Club's retired CFI, and shipped to Hong Kong where this photograph was taken from an aero club Cessna 182 flown by Ray Hanna in September 1976. via David Baker

On retirement from his colonial posting, plans to fly G-AIIZ from Hong Kong to England possibly in company with another Tiger Moth, were shelved and eventually the aircraft arrived at London Gatwick as palletised cargo on the main deck of a Cathay Pacific Boeing 747 Freighter. David Lipson

Part of the American dream: to own a comfortable house with a large garage and a big car. What then of the reality of a house alongside a communal runway, with a personal windsock and a built-in hangar capable of housing a pair of light aeroplanes? Tiger Moth N6539 on the lawn alongside Tim Jacobson's home in Port Orchard, Washington State, September 1996. Harry Repine

To celebrate the 60th anniversary of RAAF Base Pearce in July 1998, previous equipment (DH.82A Tiger Moth VH-NMD/ A17-640) cruising speed 72 knots, was flown in formation with a current RAAF trainer (Pilatus PC-9 A23-058) stalling speed 70 knots. Kirsty Chambers, RAAF

On the opposite page:

A bright and glorious day in an English winter. Wings level, throttle closed, stick back, back, back ... The pilot of G-ANEZ concentrating on a perfect three point touchdown, the most satisfying of all ways to conclude a sortie in a Tiger Moth. M J Hooks

Once the snow laden storms have passed through, the temporary exposure of clear blue skies, unlimited visibility and a stable air mass entice aviators aloft, provided the aeroplanes are properly shod. Watt Martin's DH.82C Tiger Moth CF-CKF in a blue and yellow colour scheme, February 1978. Watt Martin

Blue sky, green trees, yellow Tiger Moth on a deep carpet of white snow. The ski tracks after landing appear to be only as long as the fuselage. Experimental Tiger Moth OH-XLA on a frozen lake in Finland. Hannu Riihela

At the end of the 1985 summer season, float equipped DH.82C Tiger Moth CF-CKF was flown to his hangar/workshop at Milton, Ontario, by Watt Martin in readiness for conversion to wheel or ski undercarriage. Wind conditions on 30th September were ideal for the floatplane to be landed on the grass without any sign of fuss, bother or incredulity. Watt Martin

Although none of the world's military air arms favoured the Tiger Moth as a seaplane trainer, since the early 'fifties Watt Martin has flown a number of DH.82C Tiger Moths on floats without incident. CF-CKF was spotted with a pair of floats originally designed for a DH.60 Moth, operating from Lake Puslinch, Ontario, in September 1985. Jack McNulty

The Reading Flying Group's Tiger Moth G-ANFM appeared in a number of films but most spectacularly in a big screen production of the famous *Thunderbirds* television series, when Joan Hughes flew the aircraft accompanied by a cast of lifesize dummies. Ted Lay

What the art director wants, the art director gets. Tiger Moth ZS-BCN carried her civil registration on the fuselage side under the shadow of the tailplane when she was painted like this at Rand airport, Johannesburg, for her role in the film *King Solomon's Mines* shot in 1986. Dave Becker

Not prepared for filming, rather the private satisfaction of her owner! The colours applied to Tiger Moth G-ALUC are intended to mirror those carried by SE5s operating on the Western Front during the First World War. Intended to be rebuilt as a single seater, G-ALUC was eventually finished in standard configuration with dual controls. David Wood

Coastal flying can be more relaxed when miles of deserted sandy beaches stretch ahead. Sheer cliffs rising from a ribbon of shoreline provide an awesome backdrop and demand attention. Tiger Moth ZK-BRM, her pilot adorned with a Mae-West, operating off the coast of South Island, New Zealand. Gordon Bain

If one civil aircraft in the world is more deserving and demanding of attention than a yellow Tiger Moth, it is Concorde, a machine of enduring majesty, beauty and power. Steve Bohill-Smith, co-pilot of Concorde and captain of Tiger Moth G-ANFM, led some of his friends to Manston on 11th May 1991 as part of the Tiger Moth's Diamond Jubilee celebrations. Gordon Bain

Kurt Hofschneider ensured a place in history for his Tiger Moth N39DH when he was granted clearance by the FAA to fly over the Empire State Building in New York City, as part of the fiftieth anniversary celebrations of the legendary King Kong.
via Kurt Hofschneider

Before the craftsmanship is covered over, a chap has a family duty to ensure that his rebuilt Tiger Moth fits together and the engine works as scheduled. Barry Hills and his Australian manufactured Tiger Moth VH-AUZ in the back yard of his house near Adelaide, June 1998. Barry Hills

Kenneth Copp completely refurbished his Tiger Moth N838KC between November 1979 when the aircraft was delivered to his California home as a shambles packed inside a box van, and May 1991 when he flew her from Sonoma. As NL838, the aircraft had been sold from RAF storage in 1944 for operation by the French Air Force in Casablanca. Kenneth Copp

Two Tiger Moths of the Cambridge Flying Group painted in the pre-war colours adopted by the London Aeroplane Club at Stag Lane, formating over the misted Fenlands of East Anglia. Reg Bonner

Commander Philip Shaw RN, Squadron Commander of 360 Squadron RAF, Wyton, flying his hobby interest Tiger Moth G-AFVE, shadowed by his working day aeroplane, English Electric Canberra T.17A WD955 flown by Squadron Leader Terry Cairns. When this shot was taken from a Casa 131 Jungmann in August 1994, WD955 was the oldest operational aircraft in the RAF. Gordon Bain

When a chap has a classic aeroplane, he ought to have a classic car to get him down to the aerodrome. Tom Sumner, Seattle based restorer of quality motor cars, posed his Tiger Moth N3744M with a pair of Rolls-Royces at Martha Lake in 1983. Tom Sumner

Today, they come in a variety of colours and with some customisation to cockpits and equipment, but the airframe geometry and natural harmony with the Gipsy Major engine remains unerringly constant. Some of the 57 Tiger Moths which joined the de Havilland Moth Club's 19th International Rally at Woburn Abbey in August 1998. Darryl Cott

Anne de Havilland, grand daughter of Sir Geoffrey, with Dick Bishop, son of de Havilland Chief Designer R E Bishop, prior to flying out of Hatfield aerodrome in Tiger Moth G-APLU at mid-day on Friday 8th April 1994, the last movement before the site was closed to flying for ever. When a little girl, teddy 'Charlie Brown' had been parachuted into Anne's back garden from an aircraft operating from Hatfield, flown by her uncle, Geoffrey de Havilland Jr. Darryl Cott

In 1982, as part of the DH100 celebrations honouring the centenary of the birth of Sir Geoffrey de Havilland, multifarious Moths transited through Farnborough aerodrome and were briefly at rest adjacent to the famous black hangar, close to where Geoffrey de Havilland took his first paid employment in aviation. British Aerospace

GOING FOR A SONG

T6026, 'RUOD' of Oxford University Air Squadron, operating from Abingdon or Manor Road aerodrome, Oxford, during the late autumn of 1947. The aircraft was sold into obscurity the following April.
deHMC Archive

TOTAL WAR is as much about resources, the provision of supplies and basic economics as it is to the brutality and destruction. Supplies, services and support required to defeat the enemy must be provided regardless of cost, although accounts are dutifully and meticulously maintained in appropriate quarters. Long before any cessation of hostilities, plans will be laid by the optimists and realists of both sides engaged in the conflict, designed to cope with the continuation of trade, commerce and the freedom to prosper after the enforced interruption. Legions of artefacts and mountains of miscellaneous equipment salvaged from the material requirements of sustained modern warfare are nearly always readily adaptable to civil use following a return to peace and stability. The victor, witnessing the signature of the vanquished, could so easily become the unwitting victim of economic suicide were not the return to peace and normality managed with as much tactical care as direction of the greatest battle.

As early as 1944, the British, Canadian and American Governments were engaged in delicate discussion in Washington, aiming to establish a post-war policy for the ordered disposal of thousands of aircraft of all types in a manner politically acceptable to all parties; which did not flood the world markets with state of the art technology at insane prices, yet provided opportunities for refurbishment, operation and maintenance without degrading the prospects for research, design and manufacture.

Each camp in Washington harboured a vested interest: the Americans had a near monopoly of large transport aircraft whilst Great Britain had a major input in bombers

DX709 'AZ' of 4 FTS Heany in 1948. The aircraft was supplied from Australia against a British Government contract, and was written off after a crash on the last day of 1951. The aircraft is fitted with spin strakes and a British oil tank. David Vernon

and fighters, sharing a common interest in training aircraft with her Commonwealth partners and the USA. In 1944, with the war not won, Lend-Lease aircraft were still being provided by the United States. Intransigence on the part of the British Government during discussions concerning surplus disposals could affect agreed and future supplies, it was believed.

A view developed on the British side that suggested separate rules should be applied to aircraft bought outright rather than leased, loaned or borrowed. 'Why not scrap all surplus aircraft and have done with it?' was a bold new line tabled by the Secretary of State for Air, Sir Archibald Sinclair. There would be little financial return from such an exercise but it had merit, and would obviate the need for expensive care and storage facilities. But if a total scrapping policy was not the answer, what proportion of the surplus should be retained to guard against future emergencies, also to guarantee that closed lines for staple types like the Tiger Moth trainer, would not need to be re-activated?

The equation was complicated and grounds for endless discussion in the corridors of power. In Great Britain, implementation of whatever agreement was reached was to be the prerogative of the Ministry of Aircraft Production (MAP) rather than the Air Ministry, although in practice situations and solutions never were clear cut, and sharp inter-departmental exchanges resulted when ill defined boundaries were thought to have been transgressed.

Emphasis was placed on the interpretation of two reports published almost simultaneously in the USA. On 26th June 1944, the War Contracts Sub Committee to the Committee on Military Affairs published its paper, *'Disposal of Surplus Aircraft and Major Components Thereof'* which was followed by what became known as the Clayton Report: *'Report on Surplus Aircraft Disposal, submitted by Surplus Aircraft Advisory Sub Committee to William L Clayton, Administrator, Surplus War Property Administration, Office of War Mobilisation'*.

The Clayton Report carried a wide ranging and balanced view of the whole matter, and provided reasoned argument for construction of all the equations, but it was binding on nobody. On behalf of the MAP, the Air Ministry had on 22nd May 1944, contacted its Washington delegates before either American report had been published, requesting them to investigate claims made in the British weekly magazine *The Aeroplane,* that the United States authorities had announced they were shortly to put up for sale 5,000 war surplus training aircraft from a total of about 12,000 aircraft eventually to be offered to the market. The report stated that 3,200 aircraft had already been declared surplus, of which 1,823 were trainer and liaison types of 21 different models, and sales would be organised against a bidding process open at least initially, only to citizens of the United States.

The British delegation was reminded that *'current practice is to break down surplus RAF aircraft', but they were advised that 'we are now considering holding on to Tiger Moths and Magisters for post-war individuals and clubs, and are taking soundings as to possible bids for such aircraft from Empire or European countries'*.

At the beginning of June 1944, Canada announced that due to a reduction in the training programme, they intended to offer surplus aircraft first to the British Government and then to other Dominions.

An agreement was already in place with the United States that neither would flood the other with surplus equipment. There was no prospect that the British Government would be interested in buying Tiger Moths, having itself declared a surplus of 150 aircraft with a further 300 (plus 150 Magisters) to be released by the end of 1944, leaving 2,050 in service or in store! At the same time, an Air Ministry survey identified 600 Tiger Moths available in Canada, 660 in Australia, 235 in New Zealand, 580 in South Africa, 290 in India and a further 228 in Southern Rhodesia.

Canada was also anxious to dispose of 200 Fairchild Cornells built in Canada for shipment to South Africa, but the SAAF had refused to accept delivery on grounds that unlike the Tiger Moth, which might itself have been marginal, performance of the wooden winged Cornell was not compatible with a hot, high altitude environment, a rejection which had embarrassed the Canadians very considerably.

In a move generally accepted as being within the framework of agreements reached in Washington, the United States formally announced in July the release of 11,450 surplus aircraft for private sale within the USA, and on 23rd July, the Air Ministry confirmed the Canadian Government's proposal to sell 600 DH.82C Tiger Moths into the world market, phased at 100 aircraft per month for the next six months. This news had reached the MAP via Francis St Barbe at Hatfield whose intelligence had been gathered from the heart of the Dominion: *'The theory is that the good market for surplus war stocks will not last very long. If the government waits for a Conference with the United Nations, the opportunity will be lost'*.

The Director General of Civil Aviation (DGCA), Sir William Hildred, expressed his view that of the 450 Tiger Moths and 150 Miles Magisters due to be declared surplus by the RAF from 1st January 1945, a total of 200-300 aircraft (of which it was suggested 75-100 ought to be Magisters), should be retained for sale to allied governments, export to the colonies or sale to private owners and clubs within the British Isles. The remainder would be scrapped. As responsible selling agents, the MAP urged him to discuss the plan with the Americans, especially as 500 Cornells which had been obtained under Lend-Lease (Mutual Aid Canada), were still serving in Southern Rhodesia and India.

With the gradual deceleration of the Air Training Scheme, in mid-June South Africa declared it would have a surplus of 50 Tiger Moths from early 1945, and the Rhodesian Air Training Group (RATG) announced from Salisbury that it had declared 118 Tiger Moths surplus with immediate effect. RATG suggested selling the aircraft at £100 each; there was no covered accommodation for them and they would rapidly deteriorate if left too long in open storage. The advice offered from London was to sell immediately at any reasonable price, preferably within Africa, and whatever was left over should be scrapped. RATG were also directed not to offer any assistance for sale of surplus Cornells.

Confusion in the British approach to the still fluid disposals policy was revealed by the Air Ministry on 23rd September. MAP suggested that the Air Ministry had given permission for British Government owned aircraft damaged in South Africa to an assessment level of Category A (repairable on site), to be broken down. The Air Ministry replied politely that this report was not true. Although the normal policy on redundant aircraft was to break down, no decision on the South African based aircraft had yet been made. But some action would shortly be demanded, and following a gathering of all interested parties at the first formal meeting of the Aircraft Disposal Committee held in London on 1st November 1944, the Joint American Secretariat in Washington was cabled with the following statement, classified as 'Top Secret':

London. 8th November 1944.
To Joint American Secretariat Washington.
Re Class C light aircraft.

'Light aircraft manufacturers share the view that judicious sales (ex military) in the immediate post-war period will encourage future personal and flying club demand. Particularly so for types out of production due training cutback. We may have need of these to meet genuine civil demands until new civil types are developed. Careful watch to ensure surplus sales do not endanger new development - watch disposals in Third countries. Price and quality control required calculated to ensure the emergence of only genuine demands, to discourage speculative purchase, and to prevent the release of ill conditioned aircraft likely to discredit the manufacturer and set back the prospects for private flying. We doubt whether sale by auction is likely to achieve this'.

About 430 Tiger Moths were shipped from RAF stocks in Great Britain to Southern Rhodesia from November 1940 when the Empire Air Training Scheme (EATS) established Elementary Flying Training Schools (EFTS), at Belvedere near Salisbury, Guinea Fowl (Gwelo), Induna (Bulawayo) and Mt Hampden (Salisbury). The aircraft were sent by sea to Cape Town then via the rail link to Bulawayo and on to Induna where they were repainted yellow overall, erected, and distributed as necessary around the stations of what became the Rhodesian Air Training Group (RATG). Administratively controlled by the Rhodesian Minister of Air, the real direction was vested in the Air Ministry operating from London.

Belvedere opened on 25th May 1940, the first EFTS in the Training Scheme, beating Canada by just a few days. Under the terms of the Agreement, Southern Rhodesia was to provide buildings and facilities at a cost of about £950,000. The aircraft and staff and four fifths of the running costs were all the responsibility of the British Government.

Cranbourne Air Station had been designated an EFTS in December 1939, utilising eight Tiger Moths and some instructors from the Bulawayo and Salisbury Flying Clubs. Under these arrangements, 62 pupils qualified for advanced training with No 4 Service Flying Training School (SFTS) at Habbaniya in Iraq until the new system became operational, when Cranbourne itself took on the role of an SFTS.

Recruits arriving at the Hillside Initial Training Wing (ITW) in 1941, formerly Bulawayo's agricultural showground, found a Tiger Moth on display adjacent to the parade square, placed no doubt in an effort to raise their spirits, but on closer inspection they would have discovered it was merely a loose assemblage of parts mostly rearranged during training by their predecessors.

Although owned by the RAF, aircraft allocated to the EATS were operated on their behalf by the Southern Rhodesian Air Force, and retained RAF serial numbers. Due to the submarine threat and sinking of supplies bound for southern Africa during the summer of 1941, the British Government placed orders with de Havilland Australia to provide Tiger Moths for shipment to Southern Rhodesia from August and by the end of the year, 82 had been delivered. A further 33 from the Mascot factory scheduled for Rhodesia, were diverted to South Africa to make up for shipping losses. Tiger Moths ordered from Australia for delivery to southern Africa early in 1942 were delayed due to the sudden entry of Japan into the war and 80 aircraft were held in store in and around Sydney for almost two years before release to service with the RAAF on home ground. The United States 5th Air Force was loaned 17 Tiger Moths from the same source.

Bernie Halliday met T8113 (84425), at 26 EFTS Guinea Fowl on 22nd July 1943, *'a lovely bright yellow Tiger Moth. I had dreamed of this moment for years'*, and was soon enveloped into the ordered routine of an RAF flying training syllabus. But apart from the patient entreaties of his flying instructor, pupil pilot Halliday remembers his early flying hours for other reasons: *'The Rhodesian bush offers an uninteresting vista, but not from a Tiger Moth at 2,000ft, (6,840ft above mean sea level), for the first time. I looked around the horizon: the blue sky met a sunlit ground. Breathtaking! Only those privileged to have flown in an open cockpit aircraft on such a day would fully appreciate my feelings. The war was a long way away. My instructor asked me where we were in relation to the airfield. I had not a clue! But it was one of the first lessons to be learnt, and from early on too'.*

Guinea Fowl was the second Rhodesian EFTS to open. The whole station had been constructed in 12 weeks and was declared operational on the day 500 trainees arrived at the end of a three day train journey from Cape Town. The weather was not always so ideal, and due to a peculiar gathering of

Hatfield built Tiger Moth R4916 was shipped to the Southern Rhodesia Air Force early in 1940 and served at 25 EFTS Belvedere until scrapped in 1945. To relieve the RAF Regiment, aircraft and airfield equipment was placed under the protection of an Air Askari Corps raised for the purpose from several Central African countries. deHMC Archive

'Hoppity', constructed from scrap Tiger Moth components at Induna in 1942, and wrecked after the craft was persuaded off the ground for a moment of glory. Note the Fairchild Cornell behind the tail unit.
via Richard Riding

dust devils on the aerodrome one morning, Halliday's course picked up the dubious distinction of establishing the record for the most prangs before breakfast: nine! Tiger Moth T8113, delivered to Rhodesia in May 1941, was one of 43 flown south to the SAAF on 31st May 1944, and from whose charge she was sold as surplus in October 1946.

T7513 (83924), had been shipped on 30th November 1940, one of three paid for by Mr and Mrs G R Milne. The Tiger Moth was named *Mary Ann* after their third daughter, and in January 1942 was adopted as his personal aircraft by the 'A' Flight Commander at 28 EFTS Mt. Hampden, Flight Lieutenant C A Nepean Bishop, he of the pre-war formation team which had operated informally from Brooklands. The legendary 'Bish' was to maintain an active association with Tiger Moths for another 20 years as post-war Chief Flying Instructor (CFI) of the Tiger Club at Croydon and later Redhill. On 13th January 1944, T7513 accrued her 2,000th flying hour, and in pursuance of standing orders, was withdrawn from use and broken down for spare parts, to be replaced in RATG by one of an increasing fleet of Fairchild Cornells.

A productive use for at least one of the time-expired RATG Tiger Moths was reported to have been conceived by instructors in 1942 on behalf of the many Air Training Corps (ATC) cadets who flew with the units on a regular basis, and was featured in contemporary British magazines. A training device known as the 'Hoppity' allowed cadets the opportunity to gain valuable taxy and handling time on the ground in company with a unit instructor. A Tiger Moth fuselage with the centre section removed was fitted with a shortened undercarriage, a precaution to displace the centre of gravity and dissuade the machine from standing on her nose. Operation of the rudder on the ground, the only method of steering the craft, was made easier by the installation of a double kingpost, and fed from a one gallon fuel tank hidden underneath the front decking, the standard Gipsy Major engine was governed to reduce maximum speed to 1,400rpm, turning a cropped wooden propeller. With the exception of the oil pressure gauges, all the other instruments were painted onto flat dashboards, otherwise the cockpit controls and seats were pure Tiger Moth.

Lower mainplanes were cropped at the root end to permit standard interplane struts, attached at their normal wiring plate positions, to pick up on the fuselage top longerons and act as bracing. In this configuration, somewhat reminiscent of the 'penguins' used during the First World War to teach embryonic pilots the art of running 'straights' at speed across the aerodrome without fear of getting prematurely airborne, ATC cadets acquired useful and practical manoeuvring skills. Cadets with experience of the 'Hoppity' were actively encouraged by the RATG instructors to taxy their Tiger Moths from and to dispersal, before and after flight.

Flight Lieutenant Nepean Bishop championed the idea of turning irreparable or redundant Tiger Moths into more Hoppities for the benefit of ATC Squadrons in Great Britain and possibly elsewhere, although New Zealand provided their ATC units with a Flight of real Tiger Moths operating on a touring basis. It was hoped that Hoppities would come to represent a realistic complement to the basic gliders then in widespread use, but the idea was never taken up.

Curiously enough and almost 50 years later, a slightly different story emerged which cast some doubt on the optimism shown in the original report, and also highlighted technical differences which might have indicated that two different machines were involved. This Hoppity, built from scratch using Tiger Moth parts salvaged by engineers at 27 EFTS Induna, was offered to the Bulawayo Grammar School. Len Bracey, one of the instigators of the scheme, described how it all went together:

'A Tiger Moth fuselage was constructed complete except for the centre section and fuel tank, then fitted with a normal cockpit including controls, instruments etc. A standard tailplane, rudder and skid were fitted and a fuel tank was manufactured by the station tinsmith to fit under the fuselage decking behind the engine bulkhead. The 'powers that be' decided that, in order to make propeller swinging easier, the undercarriage was to be shortened. This was achieved by removing the main spring from the oleo leg which, when this latter part was bolted to the fuselage proper, gave the desired result.

'The bottom mainplanes only were attached in the normal way, supported by four struts from the fuselage centre section lugs to the main spar. Fittings were manufactured and the spars drilled at the required location. By doubling the length of the tailplane support struts by welding pairs together, four very suitable wing struts were manufactured. Wood and fabric fairings completed the job and the whole assembly, when completed, took on the looks of a very racy little trainer.

'A normal Gipsy Major engine was installed, minus four plugs and one magneto and fitted with a propeller reduced in diameter by 12 inches. Once the engine had been finally cowled, a ground test was declared. Several instructors tried their hand and pronounced it to be a very successful design.

'The engine, on four plugs, required some careful adjustment with the slow running which an engine fitter and I carried out. This necessitated a ground run and we saw no harm in removing the chocks and trying things out for ourselves. I found she was good fun to taxy around and we were really enjoying ourselves when an officer saw us and threatened to throw the book at us, courts martial etc. We reasoned that the Hoppity was not really an aircraft and managed to escape by the skin of our teeth.

'For some time the EFTS pilots used the trainer but the Grammar School never took up the scheme so Hoppity became the station 'fun machine' until one day a pilot tried to get her off the ground, and succeeded, gaining an altitude of about four feet before the bracing struts failed at the welds and the wings folded up'.

In England during the 'fifties, The Wiltshire School of Flying at Thruxton, having established themselves with a Tiger Moth four seat conversion to create the Jackaroo, commissioned a low wing monoplane from their associate, Jackaroo Aircraft Ltd. Called the Paragon, the layout was not dissimilar to the Hoppity, and on the engineering mock up, wings were standard Tiger Moth lower mainplanes, slightly swept and braced by externally mounted 'V' struts on the top surfaces.

Flight Lieutenant Micklethwaite, CFI at Guinea Fowl, also laid claim to a personal Tiger Moth which he graciously shared with the Station Commander: T5475 (83200), painted silver overall and named *Inez* after his wife, was another aircraft which had been presented privately to the RAF. The machine was rigged perfectly and sensitive controls lulled one pupil into applying less rudder than was necessary to get cleanly out of a test spin, earning him a private lecture. The candidate's own instructor subsequently took him to 4,000ft and demonstrated the not very gentle art of extraction from inverted spins. *Inez* later served with 4 Flying Training School (FTS) at Heany and 5 FTS at Thornhill before sale to the Government of Kenya in 1952.

Registered VP-KKA in June that year and operated by the Aero Club of East Africa from Nairobi West, she was written off on 28th August 1953. The pilot, a man of 1,800 hours experience, was cleared to fly with a false right hand, and on the day of the accident was engaged on a local sightseeing trip with a high time RAF pilot as passenger. The aircraft had no form of intercom between cockpits, and after the crash from which both men escaped relatively unscathed, the pilot made the following statement:

'It was arranged with my passenger that when I was ready to hand the aircraft over I would raise my hands above my head. The aircraft was then started up and I taxied out after normal checks and took the aircraft off on the duty runway. I climbed straight ahead to about 1,000ft, carried out a climbing turn to the left and when at approximately 1,200ft to 1,500ft, my passenger took over the controls without any pre-warning and banged the stick abruptly over to the right, whereupon I held my hands above my head to indicate that he had control.

'He then attempted to carry out a roll. This manoeuvre did not appear to be successful and the aircraft came out of the manoeuvre in a diving turn to the left. I did not attempt to interfere with the control of the aircraft at this point, believing that my passenger was demonstrating his ability prior to carrying out some further manoeuvre, and it was not until we were dangerously near the ground, that I realised that some corrective action must be taken. I made a very coarse corrective movement in an attempt to rectify the attitude of the aeroplane, but this was too late and the aircraft struck the ground'.

In the official report which was published within four weeks of the accident, highlighting a number of offences and breaches which had been committed, the Inspector suggested that it was possible that the aircraft had not been under the control of either occupant for some portion of the flight which had taken place after a heavy drinking session at lunchtime, during which the pilot admitted to having consumed at least six single gins.

Canadian built Fairchild Cornells were supplied to RATG as Tiger Moth replacements from late 1943, and all Tiger Moths with more than 2,000 airframe hours were withdrawn and scrapped. It was intended that 200 Cornells would be provided to the Joint Air Training Scheme (JATS) in South Africa, but trials with a pair of Cornells from February 1944 convinced the South African Air Force that the aircraft was quite unsuitable to their needs. While Cornells were taken on charge in Rhodesia, 81 Tiger Moths were released from RATG, ferried south and integrated into the JATS programme, taking up SAAF serial numbers in the process.

One instructor was not over-impressed with the condition of some of the aircraft, a view thoroughly endorsed by SAAF engineers who scrapped several on arrival:

'With the number of aircraft on the station after the arrival of the Cornells, there was certainly no room for Tiger Moths in the hangars, with the result that they had to stand outside, with disastrous results to their general condition, especially as regards rigging. As the decision to send them to South Africa was not made at once, they were out some weeks, so when the time came to get them ready for the flight to Induna, it needed considerable work to get them flying straight and level once again, especially level. During the first two weeks of February 1944, I made over 60 test flights to get 29 aircraft flying really to my liking. After they had been ferried down to Induna, they joined many others which were waiting in the open to be taken on the next stage to the Union, and from all reports they were still there some weeks later, so one shudders to think about the state in which they eventually arrived'.

A Tiger Moth supplied from Hatfield to the South African branch of the company in 1937 (3606), was delivered to the Aero Club de Moçambique in Lourenço Marques (Maputo) as CR-AAG, but was flown into a hillside in 1943, and effectively demolished. By whatever reasoning, the remains of the aircraft were delivered to the engineering section of 28 EFTS Mount Hampden, where they arrived in a number of sacks. Under the supervision of Flying Officer Pennant-Rea, a former de Havilland employee based in Southern Rhodesia, CR-AAG was carefully reconstructed using mostly new spares drawn from stores, and the rear fuselage of DX544, an Australian built aircraft, (DHA 605), which had been struck off charge under unknown circumstances in September 1942.

The 'new' CR-AAG was found to be faster than all other locally based Tiger Moths, even the most recently delivered, by an astonishing 20mph, and was duly returned to Mozambique where it is believed she crashed into the Zambesi River in May 1948 when operated by the Aero Club at Beira.

A better than anticipated wastage rate, improvements in the fortunes of the Allies, and the efficiency with which the training schools were producing qualified aircrew, caused an inevitable reduction in the training

The remains of Tiger Moth CR-AAG were delivered to RAF Mount Hampden, Southern Rhodesia, in a number of sacks. Nobody questioned the authority under which this 1937 civil aircraft was rebuilt and could only speculate on the reasons why she subsequently became the station's fastest Tiger Moth by a margin of 20mph.
C Nepean Bishop

programme from early 1944. Although a revision to the length of an EFTS course was a ploy previously used in the control of output, an overall reduction of 40% capacity was sought resulting in the closure of Belvedere in November 1944 and consequent redundancies in the fleet.

The first attempt by RATG Headquarters to sell a surplus Tiger Moth was under guidance from London and dragged on for six months. In October 1944, the Air Ministry (not MAP who should have been approached), cleared RATG to sell one Tiger Moth to the Southern Rhodesia Air Service Communications Squadron. It later transpired that this was for the government's Medical Officer of Health to enable him to reach outlying districts more expeditiously.

Guidance as to price was based on the original contract agreement with de Havilland which covered a new aircraft delivered in Great Britain, quoted as £1,310, a figure itemised as £880 for the airframe and £430 for the engine. RATG were advised to deduct 10% of the new price to cover the cost of a complete overhaul or ⅟₁₀₀₀ of the new price for every hour flown since the last complete overhaul. It took ten weeks for the significance of the resultant offer price of £866.15s.8d to filter through Salisbury's bureaucratic system, but the reply was much as expected in view of the fact that RATG and MAP had previously advocated quick sales for reasonable prices, and were on record as quoting £100 as a realistic expectation.

'It is not considered that the cost bears fair relation to its value under present circumstances, and the price is unacceptable to the Southern Rhodesia Government. Opportunity will be taken of the presence in the UK of AOC RATG, Air Vice-Marshal Meredith, to negotiate transfer on a different basis'.

Reacting less quickly than might have been expected to defuse an embarrassing situation, the Air Ministry replied on 3rd February 1945 suggesting that the subject aircraft should be taken from store and put to immediate good use. If the transfer of the aircraft was not catered for in the course of more comprehensive arrangements, the cost would be guaranteed at not more than £400. As the majority of the RATG aircraft were eventually sold by tender or cut up for scrap, the British Government had no mass transfer within which to shade the Medical Officer's Tiger Moth, and in spite of 'Billy' Meredith's intervention in London, £400 was the sum duly paid. This would have been somewhat less than the Southern Rhodesia Defence Department paid for No 3653, an engineless airframe exported from Hatfield in September 1937 and which is believed to have taken on the identity SR-7 the following February.

News quickly spread throughout southern and East Africa that Tiger Moths (and a large number of Avro Ansons) had been declared surplus in Southern Rhodesia, and enquiries began to flow through to RATG who passed them to MAP in London for approval. The number of Tiger Moths declared surplus rose to 138 on 13th April, and on the advice received from MAP, a minimum price of £500 each was requested, as standing. RATG was ordered not to get involved in any form of overhaul agreement with purchasers. MAP believed the aircraft were less liable to be transported out of the region if the initial purchase price was maintained at a high level, and the origin of most enquiries encouraged this view. Misr enquired after a batch of aircraft for their Flying Institute in Cairo; two aircraft in use, SU-ABX and SU-ABY (3597/3608) had been exported from Hatfield in 1937, and although six more were added to the fleet in 1944, they were recruited more conveniently from the Mediterranean Allied Air Force (MAAF). The Aero Club of East Africa asked for quotations, as did the Government of Mozambique, Quelimane Aero Club in Portuguese East Africa, and the Emperor of Ethiopia.

The supply of cheap war-surplus aircraft was still of major concern to the manufacturers, and even though Hatfield had not built a Tiger Moth since 1940, and de Havilland had no plans for light aircraft in the immediate post-war era, except perhaps a replacement for their own Tiger Moth, MAP sought the views of the company's Business Director at a meeting in his Hatfield office on 16th April 1945. Francis St Barbe stated his opinion that the manufacturers should have a greater say in the disposal of their products, and as to the suggestion that Tiger Moths should be issued free of charge to flying clubs, he was totally opposed. He believed the price for a weary Tiger Moth in Southern Rhodesia might be about £200, but no encouragement should be offered to assist with their transport, least of all back to Great Britain.

When Colonel Rod Douglas of de Havilland's South African Associated company was in London a few weeks later, it was suggested that if the re-sale prospects of the Southern Rhodesian Tiger Moths were bright, he would consider setting up a refurbishment centre, in which case he might be tempted to make an offer for the entire stock. Meanwhile, RATG reported that the condition of the aircraft was rapidly deteriorating, and on 11th May,19 were withdrawn from sale and scrapped. MAP made urgent contact with their Air Mission representatives in South Africa requesting an immediate survey of the remaining stock. The report received on 16th June grouped the surviving 119 aircraft into three categories: 22 were said to be in good condition with an average utilisation of 600 hours each; 45 were fair having accumulated about 1500 hours and the remaining 52 were described as 'indifferent', mostly due to weathered fabric.

As the Government Disposals Office in Salisbury had offered no help and shown no interest, and there was no local working facility capable of overhauling the aircraft, MAP's suggestion that in order to protect the reputation of the manufacturer, and offer the most valuable option to purchasers, only the best aircraft should be offered for sale, and this should be accomplished by tender.

With the acknowledgement of Colonel Douglas, a target price of £250 per aircraft was to be sought, and the names and addresses of all purchasers were to be supplied to de Havilland in Johannesburg for their follow-up offer of technical assistance and provision of spares.

The sale was widely advertised in Africa but by agreement, not in South Africa, and 44 tender forms were distributed including one to the de Havilland company who eventually decided not to bid.

The sealed offers were opened on 4th October 1945 and resulted in 76 firm bids for 45 aircraft from 20 prospective clients ranging from local citizens and aero clubs to the Governor General of Mozambique. Only 23 bids topped £250 posted against 15 individual aircraft, bids ranging from £50 (13 hours run on the engine) and £100 (25 minutes run on the engine), both with high airframe hours, to £425 which was probably too high for EM741 (85972), with almost 900 hours on the airframe and over 330 on the engine, when for £350 the Governor General of Mozambique bought EM786 (86003), with fewer than 190 hours total time since delivery.

Before the bid process was closed, MAP received notice of interest in 'a large number' of Tiger Moths which were required in Chile, but 4th October came and went without receipt of an offer.

In April 1946 a request for 20 Tiger Moths for Chile was received in London and rejected by one of the many proliferating civil service committees, but only on the grounds of non-availability, and eventually a number of Miles Magisters was acquired instead. The Emperor of Ethiopia did not bid either, but arrangements were made for the private sale of two aircraft which were airlifted to Addis Ababa on 16th November and erected there. Four more Tiger Moths were later sent from Great Britain: two aircraft, EM857 and EM858 (85059/85060) were supplied from RAF storage on 22nd and 15th November 1945 respectively. BB675 (3402) and T7338 (83864), were amongst 20 aircraft bought by de Havilland through MAP in England for refurbishment and resale. Following overhaul at Witney they were delivered to Addis Ababa on 6th November 1946 and both served with the Imperial Ethiopian Air Force before joining the Imperial Ethiopian Aero Club in 1949 and were written off in 1950 and 1952.

A week after the bids had been reviewed, RATG Headquarters received a visit from the proprietor of Spencer's Airways and Garage, Victoria Falls. Mr E H Spencer's total offer of £950 bid against nine individual aircraft and ranging from £50 to £150, had not been successful. He asked for favourable consideration of his plan to buy all 30 unsold aircraft, no matter what condition, all of which would be completely dismantled and reworked to as new condition by his team at Victoria Falls. As good a case as he pleaded, the decision which was referred back from London was not in his favour and no bulk deal was ever agreed. Spencer's Airways were later credited with purchase of four unidentified Tiger Moths, three of which the company themselves advertised for sale by tender in June 1947 (VP-YEA, VP-YEB and VP-YEC), all said to be in an unconverted state, whilst the fourth, VP-YDY, was offered only as a source of spare parts.

At the end of 1945, Schreiner and Co, an aircraft trading company based in The Hague, approached RATG directly enquiring after ten aircraft on behalf of the Dutch Government who were seeking to equip a new training school shortly to be established in the Netherlands. RATG advised Schreiner on 14th January 1946 that another batch of 'ancient' aircraft (*'five years old and with about 1,500 hours logged'*) was currently available against tender. The unofficial reserve level was about £200 per lot, but RATG warned that each aircraft would cost £150 to dismantle and pack, plus £50 to dispatch by rail to a South African port, plus shipping to Europe. Copies of the correspondence were sent to MAP in London who confirmed that the Director of Civil Aviation in the Netherlands had already been in contact with them, and that a deal for 12 ex-RAF Tiger Moths was being negotiated.

Sale of the second batch of 37 surplus RATG aircraft resulted in 27 contracts which raised £5,087, but eight aircraft were withdrawn and retained by the RAF. Another pair was considered not to match the quality criteria, and both were scrapped.

The Ethiopian Minister of Defence was taught to fly on a Tiger Moth by Captain Sadik Iskander Louca, contracted in from Cairo. Captain S I Louca via British Aerospace

The National Aviation School in the Netherlands operated Tiger Moths all year round, and special attention was required during bad European winters to ensure engines were kept warm. via Herman Dekker

In the circuit at RAF Heany in 1949, Tiger Moth MC542, an Australian built aircraft first delivered to the RATG in Bulawayo and subsequently sold into civilian hands as VP-YJK. David Vernon

One contented customer provided cheer for the de Havilland publicity department: Australian built '538', having somehow escaped the scrapping policy with 2,232 hours recorded on the airframe and a little over 300 hours on the engine, was sold to J H Forsythe of Gatooma for £150, and registered VP-YEE on 20th March 1946.

A need to attend two conferences in South Africa combined with a touring holiday, did not synchronise well with the aircraft's limited range, but the Shell company laid down petrol stocks at various staging fields where 'servicing facilities no longer existed'. Later reports indicated that 'in the course of their flight, Mr and Mrs Forsythe landed at 26 towns and villages, and were able to see much more of the natural beauty and wild life of the country than would have been possible in the time by other forms of transport. The total cost of the trip, including landing and hangarage, amounted to £46.10s.6d. Customs formalities were simple except at Durban, where forms in sextuplicate were required'. Less than a year after the trip, the registration was cancelled on the grounds that the aircraft had been 'withdrawn from use'.

In 1946 MAP was redefined as part of the new Ministry of Supply (MOS) and in Southern Rhodesia RATG, having trained 7,600 pilots and 2,300 navigators, bomb aimers and air gunners, reformed on a reduced scale as the Air Training Wing (ATW). An early task was to supervise disposal of a further 51 Tiger Moths. In July, six aircraft each with a spare engine, were sold to the Southern Rhodesia Government at a price which was quoted as being 'slightly less than 1/12th book value'. ATW had been requested to negotiate sale of four others to local flying clubs 'on best terms' but minimum values of £100 per aircraft and £20 per spare engine were expected to be generated.

The remaining 41 aircraft were, at the suggestion of the Air Ministry, to be offered in conjunction with the new Ministry of Civil Aviation (MCA), to flying clubs in Great Britain, provided packing and transport for each aircraft was covered by the purchasers. Even the MOS regarded this suggestion as one of severe optimism and likely to achieve nothing. Did the Air Ministry not realise the difficulties involved with individual inspection in and transport from southern Africa, and were they not aware that during the course of the next four years, their own policy would declare 1,000 British based Tiger Moths redundant?

It seems unlikely that this third batch of aircraft, all high time and badly deteriorated due to poor local storage conditions, ever did raise much interest. The previous sales had virtually saturated what was a very limited regional market, and one into which South Africa was not immediately included due to the practicalities and politics of her own disposals. As no reports of a major catastrophe have ever been uncovered, notification that the 45 Tiger Moths struck off charge on 28th October 1948 as having been 'destroyed by fire', almost certainly points to their being scrapped and burned, and probably well before that date which merely tidied the paperwork.

The 100 hand picked Tiger Moths which arrived in Rhodesia from South Africa at the end of 1946 were allocated to 4 FTS Heany and 5 FTS Thornhill. These were part of the Air Ministry's declared need for 200 high quality aircraft which were extracted from the expired JATS Agreement in South Africa, and replaced good aircraft which had already been sold or older machines relegated to scrap. The 100 Tiger Moths which were shipped across the Indian Ocean from Cape Town and into the care of the Hindustan Aircraft Company at Bangalore, were probably part of a greater overall plan for the region. Several of those which were flown up into Rhodesia from Benoni in October 1946 as urgent replacements had been sold by the following July.

The slimming down of the training system resulted in a total of just 88 Tiger Moths remaining on the ATW's inventory under RAF control from the end of 1948, to which a further 22 were added, shipped from RAF stocks in Great Britain, arriving as a trickle throughout 1950. The number was gradually eroded until July 1952 when the survivors were finally withdrawn. The CFI at Heany, Squadron Leader Hyland-Smith, inadvertently helped to get the numbers down during practice for a crazy flying display on 27th July 1948. The station was due to open to the public a few days later, and what more exciting than a Tiger Moth in unusual attitudes close to the ground! Operating from the front cockpit of EM843 (86045), the CFI dug the tip of the starboard lower wing into the ground during a tight turn at no altitude near the control tower, injuring himself and his bemused wireless mechanic passenger in the rear cockpit, and fatally wounding the aeroplane.

During the period 1948-1952, 49 Tiger Moths were scrapped or mostly crashed, 24 of those in 1951 alone. Nine aircraft had been sold to the Southern Rhodesian Government in 1948/49 to which a further seven were added in 1952. On final withdrawal, six went to the Kenyan Government and 17 were sold locally to various civilian enterprises. The Southern Rhodesian Air Force continued to use Tiger Moths in its own right at Cranbourne until the end of 1955, and the survivors were sold into the civil market in January and February the following year.

As the war seemed to be developing in favour of the Allies, the British policy of breaking down aircraft surplus to military requirements was beginning to cause concern amongst pre-war owners and operators whose assets had been impressed in 1939. Geoffrey Alington, signing himself 'Chief Test Pilot, Elmdon' enquired of the Air Ministry in August 1944 whether he could expect the early release of aircraft which had been the property of his company before the war, and which with many others, had been in store at Kemble almost ever since. He was advised in December that the aircraft were essentially redundant government property, the scrapping policy was still in effect, that 'Moth Dragon, Moth 60 and Moth Puss' had been scheduled for breaking down, and work had already started on Moth Dragon. Not until the end of 1945 was the policy adopted of selling off surplus aircraft in a state where they could be returned to flying condition, and from December of that year the 147 survivors of the 1,017 impressed civil aircraft were put up for public view and tender at Kemble, Cosford and Aston Down.

Throughout the summer of 1944, Commander Harold Perrin, Secretary of the Royal Aero Club, had been involved with the Air Ministry, Ministry of Aircraft Production (MAP), the Society of British Aircraft Constructors (SBAC) General Council, and his own Private Flying Committee, addressing the prospects for post-war private and club flying. In May 1944, a Joint Committee agreed that light aircraft of a suitable type should not be scrapped but rather handed back free of cost to the parent designing company who would undertake any necessary reconditioning in order to qualify for a Certificate of Airworthiness (C of A). The 'free of cost to the designers' provision was perhaps what caused the SBAC to approve, and to modify any concerns which Francis St Barbe for de Havilland may have expressed about plans for a suggested free of cost issue to flying clubs and similar organisations. The Committee agreed that selected surplus aircraft types which would meet the immediate post-war requirement, and the price which owners and operators might realistically be expected to pay were: Auster £100; Tiger Moth £125; Magister £125; Proctor £200; Dominie, Oxford and Anson £500.

Early the following year, Perrin's group advised MAP that the Air Ministry had told them that from March 1945, in excess of 178 Magisters would be declared surplus together with a substantial number of Austers, but no Tiger Moths would be released in quantity until a new RAF trainer was available 'in a year or so'. To emphasise their opinion, the Air Ministry were even signalling a potential need to import training aircraft from the USA. The threat was countered by the Treasury who reminded MAP that the Air Ministry were already suggesting the British Government should give away its half share of the Tiger Moths based in South Africa, that surplus aircraft were already for sale in Southern Rhodesia, and that the first of 600 Canadian owned Tiger Moths were about to be offered for sale on the world market.

The Air Ministry reacted by confirming that within the British Isles there were no surplus Tiger Moths, but supposing a new elementary trainer was in production by mid-1947, and no schools were to be relocated to Great Britain from Canada or Southern Rhodesia, then perhaps 100 Tiger Moths could be available from mid-1947, with more to follow at a later date. If Elementary Schools were to be re-located, then some of the 250 South African based Tiger Moths expected to remain on strength after disposal of 505 surplus machines, might be headed for British bases. Stocks of Tiger Moths in use or in store, they admitted, as of 1st March 1945 amounted to 2,273.

In austerity-hit Great Britain immediately post-war, the operational Tiger Moths were expected to continue to cope with equally miserable weather conditions. R5219 (83094) had been allocated to 3 EFTS Watchfield in July 1942, moving to the grass field at nearby Shellingford when the Beam Approach facilities at Watchfield became more intensively occupied by bigger and more competitive training traffic.

Charles Hastings-Winch was posted to Shellingford in December 1945 as a preliminary to undertaking a Flying Instructors' Course, (No 44), flying Tiger Moths at 10 Flying Instructor School (FIS) at nearby Woodley. The Course was scheduled to run between February and April the following year. During the previous three years he had flown a variety of aircraft in and around North Africa, India and Burma as a ferry pilot. Between November 1943 and May 1945, he had delivered 45 Republic P-47 Thunderbolts, 63 Supermarine Spitfires, 197 Hawker Hurricanes, 15 Vultee Vengeances and 15 North American Harvards, in addition to an assortment of Austers and Fairchild Argus, and four Tiger Moths. These flights involved 543 sorties and landings at 168 different airfield sites.

Some of these Tiger Moths (EM893/86087; EM951/86134, NL735/86218 and NL817/86276), had been operated on 'communication' duties from the famous Red Road airfield situated in the middle of Calcutta, and from where regular operations were conducted with Hurricanes and on one notable occasion, a Bristol Blenheim. Hastings-Winch was no stranger to Tiger Moths having trained on the type at No 5 Air School, Witbank, South Africa, in 1942. Under training and operational conditions, a major effort had been made in trying to keep cool. Now in the heart of a British winter, as he inspected R5219 prior to departure, it began to snow. But the flying programme was arranged and the detail was completed as expected.

Decorated with a witch, a black cat and a broomstick, this Tiger Moth of the Southern Rhodesia Air Force was one of a fleet in service at Cranbourne in 1954 when Rhodesian nationals were trained to fly during a five month 'Short Service Course'. Jerry Dunn

All yellow Tiger Moths wearing the post-war codes of 1 EFTS, Flying Training Command, on parade at Panshanger in 1948. Don Stoneham

The shock to the trainee instructor's system was contained. At Shellingford he flew in 13 different Tiger Moths in December and January, followed by a further 17 during his course at Woodley. The Air Ministry's posting system ensured that as a Tiger Moth trained instructor, they would extract maximum value from him, and during his 13 month posting to 28 EFTS Wolverhampton, May 1946-April 1947, he flew 39 different Tiger Moths. He met the type again on posting to Cranwell (April 1947-January 1950) where 43 aircraft were flown and at Barton (February-August 1950), where the Manchester University Air Squadron ran ten. Only the final removal of the Tiger Moth from RAF training schedules broke the link, although when posted to Debden as a Flight Commander (September 1950-August 1953) hours were flown in seven Tiger Moths on behalf of various Establishment, Command and Group Communications Flights.

Nos 6, 11 and 12 Schools of Recruit Training offered air experience in Tiger Moths in an effort no doubt, to relieve the tedium of drill. Having no aerodrome of their own, the enlightened staff at Hednesford arranged for all such activity to take place from the unrestricted centre of Hereford Racecourse.

The aeroplane which welcomed Hastings-Winch back to the English winter of 1945, R5219, had like so many, taken up a civil career when sold out of the Royal Air Force in June 1949. Registered G-ALUC, she served in a training role at Coventry until 1961 when she overturned on landing and

The scene at Scone aerodrome, Perth, immediately after the war, when the Tiger Moths of 11 EFTS were transiting from camouflage to all over yellow, unlike the hangars. Some aircraft still carry letters identifying their 'Flight' within the school. via M J Hooks

sustained damage which was then considered uneconomical to repair. The airframe was discovered on the south coast of Hampshire in 1974 and partially rebuilt as a single seat S.E.5a lookalike, although she finally emerged as a standard two seat aircraft with an S.E.5a type colour scheme, and has been maintained as such on a private aerodrome in Kent since July 1986.

Exactly a year after the first joint meeting established by the Royal Aero Club, in May 1945, Commander Perrin was in a position to report that dormant civil flying clubs and schools had been roused to respond to his enquiries about post-war equipment. He was able to confirm interest in no Magisters, but 20 Dominies and 156 Tiger Moths for British clubs together with six for Ceylon and 24 for Kenya. There was a substantial change of view on pricing with a proposal that the cost to clubs should be no greater than 25% of the original selling price, in the case of the Tiger Moth about £350 or almost three times as much as declared 12 months previously. Perhaps somebody had discovered that when the 30 civil registered Tiger Moths had been requisitioned from the British clubs pre-war, compensation of between £550 and £1,200 each had been paid to the owners.

The end of the war in Europe triggered further prodding of the Air Ministry, this time by the civilian contractors responsible for operating the Elementary Flying Training Schools (EFTS). Both Airwork and Marshall of Cambridge had reported large numbers of apparently unemployed Tiger Moths standing on their airfields, and the Air Ministry were obliged to advise the MAP that although considerable numbers of elementary trainers were 'at present' unemployed, they would be withdrawn into Aircraft Storage Units (ASU) in the near future.

'It is not possible to have any of these unemployed Tiger Moths declared surplus to combined military requirements as the existing stocks will have to meet all RAF requirements until the new elementary trainer is available. The date when the new elementary trainer will be in service is still an unknown factor. It may be months before Flying Training Command is re-equipped and before then a large number of training schools will have to be formed (probably) to deal with the intake of personnel under the National Service Act after the defeat of Japan.

'When the new trainer is approved and a definite rate of production is known it will be possible for the Director of Organisation to recast his requirements, and if it then appears that there will be after all a surplus of Tiger Moths, immediate action will be taken to have them cleared and transferred to you for disposal'.

On his desk in the offices of the de Havilland Aircraft of Canada, Wsiewolod Jakimiuk had been doodling with ideas for a new low wing monoplane since 1943; ideas which would become reality on 22nd May 1946 when the company's first independent design would fly: the DHC.1 Chipmunk. Phillip Garratt was hoping it could be his second Tiger Moth.

By the beginning of 1946, with the war finally over and the difficult transition to peace under way, the RAF was faced with storage of 22,000 military aircraft in Great Britain, and increasing as production contracts for the latest marques were honoured. Two contraction plans initiated by the Air Staff in September and December 1945, reduced the RAF's wartime squadrons from 350 to 206, under a scheme scheduled for completion by the last day of March 1946. All other units were similarly affected, including the flying training schools, and under difficult immediate post-war administrative conditions, a massive programme of storage, sale and reclamation was embarked upon, made correspondingly more complicated and urgent as some of the storage units were themselves scheduled for closure.

Foreign sales, subject to government approval, were encouraged, not only to alleviate the storage problem and to recover at least a fraction of the costs, but as a means of securing a foothold for supporting services and future exports. The regeneration of friendly air forces could be controlled by gifts straight from the political hand, and it was a device used to good effect.

Until France's manufacturing industry was in a position to cope with the country's demands, 1,383 ex RAF aircraft were to be sold to the French military under an agreement signed in November 1945. The first consignment comprising training and communications aircraft was scheduled for delivery by air from January and the 88 Tiger Moths included in the package were drawn from the 896 declared to be in store in Great Britain at the turn of the year. In the event, 101Tiger Moths were delivered beginning with 2 in January 1946 and 5 in February, followed by 42 in March, 43 in April and a final 9 in May. For the most part the aircraft were brand new, manufactured by Morris Motors between the latter part of 1943 and mid-1944. The later production aircraft had been dismantled and placed in purgatory storage in the most suitable requisitioned premises in and around Oxford. Upon sale, they were recalled to Cowley, inspected and modified where necessary before test flying and delivery to one of the designated Tiger Moth Maintenance Units (MU) at Aston Down, Colerne, Little Rissington and Llandow. Gathered in small groups at airfields in the West Country, Dunkeswell, Pershore and St Mawgan, the aircraft were flown by pilots of 16 Ferry Unit to Romorantin and Châteauroux for acceptance and allocation to establishments within the l'Armée de l'Air.

The Tiger Moths delivered into French military care as a result of the 1945 Hartemann Agreement were additional to 141 new Tiger Moths which had already been delivered in batches during the previous 18 months, a fact which may not have been fully appreciated by the Air Ministry when it was considering a recall from Africa and India, numbers of work-weary aircraft provisionally booked for British based flying schools. The refusal to declare any RAF Tiger Moths 'surplus' in March 1945, and to hint too at the prospect of American imports prior to delivery of the new elementary trainer, seems to have been the decision of a department in some degree of confusion. The first programme of French deliveries had been achieved against a regular schedule: 50 in April 1944, 2 in May 1944, 8 in June 1944, 24 in June 1945, 14 in July 1945, 41 in August 1945, 2 in September 1945.

A batch of aircraft transiting through Buc on 23rd March 1946 was hit by an overnight storm, and ten Tiger Moths were damaged after dragging their pickets and colliding with one another on the ground. The RAF sent a repair party with spares but some aircraft were delayed reaching their destination at Romorantin until after mid-April. Perhaps it was more important to service the agreement with the French Air Force by providing new aeroplanes from store, rather than supplying refurbished Tiger Moths withdrawn from Africa, or of losing the opportunity altogether which might otherwise have been filled with Cornells or canopied Tiger Moths from Canada. No records are available for public scrutiny which detail the life of the Tiger Moth in French service, but it is believed that minimal use was made of the aircraft at French military schools at Cognac and in North Africa, and most of them were directed into the hands of French civilian gliding clubs within two or three years and operated under a scheme of subsidy administered by the French Government.

The Air Ministry's grudging assertions in March 1945 that 100 surplus Tiger Moths might be available from mid-1947, subject to the international movement or not of flying schools, and the expected availability of a new elementary trainer, had clearly been overtaken by events, and the pressing need to reduce stocks of stored aircraft now that a selective scrapping, reclaim and selling policy had been agreed.

When discussing the situation in April 1946, MAP had confirmed with the Air Ministry that the Air Council's Director of Organisation was fully aware of the requests received in London following the advertised release of Tiger Moths in Southern Rhodesia. These requirements now amounted to 12 for the Dutch Government, 56 for the Dutch military, 8 for Afghanistan, 20 for Chile, 4 for Ethiopia, 3 for Trans Jordan and 1 for Ceylon.

MAP revealed that 79 Tiger Moths were expected to be declared surplus shortly, belonging to RAF units both within the British Isles and stationed overseas. From these, consideration would be given to satisfying the Dutch military order and also the 20 aircraft required by Chile, although that prospect had been temporarily blocked by a civil service committee. The Afghanistan enquiry should be covered by aircraft supplied from South Africa, suggested MAP. Only seven days after expressing this opinion, the same department signed an agreement with the Government of Afghanistan for the supply of eight Tiger Moths already stationed in India.

Records of Tiger Moths operating with the French military are closed to public scrutiny, but flight hours are thought to have been relatively slight. Sold into the civil market, white registration letters were required to show against the 'as delivered' camouflage background. Note how the bottom of the rudder has been cut away to cope with the glider towing gear. via Stan Roberts

An unidentified Tiger Moth in the R-4000 serial range, probably painted all over silver and with a gas patch at the rear of the fuselage top decking, on charge with the Royal Navy at HMS *Phoenix*, Egypt, in November 1942. There appears to be an inverted tin can over the fuel tank sight glass and non standard head rests for the occupants of both seats. Howard Levy

TJ-AAF, *Beni Kinnanah* of the Arab Airways Flying Club, was sold to the RAF Amman Flying Club in 1956, but probably never flew under their ownership.
deHMC Archive

The remaining orders were expected to be satisfied by Tiger Moths supplied by de Havilland who had recently bought 20, most of which had been held in RAF storage since delivery from Morris Motors. de Havilland did supply two aircraft to Ethiopia, T7338 (83864) and BB675 (3402), the former G-ADOI, but provided nothing for Ceylon. Two aircraft were sold to the Arab Legion Air Force in Amman on 26th April 1946: NM156 (86476) and NM205 (86513), became T-201 and T-200 respectively, and later TJ-AAG and TJ-AAF with the Arab Airways Flying Club before they both were sold back to the RAF, in a manner, joining the RAF Amman Flying Club in 1956, although it is believed neither of them ever flew with the organisation.

In August 1947 Michael Inskip was posted to Palestine on behalf of the Air Registration Board (ARB) and received a cable from the office in Cairo requesting him to travel to Amman to survey a Dragon Rapide for Arab Airways, a new company founded by a group of ex Fleet Air Arm pilots and two licensed aircraft engineers. The Club element of the business sent one of their Tiger Moths, TJ-AAF, *Beni Kinnanah*, to collect the surveyor, and the pilot, David Nowes, allowed him to occupy the back seat from where he could take photographs during the 60 mile flight, cursing occasionally as the lower mainplanes intruded into some spectacular view. Although much of the flight was at 5,000ft and at one point 6,000ft in order to clear the terrain by a small margin, the entire operation was conducted in shirt-sleeve order.

The private history and geography lesson ended with the appearance of Amman: *'... an untidy town with the large amphitheatre of Philadelfia; the Syrian desert lay beyond to the horizon. The Royal Palace to the east of the town is surrounded by trees, the first visible since passing Jerusalem. A little further on there was a rolled sand desert airfield, RAF Station Amman, 3,300ft amsl. Here again some rows of cypress trees at this outpost of the British Empire. On the approach we could clearly see the old Turkish Hejaz railway heading NE for Dera and Damascus. There was also the road leading to the headquarters of the Arab Legion and out into the desert and eventually Iraq. This was possibly the most exciting, most interesting and most enjoyable flight I have ever made ...'*

A third Tiger Moth, not included in the package, NM187 (86495), joined Arab Airways Association in August 1946 as TJ-AAH but was damaged in a desert landing on 16th January 1949. To spotlight the harsh life of a Tiger Moth based in the desert, what better than to quote from the accident report submitted by Captain Fred Terry, the pilot of TJ-AAH, to the General Technical Manager of Arab Airways, Captain Sanders. At the time, TJ-AAH was in Arab Airways' colours but actually owned by the Arab Legion under Glubb Pasha. Azraq is some 50 miles due east of Amman, and the Azraq Marshes offered winter facilities to wild duck escaping south from the Prippet Marshes in Russia. Members of the Arab Legion were partial to wild duck and a ground party had gone ahead to the Marshes by station wagon. Captain Terry followed in the Tiger Moth to act as 'beater'.

'The aircraft was flown to Azraq in fair weather conditions on Sunday 16th January 1949. Approximately half an hour after touching down, 0930 hours, a sand storm arose with winds gusting from 50 to 60mph.

'It was decided to stay with the aircraft, check it and take the necessary precautions to prevent damage until some such time as the storm showed signs of abating, and then attempt a move to some form of shelter or picketing position. For approximately one hour the aircraft remained on the open mud flats, and with the aid of Mrs Sanders and Mr Herron we were able to prevent damage.

'The storm had by now shown a slight decrease in intensity, whereupon we were able to move the aircraft to the extreme edge of the mud flats and picket her to bushes. She remained in this position until 1500 hours when it was decided after consultation with Captain Sanders that the lesser of two evils had to be chosen, i.e. either to leave the aircraft unattended and without picketing precautions being taken of sufficient quality to stand up to a sandstorm which was again increasing in violence, or, get the aircraft if possible to safe hangarage at Amman.

'On an assumption of two hours thirty minutes duration and having already flown for one hour ten minutes, we decided to refuel to the extent of four and a half gallons which was carried as spare petrol in the accompanying car. This was carried out with difficulty owing to the lack of a filter and the high wind, with the result that not more than two gallons approximately went into the tank.

'On this assumption we calculated the aircraft's duration now to be approximately one hour thirty five minutes, and at 1540 hours we set course for Amman in rather bad weather conditions. For one hour we were flying in a sandstorm with visibility reduced at times at 100-200 yards. We eventually flew out of the sand and encountered low cloud and extremely poor visibility, rain and a calculation of drift to the extent of about 25 degrees.

'At 1655 hours we flew over the Amman-Ma'am Railway line, and I assumed my position to be south of Amman, not by pinpointing which was impossible in bad visibility and falling darkness, but by a general recognition of the terrain beneath. I turned north and continued flying along the railway line with the intention of making Amman, however, due to increased adverse weather conditions and intensity of wind strength and direction, the flight had taken far longer than could possibly have been estimated, even allowing for a 25% safety margin of fuel. After a matter of five minutes, we ran into even worse conditions with low cloud, rain, and a marked and rapid failing of the light.

'In the interests of our safety I decided a forced landing was necessary to prevent loss of life and even more severe damage to the aircraft by continuing the flight with a shortage of petrol and the possibility of making a landing with a dead stick, in darkness and without knowledge of the terrain beneath. By this time we had been airborne for one hour and twenty five minutes, leaving a ten minute endurance, and at the same time having a none too reliable petrol gauge showing almost nil.

'Bearing all these facts in mind I chose the most suitable field available near habitation, ie. a railway station, and carried out a forced landing. Shortly after the landing run the aircraft's wheels became bogged in soft ploughed soil, causing it to slew to starboard and come to rest on its nose. Subsequent inspection during remaining light showed a collapsed starboard undercarriage leg and broken propeller.

'My passenger, Mr Herron, and I righted the aircraft and contacted the station, El-wadaua, some eight miles south of Amman. I then contacted the Arab Legion HQ by telephone and arranged for guards to be sent immediately. In the meantime, I sent my passenger by lorry to Amman with instructions to return as soon as possible with the guards. While awaiting their return, I stayed with the aircraft to prevent further damage by pilfering or inquisitiveness. The guards returned at 1920 hours and I duly posted them with instructions not to leave the aircraft or allow anyone to touch it until our return the following day.

'As events proved on return to the aerodrome, Amman was covered with low cloud, and the surrounding hills would have forced me down to land sooner or later, either by impact or lack of fuel. In the light of this I feel I chose the right course'.

To add insult to injury in spite of all the precautions, TJ-AAH was blown onto her back during the night even though an Arab Legion guard had been posted to remain in the rear cockpit. The aircraft was rebuilt and re-registered TJ-AAW in 1951, but was destroyed on 9th May 1951 as the result of a hangar fire at Amman.

The 16 Tiger Moths remaining from de Havilland's small investment were all sold to the Government of the Netherlands as predicted by MAP: 13 went to the National Aviation School in civil colours and were faced with the ugly appendages considered necessary as replacements for the traditionally elegant fin and rudder. The last three went straight to the Air Force. None of the 16 had ever flown with the RAF: 12 had spent all their lives in a 15MU purgatory store, or at 20 MU Aston Down from where they were collected early in 1946. The oldest aircraft, DF137 (85886), had been in storage since October 1942. The four other aircraft were all retrieved from 47 MU Sealand, more used to dispatching aircraft packed for shipping than on the back of a trailer bound for Hatfield, a pointer perhaps that these four, EM829 (85959), PG639 (86548), PG678 (86575) and PG684 (86581), had already been selected for export before de Havilland made their bid.

The Dutch military did eventually take delivery of all their 56 Tiger Moths: 36 aircraft drawn from RAF storage were air delivered between 22nd July and 26th August 1946, and a further 20 were ferried together across the North Sea packed onto the SS *Ponto*, sailing from Dagenham Docks on 12th February 1947. These were scheduled to be held in reserve but were integrated into full commission between September 1947 and August 1948.

The Dutch military shipment included the last Tiger Moth to be built at Cowley: PG746 (86632). Having graced MUs at Wroughton, Llandow and Sealand between July 1944 and September 1946, PG746 took on Royal Netherlands Air Force markings A-49 and led a varied life until March 1959 when she joined the Navy as VU-103, a serial amended to '002' the following October. By the time she was withdrawn from use in December 1965, the aircraft had accumulated only 1,348 hours, but corrosion had been discovered in the fuselage frame and by order of the Navy, some parts were donated to the Kooy Gliding Club operating from the naval air station near Den Helder, and the remainder of the aircraft, along with '001' (86589), was burned.

To confound all previous belief in the Air Ministry's statement that there would be no surplus Tiger Moths in Great Britain before mid-1947, quite apart from the substantial deliveries to France, 20 aircraft were allocated to the Yugoslav Training Flight in January and February 1945, delivered to 222 MU High Ercall, and packed for passage by ship from Glasgow Docks to Brindisi in southern Italy. The aircraft were unloaded and erected on the dockside in company with lines of Spitfires, then simply pushed a short distance the aerodrome which was immediately adjacent. RAF markings had been obliterated prior to dispatch from England, and Yugoslav mechanics quickly overlaid national stars and fin flashes onto the camouflaged background with a squirt from their paint guns, working in the open air.

The political situation in Yugoslavia was volatile. The Tiger Moths were flown across the Strait of Otranto to their new base at Zemunik to join 10 North American Harvards, where they were officially listed as operational from 26th April. The ship ferrying additional support material had been forced to sail from Brindisi on 28th March to beat a politically imposed deadline, and consequently was obliged to leave behind 1,500 cases of spares and other equipment including two Link Trainers which could not be loaded in time.

It was the brief of the RAF Element to train selected Yugoslav Air Force pilots to be instructors on the Tiger Moths, converting them onto the Harvard as soon as practicable, and then supervising the first intakes of Yugoslav pupils. Some of the Yugoslav instructors had not flown for several years having been prisoners of war, while others had had recent experience as fighter pilots in Messerschmitt Bf 109s. The RAF was not much impressed with the general situation. Apart from having to leave equipment in Italy, since frozen by the Italian authorities,

A delivery of eight (nine including the camera mount?) Tiger Moths from the southern Italian port of Brindisi to the Yugoslav Air Force, across the Strait of Otranto at Zemunik. The aircraft were assembled on the dockside where national insignia was applied and manhandled to the aerodrome for test flying. IWM

50 sets of Gosport Tubes had to be sent out from England as a personally addressed gift to prevent their confiscation in Brindisi. Inspection Schedules for the Tiger Moths had to be translated, but by the middle of June, long after their need, it was found that much of what had been done was incorrect due to the total lack of technical appreciation on the part of the interpreter.

On 16th June, whilst engaged on erecting a hangar, the Yugoslav mechanics managed to drop a door onto a parked Tiger Moth, bending the tip bow of the port upper mainplane. To the astonishment of the senior RAF engineer, under the direction of a Yugoslav officer, the mechanics produced a large hammer and set about correcting the situation, saying that once bent back into shape the tip would be bound with tape and all would be well. The RAF engineer insisted that the wing be removed and the tip bow replaced with a new part, during the course of which repair it was discovered that the internal bracing had gone loose and the wing had to be re-rigged.

The whole programme was running late and on some occasions trainees were simply not available to fly because they had been allocated to guard duty or some camp chore. The RAF Element reported back to the Air Ministry at the beginning of June:

'Instead of pupil air training starting in February as originally demanded, it is now planned that such training should start next month. The reason has been the inability of the Yugoslavs to provide competent flying instructors or ground personnel with the results that the RAF Element has had to establish an FIS Course and also a Technical Training School. Yugoslav instructors are in the main elderly men with a long flying history, mostly self-taught, and in consequence between them commit every known flying error'.

In spite of the broken Tiger Moth, the fleet managed 493 hours instructor conversion in June and once pupil training commenced on 3rd July, 640 hours were flown that month. Relations between the RAF and their hosts were always under strain, especially over the matter of who owned what. When at the beginning of the pupil programme fuel was said to be very scarce, an RAF officer stumbled upon a stock of 27,000 gallons of 100 octane petrol which had been hidden on the airfield under the pretext that it really belonged to another unit.

The Zemunik flying instructors made their first solo conversion flights on the Harvards on 16th July 1945 and two aircraft were badly damaged in wheels up landings during the first hour. Two Tiger Moths sustained damage in a storm which raged through the site on 31st July. One aircraft suffered a bent centre section strut and another was torn from its pickets and thrown 40ft into the air, crashing down into a pile of wreckage. RAF opinion was that the aircraft was a write off, but the local engineers insisted that it could and would be rebuilt. The British officers were unsure about ownership of the aircraft although they wore Yugoslav national markings and believed they were in no position to argue, a situation made no easier by a rumour that all the aircraft were shortly to be flown to Belgrade. When clarification was requested through official channels, the British Commander was advised not to raise any objections.

The end of the operations at Zemunik came swiftly. In a situation of fast deteriorating relations between the RAF and local commanders, a Tiger Moth with one of the best instructors and a pupil went missing on an early morning flight on 8th August, and in spite of an intensive air search the aircraft was not found. The following day, 351 (Yugoslav) Squadron arrived with 13 Hawker Hurricane IVs from their base at Prkos, and two days later the RAF Element was asked to withdraw as quickly as possible, but to leave all their transport. The unit Jeep had already mysteriously disappeared from inside a guarded and locked compound. On 15th August pilots from 351 Squadron flew all the serviceable Harvards to Zagreb and the following day nine Tiger Moths took off for an undisclosed destination. Two days after that the RAF Element withdrew leaving the final removal of whatever equipment they were allowed to a rearguard.

What happened to the Tiger Moths after they left Zemunik is unclear. All are believed to have been allocated local serial numbers and a June 1945 list identifies them as 'Aircraft 1-6; 12-14; 16; 18-23 and 25-30', a total of 21. A list dated July fills in all the gaps with the exclusion of '8' and '15', deletes '22' and adds '31'. Seven aircraft are known to have been transferred to the Yugoslavian civil register and one, YU-CHX (86470), was donated to the Musej Yugoslovenskog Vazouhplovsta at Surcin airport, Belgrade, where she was repainted in RAF camouflage as NM140, although her correct RAF serial was NM150.

Within the RAF, a Belgian Initial Training School had been established at Snitterfield on 1st January 1944, moving from overcrowded accommodation at Goring on Thames. In October the unit relocated to Snailwell, where the brief was 'to provide disciplinary, technical and aircrew training for Belgian personnel'. On 20th February 1945, four new Tiger Moths were delivered from Aston Down together with a further eight from Llandow. The flying element moved to the previously designated satellite station at Bottisham on 23rd November, and within a year 31 additional Tiger Moths had been delivered, all formally sold to the Belgian Government, and which eventually moved across the sea to Belgium where they took up national markings. Very much in parallel with their neighbours in the Netherlands, many of the Belgian Air Force Tiger Moths were transferred to the National Flying School, and 16 survivors took up civil identities (OO-EVA to OO-EVM, OO-EVO, OO-EVP and OO-EVR) in 1958.

Harold Perrin's determined efforts on behalf of the British civil aeroplane clubs bore fruit early in 1946 when the Ministry of Civil Aviation promulgated its views on the release and allocation of surplus military light

Displayed as Belgian Air Force Tiger Moth 'T-24' on the first floor of the National Air Museum in Brussels, this aircraft had served her entire post-war life as a civil registered trainer with the Belgian State Flying School. She was withdrawn from operations in 1971 and presented to the Museum in 1975. Barry Dowsett aircraft. The Parliamentary Secretary announced in the House of Commons on 24th January that 100 surplus light aircraft would be offered for sale on favourable terms to 'genuine' flying clubs which would need to satisfy certain conditions. The 100 aircraft were to be sold at a special low price; the offer would not be repeated, was additional to but separate from any other sales of surplus material, and there would be no prospect of an additional operating subsidy.

It was proposed that the 100 aircraft would be composed of 63 Miles Magisters and 37 Austers, but Perrin's enquiries had already established beyond doubt that the club preference would be for Tiger Moths. Coincidental with this affirmation, the Ministry was advised of 100 RAF Tiger Moths in store, all lightly damaged, but immediately available for disposal due to the contraction of repair facilities. The constituent numbers of the MCA's offer were accordingly modified to read 60 Tiger Moths, 30 Austers and only 10 Magisters.

To exactly define the eligibility of applicants as 'flying clubs' and to supervise their subsequent operations and business transactions was considered a difficult prospect, but it was decided that if aircraft distribution was to be the responsibility as hoped, of the General Council of Associated Light Aeroplane Clubs, the representative body for club flying, that organisation would be in the best position to adjudicate whether any bidding organisation was a genuine case.

The General Council would be expected to exercise authority in monitoring all conditions which the Ministry of Aviation were attaching to the sale:

1 The aircraft must be used exclusively for club flying for the benefit of club members. The aircraft must not be used for charter or other forms of commercial flying or aerial work save instructional flying for club members.
2 The aircraft should be placed in use within a reasonable period of time according to the judgement of the General Council.
3 The ownership of the aircraft should be vested in the General Council or its constituent clubs.
4 The aircraft should not be hired or resold except to clubs which have been admitted to membership of the General Council and are vouched for by the Council as genuine flying clubs. The approval of the General Council should be required to the hire or resale of the aircraft.

In recognition of the fact that 50 associated clubs could be interested in taking a share of the spoils, the Air Ministry was prepared to vary (increase) the numbers of each aircraft type on offer, all of which would be additional to those already subject to the current round of competitive tendering.

Applicants were reminded that the aircraft would need to be collected from store within a reasonable time scale and against an 'as is, where is' policy. Spares were not included in the scheme, but supplies were readily available and each club was expected to make its own arrangements. All additional costs of transport, refurbishment and certification would also fall on them.

OO-SOF was typical of the many civilian conversions for export completed by W A Rollason at Croydon: neat, tidy and silver overall. This aircraft was ordered on behalf of Sabena in 1952 and was cancelled 20 years later for reasons unknown.
M J Hooks

The estimated average market value of the aircraft was quoted at £250, but under the Ministry scheme, a nominal price of £50 was asked for each, irrespective of type, location or condition. Pre-sale inspection was not exactly encouraged, but limited access to RAF storage sites by nominated parties acting on behalf of the General Council was agreed.

The Royal Aero Club proposed that it should purchase all 100 aircraft for £5,000, completing final payment within three months of the approval, or alternatively it would guarantee purchase by the General Council. What resulted was a combination of both. During 1946, from April to August, 32 Tiger Moths were credited with 'sale' directly to the Royal Aero Club and from the end of May, five were sold to the Association of British Aero Clubs (ABAC), the new name adopted by the General Council following its annual general meeting on 20th February. All these aircraft were subsequently re-registered in the name of the recipients and in many cases within months of obtaining civil certification, had been resold within the flying club movement, or to more commercially orientated flying 'schools' who were already well established with Tiger Moths as their standard training type.

Taking into account the aircraft separately purchased by tender, approximately 130 ex-RAF Tiger Moths were registered in Great Britain alone in 1946, in addition to those bought as sources of spares, sold abroad, or broken down for scrap. At the end of the war, Dick Gliddon, Chief Engineer at W Mumford, a specialist Tiger Moth repair centre dispersed to Plymouth, was told to cut up all unserviceable aircraft into pieces that would fit inside a standard 40 gallon oil drum. The following three years were thin on British disposals as the European political situation was again uncertain, the Malayan Emergency was developing and by 1950 the United Nations was fighting a war in Korea. British civil registrations allocated to Tiger Moths during that time however, showed an increasing trend from about 20 to 50 per annum, the higher total being reached when the RAF's new trainer appeared at last. Flown by Pat Fillingham at Downsview on 22nd May 1946, the Anglicised version of the Canadian designed DHC.1 Chipmunk went into production at Hatfield in 1950, several years later than anticipated when the fate of the Tiger Moths in Southern Rhodesia was being debated in 1944.

The first post-war civilian registration of a British Tiger Moth was G-AGRA (86173), ex-RAF NL690, sold to the Ministry of Civil Aviation in July 1945, and which was pre-registered to the Minister on 30th June for operation by the MCA Flying Unit based at Croydon. The Ministry also acquired NL905 which was registered to them as G-AGRB on the same date. Marshall's Flying School at Cambridge was the first wholly civil, non-government organisation post-war to register Tiger Moths. In January 1946 they were allocated G-AGYU (85265/DE208); G-AGYV (82029/N6751); G-AGYW (3857/N6544) and G-AGZY (82287/N9176). N6544 was the only one of the quartet ever to have served in military colours with the Marshall administered 22 EFTS, Teversham. An Insurance Schedule correct to March 1942, listed 152 active Tiger Moths on charge at 22 EFTS against an agreed value of £1,200 each, plus 15 Miles Magisters which were considered to be worth more at £1,600.

Sir Arthur Marshall recalls how the return of civilian flying in Great Britain was celebrated on 1st January 1946: *'The first civilian flying pupil for six years to leave the ground on a training flight in the UK took off in Tiger Moth G-ACDG at nine o'clock on that Tuesday morning, the newly restored freedom of the air was nine hours old. A number of other pupils were in the air on that first day, and the first British 'A' Licence after the war was obtained at Cambridge on 6th January'*.

Tiger Moth 86051 (ex-RAF EM849), is credited as the first post-war club aircraft. She was registered G-AHDD to Huntingdon Aviation on 21st February 1946 (one of four), and was operated by the Luton Flying Club for two years. In 1950 she was owned by the Birmingham based 'Yellow Air Taxis' and in 1952 was registered to Chipperfield's Circus and Zoo. During her delivery flight to a new owner in West Germany in August 1955, the aircraft crashed while taking off from Calais, and the wreckage was delivered by surface as a source of spare parts for her replacement.

During the same period of planned contraction, the British Government sold Tiger Moths to a number of overseas air arms. Between October 1947 and February 1948, 13 Tiger Moths ex-stock were shipped from Birkenhead to the Burmese National Air Force; 12 new and 12 used aircraft were delivered to the Royal Hellenic Air Force between February 1947 and September 1949, satisfying an order which had been in prospect under different conditions since 1938. The Government of Iraq took 15 new aircraft between May and July 1947, having lost most of its Air Force to RAF action during the war. Eleven years later, six of the consignment were sold to the Lebanese Air Force for Air Observation duties. Malaya, a country much familiar with the performance of the Tiger Moth, accepted 18 used aircraft for its Auxiliary Air Force as a counter to the Emergency situation, over a four year period from November 1949.

The entry of the Chipmunk into service released more than 80 Tiger Moths onto the British register in 1951, but teething troubles with the type caused a certain hesitancy and probably accounted for there being only one Tiger Moth release in 1952. No 2 Reserve Flying School (RFS) based at Barton, re-equipped with Chipmunks in January 1951 but had converted back to Tiger Moths by the following December, and maintained the type until disbandment in February 1953. Two other units, 8 RFS Woodley and 22 RFS Cambridge continued to operate Tiger Moths in parallel with Chipmunks from April 1950, and two more, 7 RFS Desford and 25 RFS Wolverhampton never took delivery of the new aircraft before they were disbanded.

Having resolved the problems with their new elementary trainer, RAF storage units were permitted to turn out their residual holdings of Tiger Moths and in 1953, 380 aircraft were finally transferred to the category of 'Non Effective Stock'. The RAF now had a choice of which disposal technique to apply: outright scrapping, recovery of parts or onward sale. Fortunately, the majority of aircraft were offered for sale, and the public was invited to visit Cosford, Hullavington and Lyneham on 18th August 1953 and to deposit individual bids on 222 aircraft. The RAF wanted the storage space and the Treasury needed the funds; it was a situation tailor made for bargain hunters and finally broke down the high expectation on prices adopted by the Air Ministry and MAP's successor, the Ministry of Supply (MOS).

The degree of public interest showed without doubt that the market was far from saturated; rather it was still hungry and that at least vindicated the disposal policies adopted by the British Government before the end of the European war. It was also a stark reminder of the lack of a suitable new light aeroplane for the clubs and private owners. The protectionist attitudes adopted by Francis St Barbe and SBAC were hollow: there was nothing left to defend.

In November 1945 it was realised that some of the pre-war civil aircraft types would be difficult to maintain due to an absence of spares, manufacturing jigs and in some cases drawings and technical records, destroyed inadvertently or otherwise during the hectic activity of more imperative wartime programmes. Already limited stocks of spares had been largely consumed in keeping the impressed aircraft airworthy, after which airframes were broken down to 'produce'. Particularly badly affected were all models of the DH.60 Moth, Puss, Fox, Leopard and Hornet Moths, the Moth Minor, Dragon, Dragonfly and DH.86; no spare parts for the Gipsy Minor engine were available without cannibalisation. A crumb of comfort was supposedly offered by the assertion that *'some Tiger Moth fittings are interchangeable with those of the DH.60G Moth, and Australian Dragons can still be served by the Sydney company'*. de Havilland issued a statement in April 1948 claiming quite categorically that as the Tiger Moth *'is likely to remain in world-wide service in considerable numbers for some years to come'*, they would continue to manufacture spares for the aircraft until the end of 1949. This deadline was later extended into the early 'fifties due to the unexpected retention of the Tiger Moth in RAF service.

The much discussed notion of offering surplus aircraft to their original designers never did find favour, and at the time of the final clear out, de Havilland were busily engaged in production of their Chipmunk at Chester, but various works were to be associated with the Tiger Moth for one last official effort. A hangar at Shurlock Row, adjacent to White Waltham aerodrome, and on what might have been part of the Relief Landing Ground (RLG) at Waltham St. Lawrence, is believed to have housed a large number of Tiger Moths on behalf of de Havilland in June and July 1948. The company was well acquainted with the area having managed 13 ERFTS at White Waltham for some years prior to the war.

Most of the aircraft released from 1950 on were perfectly serviceable, and their silver doped wings and fuselages, 'aluminium' in official parlance, were adorned with broad yellow bands to indicate their recent training role, together with national insignia, unit badges and codes. It was still something of a shock to bureaucratic minds that military aircraft in airworthy condition were being sold to civilians, and capable of delivery by air rather than in tattered chunks on lorries destined for the smelter.

G-AGYU with tasteful and rounded civil registration letters anticipating trade on behalf of the Marshall Company at Cambridge. Richard Riding

Tiger Moth G-AHNX flying over a placid summer scene in 1946. Within a few years the grass acreage and modest clubhouse were swamped under the relentless development of Luton airport. deHMC Archive

Once the formalities of bids and acceptances had been acknowledged and monies paid, those aircraft scheduled for air delivery were allocated civilian registrations based on whatever documentary evidence could be provided. This often resulted in confusion as to which serial numbers identified what, and the pre-war civil identities of impressed aircraft were occasionally forgotten.

It was necessary for the civil letters to be worn for the duration of the ferry flight to wherever 'demilitarisation' was to take place, and for the most part these were crudely applied on the fuselage sides using what appeared to be creosote, applied with a three inch brush. To add the ultimate indignity, the once proud national insignia was blotted out using the same brush and bucket, achieving varying degrees of perverted artistry.

In the sealed bid auctions, some companies made offers for entire blocks of lot numbers, and substantial quantities were sold in single transactions. It was not uncommon post delivery, for aircraft to be bought or sold 'as standing', often to satisfy disappointed clients. By the time of the last sales in 1953, potential bidders had realised what good deals were being offered, and the flying clubs recognised this was their final opportunity to acquire cheap equipment. The Association of British Aero Clubs (ABAC) placed bids on behalf of constituent members in order to save them the embarrassment of bidding against one another. W A Rollason bought heavily against anticipated demand at home and overseas as did the Wiltshire School of Flying, Hants and Sussex Aviation, Muir and Adie, Marshall Flying Services, Aerocontacts and several smaller groups and individuals. None of the aircraft was sold directly to overseas customers.

A proposal to supply Tiger Moths as glider tugs to civilian clubs in France led Viscount Yves le Gallais to purchase 198 surplus aircraft which were registered to his British agent, Croydon based company A J Whittemore (Aeradio) Ltd. The bulk purchase deserved special treatment and rumours quoted the unit price to be as little as £20 each. The airworthy aircraft, about 130, were ferried to Croydon by freelancing civilian pilots and picketed out with fitted cockpit, engine and propeller covers where these were available. In most cases, wings were removed and where space permitted, fuselages shifted under cover.

The first batch of French registered Tiger Moths was ferried from Croydon to Le Touquet on 30th May 1954, but for some considerable time, lines of dismantled aircraft stood wheel by wheel on almost every square inch of hardstanding at Croydon, a situation exacerbated by the French contract running only to a fraction of the anticipated numbers.

Some airframes deteriorated sufficiently to be declared scrap while at least two went missing, believed to have been stolen. Whittemore eventually disposed of their own unintended surplus; many were absorbed on site, mainly by the Rollason company who became probably the world's biggest and most enduring supplier of Tiger Moths and spare parts, continuing their business for over 40 years.

The purchase of aeroplanes at anything between £20 and £50 in 1953, together with new engines in manufacturer's delivery crates at £5, provided scope for a complete overhaul, often including new fabric on the fuselage at least, and a repaint, for re-sale with a profit at a price of less than £600. Some dealers were more than happy merely to turn round their wares at a simple 100% mark up as one potential purchaser discovered through the range of replies to his basic enquiries:

'May 31st 1954.
We thank you for your letter of 27th instant, and are pleased to confirm that we can offer you a Tiger Moth aircraft ex RAF without Certificate of Airworthiness, but in running order complete and with all instruments etc. at £100 ex Croydon'.

'May 31st 1954.
We now confirm that we can supply a de Havilland Tiger Moth 82A without a Certificate of Airworthiness for £100. Naturally this price does not include the plane being delivered to your area, but arrangements can be made at the approximate cost of six shillings per mile, including loading and unloading, but not fitting of wings on completion.

'The particular aircraft we are offering has approximately 1,000 hours on the engine and therefore should you wish to make it airworthy at any time in the future the engine still has approximately 500 hours to run.

'Regarding your query about the instruments supplied we are prepared to include in this price the complete range of instruments as set out in the original Air Ministry specification.

'Should you wish to have the machine painted, this service can be carried out before delivery at the approximate cost of £20. Should you have any further queries the writer will be pleased to discuss the whole matter more fully on the telephone'.

Some of the bigger dealers directed their advertising at specific markets, and were particularly interested in the export trade to New Zealand where a positive requirement had been identified. Ex-surplus purchase prices, and material and labour rates for overhaul were virtually standard, the sale prices reflected how much or how little

The Southern Aero Club at Shoreham once ranked amongst its instructors Cecil Pashley. 'Pash' is believed to have taught more students to fly than any other instructor and G-AKXO, an aircraft leased in during 1955, would have featured in his logbook. via Stuart Howe

Anchored to a pair of not insubstantial marble blocks, Tiger Moth G-776 is displayed by the Greek Air Force Museum in the centre of Athens. Pre-war plans to acquire and operate Tiger Moths on the lines of the RAF's Reserve system failed to mature. Barry Dowsett

Manufactured in March 1944 and stored until August 1945, NM130 was delivered to the French Air Force in April 1946 and sold to a parachute club in 1951. By 1968 and several owners later, F-BGCA was in need of major overhaul. Acquired by a group of enthusiasts in Germany, the Tiger Moth became D-EEAJ and a vehicle with which to tow vintage gliders. David Ilott

Aircraft and staff of the London University Air Squadron photographed on what is evidently a cold day in April 1950, illustrating no unity in flying clothing. *The Aeroplane*

In attempting to take off from Tangmere in 1951, the tailskid of N6790 hooked onto a telephone cable, causing the aircraft to crash and strike a deaf workman who was erecting a new aerodrome beacon. 29 Squadron Archive

A study of the lead and port wingman in a three vic formation put up by the London University Air Squadron. Crew facemasks would indicate electric intercom was fitted. Richard Saward

work had been applied during the civil conversion. A £5 undercut here and there was significant when prices were at such standardised levels, and was just about the only avenue open to creative competition.

Aerocontacts, operating from Gatwick airport in 1951, directed their attentions at Australia, a country which had recently absorbed over 500 surplus Tiger Moths from its own resources:

'By dispatching aircraft in pairs we are able to quote the following unit prices. With 12 months' Certificate of Airworthiness and engine under 200 hours, £610 each; with engine nil hours since overhaul, £650 each; with new fuselage bag and engine with nil hours since overhaul £750.

'12 months' Certificate of Airworthiness means that the machine has received a first class complete overhaul in our own shops immediately prior to dispatch and each machine proudly bears our own name plate which is becoming known as a badge of excellence. There are Tiger Moths and Tiger Moths, but there is only one standard which we will recognise, and that is the highest.

'de Havilland Gipsy Major I engines, nil hours since complete overhaul, £155 or if ordered in pairs, £150 each'.

In January 1954, Rollason wrote to a number of prospective customers in New Zealand: *'If all the big stores in England can hold January sales, why cannot we? It is with the greatest pleasure therefore, that as a result of price slashing, we are able to make the following unprecedented offers. But before you read on, remember the old slogan, First come, First Served! So, place your orders early.*

'A quantity of DH Gipsy Major Series I engines with test bed hours only since complete overhaul, internally and externally inhibited, packed, shipped and insured, CIF main New Zealand port, delivery to docks 7 days. £145 each.

'A small number of DH Tiger Moth aircraft, with airframe hours less than 250 since new, reconditioned throughout, com-

plete with full dual control and blind flying instruments in both cockpits. All modifications complete. DH Gipsy Major engines with zero hours since complete overhaul. 12 months' C of A. Dismantled, packed, shipped and insured CIF main New Zealand port. Delivery to packers three weeks from order. £1170 per pair.

'We are offering a reduction of 10% on quoted list prices of Tiger Moth spares'.

A view held in some quarters that ex-surplus aircraft were bought for almost nothing, sprayed silver, and passed on at great profit, was entirely false. RAF Tiger Moth R4878 (82795), was acquired by W A Rollason in November 1953 and placed in store at Croydon. Pending sale to West Germany, the aircraft was issued with British civil registration G-AOBP in April 1955, a necessary qualification to see the aircraft through overhaul, certification for export and test flying. In many such similar cases the registration letters were chalked or taped on the fuselage side, and the new national identity added only with the finishing touches to the colour scheme.

R4878 was a Hatfield product of January 1940 and her first posting had been to 1 EFTS, following which she served at Wolverhampton and Cranwell before her obsolete label saw her sold from military service with 6 RFS at Sywell. Along the way she had acquired mainplanes and control surfaces manufactured, repaired or overhauled by de Havilland, Morris Motors, Taylorcraft and at least two other civilian contractors. According to the Rollason worksheets, all these items were *'opened up, cleaned down and inspected, attachments checked, all structure inspected, rectifications carried out as necessary, centre section inspected and rerigged'.*

And so the thoroughness continued: *'Undercarriage: removed, dismantled, cleaned, inspected, wheels and assemblies serviced, rectifications carried out as necessary. Flying controls: all cables removed, cleaned, inspected, reprotected and replaced. All pivots, bearings and pulleys cleaned. Controls retrued to manufacturer's requirements, movements checked and recorded. Duplicate inspection carried out. Fuel and oil system: tanks removed, inspected and pressure tested. Fuel and oil lines tested. Systems assembled and fuel flow carried out. Engine installation: firewall and bearers cleaned, inspected and reprotected. Engine No 85142 installed. Propeller BA7588 fitted. Engine run carried out. Tail skid: overhauled. Instruments: overhauled (or tested or certified) and fitted. General: all struts and wires cleaned and inspected. Mainplanes, ailerons and tail unit assembled to machine, rigged to manufacturer's specification and figures recorded. Serviceable fire extinguisher fitted. Aircraft sprayed to required scheme. Machine weighed and C of G calculated. Machine test flown and reported as satisfactory'.*

W A Rollason which had changed its name to Rollason Aircraft and Engines Ltd, produced a small brochure early in 1956 which carried a description of the Tiger Moth in terms of construction, leading particulars and performance. It was far from any recognised attempt at a hard sell. Almost apologetically, a small leaflet not much bigger than a pair of cloakroom tickets was slipped inside, reminding potential customers that completely rebuilt, nil-hour engined Tiger Moths were still available at £900 each. Readers were invited to write to Croydon aerodrome or to telephone the office to enquire about the attractive HP terms.

Harold Perrin's report to authority in May 1945 that quantified 156 Tiger Moths as a

Formation take off, all pilots solo. The lead aircraft, T6066, spent her last years in the RAF as part of No. 1 Grading Unit. She was sold to Christchurch Aero Club in 1953. The photograph was originally commissioned to illustrate a magazine article on the design of undercarriage legs. deHMC Archive

Collected from RAF Maintenance Units by recruited volunteers, some auctioned Tiger Moths were flown into Croydon. Civil markings daubed on their fuselage sides, remained until overhaul. BB748 was recognised as the pre-war G-ADIB of the de Havilland Reserve School. deHMC Archive

post-war requirement by British flying clubs proved to be a fairly accurate assessment, but once surplus aeroplanes began to trade through the system, more than twice as many could be found in daily operation in Great Britain. Employed by clubs and registered co-ownership groups, their affiliation qualified them for a healthy tax rebate on their petrol bills, a small concession from the government who viewed the drawback as an economic method of maintaining links with the most basic 'reserve'. Commercial rates for a Tiger Moth until the mid-'fifties was rarely more than £4.10s.0d per flying hour, and seemed to increase only after the approval to import American light aircraft was granted. This spelled the end of the Tiger Moth as a serious club training aeroplane. Gliding clubs who used the aircraft extensively, gradually abandoned their Tiger Moths too, mostly in favour of more efficient climbers, and so a new strata of ownership was created when private individuals bought the aeroplanes for reasons which a dedicated volume of its own could not adequately cover.

In times of national emergency, the 'Cook and Butcher's Air Force' had had to do as it was ordered, but in a country racked with post-war shortages, controls and a new level of virulent bureaucratic interference, civilian pilots now were prepared to pay to experience the privilege of Tiger Moth flight.

Maurice Marsh responded to an advertisement placed in a local newspaper by the Coventry Aero Group, and in February 1950 presented himself at Baginton aerodrome for a trial lesson, travelling the 12 miles from his home by train and bus instead of bicycle due to the snow. Outside the club hangar he made his first acquaintence with Tiger Moth G-AHKZ (83636), a surplus aircraft released in May 1946, and which now called *Barbie* was rocking on the frozen grass in a bitter easterly wind.

'The CFI welcomed me, took my money and saw the necessary forms signed before handing me over to a friendly weather beaten character. George looked after Armstrong Whitworth company aircraft in his working hours and Club aircraft when off duty. He was very concerned that he could only find an oversized flying suit for me and no boots. I was not worried and wondered what all the fuss was about.

'Eventually, I was installed in the rear cockpit of G-AHKZ wondering whether the seat belt would stand the tension George had pulled on or whether there would be a sudden crack and I should find myself sitting on the frozen grass. The CFI climbed in and chatted to me about switches on and off, and then repeated the process to George. The engine started, creating a freezing draught. We rattled across the frozen turf and after more interesting explanations, were soon climbing over the A45.

Almost every available parking space at Croydon was occupied by Tiger Moths in varying states of undress during the height of the influx in the early 'fifties.
Norman Rivett

'It was obvious now that an arctic wind was diving into the front cockpit and whistling out of the rear. A good percentage of the airflow was taking an alternative route via the legs of my flying suit and out through the neck. As I got colder and colder I realised what had concerned George. I paid less and less attention to the friendly chat from the front as I concentrated on survival. I think I held the stick for a while and remember something about ailerons, but I was really trying to calculate how many minutes more I could survive, and how much of the flight remained. Fortunately, the state of hyperthermia had not yet been invented, so I was still alive when we landed. Somehow, I was extracted from the aircraft and stood for a while to allow the cold east wind to thaw me out'.

Before the war, John Isaacs had helped to build some of the first Supermarine Spitfires by hand and living near Southampton, had joined the Hampshire Aeroplane Club at Eastleigh on a wintry morning in 1951:

A Sunbeam and a Triumph motorcycle with other classics in the Rollason hangar at Croydon. Loose stacked wings accompany a selection of very shabby fuselages, illustrating a variety of colour schemes and application of military markings.
Richard Riding

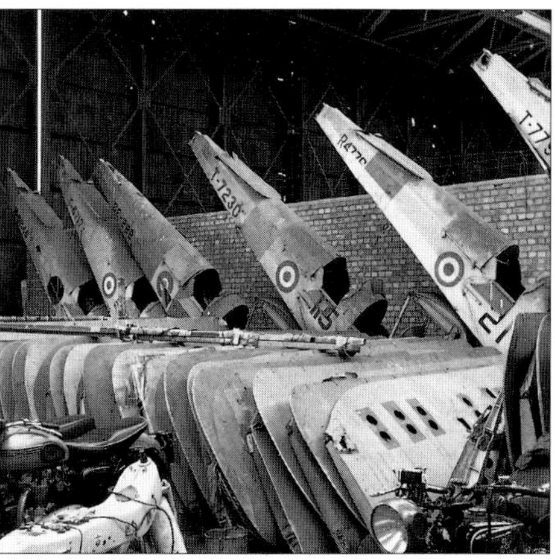

'I found the CFI, Reg Langridge, reclining in the instructors' office, chair tilted and his feet on the desk. He greeted my request to be converted to open cockpit Tiger Moth flying with singular lack of enthusiasm: his rounded jovial face resumed its friendly normality when I added that I did not necessarily wish to fly on that cold day. Like the instructors at Thruxton, he had learned to fly with the Civil Air Guard before joining the RAF as an instructor on Tiger Moths. He had also served with Bomber Command on Avro Lancasters and then flown on the Berlin Airlift.

'So in the fullness of time, like thousands before me, I flew circuits and bumps from the Tiger Moth's rear cockpit. The tired club parachutes, used to pad the bucket seats, did not inspire confidence and I never strapped one on to my backside without recalling the Cagney bush pilot film in which his associate accidentally pulled the ripcord, thereby releasing a month's dirty laundry'.

Although the aeroplanes were cheap to buy and to operate, relatively, the financial facts of life for impecuneous groups of enthusiastic aviators, were still harsh. Southport Aero Club had paid £250 in 1955 for Tiger Moth G-ANOD (84588), an aircraft whose second registered civil owner was destined to become Lord Mayor of London in 1977. Assistance with the purchase price had been in the form of a loan from the Kemsley Flying Trust, and the aircraft was collected from Honiley airfield on 9th November 1955 by David Vernon. Mist and darkness necessitated a precautionary landing near Wrexham where the aircraft was tied to a telegraph pole and left in charge of the local constable. The pilot went home to his bed by train, returning next morning to effect the delivery. G-ANOD was operated with great enthusiasm from Southport Beach at Hesketh Park, but the club could not raise sufficient cash to pay for the C of A renewal, and G-ANOD was flown south to Kidlington and sold to Peter Clifford Aviation for £109. Peter Clifford only wanted the engine, which was removed and resold, while the airframe went by road to Christchurch.

Lots 1, 4, 5, 10 and 23 offered for sale at 9 MU Cosford early in 1954 were acquired for a total price of £355 by Derby Aviation on behalf of the Norwegian Aero Club (NAK) and converted to civilian status at Burnaston.

The first aircraft to be certificated, LN-BDO (85738), was flown back to Oslo in 13 hours during the last three days of June 1954, and the remaining aircraft, LN-BDL (3443); LN-BDM (85294) and LN-BDN (85328), were all collected by members of the Drammen Flyklubb in the autumn. LN-BDP (82229), was not converted and eventually delivered by surface as a source of spare parts.

LN-BDO ran out of fuel due to an inaccurate assessment of consumption when towing an advertising banner over Skallum near Oslo on 13th September 1959 and was badly damaged in the forced landing. LN-BDM was employed as a glider tug and in 1959 was offered to Sweden in exchange for a Norwegian built aircraft then on the Swedish civil register, but the deal was rejected. LN-BDL was written off at Steinsfjorden in 1956 and LN-BDN which was damaged at Trondheim was rebuilt using parts of the dismantled LN-BDO.

Early in 1955, members of the Norsk Teknisk Hogskole Flying Club at Trondheim applied for a certificate of airworthiness for LN-BDN then owned by Jens Rolfsen, and submitted to the authorities a faked photograph showing the aircraft in a three seat tandem layout. The Civil Aviation Department was horrified and immediately sent an inspector to Trondheim having advised the club that such major structural alterations required a spectacular degree of approval paperwork. But the last laugh was with the authorities who submitted a substantial bill to cover their expenses.

A celebration of the 21st anniversary of the formal issue of a Certificate of Airworthiness to the DH.82 Tiger Moth (4th March 1932), was arranged at Denham aerodrome in 1953. The event was intended to be a show of strength if not gratitude by the clubs, nearly all equipped now with 'new' training aeroplanes acquired for very little financial outlay and not much effort. Unfortunately, acting with every good intention, the organisers chose Saturday, 7th March as the date for the party, a day blessed with winter mist and cloud and seasonal average temperatures. Fewer than 20 aircraft attended, many of which were not Tiger Moths, and as for the inter-club competitions only two teams entered, one from the RAF element of the British Army's Elementary Flying Training School at Middle Wallop, and the other from the London Aeroplane Club at Panshanger.

Intended to be light hearted and humorous, one of the Middle Wallop Tiger Moths, EM879 'BD-T' (86081), appeared covered in graffiti and fake patches, with bandaged struts, the tattiest instrument hood that could be found on the establishment, and lines of washing strung along the fuselage side. It was hardly the fanfare to the dawn of the emancipated age.

Stripping the military colours off W7955 revealed a pre-war civil identity, G-AFGT, an aircraft originally based at Luton. Although new letters G-AMEA were allocated the original registration was restored, but cancelled in 1951 when she was exported to the Royal Thai Navy. Charles Holland

Somewhat greater care than usual has been taken to cover the military markings DE454 and replace them with civil registration G-ANIW on fuselage sides and upper wing prior to delivery to the Darlington and District Aero Club at Croft. Immediately following the issue of a civil certificate in June 1954 the aircraft was sold to New Zealand. Raymond Rayner

With so many spare parts and non-airworthy airframes to choose from, what fun to create an engineering model for trainees to dabble with. The famous two-headed Tiger Moth was bred at Scone aerodrome, Perth but quickly became extinct. *The Aeroplane*

Maintained as an airworthy engineering exercise at Redhill from 1948 until 1964, Tiger Moth G-AMNN moved to Shoreham as part of Northbrook College of Aeronautical Engineering in 1991, and was airborne again in 1997. Charles Holland

At the end of the day. A collection of Tiger Moth fuselages and wings including some in French Air Force livery, abandoned on the dump at La Ferté Alais. deHMC Archive

Civilianised at Croydon, F-BGDD in service in France. Note the standard colour scheme (silver overall with black trim) and tail identification in French. deHMC Archive

Bottom: All set up for a wheeler landing, N1300D is believed to be ex-Netherlands Air Force, retrieved from the Dutch East Indies via the Philippines and registered in the USA in 1965. The vast majority of Tiger Moths in the USA were shipped in containers from Europe. Howard Levy

I-JENA was exported by Rollason Aircraft to Italy in November 1958 and has been involved in a number of major incidents since, redeemable only by the injection of many new parts. During the summer of 1996, television viewers saw her spin down into Venice Lido during a festival air display. Don Conway collection

Unlike some vintage aircraft whose cockpits reflect the latest in modern technology, most Tiger Moths around the world have maintained total authenticity, with the exception perhaps of a discreetly positioned wireless and the occasional GPS. via Colin Dodds

Tiger Moth G-ANOD in company with Foster-Wikner Wicko G-AFJB during a summer season operating from Southport Sands. David Vernon

The notorious faked photograph of Tiger Moth LN-BDN, presenting her as a three seater, which caused the Norwegian authorities to pack bags and initiate a field investigation. via K Hagby

A miserable day in March 1953 at Denham aerodrome where it was planned to celebrate the 21st anniversary of the certification of the 'A' model Tiger Moth. Very few parties attended, but the RAF Element of the Army's EFTS at Middle Wallop did their best to raise a smile, (or was it a frown?) with EM879 'BD-T'. de Havilland Aircraft Co Ltd

A famous old aeroplane flying over the equally famous but somewhat older site of Stonehenge in Wiltshire. Tiger Moth DE709 'BD-X' was operating from the Army's EFTS at Middle Wallop shortly before Chipmunks took over the role of initial pilot training. *The Aeroplane*

THE COMMONWEALTH TAKES STOCK

An awesome background at Muzzle Station, Marlborough, New Zealand. When operating under such rural and isolated conditions, the needs of the aeroplane have always to be satisfied first. John King

THE AUSTRALIAN solution to its surplus aircraft situation was quite straightforward: if the aircraft was likely to qualify for a civil certificate of airworthiness it could be sold but if not, it was scrapped. The authorities decided that the ex-RAAF DH.84 Dragons could be sold, but would only qualify for a restricted certificate; Airspeed Oxfords on the other hand would not be accepted as civil aircraft, and the entire fleet was scheduled for the bonfire.

With the war not yet concluded, the Australian Government established in November 1944 a Commonwealth Disposals Commission (CDC) acting under the direction of the Minister of Supply and Shipping. Their brief was to arrange ordered disposal of all war surplus materials, and to fix realistic levels of pricing. The Commission made full use of press advertising and the broadcasting medium to publicise its activities and was genuinely surprised at what they regarded as the exceptional public interest, particularly in the sale of aircraft.

The first 100 aircraft were offered for sale by public tender in February 1945, and included a variety of types from Tiger Moth to 'three engined flying boats'. DH.94 Moth Minors and Tiger Moths had raised between £100 and £200 each, the government actively encouraging sale to stimulate private and club flying. Pre-war, only 200 light aircraft had been registered in Australia, but in the first 14 months of their brief, the Commission sold 340 with many more still held in storage.

The CDC's pricing policy hardened due partly to the strong demand and also following advice from the British Government's Ministry of Aircraft Production (MAP) Liaison Officer in Australia, Air Commodore E R Pearce, that his masters were expecting between £250 and £500 for the Tiger Moths declared surplus in Southern Rhodesia. Pearce was asked by London to consult with de Havilland at Mascot and to elicit their views.

To provide every would-be purchaser with equal priority in obtaining a particular aircraft, should they live in the outback or the middle of Melbourne, a system was introduced linked to the date and time the bid had been lodged and recorded at the dispatching post office. It assured equality of opportunity but was time consuming, and some later sales were conducted by auction held at the storage sites.

N9135, one of the 100 ex-RAF Tiger Moths shipped to Australia in 1940 to boost the training establishment, airborne over 11 EFTS Benalla. Note the 'last three' on the engine side cowling. Robert Veitch

The maximum price for a Tiger Moth, the CDC decided, should be £500, but administration and structure of the pricing policy was to be generous and flexible. Discounts were to be granted to government subsidised aero clubs, air ambulance services and religious organisations which worked in the outback. It was also agreed that concessions would be available to what were described as 'reputable speculators' who were prepared to buy 'considerable numbers' of aircraft, thus saving on sales administration.

The Salvation Army was the first to register an ex-RAAF Tiger Moth post-war when the letters VH-ASA were allocated to A17-541 (DHA976), in September 1945. The aircraft had been purchased for £468 in August from storage at Point Cook, thanks to a donation from Red Shield units in Melbourne, and following civil conversion by the approved regional Tiger Moth centre, Victorian and Interstate Airways at Essendon, she was flown into the northern districts of Western Australia by Salvation Army Captain Victor Pederson. On 14th January 1947, the aircraft was damaged in a forced landing due to deteriorating weather conditions when flying near Wyndham, and was found three days later by a searching RAAF Dakota. To draw attention, Pederson lit a signal fire, but the flames blew back setting the aircraft alight, and the pilot could only watch helplessly as Australia's first post-war civil Tiger Moth was reduced to ashes.

In June 1945, the MAP in London signalled Air Commodore Pearce that 20 Tiger Moths in Australia, the property of the British Government, were to be included in the disposals. Would the CDC act as agents for the sale; could they arrange for the aircraft to be reconditioned; what was the state of the aircraft and were there any other known surpluses? Pearce was reminded that an agreement with the manufacturers dictated that only aircraft in good condition were to be offered for sale, providing also they were supported by an adequate spares backup. Not surprisingly, the answer was that the CDC could not act as selling or reconditioning agent: it was busy enough selling its own assets as they lay.

The CDC offered a further 200 Tiger Moths for sale in February 1946, with bids expected up to the maximum value of £500. Provision was also made to offer 48 spare Gipsy Major engines: those with full life to be offered at £150, the price declining in proportion to the recorded hours and general condition. Seven years later, during the final acts of removing the Tiger Moth from the RAF inventory in Great Britain, zero time Gipsy Majors were reportedly selling at between £5 and £20 each.

The Empire Air Training Scheme (EATS) came to a formal conclusion on 31st March 1945 at which time the British Government waived all rights and interest in the residual value of British owned aircraft stationed in Australia, although they insisted that Australia would pay for any aircraft or item of equipment contributed to the Scheme at British expense, which was diverted outside the continuing Air Training Organisation within the next 12 months, subject to the return of any stock required by the RAF. At the end of the requisite period in April 1946, a naive official at the Air Ministry in London advised the Ministry of Supply (MOS) as successor to the MAP, that 100 Tiger Moths had been shipped to Australia between June and September 1940 as part of the British contribution towards establishing the EATS, and as the RAAF was holding 639 Tiger Moths, the Air Ministry was unable to distinguish between the British and Australian owned aircraft. Having not been advised otherwise, he was forced to assume that all 100 British supplied aircraft remained accountable. Had he realised that the British Tiger had retained their RAF serial numbers in Australia, the problem would have gone away. But about two thirds of the original force had disappeared anyway, victims of five years of the attritional nature of intensive flying training.

The Air Ministry also advised MOS that the RAF had no requirement for any of the British owned aircraft in Australia to be returned home, and as the Australian Air Board had decided to scrap all surplus aircraft thought not to have an immediate post-war use, the Ministry had offered no objection to a policy of breaking down *in situ*. But the matter of the 100 British supplied Tiger Moths was still rankling with one section of the Air Ministry which was determined to balance the books. On 14th May 1946 an official request was made to RAAF Overseas Headquarters (based in London) to determine the fate of the aircraft, even though the British Government had already relinquished further claim. The reply received on 16th July came as quite a surprise: of the 100 aircraft dispatched in 1940, only 38 had survived. Furthermore, the whole of the consignment had been ordered and paid for by the Australian Government; the aircraft were not British property at all. *'Please refer to Indent 758'*, the Air Ministry was advised! The only gift had been in the supply of 200 Gipsy Major engines, and payment for a further 124 built in Australia. The Air Ministry dutifully acknowledged receipt of the information and apologised for any inconvenience their enquiry may have caused.

During 1946, 170 ex-RAAF Tiger Moths were added to the Australian civil register with 154 more in 1947, 52 in 1948 and 23 in 1949. The clubs organised themselves much as they had in Great Britain and the Australian Associated Aero Club bid successfully for 116 aircraft on behalf of constituent members. Total sales of ex-RAAF Tiger Moths between 1945 and 1949 amounted to 525 aircraft, 357 being released in 1946 alone. Until 1953, at least 85 aircraft were reported to have been sold out of Australia going mostly to India (37 confirmed) and New Zealand (22 confirmed), exported by the Newcastle Aero Club and Kingsford Smith Aviation Services in the main, who are believed jointly to have handled about 50 single shipments.

The Australian authorities went to considerable lengths to ensure that prospective purchasers of 54 Tiger Moths and 21 Gipsy Major engines scheduled for sale by auction at Western Junction, Tasmania on 18th May 1946, were well acquainted with detail and fact. In addition to the stock lists which had been circulated on request (catalogues available from the Woolgrowers Agency Co Ltd of Hobart), attendees were advised that the auctioneers had arranged special buses from Launceston and reservations (2s.6d return) were to be made with them.

Help was also available to purchasers. Petrol coupons were supplied by the Civil Aviation Department on presentation of sale receipts, and the new owners were positively encouraged to fly home. For those expecting to cross the Bass Strait heading for Melbourne and beyond, there were special preconditions: the aircraft had to be in possession of either a civil Certificate of Airworthiness issued in Tasmania, or an authorisation for the ferry flight signed on the spot by a Department representative. Pilots were only permitted to fly solo in spite of the fact that until withdrawal these same aircraft had been earning their keep by converting passengers into competent pilots, although the move was probably aimed at halving the problems if search and rescue services should need to be alerted. All departing aircraft were expected to fly in groups which would be escorted by an RAAF Catalina.

Ten days prior to the sale, the CDC announced that an additional 25 Tiger Moths were to be included in the auction, aircraft which had been intended for the RAAF Reserve, and were all serviceable. Eleven of the new lots had flown less than 50 hours since complete overhaul, and one, A17-731 (DHA 1062), which was sold to a local owner for £300, had only 18 hours logged from manufacture. As VH-AUI this aircraft was operated by the Tasmanian Aero Club until 1954 when she was sold to the mainland and converted for agricultural use.

A further 48 Tiger Moths (and 60 Consolidated Catalinas) were offered for sale in October 1946, all lying at bases scattered across the country. The CDC urged potential buyers to inspect the aircraft, and advised the public that copies of survey reports ('however it is regretted that these surveys are not complete') were available for perusal at the Commission's offices in each State Capital. On this occasion sale was to be against a fixed price dependent upon the condition of each individual machine, based on the maximum value of £500 for an aircraft considered to be in excellent condition. A priced list of lots was available along with the summarised survey sheets posted in the Commission's offices, and sales were to be made on the basis of first formal application received, the system originally notified to London in 1945.

What the Commission described as 'probably the last opportunity for the public to obtain one of these popular machines' was the announcement in November 1947 of sale of a further 12 Tiger Moths lying at Temora, Bairnsdale and Tamworth. They were to be added to more than 520 Tiger Moths already handled and their condition was described as being only 'fair' without summarising hours as had been customary. A further 25 aircraft were to be released in 1948, but as far as the Commission was concerned, when the bids closed at 2.00pm on Friday 5th December 1947, they could be satisfied that the year and their task was ending with another 130 Tiger Moths in private circulation, and almost £73,500 in the bank. The CDC had worked efficiently and fairly; aircraft had been sold from 29 sites scattered all over the country as the result of 15 separate invitations to the public to bid.

Tiger Moth and Gipsy Major spares were disposed of separately from the main aircraft sales and huge quantities were released into the market to satisfy the needs of the private owners, clubs and soon, an almost insatiable demand by the agricultural operators. They quickly realised the potential of the just adequate but cheap and plentiful Tiger Moth, an aircraft which became an essential tool for the industry in Australia and New Zealand. Harry Wallace bought 27 tons of engine and airframe spares at an auction in Sydney, although that was only part of the inventory and he continued to satisfy the demands of his clients from his store at Moorabbin for over 40 years.

In 1948, the de Havilland Company was

● If you want one or more 2-seater planes for pleasure, personal travel, or club or business use, here is an outstanding opportunity. The Commonwealth has numerous used Tiger Moths for disposal at Air Force Stations in all States. Full, detailed data of the serviceability and fixed sale price of each machine is placed in your hands as a preliminary on enquiry. Prices vary according to condition between £300 and £500. (List price of a similar machine new on today's market would be about £1,800.) Write or call at the address below for full details.

ALSO ENGINES

Used Gipsy Major Engines are also offered separately at prices varying according to condition, maximum being £150 for good used condition. The aviation industry knows the fame of the Gipsy Major for reliability, low petrol consumption, and ease of servicing.

REGIONAL MANAGER,
Commonwealth Disposals Commission,
"London House,"
321 Murray Street,
Perth, W.A.

Built as A17-746 in 1944 and sold into the civil market in 1954, VH-CEJ (sometime VH-CES) was cancelled in 1966 and extensively rebuilt by Bob Miles using all new parts. The aircraft qualified for Public Transport certification in 1983 and was enrolled into a joyriding career at Moorabbin. Keith Jose

At the end of the day. The last ten RAAF training Tiger Moths in their post-war silver with yellow bands assembled at Point Cook on 9th January 1957. The aircraft flew in formation to Tocumwal for disposal. RAAF PRO

pleased to afford publicity to the fact that the Royal Aero Club of New South Wales had a membership of 700, and was flying more than 3,500 hours per year operating 28 Tiger Moths, two taper-wing DH.87A Hornet Moths, a DH.85 Leopard Moth and a DH.84 Dragon. Freely available petrol supplies were regarded by commentators in Great Britain as a significant factor in the encouragement of such levels of activity.

A spot check on 31st July 1951, revealed that at 235, Tiger Moths represented 33% of all aircraft registered in Australia on that date. The restoration of commercial operations across the country resulted in a steady increase in the number of civil aircraft and a similar check conducted on 31st May 1959 revealed that 314 Tiger Moths were active, one in four of the total.

For a country awash with surplus aircraft, and tempting offers floating into the system from suppliers in England, Australian Aircraft Sales, a company based at Mascot, provided a sufficiency of brand new Tiger Moth spares to allow Airwork Co Pty Ltd to build four complete aircraft at Archerfield: VH-AWH (AW/TC/1), in April 1957; VH-AWJ (AW /A/16) and VH-WPP (AW/A/17), in March and June 1958, and VH-AWM (AW/A/20), in September 1959. Lawrence Engineering and Sales Pty Ltd of Camden built a Tiger Moth from all new spares and registered her as VH-KRW (LES 1), in February 1959. In June 1962, the company registered its eleventh and last new construction when VH-CRA (LES 11), was listed to Nigel Rogers of Corfield in Queensland, probably as a replacement for his VH-BCS (DHA219), which he had owned for the previous four years.

The building of new aircraft coincided with release of the last RAAF Tiger Moths; ten operational aircraft were flown from the RAAF College at Point Cook to Tocumwal on 9th January 1957 for disposal. Each civilian purchaser was required to acknowledge that sale of the Tiger Moths was conditional on their immediate availability for military requisition in times of national emergency.

At the time of the Japanese surrender, the Royal New Zealand Air Force could account for 232 Tiger Moths on the inventory, many of which where in store at Taieri or Woodbourne. During conduct of the wartime programme, 103 aircraft had been written off whilst training over 7,000 pilots to elementary standard and beyond.

The peacetime Air Force requirements indicated that about 180 Tiger Moths could be declared surplus, and an initial list of 114 aircraft was provided for action by the New Zealand Government's disposal agency, the War Assets Realisation Board (WARB). An additional 15 Tiger Moths were set aside for presentation to flying clubs as compensation for aircraft requisitioned at the beginning of the Second World War.

Unlike all other disposal programmes with roots in the EATS, the New Zealand Air Department took note of the surveys conducted by the Royal New Zealand Aero Club (RNZAC) which suggested that the country's aero clubs could accommodate between them about 60 Tiger Moths, and arrangements were made for the systematic overhaul of that number with a fixed selling price of £450 in mind, a figure negotiated down from £800 which had been the original suggestion. To establish the system, four aircraft were flown from Taieri to the de Havilland factory at Rongotai in August 1945.

On 25th September 1946, part of the Centenial Exhibition Buildings at Rongotai, previously used by the de Havilland Company as a maintenance and storage facility, was destroyed by fire. Lost in the blaze were NZ732 (3426) and NZ826 (DHNZ76), Tiger Moths then attached to the Forest Fire Patrol, a Howard DGA operated by the United States' Legation, a pair of instructional airframes and 18 engines.

Surplus stock, now identified to WARB as 98 Tiger Moths, was sold very much in line with proceedings elsewhere, and against a graduated scale of condition were offered for tender as lying, with fixed reserve prices ranging from £30 to £330. When the list closed on 9th December 1946, only 20 aircraft had been sold for between £35 and £235 each. A number of private sales reduced the number to 74 to which the Air Force added a further declared surplus of 14. A second tender operation which closed in May 1947 resulted in only 17 aircraft of the 88 aircraft on offer being sold, and a serious storage problem to be faced by somebody.

The first of the de Havilland overhauled Tiger Moths, ZK-AIC (82263), a survivor of the wartime shipments from Great Britain, was delivered to the New Plymouth Aero Club and on 11th January 1946 inaugurated civil flying in New Zealand following the end of the Second World War. Before the end of the year, 16 clubs were in operation having received 57 aircraft. From April 1946, the £450 aircraft were also available from Aircraft Service (NZ) Ltd and Airwork (NZ) Ltd at Mangere and Harewood, all delivered in the standard scheme of trainer yellow overall, except by special request.

Aircraft in storage at April 1947 were reassessed for a further sale by tender, but in view of the poor public attitude displayed the previous December and in the face of opposition from the aero clubs, the idea was abandoned. In October 1947 the Minister of Defence was prevailed upon to donate to the RNZAC 42 Tiger Moths free of charge, for issue to deserving organisations. Although there was no purchase cost, £20 per aeroplane was charged for assembly and rigging ex-storage, plus sixpence per mile air delivery by Air Force pilots. Even at these bargain prices there were objections and perhaps with reason. The 'free' aircraft would be delivered with no civil certification which would become the responsibility of the recipients, and at their own cost. Assuming no major problems, the engineering work and subsequent paperchase was expected to average some £200 per aircraft. Following quickly a £450 invoice for one overhauled Tiger Moth, some of the clubs could not afford the additional burden, and gifted aircraft were re-sold or stored for later disposal; used as a fallback reserve or even a source of free spares.

Although the rate of delivery was slow and only 28 aircraft had been provided by May 1949, the system was working, and must have caused distress to those in the industry, especially in Great Britain, who had expressed strong opinions against any suggestion of free issue. Perhaps the New Zealand Government were not aware of such objections or believed they were too far from the centre of the argument, for a year after the first allocation, a further 19 aircraft were gifted to the RNZAC. These could not be air delivered due, it was claimed, to a shortage of Air Force personnel, although it was widely believed that their condition was such that it precluded anything but delivery by surface transport anyway. All the free issue aircraft had been distributed by 1950, and at the end of the following year 27 clubs were active with almost 130 Tiger Moths on line.

The RNZAF was the last of the Commonwealth air forces to operate Tiger Moths in the primary training role. Nine aircraft were sold by tender in 1955 and the final 11 by August 1956. NZ1421 (NZ101), went to Aircraft Engineering Co of NZ Ltd for £425 and NZ1453 (NZ133), was converted to the status of Instructional Airframe and allocated to No 4 Technical Training School (TTS) at Woodbourne in September.

The average price of £363 paid for the aircraft sold into the commercial market reflected the changed public interest in the last disposal. Two damaged aircraft, NZ1425 (NZ105), which had crashed at Taieri on 19th October 1954 and NZ1427 (NZ107), which suffered an accident on the same site in March 1955, were sold for £42 and £25 respectively, almost certainly as sources of spare parts. While the aero clubs were now beginning to seek more modern equipment, the agricultural industry was almost insatiable and remained a net importer of Tiger Moths from specialist suppliers overseas.

de Havilland's Associated Company in South Africa had been responsible for the import of almost 60 Tiger Moths pre-war, mostly complete, but occasionally received less engines which were ordered independently and fitted at the company's premises on the historic aerodrome at Baragwanath near Johannesburg. In the main, these aircraft were scheduled for flying clubs where they were used as primary trainers, and the first are believed to have been ZS-AIL, ZS-AIM and ZS-AIN (3525, 3526 and 3522), operated from Baragwanath in the red and silver colours of the Johannesburg Light Plane Club. All three were impressed into the South African Air Force in 1940.

Tiger Moths of the RNZAF awaiting their visit from the 'oiler'. Unusually, serial numbers and codes applied by stencil, have not been 'filled in'. Note the aircraft log temporarily suspended below the chin cowling of '43'. deHMC Archive

Operating a military marked Tiger Moth in New Zealand also requires prominent carriage of the civil registration. ZK-BUO/ NZ795 was assembled from an imported British kit at Rongotai. John King

In 1935 and with an eye on events in Abyssinia as much as Europe, the South African Government decided to accelerate modernisation of the country's defence plans. A contract was written for the light aeroplane clubs to provide courses of 50 hours elementary flying training for pilots who would then progress to the South African Air Force's Central Flying School (CFS) for advanced training. The scheme was intended to produce 1,000 qualified pilots by 1942, and the clubs were required to standardise on their own choice from four basic aircraft types: Ryan ST-A, Miles Hawk, Miles Magister and DH.82A Tiger Moth.

The scheme became effective in 1937 and resulted in orders for 30 Tiger Moths to be shipped from Hatfield, but the SAAF reported adversely on the quality of club training although pilots were generally 'improved' by their subsequent courses at CFS. For purposes of administration, nine clubs were issued identifying numbers (1-9) as component parts of the collective Transvaal Air Training Squadron (TATS) in March 1937, but these had been amended by October 1938 when the more appropriately named Union Air Training Group (UATG) took over and expanded into 13 'Flights', all operating civil registered aircraft. At the same time the 50 hours training was expanded to 70 hours before the new pilots were posted to a network of Air Schools operated by the Air Force.

Coincident with the CFS move to Tempe near Bloemfontein in May 1940, the SAAF decided that its standard elementary trainer would be the Tiger Moth. The decision followed impressment of about 250 assorted light commercial, school, club and privately owned aircraft of some 60 different types or marques. The UATG Flights were subsequently disbanded and all elementary flying training was consolidated under control of the new SAAF Flying Training Command at seven established Air Schools.

The substantial reorganisation was partly due to South Africa's conditional agreement to take an active part in the Empire Air Training Scheme (EATS), which had been the subject of debate since October 1938. On 6th September 1939, 50 new Tiger Moths from the RAF's home reserve were allocated for shipment to South Africa. The aircraft were flown to Sealand, dismantled, packed and dispatched by sea in five separate shipments between January and April 1940. On arrival the camouflage schemes were oversprayed with trainer yellow, and each aircraft was allocated a SAAF serial number, although there appears to be no correlation between those and the RAF serials. Allocation appears to have been very much against the order in which the fuselages were unpacked and set up to receive their resprayed wings.

Although primarily intended for the training of South African nationals to operate within the confines of their own continent, the RAF was anxious to expand its own aircrew training programmes, and agreement was reached in January 1940 to allow British nationals resident in South Africa to be trained, but under SAAF control. A further 63 Tiger Moths were dispatched from England between 7th January and 8th March 1941, all brand new aircraft packed and shipped directly from the Morris Motors factory at Cowley, with just a few minutes flight test recorded in their logbooks.

A new Agreement was signed in June 1940 under the title 'Joint Air Training Plan' (JATP), allowing British cadets to train for RAF service, while permitting a gradual expansion and the introduction of seven Elementary Flying Training Schools (EFTS). The 'Joint Air Training Scheme' (JATS) was defined in June 1941, for which South Africa would provide airfields, fuel, oil and facilities while the British Government would be responsible for all instructors and staff, aircraft, spares and training equipment. In addition to the Tiger Moth, selected aircraft types were Miles Master, Hawker Hurricane, Airspeed Oxford and Avro Anson, all shipped from Great Britain. A general shortage of aircraft meant that some Elementary Schools had to share and operated with only 36 aircraft instead of the agreed establishment of 48 until deliveries caught up.

By July 1941 SAAF training units for every discipline were involved in JATS and a number of South African Government owned aircraft had been added, mostly obsolete Avro and Hawker biplanes. From December, training capacity began to exceed demand and resources were offered to train aircrew principally from Belgium, Poland, Greece and Yugoslavia. As more RAF recruits arrived, some local protest groups with grudges held since the Boer War were moved to commit murderous acts of sabotage on unguarded aircraft, with the result that some stations put up standing patrols to fly around the airfield perimeter to observe movement of people or vehicles on the otherwise nearly deserted approach roads.

Eight Air Depots (AD) were established by August 1941 to better cope with the continuing delivery of aircraft, each with responsibility for specific types. No 4 AD at Lyttelton was assigned to the reception of Tiger Moths and Miles Masters. Shipments from Morris Motors were recorded every month from January to October 1941 and during the ten month period, 250 new aircraft were accepted through Cape Town. Forty Tiger Moths shipped in April and more than 20 in July were lost at sea due to enemy action, part of the 15% losses being suffered on all shipping destined for South Africa. Six of the eight aircraft dispatched on 12th October were later recorded as being *'badly corroded due to immersion in sea water and considered beyond repair'*. They may have travelled as deck cargo and experienced a stormy passage; a more likely explanation than all six falling into the dock during unloading perhaps. On a later occasion, six airframes were condemned for identical reasons; their ship had run aground near Cape Town and suffered a flooded hold.

With the training well established, the Director of Coastal Air Force called a conference in December 1941 to identify the assistance which might be expected from the Schools by the coastal squadrons in protection of the extensive coastline. The result was that by April 1942, 30 Reserve squadrons had been formed with Nos 1-7 Air Schools constituting 101-107 Reserve Squadrons, complete with their own administration, and their Tiger Moths designated 'Light Bomber'. Apart from isolated incidents of a type expected on any wartime coastline, the main concern was fear of a possible invasion by Japanese forces following the attack on Pearl Harbor, but by December 1943 the threat was believed to have diminished, and a sufficient number of operational squadrons had been raised to tackle the job on a more permanent and professional basis.

In order to supplement British deliveries and to guard against major loss and damage caused by submarine warfare the effects of which had already been amply demonstrated, 120 Australian built Tiger Moths were added to the South African inventory from late 1941. Built against an order placed by the British Government, for 420 aircraft for southern Africa, this was reduced to 395 and finally to 214, 94 of which were dispatched up the railway line to Southern Rhodesia. The first consignment of 28 aircraft was ready for shipment from Sydney in August but not processed through the port facilities at Durban until 8th December. These aircraft were allocated RAF serial numbers but notification was received only after delivery into the South African system, where SAAF serials were applied anyway. The following 12 aircraft were dispatched from Sydney in early October and all carried RAF serials in the DX range. Seven Tiger Moths shipped in November were identified by their de Havilland Australia build numbers until SAAF serials were allocated on arrival, and the final 73 machines delivered via Durban in February, March and June 1942 all carried RAF 'DX' serials which were immediately exchanged for SAAF identification on arrival at Lyttelton. Between February and June 1943, a further 56 Tiger Moths were delivered from Great Britain, including for the first time, ten reconditioned aircraft, a few of which were included with most consignments shipped during that period.

In February 1944, 200 Canadian built Fairchild Cornells were allocated to South Africa as a Tiger Moth replacement following a trend started in Canada and Rhodesia, and a pair of aircraft was delivered for trials on loan from RATG in Southern Rhodesia. These two, 15266 and 15271, were operated as part of the Communications Flight of 24 Group based at Zwartkop Air Station during March and April 1944, and found little favour with pilots or engineers. The replacement aircraft was considered to be underpowered, especially for flying training duties at the elementary schools situated in the Highveld, where they had been deliberately placed on account of the weather record. They were also considered 'bland' and 'viceless' and consequently not ideally suited in the training role. The Air Force preferred the Tiger Moth and refused to accept its intended replacement.

With Canadian production geared up, and Southern Rhodesia's acceptance of the Cornell, one semi-solution was to move seemingly redundant Tiger Moths from RATG to South Africa. In March 1944, 26 Tiger Moths were transferred south followed by 43 on 31st May and a final 12 on 14th June. In addition, nine new Australian built aircraft were diverted to Lyttelton rather than continue on their rail journey to Bulawayo, and a quartet of Tiger Moths from Kenya's Auxiliary Air Unit (KAAU) arrived in March: a final tally of 94. But there was consternation at the condition of some arrivals which had evidently spent time picketed in the weather. As a result of post-delivery surveys, eleven Tiger Moths were immediately scrapped.

In spite of the constant build up of complete aeroplanes from RAF Maintenance Units, from Cowley and Mascot, and later from RATG and Kenya, where flying training on any scale was considered inappropriate due to the prospect of a major confrontation with Italy in East Africa, there was, or appeared to be, in concert with all other types, a constant shortage of spare parts for Tiger Moth airframes and especially for Gipsy Major engines. Always in demand were Tiger Moth mainplanes, the victims of poor ground handling, taxying accidents, ground loops and nose-overs following bounced landings. Rising to the occasion at the request of the Director General of War Supplies was G H Starck, who alleviated the problem by converted his furniture factory in The Cape to the remanufacture and repair of wooden wings.

Potentially more serious was the shortage of engine parts caused to a large degree by excessive wear, the result of the hot, dry and dusty aerodrome surfaces. During take-off and landing the Tiger Moth's tailskid spoon cut furrows in the surface topsoil, ripping out the binding grass and creating clouds of airborne dust. Other aircraft taking off flew through the hazard which was ingested by the engines, causing excessive wear in carburettors and cylinders. Australian built aircraft were fitted with engine air intake filters attached externally to the starboard side cowling, but the British aircraft had no such luxury until they were fitted as an extra precaution on site. The dust problem was equally bad for aircraft attempting to land when in addition to the suspension of abrasive particles, visibility was reduced by the effect of aircraft on the roll.

The situation was considered serious enough to warrant a detailed study of aerodrome surfaces, a task undertaken by the South African Engineer Corps (Aerodromes and Maintenance) in conjunction with the Directorate of Aerodromes and Works. Experiments with 85 different types of grass were conducted on plots at Wonderboom, but with constant over-utilisation, the problem was never completely solved. The best solution was found in fitting a small tailwheel in place of the skid, designed and trialled at 62 AS Bloemfontein and which became the standard fit on all JATS tailskid aircraft. Pilots were urged to exercise caution when taxying however, as the mainwheels still were not fitted with brakes.

Continuous efforts and organisational refinements resulted in peak output of aircrew achieved late in 1943 and maintained into 1944 when with the war outlook appearing to be brighter, the pace was allowed to slacken off. No 1 Air School at Baragwanath, home of de Havilland (South Africa) Pty Ltd was closed down on 29th February 1944 having peaked with an establishment of 58 Tiger Moths the previous July. During the past four years the school had been a willing custodian of de Havilland types having also operated Hornet Moth, Moth Major and DH.60 Moth, all disguised under military colours.

Bearing 'high visibility' serial 2471, this Tiger Moth was received by the South African Air Force from RAF stocks in June 1942 and survived to be despatched to India in 1946. Maurice Kelly

The sheer inelegance of the giant serial numbers meant there was no room for a fuselage roundel on some SAAF Tiger Moths. 4608 arrived from Great Britain in March 1943 and departed for India in July 1946. Note the tailwheel and the absence of spin strakes. Maurice Kelly

The mixture of high adventure, bravado and boredom was by no means unique to the trainee pilots and instructors of JATS, although South African weather was probably a contributing factor in some of the high jinks. To inspire their pupils to higher levels of confidence it was reported that on some occasions, instructors would climb out of their cockpits in mid-air, and inch along the line of the lower wing front spar, until they reached the interplane strut, from which position they would view the passing scrubland from varying heights. A similar story was told of an instructor in Great Britain, operating with 21 EFTS Booker, who told his pupil to hold the aircraft steady, at which point he would climb out onto one lower wing and then the other, advising the pupil that he was checking the rigging to ensure it was safely attached prior to initiating an aerobatic routine.

But it was the overconfidence of some trainees which led them to inspect the ground, and often buildings and people, from too low a level. To help identify low flying culprits, for one yellow Tiger Moth looked exactly like another yellow Tiger Moth, and stem a rising tide of accidents due to unauthorised contact with mother earth, JATS aircraft were painted with serial numbers on fuselage sides and underneath the wings, as large as could decently and practically be accommodated. A similar ploy was adopted in Canada, and for the same reasons. The Tiger Moths of No 2 AS Randfontein carried a giant '2' on the top surface of the port upper mainplane, and the school identification on the starboard upper, both of which could be easily read on a banking aircraft from some distance.

Two indulgences of the Benoni flying instructors were to run the Tiger Moth's mainwheels along the straight dirt roads, creeping up behind an unsuspecting vehicle until the aircraft filled the rear view mirror, and then to hop over the top and disappear at low level, possibly to run a tip of one lower mainplane along the surface of the water in a local stream.

Squadron Leader W L Woodward AFC was posted in as CFI at 7 AS Kroonstad in November 1941. Having survived as a soldier in the First World War he joined the RAF on a five year commission in 1919, and flew civil aircraft until re-enlisting in August 1939. The press hounds picked up the scent when it was revealed that on account of his age (and experience), King's Regulations had been altered to allow him to continue instructing, and much was made of the fact that his talents might otherwise have been lost when in 1942, an interview was published under the heading 'The Oldest Instructor in The Empire':

'People who are good horsemen almost invariably make good pilots. I noticed that when I started out as an instructor and it is still the same today. The syllabus of training is similar in outline to what it was in the early days, but it is now more thorough and of course there are more things to think about.

'More than 50% of the flying accidents at training schools are caused by disregarding regulations. Usually the cause is over confidence on the part of the inexperienced pilot; over confidence which breeds a certain carelessness and makes him boast to himself: I need not worry about this or that regulation!

'A good pilot takes no unnecessary chances! A much smaller percentage of accidents owe their cause to errors of judgement or other mistakes by the pilot. A very small number of accidents can be traced to aircraft weaknesses or failure'.

A popular story told at 5 AS Witbank concerned a pupil pilot who had damaged an aircraft during the course of normal flying training, and in consequence suffered an artificially dramatic tirade from his instructor, during which the pupil was threatened with having to pay for a new Tiger Moth. At a time when cheque books were still a fantasy of most young men's imagination, the pupil is alleged to have drawn one from an inside pocket, and with pen raised calmly asked for how much and to whom the cheque should be made payable.

The difficulties of adapting to high temperatures, high altitude and a reduced aircraft performance, especially for pupils who had begun their training in Great Britain, were sometimes demonstrated in spectacular fashion. Having flown solo on one occasion at Sealand, Paul Goddard's second solo was at Benoni where he rounded out too high, and in spite of a rapid application of full power, hit the ground hard and bounced back into the circuit. The aircraft continued to fly but the engine revs were high, there was a deal of vibration, the altimeter was stuck at 500ft, two holes had appeared in the lower wings, and there was no acceleration.

Having persuaded the aircraft round on to finals and dismissed the thought of ditching in a local lake, the aircraft made a successful touch down but taxying back to dispersal was an effort. After shut down, investigation revealed six inches missing from each propeller blade, the tips having been fired through both lower wings, and the crankshaft was bent. During the subsequent interview with his Flight Commander, Goddard, who later took up Holy Orders, was admonished for breaking the aeroplane but congratulated for managing to fly it in a 'thoroughly unairworthy condition'.

'Acclimatisation' was later recognised by establishing early in 1943 No 2 Pilot Despatch Centre (PDC) at Nigel and No 3 PDC Standerton, with the aim of providing a four week period of refresher training, but there was never enough equipment or instructional personnel to run both centres at ideal capacity.

As far as records were accurately maintained, including the civil impressments but excluding the aircraft known to have been lost at sea, believed to be a total of 93, the South African Air Force can be credited with the receipt of 698 Tiger Moths of British or Australian origin. 238 were struck off charge before the Joint Air Training Scheme was concluded on 8th March 1946.

The reduced demand for pilots allowed aircraft to be withdrawn from service and positioned to Air Depots. While the SAAF considered its future, the fate of the aircraft was being discussed 6,000 miles away in London, from December 1945, by Committees constituted by delegates from the MAP, Air Ministry, Treasury and Dominion Offices. While there had already been hectic activity surrounding surplus disposals in Southern

Rhodesia and confusion over the policy covering RAF stocks held in Great Britain, the South African question needed quiet diplomacy. Under the terms of the Agreement setting up JATS, both sides had accepted that upon termination, there would be a physical division of residual aircraft and equipment rather than cash apportionment from sales. Such an understanding would, therefore, lead to neither side demanding or suggesting minimum sale prices as elsewhere. The British Government was free to ship out its allocated stock leaving the South African authorities to raise what it could, where and how it liked, to offset the cost of aerodromes, buildings and facilities.

The fluctuation of fortunes and requirements since the Agreement was signed was now seen to have blurred the issue. A number of aircraft had undoubtedly been shipped to South Africa to help build a strategic reserve, and had now become indistinguishable from those declared surplus from JATS. London was concerned that if much was made of this issue when apportioning individual aircraft, the South African Government might retaliate by imposing high charges for storage and maintenance on all aircraft declared redundant.

An earlier suggestion made to a South African Mission visiting London in August 1945, that the Dominion might be offered the whole of the British share of surplus aircraft at a price of £100,000 had not been further discussed at the Mission's own request. Since then, the cessation of Lend-Lease supplies had caused the Air Ministry to consider withdrawal of 200 Tiger Moths from South Africa for training purposes in 'other theatres' and the sum of £100,000 was therefore, no longer appropriate.

Of the 460 Tiger Moths believed still operational, many were known to be in a 'well used' condition, and the prospect of the RAF hand-picking the 200 best examples was thought not to be diplomatic. South Africa had already declared an interest in maintaining a Tiger Moth fleet for its own defence training needs, and there was growing friction over the proposed withdrawal to Britain of 300 North American Harvards supplied under Lend-Lease, and not included under the Agreement's clause covering JATS proportional division. The SAAF had hoped to secure these aircraft at little cost for their own use, but as events moved on, 280 Harvards were shipped back to open storage in Great Britain, where the majority was eventually scrapped.

It is not clear whether the MAP or Air Ministry did have a specific destination in mind for its anticipated share of South African based Tiger Moths, but apart from a return to Great Britain it seems likely that India was the intended target, possibly to stave off any prospect of further foreign competition, evidence of which was being flagged up by RAF Commands stationed in the sub-continent during the summer of 1945.

It was London's decision to vest full rights of negotiation with their people on the spot: the British Air Liaison Mission (BALM). They were to propose South African purchase of the whole of the residual stock less the 200 Tiger Moths, and to report back to MAP before accepting any offer. In addition, and to support the selected aircraft, London asked for 50 spare Gipsy Major engines from a stock believed to number 240, spares to service 250 engines, and two fifths of all Tiger Moth airframe spares. It was appreciated that the best of the engines would already be fitted to the aircraft in service. In confirming that no other British owned aircraft would be withdrawn, the MAP were signalling their willingness to permit disposal of all other assets *in situ*, a decision made on the grounds of practicality and convenience as much as economics.

Tiger Moths were gradually withdrawn from the Air Schools between February and September 1944, and placed in storage at a number of sites: Waterkloof, Germiston, Baragwanath, Benoni, Nigel, Vereeniging, Potchefstroom, Witbank and Kroonstad, sometimes their own home station, and under the general administration of 15 AD with headquarters at Zwartkop. As more aircraft were received, especially towards the end of 1945 when Air Depots themselves were being closed and covered accommodation became scarce, Tiger Moths were

The ordered scene at 3 Air Depot, Cape Town in 1946, as some of the 100 RAF aircraft selected for a passage to India were gathered together ready for packing. W T Blick

As an 18 year old cadet, Jerry Dunn attended No 6 Short Service Course conducted by the Southern Rhodesia Air Force at Cranbourne between April and August 1954. During his subsequent service career he delivered de Havilland Vampires from Hatfield and retired as the Chief Pilot of Air Botswana. Jerry Dunn

stored with their mainplanes stowed alongside the fuselage, while a few had their engines removed.

From February 1946 the fate of most of the SAAF Tiger Moths was decided. The Air Ministry was allotted their 200 aircraft: 100 were drawn from storage and flown to Cape Town, dismantled and transferred by sea to India progressively from July, when they were delivered to the Hindustan Aircraft Company at Bangalore. Several were modified for night flying before they left their Air Depots in South Africa, and Hindustan's main task was to prepare them for local service with the Indian Air Force. Large numbers were later released and civil registered on behalf of the government by subsidised flying clubs.

A further 100 Tiger Moths were selected in February 1946 for post-war service with the SAAF Central Flying School at Dunnottar from where several were sold in August 1948 at £4.10s.0d each, prices which would have turned custodians of the British industry quite pale. It was in the wake of requirements to clear storage areas and close expensive facilities as quickly as possible that such nightmare stories resulted: 47 Avro Ansons sold to a company in Port Elizabeth at £2.0s.0d each; the 37 sold without engines were cleared at exactly half that amount. In retrospect the £6.0s.0d. each paid for serviceable Curtiss Kittyhawk IVs might still be considered a bargain, although the buyer was in the scrap metal business.

The RAF took their remaining 100 Tiger Moths from store in April 1946 which were delivered in September and October to the Air Training Wing in Southern Rhodesia, replacing the aircraft which had themselves been declared surplus and sold in batches from 1944. The replacements were gathered at Benoni and flown north to equip Nos 4 and 5 Flying Training Schools at Heany and Thornhill.

Mystery aircraft. Loaded on board HMS *Pursuer* at Durban in 1945, this apparently new Australian built Tiger Moth returned with the carrier to the Clyde where she was flown off and never seen again.
Eric Morton

The South African War Stores Disposal Board sanctioned release of Tiger Moths as surplus to requirements after the selection for India and Rhodesia had been satisfied, and sales by auction were held at many of the Air Depots in June 1946 and July 1947. Prices varied between £40 and £85 with several at £50 and the occasional extravagance such as 2152 (T8123/84435), which was sold from Benoni on 2nd June 1946 for £125.

SAAF 579 (T7814/84197), was retired from 7 AS Kroonstad on 18th December 1944 and placed in store on the same airfield. She was moved to Witbank on 1st October 1945 and later the same month transferred to Germiston where she was expected to be tagged as one of the 'RAF 100 aircraft', probably scheduled for Southern Rhodesia. On inspection the aircraft was rejected and remained in store until she was moved again, to Vereeniging, on 14th June 1947, and sold the following month.

In November 1950, 84197 took up civil markings ZS-DEU under the ownership of H E Fourie at Brixton, and following an engine overhaul by Bok Strecker, and a new red and silver paint scheme, she was flown on 7th March 1951. Several owners later in 1959, ZS-DEU was standing at Windhoek in what appeared to be an abandoned condition. A pilot from 28 Squadron, and also a member of the SAAF's Defence Flying Club (DFC) was told by a local airline engineer that the current owner would be pleased to present the aircraft to the Club. This intelligence was relayed to the Committee who sent a club engineer to inspect the aircraft, at the same time dismantling it. Almost coincidentally, an empty transport aircraft passing through Windhoek was bound for the DFC's main base at Swartkop, and not wishing to miss the opportunity, all four wings and the propeller were loaded on board and safely delivered.

Enter Mr M L Greenberg of Benoni, wondering where he might find the rest of the aeroplane he had just bought from Mr Friedrich Bohnemeier: ZS-DEU. It came as quite a shock to discover that the wings had been flown to Swartkop and Mr Greenberg politely asked the DFC to send him £300 or return the missing parts. Equally diplomatically, the Club secretary replied from a position of great embarrassment that he was empowered to offer £50 for the whole aeroplane or £25 for the four wings. *'Should you find this unacceptable,'* he wrote, *'we will return the mainplanes, reassemble the aircraft and park it where it was found'.*

The offer was refused, but to avoid any further embarrassment, a deal was struck in which the SAAF agreed to fly the fuselage of ZS-DEU from Windhoek to join the wings at Swartkop, from where the whole would be available for collection by the new owner, in addition to a veritable collection of spare parts, and compensation for legal expenses of £12.10s.0d.

Following sale of the Disposal Board's declared surpluses of 1946-1948, CFS absorbed all the remainder until they released a batch of Tiger Moths in 1955, several of which were disposed of as scrap but subsequently appeared on the civil register. CFS made a final break with the type in June 1956 when the last aircraft were sold to the SAAF Aero Club, possibly for as much as £25 each, following the Club's successful bid of £5 for an engineless airframe in 1951.

Of the 460 Tiger Moths on charge with the SAAF in September 1945, the RAF drew off 200, possibly 210, and about 220 were civil registered during the post-war years. The others were victims of accidents, scrapping and reduction to spares, or were simply lost in the system. Where for example, did the Australian built Tiger Moth that appeared on board HMS *Pursuer* come from?

The ship had been refitting in Durban, May-June 1945, in readiness for the planned invasion of Malaya, Operation *Zipper*, and the carrier's Grumman Hellcats of 898 Squadron Fleet Air Arm, were to provide air cover. The Tiger Moth appeared on board packed in a crate along with boxes of aircraft compasses and a consignment of rifles. The compasses and firearms were returned from whence they came by order of the Captain, but the aircraft stayed, believed to have been 'liberated' from a salvage yard. Durban was certainly the port through which Australian imports were received, and perhaps this example just arrived late, or missed the train, or perhaps there was no room on the train, or maybe she was damaged on unloading, her paperwork was missing or she was simply forgotten and left behind.

By the time the refit was completed, the Japanese war was over, and 898 Squadron left HMS *Pursuer* which became a Headquarters and Communications ship. The Tiger Moth was unpacked and erected on deck, and once at sea was test flown, an exercise which required the ship to reduce speed to allow her to land on. At some stage during the flight programme, the propeller was broken, and for the remainder of the voyage to the Clyde the Tiger Moth was stowed below decks. On arrival in Scotland, the aircraft was fitted with a new propeller scrounged from an unknown source, and flown away, disappearing into obscurity, and never to be recorded on any official list.

More formally, the Royal Navy was allocated ten locally manufactured Tiger Moths for use in and around Australia in 1945, all of which were written off or disposed of apart from A17-84 (DHA81). Delivered to the Royal Navy at Bankstown in November 1945 where the serial number was amended to 'A1784', the aircraft served at Schofields for two years. She was embarked on the carrier HMS *Theseus* in 1947 and was on board during the ship's arrival in Wellington, New Zealand, on 23rd August, leaving for Auckland five days later. The Tiger Moth was launched with the resident Supermarine Seafires and Fairey Fireflys on 30th August, joining the squadrons for a spot of shore leave at Whenuapai, but was first to land back prior to departure on 15th September, and was carried through to Scotland where she was held in store at a number of Royal Naval Air Stations, and last reported at Lossiemouth in 1962.

The Captain of HMS *Theseus*, Captain R K Dickson DSO RN, had previous experience of Tiger Moths. BB858 (3389), G-ADOY with the Reid and Sigrist school at Desford until impressed into the RAF in 1940, and released to the Royal Navy Directorate of Aircraft in 1943, was embarked on his ship early in 1947, but immediately after take off from the carrier on 25th March, the engine failed and Captain Dickson ditched the aircraft which was lost. Perhaps the return of 'A1784' was a means of balancing the books.

The Royal Navy had already admitted to having lost two other Tiger Moths at sea. On 7th May 1944, T6808 (85077), an aircraft delivered new into Admiralty charge in December 1941, swung to port, went over the side and crashed into the sea when landing on HMS *Ravager* during attachment to 768 Squadron FAA, and a year later, on 18th May 1945, an unidentified Tiger Moth was ditched into the sea as the result of engine failure after take off, although on this occasion the steadier platform was Kai Tak aerodrome, Hong Kong.

Early in the war, Fleet Air Arm pilots having learned to fly on Tiger Moths under the administrative care of the RAF, undertook live deck landing instruction in requisitioned DH.60 Moths painted in Navy colours. Mike Lithgow, a naval pupil at 20 ERFTS Gravesend, completed Advanced Training, again with the RAF, flying North American Harvards and Fairey Battles at Netheravon. As a post-war test pilot with Supermarines, he was to travel considerably faster in the prototype Supermarine Swift F.4, WK198, on 25th September 1953, when establishing a world air speed record of 737.3mph. Only 18 days earlier, Neville Duke, Hawker's Chief Test Pilot, trained on Tiger Moths with 13 EFTS at White Waltham in 1940, had raised the record to 727.6mph in his all-red Hawker Hunter Mk. 3, WB188.

Under the Terms of Agreement for the Empire Air Training Scheme signed in Canada on 17th December 1939, the Canadian Government would provide facilities to train Canadian, British, Australian and New Zealand aircrews, and the British Government would supply the estimated requirement of 3,540 aircraft.

Pre-war, the civil flying clubs had provided elementary training for the Royal Canadian Air Force, and to avoid delay in commencing the EATS, clubs were called upon to supply flying instructors and ground staff while operating under the jurisdiction of the RCAF. Although airfield construction made a good start, commencement of the flying programme proper was seen by local observers as lethargic.

During the summer of 1940, with Canadian approval, the Air Ministry moved a number of RAF Service Flying Training Schools (SFTS) from Great Britain to Canada, a policy that was opposed by many including some Cabinet Ministers who believed the units should remain at home as a second line of defence, and new schools should be raised as a 'reserve'. At the same time, the Canadians were showing some misgivings lest the transfer should cause an interruption in the flow of training aircraft across the Atlantic.

Repositioning of the schools was physically ponderous, but by the end of 1940, four SFTS were in commission. All flying instruction was given and received by RAF

No 8 Repair Depot, Winnipeg. Piles of DH.82C Tiger Moth fuselages, less engines and undercarriages, soon to be turned into scrap. Lloyd Carbert

A good view of the lagged oil tank on RCAF DH.82C 5810 and the invitation, mostly ignored, not to use it as a step-up to the fuel tank. Cadet pilot Ivan McLannahan about to fly with one of the civilian fitters at 19 EFTS Vinden. Ivan McLannahan

Having dumped his parachute onto a grassless, sandy surface, the instructor of DH.82C '55' took this photograph of his pupil chatting with a civilian engineer. *The Aeroplane*

personnel, although administration was a Canadian responsibility. Having seen the system into operation, Canada offered to accept more RAF schools in addition to the 36 EATS facilities which had been established by the end of 1940, but on the condition that training aircraft should be built locally.

Discussion on the merits of transferring Elementary Flying Training Schools to Canada had been a high agenda item since 1939, when the expenses surrounding an average 25% wastage rate had been sufficient to rule out the prospect.

With the establishment of SFTS in Canada, and continuous training possible in the same country, new RAF elementary units were opened from June 1941: 31 EFTS Calgary (later De Winton); 32 EFTS Swift Current (later Bowden); 33 EFTS Caron; 34 EFTS Assiniboia; 35 EFTS Neepawa and 36 EFTS Pearce. Nos 31 and 32 EFTS were established with Boeing PT-17 Stearman, but even with a cockpit canopy, the type was unsuited to the extremes of climate suffered on the Canadian Prairies, and all were eventually replaced by DH.82C Tiger Moths.

Following Japan's unexpected entry into the war from December 1941, a major review of air training policy in North America was undertaken at a conference held in Ottawa in May 1942, a conference which extended its remit to cover all Commonwealth training on a global scale. The result was signature on 1st July of a revised Agreement valid until 31st March 1945, under which the administration of all RAF schools in Canada and all EATS schools, would be merged and transferred to the RCAF under a new umbrella: The British Commonwealth Air Training Plan (BCATP). All the RAF Elementary Flying Training Schools were to be operated on a daily basis by civilian contractors, much as the EATS schools already were, although all flying instruction would be provided by RAF personnel.

DH.82C Tiger Moths were operational at 23 Canadian based Elementary Schools from 1940, in addition to four Wireless Schools, replacing the Fleet Finches at eight, an aircraft which had at one time appeared to pose a serious threat to the Tiger Moth in Canada. Having delivered 1,520 'C' models between April 1940 and September 1942, the Canadian Government was already well advanced in seeking a replacement, eventually choosing the Fairchild PT-26 Cornell, a wooden winged monoplane which was built in Canada as part of the United States' Mutual Aid Program, and introduced to the elementary schools from November 1942. The re-equipment process worked progressively through the system until June 1944, replacing Tiger Moths at eleven stations. Of the remaining 12 schools, six had disbanded during the summer of 1942, pre-Cornell, and the other six retained Tiger Moths until BCATP was to all intents closed down in 1944.

The Assistant CFI at 33 EFTS Caron early in 1942 was Leslie Gosling, a pilot who had trained on DH.60 Moths in the 'twenties with the London Aeroplane Club at Stag Lane. His personal aircraft, RCAF1120 (DHC 1323), carried a skull and crossbones on the black engine cowling, intended, he thought, to deter over-confident pupils about to take their CFI test. After Gosling nosed the aircraft into a snowbank while taxying, the death's head disappeared and was quickly replaced by a figure of an ostrich with its head in the sand, and a legend: *The Gostrich*. When 1120 was posted to 31 EFTS De Winton, replaced in January 1943 by a Cornell, she was flown by pupil pilot Roy Day who had completed Grading on Tiger Moths in England at Brough. In 1949, Gosling was captain of a British South American Airways Avro York freighter operating Heathrow to British Guiana; the First Officer was Roy Day.

In stark contrast to the heat and dust of Southern Africa which attacked and degraded fabric and engines, and the dampness of Great Britain, the Canadian aircraft which were obliged to remain picketed in the open when not in use, were the victims of attack by snow or savage temperatures which were more acceptably tolerable when the sky was blue due to the dry nature of the atmosphere. Used to such regular conditions, aircrew, groundcrew and aircraft all dressed suitably for the season. Thick coats were especially necessary when in strong, freezing wind conditions, any attempt was made to prepare Tiger Moths which were literally flying at the end of their tethering wires.

RCAF DH.82C 4329 operating from 33 EFTS Caron over a snow covered landscape with the rear canopy open, possibly during the exhaust fume scare. In compensation, the pilot has his fleecy collar turned up and is favouring sunglasses rather than goggles. John Pearson

Post war, DH.82C C-GXGS was operated for a summer season in Canada with the whole of the canopy removed excepting the windscreen, and without any apparent ill effects. Bill Wiswell

The sliding canopy of the DH.82C was a great protector from the weather, but on pleasant days one half could be slipped back on its rails. The type could be flown solo from either seat, although the rear position was the one usually occupied in this configuration. It was also possible to fly the aircraft with no canopy at all, relying on the adequately wide front windscreen for total protection. Pilots who operated the aircraft with the canopy removed likened it to flying in a bath, but the practice was not acceptable to the military users, and was mostly reserved for youthful experimentation after the war.

The canopy shielded hidden dangers too. Operating from 19 EFTS Vinden during the establishment's first winter, 1941/1942, one pupil was unlucky enough to lose his entire canopy when flying aerobatics. The aircraft was remarkably undamaged, but the pupil's unprotected face subsequently suffered frostbite to cheeks and nose. It was to be a not uncommon occurrence. The canopy was held in the closed position by two Pirelli webbing straps fixed over studs attached to the front windscreen, and any aerobatic manoeuvre with the canopy partially or accidentally open was not recommended. Part of the solo pre-flight check was to ensure that the canopy was clipped shut.

Operating at 31 EFTS De Winton in January 1943, Roy Day found his canopy had worked loose and was tending to creep back. As the temperature on the ground was -50°F, all flights were restricted to 60 minutes. At lower temperatures, flying was cancelled, and some instructors would place thermometers outside their bedroom windows to give them some warning of the morning's likely agenda. In such low temperatures and especially in high wind speeds, pupils would fly 20 minutes downwind and leave 40 minutes to claw their way back to base. Roy Day's canopy came adrift after 30 minutes' flight on a calm day. Attempting to hold the canopy closed by placing flat hands on the side panels caused extreme discomfort, even though he was wearing the equipment of the day: silk inners, woolly gloves and leather gauntlets.

Shortly after the first DH.82C Tiger Moths were delivered by school instructors from the Air Depot at Calgary to 33 EFTS Caron in December 1941, a serious accident occurred which was attributed to exhaust fumes entering the cockpit. For a time in 1942, all Tiger Moths operating from Caron did so with the rear portion of the cockpit canopy removed. John Pearson was detailed to fly an engineer carrying gas detection apparatus, and on 4th February with both parts of the canopy firmly closed, they trundled around the sky in a series of one hour trials, adopting a variety of flying attitudes. Without knowledge of any official results, Pearson was posted away, but Thomas Madigan who arrived at 33 EFTS early in 1943 realised the problem had been solved when he found that all the Tiger Moths had been replaced with Cornells. As there was no further reported trouble with suspected exhaust leakage, the theory is that the accident had occurred to a rogue aircraft, probably with a cracked heater muff.

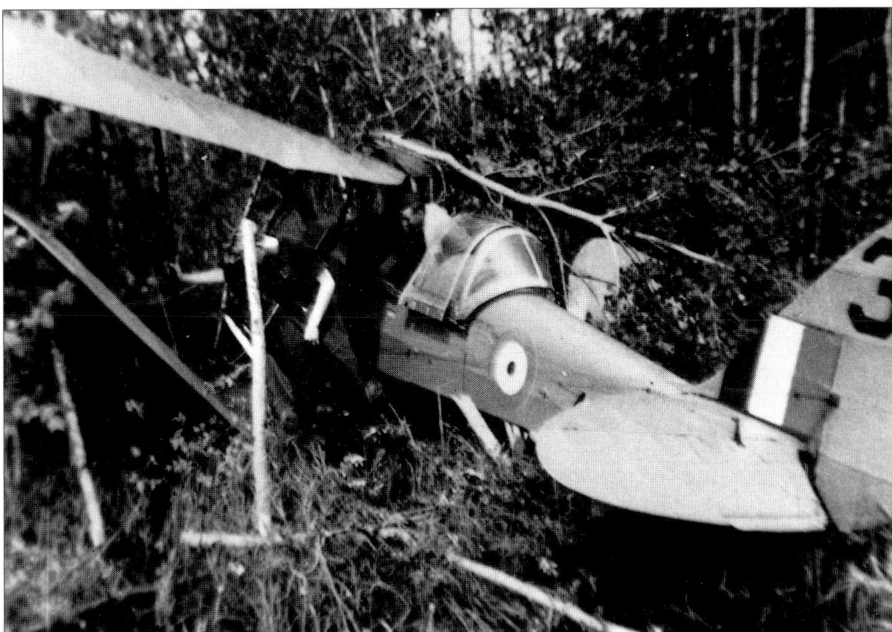

The civilian salvage crew assess the difficulty of the task before attempting to retrieve RCAF DH.82C Tiger Moth 4979, thought to have been operating with 20 EFTS Oshawa in 1941. via Watt Martin

Instead of clearing snow from grass runways, the winter temperatures permitted it to be rolled and hard packed, and wheeled operations continued as usual, with pupil pilots needing to make neat judgements when landing between the markers. The icy surfaces often resulted in completely uncontrollable but elegant ground loops with the occasional loss of an undercarriage, but otherwise the wheeled chassis was preferred. At De Winton, a Chinook wind blowing in from the Pacific and across the Rocky Mountains could quickly raise local temperatures by up to 30°F, converting rolled surfaces into lakes of slush.

In February 1943 some Tiger Moths were fitted with skis, a new challenge to pilot and instructor alike, and a configuration in which it was difficult to taxy on anything less than take-off power. Progress was erratic when attempting to travel in a straight line in any appreciable crosswind and if one ski hit a watery patch, the aircraft tended to rotate like a wounded fly until it could be broken free. Once airborne, the leading edges of the skis stabilised in a neutral position but the vibration and noise were considered to be unacceptable. Under such conditions, De Winton's remedy was to cancel flying and send everybody on leave until civilian contractors had cleared the runways, leaving some pupils to cope with their first landings on grass.

At 35 EFTS Neepawa, a rapid thaw could set in within the endurance of a short cross country flight, and touching down on a conventional undercarriage caused the wheels to break through the top of the mushy surface when the aircraft was arrested almost within its own length. From such a predicament, taxying back to dispersal was quite impossible, and it was an uncomfortable walk for any pilot not wearing regulation boots.

By the end of 1943, further expansion of the RAF was believed to be unnecessary, in favour of resources directed towards the Army, and a revised agreement was signed in February 1944 to reduce the size of the BCATP. Almost immediately, six elementary schools were served notice of closure, and in one classic case the school was advised by the local grapevine before receiving notification through official channels. The overall rundown of the training programme was effected with great rapidity, and in July 1944, all eager recruits at 20 EFTS Oshawa were paraded and advised that they would be permitted 12 hours dual instruction but no solo time. Most hours were preciously recorded in note books as official flying logs never were provided.

Canada's War Assets Corporation (WAC) took administrative charge of each aircraft following receipt of approval for its disposal, passed down through the appropriate command structure, at which time the stock was offered for sale. Many of the Tiger Moths declared surplus in 1944 did not reach new civil owners until well into 1945,

Ski equipped RCAF DH.82C Tiger Moth 5173 at 10 EFTS Pendleton, warming up against snow chocks while the low sun betrays the presence of the groundcrew and their camera. via Watt Martin

This shot of DH.82C CF-BUM was taken between 1946 and 1948. The aircraft had originally been RCAF 9654, taken on charge in July 1942 and serving at 9 EFTS St Catharines and 20 EFTS Oshawa, until sold in May 1945 with a total logged time of 1,402 hours. via Watt Martin

DH.82C Tiger Moth CF-FUG moored on Lake Winnebago sporting a pair of Edo floats. Originally fitted with a Menasco engine in RCAF service, the aircraft had accumulated only 762 hours between March 1941 and her sale in October 1946. Howard Levy

possibly as a result of official procrastination, or prolonged political discussion concerning the declared intent of the government to offer 600 DH.82C Tiger Moths to the world market at the rate of 100 aircraft per month. In the event sales were more limited: a pair went to Israel and six were sold to Iceland in 1945, via an American agent working out of New Jersey.

The Icelandic aircraft were all registered between July and October 1945, and apart from minor alterations to the colour schemes which included stencilling civil registration letters on the fuselage sides, they were operated in standard Canadian configuration by the Cumulus Flying School in Reykjavik and the Akureyrar Flying School at Akureyri in the north of the island. TF-KAV (DHC 1822), was operated as a tug by the Iceland Gliding Club at Reykjavik but crashed on take off from Sandskeid in September 1952. The aircraft was rebuilt by July 1954 but remained in commission only for one more year before her last flight in August 1955. TF-KAV was placed in store for eight years but was finally burned in 1963.

Three other aircraft were written off in 1952, 1954 and 1959. TF-KBE (DHC1353), was sold to Sweden in 1961 but was never registered there. TF-KBD (DHC1407), was stored following non renewal of her C of A in July 1955, and remained in Iceland after acquisition by an expatriate owner living in Alaska and later Texas. In December 1987, TF-KBD was sold to new owners in Akureyri for restoration to airworthy condition. A seventh DH.82C Tiger Moth, TF-ABC was registered in July 1946, although her previous Canadian identity was misquoted. Operated by the Cumulus Flying School from July 1947, and painted all over red with large white 'rounded' style registration letters on the fuselage sides, the aircraft crashed on the ice-overed Lake Ellidavatn in February the following year, and was not repaired.

By August 1945 the WAC was credited with the sale of 389 Tiger Moths each with a spare engine and sufficient parts to keep the aircraft serviceable on estimates, for two years. It was suggested that $2,400,000 had been raised from the sales, a sum far in excess of any average price demanded elsewhere. The Royal Canadian Flying Clubs Association bought 200 Tiger Moths on behalf of its 22 constituent members, and sold them on at cost.

All the Menasco engined Tiger Moths were scrapped except for a handful, as were some high time Gipsy Major examples. Following removal of engine, instruments and wheels, fuselages were piled up and burned, often within the boundary of their base airfield, several of which became storage units after operational flying had ceased. Officially struck off charge on 23rd January 1945, 50 DH.82C Tiger Moths bearing construction plates identifying them as

PT-24s of the United States Army Air Force, were destroyed in this manner at Goderich, former home of 12 EFTS. The unit was disbanded on 14th July 1944 having operated only Tiger Moths since March 1942, when Fleet Finches had been displaced. The dump site became a haven for souvenir hunters over the years especially during the winter when it was more easily accessible by ski. It was a regular attraction for John Hindmarsh, a former instructor at Goderich who still lived locally and kept his own Tiger Moth on the same airfield until as he put it, he flew it into the only tall tree in the Province. As thick vegetation grew and matured in and around the cast-off remains, a surprising number of restorable parts was liberated and carried lovingly away for re-use.

To stimulate British exports, de Havilland had opened a branch office in Karachi in 1928 to handle increasing sales of the DH.60 Moth, and before the war, some privately owned Tiger Moths were shipped to India, together with several more intended for use by the flying clubs, already good customers for de Havilland products, and which acted to some degree, in the capacity of a government sponsored reserve.

More civil registered Tiger Moths were imported at the beginning of the war following an order placed on de Havilland at Hatfield by the Indian Government. The aircraft were subsequently built and shipped by Morris Motors and test flown at Cowley wearing civil registrations in September and October 1940. The 27 aircraft order, VT-AMI to VT-ANI, had been built in seven small batches integrated with RAF orders, taking build positions between 83571 and 83746. After delivery, a handful of the aircraft was impressed and military serial numbers allocated. A few others met well-documented ends, but the majority were simply cancelled from the civil register at various times, probably recruited by the Indian Air Force.

In addition to receiving second hand civil Tiger Moths in 1940 supplied by aircraft broker W S Shackleton, the British Government re-equipped the Bristol Aeroplane Company's 10 EFTS when it relocated from Yatesbury to Weston-super-Mare in September 1940, after dispatching the whole of the old fleet to India, where the aircraft took up consecutive civil letters in the block VT-ANU to VT-AOP. An additional 33 Tiger Moths were supplied as civil registered aircraft from de Havilland Australia between January and August 1941, DHA237-249; 252-254; 361-368; 370-376 and 508-517. All were delivered via the RAF Depot at Karachi with the exception of DHA252-254 which avoided the perilous voyage round the southern tip of India and were delivered directly to the Madras Flying Club as VT-ANN, VT-ANQ and VT-ANO. Of the Karachi imports, DHA370 became VT-AQE, but was later allocated military marks LR236, and operated by the Royal Indian Air Force Volunteer Reserve with No 1 Coastal Defence Flight (CDF) at St. Thomas Mount, Madras.

Masquerading as a Royal Navy 'A' model Tiger Moth at Old Rhinebeck, New York, for many years, DH.82C N8731R, formerly RCAF 9690, was one of the last batch of DH.82Cs delivered in September 1942 to the new home of 10 EFTS at Pendleton. The aircraft flew only 580 hours with the Air Force before sale into the civil market in July 1945. deHMC Archive

Thirty three Tiger Moths, a trio of Hawker Harts, 3,000 tons of cement, 175 tons of tobacco, ten horses and a brand new Rolls-Royce listed as a Silver Phantom were part of the cargo of the SS *Breda,* a 7,000 ton Dutch ship operated during the war by the P & O Shipping Company. She had loaded at Southend with goods bound for Mombasa, Bombay and Karachi, and departed on 12th December 1940 to rendezvous with a convoy forming at the Lynn of Lorn near Oban in Scotland. Whilst marshalling there, the unprotected ships were attacked by two Luftwaffe Heinkel He 111 bombers on 22nd December 1940, and the *Breda,* badly damaged by blast from a bomb which exploded in the water alongside, was towed into the protection of Ardmucknish Bay where she sank in 100ft of water.

Although a salvage effort was attempted both before and after the ship went down, the aircraft cargo was not recovered although the horses and the Rolls-Royce were. The Tiger Moths are believed to have been scheduled originally for delivery to Kenya which would explain the call at Mombasa, but the manifest suggests the aircraft and spares were consigned to the RAF in India.

In 1975, part of the wreck was explored by members of the Royal Navy's Air Command Sub Aqua Club, more in hope than in anticipation of proving the rumour that the 33 Tiger Moths had all been packed in watertight containers, and were accompanied by a clutch of spare Gipsy Major engines. In that part of the ship the expedition managed to reach they did find the remains of seven Tiger Moth fuselages, free standing and completely corroded, plus some engines but no sign of the Harts. As evidence of their underwater adventure, a number of heavily protected Gipsy Major induction manifolds was brought to the surface, and presented to the Royal Navy Historic Aircraft Flight at Yeovilton, where underneath the grease and oiled wrapping, they were found to be in perfect order.

Several of the 208 new production Tiger Moths sent from Great Britain in RAF markings during 1943 and 1944 adopted civil letters on arrival and were operated by flying clubs on behalf of the Government of India. Unlike the losses suffered by shipments to South Africa, only one Tiger Moth, DE238 (85284), is believed to have been lost at sea, in March 1943. British deliveries were routed to Bombay where the aircraft were collected from the docks alongside crated Hawker Hurricanes, and carried by tank transporters to Santa Cruz airport, about ten miles from Juhu, where Tata Industries had been contracted to assemble them. The Tiger Moths were test flown and subsequently collected from Santa Cruz by service ferry pilots from 229 Group and air delivered into the vastness of the sub-continent.

Although some Tiger Moth spares were manufactured in India on behalf of the de Havilland Company, a plan for production of 239 new Tiger Moths in Bombay was not proceeded with, and RAF serials in the BS and BT blocks which had been set aside were neither taken up nor re-allocated to another type. Although there is no record of

DH.82C Tiger Moth CF-BHK showing a distinct flattening of the top rudder bow and cable attachment to the steerable tailskid ski, flying near Milton, Ontario during the early 'seventies. In 1984 the aircraft was sold to a 37,000 hour pilot based in Florida, and converted to open cockpit configuration. Watt Martin

Two of the few DH.82C Tiger Moths ever sold out of North America: TF-KAD and TF-KAE were registered to Flugskoli Akureyrar in Iceland during September 1945. deHMC Archive

Tiger Moths being supplied directly to the Indian Air Force before the war, in March 1940 five IAF Tiger Moths were presented to the press at the Risalpur Training School. The 'K' letter in the serial numbers (K1778, K1780, K1782, K1783 and K1784), had been applied erroneously when the aircraft were taken on charge by the IAF from whatever source, a fact which led to much historical confusion.

To some extent the aircraft at Risalpur pre-dated the post-war RAF training markings by carrying broad yellow bands around the rear fuselages, but were otherwise painted silver overall. Later, all military marked Tiger Moths operating in India took up standard brown and green camouflage, although the civil registered machines remained a rather insipid yellow.

The Indian authorities were keen to impress upon 1939's correspondents that due to a rapidly developing expansion scheme, scores of volunteers from all ethnic backgrounds would be selected and trained to the highest standards enjoyed by pilots in the Royal Air Force. To further speed the training of Indian pilots, courses were later arranged in Great Britain, and 20 ERFTS which had been closed down at Gravesend on the outbreak of war, was reformed for the purpose at Yeadon, operating Tiger Moths between March 1941 and January 1942.

The varied operational life of an RAF Tiger Moth in India was identified by the late Reginald Sansome in his book *The Bamboo Workshop*, the history of the RAF's Repair and Salvage Units (RSU) in India and Burma between 1941 and 1946. The type was used by nearly all units for the transfer of supplies and personnel, collection of urgently needed spares, and for locating aircraft reported to have put down in otherwise totally inaccessible areas. Damage reports and surveys were quickly executed by Technical Officers flown in to and out of the nearest convenient clearings, movements ripe for their own accident potential.

A Hawker Hurricane had forced landed near Kaladan early in 1944 and the Technical Officer of No 3 RSU flew out from Dhoapalong in the unit's Tiger Moth to inspect the aircraft, landing as close to the scene as was possible. During his survey a flight of RAF Dakotas arrived overhead and proceeded to drop supplies to the local army garrison, unaware of the camouflaged Tiger Moth dispersed below. The aircraft was struck squarely on the starboard upper mainplane by what her beleaguered pilot described as a crate of bully beef. The rations fell right through the wing, shearing a mainspar, and the container embedded itself in the starboard lower. The pilot managed to return to base after hitching a ride with an army convoy, and the Tiger Moth was later recovered by his own Salvage Unit.

When a mobile detachment arrived at the scene of a reported Supermarine Spitfire crash near Pyingaung, they found a second, unreported Spitfire lying alongside the first in a much better condition, and having dismantled and removed what could be reasonably expected, they set off back to base. On the banks of the Chindwin River they came across an abandoned Tiger Moth. The effects of what appeared to have been a zero option forced landing were evident in a fractured rear fuselage and a lower wing which had been torn off, but space was found on the Chevrolet transporter to carry the remains, including a valuable Gipsy Major engine. Due to a shortage of trained engineers and tradesmen, and an enormous increase in activity, technical surveys were of necessity very harsh, and more aircraft were categorised as non-repairable than might normally have been the case. The rescued Tiger Moth became a bonus supply of spare parts.

No 3 RSU's own Tiger Moth, NL708 (86191) described as being 'rather battered', was exchanged for a North American Harvard 2B, FS988, following a visit by Flying and Engineering Group Liaison Officers early in 1945. NL708 was flown away for servicing elsewhere and was one of the 14 aircraft which survived to be presented to the newly independent Indian Air Force in October 1947.

No 1 RSU (India) was established at Asanol, about 120 miles from Calcutta in February 1941, and amongst the Vickers Wellingtons, Bristol Blenheims and Westland Lysanders rotating through the unit for regular servicing and repair were sundry communications aircraft including Tiger Moths. At least one of these aircraft was always unofficially available to the Chief Technical Officer (CTO), for duty as a unit hack, and on 11th May 1941, a Tiger Moth had been despatched to Ranchi to collect spares and other essential supplies.

During their return to Asanol, the crew sighted what was not an uncommon local phenomenon in the form of a dust storm. On this occasion the swirl appeared to be of great intensity, and heading straight for the airfield. Although the Tiger Moth was landed expeditiously, there was insufficient time to warn each dispersal to take protective measures, and during its ten minute passage, what had developed into a fully developed cyclone caused considerable damage to seven Blenheims, a Wellington and a Hurricane which flew away after being lifted off its trestles. The Tiger Moth was found about a mile from where she had been parked, lying upside down with a buckled undercarriage and four broken wings: a total loss.

Not all accidents and incidents were attributable to enemy action or the sometimes precarious state of the weather in which aircraft were expected to fly. After months of work, the repair units were occasionally witness to accidents involving their most recent charges. Tiger Moth Z-02 of the Burmese Volunteer Air Force (BVAF), operating on behalf of 221 Group Communications Flight, was lost at Asanol on 6th September 1942. The engine stopped and the aircraft dived into the ground from 100ft immediately after take off for a routine air test following servicing. The pilot and his passenger were injured but the Tiger Moth was written off.

The BVAF operated four Tiger Moths, two built in Australia (DHA250/251), and two British built examples which had been exported from Hatfield as civil machines early in 1940, XY-AAB (82874) and XY-AAC (82875). The two Australian aircraft became Z-03 and Z-04 from January 1941 on delivery to the Defence Department in Rangoon, but were transferred to the RAF's 224 Group Communications Flight in 1942 and were both written off in landing accidents at Dum Dum, Calcutta, in July and September that same year. It is not known which markings were taken up by the two British built machines, but to complete the elimination of the quartet, Z-01 crashed into the sea as the result of running her wheels into sand dunes after take off from Cox's Bazaar in June 1943.

When a Dakota forced landed near Manmon on 14th March 1944, the Commanding Officer of 132 RSU together with the unit's test pilot, flew into the site from Imphal in Tiger Moth DE725 (85655), with the object of surveying the transport and assessing the possibility of flying her out. The Tiger Moth was official unit property, a new aircraft, and between them the two crew contrived to wreck her on landing, leaving them both stranded and without communication. The pair subsequently took three days to get back to base by walking, fording rivers, commandeering mules and riding in an army jeep, before collection by Dakota from Tamu. The following day, much to their chagrin, 132 RSU was advised that the stranded Dakota and the wrecked Tiger Moth had both been destroyed during target practice by one of the locally based Hurricane squadrons.

In May 1943, Squadron Leader Frank Godber finished an operational tour on Consolidated Catalinas and was posted to command RAF Vizagapatam, a large base situated between Calcutta and Madras, and which with the associated port facilities was being prepared for prospective operations against Japan. Apart from the airfield which accommodated no aircraft, the Commander was responsible for two additional aerodromes, a wireless unit and several radar sites, and in order to expedite his business, was supplied with Tiger Moth DE372 (85401), from the Communications Flight of the Air Force Headquarters at Bangalore.

'This Tiger Moth was my delight and it was not long before the Navy and the Army saw that it could be useful as well. Of course it had no wireless so the Navy made me some canvas purses with snap fasteners on them and three feet of coloured bunting to make them easy to see.

'The radar stations were beginning to get blips out to sea which they could not explain. Accordingly they would telephone me and give me a bearing and distance which could be 20 miles out to sea. I would drive down to the airfield, take off in the Tiger Moth and fly to the radar site and thence down the bearing looking for possible radar reflectors. Usually they turned out to be close gatherings of the local open fishing boats in sufficient quantity to show up on radar. On returning towards the coast I wrote details of the sighting on my note pad, put it in a purse and as I passed over the Senior Naval Officer's headquarters by the harbour, I threw the purse down on the forecourt whence a rating would retrieve it.

'In February 1944 things got more dramatic. My old squadron commander, Group Captain G A V Clayton happened to be visiting me at the time and we had a high ranking crew in a low powered aircraft doing what can only be described as operational flying. I remember trying to get an MTB to follow me to a torpedoed ship, and the following day went out to inspect an oil slick from a submarine, suspected sunk after the torpedo attack'.

The exact fate of DE372 is unrecorded, but she was struck off charge on the last day of October 1946, and was not one of the aircraft transferred to the new Indian Air Force or to the Indian Government as a civil aircraft.

The subject of disposal of RAF Tiger Moths in India was raised at the Air Ministry during a meeting on 8th August 1944 with Sir Frederick Tymms, Director General of Civil Aviation in India (DGCA). Tymms suggested that the flying club movement might require upwards of 100 Tiger Moths if the sale price was pitched at the right level. Five of the original ten pre-war clubs remained operational, working for the government, and lending their facilities to effect overhaul and repair. The five dormant clubs would probably regenerate once peace returned to the region and equipment for civil flying was available.

Two DH.82A Tiger Moths and a pair of DH.60GIII Moth Majors of the Karachi Aero Club in 1943. VT-AKS was a pre-war Indian import, impressed as MA947 in 1943. VT-AOG was registered to the Government of India in 1941, part of the Bristol Reserve School fleet exported from Yatesbury.
de Havilland Aircraft Company Ltd.

The Indian Government had formulated no policy on surpluses of its own, and in spite of the formation of an Indian Disposals Board, it was thought the government owned very little war material itself which would fall into the surplus category. The DGCA believed that the possibility that RAF Tiger Moths might be declared surplus in India was a fact that should be brought to the immediate attention of the government, and he even toyed with the prospect of some being delivered into club hands before the formal declaration of an armistice.

Having been provoked by the Ministry of Aircraft Production (MAP), the Air Ministry confirmed its long established position by a statement issued on 11th May 1945 indicating that the prospect of a surplus situation developing amongst Tiger Moths in India would only be realised as the result of re-equipment with Fairchild Cornells, and unless and until that decision was taken, it was not possible to confirm any sort of figure. By 13th July 1945 the Air Ministry had mellowed very slightly as the result of an approach by the Government of Afghanistan, forwarded through official channels in India.

Afghanistan required a number of trainer aircraft and the Air Staff had ruled out the Miles Magister as being unsuitable, leaving open the prospect for the sale of eight Tiger Moths. The Air Ministry decided it could, after all, release this number of aircraft without need of replacement, and the sale should have priority over any civilian sales in India which might have been under consideration. They assumed there would be no diplomatic or political objection as the Indian Government was aware of the request. MAP, who as primary selling agency should have been involved from the beginning of negotiations, was advised that the agreed price would have to hold good for future sales to the Indian Government, but should not be seen as setting the standard for genuine civil sales in India.

Some thought had been given to providing Afghanistan with aircraft from the surplus in South Africa, but this was countered with a suggestion that they might be supplied from the RAF pool in North Africa, from where they could be delivered by air. The geographical proximity of India made it the ideal and logical donor once the politicking had been resolved, and eight aircraft from RAF storage in India were sold, but not until 25th April 1946. The fact that three of the Tiger Moths carried sequential RAF serial numbers, NL962/3/4, (86394/5/6), must fuel speculation that they were from unissued stock, awaiting assignment. Two others, DE572 (85539) and EM986 (86169), had been delivered new to the RAF in India although no subsequent allocation to a unit can be traced unlike EM780 (85997), which had been listed in service with 1 EFTS (India) at Begumpet.

The day following the London meeting with India's DGCA, Headquarters Air Command South East Asia (ACSEA) signalled the Air Ministry to the effect that they could not release any Tiger Moths. Sir Frederick Tymms was still hopeful of a supply of ex-service aircraft to the flying clubs, and confirmed his view that the 100 Tiger Moths already owned by the Government of India had been 'flown to the limit' and were probably not suitable for economical conversion and operation as true civil aeroplanes.

Prompted, possibly, by the DGCA's further enquiries, ACSEA signalled again on 5th August with their own suggested alternative. Having re-emphasised that they had no surplus 'serviceable' Tiger Moths, they advised that the Command had loaned 30 Tiger Moths to civilian flying clubs primarily to provide targets for silent anti-aircraft gunnery practice, and added that it was open to question whether these 30 were currently being used for the furtherance of the war effort. DGCA was requested to provide confirmation that he would be willing to accept transfer of these aircraft, and to accept full responsibility for their future maintenance.

At the same time, and perhaps guided by impishness as much as genuine curiosity, ACSEA asked to be provided with details of condition and price of the Tiger Moths it understood were currently being offered in southern Africa. ACSEA's reference was probably to the aircraft being advertised in Rhodesia rather than South Africa, although plans for the extraction of 100 Tiger Moths from South Africa were almost certainly being mooted in London at the time. In the event, their transfer was not to be until July the following year, and then was principally on behalf of the Indian Air Force.

Although ACSEA was adamant that under existing responsibilities it could not afford to release a single Tiger Moth, with the exception of the special offer to DGCA, Headquarters of Base Air Forces in Delhi showed concern for the operation of the disposal procedure as practised. On 29th September 1945, they advised the British Secretary of State for Air, that already some 63 surplus American aircraft had been disposed of in the India/Burma/China theatre by the United States Foreign Liquidation Commission. All British sales were referenced through the MAP and Air Ministry in London, and the system was too cumbersome. Unless there was greater flexibility, 'it will be too late', they advised.

Attrition continued to account for some of the scattered fleet. Ferrying a Tiger Moth across India in the summer of 1946 with a passenger in the front cockpit, Derek Piggott was approaching Agra when the Gipsy Major engine failed, having given some reasonable warning of doing so. The pilot overshot his selected field and the wheels of the aircraft hit the bund of a paddy field, arresting the landing run within 30ft but forcing the aircraft onto her nose. Although the obvious damage seemed relatively slight, the sergeant in charge of the salvage party who arrived complete with Queen Mary transporter was more sceptical, and his initial diagnosis after assessing the strains, stresses and visible breakages, was that the Tiger Moth was probably a write-off, and that the pilot should have set it alight to have saved everybody a lot of trouble. Much to the surprise of the Tiger Moth crew, the salvage party cut the aircraft into manageable pieces and threw them all down a disused well.

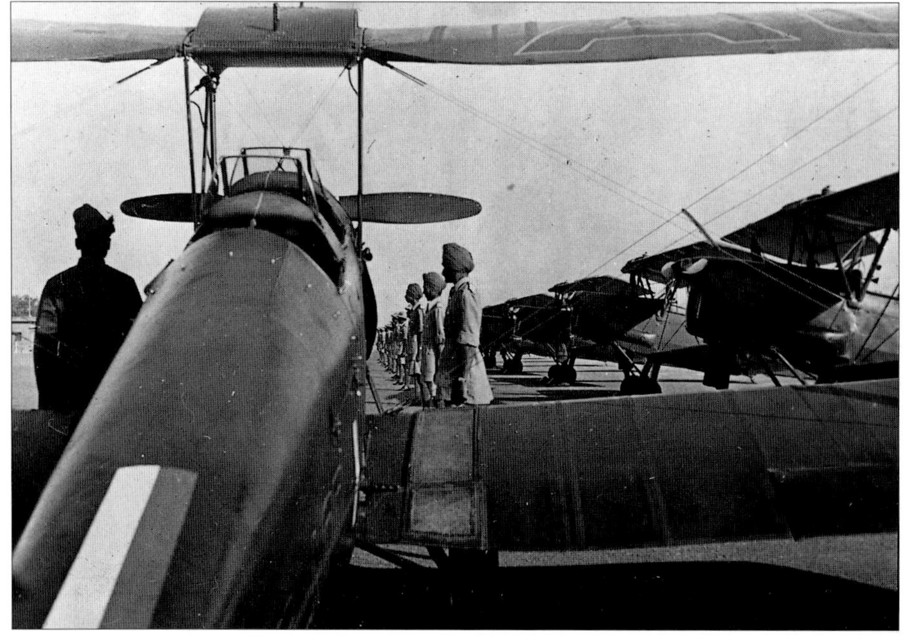

Indian Air Force officer cadet pilots awaiting inspection at a passing out parade in May 1943. All the aircraft carry Indian civil registration letters. deHMC Archive

Far from being a disposal centre, India became a net importer of Tiger Moths after the Japanese war, and there was much administrative tidying to arrange following Independence and Partition on 15th August 1947. Twenty aircraft which had been impressed into RAF service were handed over to the Indian Air Force, although in most cases their original identities had been lost. On 25th September 1947, 27 RAF Tiger Moths were transferred to the IAF followed by 14 more at the end of October. That this was largely a paper exercise is confirmed by the fact that two of the October transfers, DE357 (85379) and NL708 (86191), had already been placed on the Indian civil register as VT-ASL and VT-ATP respectively in March and December 1945.

Seven aircraft from the RAF contingent in the sub continent were transferred to the Pakistan Air Force in September 1947, and a year later six more were added, all second hand civil aircraft sourced in Great Britain by dealers W S Shackleton. Although consigned to the Pakistan Government the aircraft were almost certainly scheduled for duty with the Air Force and their civil status was a tidy manner in which to comply with some diplomatic nicety. In 1948, a further 24 Tiger Moths were supplied, purchased from RAF home stocks by de Havilland, refurbished at Witney, and shipped in May to Karachi.

Of the 207 Tiger Moths landed in wartime India from Great Britain, discounting transfers to the Air Forces of India, Pakistan and Afghanistan, 150 aeroplanes were struck off charge without any formal statement of circumstances. Of the 16 exceptions, one aircraft is credited as a donation to the Hindustan Aircraft factory at Bangalore, where almost certainly this unidentified example was used as an educational tool for the Hindustan workforce, soon to be the recipient of 100 Tiger Moths shipped from South Africa.

Some of the other 'struck off' aircraft appeared on the Indian civil register. EM846 (86048), which served with 1 EFTS (India) was supposedly on strength with Air Command South East Asia on 30th August 1945, yet she had been registered VT-ARP to the Government of India in October 1943. The aircraft was transferred to the Madras Flying Club in June 1946, cancelled in September 1959, rebuilt in August 1971 and re-registered VT-EBP against a new builder's identity: MFC-01-1971. Parts from three other aircraft, one believed to be a Jackaroo, and the engine from a fourth, were all used for the 'rebuild' which must have been comprehensive. Airworthiness was followed by sale to Canada as CF-EIO in 1972, but the aircraft passed south of the border in 1974 and was registered G-BDVI to a British owner living in Texas. The aircraft arrived in England in 1977, but negotiations over property fell through and she returned to Texas to become N982JG with a new owner in Houston in 1985.

The imports from South Africa had been gathered together in Cape Town, half of a 200 strong hand picked selection from the RAF's residual share of the assets of the Joint Air Training Scheme: 88 British built airframes and 12 of Australian origin. Although officially transferred from South Africa in July 1946, some at least of the 100 dismantled aircraft did not arrive in India until the end of February 1947, and were credited to the Hindustan Aircraft Company only from 27th November, a series of delays which might be attributed to the massive and rapid administrative changes occurring in the country.

The aircraft were overhauled at Bangalore and slowly fed into the IAF system from which the first were released to civilian use as early as 1948, and replaced in turn, many finding their way into club use in batches during 1956,1959 and throughout the early 'sixties. About 30 civilian aircraft can subsequently be identified as originating from within the South African shipment and at least three were of Australian manufacture.

A dusty looking Tiger Moth, EM918, on charge with the Indian Air Force at Comilla in August 1944, complete with primed Holt flares under the wings. Howard Levy

Part of the collection of 11 complete aircraft and tons of spares that had arrived in England from India by 1980. Most airframes were painted yellow overall with 'green trainer bands' and all were civil registered. Peter Bish

In Indian Air Force use, all these aircraft were allocated 'HU' serials, but later overhaul outside the military was often the cause for substitution of revised identities, a practice common among the flying clubs who allocated tags based on the initial letters of the club name, the date, and a numerical count of all overhaul and rebuild/repair projects previously to have gone through the shops. The Hindustan Aircraft Company is understood to have allocated overhaul of wings or fuselages to different parts of the factory, drawing main components as required from the general stock for re-assembly into whole aeroplanes. Frequently, overhaul could be defined as rigging an amalgam of parts essential to the creation of a new aeroplane with a new identity in a new logbook.

In 1947, Hangar 10 at Chakeri Air Force Base, famous as the last resting place for hundreds of Consolidated Liberators, was in receipt of numerous Tiger Moths which arrived from all over the sub-continent, delivered in a dismantled and often damaged condition on board Air Force Dakotas. From the best parts, whole aircraft were reconstructed, painted yellow overall, and delivered into the care of the Indian Air Force at 1 EFTS Begumpet and 2 EFTS Jodphur. The Tiger Moths were of mixed British and Australian manufacture in the EM, NL and DG serial batches, although there is evidence that, some of the pre-war civilian aircraft impressed into RAF service in 1941 with serials in the DP range, were still active at 2 EFTS, operating in Indian military markings.

Most of the club aircraft were flown at heavily subsidised rates by civilians aiming for a career with the Air Force or the airlines, and in late 1946 the government took whole page advertisements in national newspapers encouraging people to apply for flying training. Although there was no distinction between Indian nationals and Europeans, immediately after Independence and without warning, the flying rates for non-nationals was raised by 500%, indicating, perhaps, the level of subsidy that was being paid.

The climate encouraged pilots to fly in a relaxed manner, often wearing short sleeved, open necked shirts, and the civilian accident rate steadily rose, largely due to unauthorised low flying, often resulting in fatalities. In an effort to stop the practice, instructors randomly hid barographs on board which could be scrutinised on return, and the culprits subjected to disciplinary action. The long and unspoilt beaches of southern India were a temptation for the pilots of the Madras Flying Club, and on 16th August 1952, VT-AMC (3664), a used aircraft supplied from England by W S Shackleton in March 1940, was comprehensively wrecked when it hit the beach and turned over. The two club members were not seriously hurt, but afterwards each admitted that they thought the other was in command. One said that his admiration for the other's daring was suddenly shattered by the crash.

Not all incidents occurred at low level: VT-DBZ (84258), was another W S Shackleton import, this time from ex-RAF stocks held in England, shipped after Independence, joining the Bengal Flying Club at Barrackpore in July 1949. The aircraft made news when a collision with a soaring vulture on 5th April 1952 demolished a large portion of the port upper wing. Repairs were effected and the aircraft remained in service until December 1955 when she was written off in a landing accident at Calcutta.

A Tiger Moth registered VT-DGA to the Madhya Pradesh Flying Club in February 1952, quoted her previous identity as 'Indian Air Force' and builder's number CPF/FU /79. The aircraft subsequently passed to the Nagpur Flying Club and may have suffered an accident, for a further major rebuild was recorded in 1955 during the course of which substantial parts of the following aircraft were grafted on: VT-CUL (DHA883) and VT-CUJ (DHA890), both of which had been exported from the Newcastle Aero Club in Australia in 1948; Indian Air Force HU861, later VT-DEQ, origin unknown, written off in 1951; VT-DDQ (84477), ex T8185 from South Africa, written off in July 1958; VT-DDN (85453) ex DE457 from South Africa, not reported as cancelled; VT-DDO (85517) ex DE550 from South Africa, written off in August 1957 and VT-CUF (85526) ex DE559 from South Africa, written off in 1952.

Several of the donor aircraft remained operational after the rebuilding schedule of 1955, in which case each would have become net recipients of parts from other sources to make up the deficiency! Although cancellation dates can be purely for administrative convenience, some write-off dates are attributable to documented accidents. Laid up in 1966, VT-DGA was one of many Tiger Moths offered for sale by an Indian based aircraft sales agency, Vintair, which targeted Europe, the USA and Canada. Most of their Tiger Moth stock was scattered around the sub continent, the aircraft staked out open to the weather, with time expired engines. VT-DGA was surveyed in 1978 by an engineer flown out specially from England, as the result of which the aircraft was shipped back to Yorkshire. Following a period of storage, registration G-BHUM was allocated in June 1980 and the aircraft rebuilt in Lincolnshire from 1983, to qualify for a Certificate of Airworthiness in May 1984.

As part of a deal involving the purchase of abandoned and decoy Supermarine Spitfires, 12 whole Tiger Moths and a vast collection of new spare parts were offered for sale in India in 1979. One airframe in poor condition was donated to a childrens' playground, but the remainder was shipped to storage at Shipdham aerodrome, Norfolk, and although little effort was made to supply complete aircraft to the market, the huge volume of spares has satisfied customers on a global scale ever since, perhaps the last major source of new and original Tiger Moth parts. Perhaps!

Ex-Indian Tiger Moth VT-DOW standing in the snow at Felthorpe in March 1981 where as G-BINH she was the leased property of the local Flying Group. Badly smashed during low level aerobatics only a month later, she was rebuilt probably using an ex-India fuselage, but crashed again after engine failure in 1984 and was written off. Gordon Poulter

BACK TO THE DRAWING BOARD

Aerobatting a Tiger Moth in the southern hemisphere is no different from anywhere else! Cliff Bellingham was caught during a barrel roll in ZK-ARJ over New Zealand's Pukekohe countryside. John King

In Canada, most DH.60 Moths and later DH.82 type Tiger Moths were 'winterised', a procedure which usually implied the building on of a cockpit canopy, and the addition of other comforts. What powerful force directed some post-war owners of DH.82C model Tiger Moths to abandon their sliding canopies and heaters, and 'convert' their aeroplanes to open cockpit configuration, complete with brass framed windscreens and built-in draughts? The lure of open cockpit flying is ever present, and a Canadian summer provides just as great an opportunity for shirt sleeved enjoyment high above the madding crowd as anywhere.

Canopies fitted to Tiger Moths were essentially in aid of comfort with a bonus in efficiency due to the elimination of some drag, but at the expense of extra weight and a battle with the authorised limits for the centre of gravity (CG). Field performance was often improved.

In Great Britain during the late 'twenties, de Havilland gained experience by converting several DH.60 Moths into Coupe Moths using mostly ugly superstructures, and frequently they were used for racing. Generally, the configuration proved to be unpopular, especially with the ladies, and most were re-converted to open cockpits, including Captain Geoffrey de Havilland's personal DH.60G Moth, G-AAAA.

In New Zealand, six Tiger Moths were modified at Rongotai in1943/1944 to accept either a permanent hinged or sliding canopy structure for aircraft allocated to the Air Training Corps Touring Flight. Transiting was more comfortable for the staff pilots, but taxying the aircraft called for extra vigilance with no view immediately ahead and only limited vision through the side panels, a situation demanding energetic use of the rudder bar. For ATC cadets, often flying for the first time, a comfortable cockpit was a gentle baptism, but then there was no requirement to dress up with leather jacket, helmet and goggles which surely was all part of the ritual, although most cadets, and pilots, still did.

During the conversions at Rongotai, contact was made both with Hatfield and Downsview seeking assurances on CG positions and allowable locker loads due to the redistribution of fuselage weight. It was not possible to read Canada's limits directly across to the New Zealand built DH.82A

Super Tiger G-AOAA *The Deacon* at Hatfield for the start of the Famous Grouse Rally to Scotland in July 1979. In order to achieve the required range when carrying a passenger on a sling seat in the front cockpit, main fuel was removed to an auxiliary tank in a cradle mounted on the centre section. Air Portraits

Below: **New Zealand Tiger Moth NZ859 with the early design of side hinged canopy, photographed at Ohakea in August 1944.** RNZAF

although Downsview's advice was that with their canopied aeroplane, it was wise never to exceed a maximum load of 40lb in the locker. Rongotai's signal to Hatfield was more specific quoting a CG position with canopy of 28.9in when loaded to 1,700lb, which they achieved on paper with two crew but only half oil and petrol, a figure way aft of the approved limit in normal configuration. Also, New Zealand's figures showed that with two crew or a pilot operating from the rear seat, no load was permissible in the locker, but 60lb could be carried if the front seat only was occupied.

Any limitations imposed by the canopy appear to have been absorbed. John Neave, de Havilland New Zealand's test pilot, flew Tiger Moth NZ859 (82341), with an early design of side-hinged canopy in August 1944. The style proved more popular than the previously fitted sliding versions similar to the Canadian design, provided a quieter cockpit and was immune to partial loss in flight. The trial canopy on NZ859 was later improved by adding six times the area of perspex in the rear window and incorporating sliding panels in the port side for ventilation and 'clear view'.

Rongotai capitalised on their design postwar by selling drawings or offering to fit canopies in their works at an installed price of £50 if the job was completed during qualification for a Certificate of Airworthiness (C of A), but more than twice that if booked in at any other time. The Civil Aviation Department insisted on a series of flight tests, including spinning with strakes, and Neave was called upon to complete these with ZK-ANG (82429), in March 1947. By May 1950 the aircraft had been converted again: sold by the owner for agricultural use.

In addition to the Rongotai canopies (Mod DH/33), at least four other designs were approved within New Zealand which are known to have been fitted to 24 New Zealand registered Tiger Moths, plus others based in Australia. One aircraft owned personally by John Neave, ZK-ANE (82230), was configured with the canopy covering the rear cockpit only, and operated as an aerial seed sower and between 1948 and 1951, transportation for crayfish and whitebait.

A single position canopy was fitted to the 'Taxi Tiger' G-AOXS (85425), of 1957, when the comfort was reserved for the passenger occupying the front seat. It was another inspired development by Rollason Aircraft, but in all probability very few fares were carried as the aircraft was extensively raced and rallied by the Tiger Club, in whose hands she hit a tree during an aerobatic sortie overhead Dungate Farm near Reigate in February 1960.

At least four other post-war Tiger Moths have been fitted with canopies in Great Britain, all custom made, and all removed by subsequent owners. In 1952, G-AIZF (83635) was converted by H M Woodhams, an early employee with the de Havilland Company at Stag Lane in 1920, later a director of Sir W G Armstrong Whitworth Aircraft at Baginton. But the glazing had long since been removed before an agricultural career began in 1958 and ended in 1964 after numerous misadventures.

G-ANRN (83133), carried a canopy until it was cut off at Swanton Morley in October 1979. On 1st December the aircraft was ferried to Odiham on a day described by the pilot as 'desperately cold', which irony forced him to land at Old Warden en-route in an attempt to thaw out. In the hands of Jonathan Elwes, G-ANRN was later to make spectacularly long open cockpit flights from England to Gibraltar and North Africa, Moscow and the North Cape.

Sold as scrap, ex-RAF Tiger Moth N6944 (82194), was acquired by Doug Bianchi's Personal Plane Services in May 1954, and as G-ANSA qualified for a C of A complete with mainwheel spats and an elaborate canopy a year later. In March 1958 the aircraft was retrieved from the River Mersey by the New Brighton Lifeboat.

Engineer Chris Roberts and his commercial pilot wife Claire, initiated their own charter company 'Chrisair' in August 1957 with Tiger Moth G-AHVU (84728). Fitted with a canopy and operated from a number of sites in the Midlands, southern England and the West Country, the Tiger Moth ranged deep into Europe, aided by a long range tank and wobble pump activated by the

occupant of the front seat. Replaced by a DH.84 Dragon and DH.85 Leopard Moth, the Tiger Moth almost joined the agricultural business in 1963, but entered a long period of storage at Farnborough and Chessington, where she lost contact with her canopy and boudoir style interior decor. She was delivered to Richard Parker at Denham in 1986, joining a collection of military training aircraft, painted in a distinctive and original pre-war camouflage scheme, not recognised for its value by many unfamiliar with pre-war history.

Some of the Tiger Moths operated by the National Flying School at various sites around Belgium were fitted with canopies to improve all-weather comfort, as were a few Stampe SV-4s, all arrangements modelled on the Canadian DH.82C three piece design, built on a very light framework.

In Australia, canopies were most popular immediately after the agricultural revolution, when hinged styles similar to those developed in wartime New Zealand were rivalled only by complete sliding systems removed from surplus CAC Wacketts, an almost perfect match requiring relatively little extra engineering.

The 1,000th Tiger Moth assembled at Mascot, A17-565, had returned from a tour of duty in New Guinea in 1944 and was placed in storage at Cootamundra where she was recommended for conversion to spares in March 1946. The order was never confirmed and although sold in 1948, registration VH-FBR was not allocated until ten years later. Dutifully serving in the agricultural role for three years, the aircraft flew only 20 hours with an owner at Kelso between 1961 and 1964 during which time it is probable that the New Zealand style canopy was added. In that configuration VH-FBR was sold to the USA and registered N17565 in July 1971, and G-BCRD to British resident Richard Dent in November 1974. Both owner and aeroplane were transferred to Switzerland in 1978 and registration HB-UPP was adopted the following year, after which the aircraft was dismantled and stored until the bold decision was reached to convert her to original configuration. This was achieved by the simple expedient of taking a handsaw to the top decking, and the subsequent removal of 132lb of weight to create a new nimbleness in open cockpit Alpine revelry.

To celebrate the 25th Anniversary of Louis Blériot's successful flight across the English Channel in 1909, Geoffrey Tyson flew DH.82 Tiger Moth G-ABUL (3107), from Lympne to Calais on 25th July 1934. With the aid of the 'de Havilland inverted system', the entire 16 minute flight was made upside down, a celebration worthy of front page news. The 50th Anniversary of the Blériot crossing was marked in similar style but with less public adoration when Elwyn McAully flew Tiger Moth G-ANZZ (85834)

Once owned by John Neave test pilot for the de Havilland Aircraft Co of New Zealand, ZK-ANE was fitted with streamlined windscreens at both cockpits, and a sliding canopy over the rear seat. via A J Jackson

The side opening canopy fitted to ZK-AJB was built around a lighter structure than that employed on earlier conversions, with an increased area of glazing. Norman Eastaff

inverted from Lympne to Le Touquet in June 1959. Quite rightly, celebrations on the actual anniversary did return to the front page.

Perhaps the second of these anniversary flights was the more significant. Geoffrey Tyson was flying a relatively new aeroplane, surrounded by manufacturer's support and an inverted fuel and oil system which had been designed, manufactured, flight tested and developed specifically for the RAF. In 1957 through the good offices and financial support of Norman Jones and his controlling interest in Rollason Aircraft, the Tiger Club was born. As a result of efforts to help British pilots compete more equally in top level aerobatic competition, there evolved the Super Tiger, complete with a re-incarnation of de Havilland's tried and tested inverted system, but minus the massive industry and service support of pre-war days.

The 'inverted' system had been flown in Tiger Moth G-ANSH (86320), at Croydon in 1957. An otherwise standard aircraft operated by the Fairoaks Aero Club, another arm of Norman Jones' business interests, G-ANSH had crashed during an air race at Whitchurch in 1955, and was subsequently rebuilt by Rollason into a lightweight aircraft in a search for improved aerobatic performance. The inverted system was a straight copy made from the original de Havilland drawings but all the hardware, including the undercarriage mounted air pump, had to be won or manufactured. A description appeared in *The Aeroplane* at the beginning of the 1957 display season, on 7th June:

'The system is based on the use of a small pressurised fuel tank in the front cockpit. A small Rotherham airscrew-driven air pump mounted on the undercarriage struts provides a pressurised air feed to the tank and to the rear cockpit. At the cockpit the air supply again splits, one branch passing to

atmosphere via a Vickers on/off cock and the other to a pressure relief valve. With the Vickers cock closed, the fuel tank is pressurised to two and a half psi, at which value a relief valve starts to blow off. A pressure gauge, tapped from the tank, shows the tank pressure.

'With the tank pressurised, fuel is forced along the third tapping from the tank, to a standard Tiger Moth on/off cock mounted adjacent to the engine. For inverted flight, this is opened from the cockpit, allowing the fuel to proceed to the carburettor where it is injected into the choke section via a special metering jet.

'For the lubrication system, arrangements have to be made to scavenge the oil which drains to the crankcase top cover with the engine inverted. This is achieved by drilling the top cover webs to allow the oil to drain to the rear of the engine where an additional oil pump has been fitted. This re-directs the oil into the inlet of the main oil feed pump, the oil in this instance thus completely by-passing the oil tank. The crankcase breather pipe, which previously had been fitted where the additional oil pump is now situated, has therefore been repositioned to the front of the crankcase. The oil tank vent is also modified to use a longer pipe, such that it vents to atmosphere at a point "higher" than the tank oil level when inverted'.

Identified only by his initials, author Ken Fulton, a graduate of the de Havilland Aeronautical Technical School, had been flown in G-ANSH by Peter Langstone, a pilot contracted by Rollason to complete the trials. Following the technical description, Fulton briefly outlined his experience:

'During our flight, three inverted runs were made, the longest of these being for just under two minutes. On such occasions, the phrase time flies, seems less than apposite, and the second hand on one's watch appears to take its lead from the minute hand. In the welcome process of rolling out, the engine procedure is the reverse of the preparation for inversion, except that again the throttle has to be closed an amount to obviate the possibility of overspeeding'.

A Canadian style three piece sliding canopy fitted to ZK-BBK, an ex-RAF import of 1952, a fact accounting for the spin strakes. via Stuart Howe

Universal Flying Services converted Tiger Moth G-AOXS into a 'Tiger Taxi' at Fairoaks in 1957, enclosing only the front (passenger) cockpit. deHMC Archive

At Stapleford Tawney in 1958, Tiger Moth G-AIZF was operated with a sliding canopy built on Canadian principles and installed as a club exercise at Baginton. Ted Lawrence

What the correspondent did not reveal was that during the three inverted passes, fuel leaking from the additional tank strapped to the floor between his legs, dripped constantly, rather in the manner of a Chinese water torture, but with even more sinister prospects.

In spite of all the design and testing, the pilots who flew G-ANSH in serious competition were critical of the inverted system which they regarded as clumsy and difficult and distracting to operate. Placarded instructions were carried as a reminder of the essential sequence:

- Ensure mixture (altitude) lever is in rear position.
- Run engine at 1,900rpm or above.
- Move change-over cock to vertical position, wait until engine misfires then move mixture lever to forward position.
- When changing rpm keep throttle lever ahead of mixture lever during both closing and opening.
- The selection of the Normal System could be achieved at any engine speed simply by moving the change-over cock back to the horizontal position.

It was also their contention that however much effort had been made to reduce weight, the aircraft was seriously underpowered for satisfactory execution of some of the advanced manoeuvres increasingly expected to be within a competitor's basic ability.

David Phillips who flew G-ANSH in the 1957 Lockheed Trophy competition at Baginton was faced with the prospect of attempting an outside loop, but apprehension caused him to forget to tighten his shoulder harness before he pushed forward and he duly lifted off his seat. It may have been the tiniest fraction of an inch, but the sensation, even to an experienced pilot like Phillips, momentarily caused him to believe he was in imminent danger of involuntarily leaving the cockpit.

Bill Tomkins, a farmer from Apethorpe in Northamptonshire, had owned a civil registered Gloster Gamecock between the wars, and entered the second Lockheed Aerobatic Trophy competition in July 1956, in his modified Tiger Moth G-AHRC. Alleged to have been T6064 (84555), there was doubt about her real identity, confused even further in 1954 when she was rebuilt after turning over when being started. The damaged fuselage of 'G-AHRC' appeared in the famous Coley's scrapyard near Heathrow in May 1955, by which time she was airborne again in somebody else's new clothes.

G-AHRC's inverted system was quite simple: the aircraft was modified to accept a four gallon petrol tank attached to the cockpit side of the front bulkhead from which a pair of SU electric pumps provided fuel to an additional jet in the carburettor. During the modification programme at Sywell, extended leading edges were fitted to the undersurface of both upper mainplanes between the root end and the interplane strut, together with revised symmetrical leading edges on both lower wings, all in an effort to improve the qualities of inverted flight.

The sequence flown in the eliminating rounds of the Lockheed Trophy was later described as 'a semi aerobatic display of rock and roll flying' which was not good enough to qualify for the finals. In 1968, following re-conversion to standard configuration, G-AHRC was sold to Charles Boddington, a pilot renowned for the quality of his aerobatic and film flying. Travelling home across the Irish Sea in August 1971, the Tiger Moth spun into the water when attempting to avoid another aircraft accompanying her in loose formation, but floated long enough for Boddington and his passenger to be rescued by helicopter.

The Rollason team's experience with the inverted system and lightweight but otherwise standard G-ANSH, was developed into the first of a quartet of aircraft christened 'Super Tigers', G-APDZ (83699), in April 1958. The Super Tiger airframe was that of a standard aircraft considerably cleaned up, most noticeably by removal of the centre section fuel tank which was repositioned to the front cockpit and faired over. The leading edge slats and hinge mechanism were removed, rear cockpit door reprofiled but glued into the closed position, and a tiny windscreen substituted for the standard heavy brass frame.

Surprisingly, perhaps, a hard leading edge was not immediately applied to improve the contour of the wing, but lightweight synthetic fabric covering was used, and the elevator surface area increased by 10%. Additional power was provided by installation of a 145hp Gipsy Major IC engine turning a Fairey Reed, fixed pitch metal propeller, after which there was no requirement for the undercarriage mounted, independent air pump.

In all other respects, apart perhaps from the leather stirrups attached to the rudder pedals, the 'Super Tiger' was pure Tiger Moth and remained registered so as a basic 'type'. G-APDZ was named *The Bishop* in deference to the Club's Chief Flying Instructor, C Nepean Bishop, 'Bish', still devoted to light aeroplanes after 30 years and thousands of circuits as a wartime flying instructor in Southern Rhodesia. *The Bishop* was followed by a trio all taking an ecclesiastical line: G-ANZZ (85834), in 1959 was almost inevitably *The Archbishop*, followed by two aircraft in 1965, G-AOAA (85908), *The Deacon* and G-ANMZ (85588), *The Canon*. G-AOAA, the longest survivor in Super Tiger configuration, was eventually outclassed in her aerobatic proclivities, and spent most of her last operational seasons as a hired-out glider tug.

As a prelude to the 1960 World Aerobatic Championships in Bratislava, the Tiger Club suggested that it might prepare a trio of Super Tigers which they referred to as 'Bishop Tiger Moths', and offer six candidate pilots 50 hours' aerobatic flight training each. Following selection the three best pilots would be considered to constitute the nucleus of an official British Team. The total cost of the exercise including positioning and maintenance of the three 'Bishop' aeroplanes was carefully calculated at £5,000, and in May 1960, a correspondent with *The Aeroplane* wrote that *'The Tiger Club poses the question where the money should come from without suggesting any possible answers!'*

Following such initiative, the Club must have been considerably disheartened to read that the Czech Government was offering contestants the opportunity to lease Zlin Z.226 trainers at a cost for ten days, inclusive of fuel, servicing, insurance, practice and competition flying, of about £200. A trio of British pilots did participate in the competition with a 'Bishop' Tiger Moth, but were totally outclassed and managed to fill the last three places in the list of 29 international competitors.

In view of the non-committal opinions aired over several years by senior aerodynamicists when asked about the degradation in performance suffered as a result of sweeping the wings of the Tiger Moth, without realigning the R.A.F. Section 15 (modified) ribs, an Australian owner, Les Penna, took the opportunity to investigate. During the construction of a Tiger Moth airframe made from all new parts, *'only the instruments and engine had ever flown before'*, the owner said, Penna built wings with ribs fixed parallel to the airflow, a job he had been contemplating for over 20 years. After all the effort, the greatest benefit was gained as a result of improving the drag and reducing the weight by leaving off the 20lb encumbrance of the leading edge slats.

Built as a basic training aeroplane capable of performing the complete repertoire of standard aerobatic manoeuvres, it was unfair to expect the Tiger Moth to become a serious contender in post-war civilian competitions, especially those organised at national and international level. Competitive flying required something better than what became known perhaps unkindly as a 'cooking Tiger', and although the Super Tiger prolonged the type's active participation, Tiger Moth aerobatics increasingly became the preserve of the private owner and dedicated 'amateur'. For commercial operators, Tiger Moth joyrides produced extra revenue when commissioned to sail effortlessly round in a loop, else frighten the uninitiated when rolling through the inverted, accompanied by the faltering sounds of a fuel starved engine.

The sliding canopy superstructure fitted to G-ANRN was heavy and permitted no rear vision. The whole assembly was removed in 1979. deHMC Archive

One of the dilapidated ex-ATA hangars at White Waltham plays backdrop to Doug Bianchi's Tiger Moth G-ANSA, an aeroplane fitted with a side hinged canopy, long exhaust pipe and mainwheel spats. John Osborne

Inevitably, the docile nature of the Tiger Moth as an aerobatic platform was used to best advantage. At the 1975 Air Day organised by the Royal Navy at Yeovilton, Heron Flight's Tiger Moth T8191 (84483), was flown by Lieutenant Commander Pete Sheppard in an aerobatic routine which included 32 consecutive loops. Intoxicated by the effort, the pilot promised to fly 35 loops the following year in celebration of his birthday. During the de Havilland Moth Club's annual Woburn Abbey Rally in 1986, Henry Labouchere raised a substantial sum of money for charity by flying continuous loops for a 90 second period in his Australian built Tiger Moth G-BEWN (DHA952), and managed ten complete manoeuvres before the whistle blew. It was an exhausting exercise not only for the pilot and those watching, but especially for the spectators who had pledged cash for each loop.

The structural integrity of the Tiger Moth was tested in South Africa in 1971 where it is alleged an aircraft was successfully pushed through an outside loop, with the engine switched off! Innovation could have its drawbacks. During the Lockheed Trophy in 1956, John Pothecary attempted an inverted falling leaf in Christchurch Aero Club's G-ANPL (85624), a manoeuvre which cost him 800ft and an admission afterwards that it could be the cause of structural damage and was not, therefore, recommended for Tiger Moths. A great exponent of the erect falling leaf was Air Commodore Allen Wheeler, one of the investigating pilots of the wartime spinning trials at Boscombe Down and Farnborough. Less than a year before his death on 1st January 1984 at the age of 80, Allen Wheeler was seen effortlessly aerobatting his Tiger Moth G-ADGV (3340), in the sky above Old Warden.

A well flown aerobatic routine should exert no undue strain on engine or airframe, and a flowing sequence is a delight to behold. As part of his 1993 'Assessment' of the Tiger Moth, RAAF test pilot Tony Morris flew each of the basic manoeuvres with which the aircraft is most closely associated:

'Generally, the Tiger Moth required large control column and pedal deflections to fly acceptable aerobatics, as the control power available, especially laterally, is quite low. Engine thrust, even at maximum power, is also low, and a high power setting is normally required. 1,950rpm was used for this evaluation, although a higher power setting can be used if necessary, within the engine limitations.

Loop: *entry speed for the loop was 100 kias, (knots indicated air speed), which required lowering the nose below the horizon. As the airspeed increased from cruise toward 100 kias with 1,950rpm set, and a fixed pitch propeller, the throttle required a small reduction to ensure the engine did not exceed the limiting rpm. At 100 kias, the control column was moved centrally aft to commence a pitch rotation. As the nose pitched up, constant aft longitudinal stick pressure was required to ensure the pitching motion continued smoothly and sufficient airspeed remained to complete the manoeuvre without 'falling out' of the loop. Small rudder inputs were required as the airspeed decreased and increased throughout the loop.*

Slow roll: *entry speed for the slow roll was 95 kias. The roll was commenced by applying almost full aileron in the required direction, and introducing a small amount of rudder* in the same direction as the roll. *This application of rudder was required to assist the roll, as the lateral control circuit was designed such that at full lateral control deflection, only the up going aileron was deflected. The application of opposite rudder, as is required in some other aircraft to prevent nose drop, effectively cancelled out the rolling moment generated by the aileron and the roll ceased mid-manoeuvre, with the nose dropping rapidly. As the aircraft continued rolling towards the inverted position, forward longitudinal stick was required to prevent excessive nose drop. Past the 270 degree roll position, the amount of lateral control column was decreased to maintain a constant roll rate.*

Stall turn: *the minimum recommended speed for entry to the stall turn is 70 kias. The pull to the vertical was straightforward, with good visual cues available at the wing to ensure a level pull. Having achieved the vertical position, power was maintained, to give rudder authority, and as the airspeed decreased rudder in the desired direction was introduced such that full rudder was achieved at the point where the aircraft had* almost *stopped its climb. As the aircraft pivoted about the inner wing, a small amount of outboard aileron was required to keep a vertical attitude. The aircraft nose continued to slice down, and as the vertical position neared, a small 'check' with rudder was applied to ensure the nose did not transition past the vertical position. The power could then be reduced if required. A recovery to level flight was then simply effected.*

Barrel roll: *the entry speed for the barrel roll was 100 kias. The entry attitude and initial pull-up were similar to those required for the loop. As the nose rose to the 45 degree position above the horizon, aileron in the required direction of roll was introduced, and the aft stick force maintained. The nose was then 'flown', using continuous roll and pitch, to a previously identified 90 degrees reference point, such that at the wings level, inverted attitude, the nose was pointing at this feature. From this position, roll and pitch were continued as the nose fell below the horizon, and the aircraft returned to the wings-level, upright attitude pointed at the original feature. To maintain a constant roll rate during the manoeuvre, variation of the aileron input was required as the airspeed decreased during the climb and increased during the dive.*

Roll off the top: *entry speed for the half roll off the top of a loop was 118 kias, requiring a moderate nose-down attitude. The initial pull-up required more aft control column force than the loop, to ensure sufficient airspeed was available to complete the roll. As for the loop, the force needed to be maintained positively until an attitude just short of the inverted position was achieved, with wings level. At this position, which was adopted to cater for the nose drop during the half-roll, a positive check forward was required to prevent further nose drop. The roll was then commenced, using full deflection aileron, assisted by a small amount of rudder in the same direction, which also had the benefit of minimising nose drop.*

In-flight re-start: *occasionally during manoeuvres with low forward airspeed and a low power setting, such as a spin, the engine rpm would decay, and on one occasion the propeller stopped completely. This is understood to be a phenomenon associated with a new or 'tight' engine, or with an incorrect idle setting. In an attempt to airstart the engine, the aircraft was dived to 125 kias, requiring a steep nose down attitude. When this did not turn the propeller, a recovery to level flight using 2-3 'g' provided sufficient force to restart the engine. The total altitude loss required to restart the engine varied with airspeed; in the worst case, starting with an airspeed of 40 kias, the altitude loss required to dive, start the engine and recover to level flight was approximately 1,000ft. After further evaluation of this characteristic, it was found that occasionally increasing airspeed to 125 kias alone would restart the engine; on other occasions a positive application of 'g' was required'.*

In 1984, the de Havilland Moth Club in association with the London auction house, Christie's, sponsored an international Tiger Moth aerobatic competition with a difference. Each of the major Tiger Moth owning countries who agreed to be involved, were requested to fly local heats to choose a national candidate, and all the winners were subsequently flown to England to compete in the finals during the Club's annual rally at Woburn Abbey in August 1985. Pilots from Australia, New Zealand, South Africa, the United States and Great Britain spent several days at Old Warden practising on the aircraft each was to fly at Woburn, G-AVPJ (86322), kindly loaned by Robin Livett soon after the aircraft had been rebuilt following her dunking in the River Trent. It was an ironic twist that the British competitor, Barry Tempest, had been the pilot on that occasion too.

The Christie's competition showed a remarkable level of consistency between pilots familiar with the Tiger Moth's aerobatic capabilities and knew exactly how to exploit them. Brian Zeederberg from South Africa was a worthy winner, taking the Christie's Trophy, while Dick Nell from Australia was awarded the BAe146 Trophy for the best freestyle sequence displayed after the competition proper.

Given that the brochure figure for ultimate range of a Gipsy Major powered DH.82A Tiger Moth Landplane is 279 statute miles, it is perhaps all the more remarkable that a Tiger Moth should be chosen as the vehicle in which to undertake long distance record breaking or commemorative flights. But perhaps not! The pilots who chose the

A pleasing study of Chrisair Tiger Moth Taxi G-AHVU just airborne, showing the extended exhaust pipe, neat spats and a low profile canopy allowing a minimum of headroom for the occupant of either cockpit. Chris Roberts

A heavily glazed side hinged canopy fitted to British built Tiger Moth VH-PCI based at Wongan Hills, Western Australia in 1969. Geoff Goodall

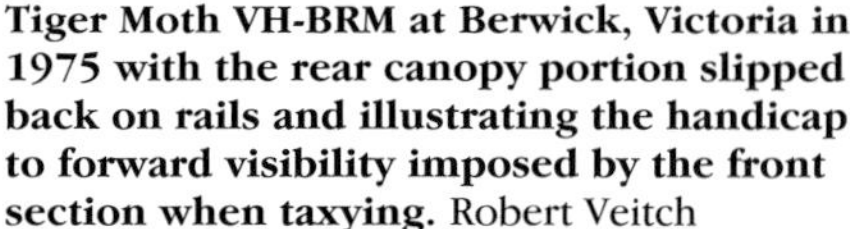

Tiger Moth VH-BRM at Berwick, Victoria in 1975 with the rear canopy portion slipped back on rails and illustrating the handicap to forward visibility imposed by the front section when taxying. Robert Veitch

Offering greater comfort when compared with a standard windscreen yet more flexibility than complete enclosure, this moulded unit with streamlined headrest was fitted to Australian built Tiger Moth VH-AUK at Griffith NSW in 1974. N K Daw

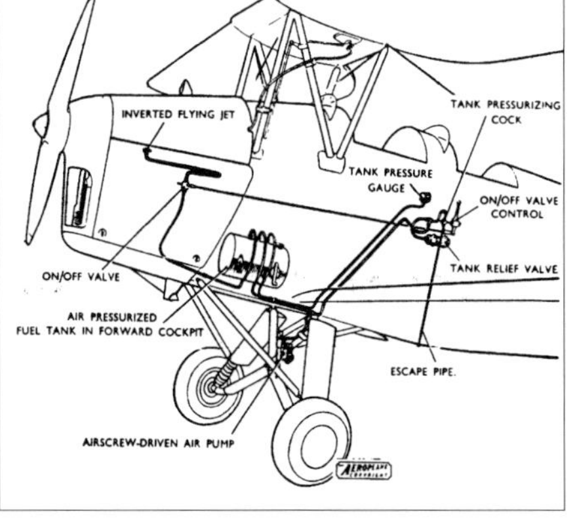

A diagrammatic scheme for the inverted fuel system fitted to Tiger Moth G-ANSH by Rollason Aircraft in 1957. *The Aeroplane*

Tiger Moth would probably have flown a DH.60 Moth if one had been available, for the majority of the many flights linking Great Britain with all parts of the Empire: Africa, India, Australia and New Zealand, had been accomplished in DH.60 Moths, modified, mostly, for the occasion. Post war, not only had the DH.60 become a rare beast, but almost all the en-route servicing facilities established by de Havilland, had disappeared, and some international boundaries had been redrawn to accompany new notices which boldly declared: keep out!

There was still adventure in flying a vintage biplane, already 50 years older than most of the Moths which had pioneered the trails. It was an affordable and meaningful challenge to fly against the elements, a task requiring physical and mental preparation and courage not to mention patience and diplomacy to cope with plans increasingly frayed by bureaucratic reluctance. Mere delivery flights within the continental masses of Australia and North America have spawned tales of adventure and grit. Aircraft not modified for long distance flying require frequent refuelling stops, and in an age of change, careful route planning. For an aircraft greatly affected by wind, weather and limited endurance, it is necessary to ensure fuel and oil of the correct specification will be available, and that arrival will be within scheduled operating hours.

Morris built Tiger Moth 86069, an ex-Indian aircraft sold to Canada in 1972, was registered N6353 the following year and rebuilt in Massachusetts, remaining in the state until 1987 when she was sold to Bud Molloy in Texas. The hilarious tale of her delivery as recounted by pilot Bob Remonte ended with a few vital statistics: 1,885 statute miles; 26 hours flight time; six days and 26 quarts of oil. Through the international network of the de Havilland Moth Club, member Arthur Whitlock realised that 86069 was the one time VT-ARQ, the aircraft in which he had flown his first solo at Madras on 17th March 1947. Through contact with the new owner Whitlock, by now a retired airline captain, flew 86069 again on 14th April 1997, and entered the *Guinness Book of Records, Aircraft Facts and Feats,* having created a world record in consideration of 50 years between solo flights in the same aircraft.

Another United States' import was 86247, an aircraft owned in England by Dr Jeremy Johnston, and which emigrated with him to Vancouver in 1972. As CF-FDQ, the aircraft was aerobatted and toured extensively, aided by a Rollason installed long range tank and inverted fuel system. A growing family necessitated replacement of the Tiger Moth by a classic Beech Staggerwing, and in 1984, 86247 became N775NL, a personalisation of her original RAF serial (NL775), following sale to Alan Lapidus in New York. The delivery flight which involved crossing the Rocky Mountains at 13,000ft was successfully accomplished by the new owner with Gerry Schwam, Chairman of the American Moth Club, acting as navigator, and against some impressive statistics: 3,000 statute miles covered in 36 flying hours and 26 stops to uplift 36 quarts of oil and 270 gallons of fuel.

Long range fuel tanks had been a standard option on Tiger Moths since the earliest days of the Persian exports from Stag Lane, and usually were tailored to fit up into the top decking between the front cockpit instrument panel and the engine bulkhead. Due to the distances involved when routinely flying in Australia, many aircraft acquired long range tanks at some time in their early civil life if not already fitted during their military lives. One pilot operating in Victoria had a shock soon after take off when he discovered flames licking round his right boot, and he subsequently discovered that the fabric covering around the starboard lower wing root and adjacent fuselage had been burned away. The aircraft had recently acquired a long range tank, and the fuel vent had been laid in line with the open stack exhaust. With great presence of mind the pilot immediately pumped fuel into the main tank to prevent further venting, and extinguished the flames by diving at 120 knots.

In order to celebrate the Golden Jubilee of Christchurch International Airport, New Zealand, in 1987, a committee was formed to organise an air race from Singapore to Christchurch. Advertised as the 'Last Great Air Race', contestants were expected to cross the line during a spectacular air show. First prize was notified as a fully restored Tiger Moth, quoted to be worth 'around $NZ45,000'. From the allocated prize fund, the committee purchased ZK-BLQ (84120), which many observers believed was bought at too high a price considering its poor condition, leaving very little resource to improve it. Registration ZK-PDL was allocated in February 1987 in deference to the main sponsors, PDL Industries, and a former de Havilland engineer, Charlie Liddell, refurbished the aircraft which was painted white and handed over to Christchurch dignitaries at a ceremony at Hobsonville. Flown by John MacDonald, ZK-PDL then began an exhaustive publicity tour which included dropping 2,000 tennis balls over South Bagley Park on 12th March, part of the 'PDL Goldair Big Prize Drop' in which collected balls were redeemable against prizes.

The Air Race itself was the subject of much controversy, the prize being awarded to Boyd Munro from Australia who had entered and flown a 'Panther Navajo'. The prize aircraft was registered in his name on 15th January 1988, reverting to the original letters, ZK-BLQ. Following meticulous preparations, which included provision for an additional 64 gallons of petrol and four gallons of oil in the front cockpit, starting on 17th January, the aircraft was flown home to Australia in six sectors, the last three of which involved long crossings of the Tasman Sea: Te Kao to Norfolk Island, 456nm; Norfolk Island to Lord Howe Island 482nm and Lord Howe Island to Sydney, 490nm. For company the Tiger Moth was accompanied during the entire journey by Munro's own circling Navajo. In case of engine failure, the plan was for the pilot to bail out and descend into the sea by parachute, from which predicament he would be picked up by rescue craft, rather than risk ditching the biplane with its fixed undercarriage. Exhaustive enquiries around the world failed to discover a pilot with knowledge of ditching a Tiger Moth in the ocean. It is alleged that safe landfall in Australia was celebrated by a quick inspection of the underside of Sydney Harbour Bridge.

In preparation for the World Vintage Air Rally from White Waltham airfield in March 1990, destination Sydney, N524R (85332), was modified on behalf of owner Bill Lusk, at Chino, California, and sent by container to England. In view of the long sector distances involved in the Rally, and the requirement to carry two crew, the aircraft was clearly expected to be heavy: an additional 70 gallons of fuel were carried in two auxiliary tanks fitted in the front cockpit, and navigational equipment included a Mode C transponder, DME, VOR, ADF, Comms radio and Magellan Nav 500 GPS. A combination strobe and navigation light system was installed on the tips of the upper mainplanes, and to carry the electrical loads, a 35 amp belt driven alternator was connected to the back cover of the Gipsy Major engine. N524R left White Waltham on schedule flown by Bill Lusk and fellow American Tiger Moth owner Lars de Jounge, but due to windshear and strong cross winds encountered during the first landing at Le Touquet, the undercarriage collapsed on touchdown and the dream was shattered along with the propeller.

Tiger Moth G-ANRF (83748), had once belonged to Air Commodore Allen Wheeler while still a serving officer at Boscombe Down, which he used to commute between there, where flight research probed daily at the frontiers of man's knowledge, and Old Warden, where Allen Wheeler was Aviation Trustee of The Shuttleworth Collection, a unique flying museum of yesterday's technology. In December 1974, G-ANRF was acquired by a farmer's son from East Sussex.

As an English Electric Lightning pilot with 56(F) Squadron RAF, Flight Lieutenant David Cyster was able to sample both ends of the flying spectrum. During a tour as an instructor on Hawker Hunters at Valley, he

Super Tiger G-APDZ *The Bishop* soon to have her metal bladed propeller swung into life. Note the heavily gloved hand of the ground crew and the latest line in private pilot protective headgear displayed in the cockpit. deHMC Archive

Super Tiger G-ANZZ *The Archbishop* playing to the camera in May 1965. Note that in spite of her purity of line, the tailskid is fitted with the lump of a glider tow hook. D W Greenacre

It would be easy to misconstrue the intentions of Spanish Tiger Moth EC-AHY, but the bomb shaped devices under each lower mainplane are streamlined canisters designed for carriage and dispersal of nothing more sinister than leaflets.
via John Pothecary

Royal Navy Tiger Moth T8191 was flown through 32 consecutive loops at Yeovilton in 1975, just two short of the pilot's age.
via Stuart Howe

conceived the idea of a Bert Hinkler commemorative flight to Australia. In some secrecy, G-ANRF was modified to accept extra fuel and oil tanks, radio, pilot comforters and other equipment considered necessary by the authorities. Much of the preparation was completed by Basil Carlin at Barton, and G-ANRF was teased out briefly at Valley before positioning to the British Aerospace Harrier flight test aerodrome at Dunsfold in Surrey.

Nagging fuel leaks and last minute electrical problems were cured by British Aerospace engineers who worked throughout the night. In spite of the frost and fog which enveloped the whole of southern England and the near continent, Cyster was able to take off on schedule early on the morning of Tuesday, 7th February 1978, flight planning direct to Marseille. The 79 gallons of petrol on board raised the endurance of G-ANRF to 10.5 hours, assuming that the tripled oil capacity was sufficient.

Fifty years after the birth of the Gipsy engine, it was left to an American engineer and Moth owner, Ed Clark, to develop a piston ring system which reduced the engine's legendary 'dripsy' reputation and factually prodigious thirst for oil, to almost nothing at all. Perhaps more than any other single modification, the reduction in oil consumption opened up whole new areas for exploration by Gipsy engined aircraft, restoring the ultimate endurance to fuel consumption metered against carrying capacity, one single and simple sum which eliminated oil entirely from the equation.

Although the flight was undertaken in a private capacity, the strength of the RAF's publicity machine ensured that regular radio reports kept the world advised of Flight Lieutenant Cyster's progress until the aircraft arrived safely in Darwin on 11th March, officially greeted from a watching Lockheed C-130 Hercules, 21,000ft above. Eleven days later, *Headwind* (a name coined by the media and not recognised by the owner), touched down at Sydney's Kingsford Smith airport at the end of her epic voyage.

G-ANRF returned to Great Britain in a dismantled state as air cargo, and following a number of air display appearances in 1978 to satisfy contractual obligations to sponsors, the Tiger Moth was flown back to Barton for re-conversion to standard configuration. Following engine overhaul by Peter Franklin at White Waltham in May 1979, G-ANRF with Cyster and his wife Cherry as crew, were declared winners of the de Havilland Moth Club's Famous Grouse Moth Rally, Hatfield to Strathallan. *Headwind's* Australia flight and the Famous Grouse victory were both well covered in classic BBC Television documentary films. In recognition of Shell's association with the Australia flight, on the 20th anniversary, G-ANRF was the central feature of the Shell stand at the 1998 Farnborough Air Show.

Following a pleasant social evening in Johannesburg, a group of Tiger Moth owners, pilots, engineers and supporters picked up on a casual suggestion and organised a flight of three Tiger Moths into the Okavango Delta region of Botswana, setting off in April 1988. Supported for the outward journey by two other aircraft carrying supplies and press reporters on behalf of the sponsors, and a cross country vehicle loaded with emergency fuel stocks, the three Tiger Moths, ZS-CKX (84869), ZS-DKY (85636) and ZS-DHR (82262), covered 1,600 miles in eleven days, flying over jungle, plains, salt pans and swamps. All three British built aircraft had been operated by the SAAF, and ZS-DHR, taken on charge in March 1940, was the oldest airworthy Tiger Moth in South Africa, taking a break from filming her most recent production, *Brutal Glory*. Two years after the adventure, ZS-CKX was dismantled and packed for emigration with her owner to Canada, but in 1991 she was out of the box again and receiving maintenance at Rand.

In March 1996, a further expedition into the Okavango was mounted from Pietersburg, when four British built Tiger Moths, all ex-SAAF imports from 1941 and 1943, pressed on to fly over Victoria Falls on 8th April: ZS-BGL (84221), ZS-BGN (84864), ZS-BXB (82709) and ZS-DNI (84454). During the flight home, operating via southern Zimbabwe, ZS-DNI broke a throttle linkage at Gwanda, home of the country's only operational Tiger Moth, and owner Ray Hollins was happy to donate the essential part on short term loan.

Tiger Moth HB-UCJ (DHA737), the former ZS-DND, left Johannesburg in February 1993 en route for Switzerland, and having travelled the length of Africa, stalled, spun and hit the ground 115 miles north of Addis Ababa, probably as the result of inattention when operating a heavy aircraft in searing temperatures, and high altitudes. Misinterpretation of the graduations on the air speed indicator (ASI) may have been a contributing factor. The wrecked aircraft was returned to South Africa for long term restoration during which the ASI was scheduled to be changed, but during the journey by transporter all the original instruments were stolen.

A Tiger Moth has a charisma: the aeroplane is not the butt of cheap jibes at the hands of the airfield jokers, neither will she ever be. Put three Tiger Moth owners together in London and announce that they will fly to Moscow, and the world stops to take notice.

Jonathan Elwes had travelled extensively in his Tiger Moth G-ANRN (83133), long before plans were conceived for the Moscow flight, and three crossings of the High Alps, trips to Gibraltar and North Africa and to Northern Finland in 1984, had proved that anything was possible providing that preparation was thorough.

During a 14 month programme of investigation and persistence, a formula for the Moscow expedition was crystallised, centring on the Tiger Moth as a privately owned vintage aeroplane of high reputation. The flight was to be regarded as one of a private touring nature, for which category all prospective applicants were made aware that every previous entreaty made to Moscow since 1932 had been refused. A British registered Zlin Z.526 Trener and two Stampe SV-4s had been granted permission to fly to Moscow in 1966, as competitors in the World Aerobatic Championships.

With the most astonishingly appropriate timing, and in the light of a continuing thaw in East-West relations, the culture of 'Glasnost' quickly was re-interpreted as 'Glasmoth', and when April 1989 was declared to be British-Soviet trade month, it provided the ideal peg on which to hang the project. The release from prison of Mathias Rust, a young German pilot who had landed his Cessna 172 in Red Square, was regarded as a friendly indication, and subsequently the pressure from Jonathan Elwes increased, all correspondence being submitted in Russian, now seeking permission not only for his own aircraft, but for two additional Tiger Moths to fly in company and suggesting that each should carry a Russian navigator. Eventually, the long awaited answer came from Moscow: Approval granted.

Selection of the two new Tiger Moth pilots was the matter of careful consideration. Not only was it vital that the team members were all compatible, they had to be reliable diplomats too, quite apart from a basic ability to provide and fly a Tiger Moth in almost all imaginable conditions, and have the facility to cope with any unforeseen eventuality, especially serious delay. Nicholas Parkhouse, an experienced Tiger Moth pilot and aerobatic competition winner, joined the team with G-ANOH (86040), an aircraft with family associations since 1966. He was followed by Roger Fiennes, businessman and genial wit, and G-BALX (82103), the last Rollason civil conversion completed at Fairoaks in 1973.

There was much to organise before the three Tiger Moths left England, part of which included confirmation of the return routing which was to be different from the outward journey. Aided by joint sponsorship from James Capel, and *The Daily Mail*, finance, communication and reliable administration was established, and the plans were given maximum exposure in the media. Anatoly Gorbatov, one of three Russian navigators, paid a short visit to England to meet the pilots and complete various formalities such as deciding sizes of boots and the specially tailored flying suits on behalf of his colleagues. All three navigators were on hand in England prior to the April departure and were to remain with the Tiger Moths until the trio touched down at White Waltham at the end of the adventure on 27th April: Anatoly Gorbatov flew with Elwes; Sasha Zaitzev with Parkhouse, and Fiennes was crewed with Andrei Izmailov, navigator on Mathias Rust's Cessna repatriation flight to Denmark.

Under glowering skies on Friday, 7th April 1989, the assembled guests at White Waltham, waved away the trio who took off on their first leg to Wevelgem in Belgium. That same night they were in Aachen and on Saturday slept in Prague. During the afternoon of the following Friday, 14th April, they were poised to leave Kaluga bound for Moscow. Fiennes penned his thoughts:

'Inbound from Briansk we landed, refuelled and re-started our engines. The control tower reported fog en-route. We stopped engines and waited, for four hours. I played chess in a ramshackle hut with an old babushka and lost quite heavily, so I was glad when the word came that the authorities had reduced the minima for Sheremetyevo to 150 metres ceiling and 1,000 metres horizontal visibility.

'We re-routed to avoid hills, electric pylons and other obstructions, took off and were soon in close to IMC conditions. Surely we must turn back? No, we pressed on, barely able at times to remain in visual contact with each other. We flew over forest, just above the tops of the trees poking through the ground mist and bumping our heads on the cloud. Just when the conditions seemed impossible we found a river valley and followed it for almost half an hour. I had no idea where we were, and neither did my navigator.

'We came across a road straight as an arrow: it lead to Moscow. None too soon the suburbs of the city could be seen in the murky distance. We descended to below 300ft and picked up the ring road which we followed around the city. I could see into the flats of the high rise buildings and people waved to us as we passed.

'All traffic had been stopped at the airport but our eyes were skinned for high tension cables that we knew surrounded the city. Without warning we were there, flying a 300ft vic formation, passing over the VIP terminal. Another low level circuit in echelon, a break and stream landing and we were down. I for one, was not sorry.

'I did not notice the welcome: just held the flowers that were thrust at me and gulped down the champagne offered until my head sang. We hugged our wives and gave thanks to our Gods'.

On 19th April 1998, Roger Fiennes flew to France for lunch, an exercise which he had enjoyed on several previous occasions. He left Dieppe and headed out over the French coast on a direct track to return to Headcorn, a water crossing of 70 miles. Following a routine radio call giving an estimated time at mid-Channel, nothing more was heard from G-BALX, and the aircraft did not arrive in England. In spite of an intensive air and sea search, no trace of the Tiger Moth or her pilot was ever found.

Brian Edwards sent his bright yellow Tiger Moth VH-HPH *Matilda* to England early in 1990, and she was assembled at the Royal

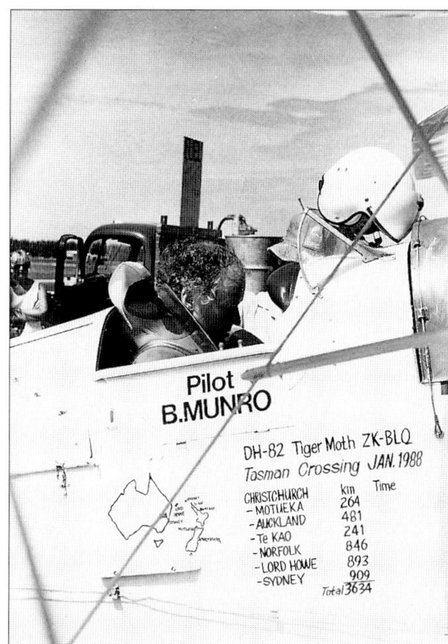

In 1987, Boyd Munro won first prize in an air race from Singapore to New Zealand: a Tiger Moth. The new owner elected to fly the aircraft home to Australia, departing Motueka on 17th January 1988. The map is not to scale. John King

Airborne from Motueka on 17th January 1988, Boyd Munro and Tiger Moth ZK-BLQ en route to Auckland during the first leg of their mostly overwater delivery flight to Sydney, Australia. John King

The cockpit of a Tiger Moth intent on serious international travel must be equipped with elaborate nav/comm equipment and the necessary power sources. California based N524R utilises every spare corner. David Watson

Aircraft Establishment (RAE) Bedford. *Matilda*, identified as build number 1375, was created from an amalgam of parts assembled by Murray Griffiths at Deniliquin, and registered in August 1988. Brian Edwards' father had been lost when captaining an RAF Avro Lancaster out of Binbrook on 3rd July 1943, and his family had been cared for in Australia by Legacy, a charitable organisation which provided assistance and education. The 1990 flight planned to start from Binbrook, was Edwards' effort to raise funds on behalf of the charity.

On the morning of 2nd March 1990, VH-HPH took off bound for Perth, Western Australia, but only two hours into the flight and a few minutes short of crossing the English coast, the Gipsy Major engine's crankshaft snapped. The propeller, full of energy, collided with the structure of the starboard upper mainplane causing major spar damage before careering off into oblivion. News of the disaster was broadcast throughout the media, reprofiling what had otherwise been a very quiet and private departure. The aircraft was further damaged when the undercarriage partially collapsed during the forced landing at Gillham Lane Farm near Smarden in Kent and again during recovery to Headcorn aerodrome.

Dismayed by the story, Michael Vaisey immediately flew to Kent in his own Tiger Moth G-APLU (85094), and by enlisting the assistance of other members of the de Havilland Moth Club, VH-HPH was removed to Hatfield where repairs were effected and a replacement engine borrowed, overhauled and fitted, all with great urgency in an attempt to maintain validity of the diplomatic clearances. Twenty days after the engine failure, Edwards resumed his journey when he left Hatfield on 22nd March 1990, and on 12th May was greeted by 16,000 delighted supporters when he landed at Langley Park, an historic old aerodrome site situated in the heart of the city of Perth. The flight raised A$50,000 for Legacy which was topped up through sales of *The Matilda Mission*, a blow by blow account of the journey as logged by the pilot, and in honour of which Edwards was awarded the Order of Australia.

More funds were raised in 1993. Starting on 26th September, *Matilda* circumnavigated Australia in a 36 day anti-clockwise circuit which began at Jandakot and again finished at Langley Park on Australia Day. Arrival was greeted by an RAAF formation aerobatic team and confirmation that not only had Edwards beaten the record for the 7,000 mile journey, set at 44 days by a Fairey IIID Seaplane in 1924, but during the course of his lectures and meetings organised for stopovers around the country at 71 aerodromes, he and *Matilda* jointly had raised a further A$70,000 for Legacy.

The Farmhand Appeal was established in August 1994 to raise urgently needed funds to assist Australian farmers battling against what in some areas was the worst drought ever recorded. Nick Gerathy, an experienced 15 year old pilot living in Queensland, too young to fly solo or to drive a car, raised more than A$40,000 for the cause by attracting sponsorship and publicity when he flew Tiger Moth VH-UVB (DHA91), on a 3,800 mile adventure involving 63 refuelling stops during 14 days.

The Tiger Moth had been provided by Barry Hempel of Archerfield, Brisbane, and began on 24th September, returning to Archerfield on 8th October, during which time Nick Gerathy was accompanied by flying instructor Paul Mikkelsen. The only delays experienced were all weather related: three hours were lost at Parafield when they were forced to return due to en route conditions; 45 knot winds and dust storms were encountered at Dubbo, but the greatest irony for a drought inspired flight was the disruption caused at Glen Innes by waves of impenetrable squally rain.

In February 1996, Tiger Moth G-ASKP (3889), was climbing out of Brindisi and over the sea when the number one big end bearing failed, and the connecting rod punched

Journey's end. David Cyster taxies G-ANRF in to a tumultuous welcome at the Qantas Engineering Base at Kingsford Smith airport, Mascot, NSW, on 22nd March 1978. Neville Parnell

An assumed soft shoe refuelling position negating the need to stand on the top of the engine cowling. Tiger Moth G-ANOH, post Glasmoth, with a long distance style comfort windscreen. Barry Peerless

a hole in the side of the crankcase. The damaged Gipsy Major engine, tough and resilient, maintained sufficient power to allow G-ASKP to return to the coast in a gradual descent, and a controlled emergency landing within the confines of a live Italian Air Force bombing range, from where she was later retrieved by courtesy of a United States Air Force helicopter. At the time of the failure, the aircraft had been heading for Greece and on to Cape Town, commemorating Alan Cobham's survey flight made on behalf of Imperial Airways in a DH.50 in 1926.

Repaired at Redhill and booked to appear in a film sequence for *The Famous Five* being shot at a narrow airstrip in Gloucestershire the following September, G-ASKP ran off the landing area in a strong crosswind, possibly due to a punctured tyre, slipped down an old railway embankment and overturned.

A more successful London to Cape Town flight occurred in 1961 when the newly overhauled G-ARMS (85698), sold to a South African customer, was air delivered from Croydon, attempting to establish a record for aircraft in the under 1,000kg category. The Tiger Moth left England on 14th May and arrived safely in Cape Town on 25th May, but only two days later hit a tree at George during a poor exhibition of low level flying, and was wrecked. To add insult to injury, on receipt of no serviceable goods, the Rollason sales invoice was declined.

Tiger Moth VH-GVA (DHA1014), was previously VH-GVE, but the amended letters were allocated on request in 1961 to reflect the identity of her new owners, Goulburn Valley Aero Club. In 1984 the aircraft was painted white overall and took the starring role in a delightful family film *Tail of a Tiger* shot at Bankstown, and given wide distribution, later to be shown on television around the world. Under the ownership of Ray Vuillermin who had learned to fly on the aircraft, and later was to instruct on her, VH-GVA was one of only three Tiger Moths in Australia to hold approval for carriage of the Stand on Wing (SOW) rig.

In 1993, VH-GVA was acquired by John Fisher with the express intention of flying her from England (London) to Australia (Sydney). In preparation for the flight, Fisher planned long solo sectors to calibrate the fuel and navigation systems, flying from Newcastle to Perth and back again, and later a return trip to Alice Springs.

On 24th August 1995, during a period of familiarisation, VH-GVA jumped her chocks on start-up, and taxied for 100 yards at high speed with the owner in hot pursuit, before turning over. Repairs were effected for test flying to begin on 21st December 1995, and on Boxing Day, VH-GVA left on the westbound sector of her transcontinental proving flight. Fifteen days later, the Tiger Moth was back at Maitland, and arrangements were made to ship her to England, from where, after local flying and a special guest appearance at the de Havilland Moth Club Rally at Woburn Abbey in August 1996, she would fly home.

Following a great send-off from White Waltham on 1st September and accompanied by the de Havilland Moth Club Diamond Nine Formation Team as far as the English coast, all ten Tiger Moths featured in a sea front air display. For all his meticulous planning, world wide support and assistance, nobody could have envisaged the delays inflicted almost immediately by ferocious storms raging in the south of France. With his schedule already tattered, Fisher discovered that apart from appalling weather, bureaucracy became his greatest enemy, together with dangerous situations created by unimaginative Air Traffic Controllers. Apart from cash which opened some doors, he discovered that his next greatest assets were the gold epaulettes and airline style cap which hastened his movements through the others.

In spite of flying extremely long sectors of up to nine hours duration, the aircraft took 35 days to reach Darwin and another seven after that before arrival in Sydney. VH-GVA was welcomed there by officials from 'Canteen', a teenage cancer charity, who were to receive substantial sponsorship funds raised by Fisher's pugnacious 42 day epic.

West Australian land agent Barry Markham acquired Tiger Moth DHA1088 in 1989, almost 30 years after the aeroplane had been substantially damaged and written off during service with the Royal Newcastle Aero Club. Registered VH-RNQ in 1955, one of the last RAAF Tiger Moths (A17-757), to be sold out of the Service, the letters were cancelled in July 1960 following a crash at Port MacQuarie.

Rebuilt by Raymond Windred at Luskintyre and registered VH-NOV in October 1991, Markham flew her home to Perth a year later taking eight days to cover the 29 sectors. In an effort to raise funds for the Royal Flying Doctor Service and commemorate the flight in August 1933 from Perth to Croydon by West Australian Jimmy Woods in DH60 Moth VH-UPD, Markam was given a rousing send off by 2,000 spectators when he left Langley Park on 26th April 1998, headed for England.

VH-NOV arrived at Cambridge on 24th June having been airborne for more than 200 hours during 45 of the 60 elapsed days, running ahead of fierce tropical storms, a political revolution in Indonesia and nuclear test explosions in India and Pakistan. In achieving his great ambition, Markham became the first Tiger Moth pilot to complete the westbound route, flying 'uphill' into the prevailing wind and weather. Modifications to VH-NOV included the luxury of mainwheel brakes and a steerable tailwheel which helped considerably when manoeuvring at major international airports. Long range fuel was carried in the same tanks previously fitted to VH-HPH during her west-east transit, generously loaned for the occasion by Brian Edwards. However, had plans worked differently, Barry Markham might have been recognised only as the first *solo* Tiger Moth flight along the route. A plan for three Tiger Moths of the Royal Aero Club of New South Wales to fly in formation from Australia to England was announced in April 1939. Scheduled to arrive on the opening day of Birmingham's new airport on 8th July, the ceremonies at Elmdon were completed without them.

Wiltshire based strawberry farmer Norman Parry had long nurtured a dream to fly from England to Australia in his Mascot built Tiger Moth G-BPHR (DHA45). An accomplished glider pilot equipped with the necessary grit and determination, Parry left a private strip near Reading on 20th September 1998, transiting via White Waltham to refuel to maximum capacity, and intending to rendezvous in France with a second Australia-bound Tiger Moth, G-ERDS (85028). A third aircraft was not airworthy in time and remained in England.

Persistent engine problems caused the husband and wife crew of G-ERDS to abandon their flight at Rome and after some weeks delay the aircraft was ferried back to England. Parry continued on his own but slipped further behind his already flexible schedule, delayed by technical problems and bad weather. Lines of communication were maintained with British based engineer Ben Borsberry, along which vital supplies and spares were shipped together with much advice for 'on the spot' maintenance and repair.

Unlike Barry Markham's east-west flight which had run ahead of weather and political disturbance, Norman Parry coincided with the worst of both. Severe delays were caused by storms and bureaucracy exacerbated by expired overflight clearances, spare parts held without reason by Customs, theft of money and a series of significant engine problems.

Ambition was achieved when G-BPHR finally touched down at Kununurra in northern-most Western Australia on New Year's Day 1999 at which point the pilot decided it was time to return home: there was a farm to run! But persuaded otherwise, he continued on to Newcastle where he arrived on 12th January, to be met by amongst other enthusiasts, John Fisher, well aware of the emotions behind the tired expression. There was some good news too: Tiger Moth VH-KRW (LES-1) had just been sold to a new owner in Great Britain and there was space in the shipping container for two dismantled aeroplanes.

Although both the RAF and Norwegian Navy had rejected the Tiger Moth as a suitable candidate for serious investment as a seaplane trainer in the early 'thirties, ten years later half a dozen Tiger Moths had been miraculously repatriated from the Dutch East Indies prior to entering service, for no other reason than that they were stored awaiting delivery of floats from the

Obviously but discreetly placarded with details of their sponsors, the Glasmoth Trio fly in close formation, each with a Russian navigator in the front cockpit. The Glasmoth Trio

United States, and could be quickly loaded on board critically scarce shipping space and whisked away from danger. Unlike the DH.60 which as a series was well endowed with floats and operated in many parts of the pre-war world, few Tiger Moths took to the water other than in isolation and mostly as one-off examples post military disposal.

Late in 1960, a group of British based marine aviation enthusiasts led by Air Commodore G J Christopher Paul, Secretary General of The Air League, proposed the formation of a Seaplane Club, and at a formal meeting held on 20th January 1961, the Club was officially constituted under a committee chaired by Britain's foremost seaplane pilot, J Lankester Parker.

Recruitment of members and raising of funds to secure a suitable aircraft, support equipment, staff and facilities, probably to be based at Gillingham on the River Medway, was slow, and the committee eventually persuaded the altruistic Norman Jones to donate a Tiger Moth from the still comfortably stocked Rollason store at Croydon. The airframe was to be mated with a pair of Edo 2000 floats which had been swapped by the owner of an Aeronca 15AC Sedan, G-AREX, imported from Canada the previous year. Norman Jones provided G-AIVW (83135), an aircraft acquired after the damage inflicted during a heavy landing at Woolsington in September 1959 had proved too expensive for the Newcastle Aero Club to repair.

G-AIVW, released by the RAF late in 1946, had earned a reputation as a very fast racing aircraft in the hands of the Newcastle airport manager, Jimmy Denyer. In the 1958 King's Cup Air Race, he flew the Tiger Moth into first place at an average speed of 118.5mph.

Painted yellow overall with matching parallel cheat lines on fuselage and floats, G-AIVW was christened *Oswald Short* as recognition of the pioneer's generous launch donation of £500, and was first flown from Lee on Solent on 20th July 1963 by Christopher Paul. Initially, utilisation was poor due to limited facilities and indifferent weather and by the following year, the Seaplane Club's brief excursion had been absorbed as the Seaplane Section of the Tiger Club.

The change of status coincided with a move to the sheltered acres of Castle Water, a disused fresh water gravel working and watersports centre near Rye, where G-AIVW, officially designated a Tiger Moth Seaplane, became universally known as the Sea Tiger.

A quick release conventional undercarriage was designed which allowed the aircraft to be flown from a short grass strip alongside the water at Rye for periodic checks at Redhill and it was there in 1968 that the enemy of all seaplanes was discovered: incurable corrosion in the tubular fuselage frame. A new fuselage was substituted, that of the repairable G-ANLR (82111), and the opportunity was taken to

The skyline of the business sector of Perth City Centre welcomes Brian Edwards on 12th May 1990 as he leads a formation of welcoming Tiger Moths at the end of his triumphant flight from Hatfield.
Reg Adkins

repaint the airframe and floats a mellow maroon and silver.

During a faster than intended touch down at Frenchman's Creek, Rye, on 14th July 1973, the floats dug into the water and G-AIVW overturned, floating upside down until salvaged. In view of the operating conditions, but guided by the small band of enthusiastic and knowledgeable instructors and volunteer helpers, there were remarkably few incidents, but on 27th August 1982, off Silver Sands, Camber, G-AIVW slipped off a low turn in poor visibility and was wrecked when she hit the sea. A marginal operation at the start, the Sea Tiger enterprise had been sustained for almost 20 years.

The level of skills required to fly a Tiger Moth accurately were magnified in the Sea Tiger. To begin with it was necessary to learn how to launch and retrieve/beach the relatively frail aeroplane, let alone how to taxy on a medium which was itself subject to ebb and flow, wind and tide. The Sea Tiger flew herself off the water at 41 knots IAS and was allowed the luxury of a climb at 44 knots to 15ft where level acceleration to 60 knots was required prior to further manoeuvring.

Perhaps the declared unsuitability of the aircraft for training pilots in the 'thirties was a result of not attempting to increase fin and rudder area to compensate for the additional side area of the floats. This reduced the tendency to weathercock when on the surface of the water, but caused directional instability in the air when heavy rudder pressure was required to overcome the additional linkage to the water rudders.

Christopher Paul remembers that general handling was considered 'clumsy' and that response to control input was delayed. Stalling was to be avoided because at the point of stall, the floats, at the increased angle of attack, provided a good deal of lift forward of the normal C of G, to a point where even full forward stick could no longer get the nose down. Speed was essential when approaching for touch down and during gliding turns, an element probably missing from the final manoeuvre of the Sea Tiger's operational life.

In 1975 Tiger Moth G-AOBX (83653), was fitted with a set of Short floats originally designed for a DH.83 Fox Moth and which used a reverse chassis geometry when compared with G-AIVW. She was successfully operated for several seasons from a gravel pit within hailing distance of Heathrow airport by Leisure Sport, together with other waterborne types, some of which were non flying replicas of famous pre-war racing seaplanes. The business was an early attempt to 'theme' a water orientated leisure facility, but a change of management saw all the marine aviation interests sold off, and G-AOBX resumed her career on a conventional undercarriage.

Both G-AIVW and G-AOBX proved that the weak points on a Tiger Moth Seaplane were the front fuselage side frames, and to prevent unnecessary damage, the strength of these became the limiting factor when assessing the condition of the water. Engine mounting bolts also required careful inspection after heavy loadings or when a seaplane alighted untidily with some degree of sideways component.

By 1980, Hannu Riihela's Finnish based 'Experimental' Tiger Moth OH-XLA, fitted with a 180hp Lycoming engine, had been placed on a set of GRP floats and struts for which much useful data had been supplied by Rollason.

The first non-European Tiger Moth ever to attend the Woburn Abbey Moth Rally was N85882 which arrived as sea cargo from San Francisco during the summer of 1986. She indulged in a continental tour including essential time in Sweden for American based owner Lars de Jounge. Safely home, N85882 attended the Chino meeting in May 1988. Jim Meads

Considered to be a very fast standard Tiger Moth, G-AIVW was a regular entrant for the National Air Races. Based at Newcastle airport, this photograph was taken at the end of the 1950 racing season. Raymond Rayner

Sea Tiger G-AIVW first time round with the Edo 2000 floats and chassis in position and a trial fitting of the port lower mainplane. *The Aeroplane*

The float chassis added over 200lb to the empty weight of the aircraft, even allowing for removal of the conventional undercarriage, although this was still 190lb lighter than the de Havilland figures quoted for a Gipsy Major powered seaplane in 1933. OH-XLA suffered from a rear C of G limit which restricted use of the luggage locker to little more than the carriage of mooring ropes, but these were mostly left tied to the front chassis struts and allowed to trail free for instant deployment on touchdown.

The GRP floats permitted operation at a maximum weight of 1,984lb and overload flight trials revealed nothing sinister at 2,050lb. Directional stability of OH-XLA was found to be far from ideal when floats were attached and plans were prepared for the addition of a ventral fin, but the aircraft was taken out of the water before the likely benefits resulting from such an experiment could be assessed.

In Canada, where some outposts survived solely through communications and resupply by waterborne aircraft, float equipped Tiger Moths found little favour before or during the war, or afterwards when 600 surplus DH.82C models were sold into the civil market. One of the rare exponents of the Tiger Moth Seaplane was Watt Martin, who in 1947 fitted a set of Short floats originally supplied for a DH.60M Moth, to DH.82C Tiger Moth CF-DGC (DHC1020). The aircraft had been sold from No 8 Service Flying Training School (SFTS) Moncton in 1946, with only 860 hours logged, to C Roper of Muskoka. Martin bought the Seaplane himself in 1954, and kept her for the next ten years. By the summer of 1958, CF-DGC was on Edo 1835 floats with Jack Arnold at Brantford.

In 1950, DH.82C CF-CKW (DHC1636), was converted onto Edo floats at Mount Hope, from where she was launched off the main runway from a purpose built dolly, a conventional operation in Seaplane circles, but one requiring a long, hard runway. Watt Martin acquired the wreck of DH.82C CF-CKF (DHC1593), in 1966, an aircraft which had been damaged at Buttonville airport during the passage of Hurricane Hazel. In between rebuilding and maintaining Moths for his customers, CF-CKF was returned to airworthiness by 1985, fitted with Edo 1835 floats and a standard wooden propeller in place of the more favourable Fairey Reed. Operated from Timmins, CF-CKF flew from numerous small lakes in the area to provide support for a film being shot on behalf of Expo 86, soon to be hosted in Vancouver.

In the hands of a skilled pilot, Martin demonstrated the ease with which a Tiger Moth Seaplane could be landed on lush grass, provided touchdown was completed with absolutely no hint of drift, when CF-CKF was positioned back to the workshops at Milton on 30th September 1985, after which the aircraft was flown on skis and floats again and a conventional undercarriage as moods and the seasons dictated.

An unexpected addition to the floatplane fraternity was Tiger Moth N41DH (84734), an aircraft registered against the personal ownership of William Arthur Rollason in September 1946, before sale to the Netherlands only two months later, and passage to the USA in 1971. N41DH was hangared at Amana airfield, Iowa, during the severe flooding suffered by the American mid-west in the summer of 1993. In anticipation, the Tiger Moth had been jacked up, and when the hangar flooded to knee height, only the lower half of the mainwheels were left submerged in the invasive brown stained goo. By placing a long wooden beam under the fuselage, parallel in theory, with the wing leading edges, and borrowing a pair of styrofoam blocks from a local marina, then attaching an inflatable children's toy to the tailwheel, the Tiger Moth became buoyant. A security fence around the airport buildings blocked the direct route to high ground, so the aircraft was floated a short distance down the main runway, around the fence, through a neighbour's back yard and out onto a dry street.

Sea Tiger G-AIVW being refuelled off the shingle beach at Lee on Solent on a cold day in September 1965. Constant effort was necessary to ensure she stayed afloat in the shallow water. Cliff Barnett

Tiger Moth G-AOBX was fitted with Short designed DH.83 Fox Moth floats in 1975 and for a limited season operated from disused gravel workings adjacent to Heathrow airport. Stuart Howe

DH.82C Tiger Moth CF-DGC at Lake Rosseau during the summer of 1947. The floats are of pre-war Short design, originally fitted to a DH.60M Moth. Jack McNulty

DH.82C CF-CKW at Mount Hope, Ontario in 1950, with Edo 1835 floats, was flown off the trolley using the paved runway in the normal way; the trolley decelerating in its own time before recovery. Watt Martin

In anticipation of severe flooding in Iowa in 1993, Tiger Moth N41DH was jacked up in her hangar. After the deluge she was floated to higher ground and eventually flown off a public highway. John R Tiffany

As the mainwheels protruded a few inches below the flotation blocks, N41DH was 'beached' on sloping ground. The problem of high guard-rails on a local canal bridge was overcome by borrowing a flatbed truck from the municipal depot, and winching the aircraft onto its back for the journey through the town to a suitable local highway. With no shortage of volunteers to stop traffic, N41DH took off from the temporary runway headed for higher ground safe from the wet.

With a glut of tired old Tiger Moths on the world market post-war, the incidence of their demise at bonfire parties and similar celebrations was only to be expected. When genuine demand began to rise again and outstrip supply, values increased to a level at which every hangar roof was scoured for the treasure that might have been long abandoned in the rafters.

The refinement of microlights quickly led to an American designed biplane, the Fisher R80 Tiger Moth, described in the company brochure as having 'the historic looks of the Tiger Moth. An 80% replica of yesterday's aircraft with today's technology'.

At Ivanovo in the former Soviet Union, Sergei Mazny built a Tiger Moth entirely from wood. A skilled model maker and regular supplier of 1/10 scale productions for the Soviet Air Force Museum, Mazny constructed the whole aircraft with the aid of magazine articles, photographs and some sketchy plans gleaned from modelling papers. Last heard of in 1993, the airframe was substantially complete with a Walter Minor M332 engine ready for installation, and the builder anxious to visit western owners to glean first hand practical data.

Recognising the need for conservation of airworthy parts, Harold Carlaw built from scratch in 1997, a full size DH.82C 'Tiger Moth lookalike' using commercial materials, intended as a children's plaything at touring country fairs. When not on the road, the 'Tiger Moth' is exhibited at the military museum at Campbellford, Ontario.

In 1998, Darci Assis, a woodworker based in Osorio, Brazil, completed a static replica Tiger Moth on behalf of the Brazilian Navy Museum. The 'aircraft' is fitted with an Alfa Romeo engine and was manufactured with the aid of manuals supplied unwittingly from Hatfield and a number of genuine Tiger Moth parts acquired for the purpose. Following roll-out, Mr Assis volunteered that he would consider building a further batch of six Tiger Moths for museum display.

Using only photographs and scale plans as reference, Sergei Mazny, model maker to the Soviet Air Force Museum, had built an almost complete wooden Tiger Moth at his home at Ivanovo by 1992. The engine, a Walter Minor M332, was ready for installation. Sergei Mazny

THE AGRICULTURISTS

A moment in the working life of Tiger Moth G-ANFP at her two foot operating altitude. Until alternative methods were developed, human field markers were faced with this view of low level Tiger Moth operations as a routine.
J Blake

THE PROTECTION and stimulation of crops is one of the fundamentals of farming and good agro-industrial economics, and the potential of using aircraft to spray or fertilise vast acreage was recognised in the USA during the 'twenties when Louisiana cotton plantations and California fruit farms were 'dusted' by low flying bugsmashers. The first recorded use of 'agricultural aviation' was in 1921 when a Curtiss Jenny spread lead arsenate dust on an infestation of caterpillars in Ohio. A de Havilland Hire Service DH.9 was involved in similar work in Kent in the mid-'twenties until the poisonous nature of its cargo was appreciated, and there is some evidence to suggest that at least one DH.60 Moth was used prewar for aerial application in the USA.

In New Zealand, soon after the First World War, when returning soldiers sought to earn themselves a living from previously unallocated land, the idea of harnessing aviation to land fertilisation was dismissed at government level as 'impractical' in spite of growing evidence from overseas that exactly the reverse was true. Advocates of the system cited numerous examples of progress made elsewhere: a 45 acre potato crop in Lincolnshire had been sprayed from the air in 29 minutes, a job which would have taken at least two days of backbreaking effort if working on the surface.

The breakthrough did not come until 1941 when a Public Works Department employee flying a government owned Miles Whitney Straight, used his initiative to redress a situation caused by weather and sowed 375 acres with lupins in two days by pouring bags of seed, at a predetermined rate, down a perforated pipe held out of the cabin window. Although admonished by his superiors, the practicability of aerial agriculture was established, and official trials were sponsored using a 75 Squadron Grumman Avenger with a hopper installed in the torpedo compartment.

The first New Zealand trials of an agricultural Tiger Moth were in March 1949 when, in an attempt to reduce the rabbit population, the front seat passenger of ZK-ASO (83533), poured poison pellets through a funnel let into the floor. In May, ZK-ASO was fitted with a hopper of 400lb carrying capacity and flown by John Brazier serviced 64 acres in the first recorded hour of such commercial activity in the country, spreading 3 tons of superphosphate on Sir Heaton Rhodes' property at Tai Tapu during 16 flights.

Once the benefits of agricultural aviation had been fully recognised in Australia, New Zealand and Great Britain, the Tiger Moth promoted her own virtues: cheap to buy and operate, available in large numbers with masses of spares, and engineers and pilots ready, willing and experienced. Converted locally as an evolving improvisation, each

Above: **Temple Martin in his workshop at Hastings, surrounded by the tools of his trade, Tiger Moth airframes, agricultural and otherwise, and Gipsy Major engines.** deHMC Archive

scheme approved on its merits, the Tiger Moth laid the foundation for a vast industry, its very success leading to its own demise as purpose-built aircraft were gradually introduced, once the industry had convinced itself they were economically viable.

In all Tiger Moth agricultural conversions, the front seat was stripped out to accommodate a hopper or a tank, depending on the business role of that aircraft: spraying, dusting, top dressing, spreading, seeding etc, and distribution of the load was achieved either through a specially designed venturi under the floor, or spraybars or atomisers under or on the lower wings, with wind driven pumps attached to the undercarriage as required. Operationally, the aircraft were pushed to the limit, and beyond. Fine pitch propellers were essential for getting out of some of the tiny unprepared landing strips most adjacent to working sites, and flying for days or weeks at a time away from base was known to cause memory lapse when engine hours were finally logged.

Before daily operations commenced, it was essential that the spray bar equipment be calibrated, and using a basic formula which included airspeed and width of the swathe, given a known system pressure, it was possible to calculate the spraying duration based on an ideal output measured in gallons per acre. Spray droplet size was critical too; coarse droplets would not wet all the crop, but too fine a measure and the spray would drift and evaporate.

British company Micronair, an associate of Isle of Wight-based Crop Culture, developed a rotary atomiser which was bolted with spar saddle plates onto the top surface of a Tiger Moth's lower wings. Liquid chemical was fed into a rotating drum and expelled by centrifugal force through a gauze cylinder where it was broken into droplets to form a spray. A major advantage of the system was that droplets were of uniform size, a feature controlled by the drum's rotational speed, governed by simply adjusting the blade pitch of the air-driven fans.

The corrosive nature of some cargoes caused a few operators to remove rear fuselage fabric to facilitate cleaning and inspection. The practice was condoned in Australia where the undressed aircraft were known as 'bare bum Tigers', but the configuration was not approved in New Zealand and at least one operator was grounded by the authorities for flying with no fabric on the underbelly of the fuselage, and loose covers attached to the sides of the rear frame by baler wire. The lack of fabric resulted in an altered spin recovery technique, and due to the general nature of the configuration, a complete ban on any form of intentional aerobatics. An approved modification to replace all fuselage fabric with plywood panels screwed to a false wooden framework found no favour.

Photographs on the opposite page:

Top left: **Doing the business in 1976. Equipped with full span spray bars and a wind driven pressure pump, Hap Neville demonstrates stripped down 'Ag-Tiger' ZK-ANL the last working example in the world. The Tiger Moth boosted the promotion of practical agricultural aviation and secured for many surplus aircraft a whole new career.** R L Ewing

Centre left: **An angled view of the hopper installation looking forward from the port side. Additional bracing takes the load and ensures that the hopper remains steadfastly in position.** AE of New Zealand

Bottom: **As an experiment, Temple Martin fitted a pair of external spray tanks to the underfloor 'bomb rack' position of Tiger Moth ZK-AIX in December 1949, but after one job the tanks were removed and discarded.** Temple Martin

Photographs on this page:

Top left: **A grader blade type spreader was fitted to Tiger Moths of Airwork (NZ) Ltd and used for dropping poisoned carrot cubes for rabbit control or superphosphate powder.** deHMC Archive

Top right: **Spray nozzles required adjustment for each individual job to ensure that the flow rate and droplet size were most ideally set for the task. Expert calibration accurately determined the volume of chemical deposited per acre.** Bill Bowker

Second from top: **Any number of locally invented loading systems was put into operation, all with the same aim: to fill the hopper to maximum capacity in the shortest possible turn-round time whilst ensuring the safety of the aircraft and the pilot.** Bill Bowker

Centre left: **The Britten-Norman rotary atomiser picked up on the rear spar of the lower mainplanes. Feed pipes ran inside the wing. Rotary atomisation was considered to be by far the most economical method of dispensing liquid chemical.** Richard Riding

Centre right: **The elaborate wind driven pumping system fitted to Tiger Moth G-AOAD. In agricultural operations, free wind power was always selected in preference to any other energy source.** Richard Riding

Bottom: **Tiger Moth G-AOAD was chosen to demonstrate the Britten-Norman rotary atomiser during a conference at the Woodstock Research Centre, Kent in October 1957. The dispensers were set to yield one gallon of chemical per acre.** via Hugh Scanlan

Tiger Moth G-ANCT fitted with a quartet of atomisers, demonstrating the emergency dump facility, a mandatory requirement for all agriculturists operating at high weight and low level. deHMC Archive

Whether appropriately registered or not, VH-BUM was one of the so-called 'bare-bum' Tiger Moths flown with rear fuselage fabric removed in 1967. Although the configuration provided easy accessibility for inspection and cleaning, the airworthiness authorities insisted on proper dress. Neville Parnell

In post-war Canada, ski-equipped Tiger Moths were used to hunt wolves when the animals could be easily tracked in the snow, and shot at with rifles fired from the back seat during low level passes. In New Zealand, pioneer crop spraying pilot Ron Bush was asked by Otago sheep farmers to assist in tracking a dog which had been worrying their flocks. The dog was duly found during a brief airborne reconnaissance, and driven towards a wall of local residents all armed to the teeth, but sensing a trap, it changed direction and headed towards cover. Not to be outsmarted, Bush dived down and hit the dog with a mainwheel, killing it instantly, but badly bending the undercarriage leg and damaging the wing leading edge too. Forced to land straight ahead, the Tiger Moth suffered further injury, but the farming community was so pleased to see the headless body of their enemy, that they carried a hat around the district and raised sufficient funds to pay for the repairs.

Even with its fine pitch propeller, at normal loaded weight, the agricultural Tiger Moth suffered a lack of climb performance, especially when operating in hot, high conditions, a deficiency countered to some extent by the type's good slow speed handling and manoeuvrability, but its carrying capacity in terms of both volume and weight was considered barely adequate to be economical.

Following a series of tests in New Zealand, representation to de Havilland in England, and a period of trial operations with selected modified aircraft, the maximum all-up take-off weight was gradually increased from the standard category 1,825lb applicable to all Tiger Moths, to 2,190lb. Part of the argument for an increase had been to divide the declared tonnage dropped by the number of logged sorties. The answer was a rough indication that almost all take offs were over the legal maximum anyway, and no spate of structural failures had been reported. By 1955, the bureaucrats had established themselves as regulators of the new industry, and decided that unless the Tiger Moth could comply with a new and admittedly practical load dump safety regulation, their maximum all-up weight would revert to standard.

In Australia, similar increases in take off weight reached a maximum of 2,000lb, and the Department of Civil Aviation (DCA), produced a take off weight graph worthy of any multi-jet Flight Manual, recognising not only the more obvious parameters of take-off distances, altitude, temperature and wind component, but put heavy emphasis on runway slope and the effect of grass, long or short, wet or dry. All performance was assumed on the basis of a propeller of 4.33ft pitch, and an engine operating at full throttle.

Peter Charles landed his agricultural Tiger Moth on an Australian farm strip and at taxy speed with the engine idling, bumped the skid over a tree stump causing the tail to lift and the propeller to strike the ground, breaking the tip of one blade where it became embedded. Hundreds of miles from base, what to do? Charles cut off the damaged tip with a hacksaw, then an equal amount from the undamaged blade. The engine ran smoothly enough on the ground and then in the air, so the spraying continued uninterrupted for a week and without any noticeable loss of performance, until the replacement propeller was delivered into the district by train.

When moving around from one contract to another, much of the support equipment was transferred by surface, but occasionally it was necessary to carry it by Tiger Moth. The loading door to the hopper was nearly always too small to allow pumps and hoses to be carried inside, and the remedy was to wrap the hoses around the lower wing root and carry the pump in the luggage locker where it put the trim well outside the CG limits. Holding the stick hard forward was considered acceptable for short duration flights, and the problem was alleviated to some extent by the practice of tying the pilot's personal kit to the root end confluence of rigging wires.

A number of reported accidents was thought to have had similar causes, two possibly due to carburettor icing, although test flights conducted in known icing conditions in New Zealand proved negative. Failures of Sutton harnesses, a style of restraint regarded purely as a military requirement for aerobatic training, resulted in the type's replacement in both New Zealand and in Australia, where a completely revised system of strap anchorage was also introduced.

In May 1961, the Australian DCA announced that turn-over trusses were to be fitted to all agricultural Tiger Moths registered in the country. This involved bolting on at four points just behind the cockpit, a welded tube pylon, a line running through the top of which and roughly parallel with the rear decking, would coincide with the top of the rudder spar. The purpose was to protect the pilot's head in case of a turn over, and some operators took the opportunity to build a framework around the pylon, creating a protective cabin with large windscreen of the type later found on purpose built agricultural aircraft. In New Zealand, a modification to save weight and drag had been to reduce the depth of the rear decking from a position immediately aft of the cockpit, affording less protection to the occupant in case of a roll over.

Tiger Moths served the British agricultural industry faithfully and well for many years, at least until the advent of more efficient tractor drawn equipment allied to the relatively small nature of the fields, rendered crop spraying by fixed wing aircraft to be relatively uneconomic. However, the country was at the forefront of invention and development of aerial spraying and spreading technology and equipment, and was a net exporter. As early as 1953, a hopper system had been designed, manufactured, tested and sold to New Zealand by a flying instructor at the Herts and Essex Aero Club at Broxbourne, all neatly packaged inside Tiger Moth G-ALZA (83589).

On a miserable day in March 1959, hundreds of farmers and officials from the National Agricultural Advisory Service and the British Sugar Corporation, assembled as guests of Fisons Pest Control at Bexwell aerodrome in Norfolk, to witness a demonstration of all the currently available types of agricultural aeroplanes and helicopters. Three Tiger Moths equipped with spray bars or venturis and included in the flying demonstrations, were singled out by the press for their special attraction of being cheap to buy and to operate. *'Despite winds that gusted up to 15 knots, the pilots achieved their object by bringing the succession of aircraft past the enclosure low, slowly and with extreme accuracy,'* wrote J W R Taylor for *The Aeroplane*.

Operators from all over the world were bidders for the annual round of contracts let to spray cotton in Egypt and the Sudan, and British companies often survived the European winter on income generated by their North African adventures. Due to the urgency of complying with contract dates or the panic call to battle without delay against some damaging infestation, some Tiger Moths travelled to the cotton fields in the holds of freighter aircraft, but more usually small gaggles of agriculturists would fly out on the long haul via the South of France, Italy and Tunisia, to follow the Mediterranean coast heading east.

Long range fuel was carried in the hopper which was fitted with rubber liners for the purpose, and transferred to the top tank by hand operated wobble pump. In this configuration it was not unknown for the endurance to be increased to 12 hours, within which sectors of eight hours would be flown without landing.

Prior to engine modifications which dramatically reduced oil consumption, a doubling of the oil capacity was often insufficient to cope with fuel range, and additional supplies were carried in cans stowed in the cockpit. Various methods were adopted for re-oiling in flight, one of which was remembered by Jim Birnie:

'The oil filler was routed to the dashboard, taming it with a cork, and assuaging the Gipsy's thirst by removing this item, inserting a funnel and upending a two gallon can into it, manipulating the whole clear of the ignition switches whilst flying by knee pressure'.

Operating basic aeroplanes with tailskids and no brakes on transit through major international airports laid out with miles of concrete taxyways and aprons was uninviting too:

'Well do I remember the sight of three Tiger Moths taxying on the main tarmac at Cairo airport, throttles set, hopefully, to a sensible taxy speed, with the three pilots outside the aircraft leaning heavily on the fin area and straining to maintain some sort of direction against a very brisk, playful crosswind, the while passing a row of Comets, Tu104s, etc. all positioned beautifully for a ghastly debacle'.

A hazard of a more unexpected nature was encountered by Peter Charles when operating in the rural idyll of Somerset. He thought little of a loud bang which occurred at the commencement of a spray run, but after landing he discovered a number of small holes in the fabric of the starboard mainplanes. Later in the day he heard two more loud reports and felt a scattering of shotgun pellets as they hit the aircraft. Locating the culprit in an adjoining field, Charles flew slowly towards him at 30ft. *'As I approached he raised the shotgun and emptied both barrels at me. Momentarily I was shocked, then angry. As I passed over him I pulled the dump lever and emptied yellow dyed spray all over him. Two months later a man was charged with unlawfully shooting at an aircraft, an offence for which he was found guilty and fined £20'.*

One of the active British operators was Bill Bowker's Farm Aviation Services, born from the financial wreckage of a concern which had gone broke after converting Tiger Moth G-AMTO (84655), to take a hopper, the same aeroplane soloed by Bowker at Panshanger on 25th August 1953 while a student at the de Havilland Aeronautical Technical School. He and two partners managed to raise enough money to liberate two Tiger Moths from the Receivers and to start their own business on a farm strip near Hitchin in the winter of 1959:

'Three seasons later we could say that we had developed systems for operating a fleet, now grown to three Tiger Moths, with a minimum of personnel, maximum mobility and efficiency of application. To do this involved designing a venturi spreader for solid materials which was powerful enough to give a wide swath and so avoid striping of the crop because of uneven application. Also loading equipment which was light, mobile, and required only one operator, and a system of field marking using disposable fluorescent paper cylinders instead of expensive and unreliable human beings, had to be evolved. By these means the company succeeded in doing as good and reliable a job as English weather permits, and staying in business where others had fallen by the wayside or abandoned British work as hopelessly uneconomic.

'With techniques perfected and ways found to deal with most of the muddles, which can only occur in a contract service involving vehicles and aeroplanes loose in a large slice of central and southern England, the aeroplanes soon became the limiting factor in developing the enterprise. Once airborne, the Tiger Moth when suitably equipped and flown, did an excellent job,

The result of pilot Reg Plane's undershoot when attempting to land ZK-ARB at Oparau on 19th August 1952 during one of his first sorties. Reg Plane went on to become Operations Manager for James Aviation. The aircraft was repaired only to be badly damaged again four months later.
via D Noble

The only obvious clue to the previous lifestyle enjoyed by seemingly conventional Tiger Moth VH-SSI is the roll-over pylon, fitted as a mandatory requirement to all Australian registered 'Ag Tigers'. deHMC Archive

Constructed from all new spares by Lawrence Engineering and Sales of Camden in 1960 and registered to Mitair Agricultural Aviation as VH-MIT, this Tiger Moth was fitted with a protective cabin, later removed when the aircraft was overhauled and prepared for commercial joyriding. Gerome Gleeson

The dexterity of the loader driver was all important in hastening the turnround of the applicator who shut down only when refuelling was necessary. Care was essential not to damage the aeroplane or to lose load to the slipstream. Tiger Moth ZK-AIE operating at Northland in April 1953. via Janic Geelan

but apart from having too small a payload it was draughty and uncomfortable for the pilot and difficult to manoeuvre on the ground. Its antique though lovely appearance was the subject of increasing prejudice on the part of the customers'.

Farm Aviation turned away from Tiger Moths and became associated fittingly, with the agricultural version of the DHC.1 Chipmunk, but it was to be a sad farewell. Having every intention of giving G-AMTO an honourable retirement and returning her to her original configuration with which Bowker was familiar, to his eternal shame he broke her beyond economical repair at Upwell, near Ely, while taking off on almost her last spraying sortie on 22nd July 1965.

Adrian Deverell, passionate supporter of the Tiger Moth through a lifetime's association with Rollason Aircraft and The Tiger Club, defended the type against the Chipmunk which in the 'fifties was still considered an upstart. He quoted the case of a taxying mishap in which a Tiger Moth and a Chipmunk had sustained precisely the same damage to propeller, port wing spar and leading edge. The Tiger Moth was returned to service in less than two days whereas the Chipmunk was unserviceable for more than two weeks. The cost of labour and materials to repair the Tiger Moth was only 8% of the bill for the Chipmunk.

And elsewhere the writing was on the wall. On 6th November 1962, the Australian Minister for Civil Aviation announced in Canberra that Tiger Moth aircraft would be banned for use in aerial agricultural work from 31st December 1965, a time scale considered sufficient for the acquisition of other more suitable aircraft types.

One of the reasons for the ban was a quoted accident rate 'three to four times higher than that of more modern aircraft engaged in low flying agricultural work'. Accepting the ban but not the reasoning, Tiger Moth supporters analysed the Australian civil register to discover 220 commercially operated Tiger Moths, outnumbering the nearest rival by 5:1, and the 'one' spent little time at modest speed at zero altitude.

In New Zealand a total of 210 Tiger Moths was engaged in aerial work reaching a peak in the mid-'fifties and reducing to just 15 by 1963. Revered and respected, the agricultural Tiger Moth earned her place in history and the museums of the world. Although New Zealand's first conversion, ZK-ASO, was written off in April 1957, her Australian counterpart VH-PCB (DHA41), survived to the end. Cancelled in October 1964, the aircraft was donated for permanent exhibition with the Walcha Historical Society of New South Wales.

James Aviation, one time operators of a fleet of eleven agricultural Tiger Moths, had owned ZK-AJO (DHA489), for ten years from October 1949, and repurchased her in August 1966. Retired to the company hangar at Hamilton in 1981 and maintained in airworthy condition as a permanent reminder of how it all began, ZK-AJO is credited with 6,914 hours of agricultural flying in addition to her Air Force and club service, during which time she spread 13,393 tons of fertiliser and lime, 42,000lb of seed, and sprayed 9,274 acres. Gross earnings until retirement amounted to £56,000 or about 160 times her Air Force surplus value.

In recognition of the sterling efforts of agricultural Tiger Moths operating in New Zealand, the country's Postal Authority issued a 50c stamp in 1993 depicting a yellow Tiger Moth mounted on a plume of dispersing 'super'. The series of which the 50c stamp was a part, celebrated notable events determined by decade and the 'Aerial Topdressing' titling of the Tiger Moth was listed under the banner of the 1940s, which it most certainly was, but only just.

The legacy of the agricultural era is a new industry from which some of the original and surviving jewels of the trade have been handed on in trust and for safe keeping to an appreciative new generation. Assets from the agricultural business are still turning up in relatively inaccessible areas in Australia where they once fell by the wayside and were not considered worthy of salvage. In 1989, a collection of redundant 'Ag Tigers' was released from over 20 years of storage in Western Australia: 14 airframes, 73 wings, 18 engines plus a treasure trove of assorted spare parts. Included as a bonus was a Royal Flying Doctor Service DH.83 Fox Moth.

The benefits of a clean aeroplane and a large blister hangar with a concrete floor were enjoyed in the early days of Bowker and Pruden Agricultural Aviation at Panshanger in the summer of 1959, facilities once the preserve of Avro Ansons of 1 RFS. Bill Bowker

The business end of the spreader box fitted to Tiger Moth G-AKXG at Panshanger during the early 'fifties. Note the fairings fitted between wing root ends and fuselage lower longerons. *The Aeroplane*

Part of the Farm Aviation air and ground fleet displaying for the camera in the snow at Rush Green during an off-season, about 1960. The agricultural conversion of the DHC.1 Chipmunk was pioneered by Farm Aviation and gradually replaced the Tiger Moth as the principal tool of the company's business. Bill Bowker

A team member guides his gantry, buffeted by the slipstream, to make precise contact with the hopper of ZK-AJO before releasing a measured load into the aircraft. via Dudley Payne

Unceremoniously dumped outside the hangars of the former RAAF Base Uranquinty after losing her undercarriage and rearranging the spray bars when landing there on 8th December 1964, VH-ACJ was stored for 20 years before transfer to a new owner at Berwick. Neville Parnell

ZK-AJO is maintained in airworthy condition by James Aviation as a reminder of how the release of military surplus Tiger Moths fuelled and accelerated the growth of the agricultural aviation business immediately after the end of the Second World War. Norman Eastaff

ALL IN A DAY'S WORK

Closed circuit air racing was and probably always will be won on the techniques employed when rounding the pylons. Super Tiger G-AOAA avoids the tree and banks round the turning point on the disused Church Lawford airfield near Coventry during the National Air Races. The grazing cattle seem to be completely oblivious. *The Aeroplane*

AIR RACING has been a competitive sport since it was discovered that one aeroplane could fly faster, or further, than another, and entrepreneurial sportsmen were persuaded to put up crocks of gold as wagers or prizes. Most prolific of the private owner types during the 'twenties, the DH.60 Moth featured heavily in high profile closed circuit racing for relatively small money prizes, although most entrants flew for the sport and honour rather than any cash reward.

It was the numerical superiority of Tiger Moths in Great Britain during the 'fifties that did much to stimulate some of the pre-war interest. Races between many aeroplanes of the same type would be won on merit: the degree of polishing and honing would be complemented only by the skill of the pilot and his ability to confuse the handicappers. There was no need to devote energy to sealing the gaps and fairing the strut ends, or to streamlining the cockpit and fitting tiny mainwheels in order to minimise the drag,

all features employed during the 'twenties. Skill in rounding pylons and assessing the best conditions for wind and drift at high or low level, and in a well rigged aeroplane with crisp controls and a good engine, would determine the winners.

A disadvantage to racing a privately owned Tiger Moth was that the engine needed to be run at nearly full throttle to qualify in the heats, and defeat the best endeavours of the handicappers in the finals, which would then be flown at full throttle all the way. A broken engine was expensive to replace. and a raced engine, unless maintained to the peak of perfection, soon lost its edge. Club owned and maintained aeroplanes were fair game: cash prizes and kudos for the organisation and no expensive maintenance charges for the competing pilot.

One of the first post-war race meetings held in Great Britain at Lympne in 1947, featured five Tiger Moths in a Scratch Race run over four laps of a ten mile course, and was won by Fred Kirk in G-AINW (83011). The Tiger Moth was sold to India the following year and was lost in 1958 when an Indian Air Force Vampire collided with her hangar, but Fred Kirk was still flying Tiger Moths 50 years later. At the same Lympne meeting, John Cunningham could only manage sixth place in the High Speed Handicap, in spite of achieving 494.63mph in a DH.100 Vampire F.1, but Pat Fillingham set up a new 100km closed circuit record of 178.33mph with the de Havilland Aeronautical Technical School's TK2, G-ADNO. In August the following year, Pat Fillingham won the Tiger Moth Race at Lympne, flying G-AHXC (85032), at 86mph, although John Cunningham's Vampire, this time an F.3, rose to second place in the High Speed Handicap, beaten by a Supermarine Spitfire Mk VIII two seat trainer.

Unlike the 'mock' air races which perambulate gently around a closed circuit in the style of a demented formation, or 'handicap' races with so many different types involved and the single seat ultra-light enjoying as great a chance of victory as the speed twin taking off half an hour behind, Tiger Moth

The pastoral scene: air racing in Great Britain during the 'fifties. The starter, wearing a lounge suit, waves away the Tiger Moth already straining on full throttle while the pilot of the Hawker Aircraft Company's 'vintage collection' Tomtit pays attention. *The Aeroplane*

de Havilland test pilot Pat Fillingham climbing aboard the London Aeroplane Club's G-AHXC at Lympne in August 1948 in preparation for a Tiger Moth race. via British Aerospace *only* races generated great rivalry and high emotion. A first wave of perhaps six Tiger Moths in a field of ten or 12, taking off with the same handicap time, and in line abreast, diving for the first pylon turn, was a sight well worth watching, accompanied by the sound of six full throttle Gipsy Major engines and their assortment of wooden and metal propellers of differing pitch and diameter, selected with infinite care. The choice of propeller was one of the few physical variations between otherwise standard machines that could greatly influence performance.

Tiger Moths have been competitors in, if not winners of, most of the recognised and prestigious air races. Jimmy Denyer's winning speed of 118.5mph flying Tiger Moth G-AIVW (83135), in the 1958 King's Cup Air Race was bettered by Dennis Hartas in G-ANZZ (85834), when he won the de Havilland Tiger Moth Challenge Trophy in 1962 at 120.5mph, a feat which contributed to his award of the Royal Aero Club Jubilee Trophy and British Air Racing Championship for that year.

Lewis Benjamin was offered friendly advice by the future Air Racing Champion before the 1959 National Air Races at Baginton in which 'Benjy' was scheduled to make his racing debut, flying his favourite Tiger Moth G-APRA (85347). His total racing qualification was, as he put it, a Competitor's Licence which he had been awarded for asking. The friendly advice of course, was to fly as fast as possible all the way, but the novice racer soon discovered that although he won the first heat by miles, he was completely handicapped out of the rest of the meeting. Following further advice from seasoned campaigners, the Tiger Moth's tyres were pumped up hard in an effort to reduce ground rolling distance on take off, 'hard' spark plugs were fitted and 'thinner' oil. But it was to no avail, and apart from the experience of legitimate low level flying at high speed through gateways and between trees, the season ended without further success.

Since Tiger Moths and especially their Gipsy Major engines have largely become privately funded icons, 'Air Racing' for the type has taken on a different meaning. In 1977, Bill Hitchcock organised the first 'Great Tiger Moth Air Race', a bi-annual event centred on the Royal Newcastle Aero Club at Maitland, New South Wales. The early sponsors promoted the event as the world's *first* Tiger Moth race and 37 aircraft took part, but the 'race' was really an intensive two day time-trial around Sydney and the Hunter Valley, and the winner was decided on a mix of navigational ability, time keeping and fuel conservation, rather than blind throttle bending.

A very similar exercise took place in Great Britain in 1979, organised by the de Havilland Moth Club, when Famous Grouse Scotch Whisky sponsored 41 Tiger Moths, seven DH.87B Hornet Moths, and a mixed fleet of supporting aircraft including four DH.89A Dragon Rapides and a DH.114 Heron, in an event sold to the media as 'The Famous Grouse Tiger Moth Air Race'.

The aircraft flew from Hatfield by way of Hucknall and Sunderland to Strathallan in Perthshire, and the winner was decided against parameters very much in parallel with those laid down in Australia. It was appropriate perhaps, that David Cyster and his wife Cherry, flying Tiger Moth G-ANRF, carried off the Grouse Trophy and a gallon jar of the sponsor's product which has remained unopened. The tenth anniversary of the 'Grouse Rally' as the event inevitably became known, operated around a curtailed circuit including Old Warden and Duxford due to the closure of both Strathallan and Sunderland in the intervening ten years. Desecration of the Hatfield site itself in1994 will ensure that the 1979 Grouse Rally will remain special and totally unique.

Perhaps one of the most challenging races in which Tiger Moths have been involved, and which really was a no-holds-barred all-out race with time as the principal challenger, was *The Daily Mail*, London (Marble Arch) to Paris (Arc de Triomphe) Air Race organised between 13th and 23rd July 1959, celebrating Louis Blériot's 1909 crossing of the English Channel, an aviation event remembered and celebrated by a greater cross section of the community perhaps, than any other. The Race stimulated the imagination of all: competitors, officials, Customs, Immigration, airlines, travel agencies, air forces, the media and sponsors. Every type of vehicle was featured: high powered motorcycles, racing and veteran cars, helicopters, hovercraft, jet airliners, bombers and military fighters operating at low level, not to mention pedal cycles, fold-up scooters and running shoes. Hugh Tansley chose a motorised lawn mower for the journey from Central London to Croydon, and from Toussous to the Arc, averaging 3.5mph on these sections. The Croydon-Lympne-Toussous sectors were completed by Tiger Moth G-ACDC (3177), whose contribution was included in Hugh Tansley's overall time of ten hours and 44 minutes. Using a combination of a fast motorcycle and RAF Hawker Hunter, the winner completed the course in less than half an hour.

Speed in the air versus speed on the ground has always been an issue worthy of publicity, and both Captain de Havilland and Hubert Broad have been featured in spectacular situations when competing against steam trains and power boats in production Moths.

To settle an argument about the relative merits of racing cars and small aircraft, a pint of beer was put up as a wager at Sunderland Flying Club in May 1964 when Tiger Moth G-AREH (85287), was entered in competition against a Lotus Ford 23B for the length of Usworth's 1,500 yard runway. Operating unfavourably into wind, the Tiger Moth started her challenge in the airborne position, but from a standing start the Lotus had achieved over 100mph within 10 seconds, and accelerated away to take the trophy with relative ease.

Placings were identical in a similar challenge mounted at Mangalore aerodrome near Sydney on 13th April 1986. The quarter mile dash was a competition between Anthony James, representing the Antique Aeroplane Association of Australia, flying his British built Tiger Moth VH-ALC (82360), one of the 1940 imports, and Graeme Lowe of the Historic Racing Car Register of Australia, who was driving a 1936, two litre, supercharged, twin OHC Alta, described as being 'very fast'. Predictably, the Tiger Moth got off to a flying start and climbed to her racing height of 5ft, but the driver of the car kept his boot pressed hard down and slowly overhauled the Tiger Moth to win by a short head.

British Army glider pilots trained with the RAF in Tiger Moths at 21 EFTS Booker after June 1941, and due to the size of the

A typical line up at the start of a Tiger Moth race during the annual jamboree that was the National Air Races at Coventry in the early 'sixties. Jackaroos were classified as 'Tiger Moths' but when flown solo had a better performance. Richard Riding

Apart from the application of much elbow grease and polish, the top speed of a Tiger Moth could generally be improved only by careful attention to detail such as this sculpted wing fillet. Bill Lusk

In the 'pits' at the Royal Newcastle Aero Club, Maitland where competitors gathered in 1978 for the locally organised 'Great Tiger Moth Air Race', in reality a test of navigational skills and fuel economy. Bill Hitchcock

establishment, it was necessary to base E and F Flights at nearby Denham as a means of relief. Although related, there was a marked degree of rivalry between the two airfields, and aerobatic competitions were regularly organised between the instructors of all the Flights.

The Glider Pilot Regiment was regarded as simply another unit of the British Army, and volunteers were lured into the ranks by the enticement of additional allowances. Serving with the Black Watch in Scotland in 1942, Bill Sarjantson was offered an extra two shillings a day to join the Parachute Regiment, but three shillings and six pence if he became a glider pilot. He opted for the additional pay, was taught to fly Tiger Moths with 3 EFTS at Shellingford in October 1942, but transferred to Booker for refresher training early in 1943. Most operational army glider flights were of necessity one way trips, and Bill Sarjentson's Tiger Moth training led him to a final landing at Arnhem in 1944, where a non-fatal shot in the head put paid to his flying career.

A peculiarity of circuit flying at Denham was that against accepted practice, it was usual to operate right hand, taking aircraft around the substantial facility that was the local film studios, and where one of the Denham based instructors, David Tomlinson, spent some of his working hours in front of the cameras. On 6th April 1985, Tomlinson was the compere at a concert in support of the Bomber Command Museum at Hendon, and between renderings of the Spitfire Prelude and the Dam Busters March, the former instructor alluded to his previous associations with Tiger Moths, at which some of the audience sniggered. Whether in anger or jest or frustration, David Tomlinson responded: 'Well I don't know what's funny about *that!*'

In action it was always believed that British trained pilots would naturally break left if attacked from behind, and one successful German fighter pilot said that his deflection shooting always assumed that would be the case. It was the built-in instinct of Denham trained pilots to break right and against convention, which unexpected reaction might have saved their lives.

Charlie Miller and his Tiger Moth VH-CES taking off from Port Macquarie during the second Great Tiger Moth Air Race in October 1978. Note the elaborate reprofiling of the cockpit surrounds. Neville Parnell

On the eve of the 1979 Famous Grouse Rally, part of the fleet drawn up at Hatfield. The buildings on the left are the first private owner hangars built in 1930, and in the distance, the classrooms, offices and hangars constructed for the Reserve School. Philip Birtles

While prospective glider pilots were learning to fly in Tiger Moths, the Airborne Forces Establishment (AFE) at Ringway kept a number of the type on charge for light tugging duties alongside Hawker Hectors and bigger birds. The Tiger Moths were used to develop new or experimental towing techniques, climbing with their charges to thousands of feet before casting off. One was fitted with a Chance sector light to enable a following glider to maintain station in darkness.

At No 1 Glider Training School (GTS), Thame in 1941, trainee army glider pilot instructors were themselves instructed whilst flying Kirby Kites towed in formation by Tiger Moths and Hawker Hectors, during which the aerial convoys were subjected to mock attack by Hawker Hurricanes. Drawn from all regiments, the situation at Thame was described by Lawrence Wright in his book *The Wooden Sword* :

'The informal air of the camp was matched by its inmates, the instructors to be, and a rum lot they were, as the devil said when he first saw the Ten Commandments. Their clothing was the opposite of uniform. All of them glider pilots, hurriedly secured by posting, by attachment, by seconding or by shadier means'.

In post-war civil life, Australian glider pilot Fred Hoinville was one of the first to be approved for towing club gliders with his ex-RAAF Tiger Moths VH-AIU (DHA398) and then VH-AYY (DHA214), the famous *Brolga*. On 27th September 1951, Hoinville left Bankstown in VH-AYY with a Grunau Baby in tow, scheduled to be delivered to Toowoomba, 500 miles away, a trip estimated to take two days divided into four sectors, and flying at 60 knots. A telephone line was attached to the tow rope to enable the Tiger Moth pilot to communicate with the glider pilot, but the exhaust note of the Gipsy Major combined with the wind noise in the open cockpit, neutralised an already weak tone, and the glider pilot fell back on the tried and tested method of hand signals transmitted with the aid of a table tennis bat.

The flight progressed through conditions of extreme turbulence, low cloudbase and at one point a wall of smoke which rose to 6,000ft from a succession of huge forest fires. In order to circumvent the worst of the smoke, the linked pair were forced to fly directly into sun where all the problems of keeping in station and with the tow line taught, were magnified by a blinding orange ball on the horizon. An unexpected headwind had cut the groundspeed after a period of rapid progress, and within 20 miles of his destination, having unexpectedly travelled almost 500 miles in the one day, Hoinville decided it would be safer to land rather than risk the prospect of running out of fuel. With a tail down attitude due to the presence of the glider, the fuel gauge was considered to be unreliable, although on estimates, about 30 minutes' worth of fuel was believed to be still in the tank. But an unexpected problem soon arose as described by Hoinville in his book *'Halfway to Heaven'*:

'It was sad to have to land so close to our goal, but the risk of going on was not justified. I selected a nice large flat paddock alongside a farmhouse on a main road, and waggled Brolga's *wings in a signal to Bob Muller. He released the rope and circled down into the paddock. I dropped the rope beside him and trundled in too.* Brolga *landed smoothly but seemed to stop rather short.*

'I stepped out, into six inches of soft, gooey Queensland black soil, wet as a swamp. It was unbelievable. Here in this drought scorched land, how the dickens did the field get wet?

'We had landed in Bill Becker's barley field, at the township of Cambooya, 15 miles from Toowoomba. Bill arrived smartly and solved our mystery. There had been a small local storm on the previous night, and alone in all Queensland, the barley paddock had got a soaking.

'Within five minutes about 20 helpers arrived, dragged the two aircraft to the end of the field, got some fuel, and passed on all the latest radio reports. All Queensland and almost all Australia were following our unusual flight with interest and goodwill. Everybody knew about us, and was desperately anxious to help us along. In a few minutes we were ready to go again. We had covered over 500 miles in one day and had only 15 to go, with half an hour of light left. We climbed in, waved good-bye, and I opened the throttle. Brolga *strained mightily, took up a little slack in the rope, and then stopped, tail up but wheels not moving.*

'Sadly and sheepishly we scrambled out again. We guessed what had happened. The Grunau had a special pair of tiny solid rubber wheels mounted on the skid. These had sunk into the mud and made a really efficient anchor. Racing against the sunset, we got out our tools and whipped the wheels and axle off, and tried again. No luck. The skid this time pushed up a mound of mud ahead of the glider. We were stuck. There was not time to take down a part of the fence to get out into the road tonight. We dragged the aircraft back to the fence and tied them down, finding great difficulty in driving the pegs into the hard earth. The end of the field had missed the heaviest rain, and although the top two inches were soft, the rest was like a rock'.

The epic journey was completed the following day after a 30ft section of wire fence was removed which enabled both aircraft to be pushed through onto a straight road three miles long. Twelve minutes after take off the Tiger Moth and its towed cargo was overhead Toowoomba Gliding Club.

Almost a year after the Toowoomba delivery, Hoinville's Tiger Moth towed a pair of gliders simultaneously from Camden to Dubbo, a distance of about 200 miles, and recorded the first double tow ever attempted in Australia.

Throughout post-war Europe, many civil and military gliding clubs and schools relied on Tiger Moth tugs as launch vehicles, apart

The Famous Grouse Rally fleet drawn up at Hatfield in June 1979. The large building at left, 'the aluminium shed', now listed and protected, was erected as Flight Test Shed for the DH.106 Comet airliner and is unique. The Clubhouse and squash courts built for the London Aeroplane Club in 1930 stand alongside the tree and marquee at right. deHMC Archive

The Famous Grouse Rally fleet safely assembled at Strathallan together with a number of local visitors and the Royal Navy Lynx helicopter which accompanied the stream along the route from Hatfield.
deHMC Archive

from basic flying training and agricultural work perhaps, the most universal of all tasks with which the aircraft was ever charged. In Scandinavia, the ability to tug targets and gliders had been a primary operational requirement since the Tiger Moth was introduced to service during the 1930s, yet this flexibility was not recognised as a selling point and was never exploited in pre-war marketing.

Earliest records lodged with the British airworthiness authorities show that clearance was granted by an Airworthiness Approval Note in March 1947 to permit Helliwells and Marshall's Flying School to tow gliders with Tiger Moths, subject to the following basic limitations which were imposed at that time:

- Maximum glider weight 650lb (but satisfactory flight trials were completed with gliders weighing 660lb, 680lb and 730lb).
- Breaking strain of towrope (or weak link), 8 cwt.
- Towing speed, 70mph.

In 1953, the British Ministry of Supply (MoS), successor to the Ministry of Aircraft Production (MAP), initiated Modification 145, possibly in respect of the minimal number of Tiger Moths scheduled to remain in service with the Royal Navy or even as support for many of the ex RAF aircraft sold to overseas governments. Mod 145 introduced the MoS request to equip the Tiger Moth Mk.II for glider towing duties, and made provision for the installation of an 'Ottley' release hook and associated controls. Engineers were advised that they were expected to provide all parts necessary for the modification by making them on site, all, that is, with the exception of the release hook which could be supplied ex stock by Ottley Motors Ltd. At first glance a simple exercise, the job was estimated to take about a week per engineer, per aircraft.

Sold from 9 MU Cosford in one of the first post-war surplus disposal sales, T6901 (85130), was re-sold in the Netherlands and registered PH-UAW in May 1947. The aircraft hit a glider towing cable while taxying at Hilversum in August 1956 and in 1963 she hit a banner towing cable while airborne at Eelde. The cable end snaked into the cockpit and wrapped itself around the pilot's hands. The aircraft was comprehensively demolished when she subsequently landed without assistance. The wreckage was sold, rebuilt into a single seat configuration at Rotterdam, and with a new identity, PH-AAB, embarked upon a career as a seaside banner tug. Within a year she was in a ditch at Zestienhoven. The aircraft had picked up the banner at too slow a speed, failed to lift it off the ground, failed to release it too, and had slowly subsided back to earth.

Banners were laid out on the ground in a manner which allowed them to be peeled back on themselves once the aircraft's tow hook had engaged on a suspended wire strop, thereby gently feeding in the drag rather than attempting a snatch. Any other method of pick up with the limited power available to a Tiger Moth would have been impossible. As a precaution against snagging the suspended strop with the main undercarriage a light cable deflection system was designed utilising the axles, the top fixing of the undercarriage radius rods, and the underside of the front cowling as anchorages.

During a banner towing flight in formation with another aircraft in July 1964, the pilot of Tiger Moth PH-UVC (84638), realised his banner had become entangled with the other, and during a manoeuvre intended to help them disengage, one tow cable broke, leaving PH-UVC in command of both. Even at full power, the Tiger Moth could not maintain height or speed and unable to cast off the tow was forced to land in a bulb field where she nosed over unceremoniously in the rich topsoil.

With the exception of an Italian Tiger Moth whose motive power was temporarily supplied by an Alfa Romeo engine, in all probability a licence-built Gipsy Major, as far as is known, all other airframes have been mated to Gipsy Major engines (of several different marques) or the Menasco Pirate. In 1970, Hannu Riihela, Finnish designer of world class PiK sailplanes, acquired the mortal remains of OH-ELA (85167), a British export of 1951 which was badly damaged at Hollola in 1954 when operating on skis and subsequently placed in store.

Riihela completely rebuilt the aircraft using alternative parts when originals could not be located, and having no Gipsy Major engine, installed a close cowled Lycoming O-360 delivering 180hp, and complete with self starter and generator. First flown on 29th April 1977 by Pekka Parssinen, the improvement in performance was phenomenal: from a 200ft take off run, a climb rate of 1,500fpm was achieved. Not surprisingly the aircraft was used for launching PiK sailplanes and was also operated on floats and skis. Later sold to a group of airline pilots, the aircraft was last seen suspended from the ceiling of the gentleman's outfitting section of a Helsinki department store, with Santa Claus waving greetings from the rear cockpit.

Standard Tiger Moths have been employed by many gliding clubs to provide aero tows to customers at the end of a 200ft nylon rope, and much of the economy of the operation was in the art of getting back down again as quickly as possible. The benefits of reduction in airborne time, due to the methods employed, were often outweighed by the cost of engine repairs. A series of full power climbs followed by the rapid cooling experienced in power off descents was not the best way to treat a Gipsy engine.

Lewis Benjamin earned some free flying by offering Tiger Club Tiger Moths to gliding clubs, and the occasions proved to be very competitive as well as financially rewarding:

'It was not that glider towing was dull, but any journey could be more exciting if, whilst on the way down, you could also have some fun. There was an element of competition amongst the tug pilots not only to see who could be down the quickest, but who could best entertain the others en route.

'We normally lost our tow around 2,000ft, and it was soon proved that the fastest way down without tangling the rope was to spin the Tiger Moth. The routine was to cast off, close the throttle and whip the nose up for a bit more altitude, then boot on rudder at the right moment and start counting the turns. Five turns in a spin were plenty, and all too soon you found yourself at 700ft or so, nicely placed for the run in. An acknowledged variation was a slow roll either way, but no one ever attempted a loop because we believed the rope might curl around and foul the controls. Just for the record we were wrong; others have done it since.

'There were two schools of thought too, about releasing the rope after the tow and prior to landing. The first was a slow run in at 30ft, to release the rope and if possible, plonk it neatly in front of the next glider all ready for the hook up. The second, because some thought the extra circuit, no matter how brief, a waste of valuable time, was to land with the rope still attached. One's landing had to be so short, that all one had to do, at least in theory, when one rolled to a stop, was to move the glider forward a few feet to hook up. The trouble was that since the prudent glider pilot wanted as long a run as possible, he would position his machine as near to the hedge as he could, and the Tiger Moth's landing run had to be very short indeed.

'It is a simple fact that the slower one flew, and the aircraft could be encouraged to fly very slowly, the more the end of the rope would dangle, aided and abetted by the metal clip at the end. To drag the rope through a tree or a hedge could prove disastrous. On one of my earlier trips I misjudged everything and dragged my rope not only through a hedge but between a couple having a picnic at the field's edge. The hook whipped away the cloth and goodies as neatly as any conjuror. The two were so shattered by this disappearing act, that by the time I got there to apologise, they had fled'.

The current generation has missed the time when almost every aerodrome boasted a club owned Tiger Moth, rocking gently in any breeze as she stood head to wind on the grass between flights, the Gipsy Major engine tinkling erratically as it gradually cooled, the aromatic odour of hot oil and petrol mingling with other unique aeroplane smells. But more than 50 years after the Tiger Moth was training the Empire to fly in times of crisis, and the Tiger Moth became too outmoded for the clubs, a whole industry grew up: operations providing 'trial lessons' and 'joyrides' in Tiger Moths. The businesses became particularly well established in Australia where the climate has much in its favour when harnessing commercial enterprise to outdoor activity, but in New Zealand and Great Britain also, the public is actively encouraged to play a fuller part by accepting the extra trappings of fleecy lined jacket, shunned by those in the know, and satirical white scarf, in addition to the essential and traditional helmet and goggles.

The customers who flock to the booking offices know that a flight in a Tiger Moth, (aerobatics optional and at extra cost), is special and significant, and is much more than a mere open cockpit circuit. The young men who flew Supermarine Spitfires and Avro Lancasters and Handley Page Halifaxes learned to fly on the Tiger Moth, did they not? Fifty years after the great conflict, many of those once young pilots wish to renew acquaintance, or to fly again in celebration of a special birthday or anniversary. Children and grand-children are encouraged to fly to experience what dad or grand-dad once did. But the first jet pilots learned to fly in Tiger Moths too, such was her service span; also the Reservists whose units retained the aeroplane into the 'fifties. A view on perspective is that nearly the whole of the first generation of British Concorde captains learned their skills on Tiger Moths.

Anthony James in his Tiger Moth VH-ALC, an ex-RAF aeroplane shipped to Australia in 1940, gradually losing his race with Graeme Lowe in a 1936 Alta at Mangalore aerodrome in April 1986. The Tiger Moth was later sold to a German owner but was badly damaged in transit when its trailer overturned into a ditch. via Anthony James

Charles Shea-Simonds and his Australian built Tiger Moth G-AGZZ down in the smoke to celebrate the 10th anniversary of the Mid-Hants Railway in 1988. The locomotive was travelling tender-first. Herbie Knott

In 1998, Commander Philip Shaw RN, a regular pilot of the Fairey Swordfish with the Royal Navy Historic Flight based at Yeovilton, and owner of Tiger Moth G-AFVE (83720), completed a civilian flying instructor course on his own aircraft which was maintained on a Public Transport category Certificate of Airworthiness. Subsequently, he arranged a contract with the Defence Research Agency (DERA), for the Tiger Moth to be flown as part of their 'handling' syllabus, by pilots attending the Empire Test Pilots School at Boscombe Down, one of the greatest compliments to the training abilities of the aircraft, perhaps.

Parachuting from Tiger Moths has always been enjoyed by those who prefer never to land in an aeroplane having taken off in one, and in the immediate post-war era, the development of parachuting as a Western sport rather than a pure military necessity, often featured a Tiger Moth as a launch vehicle. The open cockpit was sufficiently large to accommodate a seat parachute and a chest mounted reserve, providing the front stick was removed, in addition to easy egress, if standing up and stepping delicately over the door sill in a gale force slipstream can ever be considered easy.

Top: **As a glider tug based with the London Gliding Club at Dunstable, Tiger Moth G-AOEL unusually carried the extra weight of leading edge slats and spin strakes.** Richard Riding

Centre: **Tiger Moth G-AMLF climbing away from Husbands Bosworth in September 1968 with a heavy single seater on the line. The glider pilot maintained his ideal position by referencing the top wings of the Tiger Moth to the horizon.** Alfred Jenks

Above: **Tiger Moth PH-BIS was fitted with a light tubular framework picking up on undercarriage and engine mounting, almost certainly as a precaution against a misjudged cable snatch when banner towing.** via Herman Dekker

Bottom: **In 1977 Finnish PiK glider designer Hannu Riihela opted for a readily available 180hp Lycoming O-360 for his Tiger Moth OH-XLA, resulting in a phenomenal increase in performance.** Hannu Riihela

In a moment of rare inattention, it has been known for a jumper to exit by the port side, knocking off the external ignition switches as they went and leaving the pilot in a state of some embarrassment. With wires and struts to hold on to, the Tiger Moth was an ideal, steady platform and for those intending to leave the front seat in dignity, a pure vindication of the specifier's art back in 1931.

The Tiger Moth was an ideal aeroplane to drop from when parachutes were less directionally efficient, but with rapid technical development and the quest for an aircraft that could climb higher, faster and with a greater load, the type was relegated to the position of guest appearances only.

Under the terms of the Permission granted by the British authorities in compliance with the Air Navigation Order, individual aircraft were approved to drop parachutists subject to:

a. The pilot must occupy the rear cockpit.
b. The front cockpit control column must be removed.
c. The parachutist must occupy the front cockpit and exit to starboard.
d. At the time of dropping the wings must be level and airspeed between 60 and 80mph IAS.

When Charles Shea-Simonds applied in a private capacity for permission to drop parachutists from his own Tiger Moth G-AGZZ (DHA926), not influenced by his standing as Vice-President of the British Parachute Association (BPA), BPA Pilot Examiner and Private Pilot Licence X Examiner, he was advised that in addition to the existing limitations it was expected that:

1. The front rudder bar must be disconnected and the rudder bar connecting rod removed.
2. The front cockpit entry door (starboard) must be removed.

A gentle letter to the appropriate Division ensured that common sense prevailed, and the requirement to meet the additional conditions was withdrawn.

When dropping from a Tiger Moth the normal practice was to indicate the beginning of the run-up at which time the parachutist would stand up using the centre section struts for assistance, and perch half in and half out of the cockpit, in the slipstream, to ensure the best view for the final positioning. There was no necessity to open the door which could be comfortably straddled. Buffeting was considerable such that speed was reduced to less than 60mph, reducing further to just above the stall with a little power on to aid stability at the moment of departure. Facing the tail, the jumper would dive off, or facing forward merely step backwards off the walkway. In the 'fifties and 'sixties it was the done thing to follow the parachute down, exercising a degree of mother hen protection, and should the jumper descend into some predicament or foreign field, the Tiger Moth was overhead to mark the spot, ready to summon transport or necessary assistance.

RAF surplus Tiger Moth DE313 (85347), was sold as Lot 166 from 10 MU Hullavington in 1953 and delivered into the W A Rollason hangar at Croydon. In an effort to offer the best opportunities for jumping, especially during the conviviality of the Tiger Club's regular air displays of the late 'fifties, founding father Norman Jones arranged for DE313, registered G-APRA from June 1959, to be converted with the specific intention of providing airborne assistance to parachutists, and she was named *Sue Burges* in honour of Great Britain's leading lady sport parachutist of the day.

Modifications to the airframe included the removal of controls and compass bracketry from the front cockpit, fitment of a streamlined forward windscreen and a grab-handle on the starboard fuselage side. The starboard front door was removed and the exposed sill rounded and padded; the starboard walkway was widened, and a transparent panel some 12 inches square let into the trailing edge.

Flown by Lewis Benjamin, with Sue Burges as a temporary passenger, G-APRA was positioned from Croydon to Stapleford Tawney on 10th May 1959 for her first operational sortie, and with the intention of attempting to take the national free fall record past the one minute barrier. Sue Burges was dropped from 10,500ft over Stapleford in conditions of rising wind and developing cumulus, but the drop ended in disaster when she was blown into an oak tree and seriously hurt, fortunately making a full recovery.

Writing slogans or messages in the sky using smoke emitting aircraft, is an invention of the immediate post World War One era, when nimble ex-scouts were modified for the purpose. In more recent times, smoke generation for the added illumination of team or singleton aerobatic performances has become a standard expectation. Probably in all history, only one Tiger Moth has been involved professionally in skywriting, and that in 1952 when Fred Hoinville's VH-AYY (DHA214) was the first and only licensed performer in Australia.

Influenced by the size and orientation of the target towards which the message was directed, the cloud situation, position of the sun, thermal activity and wind shift, VH-AYY would operate at heights between 12,000ft and 17,000ft, and in some areas, notably over Sydney, the pilot would liaise with research meteorologists who had set up programmes to track the smoke drift on behalf of studies into clear air movements. At such heights a message in smoke can be clearly read for a radius of 20 miles covering 1,200 square miles, can be placed within ten miles of the target without loss of clarity and depending on the stability of the atmosphere, may linger overhead or drift intact for up to 30 minutes before decaying.

The employed system of smoke generation, apart from the use of firework-like smoke candles, totally inappropriate for sky writing, has always centred on the injection of liquid oil or diesel fuel, usually into a hot engine exhaust where it vaporises into billowing off-white smoke, coloured as required by the addition of concentrated dyes. On opening the Tiger Moth's smoke-oil control valve, Hoinville's aircraft immediately generated a huge plume of white smoke which just as easily and completely was cut off when the valve was closed. For total consistency in smoke quality it was necessary to operate at full throttle to achieve and maintain maximum exhaust temperature, only one of the deciding factors in determining that smoke trails should be laid in the horizontal, rather than the vertical plane.

Charity, one of the fleet of three Tiger Moth tugs maintained by the London Gliding Club at Dunstable in the early 'sixties. Two were later damaged by fire in the hangar underneath the unique 'thirties designed clubhouse. John Ellis

Australian built VH-WAP, one of a fleet of Tiger Moths operated for pleasure flying and charter work by Bruce McGarvie, based in the sub tropical environment of Queensland's Gold Coast. Stuart Howe

Inscribed 'Mount Cook Flightseeing', New Zealand built Tiger Moth ZK-BRC is used as a promotional tool by Mount Cook Airlines and operates against the breath-taking background of the southern Alps around Queenstown. John King

Tiger Moth joyriding, the new jargon for what was always a 'pleasure flight', is established business in some parts of the southern hemisphere, and the operators publish glossy, coloured brochures in parallel with any other tourist type attraction.

How does a pilot maintain orientation during a skywriting exercise? Hoinville explained:

'It is impossible to steer by compass. Once I start writing the compass will be two laps behind all the way. Even a gyro compass is no use; it would topple and stop working on the vertical turns. I must steer by eye alone. Today it can be done only by using the sun. It is 2.00pm and the sun is very high in the sky, so it will not be easy. I must fly towards the sun and towards the shadow of my head on the instrument panel for a rough west-east line. For north-south I must line up the sun with the aileron hinges either side. That sounds simple enough but it is not, for when you are coming out of a vertical turn, with 15 other things to do also, finding your head shadow and centering it where the instrument panel would be if you were flying level is a bit like doing a crossword puzzle while making a 100 yard sprint.

'When operating over Sydney the bay water was useful to me at times for observing my work as I did it. The smoke would not cast a shadow on the land, but on the grey-brown water near the city, where the muddy river stained the sea, the letters showed up very clearly. Although they still read back to front to me, the shadows gave me a perfect picture as I wrote. It was this, and some photographs, that amazed me by revealing to me the sharpness of the right angles which the Tiger Moth drew in writing such letters as L or E, using vertical turns. I had expected to see corners that were rounded somewhat, for it does not seem possible for any aircraft to change direction by 90 degrees without some skid on the corner, yet the smoke is angled as sharply as though traced with a square.

'Telling people that the letters are half a mile long does not impress them half as much as saying that one letter is the same size as six Sydney Harbour bridges piled one on top of the other, or two and a half times as high as the Empire State Building, or three times as high as the Eiffel Tower, but somewhat less enduring'.

On the occasion that Hoinville sprained his ankle by falling over a chock when moving his Tiger Moth out of the hangar, he decided he should have a deputy pilot, and lined up a suitable candidate:

'He was a first class pilot, but he had never tackled anything like skywriting before. He had two attempts and got utterly lost each time. His letters varied from very small to enormous in size, and from west to south east in direction, and either overlapped or were six miles apart. Apart from these minor points he was not bad. He got a little confused at one point halfway through the test, after he had unconsciously changed direction by 90 degrees, and proceeded to write the next bit over the top of the first. Shortly after that he lost all sight of the smoke and could not find it again.

'He landed and I showed him the sketches of his progress. We had a good laugh together and he went and got a job as an airline pilot instead'.

FRONT PAGE NEWS

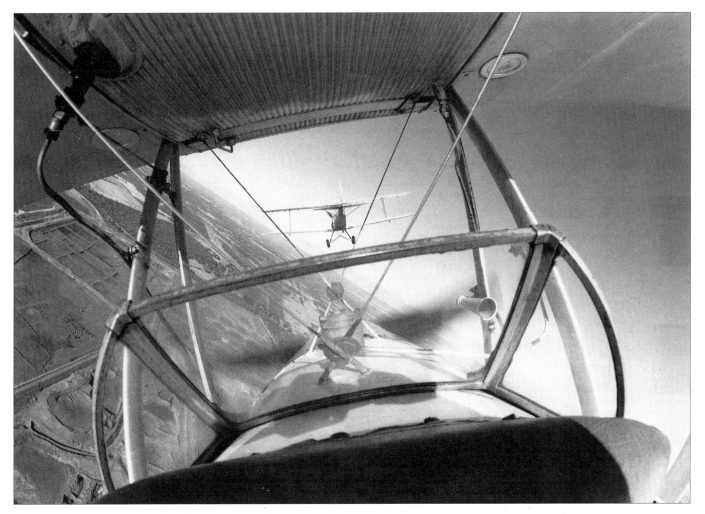

The view ahead from the front cockpit of an Australian Tiger Moth, distorted by the camera lens, but well illustrating the field of vision enjoyed by the instructor.
Kerry Berrington

DURING the communist insurgency in Malaya during the early 'fifties, the Malayan Government enlisted the aid of civil flying clubs to act in the capacity of couriers, taxi drivers and observers. Members of the Kuala Lumpur Flying Club volunteered their piloting services together with a trio of club Tiger Moths, VR-RBA (DHA25) and VR-RBB (DHA444), purchased port-war in Australia as RAAF surplus at £310 the pair, and VR-RBJ (84957), one of the first aircraft from limited RAF disposals in 1946, shipped out from Great Britain.

Travelling through the Malayan jungle with large consignments of cash, usually wages due to workers at remote mines, was hazardous, and club aircraft were chartered by banks for air drops. Pilots were not paid, but the flying was free. On one occasion, misinterpretation of a signal caused £80,000 cash to be thrown out of a Tiger Moth cockpit at the wrong location, never to be seen again. Leaflet drops and police charters to check on the positions of suspected terrorist hideouts were also regular requests.

None of the pilots wore parachutes and in case of emergency were taught to stall a Tiger Moth into the tops of trees where the aircraft was more likely to be found during a subsequent search. Although all three Kuala Lumpur Flying Club Tiger Moths were subsequently written off in local accidents, none was damaged during the political emergency, and the only lady pilot known to have volunteered was never forced to demonstrate engine out landings: her name was Joan Glyde.

Tiger Moths have been involved in their fair share of post-war scrapes, some of which made big news. On 17th May 1953, VH-BNF (DHA863), taxied out at RAAF Base Wagga following six Sea Furies which took off singly but joined together for a high speed, low level formation flight to the RAN

Joan Glyde and Tiger Moth VR-RBB of the Kuala Lumpur Flying Club. Members acted as unpaid observers and messengers during the Malayan crisis. Joan Ellis

In June 1951 Tiger Moth G-AIDS lost power during an overshoot at Broxbourne and gently subsided into a hedge of blooming may trees on the aerodrome boundary. Harry Smith

base at Nowra. The Tiger Moth was airborne and had climbed to 150ft when the Sea Fury formation appeared overhead and at 250 knots the lead aircraft collided with VH-BNF's tail unit and starboard wings. The Tiger Moth spiralled out of the sky and hit the ground hard, wrecking every component except the rear seat and propeller. The pilot brushed off the wreckage and was unhurt, continuing his interest in aviation to the stage where he was appointed senior pilot with a commercial airline in Australia.

Almost exactly 24 years later, on 15th May 1977, Tiger Moth G-ANDE (85957), was letting down into Biggin Hill when a joy riding helicopter lifted off and climbed up into her, its rotor blades shearing off the whole of the undercarriage and snapping away at the pilot's heels. While the helicopter fell back to earth fatally injured, G-ANDE flew the circuit and landed on her belly when major damage was inflicted, although neither occupant suffered more than a few scratches.

A bizarre incident with a happy ending occurred at Broxbourne aerodrome in June 1951. An ATC cadet enjoying the fruits of his flying scholarship, was letting down from high level in Tiger Moth G-AIDS (84546), without warming the engine, an operational necessity overlooked by the instructor. Finding himself too high for a safe touchdown, the cadet opened the throttle to go around, but the engine quietly died. With commendable speed, the instructor took control:

'Neatly sideslipping toward the line of trees and shrubs that separated the aerodrome from a riverside bungalow estate, he pulled the machine into a stall above a handy may tree. By luck or superb airmanship or a combination of both, the Tiger Moth slipped stern first into its warm foliated embrace, suspending itself on the tree top by the undercarriage radius rods, with the elevator trailing edge two inches above ground and brushing the grass'.

This description by Harry Smith, an engineer with the Herts and Essex Aero Club, was penned long after the event. On the day, Smith and his colleagues were called from their lunch in the famous Monty's Cafe to supervise the retrieval of G-AIDS which was painlessly accomplished with the aid of a dragline working in a neighbouring gravel pit. Ironically, Broxbourne aerodrome was itself closed and sold for gravel extraction the following year.

Damage to G-AIDS amounted to a broken propeller, two inches neatly clipped off each tip, dented cowlings, a bent port undercarriage radius rod and a broken wing rib, all repaired within a week. Closer to the event, Harry Smith had been encouraged to take up his pen:

> To think that I should ever see,
> A Tiger Moth up in a tree,
> A tree whose countenance is pressed,
> Against this Tiger's oily chest,
> A tree whose leafy arms embrace,
> This thing that came to her through space.
>
> A tree who may in summer wear,
> A battered airscrew in her hair,
> And on whose bosom did adorn,
> A set of mainplanes, somewhat torn,
> And lying close beside her heart,
> Is tightly pressed, an undercart.
>
> A tree who held with tender care,
> This navigator of the air,
> Until some men with tools and crane,
> Took this small kite back home again.
> Planes are repaired by fools like me,
> But how can we repair the tree?

Daily encounters with trees was the lot of Jim Tiffen from Griffith, New South Wales, who landed his Tiger Moth on an 800ft strip in the middle of an orchard. On approach it was essential to drag the wheels through the top of an orange tree, else an overshoot was a certain requirement. On take off one day the engine stopped, and with no prospect of escape, the Tiger Moth landed in a peach tree, breaking everything except the propeller. That same year the tree produced an outstanding crop of fruit. In later years, Tiffen established a new landing area on a dirt road with a right angle bend in it which he referred to as his cross wind runway. Most visitors revealed that they were worried at just having to taxy along the tree lined strip at just 66ft wide.

Not as fortunate as G-AIDS was Tiger Moth G-AHVY (83315), which crashed on landing at Christchurch on the morning of Sunday 12th October 1958. The Club CFI took a positive stand against unauthorised dual instruction, and he always insisted that the front control column be removed when friends of club members were taken aloft. This attitude led to at least one adaptable control column being manufactured which could be hidden as two pieces in the leg pockets of a flying suit.

During G-AHVY's fateful approach to land, the 'pilot' was seen standing up in the rear cockpit holding a cine camera. It is believed he had one foot on the control box which slipped, stabbing the base of the rear control column, and jarring the counterfeit front stick out of its unsecured housing. A witness to the accident said he believed it was the same pilot who had once become lost due to compass deviation caused by interference from the close proximity of the rogue steel column.

A private sale effected from 5 MU Kemble in May 1947 led DE943 (85814), to Thomas Cameron in Perthshire, but within the year the aeroplane had been re-sold to McDonald Aircraft Ltd at Balado and registered G-AJVE. In 1951 she joined the Edinburgh Flying Club at Macmerry but it was at Turnhouse on 24th January 1960 that John Galt, a club pilot on his first solo, sideslipped in for a landing but misjudged his descent and landed between two parallel trusses on the roof of a hangar. The entire engine bay penetrated the fabric of the structure and fuel slopped down onto the floor below, but apart from a cut lip, the pilot was uninjured. In the same hangar undergoing repairs, was a BEA Viscount which had overshot the runway on landing the previous month.

The pilot of a group-owned Tiger Moth operational in Norfolk, was once seen standing on the rear seat of a Tiger Moth in low flight over the Oulton Broad Regatta, by arrangement, playing a trumpet, but the occupant of the front seat was well in control. Perhaps spurred on by this apparent demonstration of the ease with which a Tiger Moth could be flown, a 17 year old youth removed Tiger Moth G-AMEY (85545), from her hangar at Little Snoring on 16th May 1968, somehow got her started, and attempted to take off, at which point all his ideas ran out. The aircraft was wrecked but later achieved immortality on the silver screen in a short career masquerading as a Rumpler.

Not making headlines at the time for reasons of pride as well as security, but well known to his classmates at Marlborough School, was the case of a pupil who helped himself to one of His Majesty's Tiger Moths dispersed with 29 EFTS at Clyffe Pypard. The aeroplane was wrecked, and apart from six of the best, details of further punishment are unrecorded.

Tiger Moth T7941 (84305), was shipped to Southern Rhodesia in March 1941 and was later transferred to the South African Air Force as 4695. With over 2,000 hours logged, the aircraft was stored for 10 years before sale to a scrap metal company in 1955, but was overhauled for the civil market and qualified for a C of A in 1957. Six years later the aircraft was grounded for what was described as 'poor general condition', but was made airworthy only to suffer a heavy landing at Theona in November 1965 and to turn over, after which it was discovered that the pilot had no licence. Sold to a new owner in June 1966, he subsequently noted that 'the aircraft was painted kitchen table green with a red lightning stripe along the fuselage. Everything was oil soaked, and on testing the fabric, the engineer poked his finger clean through to reveal cracked main spars in both bottom wings, bandaged and varnished over. The wings were also infested with insect life although for two years prior to sale, the previous owner had developed a relish for aerobatics'.

Rebuilt to pristine condition and operated successfully for more than 12 years, the aircraft was leaving Jan Smuts airport after a celebration of South African Airways' Golden Jubilee on 9th October 1980, when all three rocker pedestal bolts for No 4 cylinder head sheared off at 800ft over a populated area. The pilot found a clump of thatching grass amongst an estate of new houses near Edenvale High School and stalled in from a tailskid touchdown, running across a

Rebuilt between 1960 and 1984, Tiger Moth G-AIDS was called *The Sorcerer* by one of her pre-completion owners, a name that was retained as a mark of respect following sale and the achievement of airworthiness. via Terry Dann

Tiger Moth PH-UDC was landed in the main street of Middelbeers, the Netherlands, in 1948 after the pilot was overcome by air sickness. via Herman Dekker

The prototype DH.82A model Tiger Moth, G-ACDA, impaled on an electricity pylon and burned out following her engine failure in June 1979. The former de Havilland School aircraft had been stored in her camouflage paint in a barn near Exeter between 1943 and 1977. Richard Biddle

Charles Lindbergh at the controls of Cliff Robertson's Tiger Moth N524R in California. The engineer appears to be attempting to stem a leak from the fuel on/off cock. Note the chromium plated centre section struts and polished rigging wires. Henry Artof via Howard Levy

In March 1990 during the Tiger Moth Club of New Zealand's North Cape to Bluff Rally, the engine of ZK-AKC failed when crossing a river at Balclutha, but a hard shingle bank orientated into wind provided the perfect 'carrier' deck on which to put down and from which, after repairs, to take off. John King

barbed wire fence which had been squashed flat by cement lorries. A traffic patrol helicopter followed the Tiger Moth's descending flightpath and was able to report by radio that no damage was evident. Replacement bolts were discovered locally in an old Gipsy Major engine which had been standing in the open for 20 years. The day following the incident, the aircraft was towed onto Milford Road and flown off.

During a training flight on behalf of the Dutch Civil Aviation Department on 10th February 1948, the student pilot of PH-UDC (84257), suffered airsickness, and landed the aircraft in the main street at Middelbeers near Hilversum, an event greeted with enthusiasm by the local schoolchildren.

A less happy ending awaited G-ACDA (3175), the aircraft acknowledged as the prototype of the 'A' model Tiger Moth. The aircraft had been impressed into military service as BB724, but during the war with production continuing at Cowley, was sold to Bertie Arden in September 1943, and placed in secure storage on his farm at Haldon Moor near Exeter. The aircraft was viewed by few privileged visitors until 1977 when G-ACDA was accepted in lieu of fees for professional services by a local solicitor. Whether the aircraft was 'sold' or 'loaned permanently' was to be subject of legal argument at a later date.

G-ACDA was overhauled at Kemble and entered for the1979 Famous Grouse Rally but during a routine test flight on 27th June, two days before she was due at Hatfield, the engine stopped during a casual aerobatic routine and despite all efforts, failed to restart. During the forced landing within sight of Kemble aerodrome, the Tiger Moth slipped round a tree but collided with an electricity pylon which had been hidden from view, and impaled on its arms, burst into flames. Both occupants escaped by using the starboard lower wing as a stepladder to reach the ground, but the intensely original and historically significant aircraft was lost.

Charles Shea-Simonds frequently jumped from his own Tiger Moth when being piloted by a friend and had been known to arrive by parachute at summer garden parties in Bond-like style, immaculately dressed in DJ and black tie. On his last such adventure he too had the misfortune to collide with a tree.

Having gathered around him a number of like minded and experienced Tiger Moth owner/pilots, Shea-Simonds founded the de Havilland Moth Club Diamond Nine Formation Display Team in 1985, and after a period of consolidation and practice, the team's first nine Tiger Moth diamond was displayed on 26th April 1986 at Badminton. Since then the Diamond Nine has become a popular and regular attraction at many British air displays, and on two occasions in France, varying their routines annually within the limitations of their aircraft, following intensive training at the beginning of each season.

Almost inevitably, the Diamond Nine fostered excellent relations with the RAF Aerobatic Team, The Red Arrows, having modelled themselves on a similar nine-aircraft presentation, and in July 1995, nine Tiger Moths and nine BAe Hawks shared the same box of sky over the Reds' base at Scampton. It was the team's second visit to the Red Arrows, and on this occasion managed to fly a Diamond Nine with a Red Arrow team member tucked into each front seat. The experience prompted one Hawk pilot to observe that the Tiger Moth must surely have been one of the world's first 'fly-by-wire' aircraft.

In their first ten years, the Diamond Nine Team flew 149 individual shows, a heavy commitment for a group of 'amateur' pilots who flew together mostly only at weekends. In 1995, the team was asked to lead the Victory Parade at the International Air Tattoo at Fairford, and put up an expansive vic of 12 Tiger Moths on two consecutive days, all aircraft carrying a worthy 'veteran' nominated by the organisers on each occasion.

Nine Tiger Moths in a diamond formation were scheduled to pass over St Albans Abbey on the occasion of the Memorial Service for Sir Geoffrey de Havilland on 21st July 1965.

Gathered at Redhill that morning, the weather turned sour with low cloud and poor visibility, but led by Dennis Hartas, all nine aircraft struggled through to reach Hatfield safely, only for the hapless G-ASKP (3889), to run into the ILS aerial on touchdown. And then there were eight.

Although a replacement Tiger Moth was hastily summoned from Panshanger, it could not be made ready in time, and the ninth aeroplane was the willingly volunteered and entirely appropriate DH.60 Cirrus Moth G-EBLV (188), flown in the formation by de Havilland test pilot Desmond Penrose. The diamond arrived overhead the Abbey on schedule and made two passes over the congregation gathered outside. On the second run, the sun broke weakly through the cloud for the first and only time that day.

A few days after the service, Norman Jones was in receipt of a letter from Lady Joan de Havilland:

'I am writing to thank you and the members of your Club for your kindness in arranging and skill in completing the Tiger Moth fly past after the Memorial Service to my husband.

'I assure you that this act would have pleased my husband more than all the kind words that have been said and written on his work as an aviation pioneer. No fly past of jet aircraft would have pleased him so much, for he loved his little Moths.

'As for me, having got through the Service without, I hope, any sign of my feelings, I must admit I dropped some tears when your aeroplanes went over, and I was not alone.'

The weather on 30th July 1997 was bright and clear but the air was in unsettled mood as Moths again made an appearance over Hatfield in salute to Sir Geoffrey de Havilland. Denied the use of facilities at the desecrated company aerodrome a stone's throw from the Hatfield campus of the University of Hertfordshire, (there was no ILS to hit any more: it had been repositioned to Chester), a fleet of 37 aircraft, mostly Moths, operated from Old Warden in support of the ceremony to unveil a bronze statue of the founder of the Enterprise. Led by three DH.60 Moths, Group 5 was a formation of nine Tiger Moths, but on this occasion G-EBLV was not with them; she was positioned in pole position alongside Sir Geoffrey's statue, sharing the limelight.

As part of a representative formation of non-de Havilland airframes powered by Gipsy engines, Desmond Penrose was on this occasion flying his unique Arrow Active, G-ABVE. During his endeavours to return the Active to her original specification, Penrose acquired a Gipsy III engine which was fitted to the aircraft in 1988. The serial number of the engine, 3314, identifies it as that once installed in DH.82 Tiger Moth K2570, one of the first six to be delivered to the Royal Air Force in November 1931. Trained on Tiger Moths for an RAF career as a fighter pilot and later test pilot with de Havilland at Hatfield, Desmond Penrose celebrated the 50th anniversary of his first flight as an ATC cadet at Fairoaks, by visiting the site of the former Training Command station in a Tiger Moth, although on account of the shiny hard runway, he was not invited to land.

With the assistance of Desmond Penrose flying the Hatfield based DH.60 Moth G-EBLV, a nine aeroplane formation was mustered to fly over St Albans Abbey after the Memorial Service for Geoffrey de Havilland on 21st July 1965. Hawker Siddeley Aviation

The Tiger Moth has long been the vehicle with which to recognise the achievements of others, but in recent times she has increasingly celebrated her own. The Golden Jubilee of the DH.82 Tiger Moth was observed in England with two events organised by the de Havilland Moth Club in 1981. In July, six military marked Tiger Moths flew from Henlow, substituting for Stag Lane (Hatfield was suffering industrial strife), to Grantham to commemorate the anniversary of the first RAF delivery, and landed on what had become the sports field of The Prince William of Gloucester Army Barracks. Group Captain Peter Heath, one of the pilots of that first Tiger Moth formation in 1931 was taken ill just before the event and prevented from taking his rightful place in the lead aircraft, appropriately G-ANEF (83226), of the Royal Air Force College Flying Club, Cranwell. Thirty more Tiger Moths passed overhead Grantham on their way from Henlow directly to Cranwell, and a celebration banquet in College Hall.

At a 50th birthday lunch held in the old squash courts of the London Aeroplane Club at Hatfield on 21st October, the crews of seven Tiger Moths which had arrived in formation from Old Warden, greeted guest of honour Alan Butler, who as a young

It may look serene, but keeping nine low powered Tiger Moths in close formation, even on a calm day, takes considerable skill, effort and practice. The de Havilland Moth Club's Diamond Nine Team in action at Woburn Abbey. Darryl Cott

Unable to field nine aeroplanes, what the Italian team 'Le Tigri' lacked in numbers they more than made up for in charisma. The team was part of a 1987 European tour which included six Piper Cubs and a Bücker Jungmann, sponsored by Italian furniture maker Frezza. Frezza

A quartet of Australian registered Tiger Moths all flown by experienced pilots, tucked in close overhead Tooradin, Victoria in February 1975: VH-TIG; VH-SSI; VH-ULR and VH-CXY. deHMC Archive

sportsman had funded the de Havilland Company in 1922, and later gifted these same premises. In Australia only hours before, the Antique Aeroplane Association had organised a dinner limited to 50 guests, and a birthday cake complete with 50 candles. According to reports received at Hatfield, the candles generated so much heat that the squadron of model Tiger Moths which were dispersed around the culinary creation, suffered bent propellers, melted struts and broken landing gear.

Amy Johnson's 1930 flight from Croydon to Australia in her DH.60G Moth G-AAAH (804), has been compared to the achievement of man landing on the moon only 39 years later. The 50th anniversary of her arrival in Darwin was recorded on 24th May 1980 when Senja Robey, a past president of the Australian Women Pilot's Association, flew Tiger Moth VH-AWA (DHA824), back into her birthplace at Mascot, now Kingsford Smith airport, Sydney. On 5th May 1980, 50 years to the day since Amy Johnson's departure, Lewis Benjamin organised a select band of appropriate aircraft and a small Tiger Moth dominated air display on what remained of the usable grass at the closed Croydon airport. A restored green and silver DH.60G Gipsy Moth G-ABEV (1823), flown by Ron Souch, offered a privileged few the chance of a circuit. It was the last opportunity ever, for the local council refused all subsequent requests to land aeroplanes on the historic site against the pretext that they would cause nuisance to the local residents.

In London on 16th December 1931, Squadron Leader Bert Hinkler was presented with the Royal Aero Club Gold Medal in recognition of his famous flight across the South Atlantic in a DH.80 Puss Moth. The flight had its origins in Canada and the Puss Moth was the first Canadian registered aircraft to make a landing in Great Britain. On the same day as the presentation, the first Australia-Great Britain air mails to be carried by an Australian registered aircraft also arrived in London. The pilot, Sir Charles Kingsford Smith, was immediately invited to the ceremony to meet fellow Australian Bert Hinkler for the first time. To commemorate the famous meeting, in 1981 special postal covers were prepared in Australia and flown to London. Keith Palmer eyed the snow banks remaining after the first falls of the winter, put on several more layers of protection, took a deep breath and agreed to fly the covers and their courier over London in his Tiger Moth G-APMX (85645):

'After a patch of foul weather, 16th December 1981 dawned bright and clear but very cold. G-APMX really did not want to go and took 45 minutes to stir into action. Southern Television filmed every swing of the propeller but luckily showed only one attempt on the broadcast.

'We took off at 11.20am and flew straight to Thamesmead in order to join the helicopter river route to Battersea. The visibility was excellent until we reached London, and it became quite eerie flying above the cranes and chimneys. Instructions from the CAA were to ditch in the river in case of any nasties, so we wore lifejackets, just in case.

'Tower Bridge appeared through the wires, and I resisted the temptation to fly under, leaving that opportunity until later. We flew on past Westminster and turned round over the heliport where we received a wave from ATC who had been most helpful, then back along the reciprocal route to Headcorn. The flight time was only one hour, but it was the coldest Tiger Moth trip I have ever made, despite thermal underwear'.

Top left: **When landing at Hatfield in marginal visibility on 21st July 1965, Tiger Club Tiger Moth G-ASKP collided with the ILS aerial putting both the Tiger Moth and the landing system out of action.** via Michael Jones

Top right: **Painted yellow overall and displaying her military serial T5493, Tiger Moth G-ANEF pancaked into the ground after hitting trees during take off from the North Airfield at Cranwell in September 1988. The damaged aircraft was subsequently sold to Sweden and restored to airworthiness.** deHMC Archive

Right: **Owned by Swiss solicitor Roger Steck who equally could have become a professional jazz trumpeter, Tiger Moth HB-UBC was an entrant in both the Famous Grouse Rally of 1979 and the DH100 event of 1982.** RAE Farnborough

Below left: **Rebuilt in Germany in 1984 as a private owner aircraft and resident tug to a vintage glider collection, the registration D-EBKT was carefully chosen in recognition of the letters allocated to prototype DH.60 Moth G-EBKT in 1925.** David Hammond

Below centre: **The time honoured manner of righting an upturned Tiger Moth: balance her on her propeller hub and with a line fore and aft across her tail (and with the help of a few friends), gently re-establish composure.** Stan Roberts

Below right: **Alan Butler holding a model Tiger Moth in the de Havilland Museum at Hatfield on the occasion of the Tiger Moth 50th birthday celebrations, 21st October 1981.** British Aerospace

Photographs on this page:

The pastoral scene. A Tiger Moth landing long on the downslope at de Havilland Field, Crux Easton, Hampshire. Captain de Havilland frequently commuted from here to Stag Lane in pre-war days, flying mostly a DH.60G, DH.85 Leopard Moth or a DH.87 Hornet Moth, all of which could be folded and enclosed in a small compound as protection against animals. Mike Jerram

The unmistakable facade overlooking Horse Guard's Parade in London where the RAF celebrated Battle of Britain week by erecting a 1940's Operations Room and surrounding it with a representative selection of period aircraft. Tiger Moth NL985 wearing the wrong camouflage scheme for the time and spin strakes, was later almost completely destroyed in an arson attack at Hendon before the RAF Museum was declared open. deHMC Archive

The Museum of Army Flying at Middle Wallop maintains G-AHMN, a loaned civil Tiger Moth, in airworthy condition and on suitable occasions demonstrates towing techniques with Second World War training gliders. Richard Riding

Photographs on the opposite page:

Above left: **Built from unairworthy parts and carrying the letters G-MAZY in remembrance of team leader Harry Hodgson's late wife, this Tiger Moth was assembled by the Cotswold Aviation Society for display at the Newark Air Museum. The whole of the port side has been left without fabric to permit visitors to inspect the structure.** Harry Hodgson

Above right: **An RAF import from 1940 subsequently fitted with Australian built mainplanes and other local refinements, this Hatfield built Tiger Moth was registered VH-BAM when she crashed into Lake Cargelligo in 1962. Rebuilt to non airworthy standard at RAAF Base Wagga and painted to represent A17-443, the aircraft is now housed in a specially designed memorial building on the site of the former 8 EFTS at Narrandera Park.** David Tanner

Below left: **Built in New Zealand as NZ1430 the aircraft was sold into civil hands as ZK-BLN in 1955 but by 1960 had been dismantled for spares. Rebuilt in 1962 with assistance from at least three other Tiger Moths and registered ZK-CCH, she was donated to the Queenstown Motor Museum in 1971.** Neville Parnell

Below right: **Les Balla and Watt Martin at Milton, Ontario, about to fly in a DH.82C Tiger Moth with a sackful of special postal covers originated by the Mosquito Aircraft Museum, Salisbury Hall. Apart from the few in Iceland and two exports to Israel, no 'C' versions of the Tiger Moth have ever operated in Europe.** Jack McNulty

During a heavy snowstorm in Kent on 14th January 1987, the blister hangar in which G-APMX was housed, collapsed. The roof came to rest on the Tiger Moth's centre section which bore the whole weight of the snow-covered structure, and effectively prevented the crushing of many other aircraft. Extreme pressure burst a mainwheel tyre and caused severe distortion of the airframe. The insurance assessment following an independent survey declared G-APMX to be beyond economical repair, and the aircraft was sold to a third party bidder. Sold again in an incomplete condition, final restoration to airworthiness was achieved by the Newbury Aeroplane Company in November 1992.

Tiger Moth NL985 (86417), had been in continuous service from delivery to 14 EFTS Elmdon in August 1944 until withdrawn from flying duties with No 9 Advanced Flying Training School (AFTS) Wellesbourne Mountford, eight years later. Recategorised as an Instructional Airframe, 7015M, and loaned to an ATC Squadron in Birmingham, the aircraft was withdrawn to Colerne and there restored to operational configuration with a late wartime camouflage finish, to become part of the Royal Air Force Exhibition Unit. As such, NL985 was displayed at the Royal Tournament, at the annual Battle of Britain displays on Horse Guard's Parade, and most publicly at the Royal Golden Jubilee Review of the Royal Air Force at Abingdon in June 1968.

During planning for the RAF Museum at Hendon, NL985 was earmarked as the permanent representative of the type, and together with a small number of other exhibits was moved onto the site in 1972 to permit final building work to continue around them. Enter the guttersnipes who broke in through poor security and thought it awfully good sport to set fire to the Tiger Moth which was burned out. Other aircraft were attacked and damaged, but none fatally. The remains of NL985 were sold and subsequently hawked through many bazaars, but the caravan finally came to rest at Gransden for the final stages of rebuilding to airworthiness.

The RAF now had no Tiger Moth at all and turned to the Royal Navy for assistance. T6296 (84711), had served with the RAF until December 1946 when she was transferred to the Admiralty, subsequently serving at a number of shore establishments until retired from flying activity at Yeovilton in September 1973. Painted in RAF brown and green camouflage, (slime and sewage), T6296 was presented to the Museum to fill the vacant space, and in April 1990 was transferred to the Battle of Britain Hall, although her paint scheme and spin strakes are not appropriate to the period. What price a set of bomb racks?

When Tiger Moth G-ALAD was registered to the Wiltshire School of Flying at Thruxton in June 1951, the previous identity was quoted as T6296, clearly not true, and on sale of the aircraft to New Zealand in 1952, the RAF serial and history went with her. Not until 1997 and long since registered ZK-CDU, did official paperwork come to light confirming that the Tiger Moth in the RAF Museum was the genuine example, and that ZK-CDU was probably L6926 (3581), one of the 30 civil specification Tiger Moths bought 'off the shelf' by the Air Ministry in 1937.

The Museum of Army Flying at Middle Wallop have been custodians of an airworthy Tiger Moth exhibit, N6985 (G-AHMN /82223), on long term loan from Alan Curtis, since July 1984, when the aircraft was handed over by Admiral Sir Raymond Lygo. Sir Raymond, a former Royal Navy Tiger Moth flying instructor, then acting in his capacity as Chief Executive of British Aerospace, was, as he explained, making the presentation on behalf of 'the original makers'. Since N6985 will eventually be returned to her civilian owner, supporters of the Army Museum thought it prudent to have a Tiger Moth of their own and acquired a restoration project, G-AOHY (3850), a pre-war Hatfield aircraft released from the RAF in 1954.

With a growing number of privately owned Tiger Moths available for exhibition and display flying, the RAF, RAAF and Royal Navy elected not to maintain airworthy models of their own. The Fleet Air Arm Museum at Yeovilton exhibits an aircraft painted to represent G-ABUL, one of Alan Cobham's prewar display machines, in recognition of the support provided by Sir Alan's company,

Flight Refuelling Ltd. The aircraft is in reality 83805, formerly RAF T7291, sold into the civilian market in 1953 to become G-AOXG and purchased by the Royal Navy in 1956 as part of an expansion of Britannia Flight. Operated on behalf of the Royal Navy College at Dartmouth, she was allocated a new serial, XL717. On retirement from active duty, the aircraft was presented to the Museum for permanent static display. The Royal Navy retired their last working Tiger Moth T8191 (84483), to the Historic Aircraft Flight at Yeovilton, but with limited funds and the insatiable appetite of other rarer aircraft, T8191 was placed in store from 1987 until sold at public auction in November 1994.

Whilst the Tiger Moth is exceedingly well represented under private ownership and in a wide variety of museums throughout the world, very few institutions operating under the banner of government authority have the desire or the funds to maintain their charges in airworthy condition. Whilst the RNZAF Museum at Wigram has locally built Tiger Moth NZ1481 (DHNZ161), on static display, painted to represent NZ825 (DHNZ75), the real aircraft is under restoration at Mandeville. The Museum's Historical Flight maintain in airworthy condition an ex-RAF aircraft, T5773 (83502), shipped to Wellington in November 1940 and taken on RNZAF charge as NZ662. Following a post-war career in agriculture, and an assignment in Fiji, the aircraft was donated to the Flight in exchange for the restoration of ZK-BCO (83420), another ex RAF aircraft of post-war import.

The Canadian National Aviation Museum at Rockliffe inherited two DH.82C Tiger Moths from the National Museum of Science and Technology in 1967. CF-FGL (DHC724) repainted with her former RCAF serial 4394, is a Gipsy Major powered static exhibit, while 4861 (DHC1052), is maintained in airworthy condition as a rare surviving example of the type with a Menasco engine.

India, a vast sub-continent with strong Tiger Moth connections dating from before the war, appropriately maintains at least one aircraft in airworthy condition with the Indian Air Force Museum at Palam near Delhi. Cowley built 85778, was taken on RAF charge as DE893, shipped to South Africa in March 1943 and served with the SAAF as 2492. She was one of the aircraft selected for transfer to India in 1946, arriving at Bangalore in February 1947, and following overhaul by Hindustan Aircraft, joining the Air Force as HU512. In April 1963 the aircraft was registered VT-DPK to the Government of India, Civil Aviation Department, Madras, but the allocation was cancelled in 1991, and the aircraft reappeared in airworthy condition with the Indian Air Force Historic Flight, a living memorial.

Air Marshal Barry Grayson learned to fly on Tiger Moths at Point Cook, and upon his retirement as Chief of the Air Staff, Royal Australian Air Force, in 1994, he chose to leave the service on board Tiger Moth VH-SSK (DHA885). Painted in her previous RAAF colours as A17-468, the pristine aircraft was on temporary loan to the RAAF Museum at Point Cook but was withdrawn by her owner early in 1998 after sustaining damage in a careless ground handling incident.

Chile improved her internal communications in the 'twenties with a fleet of DH.60 Moths engaged on aero-postal duties, and in 1998 the Air Force Museum began a search for an airworthy example to complement the static aircraft already displayed in Santiago. In 1987, the Museum made a successful bid for British based DH.82A Tiger Moth G-BACK (85879), which had unexpectedly been offered for sale. The aircraft was airlifted by Chilean Air Force Lockheed Hercules from Hurn in December 1987 and has been maintained in airworthy condition at Santiago ever since. Painted in RAF camouflage bearing serial DF130, she was listed as a civil aircraft, CC-DMC, to the National Aeronautical Collection in 1995, and on 23rd March 1998, was part of a formation of nine vintage aircraft which proudly flew past the President of Chile at the opening of the biennial FIDAE airshow.

The difference between a collection of parts on a trailer delivered to the front door, and getting airborne in a pristine Tiger Moth can be measured in thousands of manhours and total dedication spread over several years, a feat achieved with G-AOGI by Bill Taylor. Bill Taylor

Warren Davies, an Englishman living in New York City, rebuilt the front fuselage of his Tiger Moth on the 26th storey of his apartment block and needed to choose a time when the elevators were quiet in order to achieve street level in good order. Warren Davies

G-APAO, once a Jackaroo, was reconverted to Tiger Moth configuration, and survived the flooded hangar at Newtownards to join the DH100 Celebrations at Hatfield in 1982. Bob Wall

THE DH.82 QUEEN BEE

In the sunshine at Hatfield, L5902 takes on fuel to compete with the running engines of DH.91 Albatross 'E.2'. Well illustrated is the cover over the rear compartment of the Queen Bee together with a host of external fittings. de Havilland Aircraft Company

THE DE HAVILLAND Queen Bee evolved from Air Ministry Specification 18/33 for a wireless controlled, pilotless target drone. Her primary task was to provide gunnery target practice for ships of the Royal Navy and anti-aircraft schools of the Royal Artillery, not to be intentionally shot down, but to be fired at while 'aiming off'. There was little point to the exercise if the target was destroyed by the first round of the day! As time progressed and morale improved with practice, at the end of some courses, permission was given for the aircraft to be shot at directly.

A pilot's instrumented cockpit was to be provided to allow for 'manual' test flying and occasional positioning. As British ranges mostly were situated along the coast, the Queen Bee was equipped with a Short Bros float chassis for normal operation from water and was to be launched either from the side of a cruiser at sea, or from fixed land sites close to the batteries.

The aircraft was to be considered expendable, anticipating losses due to accurate or lucky shooting and the hazards associated with waterborne operations conducted under a comparatively advanced system of remote control. A cheap, lightweight aircraft likely to float in the event of bad handling was required.

The Queen Bee amalgamated DH.82A Tiger Moth wings and empennage with some refinements and the wooden fuselage of a DH.60GIII Moth Major, powered by a standard Gipsy Major 1 engine with fully screened ignition, driving a coarse pitch de Havilland wooden propeller, DH5220/H.

A prototype aircraft was built in 1934, K3584 (5027), against contract 232902/33 and was flown at Hatfield on 5th January 1935. A further contract for the supply of 19 Queen Bees was placed with de Havilland in 1934 when production was integrated with the Moth Major. One of the first aircraft, K5055 (5116), was dispatched to the Royal Indian Air Force but served in isolation; targets for 'silent' gunnery practice were provided by the civilian flying clubs whose Moth Majors and Tiger Moths operated without fear of collision with live rounds.

Topping-up contracts against Specification 20/35 followed for the next several years: 1935 (42); 1936 (24); 1937 (30); 1938 (192) and 1939 (28). The average price of a Queen Bee ex-works in 1937 was quoted at a few pence less than £1,023 each.

Against an expected increase in attrition, an additional 75 aircraft were ordered in 1943, sub-contracted by de Havilland to their

Gipsy Major engine No 8552 installed in DH.82 Queen Bee 5384, RAF serial P4806, at Hatfield in May 1939. All the aircraft in this batch have windy ASIs fitted to the port front interplane strut.
via British Aerospace

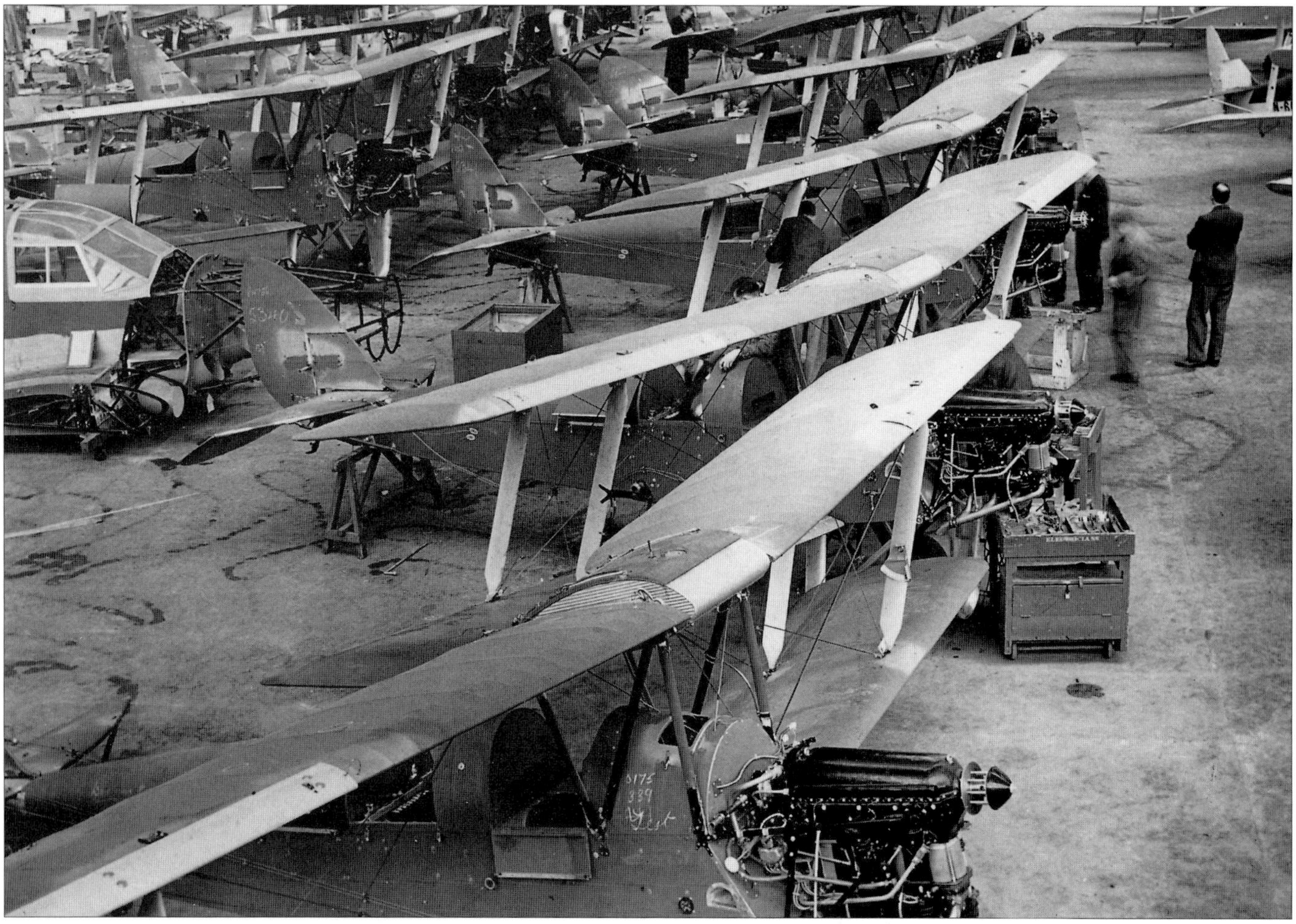

DH.82 Queen Bees in the Hatfield erecting shop in April 1939. The aircraft nearest the camera, 5175, RAF serial K8642, has a gauge let into the fuselage side adjacent to the footstep. Note the engineless DH.93 Don fuselage on a pallet at left.
via British Aerospace

associated company Scottish Aviation, who established a line in a Glasgow bus garage requisitioned from a former customer for DH.83 Fox Moths. Only 60 were delivered against a curtailed requirement. At least seven DH.82A Tiger Moths were 'converted' to the status of Queen Bees at Manorbier and several others were slated but subsequently reprieved.

Apart from the basic wooden structure of the fuselage, a number of detail and more fundamental changes were necessary in order to create a DH.82 Queen Bee from the pure DH.60/DH.82 lineage. The engine mounting feet, carburettor and wing attachments were strengthened to accept the forces of acceleration experienced during catapult launch and the whole of the rear fuselage was re-inforced to protect the integrity of the tail unit. An Eclipse hand starter was provided on the engine's starboard side.

Rudder and elevator but not ailerons were operated by pistons actuated by gyroscopically controlled air valves whose 30psi working pressure was supplied from a wind driven compressor attached by an arm to the port side of the fuselage, taking fullest advantage of the propeller slipstream. Electrical power was generated by a pair of accumulators.

One cockpit was provided, fully instrumented and fitted with standard controls except that the stick was riveted in position. An RAF 'Tiger Moth harness' was specified with 'special lugs' on account of picking up on the wooden fuselage. The cockpit was scheduled to be faired over when not in use although in practice, most aircraft were operated with an open 'front pit' and the windscreen still in place. Substituted for the rear seat, a new compartment was designed to accommodate the R1088A wireless receiving apparatus and Mk.1A Automatic Pilot. Engine controls, rudder pedals and stick were removed although an altimeter and airspeed indicator were fitted to the instrument board. The fuel tank was increased in capacity from the Tiger Moth's 19 gallons to 25 gallons. Numerous additional external fittings were necessary to assist with ground handling, lifting by ship's derrick or site crane, for tethering and catapult attachment. Spin strakes were not fitted on production or retrospectively.

In support of the Queen Bee contract, de Havilland raised their first modification to the Tiger Moth Type Record (based on the DH.60X) on 26th April 1933 as Addendum 83A, for which preparatory work had begun at the beginning of March. This called for *'Tiger Moth (wooden fuselage)'* No 5027 to be modified by the *'incorporation of wooden fuselage in RAF Tiger Moth'*.

The Addendum required certification of the aircraft at the standard weights for normal and aerobatic flight (1,825lb/1,750lb Landplane and Seaplane), on the grounds that these had been approved previously. It was the new fuselage now submitted for scrutiny and clearance:

'... this component is of 60G.III type, but has been modified by increasing the size of the centre section fuselage vertical side struts and by modifying the fuselage float chassis fittings and centre section strut fittings to accommodate increased weight. As the fuselage is ply covered, detailed stressing is not possible. Comparison, however, has been made between loads in 'Tiger' Moth metal fuselage (in Seaplane and Landplane cases) with the size of members in this centre section fuselage. The comparison indicates a fair reserve factor on all members.'

On 5th May 1933, Addendum 83B was issued, referring to revised centre of gravity (CG) limitations for aircraft fitted with Short Bros floats and chassis, identifying the type as 'Special Moth with Tiger Moth floats'. The CG was critical in view of the weight of the wireless equipment, auto-pilot and accumulators all scheduled for distribution between the rear compartment and former luggage locker.

Wireless control apparatus for the project was designed at the Royal Aircraft Establishment (RAE) Farnborough. The airborne R1088A receiver was a simple four-valve set but the ground base station, a mobile M11 unit, stood nearly six feet tall and weighed 1,500lb. Transmission frequency range was 160-180 Kcs (LW) requiring an aerial array 250ft high. At sea, base control was effected through the ship's 'wireless room'.

The M11 was fitted with nine push-button functions, each initiating a single command: left turn, right turn, climb, throttle, etc. The autopilot was set at standard rates for each manoeuvre: rate one turns, climb at 400fpm, limit normal operating height to 9,000ft amsl. Signals were similar to those produced by a 1930's state of the art telephone dialling system (dash tone followed by dots). To guard against push-button failure, a telephone hand dial was incorporated on the M11 console to duplicate signals if necessary. A similar device was included in the Queen Bee's front cockpit with which a test pilot could override ground signals to fine tune the auto controls.

The remote control system was demonstrated to the press at RAE Farnborough on 26th June 1935 when the seventh production Queen Bee, K4227 (5049), painted silver overall with blood-red outer wing panels, operating on a wheeled undercarriage, was taken off and landed.

Prior to take-off from a catapult the controlling gyroscope was spun up using an external supply of compressed air, sufficient

DH.82 Queen Bee K4227 at Farnborough in June 1935 where she was demonstrated to the press. Note the wind driven compressor above the oil tank and how the front cockpit is faired over leaving the head bumper 'crash pad' exposed. *The Aeroplane*

K8632 leaving the catapult of a Royal Navy cruiser in July 1937. Launch operations were commanded by RAF officers carried on board. Keystone

A camouflaged Queen Bee lowering onto a rotatable catapult on a cliff-top somewhere in Great Britain, November 1939. The airman at right is holding on to restraining wires to steady the tail; another wire leads off left from the underwing tethering bracket. The catapult was operated by a mixture of compressed air and glycerine fired by a cordite charge. *The Aeroplane*

to sustain erection until the on-board compressor could provide sufficient airflow. With the 'launch' valve set, controls centralised and the Gipsy Major running at full throttle, the aircraft was released Once airborne a winch box ran out a trailing aerial and contact was established with the M11 operator. It was then necessary for the controller to keep the Queen Bee in sight; there was no other indication of the aircraft's flight attitude or geographical position.

The landing sequence was set up by the controller using a visual sight mounted on a tripod. Applying a corrective allowance for wind, the aircraft could be accurately positioned on approach at the right speed. On the command 'glide', the throttle closed and the Queen Bee descended until at about 20ft, the bob weight on the trailing aerial made contact with the surface. Sensing resistance, the ignition shut off automatically, the gyro was caged and 'up elevator' was set in two distinct movements.

Should the controller lose sight of his charge or a close shell-burst disrupt wireless contact, a safety feature was automatically triggered. Having received no new command for a set time, the remote control would close the throttle and initiate a left hand descending turn and the 'glide' sequence, hopeful that the touchdown would be onto an acceptable seastate and moderately into wind.

Pre-war, the Admiralty arranged a Queen Bee demonstration in the Solent with invited VIP guests including members of the Royal Family and selected coverage by the newsreels. The combined might of naval fire-power failed to score a hit as the Queen Bee continued defiantly to cruise along its prescribed flight-line. To save further embarrassment the controller was advised by a senior officer to press the button marked 'spin' which brought the demonstration to a timely and satisfactory conclusion.

The Mediterranean Fleet was served by the RAF's No 2 Gunnery Co-operation Flight which, in April 1936, moved from Alexandria in Egypt to the RAF's main seaplane base in Malta at Kalafrana. With Queen Bees in service, the Flight was upgraded to become the aptly titled 'B Flight' of No 3 Anti-aircraft Co-operation Unit (AACU) and later spent some time in Gibraltar. Other Royal Navy units were serviced by No 2 AACU operating from Gosport and No 4 AACU at Seletar, Singapore.

In May 1937, No 1 AACU headquartered at Farnborough, formed a training unit at Henlow from where they transferred to Watchet in Somerset during July. Here, Queen Bees on floats were launched from a catapult which could be rotated on a circular concrete base to face into wind. The aircraft were flown as targets for the neighbouring army camp at Doniford and if not lost to gunfire, were put down in the Bristol Channel from where they were recovered by the SS *Radstock* operating out of Appledore or Padstow, carried back to Watchet harbour, thence by lorry for return to the launch site. Identical facilities were set up in Great Britain at Aberffraw, Aberporth, Burrow Head, Cleave, Gosport, Kidsdale, Manorbier, Morfa Towyn and Weybourne.

'V' Flight of No 1 AACU was based at Cleave in Somerset from May 1939 where the 'anti-aircraft co-operation camp' came under the command of Squadron Leader Pearce, previously with the trials unit at Henlow. The catapult was operational from June but the team believed it could launch just as easily from the grass using a wheeled undercarriage and conventional take off techniques, so the cumbersome and expensive contraption was abandoned. The first completely automatic take-off and landing in Great Britain was claimed by the unit at Cleave with Squadron Leader Pearce monitoring from the cockpit of P5743 (5413), in July 1939, although the honours had already been awarded to Farnborough some four years previously.

On the overcast morning of 13th November 1941, Squadron Leader Bill Young, Officer Commanding 'G' Flight, No 1 AACU Cleave, with eight hours logged on Hawker Henleys that month and a one hour 'silent gun' sortie in Tiger Moth T8180 (84472), was invited to sample an automatic take-off in Queen Bee V4758 (5445). He recorded his impressions:

'On the cliffs of Cornwall I found myself sitting in a Queen Bee cockpit ready for take-off, only this time things would be very different. My arms were folded across my chest; my feet away from the rudder bar and the inside of my helmet felt a little moist in spite of the cold air outside, more I think from apprehension than fear. I had flown a Tiger Moth many times before, usually on engine tests, or occasionally on ferry duties. But this time it was going to fly me!

'I adjusted my straps over my parachute harness and wondered whether I should put a bit of air into my Mae West, because at the end of the grass strip, due west, was a 600ft sheer drop from the edge of the cliff to the rolling Atlantic swell below. At least, I thought, it would give me extra height in an emergency. Would my climbing speed cope with the downdraught at the edge of the cliff fairly quickly followed by an up-current coming off the face? We would rock for a bit, that was for sure!

'I had already run up the engine against the chocks to test the magnetos and tried to give a brave wave to the wireless operator standing a few yards away. He held the black box ready to give the necessary signals that would get me airborne.

'The wind-speed had been checked half an hour ago. If it increased considerably the angle of climb would be wrong, perhaps we would just hang there with the ASI needle going off the clock. I am very much against stalling on the approach or undershooting!

'Without further warning the throttle half-opened and we were off. What was it the other pilot had said? If we veered left or right or dipped a wing or looked like going into buildings, I was to take over manually. I did not really need telling; my hands and feet were inches from the controls.

'Full throttle, the tail was off the ground and we were bumping over the rough grass gaining speed. The stick came back and we were airborne and climbing. I checked the ASI. All correct. We passed over the army's 3in guns in a gentle climbing turn to the left and levelled out at about 1,000ft. I remember thinking should I log this flight under 'pilot times' or 'passenger' until I reminded myself that I was in charge, or was I? The three little dots on the edge of the aerodrome obviously thought they were!

'The angle of glide was checked and the aircraft was now on the approach. Had the wind remained constant in speed and direction? Would the operator judge the drift correctly? This time I did the landing because the 30ft of trailing aerial with a weight on the end had a habit of snaking up and hitting the pilot on the head. Previous test pilots had been forced to wear tin hats. I pulled the stick gently back, closed the throttle, straightened up and landed'.

Some of those on the ground may have breathed just as big a sigh of relief as Bill Young. The Queen Bee could become unstable below 20ft on automatic approach, and the controller caused a warning hooter to be sounded when this happened. Little more serious than a need to replace the undercarriage was often the result.

Towards the end of the war, surviving Queen Bees were concentrated at the Pilotless Aircraft Unit (PAU) at Manorbier, South Wales, operating in support of the guns at Tenby. Sixty one examples were sold from the nearby 19 MU at St Athan in 1945. In January 1946, 39 Queen Bees in 'as new' condition were notified to be in long term storage. Declared obsolete in May 1947, all were removed from store and scrapped.

Only three Queen Bees are known to have survived. The vast majority of the aircraft sold into the civil market in 1945 were broken up for extraction of their Tiger Moth content and the remains heaped onto bonfires. Hatfield built V4760 (5447), arrived in the USA in December 1941 and was civil registered N2726A in 1955 for use by Pathé News. An ideally configured platform with the pilot in the front seat, a 180 deg. arc of almost uninterrupted view towards the tail was available to the camera operator working from his own uncluttered compartment. The aircraft was used to gather aerial footage for the film *The Spirit of St Louis* and made a brief appearance herself, re-painted as NC726A for the occasion with a DH.60M in company as set dressing. By 1977, N2726A had moved to museum storage in St Paul, Minnesota and was last heard of at Boise, Idaho, dismantled and offered for sale.

By a process of elimination a task group at the Mosquito Aircraft Museum at Salisbury Hall identified the shell they inherited in 1986 as the Scottish built LF789, sold in 1945 after storage at Manorbier where it is believed she flew on just three occasions. Restoration is planned to include stub mainplanes only, but a full set of wireless equipment and autopilot, accompanied by a replica of the M11 control unit full of authentic relays from a redundant telephone exchange.

Now painted in camouflage colours and operated on wheels as a dedicated two seater armed with a full set of duplicated controls, the world's only airworthy Queen Bee, LF858 (SAL150), was delivered to 19 MU St Athan in April 1944 and sold as surplus stock to Wales Airways at Bridgend in December 1946. The hulk was acquired from the Shuttleworth Collection by Barrie Bayes after a periodic clear out in the 'seventies, and following a restoration riddled with trauma was registered G-BLUZ in 1985 prior to her first flight in October the following year.

Apparently sold to a South African bidder as the result of a London auction in July 1995, the purchaser requested that all official documentation should refer to the aircraft as a 'Tiger Moth' to avoid foreseen difficulties with import and registration. After normal business deadlines had expired with no receipt of payment, the sale was declared void and the aircraft syndicated in England to be based, by coincidence, at Henlow.

Above: **An airman in a perilous position on the leading edge of N1846, mounted on the catapult and with the engine running. Typically, control was exercised from the wooden hut alongside the Bessonneau.** *The Aeroplane*

K8669 being launched from the catapult at Watchet, 16th August 1938. *deHMC Archive*

K8669 being launched from the catapult at Watchet, Somerset, on 16th August 1938. The occasion was a demonstration during a Territorial Army camp, to invited officers and Members of Parliament. The aircraft appears to be flying with lifting strops attached to the centre section. deHMC Archive

The SS *Radstock* in a West Country harbour with a K-serialled Queen Bee (possibly K8659) coded '69' on the deck and looking in prime condition. deHMC Archive

Queen Bee LF858, civil registered G-BLUZ, operates as a conventional two seat 'wooden Tiger Moth', a feature betrayed by the uniformity of the skinning on the rear fuselage. Darryl Cott

Queen Bee 5447 (N2726A) in the USA, painted with representative registration NC726A, which featured with DH.60M 'NC1015V' just visible at right, in the film *The Spirit of St Louis*. via Barry Dowsett

THE DH.82A (MOD) THRUXTON JACKAROO

Prototype Thruxton Jackaroo G-AOEX in flight illustrating the faired gap between standard fuel tank and upper mainplane root ends and the incongruity of the spin strakes. *The Aeroplane*

A POST-WAR shortage of dollar exchange contributed to a British Government decision to ban the import of light aircraft from the USA.

The vacuum thus created gave rise to a number of home grown projects, most of which failed due to a serious lack of development capital and a general inability to support the optimism and promotional claims made to an expectant market.

During the early 'fifties, Squadron Leader J E Doran-Webb, a former RAF Bristol Bulldog pilot and now Managing Director of the Wiltshire School of Flying, founded in 1931 at High Post but now relocated to Thruxton in Hampshire, considered building a high-wing four/five seater touring aircraft using only Tiger Moth components, by which he appeared to be surrounded.

Contacts at the Royal Aero Club (RAeC) assured Doran-Webb that his proposals would be well received and he was introduced to Ronald Prizeman, well known at the RAeC after his submissions for a 1953 design competition earned him second place only to a syndicate entry from Boscombe Down.

Prizeman soon proved that a high wing configuration incorporating the lower mainplanes and aileron of a Tiger Moth was not a practical proposition. Instead, he schemed a four seater using the same biplane layout as a Tiger Moth but with a revised fuselage. A meeting held at the Air Registration Board (ARB) on 10th October 1956 proposed an aircraft with a target all-up-weight of 2,180lb based essentially on the argument that for the Tiger Moth wing truss, a semi aerobatic loading of 4.5g at 2,180lb would be less than the DH.82A's full aerobatic loading at 1,770 lb. After a great deal of time, effort and money had been wasted in chasing tails, this view was eventually accepted by the ARB and formed the basis for certification.

At the time the project was developing, Prizeman was Chief Engineer of Baynes Aircraft Interiors, working in the old Hawker Aircraft drawing office at Langley aerodrome, busy with contracts covering Vickers Viscount and Bristol Britannia airliners.

Tiger Moth fuselages under conversion to DH.82A (Mod) Jackaroo by the Wiltshire School of Flying in an ex-RAF workshop at Thruxton aerodrome. deHMC Archive

The four seater was drawn at weekends and during the evenings. Much had to be achieved by the end of 1956 when Ron Prizeman was scheduled to take up a Fellow-ship at a leading American business school.

The name 'Jackaroo' was coined by Captain Joe Taylor who had recently spent time in Australia and returned home with the definition of a slang farming term, Jackaroo meaning a 'new chum' or 'an apprentice jack of all trades'. The name seemed apposite and was adopted without reservation.

To create sufficient elbow room with reasonable comfort for four people, the front side frames of a Tiger Moth fuselage were moved apart by 12.5in within which enlarged space four seats were installed, the starboard pair staggered slightly forward. The change called for critically important revised spaceframes at the front and rear of the parallel sided box, picking up on existing Tiger Moth joints. The basic control box was retained, sited on the port side of the cockpit floor. Centre section strut geometry was maintained, more widely spaced, also the 19 gallon fuel tank with longer carry-through spars, the gap consequently developed between wing root and tank simply faired in.

New tubular construction seats were designed by Prizeman and upholstered by the wife of the chief engineer, Australian J A Golbert. He was responsible for the canopy and new cockpit appointments. In addition to his normal school duties, Golbert also supervised manufacture of test rigs, the erection of an engineering mock-up and two flying prototypes complete with all necessary trial instrumentation.

The basic structure and rigging of wings, tail and rear fuselage were not altered but it was necessary to increase the undercarriage track by designing a new 'W' shaped centre

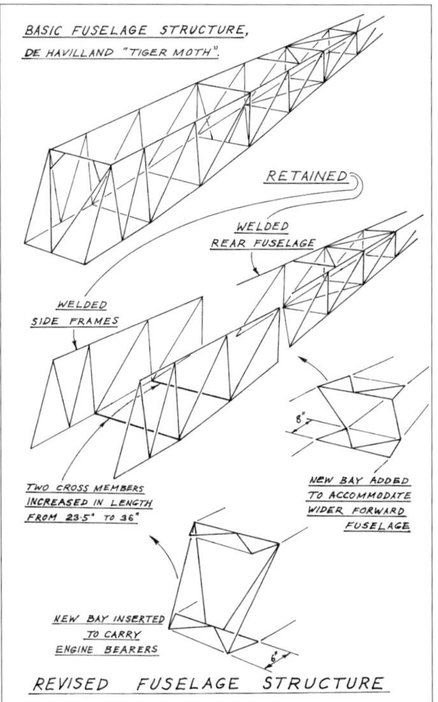

How the basic Tiger Moth frame was converted into a Jackaroo by the addition of spacer bays and an increase in width of the front fuselage. Ron Prizeman

strut, effectively doubling the Tiger Moth's 'V' system, picking up on an otherwise unchanged layout. An 8in tubular bay was added between the front fuselage box and rear pylon to facilitate joining due to the dissimilar width.

The slot locking lever was moved outside to a position on the centre section rear strut, reached through the sliding window; the ignition switches were re-positioned inside onto the panel. No provision was made for engine self-starting due to extra weight and expense.

An increase in mass aft of the certificated centre of gravity (CG) required balance and a 6in bay was added at the forward end of the front fuselage to which standard engine bearers were attached. At a much later stage, longer cowlings were built to regularise the appearance of the extended nose.

The Jackaroo was intended to be flown solo from the left front seat although it was difficult to slip into that position from the wingwalk until a pair of grab handles was strategically placed. In a reversal of the Tiger Moth role, during instructional flying the tutor sat in the back having to share the only instrument panel.

With CG restored, a refined centre section, increased wingspan and tail volume provided by the longer moment arm, spinning characteristics were expected to be better than a Tiger Moth, degraded only by the increased gyroscopic forces generated by repositioning the engine and propeller forward. Working under the close scrutiny of the ARB who only ever recognised the aircraft type as a DH.82A (Mod), the carriage of spin strakes became a mandatory but probably unnecessary requirement.

Two prototypes were built at Thruxton in 1956. G-AOEX (86483), was finished as a standard four seater with cabin and known as a Series 1. She was test flown from Thruxton by Lieutenant Commander 'Pat' Shea-Simonds on 2nd March 1957. G-AOEY (85899), a Series 2, was conceived as a cargo carrier or crop duster as an emergency business measure while waiting for the ARB's deliberations on the use of the Jackaroo for passenger carriage.

By removing the whole of the canopy structure in one easy operation, the cabin could be converted to carry a load of 550lb. A new low profile superstructure replacing the cabin, neatly converted the Jackaroo Series 2 into a single seater with open cockpit at the port side rear position and from where the pilot was expected to read instruments on the front (and only) panel, sighting below the level of the decking. For insurance and convenience, an independent Air Speed Indicator (ASI) was mounted in a teardrop housing on top of the forward decking, adjacent to the rear centre section strut. Afforded great publicity, the single seat version of the Jackaroo found no favour, and although both it and three other aircraft were used successfully as crop sprayers, all operated in the configuration of the Series 1 with the cabin structure in place.

The manufacturers claimed on launch to have received orders from agricultural contractors in New Zealand, Rhodesia and Argentina and 'earnest interest' from Germany. By July 1957 they were quoting an order book for 150 aircraft, 50 of which were for South Africa, and were anticipating production would reach at least six aircraft per month almost immediately.

Test flying duties devolved to Commander W 'Doc' Stewart after Pat Shea-Simonds left the programme. On one occasion, Stewart, a Boscombe Down test pilot, was conducting a series of full throttle climbs with Ron Prizeman as observer. During the final descent Stewart expressed his pleasure at the way the aircraft could be trimmed to land. Prizeman remembers the occasion well:

'Doc set the throttle and trim and looped his hands with fingers touching two or three inches in front of the joystick. As far as I was concerned he had proved his point when the wheels first contacted the ground. As four or five gentle, arcing bounces consumed the airfield and his hands showed no sign of moving, my anxiety and pulse rate rose in a manner I can still recall'.

To an ordinary private owner with a new licence like Kenneth Irvine, the Jackaroo was a delight. He bought G-APAO (82845) in 1976, the sole Series 3, fitted with mainwheel brakes and a metal framed cabin:

'The view from the Jackaroo is much better than from a Tiger Moth: one sits so high in the front seat that the nose is well below the horizon in level flight, she is steadier in the air (and on the ground too due to the wider undercarriage), much slower at 60 knots (1,900 revs) and much more suited to a nervous and heavy handed beginner. I do not mind her lack of aerobatic qualities as I find that the most satisfying and demanding aerobatic manoeuvre is the execution of a good landing'.

There were great hopes for the Jackaroo manufactured at Thruxton by the Wiltshire School of Flying and later an associated company, Jackaroo Aircraft. The initial price was expected to be about £900 but by July 1957 was quoted at £1,095 complete ex-works, with a nil-houred engine. An agricultural conversion kit was available at £150. Overseas owners were encouraged to convert their own Tiger Moths by purchasing a packaged kit at £600. Tiger Moths flown into Thruxton could be taken off again after ten days, fully converted, at £700. Special deals were also available for overnight engine changes or a complete engine overhaul to zero time for £150.

During her agricultural career, Jackaroo G-APHZ (82168), was operated by Airspray from Boxted where she was joined in 1959 by sister Jackaroo G-APAP (83018). The pair had been flown to Khartoum, contracted to spray the cotton crop, when the Sudanese Government fell to a military coup. Airspray sent a manager with a bag of cash but both disappeared on arrival. Airspray's owner, retired RAF pilot Percy Hatfield, flew out to investigate and discovered the two Jackaroos picketed in the desert where he was presented with a bill for 'hangared parking' which he simply tore up and took both aircraft back to England. G-APHZ found her way to Canada in 1970 having long since returned to passenger configuration, where she was upgraded by the substitution of a DH.82C Tiger Moth style undercarriage, mainwheel brakes and a tailwheel. G-APAP took up glider tugging and continued in that business after re-conversion to a Tiger Moth in 1986.

Of the other two sprayers, G-AOIV (85146), was sold to Argentina in 1959. Her subsequent career in South America is obscure. She was last reported with a group of derelict Peruvian Stearmans, probably at Don Torcuato airport in Buenos Aires in 1966. G-AOEY (85899), the sole Series 2 Jackaroo was eventually converted into a Series 1 spray-er and sold to Italy, but she was re-sold to Nigeria and registered VR-NCY before redeployment to Ghana where she was abandoned.

Ever anxious to be involved with innovation, Rollason Aircraft acquired a Thruxton built Jackaroo, G-ANZT (84176), in 1957, ostensibly for use by their employee flying group. The company incorporated a number of what they considered to be 'improvements', the most obvious of which was the 'high back', eliminating part of the tadpole-like appearance of the original fuselage shape. The slat locking control was also moved back inside the cabin. In April 1960, Rollason completed a Jackaroo of their own, G-APOV (83012), in which the decking was further modified. In plan, the rear fuselage faired smoothly from the wide cabin to the tail. Ron Prizeman was to comment wryly, *'I know of no speed, handling or weight advantage being demonstrated by the tapered tail unit.'*

Although never certificated as aerobatic, the aircraft was spun, on at least one occasion with all four seats occupied, an experience none of those on board ever wished to repeat. During early test flying, 'Doc' Stewart managed to persuade G-AOEX into a right hand spin but only with considerable difficulty. By July he had still not succeeded in creating a developed spin to the left. A world class aerobatic pilot positioning a Jackaroo with three passengers was dismayed to see his companions beginning to doze. In his hands the immaculate slow roll was effortless but not encouraged. Many solo pilots in later years admitted to looping and rolling Jackaroos without apparent harm.

As a racing, record breaking and touring aeroplane, the Jackaroo was most famously promoted by Sheila Scott who learned to fly at Thruxton in 1959 and afterwards bought G-APAM (3874). Sheila Scott named her Jackaroo *Myth* and flew her until 1964 when she was replaced by a long ranging Piper Comanche, *Myth II*. Even with such famous connections and log books full of triumph, no buyer was found when *Myth* was offered for sale in 1984 by her then owner, Tim Williams. Having a touring aeroplane already in the form of DH.80A Puss Moth G-AAZP, Williams decided he would only keep G-APAM if she was converted back to a Tiger Moth, which she was the following year.

The Wiltshire School of Flying operated the biggest fleet of Jackaroos at Thruxton in the early 'sixties, usually ten on line each day, when residential accommodation and a good summer assisted some pupils to qualify for a private licence within a fortnight

The team responsible for the Thruxton Jackaroo: left to right, Ron Prizeman, designer; J A Golbert, chief engineer, Wiltshire School of Flying; Squadron Leader J E Doran-Webb with a broken leg, managing director; Lieutenant Commander Pat Shea-Simonds, test pilot. *The Aeroplane*

The sparsely instrumented panel of the prototype Jackaroo G-AOEX and a view of the control box and remodelled front seat on the port side of the cabin. *The Aeroplane*

and then continue immediately through with commercial aspirations. When the operation finally stopped and the school was sold, the aircraft were dispersed, their training days apparently done. Not so! In 1990, husband and wife team Dennis and Tricia Neville acquired and rebuilt the Rollason 'improved' example G-ANZT which flew again in 1996. In September 1998 Tricia Neville soloed on the family aeroplane, almost certainly the first pupil to do so on type for over 30 years.

The big prospective orders never reached maturity and even the chance of exporting aircraft kits to India in 1962 was denied after G-APAK (84286), was sent as a production example. Import permits for five other Jackaroos already on the line at Thruxton were refused and each was broken up for spare parts.

Born into a situation created by government import restrictions, the Thruxton Jackaroo programme was fatally wounded when foreign light aircraft finally were allowed to flood into the country. Designer Ron Prizeman viewed it all quite dispassionately. He had achieved all that had been asked and was professionally satisfied. His total fee, an agreed royalty payment of £2 per aircraft sold, he never received.

PRODUCTION OF THRUXTON JACKAROO

List in order of aircraft laid down for conversion.

– (Mockup)	G-AMTX	83850	Completed as aircraft 13
1	G-AOEX	86483	Current. Under restoration in Hampshire.
2 (Series 2)	G-AOEY	85899	Assumed abandoned in Ghana.
3	G-ANZT	84176	Rollason 'improved'. Airworthy at Rush Green
4	G-AOIR	82882	Current. Airworthy at Little Gransden.
5	G-APAI	85838	Damaged 1964. Cancelled 1969.
6	G-ANFY	86349	Current. Dismantled and stored in Kent.
7	G-AOIX	83472	Broken up for spares at Thruxton.
8	G-APAJ	83314	Commercial joyrider in Australia as VH-KRK.
9	G-APHZ	82168	Airworthy at Guelph, Canada as C-FPHZ.
10	G-AOIO	82151	Current. Dismantled and stored in Australia.
11	G-AOIV	85146	Reported derelict in Argentina 1966.
12	G-AOIT	83190	Broken up for spares in Canada.
13	G-APJV	83850	Overturned 1960. Cancelled 1962.
14 (Series 3)	G-APAO	82845	Airworthy. Re-converted to Tiger Moth.
15	G-AOIW	85147	Broken up for spares in the Netherlands.
16	G-APAL	82102	Airworthy. Re-converted to Tiger Moth.
17	G-APAP	83018	Current. Re-converted to Tiger Moth.
18	G-APAM	3874	Airworthy. Re-converted to Tiger Moth.
19 (Rollason)	G-APOV	83012	Crashed 1961. To school playground 1964.
–	G-APAK	84286	To India as VT-DOF 1962. Cancelled 1969.
–	G-APRB	3971	Not completed. Parts to G-AOIR and Rollason.
–	G-APRC	84489	Not completed. Broken up for spares.
–	G-APSU	3879	Not completed. Broken up for spares.
–	G-APSV	85358	Not completed. Broken up for spares.
–	G-ALIV	84673	Not completed. Broken up for spares.

Difficulty in settling into the commander's seat was overcome by strategically placed grab handles. On the Series 1 Jackaroo the framework of the large door and fixed canopy was made of wood. ***The Aeroplane***

Removal of the standard canopy and three seats, installation of a hopper or container and a low profile decking, and the Series 2 Jackaroo offered opportunities for light freighting or cropspraying. ***The Aeroplane***

Prototype Series 2 Jackaroo G-AOEY was developed as an emergency business measure to counter apparent procrastination by the ARB. In spite of many public demonstrations and a short racing career, the Series 2 was not a commercial success. *The Aeroplane*

G-AOIR, most active of all privately owned Jackaroos in Great Britain, displaying the original 'economy' extension to the engine side cowling, necessary to cover the inserted bay. The wide track undercarriage was achieved with a new 'W' bracket. Tim Williams refuels G-APAM in the background. Stuart Howe

These photographs of Jackaroos G-ANFY and G-ANZT, painted in the black fuselage/silver wing scheme adopted by the Wiltshire School of Flying, allow direct comparison of the rear deckings. G-ANZT carries the high back modified by Rollason. Hugh Evans and Peter Clifton

Tim Williams and Sheila Scott leave Hatfield in Jackaroo G-APAM bound for Strathallan at the start of the Famous Grouse Rally, June 1979. *Aeroplane Monthly*

Canadian based Jackaroo C-FPHZ standing on her DH.82C undercarriage complete with a tailwheel and mainwheel brakes. Charles Holland

Australian based Jackaroo VH-KRK was used for joyriding at Cairns where high temperatures limited performance with a full load. Sold to Torqair, the aircraft moved to Torquay on the south coast of Victoria to continue her occupation. David Freeman

High-back Jackaroo G-ANZT was restored to pristine condition by Dennis and Tricia Neville between 1990 and 1996 and soloed by Mrs Neville during her PPL course in 1998 – possibly the first pupil to achieve such an ambition on this type of aircraft for more than 30 years. Barry Dowsett

THE CIRCUS COMES TO TOWN

Cheryl (Rusty) Butterworth and Tiger Moth ZK-CDU flown by Tony Renouf. The trio was airborne for 3 hours and 8 minutes in 1990, to create a world record recognised only by some. John King

THE 'NEW IDEAS' department at the Tiger Club was tasked with developing a new 'act' after their 1959 season, and on 4th March 1962, inventor Lewis Benjamin with Dennis Hartas, flew the first live trials of what became known as 'Stand on Wing' (SOW). In truth, the participant was standing on a near horizontal platform, secured above the centre section fuel tank with the aid of a stressed tubular frame which picked up on the top wing mounting bolts, and provided a backrest and anchorage for a midriff comfort strap. Although considered somewhat tame in comparison with the unsecured gambollings of true definition wing walkers who participated in pre-war air displays, particularly in the USA, the 1960's revival in Great Britain was faced not only with the use of a Tiger Moth, barely adequate due to only modest power, even when combining a Gipsy Major IC with a Fairey Reed metal propeller, but also the jungle of bureaucratic paperwork which had sprung up since the war in an effort to keep civil aviation in its proper place.

Having constructed the rig, the airworthiness authorities insisted on flight trials with a representative dummy passenger. Adrian Deverall and his fellow engineers at Redhill assembled 'Brother Ben', a 150lb mass complete with a painted face, flying helmet and a pair of the chief engineer's cast off shoes. Following a series of taxy tests, the first circuit was flown by Lewis Benjamin followed by David Phillips and Dennis Hartas when lessons were learned not only with respect to the behaviour of the aeroplane with a tall load above the fuel tank, but also the best speeds and attitudes necessary for optimum performance.

The live trials on 4th March were conducted by Lewis Benjamin on the rig with Dennis Hartas piloting Tiger Moth G-ARAZ (82867). The flight was around a Redhill aerodrome liberally sprinkled with snow, and 'Benjy' was sensibly protected by multifarious layers of flying clothing, boots, a leather helmet, goggles and an oxygen mask connected to atmosphere. Having proved that the system was safe and practical, two lady club members were enrolled, alternating with each other to stand on the wing at the club's regular displays, but it was Benjy and pilot David Phillips, performing at Rearsby in May 1962, who discovered a dark secret, and how badly a Tiger Moth in the SOW configuration performed if the aircraft was allowed to unstick at too low a speed. Their circuit at 15ft, dodging trees, hedges and washing lines, completed in style by hooking the tailskid on to the airfield boundary fence at the moment of breath

Lewis Benjamin in the reverse angle cap and Dennis Hartas together with the first SOW rig manufactured by Rollason Aircraft, and approved for live trials. deHMC Archive

The first live trials of the SOW rig at Redhill in March 1962 during which Lewis Benjamin was heavily protected against the cold. As experience was accumulated and young ladies were persuaded into the role, weatherproof clothing became less of a concern. deHMC Archive

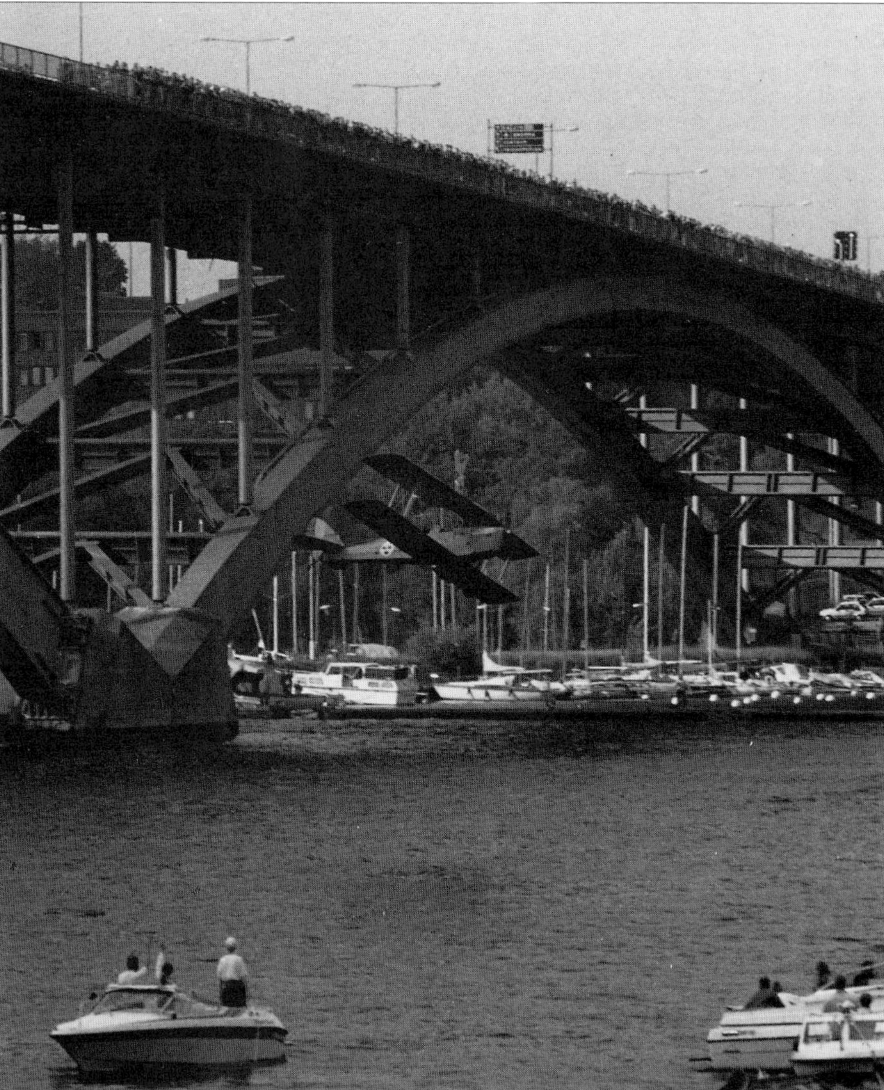

Pierre Hollander with Swedish folk character Pippi Longstocking performing acrobatics on the SOW rig at low level in the middle of Stockholm. via Pierre Hollander

relieving touchdown, promoted a close examination of the situation, and resulted in a maximum 'passenger' height of 5ft 8in and weight of 140lb, minimum fuel and flight with a suitably fine pitch propeller.

Several rigs were eventually manufactured against the original Rollason design which included a number of Tiger Moth airframe parts, and the configuration was approved for operation in Australia, New Zealand and Sweden, where Pierre Hollander carried aloft an energetic fairy-tale character, Pippi Longstocking, who was permitted to perform handstands on Tiger Moth SE-CHG (85867), as the aircraft flew around the centre of Stockholm and under some of the city's bridges. Dennis Hartas flew G-ARAZ from Lympne to Berck across the English Channel on 11th August 1963 while Allanah Campbell took in the view from her position on the top deck. In New Zealand, ZK-CDU (3581), flown by Tony Renouf with Cheryl Butterworth occupying the rig, stayed airborne for 3 hours 8 minutes on 4th March 1990, to create a feat of endurance recognised by the Guinness Book of Records but not the FAI.

The SOW routine has been used on frequent occasions as a tool for charity fund raising and has the power still, to attract a television audience when a celebrity is featured, carried aloft in pursuit of a good cause, usually to the accompaniment of much well intended guffawing. Members of the general public have been carried to celebrate special birthdays or anniversaries, or just for self satisfaction or to neutralise a bet or a dare. 'Colonel Crackshot' and 'Lolita' have ridden the rig, firing off blanks from a pistol or rifle, and mysteriously smashing all the bottles ranged in public view. The heavy protective clothing of the initial trials quickly gave way to more glamorous but practical attire when the show arena became the near exclusive domain of the girls, but the blonde stripper who was engaged during a convivial evening in the clubhouse at Rochester, failed to keep her appointment with the Tiger Moth in the cold light of the following morning.

Tiger Moth G-AVPJ (86322), operating in the SOW configuration with the Barnstormer Circus at the Nottingham Festival on 17th June 1979, hit a wire suspended above the River Trent. Aeroplane and crew were pitched into 10ft of water, 45ft from the river bank at West Bridgford, but were rescued unhurt, and both they and G-AVPJ were dried out to fly again.

G-AVPJ had been encouraged to fly over somewhat deeper water on a previous occasion when she was still in naval uniform. The Royal Navy aircraft carrier HMS *Eagle* was working up in the Western Channel following a major refit at Devonport, when a plot was hatched between naval officers attached to Britannia Flight, Royal Naval College Dartmouth, to visit the ship by Tiger Moth, and to appraise the Wardroom facilities. Approval was sought from Their Lordships of the Admiralty, and willingly gifted, with the result that NL879, the nascent G-AVPJ, and three other Tiger Moths operating from the Flight's base at Roborough, BB814 (82187), BB694 (3340) and XL714 (84566), all touched down on HMS *Eagle's* expansive flight deck on 20th June 1964. Conditions were ideal, but following good naval practise, short lengths of knotted rope were looped through the tie-down positions to ease deck handling should the need arise. While the crews availed themselves of the ship's facilities, the Tiger Moths provided practical handling experience for the deck parties, including striking down onto the capacious hangar deck with the aid of the ship's lift. A second visit was successfully accomplished on 1st July 1964, immediately after which NL879 was officially transferred to the Royal Air Force College Flying Club at Cranwell, although she was not delivered for another three years, taking up her civil letters in June 1967.

BB814 was posted to Arbroath in 1966 to serve as a tug on behalf of the Condor Gliding Club, and during the summer added a large letter 'H' to her mundane livery to commemorate her deck landing on HMS *Hermes* on 23rd June that year. Restored to her pre-war civil identity as G-AFWI in 1972, the aircraft continued her tugging career for a further ten years on behalf of the Portsmouth Naval Gliding Club at Lee on Solent until sold into private ownership – to two Royal Navy officers.

Standing on top of a Tiger Moth in flight is guaranteed to keep the adrenaline pumping, although other aircraft with greater reserves of power are capable of flying complete aerobatic sequences while one or more slinky figures lithely cavort through their choreographed programme of airborne aerobics. While a Tiger Moth would never be persuaded into a rolling manoeuvre with a passenger on the rig, moving said passenger to the walkway on a lower wing opens the door to new possibilities.

In order to demonstrate the stickability of his line of Pattex adhesives, Marketing Manager Uwe Drews arranged to be stuck to the upper surface of the port lower mainplane of Tiger Moth ZS-DND (DHA737). A detachable panel was wrapped around the wing to which Drews' flying suit was bonded with a Pattex product. On 4th June 1984, the aircraft was flown through a series of slow rolls, piloted by South African aerobatic champion Scully Levine, while the whole exercise was filmed from a helicopter. Faith in his company's products or not, Drews was equipped with a hidden parachute, just in case.

An advertisement for the Durban Wings Club 'Winter Air Pageant' scheduled for July 1982 was headed by a photograph of an anonymous Tiger Moth of Australian origin, tail high, wheels off the runway, with a man clad in open necked shirt and shorts, sitting on the hard leading edge of the starboard lower wing, midway between the fuselage and the interplane strut, and with no visible means of restraint, nor a parachute. In the publicity photograph the passenger door is open, confirming perhaps the advertised attraction of 'wing walking' at its most literal.

Cheryl Butterworth atop Tiger Moth ZK-CDU viewed from another Tiger Moth flown by ex-RNZAF pilot John Denton, trained to keep his formating really tight.
John King

From the earliest days of the movies, film makers have enjoyed the wide range of opportunities offered by photogenic biplanes. The aviation film industry was spawned in the days immediately after the First World War, when thousands of surplus aircraft could be bought for almost nothing. There was a seemingly infinite supply of 'props' for the Barnstormers and film makers, especially in the United States, to fly, stunt and crash with a spectacularly choreographed intent, mostly. But having consumed just so much cheap firewood and linen, the craze wore off, especially when the Second World War brought realism and then new inspirations for the peacetime entertainment industry.

Genuine First World War aircraft reached levels of such pricelessness that except for special consideration, they might only be released from their conditioned surroundings for guest appearances. Enter the new technicians with the talent, ability and facilities to create whole squadrons of First World War scouts, either from scratch, or more cheaply and with a greater guarantee of performance, from disguising the ubiquitous Tiger Moth.

Filming of the epic *Lawrence of Arabia* in 1961 required a Fokker D.VII and a pair of Rumpler C.Vs for filming in the Jordanian desert, and the contract to produce all three was awarded to John Crewdson's Film Aviation Services at Croydon. Ex-military surplus Tiger Moth T7438 (83817), was converted into a Turkish Air Force D.VII and the two

As SOW operations were perfected it was inevitable that some variation on the theme should be introduced. The Barnstormers enrolled 'Colonel Crackshot' who miraculously destroyed rows of bottles set up on the flightline by shooting at them during a number of low passes.
Air Portraits

HMS *Eagle*, working-up in the Western Approaches after a major refit during the summer of 1964, was host on two occasions to Tiger Moths of Britannia Flight operating out of Plymouth. Royal Navy

Rumplers were created around G-ANNF (83028) and G-ANLC (85154), both a spin-off from the A J Whittemore mass purchase of 1953. Although the Rumplers featured prominently in the film, giving Alec Guinness' horse a fright, and in all the orchestrated publicity, it is believed the pair succumbed to the accountants' whimsy and were abandoned on location. The Fokker D.VII never got further than her hangar at Croydon and was destroyed there in a fire late in 1963.

Some aura identified only by art directors, has almost always caused Tiger Moths to be cast to act with menace 'not on the Allied side'. Given a coat of dappled waterwash paint, a gas-gun mounted over a faired front cockpit, liberal application of Maltese crosses and a pilot wearing a black helmet and heavy framed goggles, the gang of Tiger Moths featured in *The Blue Max* in 1965 looked every inch as sinsiter as intended. Cheap and expendable to the film makers perhaps, all three aircraft (G-AIRI/3761; G-AIRK/82336 and G-AMTK/3985), all survived their ordeals over the Western Front, re-created in Ireland and after further cinematic excursions were eventually returned unharmed to private ownership.

To star in *The Blue Max*, the production company commissioned two full-size replicas of a 1917 Pfalz D.III. For purity of line, Vivian Bellamy's Hampshire Aeroplane Club built a Ray Hilborne-designed model starting from scratch. Doug Bianchi at White Waltham elected to build his Pfalz around a Tiger Moth in the quest for reduced workshop time. The Hampshire Pfalz flew behind an inverted Gipsy Major engine with an elaborate vertically mounted exhaust, but the aircraft required 50lb of lead hidden behind the line of the propeller spinner, to achieve a safe balance condition. In 1975, the film *Aces High* mixed Tiger Moths with Stampe SV-4s when the Western Front was created yet again, this time at Booker, but it was the thinly disguised Tiger Moths that bolstered the squadron bearing Iron Crosses to do spectacular battle with Stampe-like S.E.5s.

An earlier production with an aerial team operating from Booker was *Thunderbird 6*, a feature-length film based on the famous Thunderbirds television puppet series. Painted in multi-coloured swirls, Tiger Moth G-ANFM (83604), was required to fly with a number of dummy figures clinging to the interplane struts and the undercarriage. Piloted by the petite Joan Hughes, a former ATA pilot, who with the sole assistance of a flight engineer had delivered Lancaster bombers to wartime RAF bases, G-ANFM could be safely operated only on full throttle. Approval was given to fly low along the new but still unopened M40 Motorway which skirted the edge of Booker airfield, but because of unfavourable sidewinds in the cutting, Joan Hughes was forced to fly under a bridge, and although permission had been sought for an identical scene as part of the script, the police raised a prosecution and the film crew was taken to court, where they won their case. G-ANFM appeared in a number of other films including *Agatha, The Awakening of Emily* and *The Little Prince*, in which she took on a French disguise to play in the life story of the writer and aviator, Antoine de Saint-Exupéry .

One of the great classics of the silver screen, *King Kong,* was released in 1933, and to mark Kong's Jubilee on 14th April 1983, an eight storey, 3,000lb inflatable monster was launched from the base of the Empire State Building, to whose summit he was to be tethered for 10 days. Unfortunately, the monster impaled itself on the structure just below the roof which slightly spoiled the publicity opportunities. Kurt Hofschneider flying his camouflaged Tiger Moth N39DH (85674), in company with John Bussard in a Waco UPF-7, were hired to simulate the aerial attacks which featured in the film. Authorised to circle the Empire State Building four times, neither the Tiger Moth nor Waco was permitted to dive bomb the monster. *'It was very difficult to get FAA approval for the flight at all, let alone permission to do anything fancy. Having 50 year old biplanes flying around over New York City is not part of their procedures,'* said an otherwise highly satisfied Moth pilot.

Apart from dressing the sets, Tiger Moths have been stars in their own right, particularly in feature films made in Australia and New Zealand, and promotional material shot in Canada. They have appeared too in numerous advertisements and commercials, almost inevitably with a corny and overblown 'Biggles' angle, a view countered thankfully by highlighting a product of enduring quality or contrast, as illustrated in major promotions run on behalf of Mercedes cars and Agfa film in 1997.

The component parts of an airframe which had never flown together in ordered formation, were carried to the second floor of a factory building in Newtown, Sydney, in 1983 to make a name in *Spirit of Australia*, then the pieces were carted down the stairs again and off to Maitland, to be joined together in the interests of flight almost two years later. An abandoned Tiger Moth, supposedly the result of an accident when playing aerial farmers, stars in *Spirit of the Tiger*, when a couple discover the remarkably well preserved and complete wreckage in the bush, and fantasise about its past history and bright future. In real life and to create the set, the airframe was persuaded out of storage in Queensland, assembled in a pseudo damaged state, which was enhanced for filming, then sold on by the production company as a viable restoration project.

Perhaps the classic starring role was taken by Tiger Moth G-AMIU (83228), in the summer of 1969, when she was featured in Richard Wade's *Two in a Tiger*, a bittersweet study of teaching and learning the art of flying in a Tiger Moth. 'The Instructor' Roger Neaves, indoctrinates 'The Pupil', television actor Dudley Foster, with sufficient lore, practical expertise and self confidence to fly solo, and the whole process, although filmed against a script, is wholly believable. 'The Pupil' never flew again following his solo efforts, and after the film was completed, but not thought to be in any way connected with it, Foster committed suicide. A year later, during an attempted overshoot from an apparently bad approach when being assessed by two prospective purchasers, G-AMIU slipped into the ground and cartwheeled, each pilot believing the other had control.

In September 1996, Tiger Moth G-ASKP (3889), was contracted to play the villain's get-away vehicle in a television episode of Enid Blyton's *The Famous Five*, to be shot on a narrow strip, formerly part of a railway line, at Westbury-sub-Mendip in Somerset. An arrival in a gusting crosswind resulted in G-ASKP being blown off the strip and down an embankment, suffering grievously. The pilot later explained that he had expected the aircraft to adopt a natural weathercock attitude once settled on the ground, but the presumption was sabotaged by the possibility of a puncture coinciding with touchdown. On the same day a friend crashed the pilot's car which was being driven to the site, and the owner of the replacement aircraft, G-ADPC (3393), refused to land at Westbury, resulting in the baddies appearing on the small screen committing mayhem at Lulsgate instead.

The 1997 film *The English Patient* almost swept the board at the Hollywood Oscars. Some of the opening sequences featuring a Tiger Moth, were filmed in a studio in Rome during September 1995, with an odd-job airframe stitched together for the purpose, largely based on the remains of N6665 (3969), supplied from England. The live action was filmed in the Tunisian desert with G-AJHU (83900), an aircraft whose previous starring qualities had been witnessed in a 1985 television commercial for Windmill Bread. The two-second shot of the propeller being swung, an image fusing into the rotation of the rustic sails of a giant windmill, had taken a day and a half to shoot, but the fee paid for probably the most exhaustive overhaul ever enjoyed in the aeroplane's civil life. Just over a year later, G-AJHU was almost completely smashed when she failed to clear trees during take off, against advice, under difficult wind conditions, but was rebuilt at Membury to Public Transport standard.

G-AJHU was bought for the exclusive purpose of starring in *The English Patient*, and survived the sand and cinematic experience of being shot down in flames, to continue an airworthy post-production career in Italy. As RAF T7471, she had led a chequered life as a calibration and communications aeroplane from the start of her commission in 1941, until release in 1947. Her first 'incident' occurred in January 1943 when the curtain fastenings of her archetypal RAF blister hangar at the evocatively named Colby Grange airfield in Lincolnshire, worked loose in high winds, and the heavy cover smote her on the nose. From such beginnings, it was her destiny to star in this passionate five star drama, the creative masterpiece of an

The visit to HMS *Eagle* was a serious exercise to provide practical handling experience for the flight deck crew. In this photograph, one of the visitors is seen striking down in order to de-man out of the wind. Royal Navy

Not a limbo aircraft following collision with the bunting but one Tiger Moth tied to another Tiger Moth. The Tiger Club put up a vic of tied together aircraft which were obliged to maintain close formation from take off to landing. Stuart Howe

Left: **A rare photograph of three Super Tigers displaying identical colour layout flying a tied-together formation at White Waltham. In choppy conditions the trio experienced a tape-break for the first time. Most shows were completed successfully.** via Lewis Benjamin

Below left and right: **As a publicity stunt, the flying suit of Uwe Drews, marketing manager of an adhesive manufacturer in South Africa, was glued to a special panel wrapped around the port lower mainplane of Tiger Moth ZS-DND at Stellenbosch in 1985. Flown by aerobatic champion Scully Levine, at least four slow rolls were completed, all filmed from a chasing helicopter and later used in a series of television commercials. Not seen was a loose harness and a parachute concealed under Mr Drews' flying suit at the insistence of the local airworthiness authorities. The session was curtailed when it was discovered that the parachute had started to unfurl.** Henkel

Left: **The simple structure and basic configuration of the Tiger Moth lead to easy conversion and First World War fighter aircraft are obvious profiles to copy. The resultant 'replicas' can be flown less reverentially in display and film work.** *Aeroplane Monthly*

Opposite page:

For the film *Lawrence of Arabia*, RAF surplus Tiger Moth T7438 was converted into a Fokker D.VII by Film Aviation Services at Croydon in 1961, but was destined never to join the cast and eventually was destroyed in a hangar fire. J J Hughes internationally assembled crew working under the commercial banner of 'Tiger Moth Productions'.

The most blatant big screen exploitation of a Tiger Moth occurred in 1968 when N523R (82960), an aircraft owned by American film actor Cliff Robertson, and bought with two others whilst in England in 1965 during production of the Mosquito wrecking *633 Squadron*, was cast in a pivotal role in the Spanish-made 'western' *Villa Rides*.

The aircraft was cleverly modified to simulate what was supposed to be a stylised version of a Curtiss Jenny, with padded edges to the rounded cockpit, squared engine cowlings, dummy exhaust pipes, additional interplane struts and an array of horns and fixtures bolted to the top surfaces of the upper mainplanes in pursuit of nothing but visual effect.

In the plot, the aircraft is running guns to the army of Pancho Villa, and is requisitioned by Villa's forces together with pilot Robert Mitchum, to drop an apparently inexhaustible supply of bombs held at readiness in the cockpit, on to the opposition. All is in vain until the aircraft is hit in the engine by one of cinema's magic bullets which, as expected, causes the aircraft to gyrate wildly in the vivid blue sky, to the orchestrated tones of inebriated vacuum cleaners. Inevitably, the aircraft crashes fatally onto a section of heavy fortification, creating a breach through which Villa's army surges to victory, whilst protecting every hair of her gallant pilot.

Derek Piggott, a professional gliding instructor and ex-RAF pilot, who 20 years previously had watched a salvage party cut up and throw down an Indian well, the Tiger Moth he had only hours before forced landed into a paddy field, was contracted to crash a Tiger Moth before cameras in Spain. He had been recommended to the producers on account of considerable experience in piloting for films, including flying between narrow uprights of a bridge in *The Blue Max* and work on *Darling Lili* and *Those Magnificent Men*, for which 20 take-offs were made in a 'sabotaged' Bristol Boxkite and 20 landings successfully accomplished on the one remaining set of wheels.

For *Villa Rides*, the task was simple: crash the Tiger Moth into a barbed wire entanglement on a river bank at a precise spot where the barricade was secured by balsa wood posts; do not undershoot to land in the river or overshoot to hit a cliff face which was too close to avoid by turning either left or right in case of a fumble, and remember it is a real aircraft, in flight, and the crash contrived for the multi camera positions could be achieved only once.

Drawing on his experience with the Indian Tiger Moth incident in 1946, Piggott devised a scheme to weaken the main undercarriage to ensure certainty of total collapse on touch down, provided position and speed were absolutely correct. The main pin in the undercarriage V strut was radically reduced in diameter to create a very loose fit, and would be extracted in flight with the aid of a drawstring, leaving the axle tubes attached only by a twist of soft iron wire. The instrument panel was padded with polystyrene sheeting with holes cut to display vital dials, and all equipment in the vicinity of the rudder bars was cleared away. An additional safety harness was installed, and only four gallons of petrol put on board.

On the occasion of the shoot, Piggott flew a cautious reconnaissance then set up the aeroplane for a controlled touchdown at an intended 55mph:

'I consciously take a grip on myself and remind myself to just concentrate on the touchdown point and not to see the cliff ahead. To my surprise it all comes easily. I watch the barricade ahead and gradually reduce speed skimming over the river a few feet above the water, Then at the exact moment I close the throttle and put the aircraft down just ahead of the barrier. A spray of muddy water covers the cockpit and windscreen and I feel the jolt as we plough into the ground, slithering to a stop. The noise stops abruptly. I look round wondering if I have touched down in the right place, or if I have stopped short of the barrier. But all is well, I see the barrier behind me, although to my amazement I realise the aircraft has stopped short of the sandbag gun emplacement. I hear the director shouting 'cut' and begin to unstrap and climb out to survey the damage'.

Everybody appeared to be happy. For a screen time of about four seconds, the pilot had earned a fee equivalent to a year's salary at his gliding club, but later he learned that the shot could have been completed at a different location without the glowering menace of a cliff face acting as an impenetrable barrier to any overshoot. That made him less happy. The Tiger Moth was remarkably undamaged considering the ordeal and was eventually rebuilt to fly again, but only in order to commit a more devastatingly destructive ground loop in the opening sequence of *The Aviator*, an action drama starring her American owner.

The most salutary lesson ever to appear on film was a product of the RAF's own safety, training and education services. Tiger Moth DE685 (85626), is seen taxying towards some seemingly deserted airfield buildings, and a close up of the pilot's puckered visage reveals annoyance at being accorded no welcoming party. Leaving the engine ticking over, our hero unstraps and levers himself out of the cockpit, but he slips on the walkway, knocks the throttle lever far forward, and is distressed to watch his late mount waddling off into the distance. The moral of course: never leave an aircraft unattended with a live engine.

No matter how much energy he commits to his hot pursuit, the film makers of RAF Reserve Command ensure that the Tiger Moth 'RCVG' of 24 Reserve Flying School (RFS) Rochester, well and truly collides with the corner of a hut, neatly demolishing both port wings. How did they do it? When did they do it? According to official records, DE685 was written off after striking trees during a forced landing in Kent on 8th August 1950. Was that how the film makers disguised their dastardly deed, or was the 'RCVG' of the instructional safety presentation a ghost of the original, cobbled together for effect?

The viewers are left with an image of the grimacing face of the pilot whose agonies are blotted out in time honoured fashion with the enduring caption: The End. But for a lady with pedigree such as the de Havilland DH.82 Tiger Moth, it is merely the closing of another chapter in a story that just keeps on running. With little doubt, many more achievements and some surprises are yet in store.

Top left: **One of a pair of Albatros C.II replicas built by Jean Salis, based on cheap and discarded Tiger Moth components.** Starliner

Top right: **Still a vintage aeroplane at heart, High Technology Tiger Moth G-BPAJ, complete with 'go-faster' style registration, on her home strip at Huntingdon just after her first flight in June 1991.** Stuart McKay

Centre left: **Modern composite materials, Kevlar, fibreglass and carbon fibre, formed with the latest technology and coupled to the most effective protective treatments for both inner and outer surfaces of the steel tube structure, were incorporated into Peter Jackson's High Technology Tiger Moth G-BPAJ.** Specialised Mouldings

Centre right: **An art director's view of how a Tiger Moth can be converted into a First World War German scout by the application of a garish waterwash scheme, dominated by the identifying signal of the Cross *Patée* or *Eiserne Kreuz* - literally Iron Cross.** Geoff Green

Above: **Replica Pfalz D.III commissioned for *The Blue Max* and based on a Tiger Moth frame, was built by Doug Bianchi at White Waltham and Booker before delivery to the film set in Ireland. The British registration is applied in masking tape over the cross on the fuselage side.** Stuart McKay

Left: **A regular feature of the Royal Newcastle Aero Club flying displays of the 'seventies was a dogfight between foes distinguished only by their colours and closely observed by the news hawks of Channel 7 television hovering close by.** via Bill Hitchcock

The cheapest method of acquiring a vintage 'French' aeroplane to feature in a film covering the life of Antoine de Saint-Exupéry, was to take a vintage British aeroplane and change the national letter 'G' to the national letter 'F', with appropriate and official dispensations! Stuart Howe

A fuselage from Shobdon based on the unconverted RAF airframe N6665, mated with wings supplied from Redhill, travelled to a studio in Italy in 1995 where they were rigged to provide an airframe famously used in the opening and closing sequences of the award winning film *The English Patient*. Clive Hardiman

Tiger Moth VH-ARW was written off by the North Queensland Aero Club at Cairns in 1957 but remained in store for 20 years until used as the centrepiece for an Australian film *Spirit of the Tiger*. Post production, the aircraft was returned to airworthiness as VH-UVB at Archerfield. A Heer

Operated as a tug aircraft by the British European Airways Silver Wing Gliding Club at Booker between 1962 and 1969, Tiger Moth G-AMIU was featured in the film *Two in a Tiger* in which actor Dudley Foster was taken to solo standard. John Ellis

The Calleva Flying Group Tiger Moth G-AJHU, taking on fuel at Cranwell in 1981, was operated to spectacular effect in the Tunisian desert in 1995 during filming of the flying sequences for *The English Patient.* R A Nichols

Not part of any scripted sequence but looking all the world like a dressed set with broken propeller, lost undercarriage and shrubbery draped over the starboard lower. Canopied Tiger Moth VH-CAG was operated under those marks by the Australian Department of Civil Aviation between 1949 and 1960. Reg Adkins

Turning. Turning. Turning. Go! A trio of Tiger Moths of 1 RFS Panshanger, including DE432 coded 'RCM-C' and R5103 'RCM-T', changing heading in June 1948, but with years of service life still ahead of them. *The Aeroplane*

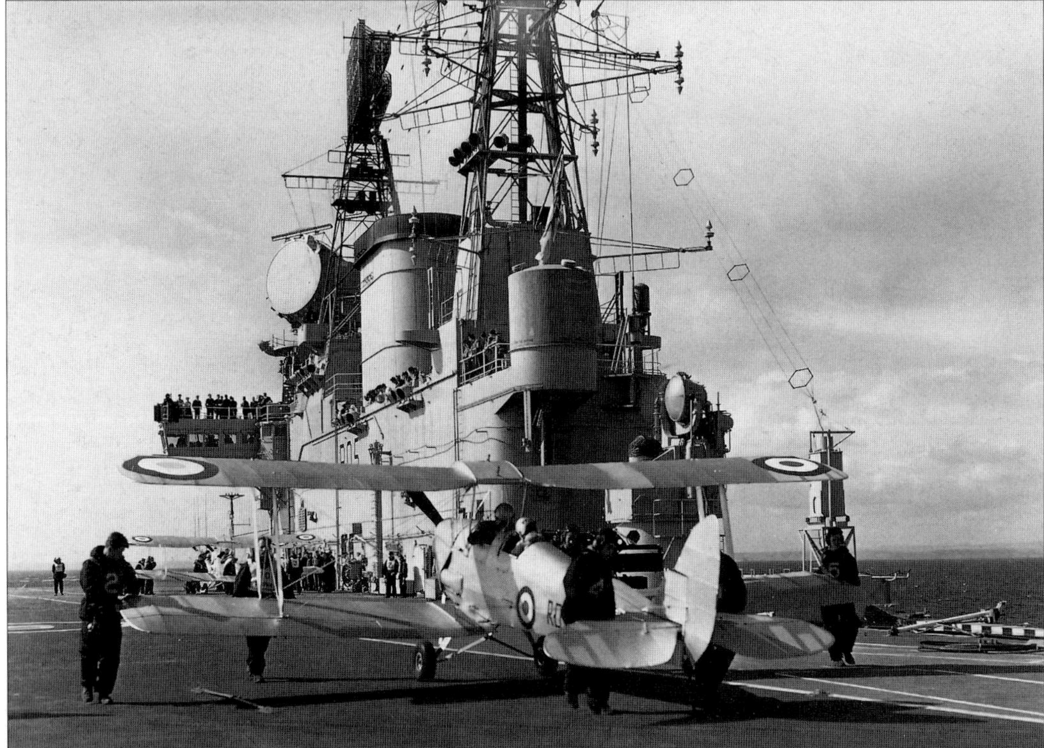

Gawpers on the flying bridge of HMS *Eagle* in June 1964 had the perfect opportunity to compare the arrival techniques of each visiting Tiger Moth. Royal Navy

VARIANT SPECIFICATIONS

On the threshold of what appeared to be an inevitable war with Germany, and during an accelerating programme of re-armament, the de Havilland Aircraft Company decided in May 1939 to issue a clarification of the differences in specification between the various civil, civil with military connections, and pure military Tiger Moths which had been manufactured until that date. Apart from relatively minor or locally inspired production modifications yet to be conceived, the list was to prove definitive:

DH.82 Tiger Moth. Civil.
Gipsy III with carburettor mounted aft.

Fuselage: The fuselage had a drop rail top longeron enabling deep front cockpit doors to be fitted. The rear fuselage cowling was of the stringer type, fabric covered. The compasses were mounted on the fuselage inner sides, adjacent to the doors.

Chassis: This was the standard split type 'Air Wheel' chassis with exception that the compression legs were of the rubber block pattern.

Empennage: The rudder had a peg type of fitting which located the tail skid to make this steerable on the ground.

Oil tank capacity 2.1 gallons; petrol tank capacity 19 gallons; short stub exhaust; fixed parachute type seats.

DH.82 Tiger Moth. RAF Mk I.

The Mk I denotes that this is the type supplied to the Royal Air Force and the main differences between that and the civil type machine are: Ailerons mass balanced; rudder mass balanced; Instruments to Air Ministry pattern; 4:1 reduction gear on the engine tachometer; fire extinguisher to Air Ministry pattern; auto slots with cockpit operated type of locking gear fitted.

DH.82A Tiger Moth. Civil.

Engine: Gipsy III and Gipsy Major Series I. Aircraft with early Gipsy III engines had the carburettor mounted aft; later models were fitted with the down draught type carburettor which entails modifications to the engine controls, fireproof bulkheads, heater pipes and engine cowling. The Gipsy Major Series I superseded the Gipsy III and is now fitted as standard. It should be noted that early models were not fitted with a flame trap carburetter.

Fuselage: Fitted with parallel type top longerons. Early models had the stringer type rear fuselage cowling fabric covered, as fitted to the DH.82. This was superseded by the ply decking extended to the stern.

Mainplanes: Spars strengthened to take a greater all up weight than on the DH.82 and DH.82 Mk I.

Chassis: Standard split type with Dowty spring legs.

Empennage: Rudder fitted with plates on the bottom for ground steering in lieu of the peg type as fitted to the DH.82 and DH.82 Mk I.

Instruments: Compasses are mounted on the centre of the instrument panel. Instrument boards of the latest type are slung on shock absorbers which allow the panels to float.

Oil tank capacity 2.1 gallons increased to 2.25 gallons on later models; petrol tank capacity 19 gallons; exhaust system, long extension type; ignition switching dual with master switch.

DH.82A Tiger Moth. RAF Mk II

The Mk II denotes that this is a type supplied to the Royal Air Force, and the main differences between that and the civil type machine are: propeller, drawing number 5220MX, finer pitch than standard; mainplanes equipped for night flying with navigation lamps on top planes and flares on bottom planes; ailerons mass balanced; rudder mass balanced; instruments to Air Ministry pattern with transmitting type oil gauges; fixed type instrument boards, 4:1 reduction drive fitted to engine tachometer; first aid stowage; battery type electrical equipment; auto slots with a locking device in the rear cockpit; dual ignition switching less a master switch; special fireproof bulkhead; oil tank capacity 2.1 gallons; short exhaust; special map case to accommodate stowage for course and height indicator, riveted to the back of the front pilot's seat; special floor incorporating a large inspection door and protective accumulator mounting.

DH.82A Tiger Moth Trainer

Thirty of these aircraft (L6920-L6949) were supplied to the Royal Air Force in full service markings. These are standard civil specification training aircraft.

The following two contracts are brought to notice as it is thought that difficulties may be experienced when dealing with items concerning the servicing, owing to their rather unorthodox construction:

DH.82A Tiger Moth machine Nos 82555-82574 inc. Gipsy Major Series II

These machines were supplied less engines to the Australian Company on behalf of the Australian Government. The Australian Company installed Gipsy Major Series II engines with fixed pitch propellers, doing all the modifications that were necessary themselves. These included the following items: Modified cross stay in the engine compartment; modified oil system; modified engine cowling; new oil tank; new carburettor heater pipe; new exhaust manifold; new fireproof bulkhead.

These items are covered on Instruction drawings Nos M.6455, sheets 1 and 2, and M.6500. With the exception of the items mentioned above plus the instruments and instrument boards, the remainder of these machines were built to DH.82A Mk II RAF drawings and specifications. The electrical system was Air Ministry pattern throughout with the exception of the accumulator which was the Rotax type.

DH.82A Tiger Moth machine Nos 82677- 82683 inc. Gipsy Major Series I

These machines for the Indian Government were built to the DH.82A Mk II RAF drawings and specification with the undermentioned exceptions:

Instruments and boards to the civil type; electrical system, wing tip, tail lamp and signal lamp to Air Ministry pattern, Rotax dash lamp, accumulator and P.T.18 switchbox. Harley landing lamp, see drawing 982044; ailerons, civil type; provision for a camera gun; provision for bomb gear and racks; oil tanks 2.1 gallons capacity, civil type; 10 gallon auxiliary petrol tank; auto slots and locking gear removed from RAF type top planes; flare brackets and fittings removed from RAF type bottom planes; civil type fire extinguisher.

The Persian Government Tiger Moth fighters had an array of additional equipment (see page 26). The synchronising disc attached to the static test propeller was used to confirm the firing sequence of the machine gun. de Havilland Aircraft Company

MODIFICATIONS INDEX

Numerical Index of modifications applicable to DH.82 and DH.82A Tiger Moth

1 Night Flying Equipment. Introduction of adapter plate for switches 5C/543.
2 Instrument panel. To introduce alternative watch holder.
3 Telephone installation. To introduce voice pipe clips.
4 Night Flying Equipment. To introduce double pole push buttons.
5 Miscellaneous
6 Miscellaneous
7 Miscellaneous
8 Miscellaneous
9 Cancelled
10 Miscellaneous
11 To increase strength of spar end plate by increasing the gauge from 14swg to 12swg.
12 Engine installation. To introduce a finer pitch propeller.
13 Miscellaneous
14 Miscellaneous
15 To introduce arrangement of a centre section strut mirror.
16 To introduce long range tankage.
17 Miscellaneous
18 Introduction of height and course indicator stowage.
19 Introduction of Mk. VIIA pressure head.
20 Introduction of increased size first aid stowage.
21 Introduction of new petrol cock.
22 Introduction of stiffening of wing tip and trailing edges.
23 Introduction of new oil tank filler cap.
24 Deletion of distance tube at joint 'K' front fuselage.
25 Introduction of longer sleeve for tail skid.
26 Introduction of new induction manifold petrol drain.
27 Introduction of new stronger springs for compression legs
28 Introduction of fibre guide for engine control rods.
29 Introduction of special washer for engine stay.
30 Introduction of packing block for luggage door catch.
31 Fuselage side member increased in gauge.
32 Introduction of alclad washers.
33 Miscellaneous
34 Stiffening of slot mounting rib, auto slots.
35 Oil tank fittings altered from Spec L32 to Spec L34.
36 Introduction of new pulley for slot locking.
37 Improved method of manufacture of mainplane external fittings.
38 Introduction of civil type RPM indicator and drives.
39 Miscellaneous
40 Deletion of engine switch covers.
41 Miscellaneous
42 D.I.S. amendments
43 Miscellaneous
44 Miscellaneous
45 Miscellaneous
46 Miscellaneous
47 Introduction of special bolt for undercarriage radius rod.
48 Miscellaneous
49 Introduction of angle washers between fore and aft levels and dashboard.
50 Miscellaneous
51 Cancelled. (Introduction of exhaust tail pipe).
52 Miscellaneous
53 Introduction of 'Woods' inspection frames in mainplanes.
54 Strengthening of safety harness.
55 Miscellaneous
56 Introduction of locking of cover plate (aileron drive).
57 Introduction of alternative airscrew (Horden Richmond 506/3).
58 Miscellaneous
59 Introduction of Grade B spruce for spars.
60 Introduction of new oil tank drain plug.
61 Miscellaneous
62 Introduction of new camouflage scheme.
63 Miscellaneous
64 Introduction of alternative airscrew (Horden Richmond LA594/2).
65 Deletion of clips from semi-rigid voice pipes.
66 Partial deletion of night flying equipment.
67 Complete deletion of night flying equipment.
68 Miscellaneous
69 Introduction of type P8 compass.
70 Modification to camouflage scheme.
71 Introduction of camouflage to airscrew and cockpit covers and to blind flying hood.
72 Miscellaneous
73 Introduction of bomb rack and mechanism for 8 x 20lb or 25lb bombs.
74 Introduction of alternative airscrew (Horden Richmond LA604/A).
75 Miscellaneous
76 Introduction of revised camouflage schemes and service markings.
77 Introduction of spring stop on bomb racks to enable 11.5lb practice bomb to be carried. (Aircraft with Mod 73).
78 Introduction of plastics.
79 Miscellaneous
80 Introduction of multi-laminated spars.
81 Introduction of dual cockpit cover.
82 Introduction of drain channel over rudder bar guide slot on fuselage side (to prevent entry of water. One man hour).
83 Introduction of a strengthened leading edge on top wings. (Strengthening of the top plane by the introduction of angle brackets on the nose web of root end ribs and replacement of the root rib stay tube by a deep wooden member. 3.5 man hours).
84 Miscellaneous
85 Introduction of an improved riblet for leading edge on top and bottom planes. (Introduction of upper and lower nose riblets of increased width and also an improved attachment of the riblets at the leading edge. 21.5 man hours).
86 Introduction of an improved drainage system. (Improvement of drainage efficiency by introduction of new drainage eyelets on the top and bottom main planes, ailerons, elevators and tailplane. 7 man hours).
87 Introduction of an improved external doping scheme and improved protection for internal members. (Partly superseded by Mod 39).
88 Introduction of modification plates.
89 Introduction of an extended 3 ply gusset at the nose end of certain mainplane ribs. (Strengthening of the nose end of certain main ribs of top and bottom planes by the introduction of a 3 ply gusset to cover the complete nose bay. 0.25 man hours per rib).
90 Introduction of a rubbing plate for tail skid shoe. (Rubbing plate reduces wear of the shoe. 1 man hour).
91 Introduction of strengthened platform ribs on bottom plane.
92 Miscellaneous
93 Introduction of revised camouflage schemes.
94 Introduction of a strengthened angle bracket for observation mirror. (0.25 man hours).
95 Introduction of an alternative method of fixing diagonal stay top planes.
96 Introduction of supports to prevent distortion of rear seat.
97 Introduction of a Sperry Horizon to instrument panel. (Superseded by Mod 130).
98 Miscellaneous
99 Introduction of a re-designed locating sleeve for compression leg.
100 Introduction of oiled silk windows to blind flying hood.
101 Introduction of improved stop for control column aileron lever. (Introduction of improved hardwood stop blocks for the control column aileron lever to reduce the occurrence of jamming and failure of the aileron controls in the bottom wing. 2 man hours).
102 Introduction of an improved tail skid spring.
103 To delete aileron mass balance.
104 Petrol system. Improved fixing for lower bell crank lever. (Introduction of an improved attachment for the lower bell crank lever situated on the port side of the front cockpit of the fuselage side panel to prevent the support bracket slipping and partially closing the petrol cock. 0.75 man hours).
105 To re-introduce night flying equipment.
106 Cancelled. (To introduce flame damping).
107 To make provision for accumulator type D in lieu of type B.
108 Miscellaneous
109 Modification to rudder spar.
110 Introduction of re-designed blind flying hood front attachment hook. (2.5 man hours).
111 To make provision for control locking.
112 Introduction of spinning strakes. (8 man hours).
113 Miscellaneous
114 Introduction of aileron cables in short replaceable lengths. (Short replaceable lengths to eliminate wastage of cable when it frays at the wing root join. 6 man hours per mainplane).
115 Miscellaneous
116 To delete wing tip forced landing flares and wiring.
117 Material of compression leg fork ends altered from dural to mild steel.
118 Introduction of a strengthened control box to prevent front seat from sagging.
119 Introduction of an eyelet lug on safety harness strap No. 1. (Provision of a leather tag with an eyelet hole on safety strap No. 1 as the existing eyelet hole frays and renders the strap unserviceable. 1 man hour).
120 Introduction of propeller No. ZD. 5220/1.

121 Introduction of clear tautening dope for light structures.
122 Introduction of cowl for air vent on centre-section strut.
123 Introduction of a re-designed tail skid shoe. (Redesigned shoe reduces wear. 0.5 man hours)
124 Modification not used.
125 Introduction of aileron sprocket chain guides and reduction of floor stop slot length.(Introduction of an improved aileron sprocket chain guide to reduce the possibility of the chain riding on the sprocket due to the sagging of slack cables. Also a reduction of the length of the slot in the cockpit floor to prevent the chain shackles riding on the sprocket when the control column is in the fully over position. 13 man hours).
126 Introduction of fabric support strip at luggage locker. (Fabric strip to prevent the starboard longeron corroding in the vicinity of the luggage locker. 1 man hour).
127 Introduction of two stage brown.
128 Miscellaneous
129 Introduction of protective cover for pressure head.
130 Instrument panel. Deletion of artificial horizon or fore and aft level ref 6A/389. (Superseding Mod 97). (Deletion of the artificial horizon, introduction of small venturies and repositioning of the turn and bank indicator on the instrument panel. 10.5 man hours).
131 Introduction of strut mirror Brown Bros No. 420 as an alternative to Brown Bros Scope Mirror M.161/134.
132 Miscellaneous
133 Introduction of improved protective treatment for the fin post. (Improved treatment for the base of the fin spar to prevent trapping of moisture. 4 man hours).
134 To seal the aileron gear box and improve inspection facilities. (Introduction of an aileron gear extension box to prevent the ingress of foreign objects. 24 man hours).
135 Introduction of additional inspection holes in aileron, tailplane and elevator. (Woods inspection frames in control surfaces to facilitate improved inspection. 3 man hours).
136 To modify oil tank to Repair Drawing R.4015 and R.4017. (Strengthening of the attachment of the dipper guide trough to the oil tank wall by the welding of three lugs to the inside of the oil tank wall and dipper guide trough. 6 man hours).
137 To delete propeller friction discs. (Aircraft with Gipsy Major engine Mod 903).
138 To prevent splitting of aileron control box side members. (Introduction of ply stiffeners to be glued into position on either side of the aileron control box side members in order to prevent splitting of the members. To be completed in conjunction with Mod 134. 12 man hours).
139 Introduction of improved materials for doping and finishing. (Superseding part of Mod 87 concerning external doping and finish).
140 To delete air speed indicator on port front interplane strut.
141 Introduction of watch holder Mk.3 ref 6A/1465. (Watch holder in lieu of a clock).
142 Introduction of General Service Watch ref 6E/50
143 Mod not used. (To introduce 20cwt cables in lieu of 15cwt for safety harness attachment.
144 Introduction of revised external colour scheme. (Aluminium with yellow bands).
145 Introduction of Ottley release hook and associated controls for glider tugging. (45 man hours).
146 Introduction of petrol filler Engine Company Part No. 83431.
147 Introduction of slow running cut out control. (Installation to prevent failures of magneto half speed wheels caused by the back firing on the engine shut down. 4 man hours).
148 Introduction of PTR.61E VHF Transmitter receiver.
149 Introduction of bowl fuel filter.
150 Introduction of Narco Comm 11A VHF Transmitter receiver and associated power supplies.
151 Introduction of a fuse in the negative supply for the VHF radio. (Aircraft with Mod 150).
152 Introduction of a 'Z' type safety harness.
153 Introduction of a BCF type fire extinguisher in lieu of existing methyl bromide type. (Aircraft 83196).
154 Introduction of A25 bolts and A27 nuts in lieu of A1 bolts and A16 nuts.
155 Introduction of a locking device for fuel on/off cock operating lever.
156 Introduction of high tensile steel bolts at cockpit harness positions.

DH.82 and DH.82A Tiger Moth Modification Drawings

March 1932	M.1791	Instructions for replacing existing slot locking lever in planes with new lever H.36776-7.
June 1933	M.2208	Modification for fixing balance weight to the horn of the rudder.
September 1934	M.2848	Stiffening of Moth seats.
March 1935	GA3223	Instructions for fitting elevator trimming flaps.
March 1935	M.3284	Modification to rudder mass balance weight.
October 1935	M.3463	Modification for the deletion of elevator tabs.
December 1935	M.3761	Modification to exhaust manifolds.
March 1935	M.3944	Addition of rubber bumpers to obviate damage to rudder rib.
October 1936	M.257	Modification to S.A.S. for test purposes only.
January 1937	M.4466	Instructions for fitting shock absorbing mountings.
January 1937	M.4420	Class 1R modification to rear spar attachment.
February 1937	M.4736	Instruction to enable DH.82A to conform with G.E. Notice 46 of 1936.
May 1937	M.4858	Conversion of Landplane to Seaplane.
May 1937	M.4863	Steerable tailskid.
June 1937		M.5120 Tailskid.
September 1937	M.5588	Compression leg.
January 1938	M.5786	Modification for arrangement of stowage box in rear fuselage for first aid equipment.
January 1938	M.5801	Wrapper plate for fuselage tube.
April 1938	M.5885	Modification to chassis radius rod eyebolt.
May 1938	M.5926	Camera gun Bowden cable clip.
June 1938	M.5961	Axle assembly U.2183-4 rivets.
September 1938	M.6310	List of oversize pins and bolts.
December 1938	M.6425	List of parts for modifying for inverted flying.
January 1939	M.6455	Tiger Moths fitted with Gipsy Major Series II engines.
February 1939	M.6500	Installation of Gipsy Major Series II engine in Tiger Moth aircraft.

Farm Aviation Tiger Moth G-AIZF with the large and protective windscreen design much favoured by pilots of long distance, high endurance Tiger Moths. Bill Fisher

Norman Jones commissioned Tiger Moth G-APRA to be converted to afford greater ease of entry and exit by parachutists. Dave Welch

AUSTRALIAN TIGER MOTH MODIFICATIONS

Principal modifications to basic DH.82A Tiger Moth design for aircraft constructed by de Havilland Aircraft Pty Ltd at Mascot, or incorporated into post-war civil aircraft at the instigation of the Australian Airworthiness Authorities.

The leading edges of all wings, except at the slat position of the port and starboard upper, have a plywood skin glued to ribs and riblets extending back to the front spar.

Main undercarriage legs have a check cable to prevent the oleo from slipping out (and down) in the event of a collapse of the internal structure. Particularly valid in the case of an undercarriage damaged during the course of a landing from which the aircraft is in a position to 'go around'.

Aluminium alloy fork ends are fitted to both ends of the main undercarriage shock struts. For operations an at increased all up weight, these were changed to steel.

Main wheel hub blanks fitted on inner and outer faces as standard to minimise ingress of foreign matter at the bearing.

The instrument panel is restrained on rubber 'Lord' shock absorbing mounts.

Fore and aft levels (inclinometers) fitted as standard instrumentation and retained following RAF modification which deleted them.

The oil pressure is read directly from the oil gallery on the crankcase rather than from a banjo fitting at the rear of the engine.

An American round type oil pressure gauge is used in preference to the vertical type, standard on most British built aircraft of the time from Avro Lancasters to Supermarine Spitfires.

Tachometer drive cables are routed through the port side of the fuselage front bulkhead rather than the starboard side.

A fail safe latch is fitted to the fuel on/off cock operating rod giving a positive indication of the fuel on/off position and resistance to the prospect of the cock vibrating into the closed or semi-closed (restricted fuel flow) position.

Front cockpit cover plate to blank off the control box position when the front control column is removed.

Rear floor inspection panel reprofiled.

The lead mass balance weight is deleted from the leading edge of the rudder.

Port and starboard aileron control cables are continuous from the operating lever under the cockpit floor to the sprocket in the wing box.

Port and starboard aileron control boxes retained at the standard of the original oblong design, prior to RAF modifications.

Aileron crank reprofiled to prevent cable chafing.

The engine air intake position on the starboard engine cowling is fitted with a removable Vokes filter element.

Fuel filter fitted to the port side of the engine bay.

Re-profiling of the engine cowling starboard panel.

Stub exhaust pipes fitted in preference to standard branch manifold.

Engine oil breather pipe extended to the bottom of the port undercarriage radius rod, deflects oil overflow away from the underside of the fuselage floor.

The oil tank fitted to bearers on the fuselage port side, is retained by quick release straps rather than a system of bolts passing through a peripheral flange, and is less liable to cracking.

Two additional fuel drain cocks, (new total of three) fitted to the underside of the centre section fuel tank.

Starboard side venturi tube serving the front cockpit, is mounted on the front arm of the inverted 'V' centre section strut.

Night flying quartered navigation light fitted to the root end of the port upper mainplane, rather than to wing tips and rudder.

Straight style pitot head in preference to the modified (kinked) RAF version, Mk. VII.

Deletion of the external fuselage drainage cover plate above the position of the rudder cable joint with the rear rudder bar extension pieces.

All ex-factory metalwork supplied in silver finish.

Spin strakes were never fitted as a production or post production modification.

A footrest is built into the starboard side fuselage frame at the position of the lower longeron, directly under the rear cockpit door.

Sutton Harness lower strap fixing point geometry revised and a new cable system introduced to pick up the rear seat shoulder harness.

Kicking boards fixed to port and starboard fuselage frames, inboard, at both front and rear rudder pedal positions.

Spacer units at the base of the rudder to improve the interface of the steering plates and the castoring tailskid, to assist with directional control during taxying.

The spotlessly clean sewing room at the Butler Air Transport Company hangar at Mascot. The relaxed supervisor appears to be enjoying a cup of tea while his young workforce get on with the job. via Barry Dowsett

An unidentified Australian built Tiger Moth operating with 10 EFTS Temora during the southern winter of 1944. Note the 'Pacific Area' roundels (less the red centre dot), hard leading edges and lack of spin strakes. Jim O'Reilly

DH.82 AND DH.82A SURVIVING AIRFRAMES

BRITISH PRODUCTION

Build No.	Previous identities – in chronological order				
3113	SE-ADF	Fv5568	Fv568	SE-ATI	SE-ADF
3139	FV594				
3175	G-ACDA	BB724	G-ACDA		
3177	G-ACDC	BB726	G-ACDC		
3182	G-ACDI	BB742	G-ACDI		
3183	G-ACDJ	BB729	G-ACDJ		
3195	33-2	EC-AGB	N182DH	G-ACMD	
3226	G-ACWB	NZ737	ZK-APM		
3255	K4259	G-ANMO	F-BHIU	G-ANMO	
3272	K4276	G-AOJX	OO-EVS		
3310	2	E.2			
3318	G-ADCG	BB731	A2126	G-ADCG	OO-TGM
3329	2-1-10	PP-DLL	PP-ZTM		
3333	2-1-14	PP-DTK			
3338	G-ADGT	BB697	G-ADGT		
3340	G-ADGV	BB694	G-BACW	G-ADGV	
3357	G-ADLU	NZ735	ZK-ARJ		
3364	G-ADLV	BB750	G-AORA	SE-CWG	
3368	G-ADIA	BB747	G-ADIA		
3375	G-ADHV	BB735	G-ANBV	D-EHYB	G-ANBV
3385	G-ADJI	BB818	F-BHII		
3386	G-ADJJ	BB819	G-ADJJ		
3393	G-ADPC	BB852	G-ADPC		
3436	G-ADXT	BB860	G-ADXT		
3450	G-ADWJ	BB803	G-ADWJ		
3455	G-ADWO	BB807	G-ADWO		
3508	VH-UVZ	A17-619	VH-BBP	VH-PCD	
3571	L6936	G-ANPK			
3581	L6926	G-ALAD	ZK-CDU		
3583	L6938	G-ANZU			
3623	VH-UYQ	A17-676	VH-CCE		
3630	ZK-AFO	NZ720	ZK-ASA	ZK-AFO	
3632	VH-UZT	A17-677	VH-AUK		
3650	111	CS-AAA			
3657	F-AQJX	30-116	EC-AIU		
3688	F-AQOX	G-AGAP	VH-ADK	A17-681	VH-UZT
	VH-PCF				
3697	ZK-AGI	NZ721	ZK-AIA		
3700	G-AFGZ	BB759	G-AFGZ		
3742	N5474	G-ANKA	I-LUNI		
3761	N5488	G-AIRI			
3763	N5490	G-ANHG	F-BHIN	N82KF	
3786	N6456	VH-BPW	VH-PCL		
3787	N6457	G-AMTG	VH-BBW	VH-ZHZ	VH-RAY
3795	ZK-AGZ	NZ704	ZK-ALK		
3803	N6466	G-ANKZ	F-BHIO	G-ANKZ	
3810	N6473	G-AOBO			
3815	N6478	G-AOGS	N82TM	OY-AJC	
3845	N6532	G-ANTS			
3850	N6537	G-AOHY			
3852	N6539	G-ASXB	N555XB	N6539 (USA)	
3858	N6545	G-AMTV	OO-SOE	G-AMTV	
3863	N6550	G-ANRX			
3874	N6580	G-APAM			
3882	G-AFNR	W7952	G-ANBU	OO-BYL	
3889	N6588	G-ASKP			
3894	N6593	G-AHUV			
3942	N6638	G-BNDW			
3946	N6642	G-ANDM	EI-AGP	G-ANDM	
3956	N6652	G-AOUX	HB-UBC		
3969	N6665				
3982	N6709	G-AMTK			
3985	N6712	G-AMMV	ZK-AZQ		
3993	N6720	7014M			
82003	N6730	D-EMWE	D-EMWT	SE-FNA	
82017	N6739	I-NONO			
82018	N6740	G-AISY	VT-CZV	G-AISY	PH-CRO
	D-ETHC				
82032	N6754	G-ANFB	ZK-BFG		
82043	N6779	D-EDON			
82067	N6797	G-ANEH			
82086	N6837	G-ANOM			
82102	N6847	G-APAL			
82104	N6849	G-AHRV	OY-DNR		
82111	N6856	G-ANLR			
82121	N6866	G-AJHS			
82138	N6900	VH-BCC			
82139	G-AFSH	X5106	G-AFSH	ZK-BAT	
82151	N6907	G-AOIO			
82155	N6911	G-ANKB	CF-CJW		
82168	N6924	G-APHZ	CF-QOT	C-FPHZ	
82186	G-AFNM	VH-ADO	A17-684	VH-BIN	VH-HVY
82187	G-AFWI	BB814	G-AFWI		
82196	N6946	G-AOEI			
82203	N6965	G-AJTW			
82210	N6972	6317M			
82216	N6978	G-AOAC			
82223	N6985	G-AHMN			
82247	N9128	G-AHLT			
82248	N9129	VH-BJV	VH-DAL	VH-NIG	
82254	N9135	VH-BDH			
82259	N9140	VH-BND	VH-SSP	VH-ABL	
82262	N9143	ZS-DHR			
82270	N9151	G-AOYU	C-GABB		
82292	N9181	G-AGHY			
82295	NZ743	ZK-ALU			
82302	N9185	NZ854	ZK-APP		
82308	N9191	G-ALND			
82309	N9192	PH-UFB	OO-GEB	OO-MEH	G-BSTJ
82332	N9215	G-APRG	OH-ELC		
82333	N9238	G-ANEL			
82335	N9240	G-ANDI	N40DH	G-ANDI	D-ENDI
82336	N9241	G-AIRK			
82346	NZ744	ZK-AJP			
82348	VH-ADH	A17-680	VH-ADH		
82355	N9254	NZ863	ZK-AQA		
82360	N9259	VH-ALC	D-EAJO		
82366	N9265	535	ZS-BUR		
82372	N9271	NZ868	ZK-API		
82387	N9306	509	ZS-CID		
82413	N9326	G-ALWS			
82439	N9369	G-ALIZ			
82442	N9372	G-ANHK			
82459	N9389	G-ANJA			
82461	N9391	PH-NGM	N9391(US civil)	N9393(US civil)	
82475	N9405	NZ874	ZK-ASM		
82494	N9440	EI-AHA			
82499	N9445	G-APOG	HB-UBH		
82512	N9458	NZ861	ZK-ANL		
82524	N9494	G-AMMK	ZK-AYY		
82530	N9503	G-ANFP			
82535	N9508	G-APCU	PH-TGR	PH-TYG	
82537	N9510	G-AOEL			
82561	A17-7	VH-BAL			
82565	A17-11	VH-RIN	VH-CFA	VH-DBE	
82568	A17-14	VH-BOR			
82569	A17-15	VH-DHR			
82573	A17-19	VH-APQ			
82592	G-AFWF	W6420	G-AMTL	OO-SOF	
82700	R4759	G-ANKN	CF-JJI	N4808	
82706	R4765	G-AOIP			
82709	R4768	4636	ZS-BXB		
82710	R4769	A-32	PH-UFK	D-EDIL	N9146
	G-AGEG				
82711	R4770	G-ALVP			
82712	R4771	ETA-29	T-29	OO-EVJ	G-BWMS
82713	(DHNZ1)	NZ751	ZK-ATN		
82720	R4776	G-ASSC	N81DH	SE-AMY	
82765	R4833	G-AOEV	D-EKUN	C-GJDO	
82768	R4836	VH-AVR	VH-BAM		
82773	R4841	VH-BMK	VT-DCC		
82776	R4844	VH-BDF	VH-LOW		
82784	R4852	G-AMVS	OO-SOJ	G-AMVS	
82793	R4876	G-AMMG	ZK-BAL		
82794	R4877	G-AMGB	21-93		
82796	R4879	VH-AIJ			
82797	R4880	VH-AMF			
82800	R4883	VH-ARM			
82807	(T.128)	R4890	VH-BKP		
82808	R4891	VH-APG	VH-BVZ		
82812	R4895	G-AOAF	ZK-BLK		
82813	R4896	G-AOJK			
82814	R4897	G-ANDC	LX-JON	D-EFYZ	G-ERTY
82824	R4907	G-ANCS			

A summer day with the Tiger Club at Redhill in 1960: a canopied Druine Turbulent, unique Arrow Active and unsuspecting Tiger Moth G-ARAZ (82867), chosen for the first SOW experiments. Michael Stroud

82838	(DHNZ6)	NZ756	ZK-ASN			
82845	R4922	G-APAO				
82852	R4944	EI-AHC				
82858	R4950	G-ANPC				
82862	R4954	G-ANOU	ZK-BFS			
82866	R4958	G-ANME				
82867	R4959	G-ARAZ				
82868	R4960	G-ANDP	D-EBEC	G-ANDP		
82869	R4961	G-APJP	SE-GXO			
82882	R4972	G-AOIR				
82887	R4977	NZ885	ZK-AJH			
82899	R4989	NZ888	ZK-ARZ			
82901	R5006	NZ899	ZK-ATI	N27WB	G-ALIW	
82906	R5011	NZ892	ZK-ANQ			
82909	R5014	G-ANSM				
82918	R5023	G-AOGY	VH-RSE	VH-FBO		
82943	R5042	G-ANEM	EI-AGN	G-ANEM		
82946	(DHNZ15)	NZ765	ZK-AUE			
82958	R5063	A-43	OO-JEU			
82960	R5065	G-ANEI	N523R			
82981	R5086	G-APIH	D-EMEX	OY-DGJ	N111DH	G-APIH
82997	R5115	G-ANZR	D-EGER	G-ANZR		
83018	R5136	G-APAP				
83026	R5144	G-AMHF				
83034	R5172	G-AOIS				
83044	R5182	VH-BMJ	VT-DBX			
83079	(DHNZ21)	NZ771				
83080	(DHNZ22)	NZ772	ZK-ASG			
83091	R5216	G-AOED	D-EKIF			
83094	R5219	G-ALUC				
83096	R5237	G-ANRA	SE-CGC			
83098	R5239	G-ANVV	OO-ACI	N8879		
83101	R5242	A-38				
83105	R5246	G-AMIV				
83109	R5250	G-AODT				
83110	R5251	G-ANXT	VH-BIC	VH-WPL		
83116	R5257	VH-BLZ	VH-AMY			
83117	R5258	VH-APX	VH-CXK			
83118	R5259	VH-AHS	VH-BHK	VH-BKS		
83120	R5261	VH-BDI	VH-RNR	VH-CKA		
83123	R5264	VH-BCB	VH-PCI			
83124	R5265	VH-BUZ	VH-WFW			
83133	T5368	G-ANRN				
83135	T5370	G-AIVW				
83145	T5378	G-ANPZ	ZK-BFX	N99108		
83152	T5409	VH-AOY	N82DH			
83153	T5410	VH-AUY				
83157	T5414	G-ALSF	PH-UDY	PH-ALG	N42DH	
83161	T5418	G-ANEE	EI-ANN			
83167	T5424	G-AJOA				
83172	T5429	G-AOCW	D-ECEF	C-GZJX		
83183	T5458	VH-AIX	VH-KBX			
83184	T5459	VT-CUP				
83185	T5460	VH-BGJ				
83202	(DHNZ25)	NZ775	ZK-AIN			
83216	T5483	VH-BCL	VH-PCE	N31191		
83222	T5489	4738	ZS-DEC			
83223	T5490	G-ANVE	D-EBUN	OY-DVR		
83226	T5493	G-ANEF	SE-AMM			
83228	T5495	G-AMIU				
83244	T5525	VH-BFO	VT-CSZ	CF-EIQ	N6463	
83247	T5528	VH-AKN	VH-PCA	VH-SDR		
83250	T5531	VH-ATD	VH-RNL	VH-CXV		
83256	T5537	G-AMAJ	ZK-BAM			
83274	T5555	VH-BEQ	ZK-AUT			
83278	T5559	VH-BBE				
83279	T5560	VH-BJT	VH-TGR			
83280	T5561	VH-ALX	VH-SSD	VH-AMT	N5560	
83283	T7025	G-AOGJ	OO-SOB	C-GWGA	N113DH	
83286	T5595					
83300	T5607	VP-YJT	ZS-EUV			
83314	T5616	G-APAJ	VH-KRK			
83323	T5625	G-AIDR	ZK-BEF			
83343	T7035	G-ANDB	ZK-BFH			
83346	T5639	G-AMEX	ZK-AYA			
83350	T5672	G-ALRI	ZK-BAB	G-ALRI		
83384	(DHNZ36)	NZ786	ZK-ASV			
83393	(DHNZ45)	NZ795	ZK-APS	ZK-BUO		
83420	T5699	G-AMTT	ZK-BCO			
83424	T5703	G-AMES	N5300			
83437	T5716	G-AODX				
83454	T5819	G-AMFN	ZK-BJQ			
83462	T5753	NZ660	ZK-AIW	N7966		
83463	T5754	NZ655	ZK-AJC			
83468	T5759	NZ669	ZK-AII			
83472	T7087	G-AOIX	G-BPAJ			
83478	T7093	G-AMMX	ZK-BAN			
83493	T5764	NZ661	ZK-AIL			
83497	T5768	NZ677	ZK-ANN			
83499	T5770	NZ676	ZK-ALJ			
83502	T5773	NZ678	ZK-AIE	VQ-FAG	DQ-FAG	NZ662
83512	T7105	G-AKXS				
83513	T7106	G-AMRM	ZK-BBI			
83536	T7109	G-AOIM				
83537	T7110	OO-SOY				
83547	T7120	G-AOEG	G-TIGA			
83557	T5845	G-AMFW	ZK-AZY			
83564	T5807	G-ANBW	ZK-BFF			
83580	T7129	G-ANTW	D-EGIT	N7404		
83589	T5853	G-ALZA	ZK-BAH			
83590	T5854	G-ANKK				
83595	T5879	6854M	G-AXBW			
83604	T5888	G-ANFM				
83607	T7148	G-ALSG	PH-UDZ	N9410		
83638	T7179	G-AKEE	VP-CAW	CY-AAB	4R-AAB	CX-123
83653	T7187	G-AOBX				
83666	T7356	E.6	D-EDUM	G-ASPZ	G-EMSY	
83673	T7363	G-AOIL				
83683	T7213	G-ANGD	D-EKAL	D-EAKP	D-EHAL	HB-UCX
83689	T7219	G-ANND	SE-CPW			
83707	T7386	G-AMMN	ZK-BCB			
83713	T7392	ZK-BJO				
83719	T7229	G-ANCX				
83720	T7230	G-AFVE				
83728	T7238	G-AMJD	OO-SOI	T24		
83738	T7397	G-ANPE	F-BHAT	G-ANPE	G-IESH	G-ANPE
83740	T7399	G-ANSK	ZK-BKF			
84745	T7404	G-ANMV				
83748	T5850	G-ANRF				
83786	T7410	D-EFPH	N8052	N82JH		
83790	T7276	G-APTV	I-MOMI			
83794	T7280	G-AHPZ	EI-AFJ			
83795	T7281	G-ARTL				
83804	T7290	G-ANNK	F-BFDO	G-ANNK		
83805	T7291	G-AOXG	XL717			
83814	T7418	G-ANNE	OO-CCI	9O-CCI	9Q-CCI	
83830	T7303	OO-SOX				
83856	T7452	G-AHUR	PH-UAT	N8224		
83866	T7340	G-AORX	HB-UBB	N82GS		
83875	T7349	G-ANJG	F-BGZT			
83896	T7467	G-ANIZ	N9714			
83900	T7471	G-AJHU				
83912	T5902	556	ZS-DLK			
83913	T5903	557	VT-DBM			
83999	T7602	A-29	JZ-ACB	PI-C586	N522R	
84013	T7611	G-ALZI	ZK-AZO			
84073	T5968	G-ANNN				
84077	T7683	2498	ZS-CTS			
84120	T7738	G-ANSL	ZK-BLQ	ZK-PDL		
84130	T7748	G-ALBD				
84134	T5983	G-AMML	ZK-AYX			
84165	T7792	G-ANLX				
84166	T7793	G-ANKV				
84167	T7794	G-ASPV				
84176	T7798	G-ANZT				
84177	T7799	G-ALTW				
84197	T7814	579	ZS-DEU	ZS-FEY	N82MT	
84207	T7842	G-AMTF	ZK-AVE	G-AMTF		
84211	T7846	G-AHUP	PH-UAU			

When the opportunity arises, a chap just has to take up the offer. Much to the astonishment of the locals, Jonathan Elwes tops up the tanks of his long range Tiger Moth G-ANRN (83133) in the forecourt of a GALP service station during one of his forays into the sunshine of southern Europe. Jonathan Elwes

In order to remain operational at Fairoaks following a change of aerodrome owner, G-AJOA (83167), which at some stage had acquired a Canadian built fuselage, was required to exchange tail skid for tail wheel, and to fit a mainwheel braking system, more applicable to parking than taxying. Peter March

84218	T7849	G-ANEZ			
84221	T7852	571	ZS-BGL		
84229	T7860	592	ZS-CGR		
84233	T6037	G-ANNB	D-EGYN	N6037	G-ANNB
84245	T7873	567	ZS-BTX	ZS-DEK	VP-YOI
	Z-YOI				
84265	T7904	2101	ZS-NHN		
84270	T7909	G-ANON			
84305	T7941	4695	ZS-DNP		
84309	T7945	ZS-CGS	N711JP		
84320	T7967	G-AIBN	EI-AOP		
84350	T7997	G-AOBH			
84412	T8100	2140	ZS-BSF	ZS-UKW	
84435	T8123	2152	ZS-BBI	ZS-DHE	
84440	T8128	2204	ZS-DFU		
84454	T8142	2213	ZS-DNI		
84478	T8186	2218	ZS-BVU	ZS-DFM	
84483	T8191	G-BWMK			
84519	T8246	4729	ZS-BJG	ZS-CNT	
84526	T8253	G-AMNE	ZK-BBK	ZK-CZX	ZK-BBK
84529	T8256	G-AOFG	VH-AWI	VH-WPK	N5676
	N38KH				
84546	T6055	G-AIDS			
84547	T6056	G-AOES			
84557	T6066	G-ANJK			
84566	T6099	G-AOGR	XL714	G-AOGR	
84567	T6100	G-APPT	OO-SOK	OO-SOW	
84569	T6102	G-ANNC	OO-SOM	F-AZCJ	N7158N
84588	T6121	G-ANOD			
84589	T6122	G-ANTV	D-EKUR	OY-DET	SE-AMG
84602	T6135	4681	ZS-BXE	OO-CEF	9O-CEF
	9Q-CEF				
84616	T6168	SE-COL	LN-KAY		
84617	T6169	G-ANFL			
84641	T6193	G-AMCK	HB-UAC	D-EGXY	SLN-05
	C-GBBF	N65N	G-AMCK		
84648	T6200	G-AMNF	ZK-BAD		
84652	T6226	G-ANJD			
84653	T6227	G-APSS			
84664	T6238	ZK-BJH			
84671	T6245	G-AMVH	ZK-BEN		
84682	T6256	G-APLR	I-JENA		
84695	T6269	G-AMOU	VR-RBZ	9M-ALJ	N200D
84711	T6296	8387M			
84726	T6311	G-ALJL			
84728	T6313	G-AHVU			
84734	T6319	G-AIJB	PH-UDB	N41DH	
84736	T6362	G-AHRL	ZK-AZH		
84748	T6374	2195	ZS-BJY	VP-RCR	VP-YMB
	9Q-CBJ	9Q-CBY			
84764	T6390	G-ANIX	D-ELOM	D-EFTF	G-ANIX
84766	T6392	G-ANJJ	F-BHIC	N54556	N639DH
84771	T6397	G-ANGJ	ZK-BEW		
84775	T6401	G-AMNP	VR-RBY	9M-ALI	
84776	T6402	2198	ZS-BXT		
84778	T6404	2167	ZS-BWO		
84811	T6457	4684	ZS-CDJ		
84812	T6458	2225	ZS-FEL		
84821	T6467	2173	ZS-BYP	VP-YPG	7Q-YPG
	N217BC				
84864	T6523	2185	ZS-BGN		
84869	T6528	2193	ZS-CKX		
84875	T6534	G-AMTP	OO-EVT		
84882	T6553	G-APIG	F-AZEI	G-APIG	F-AZEI
84887	T6558	D-ENRO	N7314	N929S	
84891	T6562	G-ANTE			
84893	T6564	G-AMKN	ZK-BAA		
84950	T6636	2292	ZS-CDN		
84959	T6645	G-AIIZ	SE-AMH		
84967	T6653	2309	VP-YJU	VP-RHU	9J-RJU
	9Q-CBO				

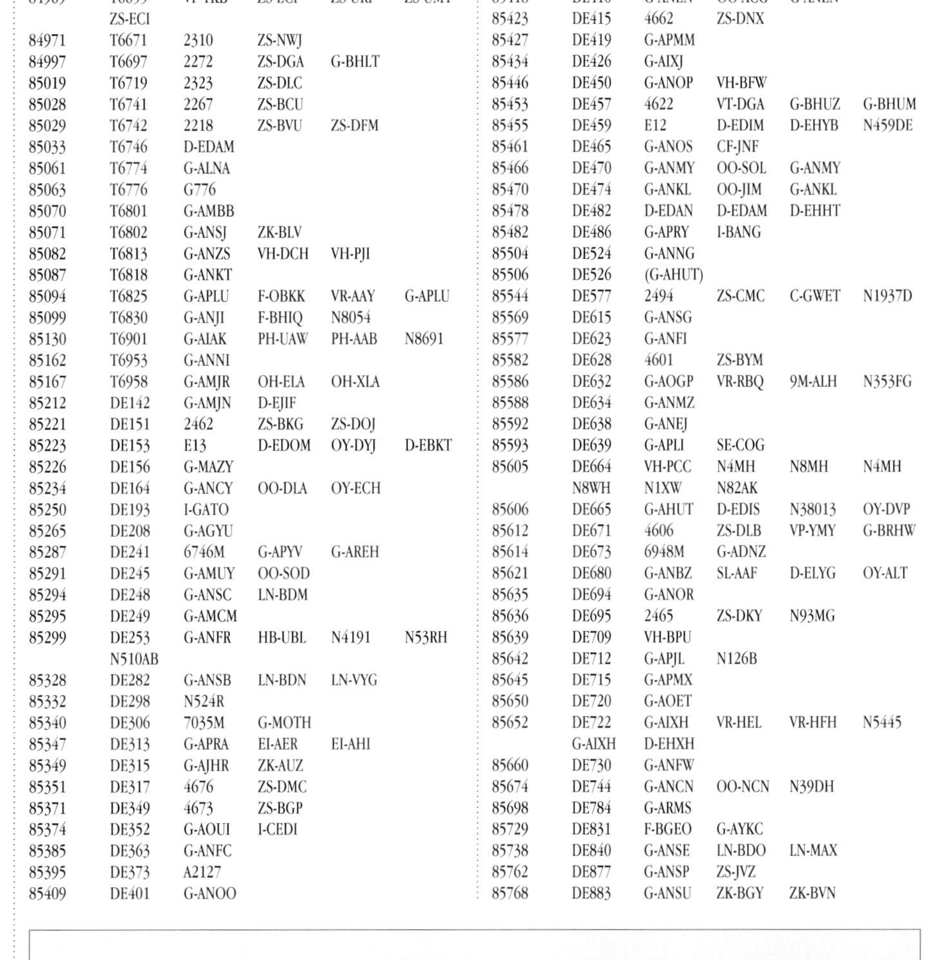

84969	T6655	VP-YKB	ZS-ECI	ZS-URP	ZS-UMY	
	ZS-ECI					
84971	T6671	2310	ZS-NWJ			
84997	T6697	2272	ZS-DGA	G-BHLT		
85019	T6719	2323	ZS-DLC			
85028	T6741	2267	ZS-BCU			
85029	T6742	2218	ZS-BVU	ZS-DFM		
85033	T6746	D-EDAM				
85061	T6774	G-ALNA				
85063	T6776	G776				
85070	T6801	G-AMBB				
85071	T6802	G-ANSJ	ZK-BLV			
85082	T6813	G-ANZS	VH-DCH	VH-PJI		
85087	T6818	G-ANKT				
85094	T6825	G-APLU	F-OBKK	VR-AAY	G-APLU	
85099	T6830	G-ANJI	F-BHIQ	N8054		
85130	T6901	G-AIAK	PH-UAW	PH-AAB	N8691	
85162	T6953	G-ANNI				
85167	T6958	G-AMJR	OH-ELA	OH-XLA		
85212	DE142	G-AMJN	D-EJIF			
85221	DE151	2462	ZS-BKG	ZS-DOJ		
85223	DE153	E13	D-EDOM	OY-DYJ	D-EBKT	
85226	DE156	G-MAZY				
85234	DE164	G-ANCY	OO-DLA	OY-ECH		
85250	DE193	I-GATO				
85265	DE208	G-AGYU				
85287	DE241	6746M	G-APYV	G-AREH		
85291	DE245	G-AMUY	OO-SOD			
85294	DE248	G-ANSC	LN-BDM			
85295	DE249	G-AMCM				
85299	DE253	G-ANFR	HB-UBL	N4191	N53RH	
	N510AB					
85328	DE282	G-ANSB	LN-BDN	LN-VYG		
85332	DE298	N524R				
85340	DE306	7035M	G-MOTH			
85347	DE313	G-APRA	EI-AER	EI-AHI		
85349	DE315	G-AJHR	ZK-AUZ			
85351	DE317	4676	ZS-DMC			
85371	DE349	4673	ZS-BGP			
85374	DE352	G-AOUI	I-CEDI			
85385	DE363	G-ANFC				
85395	DE373	A2127				
85409	DE401	G-ANOO				

85418	DE410	G-ANEN	OO-ACG	G-ANEN		
85423	DE415	4662	ZS-DNX			
85427	DE419	G-APMM				
85434	DE426	G-AIXJ				
85446	DE450	G-ANOP	VH-BFW			
85453	DE457	4622	VT-DGA	G-BHUZ	G-BHUM	
85455	DE459	E12	D-EDIM	D-EHYB	N459DE	
85461	DE465	G-ANOS	CF-JNF			
85466	DE470	G-ANMY	OO-SOL	G-ANMY		
85470	DE474	G-ANKL	OO-JIM	G-ANKL		
85478	DE482	D-EDAN	D-EDAM	D-EHHT		
85482	DE486	G-APRY	I-BANG			
85504	DE524	G-ANNG				
85506	DE526	(G-AHUT)				
85544	DE577	2494	ZS-CMC	C-GWET	N1937D	
85569	DE615	G-ANSG				
85577	DE623	G-ANFI				
85582	DE628	4601	ZS-BYM			
85586	DE632	G-AOGP	VR-RBQ	9M-ALH	N353FG	
85588	DE634	G-ANMZ				
85592	DE638	G-ANEJ				
85593	DE639	G-APLI	SE-COG			
85605	DE664	VH-PCC	N4MH	N8MH	N4MH	
	N8WH	N1XW	N82AK			
85606	DE665	G-AHUT	D-EDIS	N38013	OY-DVP	
85612	DE671	4606	ZS-DLB	VP-YMY	G-BRHW	
85614	DE673	6948M	G-ADNZ			
85621	DE680	G-ANBZ	SL-AAF	D-ELYG	OY-ALT	
85635	DE694	G-ANOR				
85636	DE695	2465	ZS-DKY	N93MG		
85639	DE709	VH-BPU				
85642	DE712	G-APJL	N126B			
85645	DE715	G-APMX				
85650	DE720	G-AOET				
85652	DE722	G-AIXH	VR-HEL	VR-HFH	N5445	
	G-AIXH	D-EHXH				
85660	DE730	G-ANFW				
85674	DE744	G-ANCN	OO-NCN	N39DH		
85698	DE784	G-ARMS				
85729	DE831	F-BGEO	G-AYKC			
85738	DE840	G-ANSE	LN-BDO	LN-MAX		
85762	DE877	G-ANSP	ZS-JVZ			
85768	DE883	G-ANSU	ZK-BGY	ZK-BVN		

The Auxiliary Squadrons of the RAF lost their aeroplanes by political decree but maintained their interest, and 600 (City of London) Squadron Flying Group bought Tiger Moth G-AOES (84547) which they operated from Biggin Hill between 1958 and 1963. Norman Rivett

During operations at their Luton airport base, Chrisair invented a novel form of Tiger Moth ground handling with G-AHVU (84728) and rubbed shoulders with flying test-beds for Napier engine research. Chris Roberts

85778	DE893	2492	HU-512	VT-DPK	
85812	DE941	G-ALSE	PH-UDX		
85814	DE943	G-AJVE			
85826	DE955	G-ANST	ZK-BGX		
85829	DE969	G-AMPN	ZK-BBG	VH-BVB	
85831	DE971	F-BGFI	G-OOSY		
85832	DE972	ETA-27	T-27	OO-EVH	
85834	DE974	G-ANZZ			
85851	DE991	F-BGJH	D-EDJH	SLN-06	C-GBBH
85852	DE992	F-BGJI	G-AXXV		
85855	DE995	F-BGFL	F-BKFL	N995DH	
85861	DF112	G-ANRM			
85862	DF113	G-ANLS			
85865	DF116	ZS-OCS			
85867	DF118	G-APOU	SE-CHG		
85873	DF124	ETA-1	T-1	OO-EVA	
85875	DF126	OO-EVR			
85877	DF128	G-AOJJ			
85879	DF130	F-BDOB	G-BACK	CC-DMC	
85882	DF133	G-ANDN	SE-COY	N85882	
85886	DF137	PH-UAG	N8232		
85904	DF155	G-ANFV			
85908	DF159	G-AOAA			
85910	DF174	F-BDOE	G-AYDI		
85922	DF186	G-AOGI	OO-SOA	G-AOGI	
85931	DF195	F-BGCL	EI-AWP		
85933	DF197	F-BDOH	G-BFHH		
85934	DF198	ETA-8	T-8	OO-EVB	G-BBRB
85939	DF203	E8	D-EDAS	OY-DGH	
85946	DF210	F-BGCS			
85951	EM720	F-BDMM	G-AXAN		
85953	EM722	ETA-25	T-25	OO-EVE	
85957	EM726	G-ANDE			
85958	EM727	G-AOXN			
85960	EM729	PH-UAO	N8233		
85962	EM731	F-BGED	N4797		
85970	EM739	F-BDMP	G-AXTY	N16645	
85980	EM749	G-AOAH	VH-BTD		
85987	EM756	HU-866	VT-DPJ		
85990	EM773	G-ANLD	OO-DPA	G-ANLD	
85995	EM778	F-BGEL	G-BAFG		
85996	EM779	VT-DKP	N8493B		
86006	EM789	4660	ZS-CTN		

86035	EM818	4655	HU-730	VT-DPI	
86040	EM838	G-ANOH			
86048	EM846	VT-ARP	VT-EBP	CF-EIO	G-BDVI
		N982JG			
86069	EM867	VT-ARQ	VT-DHB	CF-EIP	N6353
86081	EM879	G-APFU			
86097	EM903	G-APBI			
86102	EM908	G-ANEC			
86123	EM929	G-AHVV			
86128	EM945	G-APMM	ZK-BBF	VH-IVN	
86149	EM967	6940M	G-AHOO		
86166	EM973	G-ANNU	ZK-BFB	N973JS	
86221	NL750	A2123	G-AHUF		
86231	NL760	G-APJK	I-RIBI		
86243	NL772	CR-AGL	N8353	N82RD	G-BXMN
86247	NL775	G-ASET	CF-FDQ	N775NL	
86251	NL779	G-AODR	G-ISIS		
86297	NL838	F-BGEP	N4970	N838KC	
86302	NL846	F-BGEQ			
86311	NL864	F-BGJE	G-AZZZ		
86316	NL873	G-ANSH	SE-CHH		
86321	NL875	F-BGEU	G-AYHU	N5050C	
86322	NL879	G-AVPJ			
86332	NL885	F-BDNZ	N8058		
86338	NL891	ETA-15	T-15	OO-EVG	N3744N
86341	NL898	G-AOUR			
86343	NL896	F-BGEZ	G-AYIT		
86347	NL904	F-BGFA	N82DS		
86349	NL906	G-ANFY			
86366	NL923	G-ALWW			
86378	NL935	F-BGJJ	N28680	N935NL	
86403	NL971	E14	D-EDEM	PH-III	
86414	NL984	EI-AHJ	N8722		
86417	NL985	7015M			
86425	NL993	G-AOFR	SE-COX	OY-BAK	
86446	NM126	G-APJO			
86449	NM129	G-AOZH			
86450	NM130	G-BGCA	D-EEAJ		
86453	NM133	G-ANJN	F-BHIY	N6665K	
86456	NM136	F-BDOC	G-AYJV	N88816	
86457	NM137	G-AMNN			
86458	NM138	G-ANEW			
86460	NM140	G-APGL			

86470	NM150	0802	YU-CHX		
86483	NM175	G-AOEX			
86489	NM181	F-BGCF	G-AZGZ		
86498	NM190	VP-YJW	VP-RJW	9J-RJW	
86500	NM192	F-BGCJ	G-BTOJ		
86507	NM199	ETA-19	T-19	OO-EVM	
86509	NM201	F-BGCP	EI-AUB	N82JS	C-GSTP
86514	NM206	F-BGCQ	N4977	N206DH	
86515	NM207	ETA-21	T-21	OO-EVP	N3744M
86517	NM209	ETA-22	T-22	OO-EVD	
86523	PG614	ETA-24	T-24		
86526	PG617	F-BGCZ	G-AYVY	SE-AMI	
86530	PG621	F-BDOK	N28681		
86533	PG624	G-AHIZ			
86534	PG625	F-BGDC	N8872		
86536	PG627	PH-UAM	D-EBIG	N8878	N9295
86546	PG637	G-ANLH	OO-EVO	N3744F	G-ANLH
86549	PG640	G-APCC			
86550	PG641	EI-AHH	EI-AHM	G-APGM	I-JJOY
86552	PG643	F-BGDF	G-AXBZ		
86553	PG644	F-BGDG	N90406	G-AHAN	
86554	PG645	F-BDVM	N3549		
86556	PG647	F-BGDH	N3529		
86559	PG650	F-BGDJ	G-AZDY		
86560	PG651	F-BDOQ	G-AYUX	I-EDAI	
86562	PG653	G-APLV	I-RIBU	I-APLI	
86564	PG655	F-BGDL			
86565	PG656	F-BGDM			
86566	PG657	F-BGDN	N657DH	G-AGPK	
86568	PG671	F-BDOS	N82AM		
86572	PG675	G-AMLF	N675LF		
86573	PG676	F-BGDR	N5882		
86577	PG680	F-BGDS	N9TM		
86578	PG681	A-50	OO-ANY		
86580	PG683	A-56	PH-UFE	A-56	OO-MOS
86582	PG685	A-4	N1300D		
86584	PG687	F-BGDT	G-BABA		
86587	PG690	A-10			
86603	PG706	F-BFVU			
86609	PG712	A-2	OO-DJU	PH-CSL	
86610	PG713	F-BGDX			
86611	PG714	N86TM			
86618	PG732	F-BGEE			
86621	PG735	F-BGEG	G-AYVH	N45TM	

AUSTRALIAN PRODUCTION

DHA 22	A17-26	VH-AQJ	VH-OZJ	VH-AQJ	
DHA 30	A17-33	VH-AOW			
DHA 34	A17-37	VH-RJA	VH-FAS		
DHA 41	A17-44	VH-PCB			
DHA 45	A17-48	VH-BLX	N48DH	G-BPHR	
DHA 54	A17-57	VH-BGC			
DHA 55	A17-58	VH-AUG	VH-PCG	VH-BVO	VH-PCG
DHA 57	A17-60	VH-AGY			
DHA 60	A17-63	VH-KEH			
DHA 61	A17-64	VH-AQR	N9279	N282DH	
DHA 66	A17-69	VH-SJC			
DHA 75	A17-78	VH-UEQ			
DHA 77	A17-80	VH-AUA			
DHA 91	A17-94	VH-ARW	VH-ECD	VH-UVB	
DHA 94	A17-97	VH-BJE			
DHA 100	A17-103	VH-ATN			
DHA 101	A17-104	VH-APA			
DHA 104	A17-107	VH-AZD			
DHA 108	A17-111	VH-ALR	VH-RNI		
DHA 111	A17-114	VH-SSA	VH-XGZ		

A British export to the South African Air Force in 1943, DE457 was taken on charge as 4622 until routed to India in 1947. Operated latterly by the Nagpur Flying Club as VT-DGA, the aircraft was offered for sale by Vintair in 1966 and surveyed in India by an engineer acting on behalf of a prospective British customer. Overhauled in Lincolnshire in 1984 G-BHUM (85453) has since lived on a farm strip in Yorkshire. Garry Towers

In August 1985, Tiger Moth G-AVPJ (86322) was kindly loaned by owner Robin Livett to allow pilots from five countries to fly on equal terms in an acrobatic competition at Woburn Abbey, organised by the de Havilland Moth Club and sponsored by Christie's. G C Beale

DHA 113 A17-116 VH-APB
DHA 119 A17-122 VH-BKB VH-BTS VH-WFV N100MH
DHA 129 A17-132 VH-WPO
DHA 133 A17-136 VH-AMX VH-WFQ
DHA 149 A17-148 VH-ABC VH-BVX
DHA 152 A17-151 VH-AXF VH-BXF VH-BWF VH-UEF VH-BXF
DHA 154 A17-153 VH-BLK VH-BTW VH-AMD N1244T N82AZ
DHA 157 A17-156 VH-BTF VH-DHK
DHA 161 A17-160 VH-AMQ VH-JME
DHA 162 A17-161 VH-AHP
DHA 167 A17-166 VH-CKE
DHA 169 A17-168 VH-AHL VH-DDA
DHA 174 A17-173 VH-BJF VH-KYB VH-APC VH-EIE
DHA 180 A17-179 VH-APT VH-ALP
DHA 181 A17-180 VH-BAA VH-BOA VH-POL
DHA 189 A17-188 VH-AXH VH-BXH VH-RVH VH-SEC
DHA 202 A17-201 VH-AMG
DHA 205 A17-204 VH-JAU
DHA 208 A17-207 VH-AHM VH-USB
DHA 209 A17-208 VH-AMW
DHA 215 A17-214 VH-AQF
DHA 219 A17-218 VH-BCS VH-APE
DHA 221 (T.314) A17-220 VH-AZC VH-BOO VH-SNR
DHA 226 A17-225 VH-ARA VH-BTX
DHA 234 A17-233 VH-AZE VH-DDU VH-PKB
DHA 235 A17-234 VH-BKW ZK-AVA
DHA 256 A17-237 VH-ARU
DHA 258 (T.291) A17-239 VH-BDV VH-RSA VH-RTA
DHA 261 A17-242 VH-BQG VH-MPF
DHA 265 A17-246 VH-BJG
DHA 266 A17-247 VH-BAS
DHA 274 A17-255 VH-UJW
DHA 291 (T.281) A17-272 VH-AZB
DHA 292 A17-273 VH-BKX VT-CZY
DHA 296 (T.133) A17-277 VH-BNK VH-PCJ VH-BCJ VH-KLH VH-HKG
DHA 303 A17-284 VH-AFF
DHA 308 (T.124) A17-289 VH-BGE VH-UVI
DHA 309 A17-290 VH-BAE VH-BBU VH-KGS
DHA 311 A17-292 VH-BJK
DHA 319 A17-300 VH-JRS
DHA 320 (T.121) A17-301 VH-BDW ZK-BDH
DHA 325 A17-306 VH-TSD
DHA 330 (T.260) A17-311 VH-AQI VH-SSK VH-GLG
DHA 331 A17-312 VH-APN
DHA 335 A17-316 VH-BED VH-FAG
DHA 336 A17-317 VH-BCZ
DHA 341 (T.308) A17-322 VH-AYX VH-AYI
DHA 344 (T.135) A17-325 VH-BGF VH-JJB
DHA 358 A17-339 VH-AMP
DHA 375 VT-AQJ
DHA 381 A17-346 VH-BCV VH-AZG VH-RGK VH-WTM
DHA 382 A17-347 VH-AJG
DHA 392 (T.273) A17-357 VH-AZF VH-ASF
DHA 393 A17-358 VH-BXX
DHA 395 (T.257) A17-360 VH-AOU
DHA 397 A17-362 VH-AMU
DHA 400 (A17-262) A17-365 VH-AYW
DHA 402 A17-367 VH-BBR ZK-AVI VH-AQN
DHA 405 VT-COU
DHA 408 A17-373 VH-BOJ VH-RVK VH-BOJ
DHA 416 A17-375 VH-AKE
DHA 418 (T.168) A17-377 VH-AQM
DHA 425 A17-384 VH-AXZ ZK-AVK
DHA 428 A17-387 VH-BBF VH-ASC
DHA 434 A17-392 VH-ATL VH-BKB N5446
DHA 439 A17-395 VH-BKD VH-WFX VH-PVZ
DHA 459 PK-VVT A17-624 VH-AME VH-TIG
DHA 470 PK-VVU A17-626 VH-GWB VH-MDV
DHA 489 NZ1403 ZK-AJO
DHA 491 NZ1405 ZK-ATZ
DHA 501 NZ1415 ZK-BSN
DHA 503 NZ1417 ZK-AOX
DHA 568 DX491 2341 ZS-BCN
DHA 583 A17-408 VH-AUK
DHA 591 A17-416 VH-BCU
DHA 592 A17-417 VH-ART
DHA 596 A17-421 VH-AZL VH-CAG VH-TUG VH-CKF
DHA 598 (T.202) A17-423 VH-AZH
DHA 623 A17-434 VH-AYR VH-BWR VH-DAJ VH-RAC VH-CCF VH-COF VH-IHU
DHA 629 (T.192) A17-437 VH-AJA
DHA 630 DX557 2338 ZS-DEB
DHA 631 (T.173) A17-438 VH-AZS VH-PCH
DHA 635 (T.208) A17-440 VH-AYG ZK-AWB N5050 N82FD N17440
DHA 636 DX571 2351 ZS-BTP
DHA 637 A17-441 VH-ASB
DHA 639 (T.207) A17-442 VH-TWB VH-BKW N82763
DHA 645 (T.285) A17-445 VH-BGL VH-GWG
DHA 651 (T.251) A17-448 VH-ATM
DHA 660 660 2366 ZS-BGF VP-YOJ G-AGNJ
DHA 711 DX609 2397 SR94 VP-YNV Z-YNV
DHA 723 DX635 2415 ZS-CDK
DHA 728 DX640 CR-AHR ZS-FZF
DHA 732 DX644 VP-YDC 7Q-YDC VP-YDC ZS-LUE VH-WHW
DHA 735 DX647 4736 ZS-DNO ZS-URO ZS-DNO
DHA 736 DX648 4746 ZS-DNW
DHA 737 DX649 4733 ZS-DND HB-UCJ ZS-DND
DHA 742 DX654 CR-ABL ZS-DNG
DHA 746 DX658 SR26
DHA 752 DX664 2427 ZS-BUA VP-YJT ZS-LUF
DHA 759 DX684 2434 VT-CUG
DHA 767 DX692 ZS-CJM
DHA 792 A17-642 VH-RNW VH-WFP VH-TSJ VH-AKG
DHA 797 DX740 A17-647 VH-BGR
DHA 798 DX741 A17-648 VH-GMC
DHA 799 DX742 A17-649 VH-RNO VH-WFN
DHA 801 (T.042) DX744 A17-651 VH-BKE VR-RBG 9M-ALE N1978M
DHA 806 (T.022) DX749 A17-656 VH-AXU A17-656 VH-RSD VH-PSD
DHA 807 DX750 A17-657 VH-RVI
DHA 809 DX752 A17-659 VH-RVN VH-BEQ N14659
DHA 810 DX753 A17-660 INST 16 VH-CXM
DHA 812 DX755 A17-662 VH-VJW VH-CJW
DHA 813 DX756 A17-663 VH-SND VH-SNT
DHA 816 DX759 A17-666 VH-BAR
DHA 817 DX760 A17-667 VH-AJM VH-EOV VH-HSH
DHA 818 DX761 A17-668 VH-RVO VH-AMM VH-RUO
DHA 820 A17-670 VH-BWO VH-DAH VH-CKI
DHA 821 A17-671 VH-SNP
DHA 822 DX779 A17-672 VH-BGT
DHA 823 DX780 A17-673 VH-RNP VH-CCD
DHA 824 DX781 A17-692 VH-TWA VH-AWA
DHA 826 DX783 A17-694 VH-WAP
DHA 827 DX784 A17-695 VH-BVU N350JT
DHA 836 DX793 A17-704 VH-ABF
DHA 841 DX798 A17-709 VH-RSH VH-WFR
DHA 842 DX799 A17-710 VH-RSC VH-BBC
DHA 843 DX800 A17-711 VH-BFF VH-DDW VH-FHJ VH-RTB
DHA 844 DX801 A17-712 VH-BEX
DHA 848 DX805 A17-716 VH-GMB VH-BKC
DHA 849 DX806 A17-717 VH-AAR
DHA 852 DX809 A17-720 VH-BOL
DHA 853 DX810 A17-721 VH-AZT
DHA 855 DX812 A17-723 VH-CJH N10LW
DHA 861 DX829 A17-631 INST 15 VH-DFJ
DHA 864 DX832 A17-634 VH-GIL VH-BAV
DHA 865 DX833 A17-635 VH-WON N5562
DHA 867 DX835 A17-637 VH-RVG VH-TPD VH-SSI
DHA 868 DX836 A17-638 VH-RVL VH-MOC VH-KVH
DHA 870 DX838 A17-640 VH-RSB VH-BTT VH-NMD
DHA 871 DX839 A17-641 VH-SNC VH-OVL
DHA 873 (T.250) A17-456 VH-ATJ
DHA 875 A17-458 VH-BDR ZK-BDG
DHA 876 (T.267) A17-459 VH-BCN
DHA 879 A17-462 VH-LRB
DHA 880 A17-463 VH-AOC VT-CUI
DHA 881 (T.252) A17-464 VH-AKG VH-PCA VH-BCA
DHA 885 (T.257) A17-468 VH-ATE VH-SSK
DHA 901 A17-484 VH-BGG
DHA 908 A17-485 VH-BKG VH-PCO VH-AIP
DHA 914 A17-491 VH-BAI N12731
DHA 915 A17-492 VH-BGA
DHA 922 A17-499 VH-RNX VH-KNX
DHA 923 A17-500 VH-BJA
DHA 926 (T.256) A17-503 VH-BMY VH-RNM VH-BTU N3862 G-AGZZ
DHA 927 (T.258) A17-504 VH-BTH
DHA 933 A17-510 VH-BWN VH-DAI VH-CKB
DHA 941 A17-518 VH-BGX
DHA 944 (T.179) A17-521 VH-FAH VH-JLL VH-FAH
DHA 946 (T.318) A17-523 VH-BVT
DHA 950 A17-527 VH-BFD
DHA 952 (T.305) A17-529 VH-WAL G-BEWN
DHA 974 A17-539 VH-AZP VH-BLH
DHA 978 A17-543 VH-DYI
DHA 979 A17-544 VH-AZA
DHA 981 A17-546 VH-BLH N87677
DHA 986 A17-551 VH-CYA
DHA 996 A17-561 VH-AUM VH-FAH VH-TSA VH-IJM
DHA 1000 A17-565 VH-FBR N17565 G-BCRD HB-UPP
DHA 1005 A17-570 VH-WEM
DHA 1014 A17-579 VH-GME VH-GVA
DHA 1019 A17-584 VH-RSG VH-WOG VH-ULR
DHA 1022 A17-587 VH-BIT
DHA 1023 A17-588 VH-RIN
DHA 1027 A17-592 VH-BBD VH-SSB
DHA 1028 A17-593 INST15 INST17 VH-AIM VH-CDM
DHA 1033 A17-598 VH-BNZ
DHA 1034 A17-599 VH-BJD
DHA 1035 A17-600 VH-ALU P2-CTM
DHA 1039 A17-604 VH-AIN A17-604 VH-SNZ N1350 G-BWVT
DHA 1041 A17-606 VH-AZR
DHA 1043 A17-608 VH-WLK
DHA 1045 A17-610 VH-AZC VH-UNA
DHA 1048 A17-613 VH-BNI
DHA 1054 A17-619 VH-AZK VH-LSK
DHA 1056 A17-725 VH-BKF VH-PFL
DHA 1057 A17-726 VH-GMA VH-BIJ
DHA 1059 A17-728 VH-TSE
DHA 1062 A17-731 VH-AUI VH-SSH
DHA 1064 A17-733 VH-BJL VH-BJU
DHA 1065 A17-734 VH-DAC VH-SAC
DHA 1067 A17-736 VH-RQA VH-BQN
DHA 1068 A17-737 VH-BSG VH-LMF
DHA 1070 A17-739 VH-RSA VH-DEL
DHA 1072 A17-741 VH-FSS
DHA 1073 A17-742 VH-DDZ VH-WRL
DHA 1075 A17-744 VH-BTP
DHA 1076 A17-745 VH-DAD
DHA 1077 A17-746 VH-CEJ
DHA 1080 A17-749 VH-AZJ VH-CAE VH-BSD
DHA 1083 A17-752 VH-BRM
DHA 1084 A17-753 VH-DDQ VH-PUI
DHA 1085 A17-754 VH-FUQ VH-RVB
DHA 1088 A17-757 VH-RNQ VH-NOV
DHA 1090 A17-759 VH-RVE VH-COA

CANADIAN PRODUCTION

DHC 327 CF-BNF
DHC 350 4020
DHC 406 4076
DHC 468 4138 CF-EVZ
DHC 480 4150 CF-BEN C-GWKM
DHC 528 4198 CF-BQT C-GCVE
DHC 551 4221 C-GOEU C-FATG
DHC 555 4225
DHC 607 4277
DHC 636 4306 CF-CIH
DHC 640 4310 CF-CJX
DHC 644 4314 CF-DAL
DHC 649 4319 CF-GTU
DHC 698 4368 CF-COR
DHC 724 4394 CF-DTL CF-FGL
DHC 746 4947 CF-IME
DHC 829 5030 CF-CHT C-GCOE
DHC 851 5052 CF-CIK
DHC 857 5058 CF-SHB
DHC 870 5071 CF-COV
DHC 883 5084 CF-CTK
DHC 902 5103 N4030E
DHC 952 5153
DHC 986 5811 CF-CIE
DHC 991 5816
DHC 1011 4821 CF-DGB
DHC 1020 4830 CF-DGC
DHC 1051 4860 C-GXGS
DHC 1052 4861
DHC 1056 4865 CF-FUG
DHC 1060 4869 A564 CF-OQT
DHC 1101 4910 CF-DFZ
DHC 1124 4933 CF-EIX
DHC 1132 5829 CF-FEL
DHC 1133 5830 CF-CLE
DHC 1162 5859 CF-CHW
DHC 1178 5875 C-GMFT
DHC 1179 5876 CF-FDZ

DHC 1187	5884	CF-CTN			
DHC 1190	5887	CF-CKU			
DHC 1238	5935	CF-CLH	C-FCLH		
DHC 1265	5962	CF-COF	C-FCOF		
DHC 1269	5966	N3758U			
DHC 1295	5992	CF-BHJ			
DHC 1297	5994	CF-CJE			
DHC 1317	42-978	FE114	1114	CF-CSX	N18840
DHC 1325	42-986	FE122	1122	CF-COU	
DHC 1339	42-1000	FE136	1136		
DHC 1348	42-1009	FE145	1145	CF-DHS	
DHC 1373	42-1034	FE170	1170	CF-CLW	
DHC 1395	42-1056	FE192	1192	CF-COH	
DHC 1405	42-1066	FE202	1202	CF-CLK	
DHC 1407	42-1068	FE204	1204	TF-KBD	
DHC 1414	42-1075	FE211	1211	CF-CTO	C-GDWI
DHC 1417	42-1078	FE214	1214	CF-CIX	
DHC 1430	42-1091	FE227	1227	CF-CSZ	
DHC 1451	42-1112	FE248	1248	CF-CTP	
DHC 1458	42-1119	FE255	1255	CF-CHQ	
DHC 1462	42-1123	FE259	1259	CF-CSJ	
DHC 1481	42-1142	FH629	1278	CF-CVZ	
DHC 1498	42-1159	FH646	1295	CF-BEK	N882EK
DHC 1506	3845				
DHC 1508	3847	CF-BSP	C-FBSP		
DHC 1516	3855	CF-DFG	C-FDFG		
DHC 1534	3873	CF-CKN	C-GTAL		
DHC 1542	3881	CF-CLN			
DHC 1547	3886	CF-CJO			
DHC 1593	3932	CF-CKF			
DHC 1600	3939	CF-CLB	N7990	N2925	N82K
	N24SS				
DHC 1608	3947	CF-CIT	N6970		
DHC 1625	3964	CF-BTE	C-FBTE		
DHC 1636	3975	CF-CKW	N3301T		
DHC 1646	3985	CF-BZG	C-GYGU		
DHC 1667	8865	CF-IVO	N667EA		
DHC 1671	8869	CF-DHQ			
DHC 1672	8870	CF-DHR	C-FDHR		
DHC 1673	8871	CF-FYW			
DHC 1705	8903	CF-BGL	N81F	N221J	
DHC 1720	8918	CF-BUN			
DHC 1724	8922	C-GCWT			
DHC 1737	8935	CF-DHM			
DHC 1767	8965	CF-CVB	CF-FEN	N8966	
DHC 1781	8979	CF-EMT	N4446	C-GDPT	
DHC 1800	8998	CF-BUK	CF-BZH		
DHC 1819	9662	CF-BHK	N5063R	N819DH	
DHC 1848	9690	CF-BSS	N8731R	N82LN	NX82LN
DHC 1850	9692	CF-GPE			

NEW ZEALAND PRODUCTION

DHNZ 31	NZ781	ZK-AUD			
DHNZ 70	NZ820	ZK-ALX			
DHNZ 75	NZ825	ZK-AIB			
DHNZ 80	NZ830	ZK-AON			
DHNZ 88	NZ838	ZK-ATC	VH-DOC		
DHNZ 91	NZ841	ZK-ALM			
DHNZ 97	NZ847	ZK-AKC			
DHNZ 101	NZ1421	ZK-BMY			
DHNZ 103	NZ1423	ZK-DHA			
DHNZ 105	NZ1425	ZK-BJR			
DHNZ 107	NZ1427				
DHNZ 110	NZ1430	ZK-BLN	ZK-CCH		
DHNZ 115	NZ1435	ZK-BRC			
DHNZ 123	NZ1443	ZK-BRL			
DHNZ 128	NZ1448	ZK-BLI			
DHNZ 132	NZ1452	ZK-CCQ			
DHNZ 133	NZ1453	Inst 168	ZK-CYC		
DHNZ 135	NZ1455	ZK-ATM	G-BJLI	HB-UPM	
DHNZ 139	NZ1459	ZK-BRD	ZK-BRB		
DHNZ 142	NZ1462	ZK-BNC			
DHNZ 146	NZ1466	ZK-ATG			
DHNZ 147	NZ1467	ZK-BQB			
DHNZ 152	NZ1472	ZK-BRM			
DHNZ 155	NZ1475	ZK-BCZ			
DHNZ 156	NZ1476	ZK-BQC			
DHNZ 161	NZ1481	Inst 150			
DHNZ 164	NZ1484	ZK-BLM			
DHNZ 165	NZ1485	ZK-DAM	VH-JKE	VH-NVT	
DHNZ 173	NZ1493	ZK-BME			
DHNZ 175	NZ1495	ZK-ANS			
DHNZ 179	NZ1499	ZK-AQC			

NORWEGIAN PRODUCTION

158	145	
161	151	SE-ANL
172	163	SE-ALM
185	183	SE-ALP

PORTUGUESE PRODUCTION

P1	102	CS-AEF	
P12	CS-AFC		
P13	CS-AEV		
P16	CS-AFZ		
P18	CS-AFF		
P37	CS-AEO		
P65	CS-AEL		
P68	CR-AGM	ZS-FZL	G-AKUE

SWEDISH PRODUCTION

47	515	SE-BYM
49	517	SE-AMR
73	553	SE-BYL

OTHER AIRCRAFT

either constructed from new parts or rebuilt against spurious previous identities, or recorded against no notified or traced history.

Quoted Builder's Ref	Quoted Registration(s)			Current Location
1673	– (nil)			Argentina
169	VH-ABC			Australia
DH1748	VH-ADW			
120	VH-AKQ	VH-AYY	VH-BYF	
	VH-RVC	VH-ACJ	VH-AKQ	
LES 6	VH-ASD			
DHA1074	VH-AUS			
534	VH-AZE			
LES11	VH-BCI			
1035	VH-BDX			
LES 2	VH-BGO			
LES 3	VH-BRT	ZK-AOR		
LES 9	VH-BUG			
1077	VH-CES			
LES 8	VH-CXL			
LES 10	VH-CXY			
AW/TC/1	VH-DHV			
A788	VH-EFT	VH-EOB		
SA87-5	VH-HCI			
1375	VH-HPH			
LES 1	VH-KRW			
391	VH-LIZ			
LES 4	VH-MWN			
LES 7	VH-PIP	VH-RIP	VH-PIP	
	VH-EDI			
LV 1	VH-PME			
AW/A/16	VH-RJA			
DHC78	VH-TSG			
LP-5	VH-ULC			
AW/A/17	VH-UQZ			
– (nil)	VH-UTD			
399	VH-UZV			
LES 5	VH-MIT	VH-WFD		
HU-726	VT-DKN	N90277		Belgium
MFC-02/1955	VT-DHS	C-GNGS		Canada
MFC-403	– (nil)			
BFC 3	VT-DJL			
E75	– (nil)			
005	F-WZBH	F-AZAV		France
004	F-WZBG	F-AZAX		
– (nil)	F-AZCS			
– (nil)	F-AZDH			
– (nil)	F-AZDP			
– (nil)	EC-AEV	30-188		
– (nil)	EC-AFM	30-162		
– (nil)	EC-AFN	30-154		
– (nil)	EC-AHY	30-170		
– (nil)	– (nil)			Germany
OU/06/68	HU-488	VT-DOW	G-BINH	Great Britain
0482	G-BJAP			
7712	G-BJWR			
NA5100	G-BJZF			
82619	ZS-CNR	G-BMPY		
157-11095	G-DHTM			
BAPC-21	– (nil)			
BAPC-86	– (nil)			
BAPC-186	– (nil)			
– (nil)	K2572			
MOTH-1 Serial No15	N1151T			
– (nil)	SR36	VP-YOC		
MPFC-TM-2	VT-DKX			
OU/05/68	HU-483	VT-DOU		
OU/02/66	HU-492	VT-DOX		
OU/03/66	HU-498	VT-DOY		
OU/07/68	HU-504	VT-DOZ		
OU/10/69	HU-511	VT-DPA		
OU/08/69	HU-708	VT-DPB		
OU/04/67	HU-858	VT-DPE	G-BUJY	
HU-870	VT-DPG			
OU/09/69	HU-887	VT-DPH		
87427	7Q-YCA			
HU-801	VT-DHU			India
NIFC-1	VT-DHV			
HU-705	VT-DHW			
HU-856	VT-DKF			
SKG-1	VT-DKG			
HU-484	VT-DOV			
HU-187	VT-DPC			
83517	ZS-ARM			South Africa
372	ZS-BCN			
LA703	ZS-CKZ			
22-0989	ZS-DHM			
2752	ZS-LNF			
3534	ZS-MCJ			
37239	– (nil)			
1999SA/BS	ZS-FEY	N82MT		USA
3312	N5444			
T6392/RO	N54556			

Information correct to 24th July 1999.

Ex-Portuguese Air Force Tiger Moth, build No. P37, was registered CS-AEO in 1957 and operated by the Aeroclube da Costa Verde. She was acquired by the Museum at Alverca in 1995. M J Hooks

INDEX

INDEX OF NAMES

LOCATIONS INDEX

Where place and country names (e.g. Hatfield, Stag Lane, and Canada, Australia) occur profusely throughout the text, they have not been listed in this index.

GOVERNMENT & MILITARY DEPARTMENTS, Civil Clubs, Operators and Museums

BRITISH MILITARY UNITS INDEX

COMMONWEALTH MILITARY UNITS INDEX

AIRCRAFT, ENGINES, EQUIPMENT, SUPPLIES AND SERVICE INDEX

MISCELLANEOUS

June 1949:
the green fields of England in peacetime
but shadowed by Korea and the Cold War in Europe.
Pilot training for the military was still
an essential requirement, and after 18 years of service,
the Tiger Moth remained in constant use worldwide.
Today, only the colours have changed.
Bill Fisher